Religion, Personality, and Social Behavior

Psychological interest in religion, in terms of both theory and empirical research, has been constant since the beginning of psychology. However, since the beginning of the 21st century, partially due to important social and political events and developments, interest in religion within personality and social psychology has increased.

This volume reviews the accumulated research and theory on the major aspects of personality and social psychology as applied to religion. It provides a high-quality integrative, systematic, and rigorous review of that work, with a focus on topics that both are central in personality and social psychology and have allowed for the accumulation of solid and replicated and not impressionist knowledge on religion. The contributors are renowned researchers in the field who offer an international perspective that is both illuminating, yet neutral, with respect to religion.

The volume's primary audience are academics, researchers, and advanced students in social psychology, but it will also interest those in sociology, political sciences, and anthropology.

Vassilis Saroglou is Professor of Psychology at the University of Louvain (UCL) and has been a visiting professor at Arizona State University and Fulbright scholar at the College of William and Mary. He has an extensive record of publications in personality, social, and cross-cultural psychology of religion, fundamentalism, and spirituality. He currently serves as Associate Editor of the *International Journal for the Psychology of Religion*. He is a recipient of the Early Career Award (2005) and the Mentoring Award (2013) of APA-Division 36, and the Quinquennial Godin Prize (2006) of the International Association for the Psychology of Religion.

Religion, Personality, and Social Behavior

Edited by Vassilis Saroglou

Ψ Psychology Press
Taylor & Francis Group

NEW YORK AND LONDON

First published 2014
by Psychology Press
711 Third Avenue, New York, NY 10017

Simultaneously published in the UK
by Psychology Press
27 Church Road, Hove, East Sussex BN3 2FA

Psychology Press is an imprint of the Taylor & Francis Group, an informa business

Library of Congress Cataloging in Publication Data
A catalog record for this book has been requested.

ISBN: 978-1-84872-984-1 (hbk)
ISBN: 978-1-84872-665-9 (pbk)
ISBN: 978-0-203-12535-9 (ebk)

Typeset in Sabon
by EvS Communication Networx, Inc.

SFI Certified Sourcing
www.sfiprogram.org
SFI-00453

Printed and bound in the United States of America
by Edwards Brothers, Inc.

Contents

List of Contributors

Michael C. Ashton, Brock University

Christopher T. Burris, St. Jerome's University

Tom Carpenter, Baylor University

Adam B. Cohen, Arizona State University

Andrey Elster, The Hebrew University of Jerusalem

Leslie J. Francis, University of Warwick

Jochen E. Gebauer, Humboldt University of Berlin

Will M. Gervais, University of Kentucky

Pehr Granqvist, Stockholm University

Megan Haggard, Baylor University

R. David Hayward, University of Michigan

Kathryn A. Johnson, Arizona State University

Neal Krause, University of Michigan

Kibeom Lee, University of Calgary

Yexin Jessica Li, University of Kansas

Ariel Malka, Yeshiva University

Gemma Penny, University of Warwick

Raluca Petrican, Rotman Research Institute

Jesse Lee Preston, University of Illinois

Bernard Rimé, University of Louvain

Ryan S. Ritter, University of Illinois

Sonia Roccas, The Open University of Israel

Wade C. Rowatt, Baylor University

Erika Salomon, University of Illinois

Vassilis Saroglou, University of Louvain

Constantine Sedikides, University of Southampton

Patty Van Cappellen, University of North Carolina

Preface

Understanding psychologically religion, spirituality, and irreligion (for brevity, "religion") as a domain of human life involving personality, cognition, emotions, and leading to social consequences is certainly a legitimate and important task for personality and social psychology. Research on this domain, innovative in both theory and methodology, has importantly developed in the last 15 years. A volume focusing specifically on personality and social psychology of religion and synthesizing the fascinating accumulated evidence of the last years was missing.

I have been fortunate and honored to get the collaboration of highly dynamic and creative authors who contributed with chapters that offer each the best possible picture on the respective subject. The authors mostly belong to the younger generation of established experts with strong publication experience in excellent journals in personality, cognition, emotion, social psychology, cultural, political, developmental, and health psychology, as well psychology of religion and evolutionary psychology. Many of the authors have also significant expertise as editors or associate editors in journals of their respective fields. My warmest thanks go first to these colleagues who got enthusiastic about the idea and contributed happily and timely with substantial and original chapters.

It would also be a shame not to mention and thank for their ongoing contribution to my own work, research, and teaching, in psychology of religion, my students, PhD students, and postdoctoral researchers, as well as colleagues and collaborators from many places in the world, including my own department. Moreover, my early steps on this domain of research have benefited from insights, advice, and encouragement by several, today really senior, colleagues, from both Europe and the US. I also thank warmly the team in Psychology Press, and in particular Paul Dukes, who welcomed warmly the idea for this volume, and, together with Lee Transue, managed successfully and timely the whole process, from the proposal's submission, through reviewing, till publication.

The publication of this volume marks a happy coincidence. It was in 1993 that Dan Batson and colleagues published *Religion and the*

Individual: A Social-Psychological Perspective, a seminal work that thoughtfully reviewed and integrated the authors' and others' empirical, including experimental, research on religion. Batson et al.'s book focused mainly on religious orientations and their links with prosocial behavior, prejudice, and mental health. Since then, it has inspired a tremendous number of scholars and studies in the field. Twenty years later, research in personality and social psychology of religion has considerably expanded in topics, theory, methods, and accumulated knowledge. We hope the volume that is in your hands will also contribute to stimulate students and scholars in increasing the intellectual understanding of, and passion for future investigations on, religion, including spirituality and irreligion.

1 Introduction

Studying Religion in Personality and Social Psychology

Vassilis Saroglou

For centuries, even thousands of years, within each society, individuals have differed from one another in attitudes and behavior about religion. Some have been very religious, some moderately so, whereas others are not interested in religion at all or may oppose it. Additionally, within believers and non-believers, there have been different ways of expressing positive or negative attitudes towards religion. From a *personality and individual differences* psychological perspective, this raises at least two questions. First, why are there individual differences in religious attitudes and behaviors (referred to as religiousness)? Second, do religious attitudes and behaviors reflect and influence cognitions, emotions, and behaviors at the intrapersonal, interpersonal, and social levels? In other words, what is the psychological relevance—determinants, correlates, and outcomes—of religiousness and its forms?

Similarly, *social psychology* is interested in understanding the situational factors that may have an impact on individuals' religious attitudes and behaviors: how personal experiences (e.g., life events), and social events (e.g., 9/11 terrorist attacks) may impact on religious attitudes and behaviors, at personal and group levels. Can researchers understand such effects by focusing on fundamental psychological processes studied experimentally in the laboratory? Also, social psychology is interested in whether religion (religious ideas, texts, feelings, symbols, images, figures, and groups) has an influence on people's cognitions, emotions, and acts relative to other, non-religious, domains. And is this influence relevant to some, many, or all domains of human behavior? As shown in this volume, these domains comprise intra-individual functioning, interpersonal and intergroup relations, morality, prosocial and anti-social behavior, sexuality and family, political, economic, and work related behavior, as well as social processes involved in mental health and human development.

The two approaches (i.e., personality and social psychology) are in *interaction*, both theoretically and empirically. Overall, persons behave in contexts; and situations impact human behavior but not always similarly for all people (Leary & Hoyle, 2009; Rhodewalt, 2008). In particular, predictors or outcomes of religiousness may be moderated by, if not fully depend on, situational factors. For instance, religiousness's role with regard to prosocial attitudes may depend on the type of the target person (Blogowska & Saroglou, 2011). Similarly, the impact of religious ideas on social behavior (e.g., submission or rigid morality) may not be present in all persons but only among those with specific individual dispositions (Saroglou, Corneille, & Van Cappellen, 2009; Van Pachterbeke, Freyer, & Saroglou, 2011).

Research on the personality and social psychology of religion has a long history (Batson, Schoenrade, & Ventis, 1993; Beit-Hallahmi & Argyle, 1997). However, in the last 15 years, there has been a substantial increase of interest and investment in such research. Examples are the publication of special issues on religion in key personality, social, and cultural psychology journals (Baumeister, 2002; Emmons & McCullough, 1999; Saroglou & Cohen, 2011; Sedikides, 2010), the inclusion of chapters on religion and personality or culture in reference books (Ashton, 2007; Atran, 2007; Emmons, Barrett, & Schnitker, 2008), and, since 2009, the organization of preconferences on the psychology of religion and spirituality at the Society for Personality and Social Psychology annual meetings.

Moreover, as depicted in Figure 1.1, the number of published articles on religion and spirituality in journals listed in PsycINFO and whose title includes "personality" or "social psychology" has increased from 1990 to 2011. Whereas the number of articles that focus specifically on these topics (on titles) follows the more general pattern of increase in the total number of articles published in these journals, the number of articles that integrate religion/spirituality somehow in the study (in abstracts) has increased more than the total number of articles published in these journals. In 2010–2011, the number of articles that included religion/spirituality in the abstract was three times higher than in the early 1990s. Interestingly, the shape of the increase of articles integrating religion parallels the one of articles integrating political issues.

This volume aims to offer an integrated, theory-based, and systematic overview of this recently accumulated empirical research. The present introductory chapter includes five sections corresponding to five objectives. First, operational psychological definitions of religion and religiousness are provided through the description of their basic components/dimensions. Second, the "varieties of religious experiences" (forms of religiousness), to refer here to William James' seminal book (1985 [1902]), are presented by selecting key forms that reflect specific psychological processes. Third, the reader is briefly introduced to methodological issues, mainly research methods, ways of measuring religion as an independent variable in experiments, and explicit, but also implicit, measures of individual religiousness. Fourth, issues of occasional misunderstanding related to the evaluation of findings from the social

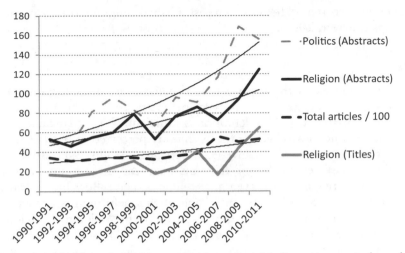

Figure 1.1 Number of articles on religion and spirituality, comparatively to the number of articles on politics and the increase of total number of articles, all published in personality and social psychology journals (1990–2011).

Note. Articles on religion were identified through the formula "relig* or spiritual* or God or prayer" (in title or abstract) and journals including in their title "personality" or "social psychology" in the PsycINFO database. Articles in politics were identified through "politic*" in abstract in the same journals. The total number of articles published in these journals was divided by 100, to facilitate comparison of tendency curves. The latter are provided, from top to down, for articles in politics (abstracts) and articles in religion (abstracts and titles).

psychological research on religion are discussed: objectivity, reductionism, religion's causal status, and generalizability. Finally, the chapter closes with a brief overview of the volume's structure and chapters.

Defining Religion, Religiousness, and their Dimensions

Throughout the history of the psychological study of religion there has been a tension between an emphasis on the *individual* dimension of the connection with what a person perceives as a transcendent entity and the acknowledgment of the *social* dimension of a religious culture (i.e., collective beliefs, rituals, and norms referring to what a group perceives as a transcendent entity). It is legitimate today to acknowledge a relative independence between these two dimensions. People may experience and express their religious attitudes—positive or negative ones—somehow independently from their own or any religious culture (Flanagan & Jupp, 2007). Yet, people deal with religious beliefs, experiences, values, and communities that have been socially shaped and legitimated. Thus, the individual and social dimensions are related (e.g., Wolf, 2005). More than two-thirds of the world population consist of believers who report belonging to established religious traditions and groups (Barrett, 2001).

Religion

I define *religion* as the co-presence of beliefs, ritualized experiences, norms, and groups that refer to what people perceive to be a transcendent to humans entity. This definition is sufficiently large to include both established and new religions; forms that are perceived as positive (e.g., recognized religions) or negative (e.g., detrimental cults, Satanism); and traditions regarded as theistic religions (e.g., the three monotheisms), non-theistic religions, or even non-religions (e.g., Buddhism, francmasonry). At the same time, the scope of this definition is not excessively large. It avoids to assimilate under the term "religion" individual and social realities such as paranormal beliefs, philosophical systems, ultimate concerns, secular rituals, self-transcendent emotions, core values, taboo trade-offs, and moral or political ideologies. These realities may be somewhat proximal to religion (thus, psychologically interesting for comparatively understanding religion; e.g., Saroglou, 2012a) but do not require the co-presence of the four components: beliefs, ritualized experiences, norms, and community.

These four components are universally present across cultures, religions, and societies. However, there is also important cultural, religious, and historical variation in the mean importance attributed to each of them, as well as in the strength of the interrelations between the four components, which leads to cultural variability of religious forms (Saroglou, 2011). For instance, beliefs and morality are more normative in mainstream Protestantism; in Judaism, this is more the case with rituals and community (Cohen, Hall, Koenig, & Meador, 2005).

This definition of religion emphasizing the co-existence of different components may be helpful to personality and social psychologists, who study basic psychological processes that operate across domains of individual and social life. Consequently, scholars may sometimes be prone to reducing the phenomenon under study (e.g., the historically and currently complex relations between Flemish and Walloons in the bilinguistic and bicultural Belgium) as simply one typical example of their preferred theory and subfield of research (e.g., intergroup conflict). Likewise, they may consider religion as simply an issue of group belongingness; or simply as a meaning-making system; or finally as just one among other conservative ideologies. Each of the above approaches is, of course, important to the understanding of a different aspect of religion. However, it is also, if not more, important to identify the combination of the various psychological mechanisms present in religion. For instance, philosophy, art, and religion all may be helpful for meaning-making or as a response to existential anxiety. Each of the above though may imply a specific combination of psychological processes involved in meaning-making or coping with existential anxiety.

Religiousness

I define here *religiousness* as the individual differences on being interested in and/or involved with religion. This includes individual differences in attitudes, cognitions, emotions, and/or behavior that refer to what people consider as a transcendent entity. Depending on whether one uses continuous or categorical variables, differences in religiousness can be observed gradually—varying from "not at all" to "totally" interested/involved—or can be summarized categorically—believers/religious and non-believers/non-religious.

Dimensions of Individual Religiousness

Like for religion as a social reality, religiousness as individual differences in attitudes towards religion is multifaceted and can be conceived of as including four major dimensions (four "Bs"): believing, bonding, behaving, and belonging (Saroglou, 2011). Specifically, religiousness includes: (a) believing specific ideas regarding the transcendent entity and its relations with humans and the world; (b) bonding emotionally through private and/or collective rituals with the transcendent entity and then with others; (c) behaving in a way to conform to norms, practices, and values perceived as established by the transcendent; and/or (d) belonging to a group that is self-perceived as eternal and as filled with the presence of the transcendent.

Within individuals, the four dimensions are importantly interrelated, but there are inter-individual and intergroup differences in the mean importance attributed to each of them (Saroglou [with 14 co-authors], 2013). Additionally, the four dimensions correspond to four major kinds of motivation for religious conversion or deconversion (exiting from or changing religion), i.e., cognitive, emotional, moral, and social motivations. Also, the dimensions point out to four major categories of possible psychological functions of religion having to do, respectively, with meaning-making, emotional regulation, moral self-transcendence, and social identity.

Additional External Indicators

Extensive sociological work distinguishes between (a) individual religiousness (as a global attitude of personal religiousness), (b) religious practice (frequency of collective and/or personal practice—i.e., most often, respectively, religious attendance and prayer/meditation) and (c) affiliation/identification with a particular religion/denomination (Voas,

2007). These three indicators (personal religiousness, religious practice, and religious affiliation) are also well-used in psychological research.

Varieties of Religious Forms

Beyond the four basic dimensions of "subjective" individual religiousness and the additional "objective" indicators of affiliation and religious practice, there exists a variety of forms through which religiousness is expressed. This has historically been a major area of investigation in the psychological study of religion, and has led to the production of a large number of religious constructs, variables, and corresponding measures. Below I will briefly overview what are the major religious forms, following specific criteria of selection and classification.

Criteria for Selecting Key Religious Forms

I followed three selection criteria. First, it is important to focus on religious expressions whose differences reflect distinct *psychological processes* (e.g., types of motivation, cognitive style, developmental trajectory, emotional quality) and not religious forms and variables that are too descriptive (e.g., "religious social support"), too theologically informed (e.g., "spiritual awareness"), or too normative (e.g., "mature religious faith").

Second, it is important for comparative and international research to focus on religious forms that have been detected or are very likely *detectable across various religions, cultures, and societies*. Specific religious expressions that reflect respective distinct psychological processes can be found in many human societies, as far as these psychological processes operate universally. This is not the case with those religious constructs and corresponding measures that are too proximal to a particular theology and spirituality of a particular denomination or religion.

Third, previous research consistently shows that, overall, the measures of various religious constructs are importantly interrelated and point out to a higher order factor of religiousness (Tsang & McCullough, 2003). Thus, these different constructs most often predict similar outcomes. This is in particular the case when a study is carried out on samples whose religiousness represents the global, average religiousness of the population and not the one of "known" groups (e.g., believers or non-believers, people high or low on fundamentalism). I opted thus to present below religious forms that are *known to predict*, at least partly, *distinct outcomes, or to follow distinct psychological predictors*, even if they may be moderately interrelated with each other in studies with samples of average religiousness.

Major Religious Forms

Intrinsic Versus Extrinsic Religious Orientation

Following a classic typology by Allport and Ross (1967), religiousness may be *intrinsic* or *extrinsic*, that is, respectively, an end in itself, motivated by inherently religious motives, or a means toward other ends, motivated by other than religious motives. Increasing one's own network of acquaintances or getting prestige by peers are just two examples of extrinsic religious motivations. This classic distinction in religious orientations has led to a large body of research (Batson et al., 1993) and has been identified in various religious and cultural contexts (see studies cited in Flere & Lavrič, 2008). Nevertheless, in recent years, the pertinence of this distinction and the validity of the extrinsic orientation and corresponding measures have been questioned (Neyrinck, Lens, Vansteenkiste, & Soenens, 2010). In addition, extrinsic orientation may have different meanings and higher normativity in non-Protestant than Protestant cultures (Cohen et al., 2005); and, across studies, the existing scales have provided null results, inconsistent results, or findings that are hard to interpret. This is likely because of the enormous variability of the underlying extrinsic motivations. Moreover, as already argued (Saroglou, 2011), measuring extrinsic religious orientation in modern secularized societies may have become less meaningful: most people are today (still) religious due to intrinsic motivation and not because of social pressure or other external factors.

Socialization Versus Conversion; Positive Versus Negative Emotionality

Religiousness may also differ depending on the underlying developmental and relational processes and life's trajectories. An important distinction exists between being religious by *socialization* (i.e. continuity in adolescence and adulthood with, often secure, parents' religiousness) or by *conversion* (discovering or rediscovering religion in discontinuity with, often insecure, parents' non-religiousness or negative religiousness) (see Granqvist, Chapter 13, this volume). Somehow similarly, religiousness may have built on, and function as a way to cope with, *negative emotionality* or may reflect or have been built on *positive emotionality*. William James (1985 [1902]) has called the former as the religion of the "sick-soul" and the latter as the "healthy-minded religion" (see, in this volume, Burris & Petrican, Chapter 5; Van Cappellen & Rimé, Chapter 6). The former religiousness often implies negative representations of God as controlling and punishing and the use of negative forms of religious coping (i.e., unsuccessful religious means to face adversity), whereas the latter is followed by positive images of God as loving and supportive and the use of positive forms of religious coping (Pargament, Fueille, & Burdzy, 2011).

Closed-Minded Versus Open-Minded Religiousness

Considerable research has focused on closed- versus open-minded forms of religiousness. These forms mainly include *religious fundamentalism*, that is, religious dogmatism combined with right-wing authoritarian structure (Altemeyer & Hunsberger, 2005; Kirkpatrick, Hood, & Hartz, 1991; see also Brandt & Renya, 2010), and *religious orthodoxy*, that is, religious conservatism characterized by literal and simplistic attachment to beliefs, practices, and norms as established by religious authority (Deconchy, 1980; Pancer, Jackson, Hunsberger, Pratt, & Lea, 1995). Somehow on the opposite pole, one can find *religion-as-quest*, that is, religiousness that is characterized by the valorization of doubt, capacity for self-criticism, including of one's own religious tradition, and openness to the possibility that one's own beliefs and faith may change (Batson et al., 1993; see also Batson, Denton, & Vollemecke, 2008).

A more extended model, based on Wulff's (1997) theorization, has resulted in a series of studies by Hutsebaut and collaborators that distinguishes between *literal* and *symbolic* ways of being either religious or non-religious (research using the Post-Critical Belief Scale; Fontaine, Duriez, Luyten, & Hutsebaut, 2003). When crossing the two axes (literal vs. symbolic thinking on religious issues; and inclusion vs. exclusion of transcendence), one obtains four quadrants. These include (a) literal believers (orthodox/fundamentalists), but also (b) literal non-believers (atheists fully despising religion as irrational, irrelevant, and dangerous); as well as (c) symbolic believers who interpret symbolically religious ideas, and (d) symbolic non-believers who acknowledge some anthropological value in religion, while rejecting it personally.

Religiosity Versus Spirituality

Ongoing theorization and research especially in the last 15 years have focused on understanding (new) forms of spirituality, namely, individuals' beliefs, emotions, and practices in reference to a reality that is perceived as transcending human existence (Belzen, 2009; Hill & Pargament, 2003; Zinnbauer & Pargament, 2005). At least in contemporary Western societies, marked by secularization, modern spirituality is perceived and experienced as mostly distinct from traditional religiosity, especially as far as the latter importantly refers to an institutionalized religious organization and collective practice through rituals validated by religious authority.

There still exists some debate on whether the two, religiosity and spirituality, should be importantly opposed or not, in terms of their definition (has not spirituality been for centuries an essential, perhaps the most intimate and intrinsic, component of religious experience?) and qualification of their respective outcomes (is spirituality only good and religiosity only bad?). Nevertheless, accumulated research, mostly in Western societies, suggests some general empirical trends. The two dimensions are moderately interrelated and most people perceive themselves as both religious and spiritual; the more a society/group is secularized, the more the two dimensions are distinct from each other (Saroglou [with 13 co-authors], 2012); and the correlates and outcomes of religiosity and spirituality (personality traits, values, social attitudes and behavior) denote several similarities as well as many differences (Saroglou & Muñoz-García, 2008; Saucier & Skrzypińska, 2006). These similarities and differences suggest that modern spirituality emerges as a new form of traditional religiosity that fits better the values of contemporary liberal societies (Saroglou, 2003; Siegers, 2011). For clarity reasons, I use the term "religiousness" as a broad umbrella that includes various forms, including traditional "religiosity"—still vibrant in many non-Western societies—and modern spirituality.

Synthesis: Devotional Versus Coalitional Religion

Integrating the various dichotomies in religious forms, a global distinction emerges between two major aspects of religion: devotional and coalitional (Hansen & Norenzayan, 2006). With the risk of being extremely polarizing and too global, but for the needs of a synthesis, one can conclude that there are forms of religion that are rather extrinsically motivated (i.e., based on social pressure and advantages), focus on the institutional and collective dimensions, and often reflect some closed-mindedness in cognition and morality. These point out to the *coalitional* part of religion. However, there are also forms of religion that are intrinsically motivated (i.e., based on internalization of belief and values), focus on the individual experience and spiritual motives for self-transcendence, and may reflect some open-mindedness in cognition and morality; these forms point out to the *devotional* part of religion.

Note that forms of religiousness reflecting negative versus positive emotionality, presented in Table 1.1 as independent from forms reflecting closed- versus open-mindedness, may in fact be in parallel with the latter. For instance, positive perception of God as supporting autonomy relates to symbolic religious thinking, whereas negative perception of God as controlling relates to literal religious thinking (Soenens et al., 2012).

Note, finally, that there is theoretically a way to consider many of the religious forms as resulting from a categorization that is orthogonal to one of the four dimensions described earlier in this section (i.e., believing, bonding, behaving, and belonging). As presented in Table

Table 1.1　Major dimensions and forms of religiousness.

	Forms			
	Closed- vs. Open-Mindedness		Negative vs. Positive Emotionality	
Dimensions[1]				
Believing	Literal thinking[2]	Symbolic thinking[2]		
Bonding			Negative emotions[3]	Positive emotions[3]
Behaving	Moral self-control	Prosociality		
Belonging	Religious ingroup	Human community		
Forms				
Motivation	Extrinsic[4]	Intrinsic[4]		
Trajectory			(Intense) conversion[5]	Socialization[5]
External indicators	Affiliation, public practice	Personal prayer/ mediation		
Global qualifications				
Common forms	Traditional religiosity[6]	Modern spirituality[7]		
	Coalitional	Devotional		
Extreme forms	Orthodoxy, Fundamentalism[8]	Religion-as-Quest[9]		
Emotional forms			"Sick-soul"	"Healthy-minded"

Note. Hereafter are examples of key measures that have been used largely in research and internationally. 1: Four Religious Dimensions Scale (Saroglou et al., 2013). 2: Post-Critical Belief Scale (Fontaine et al., 2005). 3: Religious Coping Scale (Pargament et al., 2000). 4: Intrinsic/Extrinsic Scale-Revised (Gorsuch & McPherson, 1989). 5: Socialization- and Emotionally-Based Religiosity Scales (Granqvist & Hagekull, 1999). 6: Santa Clara Strength of Religious Faith Questionnaire (Plante & Boccaccini, 1997), Attitude Toward Christianity, Judaism, Islam, and Hinduism Scales (see Francis, 2009), 3-Item Religiosity Index (Saroglou & Mathijsen, 2007). 7: Spiritual Transcendence Scale (Piedmont, 1999). 8: Religious Fundamentalism Scale (Altemeyer & Hunsberger, 1992). 9: Religion-as-Quest Scale (Batson et al., 1993; see Van Pachterbeke et al., 2011, for a scale applicable also to non-religious). Short versions exist for those of the above scales that are long (≥ 20 items).

1.1, religious people may believe literally or symbolically; have religious experience marked by negative or positive emotionality; behave ethically, being attached to a universal interpersonal morality, or moralistically by favoring a conservative, collectivistic morality; and belong strictly to their religious ingroup or identify with the larger (spiritual) human community.

Forms of Irreligion

Understanding religiousness contributes to also understanding irreligion. For instance, knowing the psychological costs and benefits of being religious may help to look for, respectively, the psychological benefits and costs of being non-religious. Although much less empirically studied, there is also a variety of forms of irreligion (Zuckerman, 2012). People who are irreligious may be agnostics, atheists, militant anti-religious, socialized as secular, "apostates" (those who exit from religion), "deconverts" (those who abandon faith through a process similar to conversion; Streib, Hood, Keller, Csöff, & Silver, 2008), or "liminals" (those inconsistent across time when declaring no religious preference; Lim, MacGregor, & Putnam, 2010).

Understanding thus religion from a personality and social psychological perspective includes, in principle, the psychological study of religion (traditional religion), spirituality (modern forms, possibly independent from traditional institutions), and irreligion. However, psychologists have been more interested in understanding religion than the lack of it. Thus, psychological research that focuses specifically on the various forms of irreligion is rare and has only recently emerged (Hunsberger & Altemeyer, 2006; Zuckerman, 2011).

Research Methods and Measures of Religion and Religiousness

Research Methods

In the past, research on the personality and social psychology of religion has been heavily based on correlational and cross-sectional studies. Experimental and quasi-experimental studies were sporadic (see Batson et al., 1993; Wulff, 1997) but have become increasingly dominant in the past 15 years. There has also been a diversification of alternative data sources and data collection methods than self-reported questionnaires administered to small samples of participants. This in turn led to higher use of complex data analytic strategies.

Today, personality and social psychological research on religion is also based on: observer ratings, implicit and behavioral measures and outcomes of religiousness, diaries and diary analytic methods, content analysis of books, websites, archival files, and interviews, psychobiographies and case studies, internet studies and experiments, field studies, priming techniques, behavioral genetic analyses of twin data, psychophysiological measures and neuroimaging, longitudinal studies, methods applied to children, quantitative meta-analyses of past studies, cross-cultural and cross-religious comparative research, and multilevel analyses distinguishing the individual and the group/country levels in large international data. A main objective of the present volume is to review evidence accumulated through this exciting body of research.

Social psychological experiments on religion typically investigate three kinds of question. First, scholars study the situational influences on religiousness and its forms—overall effects or in interaction with individual dispositional characteristics. For instance, do people more strongly attach to supernatural entities after their mortality has been salient in the laboratory? Are all or some kinds of participant sensitive to such effects? Second, researchers study the effects of religious stimulation on intra-individual functioning and social attitudes and behavior—again in general, or in interaction with participants' individual characteristics. For instance, do religious ideas (conscious or nonconscious) increase submission to the experimenter and social conformity, to do moral or immoral acts, and, if so, among whom? Third, scholars investigate the differential outcomes of religiousness and different religious forms as a function of situational variables. For instance, does religiosity (or religious fundamentalism vs. quest) lead to prosocial behavior similarly when the target person is an ingroup member, a stranger, or an outgroup member?

Below, I focus on two kinds of methodological issue that are of particular interest for those who are familiar with personality and social psychological research in general but may be unfamiliar with how to operationalize religion as an independent variable and how to measure religiousness as an individual difference construct.

Religion as Independent Variable

Religion in general (e.g., a set of various religious words or images) or specific religious ideas, images, figures, places, and symbols has been used in psychological research in order to investigate religion's capacity to activate or shape theoretically relevant cognitions, emotions, attitudes, and behaviors. In some studies, these religious materials might also vary in valence (positive or negative), moral quality (texts praising prosociality or legitimizing aggression), or the key facet of religion that is activated (coalitional versus devotional). Specifically, dozens of very recent studies in the last few years have used priming techniques to present supraliminally or subliminally participants with religious material;

in this case, religious ideas influence participants' cognitions, feelings, and behavior (Galen, 2012, Tables 2 and 3).

Various trends emerge from the accumulation of these priming studies in the last years. First, some social outcomes (e.g., prosociality) are rather consistent across studies, countries, and religions (Clobert & Saroglou, 2013; Pichon, Boccato, & Saroglou, 2007; Shariff & Norenzayan, 2007). Second, even single, distinct in content, words (e.g., "God" vs. "religion"; "prayer" vs. "mosque" or "synagogue", reflecting respectively devotional versus coalitional religion) are sufficient to activate automatically distinct social attitudes (Ginges, Hansen, & Norenzayan, 2009; Preston, Ritter, & Hernandez, 2010). Third, in several (but not all) priming studies, the effects are independent from participants' individual religiousness. In other words, they are present also among non-believers. This suggests that implicit, automatic associations between religion and some relevant constructs are part of general social cognition and produce their effects relatively independently from the correspondence between the individual centrality of religious concepts and the associated construct. Finally, there is an increasing interest for investigating the effects of "hetero-religious" priming, i.e., whether participants of a given religious background are also influenced by primes of different than their own religion (Buddhist or Muslim primes among Christians: Clobert & Saroglou, 2013; Vilaythong, Lindner, & Nosek, 2011). Similarly, there is interest on whether psychological needs manipulated in the lab will increase belief in supernatural beings from other than one's own religion (Norenzayan & Hansen, 2006; Vail et al., 2012).

Measures of Religiousness

Almost exclusively, religiousness and its forms, as well as more specific religious constructs, have been measured through questionnaires. This is not surprising, since the nature of religiousness resembles attitudes, beliefs, and values. However, even if rarely, one can also find in recent research alternative measures such as implicit and projective, quasi-behavioral measures.

Scales

There exists a large array of religious and spiritual scales. These include measures of general religious attitudes, various forms of religiousness, and various aspects of spirituality. Table 1.1 lists examples of key measures that have been widely used in research and across different cultural/religious contexts. In addition, there exist measures of more specific religious constructs studied regularly in psychological research such as religious coping, God images, attachment to God, religious and spiritual development, religious doubt, mysticism, and prayer (see for a list of measures: Hill & Hood, 1999; and for updates: Cutting & Walsh, 2008; Kapuscinski & Masters, 2010).

In addition to typical concerns for psychometric qualities, specific considerations are of interest for a researcher or a student interested in selecting a measure of religiousness. Except if one focuses on groups of known (e.g., clearly high or no) religiousness, most studies are carried out on samples whose average religiousness reflects that of the general population. It is important thus to use measures that can be applied to participants varying in religiousness, that is, both believers and non-believers. Non-believers may find it meaningless and upsetting to answer a series of long multi-item scales that distinguish between many different religious and spiritual dimensions, forms, and practices with items that, in addition, presume respondents are religious. This may not only produce inaccurate responding (the non- or low religious may react by exaggerating their negative answers), but also reduce variability in the data because of the accumulation of scores at the extreme low end of religious continuous measures.

Note also that, if studying religiousness and related psychological processes is not the unique objective of the study, then few-item indexes of religiousness may work almost equally well than multi-item and multidimensional religious measures. Indeed, in samples with participants of average religiousness, various religious measures are often interrelated and provide similar results (Tsang & McCullough, 2003; Wolf, 2005). However, if the sample includes many highly religious participants, it is also important to avoid upsetting these participants when answering to items that only include global, and probably meaningless for them, statements (e.g., "How religious are you"?). This situation too will likely decrease response variability. In this case, it is reasonable to use specific measures detailing distinct religious constructs.

Overall, I suggest that, at least in a study where religiousness takes an important part in the hypotheses, an investigator include measures of (a) general, personal, intrinsic religiousness, (b) frequency of collective vs. private religious practice, (c) closed- vs. open minded religious attitudes (e.g., fundamentalism or quest), and (d) spirituality, as being independent from traditional religiosity. The above, although considerably interrelated, have consistently been found to predict distinct patterns of personality traits (Saroglou, 2010), values (Saroglou & Muñoz-García, 2008), and social behavior (Hunsberger & Jackson, 2005; Saroglou [with 14 co-authors], 2013). An obvious additional precaution is to check for the relevance of the measure's items with respect to the participants' religious affiliation or religious background.

Finally, the positioning of measures of religiousness in a survey protocol or in an experiment is a sensitive issue. Existing research suggests that simple administration of even few-item measures of religiousness at the beginning of a study acts as a religious prime (Ginges et al., 2009). Measuring individual differences on religiousness before measuring their outcomes or correlates induces the risk of increasing social desirability and conformity to religious stereotypes (e.g., I am religious, so I want to be perceived as prosocial; or I am religious, so I am of course prosocial). Ideally, individual religiousness should be measured much earlier (weeks ago) than the main experiment (e.g., with a brief religious measure hidden in a large set of measures). Alternatively, since pre-experimental administration is not always practically possible, measures of religiousness should be administered post-experimentally but after a distractor task. In surveys, such measures should be included at the very end of session.

Implicit Measures

Explicit measures of religiousness may to some extent be affected by social desirability and, in particular, impression management (Sedikides & Gebauer, 2010). Although research also shows that the relation between explicit religious measures and external outcomes is not totally due to social desirability (results most often remain significant after controlling for social desirability; Lewis, 1999, 2000; McCullough, Emmons, & Tsang, 2002; Regnerus & Uecker, 2007; Saroglou, Pichon, Trompette, Verschueren, & Dernelle, 2005), it is of interest also to implement alternative measures of religiousness such as implicit, projective, and behavioral ones.

The Implicit Association test typically uses reaction time as an indicator of a given construct when comparing pairs congruent with the construct (targets and attributes) with pairs incongruent with the construct. Implicit measures of religiousness have been in use. For instance, LaBouff, Rowatt, Johnson, Thedford, and Tsang (2010) found that some people made the associations of religious terms with the self and of non-religious terms with others more quickly than the associations of non-religious terms with the self and religious terms with others; these people were higher in several explicit measures of religiousness. Moreover, explicit and implicit measures of religiousness predicted similar social attitudes (antigay prejudice). In another study, after exposure to an argument against the existence of God, participants associated less quickly religious target words with words denoting truth versus words denoting non-truth (e.g., *true, real, valid* vs. *fake, false, untrue*); again, this implicit measure of religious belief was related to an explicit measure of religiousness (Shariff, Cohen, & Norenzayan, 2008). Other implicit associations apply to the concept of God. Meier, Hauser, Robinson, Friesen, and Schjeldahl (2007) found that participants implicitly used the metaphor of verticality and automatically associated God with "up" and devil with "down;" these implicit associations were stronger among believers.

In the above studies, there was a correspondence between explicit and implicit measures of religiousness and their respective outcomes. Interestingly, these two kinds of measure may produce different findings, which is informative of underlying process. In a recent experiment, when primed with death, believers and non-believers explicitly defended more strongly their respective religious and non-religious beliefs (i.e., supernatural entities exist vs. not). However, when the beliefs were measured implicitly, death priming increased all participants' beliefs in religious supernatural entities, regardless of their prior religious commitments (Jong, Halberstadt, & Bluemke, 2012). In other words, even non-believers endorsed theistic belief. In another recent study, preferences of one's own religious group comparatively to other religions were found in children when measured both implicitly and explicitly. However, adults, likely being more aware of social desirability demands, showed implicit but not explicit preferences (Heiphetz, Spelke, & Banaji, in press).

Behavioral Measures

Measuring religiousness behaviorally in general, and in particular as a dependent variable in lab experiments, is difficult, as such measures are sparse. Nevertheless, like the implicit measures, they may have the advantage, comparatively to self-report measures of religious attitudes and behaviors, of providing psychologically subtler and less socially desirable information. Indeed, over-reporting religious attendance, in comparison to objective indicators, is observed in Canada and the US, countries where religion is highly socially valued (but not in Europe; Brenner, 2011; Hadaway, Marler, & Chaves, 1993).

Behavioral intentions are easier to measure. For instance, in two recent studies, participants were asked to report their willingness to visit different destinations, including spiritual ones: Tibet or the way of Saint James of Compostela. They were asked so after induction of positive emotions (Van Cappellen & Saroglou, 2012) or memories of sexual experiences (Rigo & Saroglou, 2013). Other, more direct, religious behaviors can be investigated in the lab. For instance, God's closeness after activating attachment needs was tested in 5–7-year-old children, by asking them to place a God symbol on a two-dimensional felt board (Granqvist, Ljungdahl, & Dickie, 2007).

Interpreting Findings and Drawing Conclusions

Psychological research and findings on religion sometimes raise skepticism among outsiders about objectivity and reductionism. Moreover, among "insiders" (i.e., psychology researchers, students, reviewers), there exists occasionally some confusion, or at least debate, about: the status of spirituality within individual differences; the causal status of religion/religiousness with respect to human behavior; and the universal versus culturally specific nature of religion. I will comment briefly on these issues.

Objectivity

Psychological research on religion focuses on issues that researchers, students, and the public may feel personally relevant, be they religious, agnostics, or atheists. This invites prudence in deriving hypotheses, designing a study, interpreting results, and drawing conclusions. Fortunately, the more this research involves scholars from different cultural, religious, and convictional backgrounds, and the more findings are replicated through different methods, across samples from various cultural and religious contexts, and by independent laboratories, the more the reliability of findings and conclusions increases. The present volume was attentive to the sensitivity of these issues.

Reductionism

Scholars from other scientific disciplines are sometimes suspicious on whether psychology can study successfully such a complex phenomenon as religion without reducing it; or without having a personal experience of faith and religion. Both suspicions are unjustified. First, reductionism is by definition what each behavioral and social scientific discipline is expected to do, applying its own methodology to study a particular object. No sole discipline can fully explain a complex phenomenon. Second, even science as a multidisciplinary global enterprise is reductionist by principle. Psychologists, sociologists, and other scientists investigate and arrive at principles determining, at least partly, why people fall in love and with whom. Such knowledge is not sufficient to preclude the perception of the falling-in-love process as important, personally significant, and somewhat mysterious. Finally, the psychology of religion, like for instance the psychology of sport, may benefit from the personal experience of insiders but this is neither a necessary nor a sufficient condition; and it may present disadvantages too (e.g., eagerness to accept confirming evidence and to neglect disconfirming one). The same remarks apply, of course, to outsiders, that is, scholars who do not practice religion or sport.

Religion/Spirituality's Status within Individual Differences

Scholars and the public sometimes favor the idea that spirituality, as a broad term encompassing religious and non-religious forms, is (a) a universal and fundamental dimension of human existence and (b) a basic trait of personality, possibly additional to the existing major personality traits. For several reasons (Saroglou, 2011), most personality and social psychologists agree that this is not the case. The existential quest is certainly a universal human dimension, with individual differences on intensity, frequency, and forms. The same is true for many psychological needs. Spirituality and religion may have been, at least till now, present in all human societies. However, there are many people defining themselves as non-religious and non-spiritual, which is not a sign of psychological dysfunction. In addition, spirituality constitutes a specific way to deal with, or provide specific answers to, universal existential questions. Therefore, spirituality does not constitute a fundamental dimension of human functioning—at least no more than atheism, to take the opposite end of the continuum.

Unlike individual differences in basic and fundamental human dimensions (e.g., personal identity, personality traits, emotional intelligence, attachment), being spiritual is, strictly speaking, similar to being sporty. Lack of sport practice and sport-related beliefs does not mean missing an important part of what constitutes a person. On the contrary, missing a sense of identity or attachment bond does—at least for psychology. Finally, theory and empirical evidence suggest that religiousness/spirituality is rather a sui generis individual difference, closer, even if not restricted, to values and social attitudes rather than to personality traits (Saroglou, 2010; see also Ashton & Lee, Chapter 2, this volume).

Causality

The specificity of the psychological study of religion is to understand the *psychological* mechanisms that can explain why religion or religiousness co-occurs with, follows, or precedes other psychological characteristics and behaviors. Efforts to identify the psychological variables or processes that may statistically explain (in regressions and meditational analyses) in full the relations between religion and other outcomes are more than welcome. Having a successful explanatory model in which religious variables do not have additional power constitutes an ideal and not a limitation for a researcher. As psychologists, we need to understand for what reasons religious attitudes and behavior influence human behavior. It is thus misleading to confound statistical analyses and psychological understanding and conclude, for instance, that religion has no causal role on human behavior if its power has been fully explained in meditational analyses; or, on the contrary, that religion has "unique" power if its predictiveness remained significant beyond the effects of other predictor variables. Opposing religion's causal role with "secular" psychological mechanisms (Galen, 2012) is psychologically rather meaningless (Myers, 2012; Saroglou, 2012b).

The question of uniqueness of the processes under study is an interesting issue. Indeed, it is theoretically important to understand what the specific combination of common psychological processes is that makes religion's role with regard to different outcomes to be unique (i.e., different from other combinations of common psychological processes). Other than religion, domains of human activity may lead to similar effects. For instance, both religious supernatural beings and secular authorities increase moral behavior (Shariff & Norenzayan, 2007). However, they very likely do it through different combinations of underlying psychological mechanisms.

Generalizability

Scholars may sometimes perceive religion and religiousness as too personal and intimate, too individualized; or as too culturally specific (Belzen & Lewis, 2010). Undoubtedly, there is a large variability in religious expressions across religions, cultures, and historical periods. Religion interacts with many other non-religious, country-level cultural dimensions, which results in a large variety of culturally specific outcomes (Saroglou & Cohen, 2011; see also Johnson & Cohen, Chapter 15, this volume). However, and although systematic cross-cultural psychological research on religion is only emerging, there is also evidence that, to some extent, universals may exist in the psychological characteristics, predictors, functions, and effects of religion across cultures, religions, and societies (Saroglou, 2011; Saroglou & Cohen, 2013). Adopting thus, in the psychology of religion, excessive cultural relativism or excessive cultural universalism is empirically premature and seems unjustified.

A related issue is the question of whose religiousness has been studied through decades of personality and social psychological research. As in other domains of research, most studies on religion were carried out in Western contexts with most often participants of Christian (predominantly Protestant, but also Catholic) background. Fortunately, however, in the last 10–15 years, studies, including experimental ones, with participants of other religious background and/or from non-Western cultural contexts, have started to accumulate. Finally, the main body of scientific knowledge has relied on the "average" religiousness of "average" people. This is not necessarily a problem, as it provides a reasonably good global picture. Note, however, that the psychology of champions supplies additional information to what we know from the sport psychology of the average citizen. Similarly, the psychology of central religious figures (e.g., current or historical models) could add precious knowledge.

The Present Volume

In addition to current handbooks on psychology of/and religion/spirituality (Hood, Hill, & Spilka, 2009; Paloutzian & Park, 2013; Pargament, 2013), there exist more specific reference volumes that focus on religion and spirituality from a developmental (Roehlkepartain, King, Wagener,

& Benson, 2006), health/clinical (Koenig, King, & Carson, 2012), and neurocognitive (McNamara, 2006), but not social psychological, perspective. The present book aims thus to be distinct by (a) exclusively focusing on personality and social psychology as applied to the study *of* religion, (b) providing thoughtful and integrative review of the most recent empirical, especially experimental, evidence, and (c) including many chapters that are unique in topic, content, and treatment.

The chapter titles are clear. The reader can easily anticipate with what kinds of question each chapter is concerned. Therefore, I will avoid discussing each chapter in length. Rather, I will introduce below the structure of the volume and, for each chapter, highlight key issues.

Part I concerns the psychological understanding of religion at the intra-individual level, what refers to personality traits, self-needs, cognition, and emotions. Part II extends this understanding to the interpersonal, intergroup, and social spheres. This means knowledge about how religion interferes with prosocial behavior, intergroup relations, prejudice and antisocial behavior, values and morality, sexuality and family, political preferences, as well as social factors that influence mental health and well-being. Finally, religion's psychological functions do not operate identically across all humans. Part III focuses on three typical moderators of human psychology, i.e., age and developmental changes, gender and related psychological differences, as well as culture and national contexts.

In Chapter 2, Ashton and Lee review recent research on religiousness and personality (Five-Factor and HEXACO models) and extend the scope of the chapter on other individual differences (intelligence and education) as well as on genetic influences on religious attitudes. They also clarify the status of religiousness within individual differences as a whole. In Chapter 3, Sedikides and Gebauer propose an original integration of, mostly experimental, research having focused on the key needs related to the self and the way religion seems to satisfy or at least allows dealing with them. They convincingly argue for the role of religion regarding self-enhancing and agentic needs; and they show the importance of integrating the individual level of analysis with the country level of analysis.

Religion's functions are both cognitive and emotional in nature. In Chapter 4, Gervais examines religious cognition (e.g., God perception) as being part of broader common social cognition, built on the interaction between the social cognitive mechanisms that enable humans to perceive, represent, and reason about minds in the world and social cognitive mechanisms that enable cultural learning. The links between religion and emotions are treated in two distinct chapters, one focusing on negative emotions, the other focusing on positive ones. In Chapter 5, Burris and Petrican thoughtfully integrate evidence from various research areas, including neurophysiological and neurocognitive research, that help them to detail the complex links of religion in general, and religious experience in particular, with negative emotionality and its regulation.

They astutely point out religion's capacity to transform negative emotions into positive experience and vice versa. In Chapter 6, Van Cappellen and Rimé scrutinize the individual and social effects of positive emotions and their sharing, as experienced in collective rituals that comprise music and movement synchronization. They also review recent experimental evidence that attests also for the opposite causal direction where induction of self-transcendent positive emotions influences spirituality and related outcomes.

Chapters 7 and 8 deal with the classic big questions on the bright (prosociality) and dark (prejudice) sides of social attitudes and behaviors as a function of religion. Both chapters clearly adopt an original perspective. In Chapter 7, Preston, Salomon, and Ritter propose an integrative synthesis of the existing research on the role of situational factors that importantly moderate religion's effects on prosocial attitudes and behavior; and clarify the specificities of various sub-theories on religious prosociality having recently emerged from an evolutionary psychology perspective. In Chapter 8, Rowatt, Carpenter, and Haggard integrate the existing substantial research on religion/religiousness and prejudice towards a variety of outgroups, in terms of explicit and implicit attitudes and behavior, into classic and more contemporary (e.g., terror management and evolutionary) social psychological theories on prejudice and discrimination.

Religious morality has to do with (pro)social concerns at the interpersonal and intergroup levels, but also with other concerns that have to do with societal norms emphasizing group loyalty and purity toward the divine. This is a common underlying feature in the next three chapters. Roccas and Elster, in Chapter 9, review research from a large number of studies across nations and religions that provide a coherent picture on how religiousness and forms of it reflect specific value hierarchies. They also examine the role of religion on the correspondence between values and behavior and on dealing with multiple identities implying conflicting values. Li and Cohen, in Chapter 10, focus on the way religion influences sexual attitudes and behavior, as well as family issues, mainly marriage and parenthood. They propose an evolutionary understanding of the role religion has played with regard to mating, sexuality, and family. In Chapter 11, Malka reviews key evidence from both US and international studies and analyzes important new data that clarify how individual religiousness or religious denomination lead to specific political preferences. These refer to conservatism versus liberalism in two major domains: the moral (sex and family) and economic (government intervention in economic life) spheres.

A chapter on health may be less common in social psychology books. However, it is of interest to examine how several kinds of social factor, related to the individual, the (religious) group, or the culture, may influence and explain different aspects of mental health and well-being of believers and religious practitioners. This is successfully done in Chapter

12 by Hayward and Krause who demonstrate how the religious dimensions of belonging, being, and believing impact well-being.

Religion and its psychological determinants and outcomes are not static. Important developments are observed at different age periods. In Chapter 13, Granqvist finely reviews research on religion and cognitive, emotional, and social development across the lifespan, with a particular emphasis on childhood and adolescence. He integrates the above three domains of development in order to understand how the link between religion and attachment to significant others evolves with age. In addition to age, gender also moderates religiousness. In Chapter 14, Francis and Penny review classic and contemporary psychological and sociological theories that intend to elucidate a rather pervasive phenomenon, at least in Western Christianity: Why do women seem to be more religious than men? Is it due to psychological or sociological factors? Is this gender effect independent from the aspect of religiousness measured? Does it extend to other religions? No doubt, the last question underlines the importance of having Chapter 15 dealing with religion and culture. Johnson and Cohen analyze different forms that take the relations between religion, being itself a cultural system, with other, non-religious, cultural components of the "national" culture; and they introduce intriguing questions for future research that concern the reciprocal links between religion and increasing globalization.

The concluding Chapter 16 provides an integration of psychological theory and empirical evidence that may help researchers to understand (a) what are the specificities in the way religion is involved with common and universal psychological processes and functions, and (b) why there are important and pervasive individual differences in religiousness. The chapter concludes with directions for future research.

Acknowledgments

The writing of this chapter benefited from Grant ARC08/13-013 from the Communauté Française de Belgique. I am grateful to Constantine Sedikides for very helpful comments on an earlier version of the chapter.

References

Allport, G. W., & Ross, J. M. (1967). Personal religious orientation and prejudice. *Journal of Personality and Social Psychology, 5*, 432–443.

Altemeyer, B., & Hunsberger, B. (1992). Authoritarianism, religious fundamentalism, quest and prejudice. *International Journal for the Psychology of Religion, 2*, 113–133.

Altemeyer, B., & Hunsberger, B. (2005). Fundamentalism and authoritarianism. In R. F. Paloutzian & C. L. Park (Eds.), *Handbook of the psychology of religion and spirituality* (pp. 378–393). New York: Guilford.

Ashton, M. (2007). *Individual differences and personality.* New York: Academic Press.

Atran, S. (2007). Religion's social and cognitive landscape: An evolutionary perspective. In S. Kitayama & D. Cohen (Eds.), *Handbook of cultural psychology* (pp. 417–453). New York: Guilford.

Barrett, D. A. (2001). *World Christian encyclopedia* (2nd ed.). New York: Oxford University Press.

Batson, C. D., Denton, D. M., & Vollemecke, J. T. (2008). Quest religion, anti-fundamentalism, and limited versus universal compassion. *Journal for the Scientific Study of Religion, 47,* 135–145.

Batson, C. D., Schoenrade, P., & Ventis, W. L. (1993). *Religion and the individual: A social-psychological perspective.* New York: Oxford University Press.

Baumeister, R. F. (Ed.). (2002). Religion and psychology [Special issue]. *Psychological Inquiry, 13*(3).

Beit-Hallahmi, B., & Argyle, M. (1997). *The psychology of religious behaviour, belief and experience.* London: Routledge.

Belzen, J. A. (2009). Studying the specificity of spirituality: Lessons from the psychology of religion. *Mental Health, Religion, and Culture, 12,* 205–222.

Belzen, J. A., & Lewis, C. A. (Eds.). (2010). Cultural psychology of religion [Special issue]. *Mental Health, Religion, and Culture, 13*(4).

Blogowska, J., & Saroglou, V. (2011). Religious fundamentalism and limited prosociality as a function of the target. *Journal for the Scientific Study of Religion, 50,* 44–60.

Brandt, M. J., & Renya, C. (2010). The role of prejudice and the need for closure in religious fundamentalism. *Personality and Social Psychology Bulletin, 36,* 715–725.

Brenner, P. S. (2011). Exceptional behavior or exceptional identity? Overreporting of church attendance in the U.S. *Public Opinion Quarterly, 75,* 19–41.

Clobert, M., & Saroglou, V. (2013). Intercultural non-conscious influences: Prosocial effects of Buddhist priming on Westerners of Christian tradition. *International Journal for Intercultural Relations, 37,* 391–398.

Cohen, A. B., Hall, D. E., Koenig, H. G., & Meador, K. G. (2005). Social versus individual motivation: Implications for normative definitions of religious orientation. *Personality and Social Psychology Review, 9,* 48–61.

Cutting, M., & Walsh, M. (2008). Religiosity scales: What are we measuring in whom? *Archive for the Psychology of Religion, 30,* 137–153.

Deconchy, J.-P. (1980). *Orthodoxie religieuse et sciences humaines [Religious orthodoxy and human sciences].* The Hague: Mouton.

Emmons, R. A., Barrett, J. L., & Schnitker, S. A. (2008). Personality and the capacity for religious and spiritual experience. In O. P. John, R. W. Robins, & L. A. Pervin (Eds.), *Handbook of personality: Theory and research* (3rd ed., pp. 634–653). New York: Guilford.

Emmons, R. A., & McCullough, M. E. (Eds.). (1999). Religion in the psychology of personality [Special issue]. *Journal of Personality, 67*(6).

Flanagan, K., & Jupp, P. C. (Eds.). (2007). *A sociology of spirituality.* Burlington, VT: Ashgate.

Flere, S., & Lavrič, M. (2008). Is intrinsic religious orientation a culturally specific American Protestant concept? The fusion of intrinsic and extrinsic religious orientations among non-Protestants. *European Journal of Social Psychology, 38,* 521–530.

Fontaine, J. R. J., Duriez, B., Luyten, P., Corveleyn, J., & Hutsebaut, D. (2005). Consequences of a multi-dimensional approach to religion for the relationship between religiosity and value priorities. *International Journal for the Psychology of Religion, 15,* 123–143.

Fontaine, J. R. J., Duriez, B., Luyten, P., & Hutsebaut, D. (2003). The internal structure of the Post-Critical Belief scale. *Personality and Individual Differences, 35,* 501–518.

Francis, L. J. (2009). Understanding the attitudinal dimensions of religion and spirituality. In M. de Souza, L. J. Francis, J. O'Higgins-Norman, & D. G. Scott (Eds.), *International handbook of education for spirituality, care, and wellbeing* (pp. 147–167). New York: Springer.

Galen, L. W. (2012). Does religious belief promote prosociality? A critical examination. *Psychological Bulletin, 138,* 876–906.

Ginges, J., Hansen, I., & Norenzayan, A. (2009). Religion and support for suicide attacks. *Psychological Science, 20,* 224–230.

Gorsuch, R. L., & McPherson, S. E. (1989). Intrinsic/Extrinsic measurement: I/E-revised and single-item scales. *Journal for the Scientific Study of Religion, 28,* 348–354.

Granqvist, P., & Hagekull, B. (1999). Religiousness and perceived childhood attachment: Profiling socialized correspondence and emotional compensation. *Journal for the Scientific Study of Religion, 38,* 254–273.

Granqvist, P., Ljungdahl, C., & Dickie, J. R. (2007). God is nowhere, God is now here: Attachment activation, security of attachment (SAT), and God proximity among 5–7-year-old children. *Attachment and Human Development, 9,* 55–71.

Hadaway, C. K., Marler, P. L., & Chaves, M. (1993). What the polls don't show: A closer look at U.S. church attendance. *American Sociological Review, 58,* 741–752.

Hansen, I. G., & Norenzayan, A. (2006). Between yang and yin and heaven and hell: Untangling the complex relationship between religion and intolerance. In P. McNamara (Ed.), *Where God and science meet: How brain and evolutionary studies alter our understanding of religion* (Vol. 3, pp. 187–211). Westport, CT: Praeger.

Heiphetz, L., Spelke, E. S., & Banaji, M. R. (in press). Patterns of implicit and explicit attitudes in children and adults: Tests in the domain of religion. *Journal of Experimental Psychology: General.*

Hill, P. C., & Hood, R. W., Jr. (Eds.). (1999). *Measures of religiosity.* Birmingham, AL: Religious Education Press.

Hill, P. C., & Pargament, K. I. (2003). Advances in the conceptualization and measurement of religion and spirituality: Implications for physical and mental health research. *American Psychologist, 58,* 64–74.

Hood, R. W., Jr., Hill, P. C., & Spilka, B. (2009). *The psychology of religion: An empirical approach* (4th ed.). New York: Guilford.

Hunsberger, B., & Altemeyer, B. (2006). *Atheists: A groundbreaking study of America's nonbelievers.* Amherst, NY: Prometheus Books.

Hunsberger, B., & Jackson, L. M. (2005). Religion, meaning, and prejudice. *Journal of Social Issues, 61,* 807–826.

James, W. (1985). *The varieties of religious experience: A study in human nature.* Cambridge, MA: Harvard University Press. (Original work published 1902)

Jong, J., Halberstadt, J., & Bluemke, M. (2012). Foxhole atheism, revisited: The effects of mortality salience on explicit and implicit religious belief. *Journal of Experimental Social Psychology, 48,* 983–989.

Kapuscinski, A. N., & Masters, K. S. (2010). The current status of measures of spirituality: A critical review of scale development. *Psychology of Religion and Spirituality, 2,* 191–205.

Kirkpatrick, L. A. (2005). *Attachment, evolution, and the psychology of religion.* New York: Guilford.

Kirkpatrick, L. A., Hood, R. W., Jr., & Hartz, G. W. (1991). Fundamentalist religion conceptualized in terms of Rokeach's theory of the open and closed mind: A theoretical model and its implications for mental health. In M. Lynn & D. Moberg (Eds.), *Research in the Social Scientific Study of Religion* (Vol. 3, pp. 157–170). Greenwich, CT: JAI Press.

Koenig, H., King, D., & Carson, V. B. (2012). *Handbook of religion and health* (2nd ed.). New York: Oxford University Press.

LaBouff, J. P., Rowatt, W. C., Johnson, M. K., Thedford, M., & Tsang, J. (2010). Development and initial validation of an implicit measure of religiousness-spirituality. *Journal for the Scientific Study of Religion, 49,* 439–455.

Leary, M. R., & Hoyle, R. H. (Eds.). (2009). *Handbook of individual differences in social behavior.* New York: Guilford.

Lewis, C. A. (1999). Is the relationship between religiosity and personality "contaminated" by social desirability as assessed by the Lie Scale?: A methodological reply to Michael W. Eysenck (1998). *Mental Health, Religion, and Culture, 2,* 105–114.

Lewis, C. A. (2000). The religiosity-psychoticism relationship and the two factors of social desirability: A response to Michael W. Eysenck (1999). *Mental Health, Religion, and Culture, 3,* 39–45.

Lim, C., MacGregor, C. A., & Putnam, R. D. (2010). Secular and liminal: Discovering heterogeneity among religious nones. *Journal for the Scientific Study of Religion, 49,* 596–618.

McCullough, M. E., Emmons, R. A., & Tsang, J.-A. (2002). The grateful disposition: A conceptual and empirical topography. *Journal of Personality and Social Psychology, 82,* 112–127.

McNamara, P. (Ed.). (2006). *Where God and science meet: How brain and evolutionary studies alter our understanding of religion* (3 vols.). Westport, CT: Praeger.

Meier, B. P., Hauser, D. J., Robinson, M. D., Friesen, C. K., & Schjeldahl, K. (2007). What's "up" with God?: Vertical space as a representation of the divine. *Journal of Personality and Social Psychology, 93,* 699–710.

Myers, D. G. (2012). Reflections on religious belief and prosociality: Comment on Galen (2012). *Psychological Bulletin, 138,* 913–917.

Neyrinck, B., Lens, W., Vansteenkiste, M., & Soenens, B. (2010). Updating Allport's and Batson's framework of religious orientations: A reevaluation from the perspective of self-determination theory and Wulff's social cognitive model. *Journal for the Scientific Study of Religion, 49,* 425–455.

Norenzayan, A., & Hansen, I. G. (2006). Belief in supernatural agents in the face of death. *Personality and Social Psychology Bulletin, 32,* 174–187.

Paloutzian, R. F., & Park, C. L. (Eds.). (2013). *Handbook of the psychology of religion and spirituality* (2nd ed.). New York: Guilford.

Pancer, S. M., Jackson, L. M., Hunsberger, B., Pratt, M., & Lea, J. (1995). Religious orthodoxy and the complexity of thought about religious and non-religious issues. *Journal of Personality, 63,* 213–232.

Pargament, K. I. (Ed.). (2013). *APA handbook of psychology, religion, and spirituality* (2 vols.). Washington, DC: American Psychological Association.

Pargament, K. I., Fueille, M., & Burdzy, D. (2011). The Brief RCOPE: Current psychometric status of a short measure of religious coping. *Religions, 2,* 51–76.

Pargament, K. I., Koenig, H. G., & Perez, L. M. (2000). The many methods of religious coping: Development and initial validation of the RCOPE. *Journal of Clinical Psychology, 56,* 519–543.

Pichon, I., Boccato, G., & Saroglou, V. (2007). Nonconscious influences of religion on prosociality: A priming study. *European Journal of Social Psychology, 37,* 1032–1045.

Piedmont, R. L. (1999). Does spirituality represent the sixth factor of personality? Spiritual transcendence and the five-factor model. *Journal of Personality, 67,* 985–1013.

Plante, T. G., & Boccaccini, M. T. (1997). The Santa Clara Strength of Religious Faith Questionnaire. *Pastoral Psychology, 45,* 375–387.

Preston, J. L., Ritter, R. S., & Hermandez, J. I. (2010). Principles of religious prosociality: A review and reformulation. *Social and Personality Psychology Compass, 4,* 574–590.

Regnerus, M. G., & Uecker, J. E. (2007). Religious influences on sensitive self-reported behaviors: The product of social desirability, deceit, or embarrassment? *Sociology of Religion, 68,* 145–163.

Rhodewalt, F. (Ed.). (2008). *Personality and social behavior.* New York: Psychology Press.

Rigo, C., & Saroglou, V. (2013, August). Induction of sexual thoughts and affects decreases religiousness-spirituality. In V. Saroglou (Chair), *Religion, sexuality, and sexism: Causal directions and explanatory processes.* Symposium conducted at the 121st American Psychological Association Convention, Honolulu, Hawaii.

Roehlkepartain, E. C., King, P. E., Wagener, L. M., & Benson, P. L. (Eds.). (2006). *The handbook of spiritual development in childhood and adolescence.* Thousand Oaks, CA: Sage.

Saroglou, V. (2003). Spiritualité moderne: Un regard de psychologie de la religion [Modern spirituality: A psychology of religion perspective]. *Revue Théologique de Louvain, 34,* 473–504.

Saroglou, V. (2010). Religiousness as a cultural adaptation of basic traits: A Five Factor Model perspective. *Personality and Social Psychology Review, 14,* 108–125.

Saroglou, V. (2011). Believing, bonding, behaving, and belonging: The big four religious dimensions and cultural variation. *Journal of Cross-Cultural Psychology, 42,* 1320–1340.

Saroglou, V. (2012a). Are we born to be religious? Genes and personality influence our attitudes toward religion. *Scientific American Mind, 23*(2), 52–57.

Saroglou, V. (2012b). Is religion not prosocial at all? Comment on Galen (2012). *Psychological Bulletin, 138,* 907–912.

Saroglou, V. (2013). Religion, spirituality, and altruism. In K. I. Pargament, J. J. Exline, & J. W. Jones (Eds.), *APA handbook of psychology, religion and spirituality* (Vol. 1, pp. 439–457). Washington, DC: American Psychological Association.

Saroglou, V. (with 13 co-authors of the International Project on the Psychology of Fundamentalism) (2012, July). Fundamentalism versus spirituality and readiness for existential quest: Do religions and cultures differ? In V. Saroglou & W. J. Lonner (Chairs), *Religion, culture, and acculturation: From social minds to well-being.* Symposium conducted at the 21st International Association for Cross-Cultural Psychology Congress, Stellenbosch, South Africa.

Saroglou, V. (with 14 co-authors of the International Project on the Psychology of Fundamentalism) (2013). [Measuring the four basic religious dimensions across cultures: Believing, bonding, behaving and belonging.] Unpublished raw data.

Saroglou, V., & Cohen, A. B. (Eds.). (2011). Religion and culture: Perspectives from cultural and cross-cultural psychology [Special issue]. *Journal of Cross-Cultural Psychology, 42*(8).

Saroglou, V., & Cohen, A. B. (2013). Cultural and cross-cultural psychology of religion. In R. F. Paloutzian & C. L. Park (Eds.), *Handbook of the psychology of religion and spirituality* (2nd ed., pp. 330–353). New York: Guilford.

Saroglou, V., Corneille, O., & Van Cappellen, P. (2009). "Speak, Lord, your servant is listening": Religious priming activates submissive thoughts and behaviors. *International Journal for the Psychology of Religion, 19,* 143–154.

Saroglou, V., & Mathijsen, F. (2007). Religion, multiple identities, and acculturation: A study of Muslim immigrants in Belgium. *Archive for the Psychology of Religion, 29,* 177–198.

Saroglou, V., & Muñoz-García, A. (2008). Individual differences in religion and spirituality: An issue of personality traits and/or values. *Journal for the Scientific Study of Religion, 47,* 83–101.

Saroglou, V., Pichon, I. Trompette, L., Verschueren, M., & Dernelle, R. (2005). Prosocial behavior and religion: New evidence based on projective measures and peer ratings. *Journal for the Scientific Study of Religion, 44,* 323–348.

Saucier, G., & Skrzypińska, K. (2006). Spiritual but not religious? Evidence for two independent dispositions. *Journal of Personality, 74,* 1257–1292.

Sedikides, C. (Ed.). (2010). Religiosity: Perspectives from social psychology and personality psychology [Special issue]. *Personality and Social Psychology Review, 14*(1).

Sedikides, C., & Gebauer, J. E. (2010). Religiosity as self-enhancement: A meta-analysis of the relation between socially desirable responding and religiosity. *Personality and Social Psychology Review, 14,* 17–36.

Shariff, A. F., Cohen, A. B., & Norenzayan, A. (2008). The Devil's advocate: Secular arguments diminish both implicit and explicit religious beliefs. *Journal of Cognition and Culture, 8,* 417–423.

Shariff, A. F., & Norenzayan, A. (2007). God is watching you: Priming God concepts increases prosocial behavior in an anonymous economic game. *Psychological Science, 18*, 803–809.

Siegers, P. (2011). A multiple group latent class analysis of religious orientations in Europe. In E. Davidov, P. Schmidt, & J. Billiet (Eds.), *Cross-cultural analysis: Methods and applications* (pp. 385–412). New York: Routledge.

Soenens, B., Neyrinck, B., Vansteenkiste, M., Dezutter, J., Hutsebaut, D., & Duriez, B. (2012). How do perceptions of God as autonomy supportive or controlling relate to individuals' social-cognitive processing of religious contents? The role of motives for religious behavior. *International Journal for the Psychology of Religion, 22*, 10–30.

Streib, H., Hood, R. W., Keller, B., Csöff, R., & Silver, C. F. (2008). *Deconversion: Qualitative and quantitative results from cross-cultural research in Germany and the United States of America.* Göttingen: Vandenhoeck & Ruprecht.

Tsang, J., & McCullough, M. E. (2003). Measuring religious constructs: A hierarchical approach to construct organization and scale selection. In C. R. Snyder (Ed.), *Handbook of positive psychological assessment* (pp. 345–360). Washington, DC: American Psychological Association.

Vail, K. E., III, Juhl, J., Arndt, J., Vess, M., Routledge, C., & Rutjens, B. T. (2012). When death is good for life: Considering the positive trajectories of terror management. *Personality and Social Psychology Review, 16*, 303–329.

Van Cappellen, P., & Saroglou, V. (2012). Awe activates religious and spiritual feelings and behavioral intentions. *Psychology of Religion and Spirituality, 4*, 223–236.

Van Pachterbeke, M., Freyer, C., & Saroglou, V. (2011). When authoritarianism meets religion: Sacrificing others in the name of abstract deontology. *European Journal of Social Psychology, 41*, 898–903.

Vilaythong, O. T., Lindner, N. M., & Nosek, B. A. (2011). "Do unto others": Effects of priming the Golden Rule on Buddhists' and Christians' attitudes toward gay people. *Journal for the Scientific Study of Religion, 49*, 494–506.

Voas, D. (2007). Surveys of behaviour, beliefs and affiliation: Micro-quantitative. In J. A. Beckford & N. J. Demerath, III (Eds.), *The Sage handbook of the sociology of religion* (pp. 144–166). London: Sage.

Wolf, C. (2005). Measuring religious affiliation and religiosity in Europe. In J. H. P. Hoffmeyer-Zlotnik & J. Harkness (Eds.), *Methodological aspects in cross-national research* (ZUMA-Nachrichten Spezial 11) (pp. 279–294). Mannheim: ZUMA.

Wulff, D. M. (1997). *Psychology of religion: Classic and contemporary* (2nd ed.). New York: Wiley.

Zinnbauer, B. J., & Pargament, K. I. (2005). Religiousness and spirituality. In R. F. Paloutzian & C. L. Park (Eds.), *Handbook of the psychology of religion and spirituality* (pp. 21–42). New York: Guilford.

Zuckerman, P. (2011). *Faith no more: Why people reject religion.* New York: Oxford University Press.

Zuckerman, P. (2012). Contrasting irreligious orientations: Atheism and secularity in the USA and Scandinavia. *Approaching Religion, 2*, 8–20.

Part I

Personality, Cognition, and Emotions

2 Personality and Religiousness

Michael C. Ashton and Kibeom Lee

In many contemporary societies, people differ greatly in the extent of their religious belief and practice. Some persons reject all belief in the supernatural, whereas others have deep religious convictions that influence many aspects of their lives. Understanding the psychological characteristics that predispose persons toward religiousness is an important question for psychologists of religion and for psychologists who study individual differences.

In this chapter, we will review empirical findings about the links of religiousness with personality characteristics and related individual differences.

Religiousness as Distinct from Personality

Before examining the links between religiousness and personality characteristics, it is worthwhile to consider the question of whether or not religiousness is itself a personality characteristic (see Ashton, 2013, for a similar discussion). On the one hand, religiousness does share some features of personality characteristics. For example, religiousness manifests itself across diverse situations in a consistent pattern of thought (e.g., contemplation of God), feeling (e.g., spiritual awe), and behavior (e.g., attending services).

On the other hand, however, religiousness involves several features that are not observed for personality characteristics. These features can be organized in terms of Saroglou's (2011) four dimensions of religion and individual religiosity: believing, bonding, behaving, and belonging. Perhaps the most important of these is the central role of *believing*, insofar as a religious person accepts some propositions about the spiritual or supernatural world. In contrast, a person's level of any given personality dimension does not depend on any beliefs that he or she might hold. Also central to religion is *bonding*, in the sense that religion involves efforts to unite oneself with some transcendent reality, for example through solitary meditation or through group rituals. These exercises in self-transcendence are not necessarily implicated in any personality dimension, although some forms of aesthetic appreciation or introspection may be similar. With regard to *behaving*, another important feature that differentiates religiousness from personality characteristics is that religiousness frequently involves a distinct way of living intended to achieve harmony with God or with the universe. The lifestyle prescribed by a given religious tradition may influence a wide variety of specific behaviors that have no intrinsic similarity. For example, religions may prescribe many specific rules governing one's diet, dress, spending, leisure, and sexuality. Even though a given dimension of personality may also influence a broad array of behaviors, this influence is not in the form of specific rules that may seem arbitrary to non-believers. Finally, religion involves *belonging* to a community of believers, whereas no personality dimension is concerned with this specific form of group identity.

In discussing the status of religiousness in the context of personality, Saroglou (2010) drew on the distinction made by McCrae and Costa (2008) between endogenous basic traits of personality and cultural adaptations of personality. Endogenous basic traits represent biologically based tendencies that are heavily influenced by heredity and early biological factors, whereas cultural adaptations are acquired patterns of behavior that develop as a function of social interactions. Within this framework, religiousness would represent a cultural adaptation rather than an endogenous basic trait, even if such traits might heavily influence the expression of religiousness.

Personality Correlates of Religiousness

The Big Five Personality Factors

Saroglou (2010) meta-analyzed previous studies of the links between religiousness and the Big Five personality factors. His analysis distinguished between three kinds of religiousness variable—religiosity, spirituality (and mature faith), and fundamentalism—that he conceptualized as follows (see Saroglou, 2010, p. 109):

> Religiosity involves "beliefs and practices referring to a transcendent being and legitimized through an established tradition or group."
>
> Spirituality shares with Religiosity the importance of transcendence, but also emphasizes "individual experience and independence from established religious traditions and beliefs." Also classified under Spirituality is Mature Faith, which also involves "individuation and reflectivity in faith (critical consideration of beliefs)."
>
> Fundamentalism involves "authoritarian and dogmatic religious attitudes, beliefs, and practices," following the conceptualization of Altemeyer and Hunsberger (2005).

The 71 participant samples meta-analyzed by Saroglou were drawn mainly from societies with Christian religious traditions in Europe, North America, and Oceania. The participants of most samples were adults or young (college-age) adults, and across all studies about 61% of participants were women. Data on fundamentalism were available from nine samples (N = 1894), on spirituality from 28 samples (N = 9220), and on religiosity from 49 samples (N = 15246).

The personality variables examined in Saroglou's meta-analysis were those of the well-known Big Five or Five-Factor Model of personality structure (e.g., Goldberg, 1990; McCrae & John, 1992). These five dimensions are known as Extraversion (e.g., lively, outgoing versus passive, shy), Agreeableness (e.g., kind, gentle versus cold, harsh), Conscientiousness (e.g., organized, disciplined versus sloppy, lazy), Neuroticism (e.g., anxious, irritable versus relaxed), and Openness to Experience (e.g., complex versus unimaginative).

The results of Saroglou's meta-analysis indicated that all three religiousness variables—Religiosity, Spirituality/Mature Faith, and Fundamentalism—showed modest positive correlations with the Big Five personality factors of Agreeableness and Conscientiousness. The unweighted mean correlations for Agreeableness were .20, .22, and .13 for Religiosity, Spirituality/Mature Faith, and Fundamentalism, respectively; the corresponding unweighted mean correlations for Conscientiousness were .16, .13, and .12. In addition to these links, the Big Five Extraversion showed a modest link with Spirituality/Mature Faith, with an unweighted mean correlation of .15.

In contrast to the very similar relations shown by both the Big Five Agreeableness and Conscientiousness factors with all three religiousness variables, the Big Five openness to experience factor showed strikingly different relations with those three expressions of religiousness. Openness was associated with higher levels of Spirituality/Mature Faith (unweighted mean correlation .23) but with lower levels of Fundamentalism (weighted mean correlation −.22), and was not associated with Religiosity (weighted mean correlation −.02).

Because nearly all of the studies in Saroglou's meta-analysis were based on samples of Christian participants, it is not known whether these results would generalize across religions. However, Saroglou noted that three of the studies—conducted in Hong Kong, Iran, and Israel—were based on non-Christian participants. In these samples, the associations of the Big Five factors with Religiosity were similar to those obtained in the rest of the samples, as Big Five Agreeableness and Conscientiousness showed modest positive associations with Religiosity. These results give some initial hint that the links of personality with religiousness might be rather similar across religions and cultures.

The findings of Saroglou's meta-analysis can be summarized as follows. First, there is a modest tendency for more religious persons to be higher in the Big Five Agreeableness and Conscientiousness factors. These results suggest that religious people tend to be somewhat better socialized than non-religious persons, as the combination of Agreeableness and Conscientiousness suggests a responsible and polite style of behavior. Also, the form of religious expression is to some extent a function of Openness to Experience: high-Openness people are inclined toward spirituality, mysticism, and a quest-oriented form of faith; low-Openness people are inclined toward traditionalism, orthodoxy, and fundamentalism.

The HEXACO Personality Factors

In contrast to the numerous investigations of religiousness in relation to the Big Five personality factors, fewer studies have examined religiousness in relation to the HEXACO model of personality structure. The HEXACO framework, which originated in the results of lexical studies of personality structure as conducted in various languages, consists of six factors (Ashton & Lee, 2007). The HEXACO Extraversion (X), Conscientiousness (C), and Openness to Experience (O) factors are similar to their namesakes in the Big Five. The HEXACO Agreeableness (A) and Emotionality (E) factors are somewhat similar to Big Five Agreeableness and Neuroticism, respectively, but roughly represent rotated variants of those factors, such that sentimentality is part of HEXACO Emotionality (rather than Agreeableness) and that anger or quick temper is part of (low) HEXACO Agreeableness (rather than Emotionality). The HEXACO Honesty–Humility (H) factor has some overlap with the Big Five Agreeableness factor (and somewhat more overlap with some conceptualizations of Agreeableness), but also has some content not represented in the Big Five system. Specifically, Honesty–Humility represents personality traits representing tendencies to be fair, sincere, modest, and indifferent to material wealth. Previous research has shown that the HEXACO personality factors predict certain criteria better than do the Big Five personality factors, mainly because of the Honesty–Humility factor (Ashton & Lee, 2008).

One study that examined the links of the HEXACO personality factors with religiousness was that of Lee, Ogunfowora, and Ashton (2005). In that study of Canadian respondents, the measure of religious orientation was the religiosity scale of the Supernumerary Personality Inventory (SPI; Paunonen, 2002). In terms of Saroglou's framework, this variable clearly corresponds to the religiosity category. Lee et al. included self-report measures of the HEXACO personality factors and also of the Big Five. SPI religiosity showed modest positive correlations with Big Five Agreeableness ($r = .24$) and Conscientiousness ($r = .16$) but was unrelated to the other Big Five variables. Thus, these results are very similar to those observed in Saroglou's meta-analysis. With regard to the HEXACO variables, Religiosity was related to Honesty–Humility,

Emotionality, Agreeableness, and Conscientiousness (rs = .26, .16, .16, .13). The link with Conscientiousness is unsurprising, given the similarity of the HEXACO and Big Five versions of this factor. The links with Honesty–Humility, Emotionality, and Agreeableness are also expected, given that Big Five Agreeableness is related to all three of these factors.

In two recent reports, Aghababaei (2012; Aghababaei, Wasserman, & Nannini, in press) investigated religiosity in relation to the HEXACO personality factors. In both reports, measures of intrinsically oriented religiosity were administered along with personality self-reports in samples of Iranian university students. In both samples, religiosity was associated modestly (rs in the .20s and .30s) with the HEXACO Honesty–Humility and Agreeableness factors.

Beyond the studies using personality inventories, we should also note that religiosity has been found to predict behaviors that are conceptually related to Honesty–Humility, Agreeableness, and Conscientiousness. For example, with respect to the behaviors related to Honesty–Humility and Agreeableness, Ruiter and De Graaf (2006) reported in a study involving 53 countries that people with a religious affiliation are more likely to participate in unpaid volunteering activities than did non-religious people. Brooks (2006) reported that religious Americans donated more money than did non-religious Americans even when only secular donations were considered (mean annual secular donation per person: $532 versus $467). Religiousness was found to be associated positively with some prosocial behaviors observed in laboratory studies, especially when participants were primed with religion-related cues (Shariff & Norenzayan, 2007).

Religiousness has been linked to some behaviors that are influenced by self-control (an aspect of Conscientiousness), including risky/impulsive behaviors (Welch, Tittle, & Grasmick, 2006) and substance use (Walker, Ainette, Wills, & Mendoza, 2007). In addition, a study of Texas adults found that regular churchgoers were more likely to show health-promoting behaviors, which have elsewhere been found to correlate positively with Conscientiousness. These behaviors in the Texas study included walking, strenuous exercise, not smoking, moderate drinking, and use of preventive care, seatbelt, and vitamin (Hill, Burdette, Ellison, & Musick, 2006).

Can Social Desirability Explain the Personality–Religiosity Relations?

The studies investigating personality correlates of religiousness described above were based primarily on self-reports of personality characteristics. This may raise the concern that the findings could merely reflect a tendency for persons who are more religious to describe themselves as being high in Honesty–Humility, Agreeableness, and Conscientiousness, without really having high levels of those characteristics. Although many studies have shown that self-reports of personality characteristics tend to be substantially correlated with observer reports of the target person as provided by observers who know the target person well (e.g., Ashton & Lee, 2010), few studies have examined religiousness in relation to observer reports of personality. The results of those studies suggest that religiousness is also associated with observer reports of personality: McCullough, Tsang, and Brion (2003) found that teacher and parent ratings of adolescents' Big Five Agreeableness and Conscientiousness were related modestly to the adolescents' self-reported religiousness, and a similar result was reported by Saroglou and Fiasse (2003) for mothers' reports of young adults' personality in relation to those young adults' self-reported religiousness.

Personality–Religiosity Relations: Universal Across Culture?

Although the relations between personality and religiosity described above have been demonstrated in diverse cultures involving different religions, only a few studies have investigated directly the extent to which culture moderates these relationships. In one such study, Gebauer, Paulhus, and Neberich (2013) investigated how culture-level religiosity moderates the personality–religiosity relationship at the individual level. Specifically, the authors investigated how two broad aspects of personality known as communion (warmth, relatedness, and morality) and agency (competence, uniqueness, and ambition) were related to religiosity in 11 different countries. Gebauer et al. hypothesized that people high in the communal aspects of personality should be more religious if they live in a religious culture, because "communals" seek to assimilate into the predominant norms of the society. In contrast, people high in the agency aspects were hypothesized to be more religious if they live in non-religious cultures, because "agentics" seek to be unique from many others in the society. The data generally supported these hypotheses.[1] A similar finding was reported by Gebauer, Bleidorn, Gosling, Rentfrow, and Potter (2012), who examined the relations of the Big Five personality traits with religiosity in 66 countries. Given these findings, it seems that personality correlates of religiosity will vary somewhat depending on the culture in which those variables were measured.

Tradition-Oriented Religiousness and Subjective Spirituality

One particularly informative single study of the individual difference correlates of religious and spiritual tendencies was that of Saucier and Skrzypińska (2006). Using responses from the several hundred adults of the Eugene-Springfield (Oregon) Community Sample (Goldberg, 1999),

Saucier and Skrzypińska identified markers of two factors that they called Tradition-Oriented Religiousness (TR) and Subjective Spirituality (SS). Each factor was defined by a parallel set of three markers: for TR, self-rating of *religious*, the Experiences of Spirituality Inventory (ESI; MacDonald, 2000) Religiosity scale, and the Survey of Dictionary-Based Isms (SDI; Saucier, 2004) Alpha scale (emphasizing religious orthodoxy and literalism); for SS, self-rating of *mystical*, the ESI Spiritual Experiences scale, and the SDI Delta scale (emphasizing mystical and animistic spirituality). Some of the TR markers were essentially uncorrelated with some of the SS markers, suggesting that TR and SS are roughly independent factors.[2]

Saucier and Skrzypińska (2006) went on to examine the correlates of TR and SS, drawing on the vast array of individual difference variables that had been administered to their community sample over a period of more than a decade. Their findings largely confirmed their a priori hypotheses regarding the relations of TR and SS with these criteria. Both TR and SS showed strong correlations with Self-Transcendence, a broad measure of orientation toward the supernatural. But many other variables showed sharply differing patterns of correlations. TR correlated strongly with attitude scales measuring Right-Wing Authoritarianism and Traditionalism, and also correlated negatively with drug and alcohol use; SS, by contrast, was nearly uncorrelated with these variables, actually showing very small correlations opposite in sign to those yielded by TR. SS correlated strongly with measures of Magical Ideation, Absorption, and Fantasy Proneness, whereas TR was nearly uncorrelated with those variables. In addition, SS showed moderate positive correlations with self-reported eccentricity and with Religious Quest, whereas TR showed moderate negative correlations with both variables.

The contrast between TR and SS was illustrated neatly by their correlations with several attitude variables assessing respondents' attitudes regarding causal forces and various categories of persons. For example, TR was correlated positively with belief in the power of God snd with respect for those who study scriptures and those who obey the ten commandments, and correlated negatively with respect for evolution scientists; however, SS was uncorrelated with these variables (apart from a modest positive correlation with belief in the power of God). In contrast, SS was correlated positively with belief in the power of astrological influences and of magic, and with respect for psychics; however, TR was uncorrelated with these variables. A few variables actually showed opposite patterns of correlations with TR and SS: TR was correlated negatively with respect for feminists and for gays and lesbians, whereas SS showed small positive correlations with respect for these categories of person. However, both TR and SS were correlated positively with belief in the power of miracles, in the power of the supernatural, and with respect for enlightened persons.[3]

Personality and Religiousness: Causal Influences?

The fact that religiousness consistently shows at least modest correlations with certain aspects of personality raises the question of causal direction: does religiousness influence personality trait levels, does personality predispose certain persons to be religious, or both? Saroglou (2010) addressed these questions by reviewing the results of four longitudinal studies of religion and personality (Heaven & Ciarrochi, 2007; McCullough, Enders, Brion, & Jain, 2005; McCullough, Tsang, & Brion, 2003; Wink, Ciciolla, Dillon, & Tracy, 2007). The common finding of these studies was that personality as measured at earlier time points was associated with religiosity at later time points. Moreover, as Saroglou noted, other research findings have indicated that religious conversion influences various cultural adaptations of personality (e.g., values, goals, meaning in life, life stories), but that it does not influence personality trait levels (Paloutzian, Richardson, & Rambo, 1999). If the relation between personality and religiousness represents a causal influence of the former on the latter, then it is interesting to consider why it is that certain personality characteristics tend to promote religiousness. With regard to the opposing influences of Openness to Experience on Spirituality/Mature Faith and on Fundamentalism, it is likely that higher Openness to Experience—with its philosophical depth, imagination, and curiosity—simultaneously stimulates an interest in spiritual searching and undermines conformity with established dogma. With regard to the apparent influence on religiousness from Big Five Agreeableness (or with the three altruism-related HEXACO factors) and from conscientiousness, it is plausible that non-religious persons who are organized and or who are kind and sympathetic are more strongly attracted to religious beliefs and practices. Moreover, persons who are raised in a religious household are less likely to abandon their religion if they have high levels of these characteristics, which may motivate persons to maintain order and harmony in their family relationships.

"Amazing Apostates" and "Amazing Believers"

A potentially useful strategy for future research on the effects of personality on religiousness will be to focus specifically on persons who undergo major changes in religiousness, whether by abandoning the religion in which they were raised or by adopting a religion despite a secular upbringing. Some evidence of this kind has already been provided by Altemeyer and Hunsberger (1997). Those researchers identified young adults who had either abandoned religion despite being raised in a religious family or adopted religion despite being raised in a non-religious family. These two kinds of young adult—labeled as "amazing apostates" and "amazing believers" by Altemeyer and Hunsberger—were relatively rare, each representing less than 2% of the undergraduate student populations from which they were identified. Although Altemeyer and Hunsberger did not conduct any standardized personality assessments of their research participants, they did conduct some detailed interviews aimed at gaining information about their personalities.

The interviews suggested that the amazing apostates had experienced increasing doubt about their religion, being troubled by what they perceived as moral hypocrisy in religious persons and also by what they perceived as factual inaccuracy and logical inconsistency in religious teaching. The amazing apostates, who tended to be successful in their high school studies, had eventually decided after much reflection that they no longer sincerely believed in their religion.

The interviews with the amazing believers suggested a much different trajectory. The amazing believers had tended to make sudden conversions to their religion, typically after a period of intense personal crisis, such as that involving drug or alcohol abuse or the death of someone close. The conversion was accompanied by a sense of passion and emotion, and fulfilled a need for community and meaning.

Scientific Education, IQ, and Religiousness

Given that personality characteristics have only rather modest associations with general religiousness, it is interesting to consider other individual difference variables that might predispose people to be religious. If we frame this issue in terms of the variables that make people non-religious, then one candidate is exposure to science. Because the aim of science is to find the natural laws that explain our surroundings— from matter to life to behavior—it is plausible that endorsement of and engagement in the scientific process would make people less receptive to supernatural beliefs.

Some research findings do indicate that scientists are less likely to hold religious beliefs. One study in the 1990s found that whereas only 4% of the US public did not believe in God or any other higher power, 41% of US scientists were non-believers (Larson & Witham, 1997). A similar study reported that 45% of scientists were non-believers, and that this proportion rose to 72% among the highly accomplished scientists of the National Academy of Sciences (Larson & Witham, 1998). Although there remain many scientists (and even many distinguished scientists) who are religious, the proportion of non-believers among scientists is clearly much higher than in the general population. One potential explanation of these findings is that the field of science simply attracts the kind of people who would have rejected supernatural beliefs in any case. But as noted above, the links between personality characteristics and religiousness are not very strong. Furthermore, interest in science does not show particularly strong links to personality traits that are relevant to religiousness. For example, some unpublished analyses based on Goldberg's (1999) sample of Oregon community residents indicates that interest in science (as measured by the Science Basic Interest scale of the Campbell Interest and Skill Survey) is only modestly associated with high levels of HEXACO Openness to Experience ($r = .26$) and with low levels of Honesty–Humility ($r = -.20$), Emotionality ($r = -.25$), and Agreeableness ($r = -.16$). Therefore, it seems unlikely that the distinctively high rate of non-believers among scientists could be fully explained by self-selection based on personality characteristics.

Another potential explanation for the skepticism of scientists is their high level of general mental ability, to the extent that higher IQ is associated with greater skepticism. But the link between IQ and non-religiousness is rather weak: For example, a very large sample study of US teenagers (Nyborg, 2009) found that atheists averaged about five IQ points (i.e., about one-third of a standard deviation) higher than the general population. (An even smaller difference is observed in data from the Scholastic Aptitude Test (SAT) college entrance examination that is taken by US high school students: In 1999, students who indicated "no preference" as their religious denomination averaged less than one-quarter of a standard deviation above all other students, in unpublished data from the Educational Testing Service.) A subsequent study involving a large sample of American adults (mean age over 48) showed a similar pattern of the findings (Lewis, Ritchie, & Bates, 2011). The researchers examined several aspects of religiousness, and found that IQ was negatively associated with religiousness-related variables, particularly with tradition-oriented religiousness, such as religious fundamentalism, religious identification, and private religious practice. The strongest correlation involving IQ and any religious variable, however, was only $-.25$, which was observed for religious fundamentalism.

Although the negative relationship between IQ and religiosity has robustly been found, the extent to which these two variables are related is much too small to explain the remarkably higher rate of non-believers among scientists than among the general public. The above findings suggest that the rather low level of religiousness among scientists is not chiefly due to their personality characteristics or their IQ. Their skepticism instead seems more likely to be due to their study of science and their commitment to the scientific method.

Heritability of Religiousness

A recurrent finding in research on personality and other individual differences is that much of the variation between individuals is attributable to heredity (e.g., see summary in Ashton, 2013).

Some evidence suggests that the heritability of religiousness tends to be rather low when assessed during adolescence, but then becomes considerably stronger during adulthood. Koenig, McGue, Krueger, and Bouchard (2005) examined the heritability of religiousness by studying many pairs of fraternal and identical twins. They compared the similarity in religiousness within fraternal twin pairs with the similarity in religiousness within identical twin pairs. Religiousness was assessed by current self-reports of religiousness and by retrospective self-reports of religiousness when growing up; the religiousness scale items focused on the personal importance of religion and the frequency of religious actions (e.g., prayer, scripture reading, service attendance, family discussion). The findings of Koenig et al. showed that identical twins were very similar in religiousness while growing up (correlations in the .70s), and maintained that similarity even when in their 30s (correlations in the .60s). But their findings showed a different pattern for fraternal twins, who were very similar in religiousness while growing up (correlations about .60), but then considerably less similar when in their 30s (correlations about .40). Presumably, the similarity observed for both identical and fraternal twins while growing up was due to the influence of the common environment—that is, being raised in the same family—and this influence had diminished considerably by the time that the twins had reached their 30s. By that time, genetic influences on religiousness became relatively more prominent; these influences were strong enough to maintain the similarity in religiousness for identical twins (who share 100% of their genes), but not for fraternal twins (who share 50% of their genes). Koenig et al. estimated on the basis of these results that the heritability of religiousness increased from under .15 before adulthood to above .40 during adulthood, and that the common environment influence on religiousness decreased from at least .50 before adulthood to below .20 during adulthood.

Koenig et al.'s (2005) investigation was a retrospective study where twin participants had to recall how religious they were in the past while reporting how religious they currently are. Similar findings have been reported in prospective longitudinal studies, where twin participants report on religiousness-related variables on two occasions several years apart (see Button, Stallings, Rhee, Corley, & Hewitt, 2011; Koenig, McGue, & Iacono, 2008). For example, Koenig et al. (2008) obtained self-reports of religiousness on two occasions separated by several years from a sample of twin adolescents (first at age 14 and then at age 18), and from a sample of twin young adults (first at age 20 and then at age 25). In both samples, identical twin correlations remained virtually the same (i.e., correlations in the .70s) across Time 1 and Time 2, whereas fraternal twin correlations showed noticeable decreases from Time 1 to Time 2. A larger decrease was observed for the young adult sample of fraternal twins, which may suggest that the genetic effects on religiousness start taking place from late adolescence and young adulthood.

An interesting question for future research is to examine the extent to which the genetic influence on religiousness is mediated by personality characteristics. For example, heritable influences on conscientiousness and Big Five agreeableness (or HEXACO Honesty–Humility, Emotionality, and Agreeableness) might be responsible for part of the heritability of religiousness. Also, to the extent that the religiousness variable studied by Koenig et al. included some element of fundamentalism, genetic influences on (low) Openness to Experience might also be implicated. Although there have been some previous studies examining the mediating roles that some individual difference variables play in explaining the heritability of religiousness (D'Onofrio, Eaves, Murrelle, Maes, & Spilka, 1999; Lewis & Bates, 2013), no study has yet been conducted within the framework of the FFM or of the HEXACO model of personality.

Conclusions

The findings reported in this chapter suggest the following conclusions about the links of religiousness with personality characteristics:

1. Religiousness is modestly associated with higher levels of personality dimensions relevant to being well socialized, such as Big Five Conscientiousness and Agreeableness or HEXACO Conscientiousness, Honesty–Humility, Agreeableness, and Emotionality.
2. Different forms of religiousness have opposing relations with the Big Five or HEXACO Openness to Experience factor: Higher Openness is associated with more spirituality but less fundamentalism.
3. The results of longitudinal research findings suggest that the primary causal influence is from personality to religiousness rather than the other way around.
4. Scientific education is associated with low religiousness, and this link is not explained by personality or by IQ (which is only modestly associated with low religiousness).
5. Common environment influences on religiousness decrease between adolescence and middle age, whereas genetic influences increase.

Several questions about the personality bases of religiousness remain largely unanswered and can be examined in future research. For example, we have as yet only a limited understanding of how the associations of personality with religiousness differ across cultures and across religions, but it is likely that new findings will accumulate rapidly in the years ahead. Also, it is not yet known to what extent the heritability of religiousness can be attributed to the influence of heritable personality characteristics or of other heritable psychological characteristics. And finally, beyond examining the influence of personality and other individual differences, future research can also examine the independent role of social-psychological forces (e.g., religious peer influences, religious communities, personal crises) in explaining variation in religiousness.

Notes

1 As with the findings in previous studies, the relation between positive agency and religiosity was fairly weak even in the non-religious countries included in the study (*r*s generally in the .10s), which nevertheless tends to be somewhat stronger than what was found in religious countries.

2 The content of the TR factor suggests that it is somewhat intermediate between the religiosity and fundamentalism variables of Saroglou's meta-analysis, but slightly closer to the former. Saroglou classified the TR factor as a religiosity scale.

3 Many of the variables associated with TR and SS listed here are suggestive of lower or higher levels of openness to experience, respectively. Saucier and Skrzypińska reported that NEO-PI-R openness to experience correlated −.26 with TR and .40 with SS.

References

Aghababaei, N. (2012). Religious, honest, and humble: Looking for the religious person within the HEXACO model of personality structure. *Personality and Individual Differences*, *53*, 880–883.

Aghababaei, N., Wasserman, J. A., & Nannini, D. (in press). The religious person revisited: Cross-cultural evidence from the HEXACO model of personality structure. *Mental Health, Religion, and Culture*.

Altemeyer, B., & Hunsberger, B. (1997). *Amazing conversions: Why some turn to faith and others abandon religion*. Amherst, NY: Prometheus.

Altemeyer, B., & Hunsberger, B. (2005). Fundamentalism and authoritarianism. In R. F. Paloutzian & C. L. Park (Eds.), *Handbook of the psychology of religion and spirituality* (pp. 378–393). New York: Guilford.

Ashton, M. C. (2013). *Individual differences and personality* (2nd ed.). San Diego: Academic Press.

Ashton, M. C., & Lee, K. (2007). Empirical theoretical and practical advantages of the HEXACO model of personality structure. *Personality and Social Psychology Review*, *11*, 150–166.

Ashton, M. C., & Lee, K. (2008). The prediction of honesty-humility-related criteria by the HEXACO and Five-Factor models of personality. *Journal of Research in Personality*, *42*, 1216–1228.

Ashton, M. C., & Lee, K. (2010). Trait and source factors in HEXACO-PI-R: Self- and observer reports. *European Journal of Personality*, *24*, 278–289.

Brooks, A. C. (2006). *Who really cares: The surprising truth about compassionate conservatism*. New York: Basic Books.

Button, T. M., Stallings, M. C., Rhee, S. H., Corley, R. P., & Hewitt, J. K. (2011). The etiology of stability and change in religious values and religious attendance. *Behavioral Genetics*, *41*, 201–210.

D'Onofrio, B. M., Eaves, L. J., Murrelle, L., Maes, H. H., & Spilka, B. (1999). Understanding biological and social influences on religious affiliation, attitudes, and behaviors: A behavior genetic perspective. *Journal of Personality, 67,* 953–984.

Gebauer, J. E., Bleidorn, W., Gosling, S. D., Rentfrow, P. J., & Potter, J. (2012). *Big Five personality and religiosity: Agreeableness and conscientiousness constitute the basis of religiosity only in religious cultures.* Unpublished manuscript, Humboldt-Universität zu Berlin, Germany.

Gebauer, J. E., Paulhus, D. L., & Neberich, W. (2013). Big two personality and religiosity across cultures: Communals as religious conformists and agentics as religious contrarians. *Social Psychological and Personality Science, 4,* 21–30.

Goldberg, L. R. (1990). An alternative "description of personality": The Big-Five factor structure. *Journal of Personality and Social Psychology, 59,* 1216–1229.

Goldberg, L. R. (1999). A broad-bandwidth, public-domain, personality inventory measuring the lower-level facets of several five-factor models. In I. Mervielde, I. Deary, F. De Fruyt, & F. Ostendorf (Eds.), *Personality psychology in Europe* (Vol. 7, pp. 7–28). Tilburg : Tilburg University Press.

Heaven, P. C. L., & Ciarrochi, J. (2007). Personality and religious values among adolescents: A three-wave longitudinal analysis. *British Journal of Psychology, 98,* 681–694.

Hill, T. D., Burdette, A. M., Ellison, C. G., & Musick, M. A. (2006). Religious attendance and the health behaviors of Texas adults. *Preventive Medicine, 42,* 309–312.

Koenig, L. B., McGue, M., & Iacono, W. G. (2008). Stability and change in religiousness during emerging adulthood. *Developmental Psychology, 44,* 532–543.

Koenig, L. B., McGue, M., Krueger, R. F., & Bouchard, T. J., Jr. (2005). Genetic and environmental influences on religiousness: Findings for retrospective and current religiousness ratings. *Journal of Personality, 73,* 471–488.

Larson, J., & Witham, L. (1997). Scientists are still keeping the faith. *Nature, 386,* 435–436.

Larson, J., & Witham, L. (1998). Leading scientists still reject god. *Nature, 394,* 313.

Lee, K., Ogunfowora, B., & Ashton, M. C. (2005). Personality traits beyond the big five: Are they within the HEXACO space? *Journal of Personality, 73,* 1437–1463.

Lewis, G. J., & Bates, T. C. (2013). Common genetic influences underpin religiosity, community integration, and existential uncertainty. *Journal of Research in Personality, 47,* 398–405.

Lewis, G. J., Ritchie, S. J., & Bates, T. C. (2011). The relationship between intelligence and multiple domains of religious belief: Evidence from a large adult US sample. *Intelligence, 39,* 468–472.

McCrae, R. R., & Costa, P. T., Jr. (2008). The five-factor theory of personality. In O. P. John, R. W. Robins, & L. A. Pervin (Eds.), *Handbook of personality: Theory and research* (3rd ed., pp. 159–181). New York: Guilford.

McCrae, R. R., & John, O. P. (1992). An introduction to the five-factor model and its applications. *Journal of Personality, 60,* 175–215.

McCullough, M. E., Enders, C. K., Brion, S. L., & Jain, A. R. (2005). The varieties of religious development in adulthood: A longitudinal investigation of religion and rational choice. *Journal of Personality and Social Psychology*, *89*, 78–89.

McCullough, M. E., Tsang, J.-A., & Brion, S. (2003). Personality traits in adolescence as predictors of religiousness in early adulthood: Findings from the Terman Longitudinal Study. *Personality and Social Psychology Bulletin*, *29*, 980–991.

MacDonald, D. A. (2000). Spirituality: Description, measurement, and relation to the five-factor model of personality. *Journal of Personality*, *68*, 153–197.

Nyborg, H. (2009). The intelligence–religiosity nexus: A representative study of white adolescent Americans. *Intelligence*, *37*, 81–93.

Paloutzian, R. F., Richardson, J. T., & Rambo, L. R. (1999). Religious conversion and personality change. *Journal of Personality*, *67*, 1047–1079.

Paunonen, S. V. (2002). *Design and construction of the Supernumerary Personality Inventory* (Research Bulletin 763). London, Ontario: University of Western Ontario.

Ruiter, S., & De Graaf, N. D. (2006). National context, religiosity, and volunteering: Results from 53 countries. *American Sociological Review*, *71*, 191–210.

Saroglou, V. (2010). Religiousness as a cultural adaptation of basic traits: A five-factor model perspective. *Personality and Social Psychology Review*, *14*, 108–125.

Saroglou, V. (2011). Believing, bonding, behaving, and belonging: The big four religious dimensions and cultural variation. *Journal of Cross-Cultural Psychology*, *42*, 1320–1340.

Saroglou, V., & Fiasse, L. (2003). Birth order, personality, and religion: A study among young adults from a three-sibling family. *Personality and Individual Differences*, *35*, 19–29.

Saucier, G. (2004). *Personality and ideology: One thing or two?* Unpublished manuscript, University of Oregon.

Saucier, G., & Skrzypińska, K. (2006). Spiritual but not religious? Evidence for two independent dispositions. *Journal of Personality*, *74*, 1257–1292.

Shariff, A. F., & Norenzayan, A. (2007). God is watching you: Priming God concepts increases prosocial behavior in an anonymous economic game. *Psychological Science*, *18*, 303–809.

Walker, C., Ainette, M. G., Wills, T. A., & Mendoza, D. (2007). Religiosity and substance use: Test of an indirect-effect model in early and middle adolescence. *Psychology of Addictive Behaviors*, *21*, 84–96.

Welch, M. R., Tittle, C. R., & Grasmick, H. G. (2006). Christian religiosity, self-control and social conformity. *Social Forces*, *84*, 1605–1623.

Wink, P., Ciciolla, L., Dillon, M., & Tracy, A. (2007). Religiousness, spiritual seeking, and personality: Findings from a longitudinal study. *Journal of Personality*, *75*, 1051–1070.

3 Religion and the Self

Constantine Sedikides and Jochen E. Gebauer

People go to church for the same reasons they go to a tavern: to stupefy themselves, to forget their misery, to imagine themselves, for a few minutes anyway, free and happy.

Bakunin (1953 [1871], p. 120)

We are both in agreement and in disagreement with the above claim. We agree that religion confers benefits to the self. However, we disagree with the suggestion that such benefits are ephemeral or shallow. Instead, we argue that the functions that religiosity serves for the self are long lasting and important.

We address, in this chapter, the interface between religion and the self. We ask how religiosity—defined as belief in deity and engagement in deity-worshiping practices—interjects with components of the self-system (i.e., the individual, relational, and collective self). We present briefly a theoretical framework, the *hierarchical self model*, that articulates these components. We then discuss how religiosity satisfies psychological needs that are linked to the said self-components. We conclude by arguing that the fulfillment of multiple self-needs is a key reason for the worldwide and enduring appeal of religion.

The Hierarchical Self Model

As mentioned above, the self-system entails three major components: the individual self, the relational self, and the collective self (Sedikides & Brewer, 2001a). The *individual self* represents a person's uniqueness. This type of self consists of attributes (e.g., characteristics, preferences, goals) that differentiate the person from others. This self is a distinct entity from (albeit interconnected with) dyadic relationships or group memberships. The *relational self* represents dyadic interpersonal bonds (e.g., romantic partners, close friends). This type of self consists of attributes that are shared by dyad members and may define roles within the relationship. These attributes differentiate one's relationships from the relationships other persons have. The *collective self* represents group membership, that is, similarity and affiliation with valued groups. This type of self consists of attributes that are shared among group members and may define roles within the ingroup. These attributes differentiate one's ingroup(s) from relevant or antagonistic outgroups.

Each type of self is inherently social (Sedikides, Gaertner, & O'Mara, 2011). Also, each type of self is partly sustained through social comparison processes, namely assimilation and contrast. In particular, the individual self is compared with other persons, the relational self is compared with other relationships, and the collective self is compared with outgroups (Gaertner, Sedikides, Luke, & Iuzzini, 2008). In addition, each type of self is important to human functioning (Hawkley, Browne, & Cacioppo, 2005; Sedikides & Brewer, 2001b; Sedikides et al., 2011). For example, having a strong individual self (e.g., high self-concept clarity, personal self-esteem, or resilience), having a strong relational self (e.g., high relational self-esteem), and having a strong collective self (e.g., high collective self-esteem) is uniquely associated with psychological and physical well-being (Chen et al., 2006; Haslam, Jetten, Postmes, & Haslam, 2009; Ritchie, Sedikides, Wildschut, Arndt, & Gidron, 2011; Taylor, Lerner, Sherman, Sage, & McDowell, 2003a, b). Finally, each self is meaningful to human experience. Meaning in life can originate from personal goals (individual self), satisfying relationships (relational self), or group belongingness (collective self) (Hicks & Routledge, in press).

Nevertheless, not all selves are equally important and vital. The selves differ in their motivational potency. The individual self is more central to human experience, lies closer to the motivational core of the self-system, and reflects more pointedly the psychological "home base" of selfhood. The individual self is motivationally primary, followed in the pyramidal structure by the relational self and trailed by the collective self (Gaertner, Sedikides, Gaertner, Luke, O'Mara, & Gebauer, in press). For example, people anticipate that their life will be more negatively impacted if they "lose" (say, through surgical removal) their individual self than either their relational or collective self (Gaertner et al., 2012, Study 1). They also feel their individual self as most true or "at home" compared to the other two types of self (Gaertner et al., 2012, Study 1). In addition, they allocate a larger monetary sum toward bettering their individual self than their relational or collective self, price the value of their individual self as higher than the value of the other two selves, and expect to receive more money for selling the individual than any of the other two selves; notably these result patterns are obtained both in Western and Eastern culture (Gaertner et al., 2012, Study 3). Finally, people attribute more goals to their individual than relational or collective self, and this is the case both in Eastern and Western culture (Gaertner et al., 2012, Study 4).

The Hierarchical Self and Psychological Needs

Many psychological needs rely, to a great degree, on the self for their satisfaction. Such needs include self-esteem (Rosenberg, 1965), control (Kelley, 1971), uncertainty reduction (Van den Bos, 2001), meaning (Park, 2010), attachment (Bowlby, 1982), and belongingness (Baumeister & Leary, 1995).

We propose that these needs are linked differentially to the three selves. The needs for self-esteem, control, uncertainty reduction, and meaning are linked predominantly to the *individual self*. The need for attachment is linked predominantly to the *relational self*. And the need for social belonging is linked predominantly to the *collective self*. The dependency of most of these needs (i.e., self-esteem, control, uncertainty reduction, meaning) for satiation by the individual self reflects the motivational primacy of this type of self. But how does each type of self meet these needs? We propose that it does so, in part, through religiosity.

Religiosity and Satisfaction of Self-Needs

We assume that religiosity stands partially in the service of need satisfaction (Sedikides, 2010a, b). We now discuss how religiosity fulfills the above mentioned self-needs.

Self-Needs and the Individual Religious Self

We posit that religiosity satisfies (in some measure) the individual-self needs for self-esteem, control, uncertainty reduction, and meaning. We now turn to illustrative empirical examples.

Self-Esteem

The idea that religiosity is partly in the service of self-esteem (or self-enhancement) was introduced by William James (1902), advocated by Gordon Allport (1950), and embellished by Batson and Stocks (2004), who stated: "Feeling good about oneself and seeing oneself as a person of worth and value play a major role in much contemporary religion" (p. 47). Two contemporary theoretical frameworks have capitalized on this idea: the religiosity as self-enhancement hypothesis and terror management theory.

RELIGIOSITY AS SELF-ENHANCEMENT HYPOTHESIS

Sedikides and Gebauer (2010) based their theoretical proposal on two assumptions. First, persons across cultures deploy an inventive array of means for elevating their self-esteem or for self-enhancement (Alicke &

Sedikides, 2011; Hepper, Gramzow, & Sedikides, 2010). These means include facets of the sociocultural context (e.g., institutions, norms, values, traditions; Hepper, Sedikides, & Cai, 2013; Sedikides & Gregg, 2008). Religion is typically a pivotal facet of the sociocultural context. As such, persons will likely capitalize on religion to increase their self-esteem or to self-enhance. Second, self-esteem or self-enhancement is a disposition. Religiosity, however, is largely regarded as a cultural adaptation (Saroglou, 2010). As such, self-enhancement is a more basic psychological structure than religiosity: it has chronological priority over religiosity and is likely to drive it.

According to the religiosity as self-enhancement hypothesis, self-enhancement (operationalized conventionally in terms of socially desirable responding; Paulhus & Holden, 2010), is associated with higher religiosity. In particular, the hypothesis posits that the relation between self-enhancement and religiosity is stronger in cultures that ascribe a notably positive value on religiosity. In such cultures, being religious means "being a good, moral, decent person." It follows that people with a higher self-enhancement need (i.e., those scoring higher on socially desirable responding) will satisfy this need through greater levels of religiosity.

The hypothesis was confirmed in a meta-analysis (Sedikides & Gebauer, 2010) examining both macro-level culture and micro-level culture. Macro-level culture involved countries varying in religiosity (from higher to lower: USA, Canada, UK). Micro-level culture involved US universities varying in religiosity (from higher to lower: religious universities, secular universities). The relation between self-enhancement and religiosity was stronger in cultural contexts that placed particularly high value on religiosity. That is, this relation was stronger in the US than in Canada than in the UK, and it was also stronger in religious than secular US universities. In all, this meta-analysis, alongside an earlier relevant meta-analytic synthesis (Trimble, 1997), presents evidence consistent with the idea that religiosity partially realizes self-enhancement or self-esteem concerns.

A survey of 11 European nations offered additional support to the religiosity as self-enhancement hypothesis (Gebauer, Sedikides, & Neberich, 2012). In particular, believers' social self-esteem was higher than that of non-believers in countries that bestowed relatively high merit on religiosity. In contrast, believers' and non-believers' social self-esteem did not differ in countries that bestowed relatively low merit on religiosity.

Another demonstration of the relevance of cultural context for religiosity can be found in research linking culture to religiosity through personality (Gebauer, Paulhus, & Neberich, 2013). This research focuses in part on agentic persons, that is, persons with a chronically high need for uniqueness (e.g., independence, ambition, competence; Abele, Cuddy, Judd, & Yzerbyt, 2008; Bakan, 1966). Agentic persons, then, derive self-esteem from their uniqueness. This need for uniqueness would be best satisfied through religiosity in cultures that are non-religious: it is in those cultures that an agentic person would feel set apart from others. Agentic persons, then, would be most religious in non-religious countries. However, agentic persons would be least religious in religious countries: in those countries, agentic persons would feel similar to others and, hence, their need for uniqueness would be stifled rather than nurtured. The results of a large-scale survey were consistent with these predictions (Gebauer et al., 2013).

TERROR MANAGEMENT THEORY

Evidence for the idea that religiosity partially satisfies self-esteem concerns is also supplied by research on terror management theory (Greenberg, Pyszczynski, & Solomon, 1986; Vail et al., 2010). This theory proposes that a major function of religion is to assuage existential concerns that arise from humankind's awareness of their mortality. Religion soothes fear of death via literal and symbolic immortality. Literal immortality refers to promises for afterlife. Symbolic immortality refers to the cultural or religious worldview (e.g., norms, values, contributions or achievements) that transcend one's physical demise.

People strive to live up to the standards of value prescribed by the cultural or religious worldview. This sense of value is what terror management theory refers to as self-esteem. Self-esteem, then, allows people to manage existential or death anxiety and affords psychological equanimity. Religion serves to lift self-esteem.

Several lines of research are relevant to the propositions of terror management theory. One such line brings to the fore the problem of death by reminding participants in the experimental condition of their own mortality ("Briefly describe the emotions that the thought of your own death arouses in you" and "Jot down, as specifically as you can, what you think will happen to you physically as you die and once you are physically dead") while reminding participants in the control condition of an averse experience (e.g., dental pain, exam failure). This is known as the *mortality salience manipulation*. Compared to their control condition counterparts, participants who receive the mortality salience manipulation:

- show an increase in beliefs in afterlife (Osarchuk & Tatz, 1973)
- report higher anxiety when using a respected religious symbol (i.e., a crucifix) in an irreverent manner (Greenberg, Simon, Porteus, Pyszczynski, & Solomon, 1995)
- manifest unaltered levels of self-esteem, provided that ostensible scientific evidence has proved the existence of afterlife (Dechesne et al., 2003).

In addition, challenges to religious belief (e.g., arguing in favor of evolution, highlighting inconsistencies in the Bible) increase death-related thoughts, but not other types of thought, among believers (Friedman & Rholes, 2007).

Another line of research demonstrates that mortality salience augments faith in deity, possibly also deity of other religions. Persons may view deities of other religions as different manifestations of the deity (or deities) of their own religion. As such, other deities are appealing, because they increase the plausibility of faith in one's own deity. Deities are gatekeepers to an afterlife. Indeed, mortality salience increases among participants of Christian background the endorsement and perceived gravitas of scientific articles that presumably furnish support for the effectiveness of prayer not only to the Christian God, but also to the Buddha and shamanic spirits of faith; this effect, however, is observed for believers only (Norenzayan & Hansen, 2006; see also Vail et al., 2012). More generally, deities and norms will impact on one's behavior only when they are incorporated in one's worldview. Rothschild, Abdollahi, and Pyszczynski (2009) illustrated elegantly this point. They found that, following mortality salience, persons high on religious fundamentalism (e.g., American Christian and Iranian Shiite Muslim) became more compassionate but only when compassionate values were embedded in a religious framework (i.e., respectively, Bible and Koran). Such persons, however, were unaffected on compassion by mortality salience, when compassionate values were portrayed in a non-religious context.

Still a third line of research (Jonas & Fischer, 2006) shows that religiosity conduces to religious persons' management of their fear of death. Following mortality salience, persons low on religiosity engage in worldview defense, whereas persons high on religiosity refrain from worldview defense especially when they have the opportunity to affirm their religiosity. In addition, religiosity affirmation, following mortality salience, reduced death-thought accessibility but only for persons high on religiosity. Religiosity affirmation, then, decreased the implementation of terror management defenses and death-thought accessibility among the faithful. In all, research inspired by terror management theory establishes that religiosity helps people cope with the problem of death, and it does so in part by bolstering their self-esteem.

Control

We begin by distinguishing between personal and compensatory control. The need for personal control refers to the belief that one can predict, influence, and direct present and future events in a desired manner. Personal control protects from the anxiety resulting from randomness and disorder. Compensatory control, by the same token, functions to maintain nonrandomness and order even in the absence of personal control—the former substitutes for the latter.

Personal control underlies religiosity. Specifically, low personal control stirs an upsurge in religiosity. This effect has been illustrated in the laboratory. Participants in the experimental condition are instructed to "think of something positive that happened to you in the past few months that you had absolutely no control over" and to "describe this event in more than 100 words." Participants in the comparison condition are instructed to think of a positive event over which they had control and describe it accordingly. This manipulation decreases personal control without influencing mood or self-esteem. Subsequently, participants state their level of religiosity—specifically, their beliefs in a controlling deity (e.g., "to what extent do you think that the events that occur in this world unfold according to God's plan?"). Participants in the experimental condition report stronger beliefs in God's existence (Kay, Gaucher, Napier, Callan, & Laurin, 2008). In a similar vein, participants primed with words that denote uncontrollability (e.g., "random," "uncontrollable") report stronger beliefs in God compared to participants primed with words that denote negativity (e.g., "terrible," "slimy") (Kay, Moscovitch, & Laurin, 2010).

The upsurge in religiosity is indeed due to decrease in personal control. For example, the abovementioned personal control manipulation (Kay et al., 2008) yields stronger beliefs in God when God is thought to exert a mighty controlling influence on the universe. Also, personal control undermines perceptions of order, and this undermining in turn raises belief in God (Kay et al., 2008). Finally, both direct anxiety inductions—through loss of personal control in a highly stressful situation (Laurin, Kay, & Moscovitch, 2008) or through swallowing a pill purported to create anxiety (Kay et al., 2010) —lead to firm beliefs in the existence of a controlling deity.

Compensatory control also underlies religiosity (Shepherd, Kay, Landau, & Keefer, 2012). This type of need for control is satisfied by having faith in institutions that represent consistency and structure (Antonovsky, 1979; Rothbaum, Weisz, & Snyder, 1982). If one type of institution (e.g., government) fails to restore order and structure, another type of institution (e.g., religion) will come to the rescue. In that case, faith will rest on deities who are in charge of earthly endeavors and can intervene appropriately.

This idea has received empirical support. Participants who learn that their government is about to fall requiring urgent elections (vs. their government is stable with no elections required) declare firmer beliefs in the existence of a controlling God. The same pattern is obtained when participants learn that their government is failing to procure control and order to its citizens. Finally, beliefs in a controlling deity become stronger before a national election (when the government is unstable) than after a national election (when the government is stable) (Kay, Shepherd, Blatz, Chua, & Galinsky, 2010). In all, religiosity fulfills the needs for both personal and compensatory control.

We would like to refer to another type of control, impulse control (i.e., delayed gratification). Research has started to show that religious individuals are characterized by good impulse control (McCullough & Willoughby, 2009; see also Burris & Petrican, Chapter 5, this volume). For example, religiosity is positively related to the relinquishment of smaller rewards in the present in favor of larger awards in the future (Carter, McCullough, Kim, Corrales, & Blake, 2012). Also, experimental inductions of religiosity in men decrease both impulsivity and their motivation to display their physical prowess. In this research, male participants who were primed with religious concepts (e.g., implicit exposure to religious words, reading argument for the existence of afterlife, writing religion-relevant essays) became less impulsive with money and physical endurance on a manual (i.e., hand gripping) task (McCullough, Carter, DeWall, & Corrales, 2012). The impulse control benefits of religiosity are partly due to the higher state of self-monitoring that it induces. That is, religious people monitor closely their goals, as they believe that they are monitored not only by others but also by God. Self-monitoring, in turn, is positively linked to impulse control (Carter, McCullough, & Carver, in press).

Uncertainty Reduction

Uncertainty about the self and the world can breed religiosity. A case in point is religious participants who are either dispositionally uncertain or transiently (i.e., through priming) uncertain. These participants, compared to their relatively certain counterparts, express strong support for a religious leader who endorses an orthodox (rather than moderate) view of their faith (Blagg & Hogg, 2012). However, uncertainty per se may not be sufficient to bolster religiosity. Dispositionally and transiently uncertain participants react angrily toward highly critical statements about their religion only when these participants consider uncertainty as a personally threatening emotional experience (Van den Bos, Van Ameijde, & Van Gorp, 2006).

Moreover, uncertainty can spawn religious extremism. Anecdotal observations or interviews point to periods of cultural uncertainty as giving rise to radical forms of religiosity (Armstrong, 2009; Stern, 2003). Experimental research buttresses this point. Regardless of how participants are made transiently uncertain (i.e., through either an academic uncertainty or a relational uncertainty manipulation), they report heightened religious conviction, more acute derogation of a religion perceived as rival to their own, and more fervent support for religious warfare (McGregor, Haji, Nash, & Teper, 2008). Furthermore, participants with stronger religious identities are more supportive of violent action (Hogg & Adelman, in press).

Reactive approach motivation is a mechanism that steers uncertainty to religious extremism (McGregor, Nash, Mann, & Phills, 2010). Threat (accompanied by anxiety) stemming from uncertainty engenders heightened vigilance about the threat domain, thus giving way to a preparatory fight (e.g., dispute, argue) or flight (e.g., rationalize, withdraw) reaction as well as to alternative means for protection. Identification and selection of such a means instigates approach motivation, a surge toward that means, and, in the end, a restoration of certainty. As such, uncertainty-caused reactive approach motivation may express itself as extremism or, as the case may be, religious extremism.

Not only uncertainty, but also certainty (about the world), is related to religiosity. This is the other side of the equation. To explicate, religious certainty is positively linked to religious satisfaction (Puffer et al., 2008). Also, religious conviction soothes brain centers linked to anxiety underlying uncertainty. For example, religious devotees manifest decreased reactivity in the anterior cingulate cortex, a cortical structure implicated in the experience of anxiety and in self-regulation (Inzlicht, McGregor, Hirsh, & Nash, 2009). In all, religious conviction insulates the faithful from a drop in their feelings of uncertainty (McGregor, 2006).

Meaning

Religiosity is thought to satisfy the human quest for meaning (Baumeister, 1991; Park, 2005). It is considered an aid to the comprehension of the deepest existential problems (Geertz, 1966), of the core issues surrounding the self, the world, and their interplay (McIntosh, 1995), and of both mundane and extraordinary circumstances (Spilka, Hood, Hunsberger, & Gorsuch, 2003). Religiosity is also regarded as a gateway to understanding loss and suffering (Kotarba, 1983).

Religiosity helps to cope with traumatic life events and regain meaning in life (Wortmann & Park, 2011). To begin with, religion is implicated in appraising the meaning of various stressors. For example, a portion of spinal cord injury victims (Bulman & Wortman, 1977) as well as bereaved college students (Park & Cohen, 1993) attribute their predicament to a caring and loving God. Religiosity also influences coping with stressors through religious reappraisal, such as prayer, religious support, and religious forgiveness (Pargament, Koenig, & Perez, 2000). In addition, religiosity partakes in reappraising the meaning of stressors by refocusing the individual on seeking positive implications and by purveying the forum for benign attributions (Park, Edmondson, & Blank, 2009), which can be psychologically beneficial (Emmons, Colby, & Kaiser, 1998).

Yet, sometimes overwhelmingly stressful life events occur that render people incapable of coping and shatter their sense of meaning. In those occasions, people will resort to any of a variety of behaviors or strategies in their attempt to re-establish meaning. They may come to see God as less powerful, see the devil as more powerful, or see themselves as sinners (Pargament, 1997). They may feel victimized, perceive God as cruel, experience and direct anger toward God, and hold God responsible for their plight (Exline, Park, Smyth, & Carey, 2011). They may switch to another congregation or denomination (Paloutzian, Richardson, & Rambo, 1999). They may become agnostics or atheists (Pargament, 1997). Or, on the other end of the continuum, they may rededicate themselves to their faith and pledge even higher devotion to it (Emmons et al., 1998). This is a rather bewildering set of behaviors and strategies, and a task of future research would be to sort out which strategies are likely to be undertaken by whom and when. We will speculate on this issue in the following section.

In all, there is some evidence that religiosity serves a meaning function. However, more rigorous research is necessary to establish this otherwise plausible and intuitive function of religiosity. For example, experimental studies would need to induce meaninglessness and assess ensuing levels of religiosity among the faithful. Furthermore, meaninglessness would need to be distinguished empirically from other "competing" mechanisms, such as low self-esteem, weak personal control, and uncertainty.

Self-Needs and the Relational Religious Self

The innate attachment behavioral system motivates humans to seek proximity to significant others especially in times of distress (Bowlby, 1982). These significant others are called attachment figures. God qualifies as a crucial such figure (Freud, 1961 [1927]; Kirkpatrick, 2005).

In surveys, believers state that having a relationship with God best describes their view of faith (Gallup & Jones, 1989). The notion that one can have a personal relationship with God is well-established in theistic religions (Granqvist & Kirkpatrick, 2008), and belief in such a relationship predicts lower loneliness (Kirkpatrick, Shillito, & Kellas, 1999). Also, this relationship resembles a classic attachment bond. God is seen as benevolent (e.g., warm hearted, comforting, and caring about one's safety), omnipotent (e.g., always available for one's comfort and protection), and omniscient (e.g., all knowing) (Gorsuch, 1986; Tamayo & Desjardins, 1976). In addition, God is also seen as emotionally similar, that is as sharing higher level and otherwise uniquely human emotions (Demoulin, Saroglou, & Van Pachterbeke, 2008). Moreover, believers strive to maintain proximity to God, as they would to an attachment figure. They maintain proximity to God through singing, visiting the place of worship (God's home), praying, talking to, or being emotionally involved with God.

When surveyed, theists who hold an accepting image of God report that their belief is motivated by the need for attachment (Gebauer & Maio, 2012, Study 4). Experimental studies corroborate this point further (Gebauer & Maio, 2012, Studies 1–3). Participants who read bogus proof for God's existence (compared to those who do not do so) indicate stronger belief in deity, especially when they imagine God as accepting. However, this pattern is cancelled out when these participants' attachment need is met a priori through exposure to primes of a close other. Finally, theists who chronically imagine God as rejecting manifest reduced desire for closeness with God, which in turn leads to lower stated likelihood of religious practices.

Importantly, as an attachment figure, God offers a safe haven in times of distress or threat. In those times (e.g., physical illness or injuries, death of a loved one, separation from close others), people may turn to God through prayer (Argyle & Beit-Hallahmi, 1975) or by reinforcing their religiosity (Brown, Nesse, House, & Utz, 2004). Personal crises also may sometimes precipitate religious conversion (Kirkpatrick, 2005). In addition, subliminal exposure to threatening words (e.g., "death," "failure") activates the concept of God (Granqvist, Mikulincer, Gewirtz, & Shaver, 2012), and subliminal exposure to separation threat (e.g., "mother is gone") strengthens the desire to be close to God (Birgegard & Granqvist, 2004).

In the preceding *meaning* section, we stated that, under overwhelming crises, the faithful manifest an impressive repertoire of reactions ranging from deepening their belief in God (Emmons et al., 1998) through being angry at God (Exline et al., 2011) to abandoning God (Pargament, 1997). We speculate that which reaction the faithful will manifest may depend on the specific attachment style they hold regarding God (Rowatt & Kirkpatrick, 2002). Secure attachment to God may be related to a deepening of one's religiosity, an anxious attachment style may be linked to anger toward God, and an avoidant attachment style may be associated with distancing from God.

Regardless, the proposition that God is an attachment figure is also supported by responses to perceived separation from God. Typical responses following separation from close others involve protest about the breakup of the relationship, despair about one's present state or future prospects, and reorganization of one's emotional life (Shaver & Fraley, 2008). Perceived separation from God involves protestation (reminiscent of Jesus's proclaim from the cross "*My God, My God, why hast Thou forsaken me?*"), felt as torturous (referred to as "wilderness experience" or "a dark night of the soul"; St. John of the Cross, 1990), and may herald adherence to alternative worldviews such as other denominations, agnosticism, or atheism (Pargament, 1997). In all, the self-need for attachment to a caring, powerful, and omnipresent other can be met through religiosity and, in particular, through God as attachment figure. (For a discussion of developmental trajectories in the relational religious self, see Granqvist, Chapter 13, this volume.)

Self-Needs and the Collective Religious Self

Durkheim (1965 [1915]) observed that shared social practices, or the worshipping of the group, is the aim of religiosity. He famously stated that "to its members [society] is what a god is to his worshippers" (p. 237). Indeed, people agree strongly with "enjoy the religious services and style of worship" as a reason for joining a faith (Pew Research Group, 2011).

We argue that religiosity satisfies the human need for social belonging through several channels. To begin with, social exclusion activates the need to belong, which, in turn, sparks religiosity. Immigrants who experience social exclusion report higher levels of religiosity than their compatriots in the home country, controlling for socioeconomic status (Aydin, Fischer, & Frey, 2010, Study 1). The results of several experimental studies converge with this empirical pattern. Feelings of social exclusion are induced by asking participants to write about an incident in which they were socially excluded; in the control conditions, participants write about an incident in which they are accepted or just record their daily activities. Social exclusion generates stronger religiosity—in terms of both belief and intended practices (Aydin et al., Studies 2–4). Similarly, chronically or transiently lonely persons (who presumably feel socially excluded) report higher religiosity, an effect that cannot be accounted for by negative affect (Epley, Akalis, Waytz, & Cacioppo, 2008).

Moreover, religiosity strengthens one's social identity (Ysseldyk, Matheson, & Anisman, 2010). Religious identification is special, as it offers eternal membership to a sacred mission and accompanying psychosocial value. Religious identification is maintained and reinforced through collective rituals such as singing and dancing— rituals that may foster liking, trust, cooperation, and self-sacrifice (Wiltermuth & Heath, 2009) These rituals and communal participation may be linked to group morality, and in particular to such values as ingroup/loyalty, authority/respect, and purity/sanctity (Graham & Haidt, 2010).

Culture can also shape the way in which religiosity satisfies the need for social belonging. An example is research that links culture to religiosity through personality (Gebauer et al., 2013). Communal persons have a high need for social belonging (e.g., interdependence, warmth, social propriety; Abele et al., 2008; Bakan, 1966). This need would be best fulfilled through religiosity in cultures that are religious: it is in those cultures that communal persons would feel similar to others. It follows that communal persons would be most religious in religious countries. However, such persons would be least religious in non-religious countries: in those countries, they would feel least similar to others and, hence, their need for social belonging would be thwarted. Their predictions were empirically backed (Gebauer et al., 2013).

Increased social belongingness as a function of religiosity is associated with higher psychological health (Ysseldyk et al., 2010; see also Hayward & Krause, Chapter 12, this volume) and a more magnanimous response to subsequent provocations having to do with social rejection (Aydin et al., 2010, Study 5). However, the social belongingness function of religiosity is also associated with negative social consequences such as racial intolerance, prejudice, and discrimination against members of other religions (Bulbulia & Mahoney, 2008; Hall, Matz, & Wood, 2010; Widman, Corcoran, & Nagy, 2009; Ysseldyk et al., 2010) and against atheists (Gervais, Shariff, & Norenzayan, 2011; Harper, 2007; Jackson & Hunsberger, 1999; Johnson, Rowatt, & LaBouff, 2012).

Broader Considerations

In this final section of the chapter, we provide a synopsis, discuss unresolved issues surrounding our approach, and discuss how the cultural level of analysis can inform our approach.

Synopsis

We acknowledged that religion is a multiply determined and, for some, an intractable phenomenon. Religion, as this volume illustrates, can be approached from an assortment of perspectives and levels of analyses, such as the neuronal, psychological, group, societal or cultural, interethnic, and evolutionary. We focused in this chapter on the psychological level of analysis and adopted a self-needs perspective.

Our point of departure was the hierarchical self model (Sedikides et al., 2011). The model distinguishes between three fundamental self-components: the individual self, the relational self, and the collective self. The model further states, and is propped by evidence, that the individual self sits at the top of the hierarchy, followed by the relational self, and trailed at the bottom by the collective self (Sedikides et al., in press). We posited that each self is associated with different psychological needs. The individual self is associated with the needs for self-esteem, control, uncertainty reduction, and meaning. The relational self is associated with the need for attachment. Finally, the collective self is associated with the need for social belonging. More importantly, we suggested that each type of self meets these needs through religiosity. We proceeded to argue and show that religiosity satisfies (a) the individual self-needs for self-esteem, control, uncertainty reduction, and meaning, (b) the relational self-need for attachment, and (c) the collective self-need for social belonging.

Unresolved Issues Surrounding Our Approach

Several conceptual and empirical issues remain unresolved. They all center around the nature of the discussed self-needs. For example, are these needs independent of one another? Concurrently assessing the self-needs in a large sample of devout participants and subjecting the results to factor analyses would begin to address this question. Relatedly, how do the self-needs interact with one another? Here, theoretical development is needed before delving into the empirical arena. For example, it may be that religiosity reduces uncertainty and increases control, a process that elevates a sense of meaning and self-esteem, with an ensuing strengthening of attachment to God and belongingness to a community. Other causal sequences are, of course, plausible. Also, are the self-needs differentially related to psychological health? Moreover, do the needs seem to contribute differently to psychological health and well-being? And what are the pathways through which the intrapsychic needs (self-esteem, control, uncertainty reduction, meaning) impact on belongingness?

Our self-needs perspective capitalizes on the self-regulatory function of religiosity (Fischer, Greitemeyer, Kastenmüller, Jonas, & Frey, 2006). But can religiosity satisfy all self-needs at once? It is possible that religiosity facilitates implicit self-regulation, defined as "a process in which a central executive (i.e., the implicit self) coordinates the person's functioning by integrating as many subsystems and processes as possible for supporting a chosen course of action" (Koole, McCullough, Kuhl, & Roelofsma, 2010, p. 96). This flexible and efficient, yet unconscious, self-regulatory mode may allow persons to strive living up to their religious standards while sustaining relatively high emotional well-being through the simultaneous satisfaction of the self-needs.

There are other notable ways in which religiosity operates at the psychological level. Religiosity influences family dynamics and childhood experiences (Mahoney, 1995: see also Li & Cohen, Chapter 10, this volume), goals (Emmons, 2005), and values (Roccas, 2005; see also Roccas & Elster, Chapter 9, this volume). Also, personality shapes religiosity (Saroglou, 2010; see also Ashton & Lee, Chapter 2, this volume). Future research would do well to examine the interplay between these factors and the self-needs.

Finally, our account focused mainly on Christianity, reflecting the fact that most research on the topic has used Christian samples. Religions, however, differ in the way they conceptualize deity or the way in which they justify God's goodness in the face of evil (Donahue, 1989), with accompanying implications for self-needs. For example, Christians usually consider suffering (e.g., disease, sin, death) illusions of a mortal mind and hence not a cause for grief (Allen, 1994), whereas Buddhists typically consider suffering to be caused by craving for wrong things or craving for right things but in the wrong way (Drumont, 1994). Need satisfaction, then, may take a different route, depending on one's faith. The need for meaning is an example. A Christian may justify suffering in terms of God's will, whereas a Buddhist may justify suffering as grasping for the wrong things. Furthermore, the search and acquisition of meaning (and, probably the satisfaction of other needs) may differ depending on Christian denominations such as Protestant and Catholic (Tix & Frazier, 1998).

Religion and Culture

As we have argued previously (Gebauer et al., 2012; Sedikides & Gebauer, 2010), more general levels of analyses, such as the cultural level, can inform our need-based approach. An additional recent example involves Gallup Polls both in the US (Diener, Tay, & Myers, 2011, Study 1) and in 154 nations (Diener et al., 2011, Study 2). These surveys have shown that religiosity is associated with feeling respected (arguably a proxy of self-esteem), perceiving life as meaningful, and having a sense of social support (a proxy of social belonging). These benefits are in turn linked to increased subjective well-being. However, the relation between religiosity and well-being depends on whether societal circumstances are difficult or easy. Societal circumstances refer to the accommodation of basic needs (i.e., food and shelter), to safety (i.e., feeling safe to walk alone at night), to income, to education, and to life expectancy at birth. Difficult circumstances are defined as having relatively low basic need fulfillment, safety, income, education, and life expectancy. People in US states and nations that encounter difficult circumstances are more likely to be religious, and religiosity is associated with higher self-esteem, meaning, and belongingness. However, people in US states and nations who encounter easy circumstances are less religious, and religiosity does not confer benefits in terms of fulfillment of self-needs (i.e., self-esteem, meaning, belongingness).

Another example of how the cultural level of analysis can inform a needs-based approach is research on the role of religiosity in the relation between income and psychological adjustment. In general, higher income is associated with better psychological adjustment. Gebauer, Nehrlich, Sedikides, and Neberich (in press) proposed that religiosity attenuates this association. They hypothesized that religious teachings convey anti-wealth norms, which decrease the psychological benefits of income. They used survey data from approximately 190,000 individuals originating in 11 religiously diverse European countires. Consistent with their hypothesis, income and psychological adjustment were virtually unassociated in religious cultures (if not negatively associated), whereas they were positively associated in non-religious cultures. The need for self-esteem, and in particular performance self-esteem, mediated this relation.

The cultural level of analysis is also relevant to control. Sasaki and Kim (2011) were interested in the concept of secondary control, defined as acceptance of, and adjustment to, difficult situations. They tested the role of culture and religion on secondary control. Specifically, they focused on Westerners (i.e., European–Americans), thought to be relatively agentic, and East Asians (i.e., Koreans), thought to be relatively communal. US church websites featured more themes of secondary control in their mission statements than Korean websites, whereas Korean church websites featured more themes of social affiliation than US church websites. Further, experimental priming of religion resulted in acts of secondary control for European–Americans but not for Koreans. Finally, religious coping predicted higher levels of secondary control for European–Americans but not for Koreans, whereas religious coping predicted higher levels of social affiliation for Koreans and European–Americans. In all, the effects of religion were moderated by cultural context.

We have maintained that threat to one's social belonging (e.g., social exclusion or loneliness; Aydin et al., 2010; Epley et al., 2008) heightens one's religiosity. This principle is observed at the cultural level as well. Stress resulting from parasite threat raises ingroup or family ties as well as religiosity. In contrast, low levels of parasite stress lower social ties and religiosity (Fincher & Thornhill, 2012). On the face of it, this would be an alternative explanation for the Diener et al. (2011) findings: cultures characterized by easy circumstances also boast low parasite threat, and hence this effect would account partially for low religiosity in such countries. However, the relation between parasite threat, on the one hand, and social belonging and religiosity, on the other, holds even when controlling for economic development and human freedom (arguably, a proxy of safety).

The relevance of culture for religiosity opens up another issue. Can religiosity be replaced with other worldviews, such as atheism, especially in countries where religiosity has relatively low currency? A preliminary investigation in the non-religious United Kingdom answers this question in the affirmative (Wilkinson & Coleman, 2010). The investigation involved interviewing persons over the age of 60 who were facing stresses and losses associated with aging. Theists and atheists alike reported coping well, suggesting that an atheistic belief system can provide the same psychological benefits to its holders as a theistic belief system can provide to its holders (Dawkins, 2006, p. 347). Similarly, atheism too can satiate attachment and social belongingness needs, for example via connection with likeminded others over the internet (Sproull & Faraj, 1995). Nevertheless, more systematic investigation will need to follow these preliminary findings.

Concluding Notes

Religiosity can be costly. It involves labor in familiarizing oneself with religious doctrines and practices, effort in continuing to display belief in the power of supernatural phenomena that often contradict sensory experiences, extended fasting, missed opportunities to expand one's social circle with persons outside one's religious group, and disadvantages resulting from refusal of modern medical care (Irons 2008; Sosis et al., 2007). How do religious people compensate for these seemingly large costs?

We argued that religiosity entails remarkable compensatory potential. It allows the faithful to fulfill fundamental self-needs: self-esteem, control, uncertainty reduction, and meaning (connected with the individual self), attachment (connected with the collective self), and social belonging (connected with the collective self). Need fulfillment is associated with improved psychological adjustment in cultures that particularly value religion (Diener et al., 2011; Gebauer et al., 2012; Sedikides & Gebauer, 2010).

Our need-based approach, albeit limited, grants the advantage of linking religiosity to broader psychological and social-behavioral phenomena (Baumeister, 2002; Sedikides, 2010b). Our approach also offers an account for the enduring appeal of religiosity. This appeal, culturally circumscribed as it may be, is due, in part, to the concurrent satisfaction of many psychological needs that span the entirety of the self-system. Voltaire (1694–1778) may have had a point when he professed: "If God did not exist, it would be necessary to invent him."

References

Abele, A. E., Cuddy, A. J. C., Judd, C. M., & Yzerbyt, V. Y. (2008). Fundamental dimensions of social judgment. *European Journal of Social Psychology*, 38, 1063–1065.

Alicke, M. D., & Sedikides, C. (2011). (Eds.). *The handbook of self- enhancement and self- protection*. New York: Guilford Press.

Allen, J. (1994). The spiritual search. In R. P. Beaver (Ed.), *Gerdman's handbook to the world's religions* (pp. 399–405). Grand Rapids, WY: W. B. Gerdman's Publishing Co.

Allport, G. W. (1950). *The individual and his religion*. New York: Macmillan.

Antonovsky, A. (1979). *Health, stress and coping*. San Francisco, CA: Jossey-Bass.

Argyle, M., & Beit-Hallahmi, B. (1975). *The social psychology of religion*. London: Routledge.

Armstrong, K. (2009). *The case for God*. New York: Alfred A. Knopf.

Aydin, N., Fischer, P., & Frey, D. (2010). Turning to God in the face of ostracism: Effects of social exclusion on religiousness. *Personality and Social Psychology Bulletin*, 36, 742–753.

Bakan, D. (1966). *The duality of human existence: Isolation and communion in Western man.* Boston, MA: Beacon Press.

Bakunin, M. (1953). Man had to look for God within himself. In G. P. Maximoff (Ed.), *The political philosophy of Bakunin* (pp. 114–120). London: Free Press. (Original work published 1871)

Batson, C. D., & Stocks, E. L. (2004). Religion: Its core psychological functions. In T. Pyszczynski, S. L. Koole, & J. Greenberg (Eds.), *Handbook of experimental psychology: An emerging synthesis* (pp. 141–155). New York: Guilford.

Baumeister, R. F. (1991). *Meanings of life.* New York: Guilford.

Baumeister, R. F. (2002). Religion and psychology: Introduction to the special issue. *Psychological Inquiry, 13*, 165–167.

Baumeister, R. F., & Leary, M. R. (1995). The need to belong: Desire for interpersonal attachments as a fundamental human motivation. *Psychological Bulletin, 117*, 497–529.

Birgegard, A., & Granqvist, A. (2004). The correspondence between attachment to parents and God: Three experiments using subliminal separation cues. *Personality and Social Psychology Bulletin, 30*, 1122–11135.

Blagg, R. D., & Hogg, M. A. (2012). *Religious leadership and follower uncertainty: Implications for religiousness and identity.* Unpublished manuscript, Claremont Graduate University.

Bowlby, J. (1982). *Attachment and loss: Vol 1. Attachment* (2nd ed.). New York: Basic Books.

Brown, S. L., Nesse, R. M., House, J. S., & Utz, R. L. (2004). Religious and emotional compensation: Results from a prospective study of widowhood. *Personality and Social Psychology Bulletin, 30*, 1165–1174.

Bulbulia, J., & Mahoney, A. (2008). Religious solidarity: The hand grenade experiment. *Journal of Cognition and Culture, 8*, 295–320.

Bulman, R. J., & Wortman, C. B. (1977). Attributions of blame and coping in the "real world": Severe accident victims react to their lot. *Journal of Personality and Social Psychology, 35*, 351–363.

Carter, E. C., McCullough, M. E., & Carver, C. S. (in press). The mediating role of monitoring in the association of religion with self-control. *Social Psychological and Personality Science.*

Carter, E. C., McCullough, M. E., Kim, J., Corrales, C., & Blake, A. (2012). Religious people discount the future less. *Evolution and Human Behavior, 33*, 224–231.

Chen, S., Boucher, H. C., Tapias, M. P., Chen, S., Boucher, H. C., & Tapias, M. P. (2006). The relational self revealed: Integrative conceptualization and implications for interpersonal life. *Psychological Bulletin, 132*, 151–179.

Dawkins, R. (2006). *The God delusion.* London: Bantam.

Dechesne, M., Pyszczynski, T., Arndt, J., Ransom, S., Sheldon, K., van Klippenberg, A. et al. (2003). Literal and symbolic immortality: The effect of evidence of literal immortality on self-esteem striving in response to mortality salience. *Journal of Personality and Social Psychology, 84*, 722–737.

Demoulin, S., Saroglou, V., & Van Pachterbeke, M. (2008). Infra-humanizing others, supra-humanizing Gods: The emotional hierarchy. *Social Cognition, 26*, 235–247.

Diener, E., Tay, L., & Myers, D. G. (2011). The religion paradox: If religion makes people happy, why are so many dropping out? *Journal of Personality and Social Psychology, 101,* 1278–1290.

Donahue, M. J. (1989). Disregarding theology in the psychology of religion: Some examples. *Journal of Psychology and Theology, 17,* 329–335.

Drumont, R. (1994). The Buddha's teaching. In R. P. Beaver (Ed.), *Gerdman's handbook to the world's religions* (p. 231). Grand Rapids, WY: W. B. Gerdman's Publishing Co.

Durkheim, E. (1965). *The elementary forms of religious life* (J. W. Swain, Trans.). New York: Free Press. (Original work published 1915)

Emmons, R. A. (2005). Striving for the sacred: Personal goals, life meaning, and religion. *Journal of Social Issues, 61,* 731–746.

Emmons, R. A., Colby, P. M., & Kaiser, H. A. (1998). When losses lead to gains: Personal goals and the recovery of meaning. In P. T. P. Wong & P. S. Fry (Eds.), *The human quest for meaning* (pp. 163–178). Mahwah, NJ: Erlbaum.

Epley, N., Akalis, S., Waytz, A., & Cacioppo, J. T. (2008). Creating social connection through inferential reproduction: Loneliness and perceived agency in gadgets, Gods, and greyhounds. *Psychological Science, 19,* 114–120.

Exline, J. J., Park, C. L., Smyth, J. M., & Carey, M. P. (2011). Anger toward God: Social-cognitive predictors, prevalence, and links with adjustment to bereavement and cancer. *Journal of Personality and Social Psychology, 100,* 129–148.

Fincher, C. L., & Thornhill, R. (2012). Parasite-stress promotes in-group assortative sociality: The cases of strong family ties and heightened religiosity. *Behavioral and Brain Sciences, 31,* 1–19.

Fischer, P., Greitemeyer, T., Kastenmüller, A., Jonas, E., & Frey, D. (2006). Coping with terrorism: The impact of increased salience of terrorism on mood and self-efficacy of intrinsically religious and nonreligious people. *Personality and Social Psychology Bulletin, 32,* 365–377.

Freud, S. (1961). *The future of an illusion* (J. Strachey, Trans.). New York: Norton. (Original work published 1927)

Friedman, M., & Rholes, W. S. (2007). Successfully challenging fundamentalists' beliefs results in increased death awareness. *Journal of Experimental Social Psychology, 43,* 794–801.

Gaertner, L., Sedikides, C., Luke, M. A., & Iuzzini, J. (2008). Hierarchy among selves: An implication for relations with persons versus groups. In H. A. Wayment & J. J. Bauer (Eds.), *Transcending self-interest: Psychological explorations of the quiet ego* (pp. 127–135). Washington, DC: American Psychological Association.

Gaertner, L., Sedikides, C., & O'Mara, E. (2008). On the motivational primacy of the individual self: "I" is stronger than "We." *Social and Personality Psychology Compass, 2,* 1913–1929.

Gallup, G., Jr., & Jones, S. (1989). *One hundred questions and answers: Religion in America.* Princeton, NJ: Princeton Religious Research Center.

Gebauer, J. E., & Maio, G. R. (2012). The need to belong can motivate belief in God. *Journal of Personality, 80,* 465–501.

Gebauer, J. E., Nehrlich, A. D., Sedikides, C., & Neberich, W. (in press). The psychological benefits of income are contingent on individual-level and culture-level religiosity. *Social Psychological and Personality Science.*

Gebauer, J. E., Paulhus, D. L., & Neberich, W. (2013). Big Two personality and religiosity across cultures: Communals as religious conformists and agentics as religious contrarians. *Social Psychological and Personality Science, 4,* 21–30.

Gebauer, J. E., Sedikides, C., & Neberich, W. (2012). Religiosity, self-esteem, and psychological health: On the cross-cultural specificity of the benefits of religiosity. *Psychological Science, 23,* 158–160.

Geertz, C. (1966). Religion as a cultural system. In M. Banton (Ed.), *Anthropological approaches to the study of religion* (pp. 1–46). London: Tavistock.

Gervais, W. M., Shariff, A. F., & Norenzayan, A. (2011). Do you believe in atheists? Distrust is central to anti-atheist prejudice. *Journal of Personality and Social Psychology, 101,* 1189–1206.

Gorsuch, R. L. (1986). The conceptualization of God as seen in adjective ratings. *Journal for the Scientific Study of Religion, 7,* 56–64.

Graham, J., & Haidt, J. (2010). Beyond beliefs: Religions bind individuals into moral communities. *Personality and Social Psychology Review, 14,* 140–150.

Granqvist, P., & Kirkpatrick, L. A. (2008). Attachment and religious representations and behavior. In J. Cassidy & P. R. Shaver (Eds.), *Handbook of attachment: Theory, research, and clinical applications* (2nd ed., pp. 906–933). New York: Guilford.

Granqvist, P., Mikulincer, M., Gewirtz, V., & Shaver, P. R. (2012). Experimental findings on God as an attachment figure: Normative processes and moderating effects of internal working models. *Journal of Personality and Social Psychology, 103,* 804–818.

Greenberg, J., Pyszczynski, T., & Solomon, S. (1986). The causes and consequences of a need for self-esteem: A terror management theory. In R. F. Baumeister (Ed.), *Public self and private self* (pp. 189–212). New York: Springer.

Greenberg, J., Simon, L., Porteus, J., Pyszczynski, T., & Solomon, S. (1995). Evidence of a terror management function of cultural icons: The effects of mortality salience on the inappropriate use of cherished cultural symbols. *Personality and Social Psychology Bulletin, 21,* 1221–1228.

Hall, D. L., Matz, D. C., & Wood, W. (2010). Why don't we practice what we preach? A meta-analytic review of religious racism. *Personality and Social Psychology Review, 14,* 126–139.

Harper, M. (2007). The stereotyping of nonreligious people by religious students: Contents and subtypes. *Journal for the Scientific Study of Religion, 46,* 539–552.

Haslam, S. A., Jetten, J., Postmes, T., & Haslam, C. (2009). Social identity, health and well-being: An emerging agenda for applied psychology. *Applied Psychology, 58,* 1–23.

Hawkley, L. C., Browne, M. W., & Cacioppo, J. T. (2005). How can I connect with thee? Let me count the ways. *Psychological Science, 16,* 798–804.

Hepper, E. G., Gramzow, R. H., & Sedikides, C. (2010). Individual differences in self-enhancement and self-protection strategies: An integrative analysis. *Journal of Personality, 78,* 781–814.

Hepper, E. G., Sedikides, C., & Cai, H. (2013). Self-enhancement and self-protection strategies in China: Cultural expressions of a fundamental human motive. *Journal of Cross-Cultural Psychology, 44*, 5–23.

Hicks, J., & Routledge, C. (2013). *The experience of meaning in life: Classical perspectives, emerging themes, and controversies*. New York: Springer.

Hogg, M. A., & Adelman, J. (in press). Self-uncertainty, social identity and support for political and religious violence. *Journal of Social Issues*.

Inzlicht, M., McGregor, I., Hirsh, J. B., & Nash, K. (2009). Neural markers of religious conviction. *Psychological Science, 20*, 385–392.

Irons, W. (2008). Why people believe (what other people see as) crazy ideas. In J. Bulbulia, R. Sosis, C. Genet, R. Genet, & K. Wyman (Eds.), *The evolution of religion: Studies, theories, and critiques* (pp. 51–57). Santa Margarita, CA: Collins Foundation Press.

Jackson, L. M., & Hunsberger, B. (1999). An intergroup perspective on religion and prejudice. *Journal for the Scientific Study of Religion, 38*, 509–523.

James, W. (1902). *The varieties of religious experience: A study in human nature*. New York: Random House.

Johnson, M. K., Rowatt, W. C., & LaBouff, J. P. (2012). Religiosity and prejudice revisited: Ingroup favoritism, outgroup derogation, or both? *Psychology of Religion and Spirituality, 4*, 154–168.

Jonas, E., & Fischer, P. (2006). Terror management and religion: Evidence that intrinsic religiousness mitigates worldview defense following mortality salience. *Journal of Personality and Social Psychology, 91*, 553–567.

Kay, A. C., Gaucher, D., Napier, J. L., Callan, M. J., & Laurin, K. (2008). God and the government: Testing a compensatory control mechanism for the support of external systems. *Journal of Personality and Social Psychology, 95*, 18–35.

Kay, A. C., Moscovitch, D. M., & Laurin, K. (2010). Randomness, attributions of arousal, and belief in God. *Psychological Science, 21*, 216–218.

Kay, A. C., Shepherd, S., Blatz, C. W., Chua, S. N., & Galinsky, A. D. (2010). For God (or) country: The hydraulic relation between government instability and belief in religious sources of control. *Journal of Personality and Social Psychology, 5*, 725–739.

Kelley, H. H. (1971). *Attributions in social interaction*. Morristown, NJ: General Learning Press.

Kirkpatrick, L. A. (2005). *Attachment, evolution, and the psychology of religion*. New York: Guilford.

Kirkpatrick, L. A., Shillito, D. J., & Kellas, S. L. (1999). Loneliness, social support, and perceived relationships with God. *Journal of Social and Personal Relationships, 16*, 13–22.

Koole, S. L., McCullough, M. E., Kuhl, J., & Roelofsma, P. H. M. P. (2010). Why religion's burdens are light: From religiosity to implicit self-regulation. *Personality and Social Psychology Review, 14*, 95–107.

Kotarba, J. A. (1983). Perceptions of death, belief systems and the process of coping with chronic pain. *Social Science and Medicine, 17*, 681–689.

Laurin, K., Kay, A. C., & Moscovitch, D. M. (2008). On the belief in God: Towards an understanding of the emotional substrates of compensatory control. *Journal of Experimental Social Psychology, 44*, 1559–1562.

Mahoney, A. (2005). Religion and conflict in marital and parent–child relationships. *Journal of Social Issues, 61*, 689–706.

McCullough, M. E., Carter, E. C., DeWall, C. N., & Corrales, C. M. (2012). Religious cognition down-regulates sexually selected, characteristically male behaviors in men, but not in women. *Evolution and Human Behavior, 33,* 562–568.

McCullough, M. E., & Willoughby, B. L. B. (2009). Religion, self-control, and self-regulation: Associations, explanations, and implications. *Psychological Bulletin, 135*, 69–93.

McGregor, I. (2006). Zeal appeal: The allure of moral extremes. *Basic and Applied Social Psychology, 28*, 343–348.

McGregor, I., Haji, R., Nash, K. A., & Teper, R. (2008). Religious zeal and the uncertain self. *Basic and Applied Social Psychology, 30*, 183–188.

McGregor, I., Nash, K., Mann, N., & Phills, C. E. (2010). Anxious uncertainty and reactive approach motivation (RAM). *Journal of Personality and Social Psychology, 99*, 133–147.

McIntosh, D. N. (1995). Religion as schema, with implications for the relation between religion and coping. *International Journal for the Psychology of Religion, 5*, 1–16.

Norenzayan, A., & Hansen, I. G. (2006). Belief in supernatural agents in the face of death. *Personality and Social Psychology Bulletin, 32*, 174–187.

Osarchuk, M., & Tatz, S. J. (1973). Effect of induced fear of death on belief in afterlife. *Journal of Personality and Social Psychology, 27*, 256–260.

Paloutzian, R. F., Richardson, J. T., & Rambo, L. R. (1999). Religious conversion and personality change. *Journal of Personality, 67*, 1047–1079.

Pargament, K. I. (1997). *The psychology of religion and coping.* New York: Guilford.

Pargament, K. I., Koenig, H. G., & Perez, L. M. (2000). The many methods of religious coping: Development and initial validation of the RCOPE. *Journal of Clinical Psychology, 56*, 519–543.

Park, C. L. (2005). Religion as a meaning-making framework in coping with life stress. *Journal of Social Issues, 61*, 707–729.

Park, C. L. (2010). Making sense of the meaning literature: An integrative review of meaning making and its effects on adjustment to stressful life events. *Psychological Bulletin, 136*, 257–301.

Park, C. L., & Cohen, L. H. (1993). Religious and nonreligious coping with the death of a friend. *Cognitive Therapy and Research, 6*, 561–577.

Park, C. L., Edmondson, D., & Blank, T. O. (2009). Religious and non-religious pathways to stress-related growth in cancer survivors. *Applied Psychology: Health and Well-Being, 1*, 321–335.

Paulhus, D. L., & Holden, R. R. (2010). Measuring self-enhancement: From self-report to concrete behavior. In C. R. Agnew, D. E. Carlston, W. G. Graziano, & J. R. Kelly (Eds.), *Then a miracle occurs: Focusing on behavior in social psychological theory and research* (pp. 227–246). New York: Oxford University Press.

Pew Research Group. (2011). *Faith in flux: Changes in religious affiliation in the U.S. The Pew Forum on Religion and Public Life.* Retrieved February 7, 2012, from http://pewforum.org/docs/?DocID=409.

Puffer, K., Pence, K., Graverson, T., Pate, E., Clegg, S., & Wolfe, M. (2008). Religious doubt and identity formation: Salient predictors of adolescent religious doubt. *Journal of Psychology and Theology, 36*, 270–284.

Ritchie, T. D., Sedikides, C., Wildschut, T., Arndt, J., & Gidron, Y. (2011). Self-concept clarity mediates the relation between stress and subjective well-being. *Self and Identity, 10*, 493–508.

Roccas, S. (2005). Religion and value systems. *Journal of Social Issues, 61*, 747–759.

Rosenberg, M. (1965). *Society and the adolescent self-image*. Princeton, NJ: Princeton University Press.

Rothbaum, F., Weisz, J. R., & Snyder, S. S. (1982). Changing the world and changing the self: A two-process model of perceived control. *Journal of Personality and Social Psychology, 42*, 5–37.

Rothschild, Z., Abdollahi, A., & Pyszczynski, T. (2009). Does peace have a prayer? The effect of mortality salience, compassionate values, and religious fundamentalism on hostility toward out-groups. *Journal of Experimental Social Psychology, 45*, 816–827.

Rowatt, W. C., & Kirkpatrick, L. A. (2002). Two dimensions of attachment to God and their relation to affect, personality, and religiosity constructs. *Journal for the Scientific Study of Religion, 41*, 637–651.

Saroglou, V. (2010). Religiosity as a cultural adaptation of basic traits: A five-factor model perspective. *Personality and Social Psychology Review, 14*, 108–125.

Sasaki, J. Y., & Kim, H. S. (2011). At the intersection of culture and religion: A cultural analysis of religion's implications for secondary control and social affiliation. *Journal of Personality and Social Psychology, 101*, 401–414.

Sedikides, C. (Ed.). (2010a). Religiosity: Perspectives from social and personality psychology [Special issue]. *Personality and Social Psychology Review, 14*(1).

Sedikides, C. (2010b). Why does religiosity persist? *Personality and Social Psychology Review, 14*, 3–6.

Sedikides, C., & Brewer, M. B. (2001a). *Individual self, relational self, collective self*. Philadelphia, PA: Psychology Press.

Sedikides, C., & Brewer, M. B. (2001b). Individual, relational, and collective self: Partners, opponents, or strangers? In C. Sedikides & M. B. Brewer (Eds.), *Individual self, relational self, collective self* (pp. 1–4). Philadelphia, PA: Psychology Press. Advance online publication. doi:10.1177/1948550612469819.

Sedikides, C., Gaertner, L., Luke, M. A., O'Mara, E. M., & Gebauer, J. E. (in press). A three-tier hierarchy of self-potency: Individual self, relational self, collective self. *Advances in Experimental Social Psychology*.

Sedikides, C., Gaertner, G., & O'Mara, E. M. (2011). Individual self, relational self, collective self: Hierarchical ordering of the tripartite self. *Psychological Studies, 56*, 98–107.

Sedikides, C., & Gebauer, J. E. (2010). Religiosity as self-enhancement: A meta-analysis of the relation between socially desirable responding and religiosity. *Personality and Social Psychology Review, 14*, 17–36.

Sedikides, C., & Gregg, A. P. (2008). Self-enhancement: Food for thought. *Perspectives on Psychological Science, 3*, 102–116.

Shaver, P. R., & Fraley, R. C. (2008). Attachment, loss, and grief: Bowlby's views and current controversies. In J. Cassidy & P. R. Shaver (Eds.), *Handbook of attachment: Theory, research, and clinical applications* (2nd ed., pp. 48–77). New York: Guilford.

Shepherd, S., Kay, A. C., Landau, M. J., & Keefer, L. A. (2012). Evidence for the specificity of control motivations in worldview defense: Distinguishing compensatory control from uncertainty management and terror management processes. *Journal of Experimental Social Psychology, 47*, 949–958.

Sosis, R., Kress, H. C., & Boster, J. S. (2007). Scars for war: Evaluating alternative signaling explanations for cross-cultural variance in ritual costs. *Evolution and Human Behavior, 28*, 234–247.

Spilka, B., Hood, R. W., Jr., Hunsberger, B., & Gorsuch, R. (2003). *The psychology of religion: An empirical approach* (3rd ed.). New York: Guilford.

St. John of the Cross. (1990). *Dark night of the soul.* New York: Doubleday.

Sproull, L. S, & Faraj, S. (1995). Atheism, sex and databases. In B. Kahin & J. Keller (Eds.), *Public access to the internet* (pp. 62–81). Cambridge, MA: MIT Press.

Stern, J. (2003). *Terror in the name of God: Why religious militants kill.* New York: HarperCollins.

Tamayo, A., & Desjardins, L. (1976). Belief systems and conceptual images of parents and God. *Journal of Psychology, 92*, 131–140.

Taylor, S. E., Lerner, J. S., Sherman, D. K., Sage, R. M., & McDowell, N. K. (2003a). Portrait of the self-enhancer: Well adjusted and well liked or maladjusted and friendless? *Journal of Personality and Social Psychology, 84*, 165–176.

Taylor, S. E., Lerner, J. S., Sherman, D. K., Sage, R. M., McDowell, N. K. (2003b). Are self-enhancing cognitions associated with healthy or unhealthy biological profiles? *Journal of Personality and Social Psychology, 85*, 605–615.

Tix, A. P., & Frazier, P. A. (1998). The use of religious coping during stressful life events: Main effects, moderation, and mediation. *Journal of Consulting and Clinical Psychology, 66*, 411–422.

Trimble, D. E. (1997). The religious orientation scale: Review and meta-analysis of social desirability effects. *Educational and Psychological Measurement, 57*, 970–986.

Widman, D. R., Corcoran, K. E. & Nagy, R. E. (2009). Belonging to the same religion enhances the opinion of others' kindness and morality. *Journal of Social, Evolutionary, and Cultural Psychology, 3*, 281–289.

Wilkinson, P. J., & Coleman, P. G. (2010). Strong beliefs and coping in old age: A case-based comparison of atheism and religious faith. *Aging and Society, 30*, 337–361.

Wiltermuth, S. S., & Heath, C. (2009). Synchrony and cooperation. *Psychological Science, 20*, 1–5.

Wortmann, J. H., & Park, C. L. (2011). Religion/spirituality and change in meaning after bereavement: Qualitative evidence for the meaning making model. *Journal of Loss and Trauma, 14*, 17–34.

Vail, K. E., III, Juhl, J., Arndt, J., Vess, M., Routledge, C., & Rutjens, B. T. (2012). When death is good for life: Considering the positive trajectories of terror management. *Personality and Social Psychology Review, 16*, 303–329.

Vail, K. E., III, Rothschild, Z. K., Weise, D. R., Solomon, S., Pyszczynski, T., & Greenberg, J. (2010). A terror management analysis of the psychological functions of religion. *Personality and Social Psychology Review, 14,* 84–94.

Van den Bos, K. (2001). Uncertainty management: The influence of uncertainty salience on reactions to perceived procedural fairness. *Journal of Personality and Social Psychology, 80,* 931–941.

Van den Bos, K., Van Ameijde, J., & Van Gorp, H. (2006). On the psychology of religion: The role of personal uncertainty in religious worldview defense. *Basic and Applied Social Psychology, 28,* 333–341.

Ysseldyk, R., Matheson, K., & Anisman, H. (2010). Religiosity as identity: Toward an understanding of religion from a social identity perspective. *Personality and Social Psychology Review, 14,* 60–71.

4 Religious Cognition

Will M. Gervais

In the early years of the 20th century, William James delivered the lectures that would turn into his classic *The Varieties of Religious Experience: A Study in Human Nature*. Within, James argued that the sciences had largely overlooked religion as a topic of legitimate study, despite the fact that religion has played a major role in many, if not most, human lives throughout history. Throughout the remainder of the century, interest in the psychological factors that contribute to people's religious beliefs waxed and waned. However, the past decade or so has brought consistently renewed interest in questions related to the *cognitive* factors that enable and constrain religious beliefs, as well as the ways that people's religious beliefs in turn affect cognitive processes.

This chapter's central argument is that religious cognition does not represent a "special" category of cognition, although it may represent a specific configuration of (common) cognitions and beliefs. Instead, religious cognitions emerge largely through the workings of cognitive mechanisms devoted to other specific purposes. And specifically, many different aspects of religious cognition can be productively viewed and studied from within a conceptual framework highlighting the interaction between the social cognitive mechanisms that enable humans to perceive, represent, and reason about minds in the world and the potentially related social cognitive mechanisms that enable cultural learning. The interplay between social cognitive mechanisms for mind perception and cultural learning offers insights into diverse domains of religious cognition, including belief in supernatural agents, mind–body dualism, afterlife beliefs, and beliefs about the origins of species. In addition, an integrative perspective incorporating both cognition and culture can help explain large-scale patterns in the epidemiology and ontogenesis of *both* religious belief and religious disbelief.

Is Religious Cognition Special?

Humans possess a variety of different cognitive mechanisms devoted to performing a variety of specific tasks (e.g., Wellman & Gelman, 1992).

Is religious cognition itself a core cognitive domain in which children reliably develop similar intuitive expectations across cultural contexts, or is religious cognition instead a product of the workings of other cognitive capacities?

Most of the people who have ever lived—including most of the people alive today—have adopted various religious beliefs, and in many ways these beliefs appear to be constrained in specific ways. While the recurrence of similar themes—such as more-or-less anthropomorphic supernatural agents—across different religions might indicate the workings of specific mechanisms devoted to religious cognition, there is an emerging consensus that, rather than being its own core domain, religious cognition instead emerges as a byproduct of the workings of other cognitive faculties (e.g., Atran & Norenzayan, 2004; Barrett, 2000; Boyer, 2003).

We do not have cognitive mechanisms *for* religious cognition, but rather religious cognition tends to be a good fit for the types of mind that humans have. Successful religious beliefs and practices are able to mesh well with humans' existing cognitive architecture, even though this cognitive architecture is not specifically devoted to religious cognition. In this view, a central goal in studying religious cognition is exploring which specific cognitive faculties are especially likely to enable and interact with religious concepts. This perspective helps researchers to draw on existing cognitive literatures in order to "carve nature at the joints," and form productive hypotheses about the phenomena they study.

What Needs Explaining?

Religious cognition includes a rather disparate group of separate types of belief that people hold about the world. This section highlights some questions that a comprehensive model of religious cognition should consider, and subsequent sections will evaluate the explanatory power a mind perception framework offers for conceptually uniting these seemingly disparate phenomena. Of central importance to most (arguably *all*) religions, supernatural agent beliefs are an ideal point in which to begin exploring religious cognitions. Throughout history, most people have believed in the existence of at least one supernatural agent. To a researcher from another planet, this might provoke some genuinely puzzling inquiries. Why have the vast majority of people who have ever lived endorsed the existence of empirically unverifiable supernatural agents? Why do the endorsed supernatural agents of disparate peoples tend to be fairly similar in some ways, and incredibly different in others? What cognitive processes enable and constrain beliefs about supernatural agents?

Of course, not all religious concepts center on beliefs about gods. Many religions also include beliefs about the origins of the world and its inhabitants, or about purpose and apparent order in the world, or about mysterious existential quandaries such as what happens when people die. Do these types of religious concept depend on the same types of cognitive process as do supernatural agent beliefs?

Finally, although most of earth's human inhabitants have adopted religious beliefs of one sort or another, there are currently more than half of a billion people who do not adopt belief in gods (e.g., Zuckerman, 2007). What brings most people to belief, but a sizeable minority to disbelief?

On the surface, these appear to be a diverse set of questions about relatively unrelated phenomena. However, at their core, most of these questions are social in nature, focusing in some way on people's supposed interactions with other intentional social agents, be they human or supernatural. In addition, questions about apparent purpose and design in nature again center on the theme of intentionality. Finally, I will argue that much of the answer to why some people are not believers again comes down to social cognitive factors influencing either people's abilities to mentally represent intentional supernatural agents, or to the end result of the workings of social cognitive processes devoted to cultural learning.

Religious Cognitions as Inherently Social Phenomena

To illustrate how various forms of religious cognition are inherently social in nature, consider three distinct types of cognition: afterlife beliefs, beliefs about the origins and apparent functions of living things, and supernatural agent beliefs. Of course, these three types of cognition are not exclusively religious. For example, people may believe in a variety of supernatural agents not explicitly endorsed by their culture's dominant religion (e.g., ghosts or garden fairies). Nevertheless, all three of these types of belief are central to religions around the world. And all three fundamentally depend on social cognitive processes.

Many (if not most) religions include various afterlife beliefs (e.g., Bering, 2006). Not all faiths include afterlives in which people are allocated to either a good place or a bad place in reward (or punishment) for deeds committed while alive. But most faiths do include notions of what lies beyond the present life. But why should afterlife beliefs be viewed as social phenomena? Ultimately, belief in an afterlife depends on a form of mind–body dualism. People tend to view themselves as composed of two distinct, yet interacting, elements: a physical body, and a more ethereal mind or self (e.g., Boyer, 2001; Bloom, 2004). A body is what we are made of, but a mind is who we *are*. Bloom (2004) has argued that this type of folk dualism results from the distinct ways in which our minds perceive the world. According to this argument, we have distinct cognitive mechanisms for representing physical stuff in the world and for representing the social world, and the minds on which social interactions depend. Because separate cognitive mechanisms track physical objects and perceive the contents of other minds, it is easy to represent the two as fundamentally distinct elements of people. People are innate folk dualists because we use different cognitive mechanisms to track physical and social relations. And, although we might be able to see a body and represent that part of a person as dead, it may be harder to represent the (easily dissociable) mental aspects of a person as entirely absent from the world (e.g., Bering, 2006). So, without cognitive mechanisms that enable us to easily track the social world around us, dualism might not be intuitively compelling. And without dualism, afterlife beliefs make little sense. As with supernatural agent beliefs, afterlife beliefs depend directly on social cognition.

Many religions also deal with questions of teleology. Is there an underlying purpose or design to the world? Where did efficiently operating, apparently well-designed things like plants and animals come from? Even as children, people make teleological judgments about the natural world: clouds don't merely emit rain, clouds *are for* raining (e.g., Kelemen, 2004). Teleological thinking—ascribing functionality and purpose to the world—appears to be an intuitive default stance. For example, teleological thinking increases among people whose executive functions are disrupted, either by experimental manipulations (Kelemen & Rosset, 2009) or by Alzheimer's disease (Lombrozo, Kelemen, & Zaitchik, 2007). If people intuitively find it plausible to view the world as having purpose and function, it is a small step to believing in an intentional basis to this purpose and function. Indeed, there is evidence that children quite readily ascribe intentional causes (e.g., supernatural creators) as the ultimate origins of animal species (Evans, 2000, 2001). As with afterlife beliefs, social cognitive processes appear to be the bedrock on which (oftentimes) religious cognitions regarding teleology and the origins of species lie.

Across religions, supernatural agents play a prominent role. The supernatural agents in which people believe vary greatly across contexts, from the ancestor spirits common among many small-scale societies to the powerful morally concerned gods of most world religions. Yet despite these differences, the gods of most religions tend to be described and represented as intentional social agents with whom believers can interact. Indeed, a central point of many religions is that people can interact with their gods in order to assuage existential anxieties (e.g., Atran & Norenzayan, 2004). As intentional agents, the gods of most religions tend to be described in social, mentalistic terms. God can experience *anger* when his dictates are not adhered to. The Norse trickster god Loki *schemes* to interrupt the *goals* and *wishes* of Odin. Zeus becomes *upset* when his wife Hera *intends* to act in opposition to his *plans*. Some gods might be explicitly described as an abstract force, but implicitly, people tend to represent their gods as anthropomorphic social agents (e.g., Barrett & Keil, 1996). As I will argue in more detail in subsequent sections, the common anthropomorphic social aspects of supernatural agent beliefs around the globe may result from these beliefs emerging as byproducts of humans' basically similar social cognitive mechanisms that evolved for dealing with other human social agents.

In sum, many types of cognition fundamental to religions—including afterlife beliefs, beliefs about function and purpose in the world, and supernatural agent beliefs—variously depend on basic social cognitive processes. In the next section, I will explore supernatural agent beliefs in more detail, to highlight how certain religious cognitions can be viewed as extensions of everyday social cognition.

Mind Perception, God Perception

Supernatural agent beliefs are not exclusive to religions, but they are endemic to them. Believers typically describe (Guthrie, 1993) or implicitly represent (Barrett & Keil, 1996) their gods as anthropomorphic intentional agents with whom humans can meaningfully interact. Given that people's gods are seen as social agents, it is perhaps unsurprising that there are certain commonalities between ordinary social cognition and supernatural agent beliefs. However, a much stronger claim may also be made: that supernatural agent beliefs actually are directly derived byproducts from ordinary social cognition. Specifically, the cognitive capacity to represent and reason about other (human) minds in the world—variously termed mentalizing, mind perception, or theory of mind—is the specific cognitive faculty that both enables and constrains supernatural agent beliefs. This view makes a number of specific claims about supernatural agent beliefs that can be evaluated against currently available evidence. If supernatural agent beliefs are byproducts of everyday social cognitive processes in general, and mind perception abilities in particular, then it follows that:

1. Neurologically, the same brain regions known to underpin mind perception and social cognition should also be recruited when people are thinking about supernatural agents.
2. Developmentally, children's abilities to reason about supernatural agents should closely track developmental changes in children's mind perception abilities.
3. The same cognitive biases known to constrain mind perception in adults should constrain supernatural agent beliefs.
4. The same social contexts that lead people to seek out social connection with other minds should also lead people to seek out gods.
5. The same types of response triggered when people perceive other minds should also be triggered when people are thinking about supernatural agents.

What is Mind Perception?

Before exploring in detail the connections between mind perception and people's representations of supernatural agents, it is worth briefly discussing and defining mind perception. Just as people need to be able to form spatial representations of objects in order to navigate the physical landscape, individuals must be able to form representations of other people's minds in order to navigate the social landscape. The ability to perceive other minds allows people to gauge the intentions of others (e.g., "Is this big fellow smiling because he is about to hug me, or smiling because he is about to rob me?"), the knowledge states of others (e.g., "Is she a good source of information about where I should go to eat tonight?"), and to ease communication in ambiguous circumstances (e.g., "Was that a joke, or a serious business proposal?"). This is a challenging endeavor, of course, because people cannot directly witness the contents of others' minds, but must instead infer their contents based on indirect cues. Oftentimes, these inferences must be made with partial and inconsistent information. Nevertheless, most of us are able to easily survive the pitfalls of social life (i.e., most of the time, we do well enough).

Without providing a comprehensive summary of mind perception (which can be obtained instead in Epley & Waytz, 2010), there are several relevant and basic features. First, although there is vigorous debate about the exact timing of various developmental milestones, children's abilities to mentally represent other minds and their contents—termed theory of mind (Premack & Woodruff, 1978) or mentalizing (Frith & Frith, 2003)—follows a regular developmental trajectory during the first several years of most children's lives. By about the end of the second year of life, children are able to explain the behavior of others in mentalistic terms and know that people get upset when their desires are thwarted (e.g., Bartsch & Wellman, 1995). While this type of reasoning demonstrates holding a representation of another person's mental states (e.g., "I *know* what Mina *wants*"), a more complicated feat involves mentally representing cases in which another's mental states differ from one's own (e.g., Dennett, 1978; Flavell, 1986; Wimmer & Perner, 1983).

While the exact timing of developmental milestones is hotly debated, by mid-childhood most people can reason well about the beliefs of others, even when those beliefs differ from their own. However, even as adults, there are stable individual differences in advanced mind perception abilities. Most notable is the case of the autism spectrum, which is associated with deficits in advanced mentalizing abilities (e.g., Baron-Cohen, 1997; Frith, 2001). In addition, there is a reliable gender difference such that women tend to be better than men at advanced mentalizing tasks (e.g., Baron-Cohen, Joliffe, Mortimore, & Robertson, 1997; Baron-Cohen, Wheelwright, Hill, Raste, & Plumb, 2001; Stiller & Dunbar, 2007). So, although most adults have little trouble perceiving other minds (although see Birch & Bloom, 2007 for cases in which even adults fail false belief tasks), not all adults seem to be quite as adept in this regard.

Finally, there is a suite of social cognitive consequences triggered when people feel that they are targets of another mind's attention. Indeed, a classic study commonly cited as the first social psychological investigation (Triplett, 1898) studied what is essentially a question about mind perception: How does performance vary with the presence of an attentive audience? Perceived social surveillance (i.e., feeling that other minds are attending to oneself) typically leads people to worry about their appearances. That is, when people feel watched, they tend to experience a state of public self-awareness (e.g., Duval & Wicklund, 1972) that often interferes with performance on various tasks (e.g., Beilock & Carr, 2005; Savitsky & Gilovich, 2003). However, only agents perceived as mindful produce this effect (Allen, Blascovich, Tomaka, & Kelsey, 1991). And as people worry about how they appear to others, they may take steps to ensure that they look better. This leads both to increased socially desirable responding (Sproull, Subramani, Kiesler, Walker, & Waters, 1996) and increased prosocial behavior (Bateson, Nettle, & Roberts, 2006; Haley & Fessler, 2005) when people feel that they are being watched.

This brief discussion of mind perception sets the stage for a critical evaluation of the connections between mind perception and supernatural agent beliefs. If god perception "piggybacks" on social cognitive mechanisms primarily devoted to mind perception, then there should be intimate commonalities between the two at the levels of neurology, development, bias and constraint, context-dependent effects, and consequences. The following sections treat each of these cases individually, testing them against extant evidence from respective literatures.

Empirically Evaluating the Five Predictions

Neural Bases of Mind Perception and God Perception

In recent years, a number of researchers have used neuroimaging techniques in an attempt to elucidate which brain regions underlie religious cognition. If, as outlined in the present chapter, thinking about supernatural agents depends on cognitive machinery primarily devoted to ordinary, everyday mind perception, then one would predict substantial overlap in activation when participants are either thinking about God or performing more basic social cognition tasks. At least two research teams have independently found suggestive evidence that this is, indeed, the case. Schjoedt and colleagues (2009) explored patterns of neural activation in strongly religious Danish Christians as they either prayed to God (a supernatural agent these participants believe to be real) or made a wish to Santa Claus (a supernatural agent that no participants believed to be real). Relative to wishing to Santa, praying to God produced increased activation in the temporo-parietal junction, the temporopolar region, the anterior medial prefrontal cortex, and the precuneus, all regions classically identified with mind perception (see, e.g., Castelli, Frith, Happé, & Frith, 2000). These authors pithily summarized the implications of these findings (p. 205), that for believers "praying to God is an intersubjective experience comparable to 'normal' interpersonal interaction." Corroborating these findings, Kapogiannis and colleagues (2009) investigated the brain regions activated when participants were asked to think about God's mental states. Unsurprisingly (in the context of the present conceptual framework), the authors found heightened activity in the same brain regions known to underpin social cognition and mind perception. Combined, these studies demonstrate that thinking about gods and thinking about social interactions with other humans are entirely comparable activities, at a neurological level.

Developmental Trajectories of Mind Perception and God Perception

Children display developmental regularities in their understanding of other minds. Typically, this regularity is seen as a series of developmental milestones in which children are able to overcome a given error in their thinking about other minds (e.g., not being able to recognize that other minds can hold different knowledge than their own). If mind perception abilities underpin mental representation of supernatural agents, then the errors children make when thinking about other people's minds should also influence children's descriptions of God's mental capabilities. This is a particularly interesting prediction because many gods, the Judeo-Christian deity being a prime example, are described as omniscient—without mental limitations. Yet if children describe God in terms that reflect their own waxing understanding of other human minds, rather than in the explicitly omniscient terms that reflect what they most likely have heard about God, this would represent strong evidence that children's conceptions of supernatural agents are driven more by their own core social cognitive capabilities than by explicit religious indoctrination.

To investigate this question, Lane, Wellman, and Evans (2010) took advantage of a well-known limitation in children's developing mind perception abilities. Young children typically demonstrate a *reality bias*; that is, they assume that other people's minds have accurate knowledge about the world. As they get older, children come to appreciate that other minds can have false beliefs—they can be mistaken about the true state of the world. A classic test of this developmental step is the use of a task whereby children see a container that appears to contain one type of object (e.g., a Crayola crayon box usually holds crayons). Next, children are shown that the box in fact contains a different type of object (e.g., marbles). When asked what a naïve agent would predict as the contents of the box, young children report that the naïve agent would think that the container contains what it actually contains (marbles), while older children understand that the naïve agent would be fooled by the appearance of the container and therefore guess based on the apparent (rather than actual) contents (e.g., crayons). Lane and colleagues performed these sorts of task, only they asked children what God would think is in the box, and found an intriguing developmental trend. The youngest children reported that God would know the true contents of the box, consistent with either reality bias or an accurate representation of God's omniscience. During the age range in which children first begin to attribute false beliefs to others, they also attributed false beliefs to God! Only the oldest children were able to override this intuitive response and give a theologically correct description of an omniscient God. The most parsimonious interpretation of these findings is that children's representations of God's mental abilities closely mirror their representations of other human minds, with expectations of divine omniscience only explicitly coming online later, likely through enculturation rather than development. At the same time, this explicitly elaborated representation of an omniscient God is not without its flaws, as even adults will implicitly describe God as having anthropomorphic mental constraints, such as needing to have perceptual access to events to know that they are occurring (Barrett & Keil, 1996). Let us turn now to other ways that adults' intuitive representations of God diverge from explicitly espoused theological representations.

Adult Biases in Mind Perception and God Perception

As children develop, they become ever more adept at inferring and reasoning about the contents of other minds. However, this developmental trajectory does not arrive at an end point of perfectly accurate mind perception, and adults exhibit a number of biases in the ways that they reason about other minds. If mind perception abilities underpin mental representation of supernatural agents, then systematic biases in adult mind perception should also be reflected in adults' representations of God.

Among other biases, adults tend to assume that others hold similar beliefs as themselves, and only adjust this initial *egocentric bias* with additional processing (e.g., Krueger & Clement, 1994). To the extent that this mind perception bias also influences religious cognition, people should tend to have an egocentric bias when thinking about God's beliefs. Across an elegant series of studies, Epley and colleagues (2009) found converging evidence to support this hypothesis. On a variety of issues (e.g., abortion), people tend to report that God holds opinions similar to their own. Additionally, experimental manipulations of people's beliefs on various issues also caused them to change how they viewed God's beliefs. Strikingly, Epley and colleagues (2009) also compared brain activation while participants were thinking about their own beliefs and while participants were thinking about God's beliefs ... and found no differences. Combined, these studies do not merely indicate that people hold egocentric representations of God's mind (just as they hold egocentric representations of other human minds). Instead, Epley and colleagues found that representations of God's mind were even more egocentrically biased than were representations of the minds of other humans. This startling finding may be driven by the fact that people can adjust their initial egocentric representations of others' beliefs as they learn more about each other, yet people do not seem to frequently receive behavioral confirmation or disconfirmation of where God stands on things. Thus basic mind perception processes—along with their inherent biases—are all people have to go on.

Social Contexts Triggering Mind Perception and God Perception

Social cognition and mind perception processes are not always activated. Rather, they tend to be elicited in certain situations. If mind perception abilities underpin mental representation of supernatural agents, the same social contexts that lead people to seek out other minds in the world should also lead people to seek out affiliation with supernatural agents. What situations lead people to seek out other minds, however?

As inherently social creatures, humans have a need to belong (Baumeister & Leary, 1995), and people experience a variety of negative consequences when this need is thwarted, either through ostracism or loneliness (e.g., Williams, 2007). However, when people's need to belong is thwarted, they can seek out contact with other human minds through either seeking new friendships (Maner, DeWall, Baumeister, & Schaller, 2007) or in imagining new social contacts (Twenge, Catanese, & Baumeister, 2003). Epley, Akalis, Waytz, and Cacioppo (2008) investigated whether loneliness might lead people to increased belief in various supernatural agents. In one study, they had participants complete a questionnaire that purportedly predicted future life outcomes, but in reality was an experimental manipulation designed to make some participants feel lonely. After completing the questionnaire, participants received fake feedback that either made them feel okay about their future life prospects (e.g., "You're the type who has rewarding relationships throughout life") or made them feel as if they would live lonely lives (e.g., "You're the type who will end up alone later in life"). After receiving the good or bad news, participants—in an ostensibly separate task—filled out demographic questionnaires, including one that measured belief in supernatural agents, including God, angels, ghosts, and the devil. Participants who were made to feel lonely via the fake feedback given after the initial questionnaire reported greater belief in supernatural agents than did participants who were not made to feel lonely. This result was not merely the result of the manipulation making participants feel negative affect, as a subsequent study compared two experimental conditions that made participants feel negatively, albeit in different ways. There was a similar increase in belief in supernatural agents among participants who were made to feel lonely by watching a clip of Tom Hanks in *Cast Away*, relative to participants who were made to feel afraid by watching a clip from *Silence of the Lambs*.

Furthermore, there is evidence that thinking about supernatural agents can, in fact, buffer people against the ill effects of ostracism. After an experimental manipulation that made participants feel ostracized, participants who received a subtle religious prime were less susceptible to negative consequences then were participants who received no such prime (Aydin, Fischer, & Frey, 2010). Loneliness and ostracism leads people to seek out other minds in the world; however this basic affiliative motive to seek out other minds can lead either to people seeking new friendships, or to people seeking God. Both strategies help ease the sting of social pain.

Social Cognitive Consequences Triggered by Mind Perception and by God Perception

People are quite sensitive to the presence of other minds. However, other minds are not merely passive pieces of furniture in the social landscape. The minds of others can direct their attention on our own minds. Knowledge (or supposition) that we are targets of other minds' attention is known to trigger a host of social cognitive consequences. As already discussed, perceived social surveillance (i.e., feeling watched) leads to increased public self-awareness (e.g., Duval & Wicklund, 1972), socially desirable responding (Sproull et al., 1996), and prosocial behavior (e.g., Bateson et al., 2006; Haley & Fessler, 2005). If mind perception abilities underpin mental representation of supernatural agents, then thinking about gods should trigger these same consequences for believers. Indeed, thinking about a watchful, morally concerned god might be a particularly potent cue to trigger feelings of being watched, and thus a potent trigger for public self-awareness, socially desirable responding, or prosocial behavior.

The present conceptual framework provokes two interrelated questions. First, does thinking of God cause increased public self-awareness among believers? Second, is this effect comparable with the effect of feeling watched and judged by one's human peers? Some of my own work (Gervais & Norenzayan, 2012b) yields suggestive supporting evidence for both possibilities. In one study, we had participants rate a series of adjectives (e.g., loving, distant) based on different criteria. In a control condition, participants rated how common each adjective is in everyday speech. In a second condition aimed at eliciting public self-awareness through making participants think of human social surveillance, participants rated each adjective according to how much each participant felt that the word might be used by peers to describe the participant. In a final condition aimed at triggering thoughts of God, participants rated the degree to which they felt each adjective described God. After completing the adjective rating task, participants completed a brief measure of state of public self-awareness (sample item: "Right now I am self-conscious about the way I look"; Govern & Marsch, 2002). Among those participants who were high in belief in God, thinking about other people's judgments increased public self-awareness, as expected. More interestingly, however, thinking about God produced a comparable effect. For strong believers, thinking about judgment by one's peers and thinking about God appear to have psychologically similar results. For participants low in belief in God, the story was different, as thinking about judgment by one's peers elicited significantly more public self-awareness than did thinking about God (which, incidentally, produced the lowest public self-awareness of the three conditions).

Similar results emerge when looking at socially desirable responding. In terms of stable, trait-level associations, Trimble (1997) found a reliable positive association between religious beliefs and socially desirable responding in a meta-analysis of the correlates of religiosity. Although suggestive, this evidence cannot answer questions of causation. As with public self-awareness, there is experimental evidence linking thoughts of God to socially desirable responding. Gervais and Norenzayan (2012b) performed an experiment in which participants were given an opportunity to engage in socially desirable responding after receiving either a subtle prime to think about God or a control prime. Those participants primed to think about God were significantly more likely to agree with socially desirable (although likely untrue) statements such as "No matter who I'm talking to, I'm always a good listener." This effect was entirely driven by strong religious believers in this study, although it should be noted that the effects of priming religious concepts among nonbelievers are inconsistent across the literature.

Finally, just as people engage in more prosocial behavior when they feel watched, they are also more likely to engage in prosocial behavior when they are primed with religious and God concepts. Specifically, subtly priming thoughts of God and religion leads to increased honesty (Randolph-Seng & Nielsen, 2007), willingness to volunteer (Pichon, Boccato, & Saroglou, 2007), and anonymous generosity and fairness (Shariff & Norenzayan, 2007). Although there are possible alternative and complementary explanations for these effects, all are broadly consistent with the possibility that thinking of God leads to prosocial behavior in part by reminding people of a morally concerned, mindful agent who is monitoring their behavior. Future research should more directly address the potential mechanisms underlying the religion–prosociality link. However, given that God primes trigger a number of other social cognitive consequences associated with perceived social surveillance, mind perception does provide one framework within which such future research may prove fruitful.

Summary

A conceptual framework that views mind perception as a key cognitive foundation of religious belief leads to a number of empirically testable hypotheses. Although research on the foundations of religious cognition is still developing, current evidence largely converges to support hypotheses drawn from this perspective. Mind perception and god perception share substantial overlaps in neural activation, child development, and adult biases. Further, the same social contexts that prod people to seek out other minds in the world also promote belief in supernatural agents. Finally, thinking about other minds monitoring us triggers many of the same social cognitive consequences as does thinking about God, at least for believers. Thus far, most of this chapter's discussion has focused on ways that mind perception processes affect individual religious representations and concepts. The remainder of the chapter turns to instead view social cognition and religious cognition in the larger context of human interactions.

Religious Cognition in a Cultural Context

The preceding sections largely discussed the ways in which social cognitive mechanisms devoted to mind perception also underpin the mental representation of supernatural agents. However, it is a far step from being able to mentally represent a given supernatural agent and coming to believe that that agent actually exists. This is empirically and theoretically problematic, because even children are able to reliably distinguish between agents that actually exist and fictional agents, while being able to easily mentally represent both (e.g., Sharon & Woolley, 2004). Furthermore, children are can also reliably tell the difference between what actually exists and what only exists in pretense (e.g., DiLalla & Watson, 1988; Golomb & Galasso, 1995; Harris, Brown, Marriott, Whittal, & Harmer, 1991; Morison & Gardner, 1978; Samuels & Taylor, 1994). This should come as little surprise to any parent, who will no doubt notice his or her children readily engaging in pretend play, without confusing the pretense for reality. Indeed, many children mentally represent and "interact with" imaginary friends—often described as supernatural agents—while entirely understanding that the imaginary friends are not, in fact, real (Taylor, 1999). Given that it is easy for people to represent a wide variety of agents—supernatural and natural—without coming to believe that they are real, what mechanisms enable people to selectively come to believe in some agents, but not others?

One straightforward potential answer to this question is that people might find many supernatural agent concepts interesting or memorable, but they only come to believe in those supernatural agents who tend to be supported by a given cultural context (e.g., Gervais & Henrich, 2010; Gervais, Willard, Norenzayan, & Henrich, 2011). Cultural learning, rather than anything special about the cognitive content of a given supernatural agent, may explain the patterns of belief in given supernatural agents, as well as other facets of religious cognition. On one level, this claim seems obvious, almost to the point of tautology. Why else would children growing up in a primarily Christian region probably grow up to be Christians (or, perhaps, atheists who only produce arguments against a Christian God), rather than worshippers of Zeus and the ancient Greek pantheon (see Gervais & Henrich, 2010 for more discussion on this dilemma)?

Despite the prima facie plausibility of cultural learning as a belief mechanism in religious cognition, the issue is actually somewhat contentious within the literature. After all, following the logic of religion as a cognitive byproduct, might not cultural learning perhaps be unnecessary to produce belief in supernatural agents? In this view, belief is a default stance, and culture may operate only to produce disbelief (e.g., Bering, 2010). For example, Barrett (2010, p. 171) claims "little cultural scaffolding is necessary" to produce belief in supernatural agents. While there is much to recommend a perspective viewing much about religious cognition as a cognitive byproduct (indeed, as much of this chapter indicates, it is a perspective recommended by this author), it is insufficient to explain patterns of belief in supernatural agents. Furthermore, it fails to recognize a rich literature that has emerged in the past couple of decades recognizing culture as a potent force driving human cognition, cooperation, and evolution (e.g., Boyd, Richerson, & Henrich, 2011; Chudek & Henrich, 2011).

Cultural Learning and Religious Cognition

Humans inhabit a cultural niche, relying on information from conspecifics to an *unprecedented* degree in order to survive (Boyd et al., 2011). However, humans are not simple culture sponges who passively soak up information from their surrounding contexts. Rather, people possess a variety of specific social cognitive adaptations that allow them to pursue different specific cultural learning strategies (see Rendell et al., 2011, for a review). For example, a naïve cultural learner in a new environment may try to haphazardly learn vital skills through trial-and-error learning. Alternatively (and likely with more success), he or she could attempt to learn from other individuals in the area. For example, a learner could observe other people in the area and try to imitate what most other people are doing by adopting a *conformist learning* strategy (e.g., Boyd & Richerson, 1985; Henrich & Boyd, 1998). Rather than indiscriminately copying the majority of people, our cultural learner could instead selectively target and emulate cultural models who appear to be more successful or prestigious (e.g., Gil-White & Henrich, 2001). In order to figure out who is successful, our cultural learner could even simply see which other individuals seem to have a larger number of people imitating them—the imitation of others, after all, might be a good cue to who is worth imitating (e.g., Chudek, Heller, Birch, & Henrich, 2012; Gil-White & Henrich, 2001).

Naïve cultural learners cannot simply attend to information likely to have an immediate survival payoff. After all, a naïve learner, by definition, does not know which information is likely to be important. As a result, learners may generally use these learning strategies to adopt entire repertoires of behaviors, beliefs, norms, dress codes, food preferences, and so on from their surrounding cultural contexts. However, learners are likely to adopt beliefs that are backed up by actions. After all, talk is cheap, and learners can be more confident that a cultural model actually holds a belief if he or she is willing to engage in actions likely to be costly if the model did not actually hold the given belief (e.g., Henrich, 2009). For example, if a model informs a learner that bright red mushrooms are delicious and nutritious, the learner would likely be more persuaded if the model actually were willing to eat said mushrooms. That is, learners should pay keen attention to beliefs that are backed up by *credibility-enhancing displays* diagnostic of underlying belief (Henrich, 2009).

How might cultural learning strategies influence religious cognitions? Although this question has received more detailed treatment elsewhere (e.g., Gervais et al., 2011; Harris & Koenig, 2006), one general answer is possible. Imagine that our fictitious cultural learner is not trying to learn how to survive, but rather learning what to believe about the world. If savvy, the learner will use a variety of cultural learning strategies to assess the beliefs of others, including assessments of what most people (conformist transmission) or successful people (prestige-biased transmission) believe. In addition, the learner should pay special attention to beliefs backed up by actions (credibility-enhancing displays). In this latter case, religions around the world often include a variety of costly and painful rites that allow people to prove their faith—rites including ritual scarification, male and female genital mutilation, self-flagellation, dress codes, dietary restrictions, and even martyrdom. These costly credibility-enhancing displays likely help to ratchet up belief in and commitment to the tenets of a given religion (e.g., Atran & Henrich, 2010; Henrich, 2009). As an end result, our naïve cultural learner would most likely come to believe in the religion common to their own particular cultural milieu. By recognizing the specific cultural learning mechanisms underlying the formation of beliefs, researchers are able to more clearly specify the conditions under which individuals will come to believe in— rather than merely mentally represent—a given religious tenet.

Little about human nature makes sense without culture, and there is little reason—empirical or theoretical—to expect that something as fundamentally culturally bound as religious belief would be an exception. Indeed, there is evidence indicating that cultural learning strategies influence a wide array of religious cognitions, including afterlife beliefs, beliefs about the origins of species, and belief in supernatural agents (see, e.g., Gervais et al., 2011, for a more extended discussion of these topics.). The study of religious cognition may benefit greatly by more fully incorporating rigorous models of cultural learning strategies—and the social cognitive mechanisms that facilitate them—into the cognitive study of religion.

Non-Religious Cognition

It may seem odd to close a chapter on religious cognitions with a discussion of non-religious cognition. However, the rich theoretical landscape of religious cognition must also accommodate the cognitions of religious nonbelievers. After all, there are currently more than half of a billion nonbelievers in the world, making them the fourth largest "religious" group in the world (Zuckerman, 2007). The bulk of this chapter has focused on the ways in which social cognitive mechanisms—mind perception and cultural learning in particular—enable religious cognition to flourish. If these social cognitive mechanisms are largely universal to humans, and are also fundamental to religious cognition, why then are there so many nonbelievers (or any at all)? Or, to frame the question differently, if religious cognition is built on universal social cognitive foundations, then what are potential sources of individual differences in belief? The two main foci of this section present two candidate explanations for variability in religious cognition: individual differences in mind perception and differences in cultural learning inputs. I will now discuss relevant evidence pertaining to these two possibilities, with a specific focus on belief in God.

Individual Differences in Mind Perception and Belief in God

Most mentalizing tasks are designed to gauge whether or not children of various ages have passed various developmental milestones, and the measurement of advanced adult mentalizing is still a contentious issue. Nonetheless, as already discussed, available measures indicate that there are stable and appreciable differences in adults' advanced mind perception abilities. If mind perception abilities underpin mental representation of supernatural agents, then individual differences in advanced mentalizing abilities should predict variation in belief in God.

As previously noted, autism is associated with, among other things, deficits in mentalizing abilities. This raises the possibility that people with autism spectrum disorders might lack intuitive support for belief in God and, therefore, exhibit reduced belief. Indeed, one study (Norenzayan, Gervais, & Trzesniewski, 2012, Study 1) found that adolescents diagnosed with autism are only 11% as likely as neurotypical control participants to report strong belief in God. Subsequent tests examined whether the autism spectrum—the suite of traits that underlie autism, yet also vary considerably in nonclinical samples—was negatively correlated with belief in God. Across three studies drawing large samples in Canada and the United States (Norenzayan et al., 2012, Studies 2–4), the autism spectrum was, indeed, negatively associated with religious belief. This relationship was fully and significantly mediated by various measures of mentalizing, and held up as controlling for a whole slew of other factors that covary with the autism spectrum, religious belief, or both (e.g., education, income, interest in science, systemizing, personality). In sum, the mentalizing deficits associated with the autism spectrum also constrain the degree to which people believe in God.

In addition, there are reliable gender differences in advanced mentalizing abilities, as previously discussed. Interestingly, there are also reliable gender differences in belief in God: women tend to be more religious than men (e.g., Argyle & Beit-Hallahmi, 1975; Lenski, 1953; Miller & Hoffman, 1995; see also Chapter 14 in this volume). It is possible that gender differences in advanced mentalizing abilities explain the gender gap in belief in God. Indeed, across three studies (Norenzayan et al., 2012, Studies 2–4), mentalizing fully and significantly mediated gender differences in belief in God.

These findings—that advanced mentalizing abilities constrain belief in God—suggest a few avenues for future research. First, although autism is associated with mentalizing deficits, Crespi and Badcock (2008) argue that autism and schizophrenia can be seen as two endpoints on a spectrum, with hyperactive mind perception on the schizophrenic end. It is therefore possible that schizophrenic individuals might exhibit hyperreligiosity. Although there is no firm scientific consensus regarding relationships between schizophrenia and religiosity, and there is both active research and debate, there is at least some evidence (albeit somewhat tangential) that is consistent with a link between schizophrenia and religiosity: schizophrenic patients do tend to report higher belief in supernatural agents than do patients with anxiety disorders or depression (Kroll & Sheehan, 1989), and religious ideation is most common among those experiencing many other severe symptoms of schizophrenia (Siddle, Haddock, Tarrier, & Faragher, 2003). Second, the ability to mentalize is partially heritable (Hughes & Cutting, 1999), and the relationship between mentalizing and belief in God may help explain why religiosity is partially heritable (Bouchard, McGue, Lykken, & Tellegen, 1999).

Cultural Learning and Belief in God

Most people are able to easily mentally represent a whole host of supernatural agents, but they tend to only believe in some. I have argued that specific cultural learning strategies—including conformist learning, prestige-biased learning, and credibility-enhancing displays—lead people to selectively believe in some gods but not others. For example, somebody growing up in a cultural context in which cultural inputs support belief in Zeus is likely to believe in Zeus, rather than in Papa Gede, Vishnu, or Yahweh. And the converse is true for individuals growing up in cultural contexts supporting Papa Gede, Vishnu, or Yahweh, respectively. However, there are hundreds of millions of people on earth who do not endorse any of these gods, or any others for that matter. How might cultural learning explain these people?

Simply, if cultural input supporting a given god is necessary to instill belief in that god, then disbelief in all gods might simply result from contexts in which individuals do not receive clear cues to believe in any specific gods. Indeed, this appears to be the case for many, if not most, current inhabitants of Scandinavian countries such as Sweden and Denmark (Zuckerman, 2008). More detailed investigation lends further support.

In perhaps the most comprehensive test of the role cultural learning plays in supernatural agent beliefs, Lanman (2012) conducted widespread research to tease apart different potential sources of religious disbelief, particularly focusing on the role of credibility-enhancing displays. He queried believers and nonbelievers alike on the number of credibility-enhancing displays of their parents' religious faith they witnessed while growing up. While growing up, current believers witnessed almost twice as many credibility-enhancing displays of faith in supernatural agents than did nonbelievers. What is particularly striking, however, is that this staggering difference even holds up only when looking at participants whose parents espoused belief in God or gods. Far from belief in God or gods being a cognitive default that requires little cultural scaffolding, even children of religious believers who do not act on their faith are likely to grow up to be nonbelievers! Given these striking results, future research examining the contribution of other specific cultural learning to religious beliefs would be welcome.

Mentalizing deficits and cultural learning might be two distinct pathways to atheism, but they are not the only such pathways, and there are likely many distinct origins of religious disbelief (e.g., Norenzayan

& Gervais, 2013). Two likely pathways stem from existential security and cognitive style. First, religion tends to flourish in areas where everyday life is difficult and unpredictable (e.g., Norris & Inglehart, 2004). In the lab, presenting people with a variety of existential threats (loss of control, awareness of death, etc.) bolsters religious faith (e.g., Kay, Gaucher, McGregor, & Nash, 2010; Norenzayan & Hansen, 2006). Conversely, under conditions of existential security, or conditions in which the government provides stability, religious zeal fades (e.g., Kay, Shepherd, Blatz, Chua, & Galinsky, 2010; Norris & Inglehart, 2004) as witnessed in, for example, modern Scandinavia (e.g., Zuckerman, 2008). Second, people possess both intuitive and analytic systems for processing information, and religion looks to rest on largely intuitive foundations. As a result, increased reliance on analytic thinking predicts lower levels of religious and paranormal belief (Gervais & Norenzayan, 2012a; Pennycook, Cheyne, Seli, Koehler, & Fugelsang, 2012; Shenhav, Rand, & Greene, 2012), and experimental manipulations that trigger analytic thinking also reduce religious belief (Gervais & Norenzayan, 2012a; Shenhav et al., 2012).

Summary

The present conceptual framework identifies two potential sources of variability in religious cognition. Individual differences in mind perception abilities may be one source of variable religious belief. To the extent that the mental representation of gods requires adept abilities to represent and reason about the minds of others, then people's advanced mentalizing abilities may place a constraint on degrees of religious belief. Of course, most religious nonbelievers worldwide likely have intact mentalizing abilities, suggesting that other factors likely have major influences on religious belief and disbelief. Cultural learning appears to be one such factor, as credibility-enhancing displays greatly contribute to the development of belief in God or gods. However, research on both of these areas is still in its infancy, and much more empirical work is needed. In addition, it is likely that there are many more sources of variability in religious cognition than the two outlined here, and hopefully the coming years will bring further research into this gap in the literature.

Conclusions

The scientific study of religion has flourished in recent years. As this volume illustrates, social and personality psychology have been at the vanguard of a recent resurgence of empirically based approaches for understanding religion. This movement has in part been successful because it has been able to import successful research programs and theoretical frameworks from social and personality psychology. By drawing on existing literatures, researchers interested in understanding religion can pick from well-understood methodological tools and increasingly well-articulated models of human cognition.

The present chapter highlights mind perception as one cognitive foundation of religion. By viewing religions as inherently social phenomena that recruit and depend on the same cognitive mechanisms that govern everyday social interactions, a number of predictions come into sharp focus. Mind perception and religious cognition 1) depend on the same neural substrates, 2) track the same developmental patterns, 3) are influenced by the same sorts of bias, 4) are triggered by the same situations, and 5) trigger the same types of cognitive and behavioural response. In addition, cultural learning—which ultimately depends on mind perception—appears to be intimately intertwined with religious belief and disbelief. Mind perception and cultural learning explain some, but not all, pathways that lead some folks towards religion and other folks away from religion.

Social cognition provides one productive lens through which to view religious cognitions in general—and representations of supernatural agent beliefs in particular—deriving from ordinary social cognitive capacities for perceiving other minds in the world. These representations interact with still other social cognitive capacities devoted to cultural learning to help explain variation in religious cognition. Above all, however, the present chapter hopefully highlights how viewing religion in terms of more basic cognitive mechanisms may illuminate the rich tapestry of both religious and non-religious cognition.

References

Allen, K. M., Blascovich, J., Tomaka, J., & Kelsey, R. M. (1991). Presence of human friends and pet dogs as moderators of autonomic responses to stress in women. *Journal of Personality and Social Psychology, 61*, 582–589.

Argyle, M., & Beit-Hallahmi, B. (1975). *The social psychology of religion*. London: Routledge & Kegan Paul.

Atran, S., & Henrich, J. (2010). The evolution of religion: How cognitive by-products, adaptive learning heuristics, ritual displays, and group competition generate deep commitments to prosocial religions. *Biological Theory: Integrating Development, Evolution, and Cognition, 1*, 18–30.

Atran, S., & Norenzayan, A. (2004). Religion's evolutionary landscape: Counterintuition, commitment, compassion, communion. *Behavioral and Brain Sciences, 27*, 713–770.

Aydin, N., Fischer, P., & Frey, D. (2010). Turning to God in the face of ostracism: Effects of social exclusion on religiousness. *Personality and Social Psychology Bulletin, 36*, 742–753.

Baron-Cohen, S. (1997). *Mindblindness: An essay on autism and theory of mind*. Boston, MA: MIT Press.

Baron-Cohen, S., Joliffe, T., Mortimore, C., & Robertson, M. (1997). Another advanced test of theory of mind: Evidence from very high functioning adults with autism or Asperger Syndrome. *Journal of Child Psychology and Psychiatry, 38*, 813–822.

Baron-Cohen, S., Wheelwright, S., Hill, J., Raste, Y., & Plumb, I. (2001). The 'Reading the mind in the eyes' test revised version: A study with normal adults, and adults with Asperger Syndrome or high-functioning autism. *Journal of Child Psychology and Psychiatry, 42*, 241–252.

Barrett, J. L. (2000). Exploring the natural foundations of religious belief. *Trends in Cognitive Science, 4*, 29–34.

Barrett, J. L. (2010). The relative unnaturalness of atheism: On why Geertz and Markusson are both right and wrong. *Religion, 40*, 169–172.

Barrett, J. L., & Keil, F. C. (1996). Anthropomorphism and God concepts: Conceptualizing a non-natural entity. *Cognitive Psychology, 31*, 219–247.

Bartsch, K., & Wellman, H. M. (1995). *Children talk about the mind*. Oxford: Oxford University Press.

Bateson, M., Nettle, D., & Roberts, G. (2006). Cues of being watched enhance cooperation in a real-world setting. *Biology Letters, 2*, 412–414.

Baumeister, R. F., & Leary, M. R. (1995). The need to belong: Desire for interpersonal attachments as a fundamental human motivation. *Psychological Bulletin, 117*, 497–529.

Beilock, S. L., & Carr, T. H. (2005). When high-powered people fail: Working memory and "choking under pressure" in math. *Psychological Science, 16*, 101–105.

Bering, J. M. (2006). The folk psychology of souls. *Behavioral and Brain Sciences, 29*, 453–498.

Bering, J. (2010). Atheism is only skin deep: Geertz and Markusson rely mistakenly on sociodemographic data as meaningful indicators of underlying cognition. *Religion, 40*, 166–168.

Birch, S. A. J., & Bloom, P. (2007). The curse of knowledge in reasoning about false beliefs. *Psychological Science, 18*, 382–386.

Bloom, P. (2004). *Descartes' baby*. New York: Basic Books.

Bouchard, T. J., McGue, M., Lykken, D., & Tellegen, A. (1999). Intrinsic and extrinsic religiousness: Genetic and environmental influences and personality correlates. *Twin Research, 2*, 88–98.

Boyd, R., & Richerson, P. J. (1985). *Culture and the evolutionary process*. Chicago, IL: University of Chicago Press.

Boyd, R., Richerson, P. J., & Henrich, J. (2011) The cultural niche: Why social learning is essential for human adaptation. *Proceedings of the National Academy of Sciences of the United States, 108*, 10918–10925.

Boyer, P. (2001). *Religion explained: Evolutionary origins of religious thought*. New York: Basic Books.

Boyer, P. (2003). Religious thought and behaviour as by-products of brain function. *Trends in Cognitive Sciences, 7*, 119–124.

Castelli, F., Frith, C. D., Happé, F., & Frith, U. (2002). Autism, Asperger syndrome and brain mechanisms for the attribution of mental states to animated shapes. *Brain, 125*, 1839–1849.

Chudek, M., Heller, S., Birch, S., & Henrich, J. (2012). Prestige-biased cultural learning: Bystander's differential attention to potential models influences children's learning. *Evolution and Human Behavior, 33*, 46–56.

Chudek, M., & Henrich, J. (2011) Culture-gene coevolution, norm-psychology and the emergence of human prosociality. *Trends in Cognitive Sciences, 15*, 218–226.

Crespi, B. J., & Badcock, C. (2008). Psychosis and autism as diametrical disorders of the social brain. *Behavioral and Brain Sciences, 31*, 284–320.

Dennett, D. C. (1978). Beliefs about beliefs. *Behavioral and Brain Sciences, 1*, 568–570.

DiLalla, L. F., & Watson, M. W. (1988). Differentiation of fantasy and reality: Preschoolers' reactions to interruptions in their play. *Developmental Psychology, 24*, 286–291.

Duval, T. S., & Wicklund, R. A. (1972). *A theory of objective self-awareness.* New York: Academic Press.

Epley, N., Akalis, S., Waytz, A., & Cacioppo, J. T. (2008). Creating social connection through inferential reproduction: Loneliness and perceived agency in gadgets, gods, and greyhounds. *Psychological Science, 19*, 114–120.

Epley, N., Converse, B. A., Delbosc, A., Monteleone, G., & Cacioppo, J. (2009). Believers' estimates of God's beliefs are more egocentric than estimates of other people's beliefs. *Proceedings of the National Academy of Sciences, 106*, 21533–21538.

Epley, N., & Waytz, A. (2010). Mind perception. In S.T. Fiske, D.T. Gilbert, & G. Lindsay (Eds.), *Handbook of social psychology* (5th ed., pp. 498–541). New York: Wiley.

Evans, E. M. (2000). The emergence of beliefs about the origins of species in school-age children. *Merrill-Palmer Quarterly: A Journal of Developmental Psychology, 46*, 221–254.

Evans, E. M. (2001). Cognitive and contextual factors in the emergence of diverse belief systems: Creationism versus evolution. *Cognitive Psychology, 42*, 217–266.

Evans, J. S. B. T. (2003). In two minds: Dual-process accounts of reasoning. *Trends in Cognitive Sciences, 7*, 454–459.

Flavell, J. H. (1986). The development of children's knowledge about the appearance-reality distinction. *American Psychologist, 41*, 418–425.

Frith, U. (2001). Mind blindness and the brain in autism. *Neuron, 32*, 969–979.

Frith, U., & Frith, C. (2003). Development and neurophysiology of mentalizing. *Philosophical Transactions of the Royal Society of London B, 358*, 459–473.

Gervais, W. M., & Henrich, J. (2010). The Zeus problem: Why representational content biases cannot explain faith in gods. *Journal of Cognition and Culture, 10*, 383–389.

Gervais, W. M., & Norenzayan, A. (2012a). Analytic thinking promotes religious disbelief. *Science, 336*, 493–496.

Gervais, W. M., & Norenzayan, A. (2012b). Like a camera in the sky? Thinking about God increases public self-awareness and socially desirable responding. *Journal of Experimental Social Psychology, 48*, 298–302.

Gervais, W. M., Willard, A., Norenzayan, A., & Henrich, J. (2011). The cultural transmission of faith: Why natural intuitions and memory biases are necessary, but insufficient, to explain religious belief. *Religion, 41*, 389–411.

Gil-White, F., & Henrich, J. (2001). The evolution of prestige: Freely conferred deference as a mechanism for enhancing the benefits of cultural transmission. *Evolution and Human Behavior, 22*, 165–196.

Golomb, C., & Galasso, L. (1995). Make believe and reality: Explorations of the imaginary realm. *Developmental Psychology, 31*, 800–810.

Govern, J. M., & Marsch, L. A. (2002). Development and validation of the Situational Self-Awareness Scale. *Consciousness and Cognition, 10*, 366–378.

Guthrie, S. (1993). *Faces in the clouds.* Oxford: Oxford University Press.

Haley, K. J., & Fessler, D. M. T. (2005). Nobody's watching? Subtle cues affect generosity in an anonymous economic game. *Evolution and Human Behavior, 26*, 245–256.

Harris, P. L., Brown, E., Marriott, C., Whittall, S., & Harmer, S. (1991). Monsters, ghosts and witches: Testing the limits of the fantasy–reality distinction in young children. *British Journal of Developmental Psychology, 9*, 105–123.

Harris, P. L., & Koenig, M. A. (2006). Trust in testimony: How children learn about science and religion. *Child Development, 77*, 505–524.

Henrich, J. (2009). The evolution of costly displays, cooperation, and religion: Credibility enhancing displays and their implications for cultural evolution. *Evolution and Human Behaviour, 30*, 244–260.

Henrich, J., & Boyd, R. (1998). The evolution of conformist transmission and the emergence of between-group differences. *Evolution and Human Behavior, 19*, 215–242.

Hughes, C., & Cutting, A. L. (1999). Nature, nurture, and individual differences in early understanding of mind. *Psychological Science, 10*, 429–432.

Kapogiannis, D., Barbey, A. K., Su, M., Zamboni, G., Krueger, F., & Grafman, J. (2009). Cognitive and neural foundations of religious belief. *Proceedings of the National Academy of Sciences, 106*, 4876–4881.

Kay, A. C., Gaucher, D., McGregor, I., & Nash, K. (2010). Religious conviction as compensatory control. *Personality and Social Psychology Review, 14*, 37–48.

Kay, A. C., Shepherd, S., Blatz, C. W., Chua, S. N., & Galinsky, A. D. (2010). For God (or) country: The hydraulic relation between government instability and belief in religious sources of control. *Journal of Personality and Social Psychology, 5*, 725–739.

Kelemen, D. (2004). Are children "intuitive theists"? Reasoning about purpose and design in nature. *Psychological Science, 15*, 295–301.

Kelemen, D., & Rosset, E. (2009). The human function compunction: Teleological explanation in adults. *Cognition, 111*, 138–143.

Kroll, J., & Sheehan, W. (1989). Religious beliefs and practices among 52 psychiatric inpatients in Minnesota. *American Journal of Psychiatry, 146*, 67–72.

Krueger, J., & Clement, R. W. (1994). The truly false consensus effect: An ineradicable and egocentric bias in social perception. *Journal of Personality and Social Psychology, 67*, 596–610.

Lane, J. D., Wellman, H., & Evans, E. M. (2010). Children's understanding of ordinary and extraordinary minds. *Child Development, 81*, 1475–1489.

Lanman, J. A. (2012). The importance of religious displays for belief acquisition and secularization. *Journal of Contemporary Religion, 27*, 49–65.

Lenski, G. E. (1953). Social correlates of religious interest. *American Sociological Review, 18*, 533–544.

Lombrozo, T., Kelemen, D., & Zaitchik, D. (2007). Inferring design: Evidence of a preference for teleological explanations in patients with Alzheimer's disease. *Psychological Science, 18*, 999–1006.

Maner, J. K., DeWall, C. N., Baumeister, R. F., & Schaller, M. (2007). Does social exclusion motivate interpersonal reconnection? Resolving the "porcupine problem." *Journal of Personality and Social Psychology, 92*, 42–55.

Miller, A., & Hoffman, J. (1995). Risk and religion: An explanation of gender differences in religiosity. *Journal for the Scientific Study of Religion, 34*, 63–75.

Morison, P., & Gardner, H. (1978). Dragons and dinosaurs: The child's capacity to differentiate fantasy from reality. *Child Development, 49*, 642–648.

Norenzayan, A., & Gervais, W. M. (2013). The origins of religious disbelief. *Trends in Cognitive Sciences, 17*, 20–25.

Norenzayan, A., Gervais, W. M., & Trzesniewski, K. (2012). *Mentalizing deficits constrain religious belief in a personal God*. PLOS One, 7, e36880.

Norenzayan, A., & Hansen, I. G. (2006). Belief in supernatural agents in the face of death. *Personality and Social Psychology Bulletin, 32*, 174–187.

Norris, P., & Inglehart, R. (2004). *Sacred and secular: Religion and politics worldwide*. Cambridge: Cambridge University Press.

Pennycook, G., Cheyne, J. A., Seli, P., Koehler, D. J., & Fugelsang, J. A. (2012). Analytic cognitive style predicts religious and paranormal belief. *Cognition, 123*, 335–346.

Pichon, I., Boccato, G., & Saroglou, V. (2007). Nonconscious influences of religion on prosociality: A priming study. *European Journal of Social Psychology, 37*, 1032–1045.

Premack, D., & Woodruff, G. (1978). Does the chimpanzee have a theory of mind? *Behavioral and Brain Sciences, 1*, 515–526.

Randolph-Seng, B., & Nielsen, M. E. (2007). Honesty: One effect of primed religious representations. *International Journal for the Psychology of Religion, 17*, 303–315.

Rendell, L., Fogarty, L., Hoppitt, W., Morgan, T., Webster, M. M., & Laland, K. N. (2011). Cognitive culture: Theoretical and empirical insights into social learning strategies. *Trends in Cognitive Sciences, 15*, 68–76.

Samuels, A., & Taylor, M. (1994). Children's ability to distinguish fantasy events from real-life events. *British Journal of Developmental Psychology, 12*, 417–427.

Savitsky, K., & Gilovich, T. (2003). The illusion of transparency and the alleviation of speech anxiety. *Journal of Experimental Social Psychology, 39*, 618–625.

Schjoedt, U., Stodkilde-Jorgensen, H., Geerts, A. W., & Roepstorff, A. (2009). Highly religious participants recruit areas of social cognition in personal prayer. *SCAN, 4*, 199–207.

Shariff, A. F., & Norenzayan, A. (2007). God is watching you: Priming God concepts increases prosocial behavior in an anonymous economic game. *Psychological Science, 18*, 803–809.

Sharon, T., & Woolley, J. D. (2004). Do monsters dream? Young children's understanding of the fantasy/reality distinction. *British Journal of Developmental Psychology, 22*, 293–310.

Shenhav, A., Rand, D. G., & Greene, J. D. (2012). Divine intuition: Cognitive style influences belief in God. *Journal of Experimental Psychology: General, 141*, 423–428.

Siddle, R., Haddock, G., Tarrier, N., & Faragher, E. B. (2002). Religious delusions in patients admitted to hospital with schizophrenia. *Social Psychiatry and Psychiatric Epidemiology, 37*, 130–138.

Sproull, L., Subramani, R., Kiesler, S., Walker, J., & Waters, K. (1996). When the interface is a face. *Human–Computer Interaction, 11*, 97–124.

Stiller, J., & Dunbar, R. I. M. (2007). Perspective-taking and memory capacity predict social network size. *Social Networks, 29*, 93–104.

Taylor, M. (1999). *Imaginary companions and the children who create them.* New York: Oxford University Press.

Trimble, D. E. (1997). The religious orientation scale: Review and meta-analysis of social desirability effects. *Educational and Psychological Measurement, 57*, 970–986.

Triplett, N. (1898). The dynamogenic factors in pacemaking and competition. *American Journal of Psychology, 9*, 507–533.

Twenge, J. M., Catanese, K. R., & Baumeister, R. F. (2003). Social exclusion and the deconstructed state: Time perception, meaninglessness, lethargy, lack of emotion, and self-awareness. *Journal of Personality and Social Psychology, 85*, 409–423.

Wellman, H. M., & Gelman, S. A. (1992). Cognitive development: Foundational theories of core domains. *Annual Review of Psychology, 43*, 337–375.

Williams, K. D. (2007). Ostracism: The kiss of social death. *Social and Personality Psychology Compass, 1*, 236–247.

Wimmer, H., & Perner, J. (1983). Beliefs about beliefs: Representation and constraining function of wrong beliefs in young children's understanding of deception. *Cognition, 13*, 103–128.

Zuckerman, P. (2007). Atheism: Contemporary numbers and patterns. In M. Martin (Ed.), *The Cambridge companion to atheism* (pp. 47–65). Cambridge: Cambridge University Press.

Zuckerman, P. (2008). *Society without God: What the least religious nations can tell us about contentment.* New York: New York University Press.

5 Religion, Negative Emotions, and Regulation

Christopher T. Burris and Raluca Petrican

"Let us ... turn towards those persons who cannot so swiftly throw off the burden of the consciousness of evil, but are congenitally fated to suffer from its presence." With these words and his characteristic flourish, William James (1961 [1902], pp. 118–119) began his exposition of the "sick-souled"—individuals whom he characterized as having a "neurotic constitution" (p. 127) and "born close to the pain-threshold, which the slightest irritants fatally send them over" (p. 120), and who are thus at risk for "becoming prey of a pathological melancholy" (p. 127). Although by no means inevitable, James goes on to suggest that such individuals may be predisposed to seek relief from their deep-seated unrest in the context of religion.

In broad terms, James's postulations set the agenda for this chapter. That is, we will first examine the evidence suggestive of a "sick-souled" neural profile typified by a predominance of negative emotionality that might predispose some individuals to seek out religion as a means of coping with such tendencies. More specifically, we will review neurophysiological research linking the same pattern of hemispheric functional dominance and neurotransmitter activity to both a predisposition towards spirituality/religiosity and a tendency to experience negative mood states and more global difficulties in cognitive-affective regulation. With this as a backdrop, we will suggest that some individuals who possess such a "sick-souled" neural profile may be inclined therefore to turn to religion as a means of coping with their negative affective states.

Subsequently, we will consider the ways in which religion can assist such individuals as they attempt to regulate and cope with a variety of negative emotions. In particular, we will present suggestive evidence that regular engagement in spiritual or religious activities does indeed lead to neurocognitive changes that may foster superior self-regulatory skills and, consequently, may be capable of offsetting the malignant consequences associated with a "sick-souled" neural profile. We will then explore the functionality of religion as a regulatory system from a social-cognitive perspective, with a particular focus on emotion regulation—which, we will argue, is in the service of maintaining one's religious identity. We will also consider some of the limitations and risks associated with this process.

A word of caution as we begin: Despite Exline's (2002) call for more research directed toward understanding the relationship between religion and negative emotions a decade ago, empirical investigations that tackle this question directly remain rather scarce. Consequently, although we cite empirical work wherever possible as we build our arguments, the links are often indirect and must be supplemented by reference to previous conceptual analyses and exemplars from the literatures of various faith traditions.

The Neurophysiological Profile of the "Sick Soul"

We begin by considering two lines of research suggestive of a "sick-souled" neural profile. First, we review evidence linking right hemispheric functional dominance both to a tendency to experience negative affect and be more reactive to negative events, and to a predisposition towards engaging in spiritual or religious experiences. Second, we present neurophysiological evidence concerning the effect of serotonergic hypofunction, and the ensuing dopaminergic hyperfunction, on both affective-behavioral regulation and a predisposition towards spirituality/religiosity, ranging from healthy to more pathological manifestations.

Right versus Left Hemispheric Dominance: Negative Affect

Research on the asymmetric involvement of the two hemispheres in supporting positive versus negative affective states has a long tradition in the neuropsychological literature (for a review, see Harmon-Jones, Gable, & Peterson, 2010). For example, studies dating as far back as the 1970s document depressive symptomatology following left hemispheric damage and manic symptomatology following right hemispheric lesions (Gainotti, 1972; Robinson & Price, 1982). With modern electrophysiological measures, researchers have been able to show that greater right (versus left) resting frontal activity, likely suggestive of right hemispheric functional dominance, may be a clinical marker of vulnerability to chronic negative affect, for it is evidenced by clinically depressed patients (Jacobs & Snyder, 1996; Schaffer, Davidson, & Saron, 1983) even when they are in remission (Henriques & Davidson, 1990). This effect extends to the general population: Tomarken, Davidson, Wheeler, and Doss (1992) documented a significant association between trait negative affect and greater right (versus left) resting frontal activity within the general population, and the opposite for trait positive affect and asymmetric resting state brain activity.

The aforementioned findings are by no means ubiquitous (e.g., Reid, Duke, & Allen, 1998; but see also Peterson & Harmon-Jones, 2009, for evidence regarding factors that may obstruct the detection of such effects). Nonetheless, evidence is accruing that greater right versus left resting frontal activity is not merely a correlate of higher levels of dispositional negative affect and heightened emotional reactivity to negative events (see Harmon-Jones et al., 2010), but is instead a causal contributor to the emergence of momentary negative affective states (Harmon-Jones, 2006). Recently, it has been suggested that the motivational value of the associated affective states as well as their valence predicts asymmetric resting frontal activity, with greater right activity being associated with withdrawal-focused affective states and greater left activity being linked to approach-focused affective states (see Harmon-Jones et al., 2010).

In sum, the current literature suggests that left versus right hemispheric functional dominance is associated with distinct affective profiles. That is, greater left (versus right) resting frontal activity, likely suggestive of left hemispheric functional dominance, predisposes one towards experiencing positive—particularly approach-focused—affective states such as joy. In contrast, greater right (versus left) resting frontal activity, likely suggestive of right hemispheric functional dominance, appears to render one more reactive to negative events and, thus, more likely to experience negative—particularly withdrawal-focused—affective states such as sadness.

Right versus Left Hemispheric Dominance: Spirituality/Religiosity

The literature concerning hemispheric dominance and predisposition towards spirituality/religiosity is rather mixed. On one hand, studies conducted with clinical populations—mostly temporal lobe epilepsy patients—identify greater left (versus right) hemispheric activity as a neurophysiological correlate of religiosity or inclination towards spirituality. For example, Wuerfel et al. (2004) reported a significant correlation between religiosity scores and reduced right, but not left, hippocampal volume (implying greater left versus right hemispheric activity) in temporal lobe epilepsy. Similarly, Britton and Bootzin (2004) confirmed that left, rather than right, temporal epileptiform activity predicts the occurrence of transcendental ("near death") experiences.

On the other hand, research conducted with neurologically intact individuals points to right hemispheric functional dominance as a neurophysiological marker for inclination towards spiritual activities. For example, a number of studies have documented greater right hemispheric activity in individuals predisposed to magical ideation and paranormal beliefs (e.g., Brugger, Gamma, Muri, Schafer, & Taylor, 1993; Leonhard & Brugger, 1998; Mohr, Rohrenbach, Laska, & Brugger, 2001; Persinger, 1993, 1994; Taylor, Zach, & Brugger, 2002). It should be noted, however, that all of these studies used behavioral instruments to assess laterality, and these are prone to contamination by various extraneous factors (see Previc, 2006). Nonetheless, right hemispheric dominance as a neural marker of religiosity has received additional support in studies that used more neurophysiologically focused measures of laterality. Specifically, based on an analysis of neurotransmitter catabolic patterns revealed through blood work, Kurup and Kurup (2003) documented that their small sample of atheists exhibited a neurophysiological profile that matched that of a left hemispheric chemical dominance comparison group, whereas the profile of their monastic sample was more consistent with a right hemispheric chemical dominance comparison group.

In sum, although the broad literature on hemispheric dominance and predisposition toward spirituality/religiosity is mixed, studies conducted with neurologically intact individuals suggest that right hemispheric functional dominance may be a neurophysiological marker of the religiously or spiritually inclined soul. Such a proposal is particularly intriguing in light of prior findings linking greater right (versus left) hemispheric activity to higher dispositional negative affect levels and heightened reactivity to negative events (Harmon-Jones et al., 2010). That negative affect and a predisposition towards spirituality/religiosity may both be linked to right hemispheric functional dominance suggests a neural profile reminiscent of James's (1961 [1902]) "sick soul," typified by a predominance of negative emotionality as a predisposing factor for engaging in religious activities as a potential "treatment" for such a state.

To the best of our knowledge, such a proposal has yet to be investigated empirically, but Burris and Petrican (2011) took a first step in that direction. As previously noted, Kurup and Kurup (2003) offered evidence suggesting that, relative to atheists, religious individuals are more likely to be right hemispheric dominant. Elsewhere, greater right (versus left) baseline frontal activity has been shown to predict heightened reactivity to negative emotion-inducing movies (Harmon-Jones et al., 2010). Drawing on these reports, Burris and Petrican (2011) documented that, among their age-traditional university sample, individuals who identified with religion reported greater sadness in response to a tragic news story than did self-identified atheists. This finding is certainly consistent with the suggestion that individuals who identify with religion are typified by right hemispheric dominance, but this group was also more capable of accessing positively as well as negatively valenced personal memories compared to atheists. Thus, more research is needed to clarify the links between right hemispheric functional dominance, predisposition towards negative affective states, and religiosity/spirituality.

Serotonergic and Dopaminergic Activity: Negative Affect

Deficient serotonergic functioning is currently considered to be a major risk factor for a number of mood disorders (Young, 2007), and reduced serotonin levels are regarded as a neurophysiological marker of clinical depression (Mulder, Porter, & Joyce, 2003). Reduced serotonin levels also have been linked to a host of other adverse socioaffective outcomes, both in humans and in animals, among which aggression—particularly in its impulsive forms (Coccaro, 1989)—figures most prominently (for a meta-analysis, see Moore, Scarpa, & Raine, 2002).

Moreover, because the serotonergic system seems to play a crucial role in regulating the functioning of the dopaminergic system (Sorensen et al., 1993), deficient functioning of the former results in a cascade of neurochemical dysfunctions. In particular, because the serotonergic system exerts an inhibitory effect on frontal dopamine activity (Millan, Dekeyne, & Gobert, 1998), reduced serotonin levels result in extremely high levels of frontal dopamine, which impact adversely one's capacity to self-regulate. The net behavioral effect of dopaminergic hyperfunction is a higher incidence of dysregulated behaviors—from addictions to impulsive and aggressive behaviors directed toward the self (e.g., violent suicidal attempts) and others (for a review of both human and animal findings, see Seo, Patrick, & Kennealy, 2008). The serotonergic hypofunction/dopaminergic hyperfunction profile has been identified as a neurophysiological marker of risk for Type 2 alcoholism, typified by early onset among anxiety-prone individuals who show general deficits in impulse control and a predisposition to engage in risky behaviors (see Seo et al., 2008).

Serotonergic and Dopaminergic Activity: Spirituality/Religiosity

A link between serotonergic system activity and propensity towards spiritual or religious experiences has also been documented. For example, reduced serotonin activity predicts higher self-reported spiritual acceptance scores (Borg, Andree, Soderstrom, & Farde, 2003), as well as more extreme religious beliefs and practices, resembling obsessive-compulsive symptoms (Fallon et al., 1990). Complementarily, drugs that inhibit serotonergic activity foster mystical states and religious experiences (Previc, 2006). Serotonergic hypofunction and the resulting dopaminergic hyperfunction have also been linked to higher incidence of quasi-religious behaviors: Surges in superstitious behaviors following hippocampal damage have been reported (Davenport & Holloway, 1980), presumably because of the associated loss in serotonergic (and cholinergic) inhibitory signals from the medial temporal lobe structures over the mesolimbic dopaminergic activity (Gray, Feldon, Rawlins, Hemsley, & Smith, 1991; Weiner, 2003).

The role of dopaminergic hyperfunction in religion has received extensive attention, and there is consensus concerning a positive relationship between variations in religiosity and dopaminergic activity.

For example, behavioral genetics studies have linked polymorphisms of a dopamine D4 receptor gene (linked to dopaminergic hyperfunction) to individual differences in spiritual acceptance (Previc, 2006) as well as novelty seeking and substance abuse liability (Vanyukov & Tarter, 2000). Experimental evidence of the role of dopamine in spiritual/religious experiences has also been reported in neurologically intact participants. Essentially, optimal dopamine activity levels foster superior perceptual and cognitive processing, but dopamine overactivity makes both perceptual and cognitive processing less precise and more error prone, thereby increasing susceptibility to paranormal ideation: Krummenacher, Mohr, Haker, and Brugger (2009) showed that, when administered a dopamine precursor, the perceptual sensitivity of their skeptic group approached the level of their paranormal believer group, which rendered the former more susceptible to paranormal thinking patterns typified by loosened associations and superstitious beliefs (Brugger, 2001; Brugger, Dowdy, & Graves, 1994).

Complementing these findings with neurologically intact individuals is a substantial body of research with clinical populations, characterized by dopaminergic hyperfunction, who exhibit behaviors suggestive of hyperreligiosity. Of these, schizophrenic patients (especially those who are paranoid) have received the most attention: They report stronger religious beliefs and more religious experiences compared to controls (Brewerton, 1994) as well as religious delusions ranging from the "messiah complex" (Goldwert, 1993) to the "passivity" delusion (feeling that one's thoughts and actions are controlled by God or another powerful spiritual entity: Frith, Blakemore, & Wolpert, 2000). Mania patients are likewise characterized by dopaminergic hyperfunction and, relative to controls, are much more likely to profess a belief in major religious tenets; they, too, often manifest religion-related delusions of grandiosity (Brewerton, 1994).

Additional evidence of the link between dopaminergic hyperfunction and predisposition to religiosity/spirituality comes from complementary investigations on patients who evidence extremely low dopaminergic activity levels, such as Parkinson's Disease patients. Impaired functioning of the prefrontal dopaminergic pathway, associated with Parkinson's Disease progression, has been linked to patients' apparently reduced capacity to access religiously relevant constructs and experiences (Butler, McNamara, & Durso, 2009; McNamara, Durso, & Brown, 2006).

In sum, research points to meaningful interrelationships among serotonergic hypofunction and the consequent dopaminergic hyperfunction, affective-behavioral regulation failures, and predisposition towards spirituality/religiosity, ranging from healthy to more pathological manifestations. The overarching theme is that increased dopaminergic activity levels, which can result from decreased serotonin levels linked to a higher incidence of negative affect, render one more receptive to spiritual/religious experiences and activities. Mild elevation of dopaminergic activity appears to increase susceptibility to paranormal ideation and increased belief in the relatedness of random events while decreasing the propensity to test those beliefs. More extreme dopaminergic hyperfunction leads to bizarre attributions of causality and relatedness that characterize the pathological thinking evidenced by clinical populations, such as mania or schizophrenic patients, who exhibit extreme forms of religiosity (Brugger et al., 1994).

Religion and Regulation: A Neuroscientific Perspective

The literature reviewed thus far suggests a neural profile of a spiritually/religiously inclined individual reminiscent of the "sick soul" (James, 1961 [1902]) —that is, one who is predisposed to bouts of negative affect and heightened reactivity to negative events, and who tends to show a "fuzzier" subjective representation of the world that makes him/her particularly receptive to paranormal ideation. Neurochemically speaking, increased dopaminergic activity seems to be the main mechanism underlying a cognitive-perceptual predisposition towards religion (e.g., Krummenacher et al., 2009). This link is intuitively appealing in light of prior neuroimaging studies documenting increased dopaminergic activity during religious experiences, suggesting that religious practices such as meditation and prayer depend critically on dopaminergic systems, encompassing the basal ganglia and prefrontal lobe structures (Azari et al., 2001; Beauregard & Paquette, 2006; Kapogiannis et al., 2009; Newberg, Pourdehnad, Alavi, & d'Aquili, 2003). There is also indirect evidence of increased dopaminergic activity during meditation and other religious behaviors in neurologically intact individuals, with most studies to date suggesting that meditation leads to an increase in primarily parasympathetic activity in the autonomic nervous system, reflected in lowered heart rate, blood pressure, and core body temperature (e.g., Hoffman et al., 1982; Newberg & Iversen, 2003; Schuman, 1980). This effect is similar to that observed following the administration of dopamine-enhancing drugs for controlling hypertension (see Previc, 2006) and is consistent with observations of increased parasympathetic activity during states that are characterized by high dopaminergic activity levels, such as dreaming (Miller & Horvath, 1976) and depersonalization reactions (Sierra & Berrios, 1998).

Previc's (2006) neurocognitive model of spiritual/religious experiences postulates that religious behaviors are supported by ventral dopaminergic pathways, encompassing temporal and frontal regions, that align most closely with the action-extrapersonal system; elsewhere, Previc (1998) has suggested that these support perceptual and motor sequences directed towards distant (particularly, upper) space. Thus, the engagement of ventral dopaminergic pathways during religious experiences is consistent with the experiential nature of religious entities, which are distant in time and place from the perceiver, paralleling the "real-life" entities that are normally processed by the dopaminergic extrapersonal system. This posited perceptual-experiential link between distant, upper space and religion may help account for religious experiences reported by pilots and astronauts while flying high above the ground (e.g., Gawron, 2004).

Thus, research suggests that engagement in religious/spiritual activities, such as prayer and meditation, is associated with recruitment of dopamine-rich prefrontal areas. Frequent activation of these areas, in turn, may increase their functional efficiency (see McNamara, 2001), thereby facilitating implementation of other behaviors supported by these structures, such as emotion regulation (Urry, Roeser, Lazar, & Poey, 2012). Engagement in religiously relevant activities such as meditation may also have a direct impact on the efficiency of the executive attentional mechanisms that are crucial to all self-regulatory processes (see Braboszcz, Hahusseau, & Delorme, 2010). Frequent engagement in spiritual/religious activities may thus yield structural and functional neural changes that increase the practitioner's capacity to ward off negative emotions and increase positive emotions—which may help to offset the adverse hedonic consequences associated with the "sick-souled" neural profile.

To illustrate, there is accumulating evidence that regular engagement in spiritual activities, specifically those that entail training of attentional mechanisms (i.e., meditation), is associated with structural changes in brain regions such as the anterior cingulate cortex and the dorsolateral prefrontal cortex (PFC) that support emotion regulation processes (Cahn & Polich, 2006). For example, Lazar et al. (2005) documented greater cortical thickness in regions of the dorsolateral PFC in expert meditators relative to control participants. Spiritual practice also leads to increased functional efficiency of emotional control-relevant neural areas: Urry et al. (2012) showed that higher levels of meditation practice predicted greater engagement of PFC cognitive control areas (i.e., left lateral PFC and dorsomedial PFC) during cognitive attempts to increase the level of positive emotions, which, in turn, predicted higher levels of daily positive affect.

Moreover, frequent engagement in spiritual activities seems to be associated with reduced neural reactivity to the affectively aversive aspects of stimuli. For example, long-term meditators, relative to non-meditators, have weaker anterior cortical responses to aversive movie clips (Aftanas & Golosheykin, 2005). Likewise, a five-month span of meditation training yielded decreased affective reactions to acute pain, as revealed by reduced recruitment of brain regions (i.e., thalamus, anterior cingulate cortex) involved in processing the emotional (versus purely physical) aspects of pain (Orme-Johnson, Schneider, Son, Nidich, & Cho, 2006). Suggesting that meditation is associated with superior capacity to regulate both negative and positive emotions, long-term Tibetan expert practitioners (versus novices) exhibit reduced neural activity in the amygdala in response to emotional stimuli of either valence when engaged in focused attention meditation (Brefczynski-Lewis, Lutz, Schaefer, Levinson, & Davidson, 2007). Suggesting that engagement in spiritual activities may train one's ability to respond flexibly (rather than indiscriminately) to affective stimuli, expert meditators from the same tradition (versus novices) exhibited greater amygdala responsiveness to affective stimuli when engaged in focused compassion meditation (Lutz, Brefczynski-Lewis, Johnstone, & Davidson, 2008).

Moving beyond meditation research, there is an emerging body of work attesting to the importance of religious symbols in promoting *situation-specific* self-regulatory success. For example, a recent study by Inzlicht and Tullett (2010) showed that increasing the cognitive accessibility of religious symbols among theists (but not atheists) via priming resulted in reduced neural responsivity (i.e., reduced anterior cingulate cortex activity) to errors on a Stroop color-naming task, suggesting that—among believers—religion can buffer against the anxiety provoked by making a mistake (see also Inzlicht, McGregor, Hirsh, & Nash, 2009). Findings such as these dovetail previous theoretical proposals that religious symbols possess unique emotional and motivational value. Indeed, Deeley (2004) suggested that an important function of religious rituals is to imbue ordinary objects with special significance, thereby transforming them into the emblematic or "sacred" among ritual participants. Importantly, this process depends on dopamine-mediated mechanisms that consequently come to be reliably recruited during subsequent presentations of the now "consecrated" symbols (cf. Deeley, 2004). This intriguing proposal carries significant implications concerning how religious symbols may foster self-regulation. For example, religious symbols may play a similar role to the one documented (e.g., Eisenberger et al., 2011) for attachment figures—that is, the triggering of safety signals, neurally supported by dopaminergic ventromedial prefrontal structures, that counteract the deleterious effects of immediate stressors. Alternatively (or additionally), because *self-regulation is linked to one's identity as a religious person* (see later), presentation of religious symbols under threatening circumstances may render more salient one's identity as a religious person, thereby triggering automatic emotion regulation processes, supported by dopaminergic prefrontal structures (for a review, see Mauss, Bunge, & Gross, 2007).

Although we are not aware of any studies testing the safety signal proposal, there is some recent empirical evidence supportive of the automatic emotion regulation proposal. Specifically, Wiech et al. (2009) documented that presentation of an image of the Virgin Mary (but not a non-religious image) led to lower pain ratings in practicing Catholics (but not non-religious individuals), and that the reported pain reductions correlated significantly with recruitment of prefrontal areas (i.e., the right ventrolateral prefrontal cortex) relevant to emotion regulation. Practicing Catholics' descriptions of their image exposure experience as "calm" and "meditative" was likewise suggestive of automatic emotion regulation, and hints that those participants may have engaged in self-focused reappraisal strategies that helped create a sense of detachment from the painful, immediate experience.

Earlier we presented evidence linking right hemispheric functional dominance and reduced serotonergic activity to tendencies to experience negative affect and be more reactive to negative events, as well as to a predisposition towards engaging in spiritual/religious experiences. We suggested that this neural profile maps well onto James's (1961 [1902]) description of a "sick soul." We also presented evidence that frequent engagement in spiritual/religious activities such as meditation or ritual may improve the practitioner's capacity to regulate emotions by boosting the functioning of neurocognitive mechanisms supporting self-regulation. Is it reasonable to suggest, then, that spiritual practice can help "treat"—or even "cure"—the "sick soul" by altering his/her neural profile? Pertinent data appear scarce. There is some evidence that spiritual activities may have a "therapeutic" effect on serotonin activity, i.e., increased serotonin activity during and after meditation (Bujatti & Riederer, 1976). Davidson et al. (2003) reported that, following six months of mindfulness meditation practice, participants exhibited enhanced left-sided prefrontal activity after induction of both positive and negative feelings—a pattern of neural activity that, in turn, predicted both reduced anxiety and negative emotional reactivity as well as higher levels of positive affect. Thus, spiritual practice—meditation, at least—may both enhance responsiveness to positive stimuli and decrease the original heightened responsiveness to negative stimuli that seems to typify religiously inclined individuals (Burris & Petrican, 2011). Nevertheless, a more comprehensive understanding of the spiritual/religious facilitators of such possible alterations and their resilience will require much additional research.

Religion and Regulation: A Social-Cognitive Perspective

Complementing these neurological considerations are social-cognitive considerations concerning the experience, expression, and regulation of emotion in religious contexts. Perhaps the most foundational is the explicit or implicit recognition within religion that *self-regulation is a moral issue* (cf. Baumeister & Exline, 1999), exemplified in the (predominantly Christian) US South by referring to the loss of one's temper or composure as "losing one's religion." By extension, we suggest that *self-regulation is linked to one's identity as a religious person* (Burris & Jackson, 2000) and is bolstered by a combination of external (e.g., like-minded religious peers and elders: Wilkins, 2008) and internal forces (e.g., the implicit audience of one's religious peers or the "watchful eye" of a deity: Burris & Navara, 2002; Shariff & Norenzayan, 2007).

The most concrete form of self-regulation, of course, is *behavioral* self-regulation, and religious traditions are rife with tales and teachings—from ancient Egypt's "weighing of the heart" to karma in Eastern traditions—that underscore the importance of engaging in prescribed behaviors and avoiding proscribed ones. Indeed, McCullough and Willoughby (2009) reviewed a broad range of research documenting the adaptive correlates of religious involvement—for example, "religious people tend to live slightly longer lives; suffer less from depressive symptoms; avoid trouble with sex, drugs, and the police; do better in school; enjoy more stable and more satisfying marriages; and more regularly visit their dentists" (p. 70).

At this point, the causal effects of personal religious involvement on such real-world behavioral markers of self-control are by no means clear. Nevertheless, Rounding, Lee, Jacobson, and Ji (2012) recently showed that subtly increasing the salience of religion in an experimental setting yielded a variety of behavioral effects on lab tasks that were consistent with putative markers of self-control such as "enduring discomfort, delaying gratification, exerting patience, and refraining from impulsive responses" (p. 636). Moreover, McCullough and Willoughby (2009) asserted that evidence is much more solid concerning religion's role in shaping the adherent's selection, pursuit, and management of personal goals, which can take the form of ascribing differential value to elements of one's inner experience, such as one's *motives*. For example, Christians tend to judge the intent to engage in proscribed behaviors as negatively as the behaviors themselves, whereas Jews from various subgroups (e.g., Orthodox, Conservative, Reform) do not (Cohen & Rankin, 2004). This difference appears linked to consonant teachings within these two traditions—in particular, the greater belief among Christians that one's inner experience will eventuate in behavior—and is more pronounced when the motive/behavior in question is proscribed (e.g., an extramarital affair) rather than prescribed (e.g., a charitable act).

Likewise, *emotions* can be targeted for regulation in religious contexts: Watts (1996; cf. Emmons, 2005; Watts, 2007) suggested that two primary approaches have manifest historically across various faith traditions. In one, as signifiers of the authenticity and depth of one's religious devotion, emotions and their expression are to be enhanced: Corrigan (2000) cited Hindu bhakti and Christian revivalism as examples of this approach. In the other, the devotee seeks to quiet his or her emotional state, possibly assisted by the suppression of outward emotional expression: Buddhist nirvana represents one idealized conception of such a state.

Notwithstanding the fact that these amplification and dampening approaches make opposing prescriptions, both reflect the same underlying assumption that emotions do not simply reflect one's motives, but also direct them. Thus, in a Christian revivalist context, intense guilt for one's misdeeds motivates repentance and a desire to seek forgiveness from God; likewise, in a Buddhist framework, strong emotion (positive or negative) maintains the attachments understood to be the root cause of human suffering. Consequently, intervening at the emotional level can be understood as facilitating the attainment of religiously approved goals (cf. Saroglou, Buxant, & Tilquin, 2008; Wilkins, 2008). Offering some support for this characterization, Tsai, Miao, and Seppala (2007) found that a (mostly Protestant) Christian student sample was more likely to idealize high-arousal positive affect (e.g., "excited"), whereas a comparable Buddhist sample was more likely to idealize low-arousal positive affect (e.g., "serene")—a difference that was also evident in both classical and contemporary texts representing the respective traditions. Moreover, the Buddhist sample also tended to devalue high-arousal negative affect (e.g., "fearful") compared to the Christian sample.

Complementing Tsai et al. (2007), the self-identified Christians in Kim-Prieto and Diener's (2009) large, multinational student sample reported experiencing love more frequently than did Muslims, Buddhists, and Jews; Muslims reported experiencing sadness and shame more than the other religious groups (which included Hindus in the latter case); Buddhists tended to report lowest frequencies of experienced emotions (positive and negative) among the groups represented. In a follow-up study with a much smaller student sample, Christians were especially likely to rate love as desirable relative to other religious groups; Muslims were more likely to enshrine sadness (with shame and jealousy trending similarly). Conceptually replicating Tsai et al. (2007), Buddhists' ratings of the desirability of both positive and negative emotions were muted overall. Lastly, Christians were more likely to characterize their current emotional state in terms of "love" when their religious identity was made salient experimentally.

Kim-Prieto and Diener (2009) are to be commended for what appears to be the most expansive investigation of the relationship between faith traditions and emotions to date; nevertheless, there are constraints with respect to the questions that their data can answer. First, we must note that the negative emotions sampled were an eclectic mix of basic (sadness, anger) and more complex (guilt, shame, and [romantic] jealousy). Missing were basic emotions such as fear and disgust, as well as more complex emotions such as existential anxiety that may be especially pertinent in multifaith contexts (see Tomás-Sábado & Limonero, 2009, for a partial review).

Kim-Prieto and Diener's (2009) results *do* suggest some correspondence between the religious tradition with which one identifies and both the specific emotions that one values and the self-reported frequency of specific emotions that one experiences. Asserting that religious differences *cause* emotion differences oversteps the limits of these cross-sectional data, however, so longitudinal studies that track the emotions idealized and experienced by apostates from, and converts into, the faith traditions represented could prove useful in addressing the causality issue (see Kim, Seidlitz, Ro, Evinger, & Duberstein, 2004, for a cross-sectional exploration of links between religious change and predominant emotions in a Korean sample).

That declaration of one's religious identity on a demographic questionnaire increased Christian respondents' state self-reports of "love" in Kim-Prieto and Diener (2009) is likewise intriguing, but difficult to interpret. Did this salience manipulation cue feelings of affection for like-minded believers and/or their deity so that increased self-reports of love accurately reflected respondents' online experience? Alternatively, did the manipulation evoke a sense of "ought" linked to that tradition's teachings that influenced self-reports, but did not necessarily accurately reflect state emotions (cf. Wilkins, 2008; see also Kim-Prieto & Diener, 2009, p. 456, for additional interpretive possibilities)? Given multiple plausible interpretations and a restricted focus (i.e., Christians and "love"), the results of this provocative study by themselves do little to clarify the relationship between religion and emotions (positive or negative).

Instead, the most pertinent findings from Kim-Prieto and Diener (2009) concerned the greater ascribed importance and self-reported frequencies of negative emotions (particularly sadness) among Muslims. Unfortunately, as those authors conceded, it is unclear whether these results were attributable to a melancholic ethos that is possibly endemic to Islam, or were instead an artifact of the cultural, political, and economic strains currently facing Muslims in many areas of the world. A definitive interpretation seems even more elusive in light of Abu-Raiya and Pargament's (2011) conclusion, based on a comprehensive review of the empirical psychological literature concerning Islam, that although pockets of maladaptive coping indeed exist therein, "most Muslims adopt types of religiousness that enhance their lives and foster their well-being" (p. 106). Moreover, these authors noted an "unwillingness of many Muslims to admit negative consequences of Islam" for "admitting religious struggles and doubts might be considered by some Muslims as an offence to Allah" (p. 107). This suggests, if anything, that Muslims would be prone to underreporting (rather than exaggerating the prevalence of) negative emotions.

Emotion Regulation in the Service of Religious Identity: The Sovereign Principle?

Abu-Raiya and Pargament's (2011) observations point to what may be the sovereign principle that guides individual emotion regulation in religious contexts: *Emotion regulation is in the service of preserving and promoting the religious identity of the individual.* That is, we suggest that both the dampening and the amplification strategies (Watts, 1996) are impractical if utilized inflexibly. Indeed, although Buddhists are averse to a wide range of intense emotions, bliss seems to be accorded an exceptional status. Likewise, as we will see later, the meaning that Christians ascribe to intense states of happiness or sadness is highly situation specific. This sort of selectivity instead seems to parallel the third way described by Watts (1996), an approach that he labeled "emotional refinement." That is, the correspondence between the usual experiential valence of an emotional state and its appraised significance is straightforward in some instances ("positive is positive, and negative is negative"), but subverted in others ("positive is negative, and negative is positive")—all in the service of maintaining religious identity.

"Positive is Positive; Negative is Negative"

One of the most suggestively documented illustrations of the first principle concerns the differential significance accorded to happiness and sadness within (particularly the evangelical) Christian tradition. We have already noted Tsai et al.'s (2007) finding that a (mostly Protestant) Christian student sample was more likely to idealize high-arousal positive affect (i.e., excited, enthusiastic, elated, euphoric) relative to a Buddhist student sample, a difference that was reflected in both classical and contemporary texts representative of those traditions. Based on participant observation and interviews with members of an American evangelical Christian student organization that she dubbed "Unity Christians," Wilkins (2008) concluded that "happiness is compulsory" within that group. For example, she observed that "Unity's formulation limits (if not eliminates) participants' access to negative emotions like anger and sadness, while requiring them to relentlessly generate a wide range of socially desirable emotions, including love and peacefulness, regardless of life circumstance" (p. 283). Thus, happiness is set forth explicitly by the religious group as a signifier of one's religious identity, i.e., that one believes and behaves correctly. Indeed, Wilkins described many of her interviewees' conversion narratives as "retroactive and formulaic": "Just as participants learn to talk about good emotions, they also learn to refer to their pre-Christian lives in terms of bad emotions" (p. 288).

It should be noted, moreover, that the pursuit of "authentic happiness" among Unity Christians manifested in behavior as well as self-report. Indeed, devotees were encouraged to engage in daily introspection, often with the express purpose of developing consistent emotion regulation strategies. Such inner work appears to be undertaken—or at least reported—in broader contexts as well. For example, Paek (2006) found devout, intrinsic religious orientation to be positively correlated with self-reported "clarity of emotions" (i.e., the ability to understand one's moods) in a Christian sample wherein 80% self-identified as evangelical, Pentecostal, or nondenominational.

Wilkins' (2008) interviewees were also encouraged by their group's leadership to discuss their regulatory efforts with one another as a means of fostering individual accountability. She relayed a particularly striking story of a young woman ("Hannah") who described "calling on Jesus" while sitting, alone and bleeding, in the aftermath of a serious car accident: "It was one of the sweetest days of my life. It should have been traumatic but it was just Him." According to Wilkins, "Hannah's ability to control her more difficult emotions and to generate more desirable feelings helped her get through a bad situation, but it also made her feel good about herself, as it confirmed her Christian identity" (pp. 293–294). Suggesting that Hannah's experience is not unique, Friedman (2008) found that higher scores on a fundamentalism measure predicted more frequent use of positive emotion words in response to a prompt to write about one's own death. More broadly, Bamford and Lagattuta (2010) showed that, by 8 years of age, children understand the experience of negative emotion (especially sadness and fear, versus anger) to be a viable motive for prayer, and that prayer can have ameliorative effects on one's emotional state (cf. Kashdan & Nezlek, 2012).

Among those for whom positive emotion is a signifier of "authentic" religious experience, the presence and pervasiveness of negative emotion is a spiritual warning sign. For example, Wilkins (2008) noted the "relentless exclusion of bad emotions" among Unity Christians in the service of identity maintenance. More specifically, she claimed that securing one's place in the group "depends on multiple exclusions: the exclusion of emotions like anger and anxiety, the exclusion of people who do not share their emotional repertoire, the exclusion of behaviors that might create bad feelings, and so forth" (p. 288). Suspicion of recurrent negative emotions is not exclusive to Unity Christians. For example, based on content analysis of representative texts, Webb, Stetz, and Hedden (2008) found that contemporary (mostly evangelical) Christian self-help authors frequently singled out depression as arising from demonic influence and oppression, and/or the spiritual shortcomings of the afflicted individual. We suspect that such attributions may seem all the more compelling to some religious group members given Exline, Yali, and Lobel's (1999) finding that "anger at God"—a stance likely regarded as unjustifiable by those who assume that God is irrefutably good—was correlated with depressed/anxious mood among their mostly Christian student sample.

Along with the chronic, negative emotional states that typify depression, disgust also nicely fits the "negative is negative" designation. Core disgust seems to have originated as the body's rejection response to potential toxins or contaminants, but has since been co-opted by cultural systems (including religious ones) as an input for moral judgments (e.g., Haidt, Rozin, McCauley, & Imada, 1997). Although conceptually distinct, "core disgust" and "moral disgust" are often intertwined. For example, Jones and Fitness (2008) showed that greater sensitivity to core disgust elicitors predicted "moral hypervigilance," manifest in part as punitive responses to criminals—including a greater willingness to label them as "evil."

Of even greater relevance is Ritter and Preston (2011), who found that Christian participants who manually transcribed a passage from either the Koran or an atheist manifesto (versus a neutral text) showed increased sensitivity to a core disgust elicitor (i.e., the taste of an unsweetened lemon-water solution). In a follow-up study, this effect was neutralized if participants were given the opportunity to wash their hands, thereby symbolically purifying themselves after contact with the contaminating (outgroup) text. In those contexts, although clearly an aversive state, disgust seemed to function as a sort of "border patrol agent," reinforcing the boundary between "good" and "bad" people and deeds.

In a curious innovation, core disgust has also been used symbolically to illustrate the virtues of moral exemplars (saints) in the lore of historic Christianity. For example, Miller (1997, pp. 149ff.) presented the story of a leper healed by drinking the water in which St. Anselm had washed his own hands. Thus, what would be regarded as unclean under normal circumstances (i.e., discarded wash water) was purifying rather than contaminating: A horridly disfiguring disease of biblical vintage—a core disgust elicitor—was no match for a saint's sanctity. Miller (1997, pp. 158ff.) also recounted a story from the life of Catherine of Siena, who inhaled the odor of the cancerous sores afflicting a fellow sister, and even drank the pus-filled water that had washed those sores. Critical was Catherine's alleged appraisal: She framed her initial (core) disgust reaction as the work of the Devil, and persisted until she was able to perceive her acts as pleasurable. Thus, much like Wilkins' (2008) "Hannah," Catherine of Siena demonstrated her closeness to God via a Herculean act of emotion regulation— that is, overcoming an intense negative and replacing it with a positive (cf. Ellis's, 2011, analysis of the "left-hand path" in Hindu tantra).

"Positive is Negative; Negative is Positive"

This second principle—that, in the service of preserving and promoting religious identity, positively valenced emotions should not always be appraised as "good," and negatively valenced emotions should not always be appraised as "bad"—is no less important than the first principle. Indeed, its inherent subversiveness may contribute substantially to religion's flexibility and utility as a regulatory system. Illustrating the "positive is negative" aspect, Wilkins's (2008) Unity Christians regarded happiness as indicative of the correctness of one's moral and spiritual state *only* if it is "authentic," and it is only authentic if one is a believer. Thus, nonbelievers who think they are happy are either deceiving themselves or settling for an inferior experience.

Illustrating the "negative is positive" aspect, although depression is regarded as spiritually suspect by many contemporary evangelical Christian authors (Webb et al., 2008), Rubin (2007) provided numerous examples—from evangelical Christian Pietism as well as from the apophatic mystical traditions in Christianity, Hasidic Judaism, and Sufi Islam—of "godly sorrow." Each of these traditions, he claimed, has "structured religious ethics where the path to God and salvation has an elective affinity to melancholy" (p. 303), which is understood as an experiential state typified by a fusion of "fear, sadness, [and] hopelessness" (p. 292). Thus, there is a place for the "sick soul"—as long as that soul is moving toward God.

Likewise, fear and disgust, and guilt and anger, have their place—provided that they are harnessed in the service of religious ends. For example, Alcorta and Sosis (2005) noted that the evocation of negative affective states—especially fear and pain—is central to many religious rituals, particularly those involving initiates. Regarding these "rites of terror," Whitehouse (2007, p. 259) argued that "[i]t is not so much that one's beliefs inspire fear but that fear is a major part of the psychological processes that *give rise* to the gradual formation of mystical knowledge." Miller (1997, p. 93) cited St. John Chrysostom's meditations on mucus contained within as a means of defusing desire for another's (beautiful) body—thereby using core disgust to curb lust.

Walinga, Corveleyn, and van Saane (2005) found that both orthodox Protestants and orthodox Roman Catholics in their Belgian adolescent sample reported more frequent guilt than their less orthodox peers. Moreover, whereas the orthodox Catholics scored higher than orthodox Protestants on "constructive" (reparative, other-focused) guilt, the latter did not outscore the former on "non-constructive" (ruminative, self-reproachful) guilt as expected. Although we hesitate to make too much out of the latter null finding, because orthodox Protestants were more likely than orthodox Catholics to endorse statements concerning humans' inherent sinfulness and imperfection and need to rely on God's mercy, they may have had a "roadmap" for dealing with their own perceived moral shortcomings that is the analog to the Catholic sacrament of reconciliation. The plausibility of this interpretation would be bolstered, perhaps, by differential correlations among frequency of self-reported guilt, constructive and non-constructive guilt reactions, and endorsement of these guilt-related doctrines within the two religious groups—which, unfortunately, Walinga et al. did not report.

Although "anger at God" (Exline et al., 1999) may be judged as problematic, anger can be "righteous" as well—and identification with one's religious group figures centrally in this framing. For example, Ysseldyk, Matheson, and Anisman (2011) recently demonstrated experimentally that higher intrinsic orientation predicted greater anger and confrontational motivation in response to perceived threat directed toward one's own religious group (Protestant, Catholic, or Muslim in their sample). Curiously, this response manifested alongside both sadness and positive emotion (cf. Kim-Prieto & Diener, 2009) in that condition, but did not appear when a self-relevant group that was not relevant to religious identity (i.e., the student's home university) was threatened.

Corrigan (2007, p. 333) asserted that "[r]eligious hatred has appeared throughout history and in virtually every culture where encounter between different religious groups has taken place." A consensus has yet to emerge concerning whether hate is better conceptualized as an *emotion* with destructive motivational implications or as a *motive*—typified by the goal of diminishing the target's well-being—with a range of possible emotional antecedents such as anger (see Rempel & Burris, 2005). In either case, Ginges, Hansen, and Norenzayan's (2009) finding that increasing the salience of religious group identity increased support for suicide attacks among both Palestinians and Israelis certainly seems consistent with the main thrust of Corrigan's assertion, even though Ginges et al. made no attempt to measure self-reported "hate" or associated emotions. Again illustrating the "negative is positive" principle, Burris and Rempel (2012) argued that destructive intentions—such as those condoned by some of Ginges et al.'s religious participants, for example— are often valorized rather than condemned, *provided that the target is regarded as evil* (for empirical evidence concerning the link between labeling a target "evil" and intensity of desire that harm befall that target [i.e., hate], see Burris & Rempel, 2011).

Conclusions and Future Directions

Research on religion and emotion is expanding: At the time of writing, 58% (627 of 1078) of the hits in a PsycINFO search for the terms "religio*" and "emotion" dually appearing in abstracts have appeared since 2000. Despite Exline's (2002) plea, research focusing on links between religion and *negative* emotion remains sparse and unsystematic, however. Thus, we cast our net rather broadly and attempted to sort our catch around two central ideas. First, disparate neuroscientific investigations seem to converge on a neural profile that is suggestively consistent with James's (1961 [1902]) "sick soul"—that is, one who is simultaneously predisposed to negative affect and to an experiential mindset typified by an "openness to the extraordinary" that is amenable to spiritual/ religious interpretations: "A mystery is concealed, and a metaphysical solution must exist. If the natural world is so double-faced and unhomelike, what world, what thing is real?" (p. 132). Second, once in place, we suggested that religion functions as an astonishingly flexible regulatory mechanism, nimbly managing both negative and positive emotions in the service of maintaining religious identity.

Although we contend that there is enough evidence to set forth both ideas as reasonable hypotheses, more direct tests are certainly warranted. When doing so, we recommend that researchers carefully attend to the level of analysis—that is, whether comparisons involve: 1) religiously identified versus non-identified individuals (recognizing that the latter group, like the former, is heterogeneous: see Burris & Petrican, 2011); 2) individuals from different religious groups; or 3) individuals within religious groups. For example, in their Canadian university sample, Burris and Petrican (2011) found that heterogeneously religiously identified individuals scored higher on a measure of alexithymia (i.e., difficulty identifying and describing one's emotions) compared to atheists, yet Watson et al. (2002) found higher intrinsic religious orientation within American Christian and Iranian Muslim samples to predict *lower* alexithymia. Similarly, Kim-Prieto and Diener (2009) found Muslims to be more prone to sadness compared to other religious groups, yet Abu-Raiya and Pargament (2011, p. 105) concluded that "Islam's role in the lives of Muslims seems mostly positive." Superficially contradictory findings such as these clearly merit close scrutiny.

Likewise, future researchers ought also to make concerted efforts to determine causal relationships via more extensive utilization of experimental, longitudinal, and mediational analyses. For example, although Walinga et al. (2005) reported that both orthodox Protestants and orthodox Roman Catholics reported more frequent guilt than their less orthodox peers, they did not indicate whether endorsement of so-called "depressogenic" doctrines concerning human sinfulness accounted for this difference: Mediational analyses such as this one could either retain or rule out potential causal mechanisms at relatively low cost to the researcher.

Similarly, longitudinal studies could shed some light on the neurocognitive implications of regular engagement in religious activities, such as the development of compensatory mechanisms or even the reversal of the "sick-souled" neural patterns that we documented herein. Moreover, investigations of whether religious symbols function more like attachment figures or merely as triggers of automatic emotion regulation processes are definitely warranted. Further, among individuals who fit the neural profile of the "sick soul," might some seek to "treat" themselves via religion, whereas others opt for a "different kind of medicine" in the form of substance abuse (cf. Seo et al., 2008)? Might a common neural profile help account for the popularity and success of quasi-religious (e.g., 12 Step) groups in promoting chemical abstinence among some recovering individuals (e.g., Kelly, Pagano, Stout, & Johnson, 2012)?

Although we have pointed to evidence suggestive of the flexibility of religion as a regulatory mechanism in the service of maintaining religious identity, the potential for maladaptive inflexibility also warrants consideration. For example, although findings are mixed and causal direction remains uncertain, Himle, Chatters, Taylor, and Nguyen (2011) concluded that there is at least some evidence of a link between greater religiosity and obsessive compulsive disorder (OCD) and related tendencies (e.g., scrupulosity, which is typified by obsessions and compulsions of a moral/religious nature); for reasons yet to be determined, Muslims especially may be at increased risk for religious manifestations of OCD.

Finally, although the "sick soul" has occupied most of our attention—a logical enough choice given our focus on religion and *negative* emotions—James (1961 [1902]) also discussed the so-called "healthy-minded" religious individual who does not seem to be similarly afflicted by "morbid repining at his distance from the infinite" (p. 90). To the best of our knowledge, data pertaining to the differentiation between "sick-souled" and "healthy-minded" religion are nonexistent (but see Burris & Tarpley, 1998, and Petrican & Burris, 2012, for a potentially relevant conceptualization). Could a "healthy-minded" articulation of spiritual/religious inclinations likewise be linked to a distinct neural profile? What are the implications of such an articulation for the experience, expression, and regulation of emotion—and for self-regulation more generally? Regarding answers to such questions, we hope that William James would be as curious as we are.

References

Abu-Raiya, H., & Pargament, K. I. (2011). Empirically based psychology of Islam: Summary and critique of the literature. *Mental Health, Religion, and Culture, 14*, 93–115.

Aftanas, L., & Golosheykin, S. (2005). Impact of regular meditation practice on EEG activity at rest and during evoked negative emotions. *International Journal of Neuroscience, 115*, 893–909.

Alcorta, C. S., & Sosis, R. (2005). Ritual, emotion, and sacred symbols. *Human Nature, 16*, 323–359.

Azari, N. P., Nickel, J., Wunderlich, G., Niedeggen, M., Hefter, H., Tellmann, L. et al. (2001). Neural correlates of religious experience. *European Journal of Neuroscience, 13*, 1649–1652.

Bamford, C., & Lagattuta, K. H. (2010). A new look at children's understanding of mind and emotion: The case of prayer. *Developmental Psychology, 46*, 78–92.

Baumeister, R. F., & Exline, J. J. (1999). Virtue, personality, and social relations: Self-control as the moral muscle. *Journal of Personality, 67*, 1165–1194.

Beauregard, M., & Paquette, V. (2006). Neural correlates of a mystical experience in Carmelite nuns. *Neuroscience Letters, 405*, 186–190.

Borg, J., Andree, B., Soderstrom, H., & Farde, L. (2003). The serotonin system and spiritual experiences. *American Journal of Psychiatry, 160,* 1965–1969.

Braboszcz, C., Hahusseau, S., & Delorme, A. (2010). Meditation and neuroscience: From basic research to clinical practice. In R. A. Carlstedt (Ed.), *Handbook of integrative clinical psychology and behavioral medicine: Perspectives, practices, and research* (pp. 755–778). New York: Springer.

Brefczynski-Lewis, J. A., Lutz, A., Schaefer, H. S., Levinson, D. B., & Davidson, R. J. (2007). Neural correlates of attentional expertise in long-term meditation practitioners. *Proceedings of the National Academy of Sciences, 104,* 11483–11488.

Brewerton, T. D. (1994). Hyperreligiosity in psychotic disorders. *Journal of Nervous and Mental Disease, 182,* 302–304.

Britton, W. B., & Bootzin, R. R. (2004). Near-death experiences and the temporal lobe. *Psychological Science, 15,* 254–258.

Brugger, P. (2001). From haunted brain to haunted science: A cognitive neuroscience view of paranormal and pseudoscientific thought. In J. Houran & R. Lange (Eds.), *Hauntings and poltergeists: Multidisciplinary perspectives* (pp. 195–213). Jefferson, NC: McFarland & Company.

Brugger, P., Dowdy, M. A., & Graves, R. E. (1994). From superstitious behavior to delusional thinking: The role of the hippocampus in misattributions of causality. *Medical Hypotheses, 43,* 397–402.

Brugger, P., Gamma, A., Muri, R., Schafer, M., & Taylor, K. I. (1993). Functional hemispheric asymmetry and belief in ESP: Towards a "neuropsychology of belief." *Perceptual and Motor Skills, 77,* 1299–1308.

Bujatti, M., & Riederer, P. (1976). Serotonin, noradrenaline, dopamine metabolites in transcendental meditation-technique. *Journal of Neural Transmission, 39,* 257–267.

Burris, C. T., & Jackson, L. M. (2000). Social identity and the true believer: Responses to threatened self-stereotypes among the intrinsically religious. *British Journal of Social Psychology, 39,* 257–278.

Burris, C. T., & Navara, G. S. (2002). Morality play, or playing morality?: Intrinsic religious orientation and socially desirable responding. *Self and Identity, 1,* 67–76.

Burris, C. T., & Petrican, R. (2011). Hearts strangely warmed (or cooled): Emotional experience in religious and atheistic individuals. *International Journal for the Psychology of Religion, 21,* 183–197.

Burris, C. T., & Rempel, J. K. (2011). "Just look at him": Punitive responses cued by "evil" symbols. *Basic and Applied Social Psychology, 33,* 69–80.

Burris, C. T., & Rempel, J. K. (2012). Good and evil in religion: The interpersonal context. In L. Miller (Ed.), *The Oxford handbook of the psychology of religion and spirituality* (pp. 123–137). New York: Oxford University Press.

Burris, C. T., & Tarpley, W. R. (1998). Religion as being: Preliminary validation of the Immanence scale. *Journal of Research in Personality, 32,* 55–79.

Butler, P. M., McNamara, P., & Durso, R. (2009). Deficits in the automatic activation of religious concepts in patients with Parkinson's disease. *Journal of the International Neuropsychological Society, 16,* 252–261.

Cahn, B. R., & Polich, J. (2006). Meditation states and traits: EEG, ERP, and neuroimaging studies. *Psychological Bulletin, 132,* 180–211.

Coccaro, E. F. (1989). Central serotonin and impulsive aggression. *British Journal of Psychiatry Supplements, 8*, 52–62.

Cohen, A. B., & Rankin, A. (2004). Religion and the morality of positive mentality. *Basic and Applied Social Psychology, 26*, 45–57.

Corrigan, J. (2000). A critical assessment of scholarly literature in religion and emotion. In J. Corrigan, J. Kloss, & E. Crump (Eds.), *Emotion and religion: A critical assessment and annotated bibliography* (pp. 1–19). Westport, CT: Greenwood Publishing Group.

Corrigan, J. (2007). Religious hatred. In J. Corrigan (Ed.), *The Oxford handbook of religion and emotion* (pp. 333–345). New York: Oxford University Press.

Davenport, L. D., & Holloway, F. A. (1980). The rat's resistance to superstition: Role of the hippocampus. *Journal of Comparative and Physiological Psychology, 94*, 691–705.

Davidson, R. J., Kabat-Zinn, J., Schumacher, J., Rosenkrantz, M., Muller, D., Santorelli, S. F. et al. (2003). Alterations in brain and immune function produced by mindfulness meditation. *Psychosomatic Medicine, 65*, 564–570.

Deeley, P. Q. (2004). The religious brain. *Anthropology and Medicine, 11*, 245–267.

Eisenberger, N. I., Master, S. L., Inagaki, T. I., Taylor, S. E., Shirinyan, D., Lieberman, M. D. et al. (2011). Attachment figures activate a safety signal-related neural region and reduce pain experience. *Proceedings of the National Academy of Sciences, 1081*, 11721–11726.

Ellis, T. B. (2011). Disgusting bodies, disgusting religion: The biology of Tantra. *Journal of the American Academy of Religion, 79*, 879–927.

Emmons, R. A. (2005). Emotion and religion. In R. F. Paloutzian & C. L. Park (Eds.), *Handbook of the psychology of religion and spirituality* (pp. 235–252). New York: Guilford.

Exline, J. J. (2002). The picture is getting clearer, but is the scope too limited? Three overlooked questions in the psychology of religion. *Psychological Inquiry, 13*, 245–247.

Exline, J. J., Yali, A. M., & Lobel, M. (1999). When God disappoints: Difficulty forgiving God and its role in negative emotion. *Journal of Health Psychology, 4*, 365–379.

Fallon, B. A., Liebowitz, M. R., Hollander, E., & Schneier, F. R., Campeas, R. B., Fairbanks, J. et al. (1990). The pharmacotherapy of moral or religious scrupulosity. *Journal of Clinical Psychiatry, 51*, 517–521.

Friedman, M. (2008). Religious fundamentalism and responses to mortality salience: A quantitative text analysis. *International Journal for the Psychology of Religion, 18*, 216–237.

Frith, C. D., Blakemore, S.-J., & Wolpert, D. M. (2000). Explaining the symptoms of schizophrenia: Abnormalities in the awareness of action. *Brain Research Reviews, 31*, 357–363.

Gainotti, G. (1972). Emotional behavior and hemispheric side of the lesion. *Cortex, 8*, 41–55.

Gawron, V. (2004). Psychological factors. In F. H. Previc & W. R. Ercoline (Eds.), *Spatial disorientation in aviation* (pp. 145–195). Reston, VA: American Institute of Astronautics and Aeronautics.

Ginges, J., Hansen, I., & Norenzayan, A. (2009). Religion and support for suicide attacks. *Psychological Science, 20,* 224–230.

Goldwert, M. (1993). The messiah-complex in schizophrenia. *Psychological Reports, 73,* 331–335.

Gray, J. A., Feldon, J., Rawlins, J. N. P., Hemsley, D. R., & Smith, A. D. (1991). The neuropsychology of schizophrenia. *Behavioral and Brain Sciences, 14,* 1–20.

Haidt, J., Rozin, P., McCauley, C., & Imada, S. (1997). Body, psyche, and culture: The relationship of disgust to morality. *Psychology and Developing Societies, 9,* 107–131.

Harmon-Jones, E. (2006). Unilateral right-hand contractions cause contralateral alpha power suppression and approach motivational affective experience. *Psychophysiology, 43,* 598–603.

Harmon-Jones, E., Gable, P. A., & Peterson, C. K. (2010). The role of asymmetric frontal cortical activity in emotion-related phenomena: A review and update. *Biological Psychiatry, 84,* 451–462.

Henriques, J. B., & Davidson, R. J. (1990). Regional brain electrical asymmetries discriminate between previously depressed and healthy control subjects. *Journal of Abnormal Psychology, 99,* 22–31.

Himle, J. A., Chatters, L. M., Taylor, J., & Nguyen, A. (2011). The relationship between obsessive-compulsive disorder and religious faith: Clinical characteristics and implications for treatment. *Psychology of Religion and Spirituality, 3,* 251–258.

Hoffman, J. W., Benson, H., Arns, P. A., Stainbrook, G. L., Landsberg, L., Young, J. B. et al. (1982). Reduced sympathetic nervous system responsivity associated with the relaxation response. *Science, 215,* 190–192.

Inzlicht, M., McGregor, I., Hirsh, J. B., & Nash, K. (2009). Neural markers of religious conviction. *Psychological Science, 20,* 385–392.

Inzlicht, M., & Tullett, A. M. (2010). Reflecting on God: Religious primes can reduce neurophysiological response to errors. *Psychological Science, 21,* 1184–1190.

Jacobs, G. D., & Snyder, D. (1996). Frontal brain asymmetry predicts affective style in men. *Behavioral Neuroscience, 110,* 3–6.

James, W. (1961). *The varieties of religious experience.* New York: Macmillan. (Original work published 1902)

Jones, A., & Fitness, J. (2008). Moral hypervigilance: The influence of disgust sensitivity in the moral domain. *Emotion, 8,* 613–627.

Kapogiannis, D., Barbey, A. K., Su, M., Zamboni, G., Krueger, F., & Grafman, J. (2009). Cognitive and neural foundations of religious belief. *Proceedings of the National Academy of Science of the United States of America, 106,* 4876–4881.

Kashdan, T. B., & Nezlek, J. B. (2012). Whether, when, and how is spirituality related to well-being? Moving beyond single occasion questionnaires to understand daily process. *Personality and Social Psychology Bulletin, 38,* 1523–1535.

Kelly, J. F., Pagano, M. E., Stout, R. L., & Johnson, S. M. (2012). Influence of religiosity on 12-step participation and treatment response among substance-dependent adolescents. *Journal of Studies on Alcohol and Drugs, 73,* 1000–1011.

Kim, Y., Seidlitz, L., Ro, Y., Evinger, J. S., & Duberstein, P. R. (2004). Spirituality and affect: A function of changes in religious affiliation. *Personality and Individual Differences*, 37, 861–870.

Kim-Prieto, C., & Diener, E. (2009). Religion as a source of variation in the experience of positive and negative emotions. *Journal of Positive Psychology*, 4, 447–460.

Krummenacher, P., Mohr, C., Haker, H., & Brugger, P. (2009). Dopamine, paranormal belief, and the detection of meaningful stimuli. *Journal of Cognitive Neuroscience*, 22, 1670–1681.

Kurup, R. K., & Kurup, P. A. (2003). Hypothalamic digoxin, hemispheric chemical digoxin, and spirituality. *International Journal of Neuroscience*, 113, 383–393.

Lazar, S. W., Kerr, C. E., Wasserman, R. H., Gray, J. R., Greve, D. N., Readway, M. T. et al. (2005). Meditation experience is associated with increased cortical thickness. *Neuroreport*, 16, 1893–1897.

Leonhard, D., & Brugger, P. (1998). Creative, paranormal, and delusional thought: A consequence of right hemisphere semantic activation? *Neuropsychiatry, Neuropsychology, and Behavioral Neurology*, 11, 177–183.

Lutz, A., Brefczynski-Lewis, J. A., Johnstone, T., & Davidson, R. J. (2008). Regulation of the neural circuitry of emotion by compassion meditation: Effects of meditative expertise. *PLoS One*, 3, e1897. *Psychology Compass*, 1, 146–167.

McCullough, M. E., & Willoughby, B. L. B. (2009). Religion, self-regulation, and self-control: Associations, explanations, and implications. *Psychological Bulletin*, 135, 69–93.

McNamara, P. (2001). Religion and the frontal lobes. In J. Andresen (Ed.), *Religion in mind* (pp. 237–256). Cambridge: Cambridge University Press.

McNamara, P., Durso, R., & Brown, A. (2006). Religiosity in patients with Parkinson's disease. *Neuropsychiatric Disease and Treatment*, 2, 341–348.

Mauss, I. B., Bunge, S. A., & Gross, J. J. (2007). Automatic emotion regulation. *Social and Personality Psychology Compass*, 1, 146–167.

Millan, M. J., Dekeyne, A., & Gobert, A. (1998). Serotonin (5-HT)2C receptors tonically inhibit dopamine (DA) and noradrenaline (NAD), but not 5-HT, release in the frontal cortex in vivo. *Neuropharmacology*, 37, 953–955.

Miller, J. C., & Horvath, S. M. (1976). Cardiac output during human sleep. *Aviation, Space, and Environmental Medicine*, 47, 1046–1051.

Miller, W. I. (1997). *The anatomy of disgust*. Cambridge, MA: Harvard University Press.

Mohr, C., Rohrenbach, C. M., Laska, M., & Brugger, P. (2001). Unilateral olfactory perception and magical ideation. *Schizophrenia Research*, 47, 255–264.

Moore, T., Scarpa, A., & Raine, A. (2002). A meta-analysis of serotonin metabolite 5-HIAA and antisocial behavior. *Aggressive Behavior*, 28, 299–316.

Mulder, R. T., Porter, R. J., & Joyce, P. R. (2003). The prolactin response to fenfluramine in depression: Effects of melancholia and baseline cortisol. *Journal of Psychopharmacology*, 17, 97–102.

Newberg, A. B., & Iversen, J. (2003). The neural basis of the complex mental task of meditation: Neurotransmitter and neurochemical considerations. *Medical Hypotheses*, 61, 282–291.

Newberg, A., Pourdehnad, M., Alavi, A., & d'Aquili, E. (2003). Cerebral blood flow during meditative prayer: Preliminary findings and methodological issues. *Perceptual and Motor Skills, 97*, 625–630.

Orme-Johnson, D. W., Schneider, R. H., Son, Y. D., Nidich, S., & Cho, Z. H. (2006). Neuroimaging of meditation's effect on brain reactivity to pain. *Neuroreport, 17*, 1359–1363.

Paek, E. (2006). Religiosity and perceived emotional intelligence among Christians. *Personality and Individual Differences, 41*, 479–490.

Persinger, M. A. (1993). Vectorial cerebral hemisphericity as differential sources for the sensed presence, mystical experiences and religious conversions. *Perceptual and Motor Skills, 76*, 915–930.

Persinger, M. A. (1994). Sense of a presence and suicidal ideation following traumatic brain injury: Indications of right-hemispheric intrusions from neuropsychological profiles. *Psychological Reports, 75*, 1059–1070.

Peterson, C. K., & Harmon-Jones, E. (2009). Circadian and seasonal variability of resting frontal EEG asymmetry. *Biological Psychology, 80*, 315–320.

Petrican, R., & Burris, C. T. (2012). Am I the stone?: Overattribution of agency and religious orientation. *Psychology of Religion and Spirituality, 4*, 312–323.

Previc, F. H. (1998). The neuropsychology of 3-D space. *Psychological Bulletin, 124*, 123–164.

Previc, F. H. (2006). The role of the extrapersonal brain systems in religious activity. *Consciousness and Cognition, 15*, 500–539.

Reid, S. A., Duke, L. M., & Allen, J. J. B. (1998). Resting frontal electroencephalographic asymmetry in depression: Inconsistencies suggest the need to identify mediating factors. *Psychophysiology, 35*, 389–404.

Rempel, J. K., & Burris, C. T. (2005). Let me count the ways: An integrative theory of love and hate. *Personal Relationships, 12*, 297–313.

Ritter, R. S., & Preston, J. L. (2011). Gross gods and icky atheism: Disgust responses to rejected religious beliefs. *Journal of Experimental Social Psychology, 47*, 1225–1230.

Robinson, R. G., & Price, T. R. (1982). Post-stroke depressive disorders: A follow-up study of 103 patients. *Stroke, 13*, 635–641.

Rounding, K., Lee, A., Jacobson, J. A., & Ji, L.-J. (2012). Religion replenishes self-control. *Psychological Science, 23*, 635–642.

Rubin, J. (2007). Melancholy. In J. Corrigan (Ed.), *The Oxford handbook of religion and emotion* (pp. 290–309). New York: Oxford University Press.

Saroglou, V., Buxant, C., & Tilquin, J. (2008). Positive emotions as leading to religion and spirituality. *Journal of Positive Psychology, 3*, 165–173.

Schaffer, C. E., Davidson, R. J., & Saron, C. (1983). Frontal and parietal electroencephalogram asymmetry in depressed and non-depressed subjects. *Biological Psychiatry, 18*, 753–762.

Schuman, M. (1980). The psychophysiological model of meditation and altered states of consciousness: A critical review. In J. M. Davidson & R. J. Davidson (Eds.), *The psychobiology of consciousness* (pp. 333–378). New York: Plenum.

Seo, D., Patrick, C. J., & Kennealy, P. J. (2008). Role of serotonin and dopamine system interactions in the neurobiology of impulsive aggression and its comorbidity with other clinical disorders. *Aggression and Violent Behavior,* *13,* 383–395.

Shariff, A. F., & Norenzayan, A. (2007). God is watching you: Priming god concepts increases prosocial behavior in an anonymous economic game. *Psychological Science, 18,* 803–809.

Sierra, M., & Berrios, G. E. (1998). Depersonalization: Neurobiological perspectives. *Biological Psychiatry, 44,* 898–908.

Sorensen, S. M., Kehne, J. H., Fadayel, G. M., Humphreys, T. M., Ketteler, H. J., Sullivan, C. K., et al. (1993). Characterization of the 5-HT2 receptor antagonist MDL100907 as a putative atypical antipsychotic: Behavioral, electrophysiological and neurochemical studies. *Journal of Pharmacology Experimental Therapeutics, 266,* 684–691.

Taylor, K. I., Zach, P., & Brugger, P. (2002). Why is magical ideation related to leftward deviation on an implicit line bisection task? *Cortex, 38,* 247–252.

Tomarken, A. J., Davidson, R. J., Wheeler, R. E., & Doss, R. (1992). Individual differences in anterior brain asymmetry and fundamental dimensions of emotion. *Journal of Personality and Social Psychology, 62,* 676–687.

Tomás Sábado, J. & Limonero, J. T. (2009). Religiousness and death anxiety. In S. D. Ambrose (Ed.), *Religion and psychology: New research* (pp. 107–122). New York: Nova Science Publishers.

Tsai, J. L., Miao, F. F., & Seppala, E. (2007). Good feelings in Christianity and Buddhism: Religious differences in ideal affect. *Personality and Social Psychology Bulletin, 33,* 409–421.

Urry, H. L., Roeser, R. W., Lazar, S. W., & Poey, A. P. (2012). Prefrontal cortical activation during emotion regulation: Linking religious/spiritual practices with well-being. In A. E. A. Warren, R. M. Lerner, & E. Phelps (Eds.), *Thriving and spirituality among youth: Research perspectives and future possibilities* (pp. 19–31). New York: Wiley.

Vanyukov, M. M., & Tarter, R. E. (2000). Genetic studies of substance abuse. *Drug and Alcohol Dependence, 59,* 101–123.

Walinga, P., Corveleyn, J., & van Saane, J. (2005). Guilt and religion: The influence of orthodox Protestant and orthodox Catholic conceptions of guilt on guilt-experience. *Archive for the Psychology of Religion, 27,* 113–136.

Watson, P. J., Ghorbani, N., Davison, H. K., Bing, M. N., Hood, R. W., Jr., & Ghrarmaleki, A. F. (2002). Negatively reinforcing personal extrinsic motivations: Religious orientation, inner awareness, and mental health in Iran and the United States. *International Journal for the Psychology of Religion, 12,* 255–276.

Watts, F. (1996). Psychological and religious perspectives on emotion. *International Journal for the Psychology of Religion, 6,* 71–87.

Watts, F. (2007). Emotion regulation and religion. In J. J. Gross (Ed.), *Handbook of emotion regulation* (pp. 504–520). New York: Guilford.

Webb, M., Stetz, K., & Hedden, K. (2008). Representation of mental illness in Christian self-help bestsellers. *Mental Health, Religion, and Culture, 11,* 697–717.

Weiner, I. (2003). The "two-headed" latent inhibition model of schizophrenia: Modeling positive and negative symptoms and their treatment. *Psychopharmacology, 169,* 257–297.

Whitehouse, H. (2007). Terror. In J. Corrigan (Ed.), *The Oxford handbook of religion and emotion* (pp. 259–275). New York: Oxford University Press.

Wiech, K., Farias, M., Kahane, G., Shackel, N., Tiede, W., & Tracey, I. (2009). An fMRI study measuring analgesia enhanced by religion as a belief system. *Pain, 139*, 467–476.

Wilkins, A. C. (2008). "Happier than non-Christians": Collective emotions and symbolic boundaries among evangelical Christians. *Social Psychology Quarterly, 71*, 281–301.

Wuerfel, J., Krishnamoorthy, E. S., Brown, R. J., Lemieux, L., Koepp, M., Tebartz van Elst, L. et al. (2004). Religiosity is associated with hippocampal but not amygdala volumes in patients with refractory epilepsy. *Journal of Neurology, Neurosurgery and Psychiatry, 75*, 640–642.

Young, S. N. (2007). How to increase serotonin in the human brain without drugs. *Journal of Psychiatry and Neuroscience, 32*, 394–399.

Ysseldyk, R., Matheson, K., & Anisman, H. (2011). Coping with identity threat: The role of religious orientation and implications for emotions and action intentions. *Psychology of Religion and Spirituality, 3*, 132–148.

6   Positive Emotions and Self-Transcendence

Patty Van Cappellen and Bernard Rimé

This chapter intends to examine existing relationships between positive emotional states, self-transcendence, spirituality, and religion. It will be divided into three parts. The first two parts will document proper conditions to dissolve rigid boundaries between the self and the outer world, and thus to favor the emergence of self-transcendence. The first part will focus on the effect of positive emotional states at an intra- and an inter-individual level. The second part will examine positive emotions at a collective level through the study of rituals. In particular, we will scrutinize human practices such as movement synchronization and music often observed in social and religious rituals and known to spread positive emotions and enhance feelings of rapport. In the third part, we will examine the role of positive emotions in religion/spirituality, as it is a manner in which people, throughout history and across many societies, have been expressing their aspirations toward self-transcendence. In this regard, a rationale for taking into account the properties of specific positive emotions will be proposed and a family of positive emotions called self-transcendent will be at the center of our attention. Research concerning both directions of causality, i.e., positive emotions as consequences and as possible antecedents of religion and spirituality, will be presented.

Positive Emotions and Transcendence of the Self

Self-transcendence is the experience of seeing oneself and the world in a way that is not hindered by the boundaries of one's ego identity (Erikson, 1982). It involves a heightened sense of meaning and connectedness with others and with the world (Frankl, 2000). Hereafter, we will first concentrate on observations suggesting that positive emotional states create an opened and broadened mindset favorable to self-transcendence. We will then see that these effects persist and expand beyond the sole individual through the *sharing* of positive emotions.

Positive Emotion and Self-Transcendence are Intertwined

Carver and Scheier (1990) posited that for positive affect to occur, the current action should bring the person closer to an active goal. Yet, in their view, positive affect will hardly occur if the progress toward the goal simply conforms to what was anticipated. The unexpectedness of the positive outcome, the effort spent in achieving it, and the uncertainty that preceded it, are all predictors of the intensity and duration of the emotion (Frijda, 1986). Importantly, positive emotions begin with curiosity and interest. These responses develop when detected novelties remain within acceptable limits (Berlyne, 1960). Positive emotions encourage individuals to enhance their contacts with the new element, to explore it and to work out an appropriate cognitive scheme. Such an operation leads to an extension of the person's potential. New meanings are acquired and connections with the outer world are broadened. In sum, positive emotions do sustain a cognitive-behavioral process conducive to self-transcendence.

Isen (2000) reviewed data showing that positive emotions entail important cognitive and social effects. As for cognitive effects, compared to individuals in a negative or neutral state, those in a positive emotional state are found to be more creative, more open to surrounding information and more inclined to exploration and discovery. They also perform better in tasks requiring synthesis and in problem resolution. As for social effects, individuals in a positive emotional state adopt the perspective of others more than those in a negative state. They are also more sociable, more cooperative, more generous, more inclined to social responsibility, and more apt to negotiation.

Such observations led Fredrickson (1998, 2001) to develop the "broaden-and-build theory" of positive emotions: the latter broaden people's momentary thought–action repertoires and build their enduring personal resources over time. Abundant data supported the broadening effect. Positive emotions induce holistic attention (Fredrickson & Branigan, 2005), greater attention to peripheral stimuli (Wadlinger & Isaacowitz, 2006), and feelings of oneness and enlargement of the ingroup (Johnson & Fredrickson, 2005; Waugh & Fredrickson, 2006). In sum, positive emotions are intertwined with experiences of growth and they stimulate both cognitive expansion and social communion. They thus open the way to further self-transcendence.

An extreme form of positive emotion is found in "states of flow" that one might develop when acting in a well-mastered field. When action takes an optimal course, powerful positive emotions can be experienced. This happens when the various systems at work—active cognitions, action in progress, and related information—are temporarily aligned (Csikszentmihalyi, 1990). Flow is characterized by strong concentration, feeling of control, euphoria and transcendence. Tasks best suited to induce flow are those in which people are completely immersed in the experience, involved in a different reality, and pushed at higher levels of performance, thus becoming more complex. In addition to play and games, common triggers include: creativity and research at the frontier; transcendental, peak, or religious experiences; collective ritual; and zen, yoga, and other meditative states. Flow shares many qualities with peak experiences including absorption, involvement, joy, and a sense of power (Privette, 1983). In these extreme forms of positive experiences, the overlap of positive affect, growth or expansion of the individual, and self-transcendence becomes maximal.

In conclusion, even when examining solely the intra-individual level, positive emotions can hardly be dissociated from self-transcendence. Thus, curiosity and interest encourage individuals to enhance their contacts with new facets of their environment and to expand their potential. Positive emotions in general are linked with broadened thought–action repertoires and with openness to other people and to the world. Optimal states result from a temporary alignment of the individual's thought–action systems and the outer world, and they involve the experience of both joy and oneness.

Social Sharing of Emotions

Contrary to popular belief, emotions are not limited to diffuse feelings that people experience in intimate facets of the phenomenal world and bound to remain private. The broadening effect of positive emotions is also found at the interpersonal level through the sharing of emotions. People who experienced an emotion talk about it and, like any emotion, positive emotions are thus socially shared, which further dampens the boundaries between the self and the others. The social sharing of emotion develops in 80 to 95% of emotional episodes (for review, see Rimé, 2009). Positive and negative emotional events are shared at comparable frequency. More intense emotions are shared more repetitively and for a longer period. Listeners engage a *secondary* sharing in nearly 80% of shared episodes (Christophe & Rimé, 1997) and a *tertiary* sharing occurred for two-thirds of secondary listeners (Christophe, 1997). Emotional episodes thus spread across social networks (Harber & Cohen, 2005).

People's willingness to talk about their emotional experiences suggests important benefits. Strong interest and empathetic emotional responding were observed in listeners (Christophe & Rimé, 1997). Sharing an emotion with a supportive listener provides a feeling of rapport (Nils & Rimé, 2012; Zech & Rimé, 2005). Self-disclosure of emotion emerged as a more important predictor of intimacy than did self-disclosure of facts and information (Laurenceau, Feldman-Barrett, & Pietromonaco,

1998). In sum, the social sharing of emotion has the power to bring sender and receiver closer together.

The social bonding effect of emotion sharing is particularly strong and now well documented for positive emotions. Their sharing activates pleasurable emotional images and feelings and thus generates immediate benefits. Positive emotions are opportunities on which to "capitalize," or achieve benefits by letting others know about the event (Langston, 1994). Communicating positive events is indeed associated with an enhancement of positive affect largely exceeding benefits due to the valence of the positive events themselves. When one's partner typically responds enthusiastically to capitalization, relationship well-being as assessed by intimacy or by daily marital satisfaction is higher (Gable, Reis, Impett, & Asher, 2004). In consistency with Fredrickson's (1998, 2001) broaden-and-build functional theory of positive emotions, capitalization attempts and the responses to them build relationship resources. The resources take the form of increased intimacy, satisfaction, love, and commitment (Gable, Gonzaga, & Strachman, 2006). Thus, sharing positive emotions does not only augment positive affect at the intrapersonal level, it also enhances bonds in interpersonal relationships.

The positive emotions of a single individual can stimulate analogous states among people around and thus elicit emotional fusion or communion. This typically happens in "triumph" displayed by sport winners when they meet success or victory. Signals of triumph generally consist of: (1) facial and bodily expression of anger manifesting that major obstacles were transcended, (2) expansion gestures—arm rising, jumping, shouting—reflecting the feeling of growth and enhancing the winner's social visibility, and (3) expressive manifestations openly addressed to the audience, with smiles, laughter, cries, calls, body contacts, hugs, and sketched celebration. The last invite spectators to join the winner and/or to come closer to one another. These manifestations elicit empathetic positive emotional states among witnesses of the victorious action. Festivities start and indicate the consolidation of group members' bonds thus evidencing the strong impact a victory has on social integration and group cohesion.

In conclusion, the self-transcending effect of positive emotions occurs not only at an intra-personal level, but also at an inter-personal, and more largely, at a collective level. Just like any emotion, positive ones push people to share their experience and connect with others. Sharing positive experiences builds additional resources that are important for both the sender and the listener. The sharing process propagates at very high speeds across a community, placing positive emotions at the heart of a collective phenomenon. Although both positive and negative emotional states are shared and propagated, positive ones are specific in that they are intertwined with the broaden-and-build and self-transcendence effects described earlier in this chapter.

Collective Rituals and Self-transcendence

Collective rituals and, among them, religious rituals, are particular settings in which the sharing of positive emotions can be intense. Ritual indoctrination and practice also create believers: without participation in rituals, religious beliefs lack both emotional salience and motivational force (Sosis, 2003). In this context, we will examine music, entrainment, and synchronization in more detail as they are powerful means to induce positive emotions and blur the self–other distinction.

Rituals

The emotional, social, and cognitive effects of collective rituals are described in Durkheim's (1912) classic model of the socially functional nature of rituals. Though primarily focused on religions, his analysis addressed any collective manifestations. Collective rituals generally involve the presence of the group's symbols (e.g., flags, emblems) and collective expressions (singing, yelling, telling words or sentences, shared movements, music and dance) that aptly awaken the latent social dimension of every human being. Shared beliefs and collective representations are set at the foreground, thus consolidating participants' faith in their cultural beliefs. Particularly central to Durkheim is that individuals' consciousnesses echo one another in such a context. Thus, any expression of emotions among participants vividly elicits analogous feelings in people around them so that a reciprocal stimulation of emotion follows, leading to an "emotional effervescence." Such a circular process ends up in a collective state of emotional communion in which participants experience unity and similarity. Salience of participants' self is lowered and their collective identity is enhanced. This is how, according to Durkheim, social rituals have the capacity to boost participants' feelings of group belonging and of social integration. Emotions elicited during a religious or secular ritual have effects on the collective level that largely exceed the effects on the individual level. Rituals indeed entail holistic effects on participants. They end up globally dissolving the boundaries separating individuals. They unite them all by substituting their group identity for their preexisting self-identity.

Music and Entrainment

Music is inseparable from religious rituals (Alcorta & Sosis, 2005). Among the African Igbo for example, there is a single word to say religion and music (Becker, 2001). Music is a consistent feature of contemporary religious services in the US (Chaves, Konieczny, Beyerlein, & Barman, 1999) and in ritually constrained religions (Atran, 2002). Cross-culturally, happiness is the most frequently reported emotion evoked by music in religious rituals. When intensified through the social aspects of the ritual, happiness can reach ecstasy (Becker, 2001). Music may therefore provide the catalyst for a strong emotional response that may lead to trance or a similar sense of transcendence in religious practice (Penman & Becker, 2009). For example, in Pentecostal churches, music is used as a facilitator of religious experience (Miller & Strongman, 2002). It even emerged as the single most important elicitor of such an experience (Greeley, 1975).

Alcorta and Sosis (2005) stressed that music acts as a "rhythmic driver." Music impacts autonomic functions and synchronizes "internal biophysiological oscillators to external auditory rhythms" (Scherer & Zentner, 2001, p. 372) and amplifies this "coupling effect" by synchronizing individual body rhythms within a group. Levenson (2003) showed that synchronized autonomic functions, including pulse rate, heart contractility, and skin conductance, are positively and significantly associated with measures of empathy. Music in religious ritual promotes such empathy. According to Alcorta and Sosis (2005), the capacity of music to entrain autonomic states and evoke congruent emotions in listeners provides the basis for creating and synchronizing motivational states in ritual participants and for evoking communal emotions among them. In this regard, effects of music resemble those of flow experiences examined earlier in that they favor an alignment of internal states and external conditions.

Anthropologists and psychiatrists have long observed how the rhythmic behavioral activities induced by music can lead to altered states of consciousness, through which mutual trust among members of societies is engendered. Music has the power to entrain others and engage them in movement. Most of the contexts in which music occurs are not only active but also participatory, involving overt active engagement of persons in musical activities of the group (Clayton, Sager, & Will, 2004; Cross & Morley, 2008). This entrainment effect of music is an important mechanism since social rituals may involve a large number of participants. Human beings share with many other species the double ability to detect rhythmic signals that are produced in nature (e.g., day/night cycles, lapping waves on the shore, approaching footsteps) and to produce rhythmic output (e.g., physical locomotion, respiration). Once these two abilities are coordinated, motor output can be adjusted on rhythmic input, and the capacity for entrainment emerges (Philips-Silver, Aktipis, & Bryant, 2010; Todd, Lee, & O'Boyle, 2002). Individuals indeed manifest spontaneous coordination resulting from rhythmic responsiveness to a perceived rhythmic signal (Philips-Silver et al., 2010).

Because of its entrainment effect, music can mobilize joint intentionality and thus arouse a feeling of oneness among performers. Dissanayake (2008) argued that musicians use tones, chords, motifs, rhythms, timbres, and so forth in order to attract attention and hold interest as well as to create, sustain, and mold emotion. Participation with others in such sequences of exaggerated and formalized kinetic, visual, and vocal behaviors can engender and sustain affinitive emotion and accord among members of a group. Freeman (2000) argued that music and dance have co-evolved biologically and culturally to serve as a technology of social bonding. For example, joint music making increases spontaneous cooperative and helpful behavior already among 4-year-old children (Kirschner & Tomasello, 2010).

When a collective activity is experienced as coordinated, it engenders a strong feeling of group identity with the communication of pleasure and positive emotions (Cross & Morley, 2008). Music can transmit emotional information to many people at once, equalizing the emotional state of the group and thus creating bonding effects among group members (Roederer, 1984).

Movement Synchronization

Beyond music, religious rituals are also characterized by gestures and behaviors performed all together. Human beings can coordinate their movements with one another quickly and with little effort. Dyads synchronize their movements when they walk side by side, rock in chairs side by side, swing pendulums together, tap fingers jointly, or are immersed in conversation (for review, see Konvalinka, Vuust, Roepstorff, & Frith, 2010). Graham and Haidt (2010) speculated that acting in synchrony triggers a kind of "off switch" for self-representations in the brain, allowing for a self-transcendent experience. Across many studies, movement synchrony was found to lessen self's boundaries, to enhance rapport, cooperation, and prosociality, and to favor the emergence of a social unit (Chartrand & Bargh, 1999; van Baaren, Holland, Kawakami, & van Knippenberg, 2004). Across three experiments, Wiltermuth and Heath (2009) found that compared to people in control conditions, those who acted in synchrony with others (walking around campus in groups of three; listening to music in groups of three while performing a task requiring some degree of synchrony) cooperated more in subsequent group economic exercises, even in situations requiring personal sacrifice. Their results also showed that bodily movements are not a precondition to such effects as they were found under simple synchronization achieved through singing.

Paladino, Mazzurega, Pavani, and Schubert (2010) recently demonstrated that synchronous movement can actually blur self–other boundaries. In a study using synchronous multisensory stimulation, an experimenter brushed a participant's cheeks as the latter watched a stranger's cheek being brushed in the same way, either in synchrony or in asynchrony. Compared to participants exposed to asynchronous stimulation, those who received synchronous stimulation showed more merging of self and the other on a set of indicators involving body sensations, perception of face resemblance, judgment of the inner state of the other, closeness felt toward the other, and conformity behavior. The authors concluded that synchronous movement both implements and communicates a communal relationship that is characterized by feelings of sameness and unity. Acting in synchrony can thus easily lessen the self's boundaries and thus elicit the cognitive phenomenon of self–other overlap that is typically experienced with close others and ingroup members. Movement synchrony thus opens up the self to experiences of self-transcendence in the form of feelings of oneness and social fusion.

Positive Emotions and Religion/Spirituality

As described earlier, positive emotions push people to consider the world and others in a more holistic, flexible, and integrative way. By doing this, they allow for self-transcendence. Through their sharing, they unexpectedly open up to others and benefit everyone in the chain. This social aspect of positive emotions also takes place in a very central motivational part of religion: collective rituals. Moreover, music and behavioral synchrony present in rituals have been shown to dissolve the rigid boundaries between the self and the others. We will now take a step further by examining not the self–others overlap increased by positive emotions, but whether this sense of heightened connectedness to others could lead to the *belief in* a transcendent being heading this collectivity.

Religion/spirituality is one particular way through which, historically and widely across many societies, people have been expressing their aspirations toward self-transcendence by assuming the existence of a being transcendental to human reality. Religion and spirituality are multidimensional constructs that have been variously defined. Even if there is no consensus among researchers, they share different elements (see Zinnbauer & Pargament, 2005). Religion and spirituality can be defined as (1) one's *personal* affirmation of an external transcendent force and (2) one's *relationship to a higher entity*. Additionally, they typically imply (3) *belief in* a life infused with *meaning and purpose* and (4) *belief in* relatedness and *interconnectedness* with the world and living beings. In the case of religion, the higher entity refers to a denominational God, and many researchers add a supplementary element of definition referring to the institutionalized aspect of religion: one's *commitment to practices* characteristic of a particular tradition.

Several authors, philosophers, and theologians, such as Jonathan Edwards (1959 [1746]), Schleiermacher (1799), and Otto (1958 [1917]) have recognized the core importance of emotions, including positive emotions, in religion. The presence of positive emotions is also confirmed in religious texts such as the Old Testament, which provides to the readers descriptions of joyous feasts, experiences of various positive emotions, and even invitation to experience them (Anderson, 1991; Van Cappellen, 2011, 2012). As we have seen, positive emotions are also very present in religious rituals (Becker, 2001). An intriguing question, which will be addressed in the following sections, is what role might positive emotions play regarding religion and spirituality? In this regard, we will first present a group of positive emotions that could be particularly relevant for the religious and spiritual domains: the self-transcendent positive emotions.

Introduction to the Self-Transcendent Positive Emotions

When studying the interplay between positive emotions and religion/ spirituality, one intriguing question is whether one should consider general positive emotionality or address discrete positive emotions. Authors have claimed that just like for negative emotions, positive emotions do not all have the same appraisals and functions (Griskevicius, Shiota, & Nowlis, 2010; Sauter, 2010). This specificity is therefore important to take into account when studying the effects of positive emotions.

One meaningful way of taking into account different types of positive emotion is a model from Haidt (2003) that distinguishes positive emotions called "moral" or "self-transcendent." These emotions are *elevation, compassion, admiration, gratitude, love,* and *awe.* Haidt (2003) proposed a preliminary definition of self-transcendent emotions as "those emotions that are linked to the interests or welfare either of society as a whole or at least of persons other than the judge or agent" (p. 853). Therefore, emotions such as *amusement, joy,* or *pride* are rather self-relevant.

Two characteristics help to identify self-transcendent emotions. The first relates to the elicitors, which are disinterested. The stimulus causing these emotions is not directly related to the person and to his/her direct interests. A simple picture of an unknown child who suffers, for example, can trigger the emotion of compassion. As a potential consequence, self-transcendent positive emotions are more stimulus focused and directed toward the environment of the self than self-focused. This has been shown for the emotion of *awe,* for example in comparison with amusement and pride (Shiota, Keltner, & Mossman, 2007). However, an emotion such as *joy* occurs when something good happens to the self or to someone related to the self (Haidt, 2003). It is the same for *pride,* which is typically a self-conscious and self-oriented emotion (Tracy & Robins, 2007). The more an emotion is elicited by disinterested stimuli, the more it can be considered as a self-transcendent emotion. Importantly indeed, that one emotion is more on the self-transcendent or the self-relevant side is more a question of continuum than of clear limitation.

The second characteristic of self-transcendent emotions concerns their activation of care for others. The latter emotions push the individual to engage in actions that may benefit others or society. For example, induction of elevation (Schnall, Roper, & Fessler, 2010), gratitude (DeSteno, Bartlett, Baumann, Williams, & Dickens, 2010), and awe (Rudd, Vohs, & Aaker, 2012) have been shown to increase volunteer time and helping behavior even toward strangers. According to Haidt's (2003) model, self-relevant emotions of amusement, joy, or pride, may activate a positive focus on others to a certain extent, but self-transcendent positive emotions more strongly activate a self-disinterested behavior of care.

Saroglou, Buxant, and Tilquin (2008) proposed that self-transcendent emotions, which imply the "experience of marvel, wonder, appreciation, or respect for something that is perceived as larger, higher or more important than the self, or something that is beautiful, pure, or implying some mystery" (p. 166–167), might be particularly relevant when one studies the interplay between positive emotions and religion or spirituality. We have (Van Cappellen, Saroglou, Iweins, Piovesana, & Fredrïckson, in press) extended that claim by arguing that the core appraisals of self-transcendent emotions are related to important characteristics of religion and spirituality. Indeed, when self-transcendent positive emotions occur, the event is appraised as positive, self-disinterested/other focused, and praiseworthy. In other words, witnessing greater good or beauty outside the self elicits a self-transcendent emotion. Importantly, according to the Appraisal Tendency framework, such cognitive appraisals persist beyond the eliciting situation and predispose the individual to appraise subsequent, unrelated situations in line with those appraisals. Therefore, self-transcendent positive emotions might be particularly apt to elicit cognitions conducing to spiritual/religious belief as defined earlier. Importantly, self-transcendent emotions are not religious or sacred emotions per se. They can be experienced as fully secular and by all people, independently of their religiousness.

We will now review the empirical findings related to the study of positive emotions and religion/spirituality, distinguishing between the two directions of relations that have been investigated in past research: religion/spirituality as leading to positive emotions, and positive emotions as influencing religion/spirituality. We will pay particular attention to the types of positive emotion considered, i.e., whether they are more self-transcendent or self-relevant.

Religion/Spirituality as Leading to Positive Emotions

Several correlational studies show a positive association of religiosity/spirituality with positive emotions (for a review, see Smith, Ortiz, Wiggins, Bernard, & Dalen, 2012). Concerning more specific positive emotions, religiosity and spirituality were found to be modestly but consistently positively correlated with dispositional *gratitude* as well as with a daily report of feeling grateful (Emmons & Kneetzel, 2005; McCullough, Emmons, & Tsang, 2002). Kim-Prieto and Diener (2009) showed that Christians more frequently experience the emotion of *love* and also find love more desirable in comparison to the other major religions. In addition, we can notice that in that study the positive emotions of happiness, love, and gratitude were felt with greater frequency and found to be more desirable by Christians than that of pride or negative emotions. In sum, even if not directly testing the specific causal direction, i.e., religion/spirituality as leading to positive emotions, the existing correlational studies have been interpreted as showing that religion/spirituality increase positive emotions.

More recently, research has shown that religious and spiritual practices do indeed increase positive emotions. Using longitudinal designs, meditation has been shown to increase positive emotions (Fredrickson, Cohn, Coffey, Pek, & Finkel, 2008) and prayer to increase gratitude (Lambert, Fincham, Braithwaite, Graham, & Beach 2009). Interestingly, manipulating religious salience (asking participants to indicate their religious affiliation at the beginning of the study) makes Christian participants reported to feel more love than those whose religious identity has not been activated (Kim-Prieto & Diener, 2009).

Even if previous research did not explicitly take into account the difference between self-transcendent and self-relevant positive emotions, results show a clearer affinity between religion/spirituality and self-transcendent emotions such as love or gratitude than with self-relevant emotions such as amusement or pride. Joy and happiness are also felt with higher frequency by religious and spiritual people maybe because these emotions reflect a general positive state, rather than discrete emotions (Herring, Burleson, Roberts, & Devine, 2011).

Positive Emotions as Influencing Religion and Spirituality

In this section, we will report recent existing research that has investigated the other side of the picture, i.e., positive emotions influencing religious and spiritual beliefs, people, and related behaviors and cognitions. The first question addresses whether positive emotions may be an *antecedent* of religious or spiritual beliefs. The second question addresses the benefits of feeling such positive emotions for religious/spiritual people. In addition, concerning these two questions, we will examine whether the effects found are driven by self-transcendent positive emotions and not by self-relevant emotions.

Positive Emotions and Openness to Spirituality and Religion

In previous research on the emotional antecedents of religiosity and spirituality, mainly negative emotions and negative experiences have been investigated. Numerous cross-sectional, longitudinal, and experimental evidences show that religiousness and/or spirituality increases following negative experiences (Spilka, Hood, Hunsberger, & Gorsuch, 2003) such as socioeconomic distress (e.g., Wimberley, 1984), the death of a loved one (e.g., Michael, Crowther, Schmid, & Allen, 2003), and difficult relationships with significant others, in either adulthood or childhood (Kirkpatrick, 2005). Religion is therefore mostly thought to serve as a compensatory function for various negative experiences (see also Burris & Petrican, Chapter 5, this volume).

Nevertheless, is religion/spirituality only a matter of previous vulnerability overcome by positivity and meaning in life? Is it not possible that positive emotions and experiences may also push people to believe in transcendence?

To our knowledge, the first experimental evidence comes from Saroglou et al. (2008). These authors addressed the question of whether feeling self-transcendent positive emotions could make people more religious and more spiritual. In two experiments using the same design, participants were randomly assigned to one out of four conditions implying emotional inductions: two self-transcendent positive emotions (awe of nature or awe at childbirth), one self-relevant positive emotion (amusement), or no specific positive or negative emotion (control condition). The self-transcendent emotion of awe corresponds to a feeling of wonder experienced by the self when facing something vaster, greater, beyond current understanding (Keltner & Haidt, 2003). After the emotional induction, participants completed measures of religiousness (Saroglou et al., 2008) and spirituality (Piedmont's (1999), Spiritual Transcendence Scale). Results showed that participants who watched the videos inducing awe at childbirth and awe of nature reported to be more religious and more spiritual than participants who watched the control video. They were also more spiritual than participants who watched the humor video. Awe, a self-transcendent positive emotion, induced in the lab, thus made people more spiritual. This was not the case with humor/amusement, a self-relevant positive emotion.

Are the findings of these two studies specific to the emotion of awe or can they be generalized to other self-transcendent positive emotions? In two subsequent studies, Van Cappellen et al. (in press) extended that previous research by investigating the impact of two other self-transcendent positive emotions, i.e., elevation (Study 1 and 2) and admiration (Study 2), whose relations to religion and spirituality are less obvious and less direct than the one of awe. Elevation corresponds to the emotional response to human exemplars of kindness and virtue and admiration is produced by exemplars of talent and skill (Algoe & Haidt, 2009). These emotions were again compared with amusement and neutral conditions.

Two other objectives were also pursued. First, the authors tested whether the impact of positive emotions on spirituality constitutes a totally positive process by investigating changes in meaning in life (Study 1). Second, in Study 1, the authors looked for a possible moderation by previous religiousness, or to put it in different words, whether the effect of self-transcendent positive emotions on spirituality occurs for all participants or occurs more for the more or less religious people.

Results showed that induction of self-transcendent emotions of elevation (through a video clip and a recall task) and admiration (through a video clip) made participants more spiritual than in the control condition. This was not the case for the self-relevant (amusement) emotion. The basic belief in the benevolence of others and the world and finding meaning in life turned out to be two significant mediators of this effect. In Study 2, where authors have also assessed religiosity, results were in the same direction, although not significant. Study 1 also revealed a significant moderation by personal religiosity, as measured prior to the experiment: the effect of elevation on spirituality held for the less religious participants. Thus, being religious is not a requirement for a self-transcendent emotion to increase spirituality; even non- or less religious people endorse a more spiritual belief after experiencing a self-transcendent positive emotion. For the highly religious participants, a ceiling effect may be responsible for the lack of results, meaning that these participants may have higher scores on spirituality that cannot be further increased when experiencing a self-transcendent positive emotion.

Thus, across four different studies (Saroglou et al., 2008; Van Cappellen et al., in press) using different methodologies to induce positive emotions and using different samples in ethnicity and age, the induction of various self-transcendent positive emotions (awe at childbirth, awe of nature, elevation, and admiration) made people endorse more a spiritual belief. The effect of self-transcendent emotions on spirituality was partially explained by two positive and "secular," not religious/spiritual, mechanisms: belief that there is meaning in life and belief in benevolence of others and the world. In sum, secular positive emotions, elicited by non-religious stimuli and experienced in nonreligious contexts, can, via their particular effects, open people up to a certain belief in transcendence external to humans.

Results for religiosity were less clear-cut. One explanation for this is that the (European) countries in which the experiments were conducted are secularized and that participants tended to score low on religiosity. Therefore, it may be that changes toward higher religiousness (attachment to religious beliefs, practices, and attitudes in reference to a religious institution) presuppose more effort, motivation, and engagement than changes toward higher spirituality (feeling connected with a sacred external transcendence).

Pursuing that work, Van Cappellen and Saroglou (2012) investigated through two additional studies whether self-transcendent positive emotions provide a facilitative context for religious and spiritual people to express relevant behaviors and feelings: one's propensity for spiritual behavior and feelings of closeness with others.

In Study 1, participants were randomly assigned to one of three conditions: induction (through a recall task) of awe, pride, or no emotion in particular (control condition). Then, willingness to visit Tibet (a spiritual destination) and willingness to visit Haiti (a rather hedonistic destination) were assessed. Finally, religiousness and spirituality were also assessed. Results showed that when awe was induced, religious and spiritual people were more willing to visit Tibet but not Haiti, in comparison to an emotionally neutral control condition. This effect did not occur after the elicitation of pride, a self-relevant positive emotion. In Study 2, the same design was used. The emotions induced (as in Saroglou et al., 2008) were either awe of nature (rather impersonal), awe at childbirth (interpersonal), or amusement. Feelings of oneness with friends and with people in general were assessed afterwards using modified versions of the Inclusion of Other in the Self Scale (Aron, Aron, & Smollan, 1992). Results showed again that, comparatively to a neutral (no emotion induction) condition, when awe of nature and awe at childbirth were induced, religious and spiritual people expressed, respectively, strong feelings of oneness with people in general and with friends. However, induction of a self-relevant positive emotion, amusement, had no such effect. Thus, in these two studies, self-transcendent positive emotions were shown to make participants scoring high on religiosity and spirituality feel and behave more in accordance to their beliefs. Again, for both studies, the results found were not independent of participants' level of religiosity and spirituality.

In sum, across the six studies just described, self-transcendent positive emotions were shown to (1) increase spirituality through positive, cognitive, and socio-affective mechanisms, and especially among less religious people, and (2) provide a facilitative context to express spirituality-related feelings and behaviors among religious and spiritual people. The use of emotional induction has allowed the authors to test and provide first empirical evidence in favor of a specific causal direction, i.e., from positive emotions to religious and spiritual beliefs.

Benefits of Positive Emotions for Religious People

As outlined in a prior section of the present chapter, positive emotions are very present in religious rituals and promoted by religious and spiritual practices. One important remaining question is what the consequences for religious and spiritual people feeling such positive emotions are. More specifically, in the next studies to be presented, self-transcendent positive emotions have been investigated as possible explanatory mechanisms of two positive and well-studied correlates of religion and spirituality, i.e., well-being (see Hayward & Krause, Chapter 12, this volume) and prosociality (see Preston, Salomon, & Ritter, Chapter 7, this volume).

A plethora of empirical evidence supports that religion fosters well-being and that religious attendance more specifically might be a particularly strong predictor (Koenig, King, & Carson, 2012). Different mechanisms have been studied to understand how religion affects well-being (see Hackney & Sanders, 2003). However, positive emotions have been neglected in empirical research. And yet positive emotions can be triggered by religion and are also known to promote well-being (Cohn, Fredrickson, Brown, Mikels, & Conway, 2009). In a survey about the mechanisms by which religious attendance might benefit well-being, Van Cappellen, Saroglou, and Toth (2011) investigated positive emotions. A total of 548 participants completed a questionnaire distributed in 15 Belgian Catholic parishes on the same Sunday. The questionnaire was composed of measures of religiosity, well-being, and a list of positive emotions felt during mass. Results showed first that, as found in previous research, all religious measures (and also a measure of spirituality) were positively related to well-being, i.e., life satisfaction and meaning in life. Second, and more importantly, positive emotions were one of the significant mediators of this relation. When the positive emotions were split into two groups, self-transcendent and self-relevant emotions, the meditational analyses confirmed the expectations: only self-transcendent positive emotions emerged as the active ingredient in the religion–well-being relation. In conclusion, the increase in positive emotions during religious rituals is not to be neglected as it is one of the mechanisms by which religious attendance benefits the attendees' well-being.

In a rather similar vein, Van Cappellen, Saroglou, and Cara (2012) investigated, in another study, whether positive emotions felt during regular religious rituals (Catholic mass) could boost religious people's prosociality. The links between religion and prosociality have a prolific history of research (see for reviews, Preston et al., Chapter 7, this volume; Saroglou, 2013). An intriguing study has shown that religious people are more prosocial than non-religious people, *but only on Sundays* (Malhotra, 2010). Van Cappellen and colleagues (2012) hypothesized that some self-transcendent positive emotions activated during mass may explain, at least in part, Sunday's prosociality. As described earlier in this chapter, self-transcendent positive emotions are characterized by a high concern for others, which can ultimately lead to prosociality.

To test the hypothesis that self-transcendent emotions constitute one of the mechanisms by which religious attendance increases prosociality, the authors collected 196 questionnaires distributed at the end of the Sunday mass to churchgoers from three Belgian Catholic parishes. The questionnaire was composed of measures of religiosity, a list of positive and negative emotions felt during mass, and a measure of prosociality, i.e., the spontaneous tendency for sharing a monetary prize with others (participants mainly mentioned kin members and friends; or distant targets, e.g., donations to charity).

Intrinsic religiosity was found to be positively related to spontaneous sharing with others and, more specifically, to donations to charity. Self-transcendent positive emotions of awe, respect, and love were related both to donations to charity and to intrinsic religiosity. This was not the case for any of the self-relevant positive emotions, or of the negative emotions (such as guilt or fear). Mediational analyses revealed that intrinsic religiosity mediated the effect of awe, respect, and love on donations to charity. This shows that self-transcendent positive emotions felt during Sunday mass promote willingness to donate to charity through the enhancement of religiosity.

The studies presented in this last section were correlational and cannot address issues of causality. However, they show that it is important to consider the role of self-transcendent positive emotions in the link of religion with broader related concepts such as well-being and prosociality. Positive emotions triggered during the religious ritual are not inconsequential; they may have important positive consequences in the life of the attendees.

We conclude, following Van Cappellen et al. (in press), that there is a reciprocal causality between positive emotions and spirituality. Previous and very recent research provides evidence for the two directions of causality: one from self-transcendent positive emotions to religion/spirituality and another from religion/spirituality to positive emotions. Taking a broader perspective, we suspect that religion/spirituality can be part of two very different trajectories. The first is a coping trajectory that goes from negative emotions to positive emotions and well-being through religiousness and spirituality. The second is a positive growth trajectory: an upward spiral where positive emotions make people see the world and others as more benevolent and life as more meaningful. This, in turn, makes people more religious/spiritual and, therefore, again more prone to feel positive emotions, to have greater well-being, and be more prosocial.

Conclusion

Self-transcendence corresponds to the experience of self-concerns being pushed into the background, a heightened sense of connection to others, and a sense of meaning that could ultimately lead to the belief in transcendence per se. Positive emotions are powerful means for self-transcendence at different levels. At the intra-individual level, as outlined in the broaden-and-build model, positive emotions have been shown to promote broadened mindsets, approach behaviors, interest and curiosity for what happens outside the self, and a feeling of oneness with others. However, the breakdown of rigid boundaries between the self and others might occur even more strongly when positive emotions are shared at an inter-individual level or at a collective level such as in rituals.

Sharing a positive emotion promotes a very direct sense of rapport with the listener and may induce positive emotions in the listener as well. In turn, the latter may share his or her positive emotions with others, creating a chain of social sharing. Therefore, the effects of positive emotions spread beyond the initial person and occur for each member in the chain.

Collective rituals, in which positive emotions are important ingredients, are also places in which emotions spread and their effects even amplify. Music, entrainment, and synchrony have been studied as powerful means by which rituals allow for self-transcendence. Music is a common component of collective rituals and is inseparable from religious rituals in which it has been shown to provoke mostly positive emotions. Music may provide the catalyst for a strong emotional response that may lead to a sense of transcendence in religious practice. Music also has the ability to entrain others. Because collective rituals may involve a large number of participants, music is one of the mechanisms by which rituals promote a sense of social bonding among all of them. Synchrony, in movements, singing, or speaking, is another means by which rituals allow for self-transcendence. Rituals thereby have been shown to heighten a sense of group identity instead of self-identity by lessening the self's boundaries. In addition, rituals create emotional effervescence so that if positive emotions are present, they will be experienced at very high levels.

If positive emotions open a path to the *experience* of self-transcendence, can they also push people to *believe* in a self-transcendent being? To investigate the role of positive emotions in regard to religion and spirituality, a family of positive emotions, the self-transcendent positive emotions, has been presented as particularly relevant to consider in the religious and spiritual domains. Indeed, self-disinterested elicitors and prosocial action tendencies characterize these emotions. Their appraisals are already, in a way, self-transcendent as they correspond to watching greater good or beauty outside the self.

Research has shown that there is a clear affinity between positive emotions and religion/spirituality. Confirming what philosophers and theologians have said for a long time, research has shown that religious practices and rituals enhance positive emotions. Importantly however, in this chapter, we also reported studies showing that positive emotions are not only consequences of religion and spirituality but they may also be an antecedent. Across four studies, induced self-transcendent positive emotions (awe, elevation, and admiration) were found to increase participants' belief in transcendence as assessed by scales of spirituality and religiousness. This effect was explained by the increase of belief in benevolence of others and the world and in meaningfulness of life. In two other studies, self-transcendent positive emotions also pushed the more religious and spiritual participants to act according to their faith. Finally, it was shown in two other studies that positive emotions are not to be considered as end states in themselves. They are one of the means by which religious rituals enhance important life domains such as well-being and prosociality.

For the last 15 years, research in positive emotions has exploded. However, more integrative and direct investigation of their self-transcendent effect is still needed. The literature we referred to in this chapter comes from very different areas of research for which more dialogue would be worthy. Many avenues for future research are still open. Researchers should further investigate the specificity of the role of positive emotions compared to that of negative emotions in social sharing and rituals. What are the implications of sharing a positive rather than a negative emotion with someone, or of going to a mourning or celebratory ritual? We can already presume their distinct intra-individual effects, but one intriguing question is whether the valence might also have an impact on the collective level. Moreover, having a better understanding of the differences between *discrete* positive emotions is another important step that needs to be taken. Specific self-transcendent positive emotions are particularly important in the religious and spiritual domains, but they have remained understudied. More research is needed to determine the exact role of these emotions in religious and spiritual people's lives. Importantly, both sides of causality and related processes need to be further investigated as well as long-term effects of positive emotions on religiousness/spirituality.

References

Alcorta, C., & Sosis, R. (2005). Ritual, emotion, and sacred symbols: The evolution of religion as an adaptive complex. *Human Nature, 16*, 323–359.

Algoe, S. B., & Haidt, J. (2009). Witnessing excellence in action: The "other-praising" emotions of elevation, gratitude, and admiration. *Journal of Positive Psychology, 4*, 105–127.

Anderson, G. A. (1991). *A time to mourn, a time to dance: The expression of grief and joy in Israelite religion.* University Park, PA: Pennsylvania State University Press.

Aron, A., Aron, E. N., & Smollan, D. (1992). Inclusion of Other in the Self Scale and the structure of interpersonal closeness. *Journal of Personality and Social Psychology, 63,* 596–612.

Atran, S. (2002). *In gods we trust: The evolutionary landscape of religion.* Oxford: Oxford University Press.

Becker, J. (2001). Anthropological perspectives on music and emotion. In P. Juslin & J. Sloboda (Eds.), *Music and emotion* (pp. 135–160). Oxford: Oxford University Press.

Berlyne, D. E. (1960). *Conflict, arousal and curiosity.* New York: McGraw-Hill.

Carver, C. S., & Scheier, M. F. (1990). Origins and functions of positive and negative affect: A control-process view. *Psychological Review, 97,* 19–35.

Chartrand T. L., & Bargh, J. A. (1999). The chameleon effect: The perception-behavior link and social interaction. *Journal of Personality and Social Psychology, 76,* 893–910.

Chaves, M., Konieczny, E., Beyerlein, K., & Barman, E. (1999). The national congregations study: Background, methods, and selected results. *Journal for the Scientific Study of Religion, 38,* 458–476.

Christophe, V. (1997). *Le partage social des émotions du point de vue de l'auditeur [Social sharing of emotions under the angle of the listener].* Unpublished doctoral dissertation, Université de Lille III, France.

Christophe, V., & Rimé, B. (1997). Exposure to the social sharing of emotion: Emotional impact, listener responses and the secondary social sharing. *European Journal of Social Psychology, 27,* 37–54.

Clayton, M., Sager, R., & Will, U. (2004). In time with the music: The concept of entrainment and its significance for ethnomusicology. *ESEM Counterpoint, 1,* 1–45.

Cohn, M. A., Fredrickson, B. L., Brown, S. L., Mikels, J. A., & Conway, A. M. (2009). Happiness unpacked: Positive emotions increase life satisfaction by building resilience. *Emotion, 9,* 361–368.

Cross, I., & Morley, I. (2008). The evolution of music: Theories, definitions and the nature of the evidence. In S. Malloch & C. Trevarthen (Eds.), *Communicative musicality* (pp. 61–82). Oxford: Oxford University Press.

Csikszentmihalyi, M. (1990). *Flow: The psychology of optimal experience.* New York: Harper & Row.

DeSteno, D., Bartlett, M. Y., Baumann, J., Williams, L. A., & Dickens, L. (2010). Gratitude as moral sentiment: Emotion-guided cooperation in economic exchange. *Emotion, 10,* 289–293.

Dissanayake, E. (2008). If music is the food of love, what about survival and reproductive success? *Musicae Scientiae, 12,* 169–195.

Durkheim, E. (1912). *Les formes élémentaires de la vie religieuse [The elementary forms of religious life].* Paris: Alcan.

Edwards, J. (1959). Religious affections. In J. E. Smith (Ed.), *The works of Jonathan Edwards* (Vol. 2). New Haven, CT: Yale University Press. (Original work published 1746)

Emmons, R. A., & Kneetzel, T. T. (2005). Giving thanks: Spiritual and religious correlates of gratitude. *Journal of Psychology and Christianity, 24,* 140–148.

Erikson, E. H. (1982). *The life cycle completed.* New York: Norton.

Frankl, V. E. (2000). *Man's search for ultimate meaning.* New York: Perseus.

Fredrickson, B. L. (1998). What good are positive emotions? *Review of General Psychology, 2,* 300–319.

Fredrickson, B. L. (2001). The role of positive emotions in positive psychology: The broaden-and-build theory of positive emotions. *American Psychologist, 56,* 218–226.

Fredrickson, B. L., & Branigan, C. (2005). Positive emotions broaden the scope of attention and thought-action repertoires. *Cognition and Emotion, 19,* 313–332.

Fredrickson, B. L., Cohn, M. A., Coffey, K. A., Pek, J., & Finkel, S. M. (2008). Open hearts build lives: Positive emotions, induced through loving-kindness meditation, build consequential personal resources. *Journal of Personality and Social Psychology, 95,* 1045–1062.

Freeman, W. (2000). A neurobiological role of music in social bonding. In B. Merker, N. L. Wallin, & S. Brown (Eds.), *The origins of music* (pp. 411–424). Cambridge, MA: MIT Press.

Frijda, N. H. (1986). *The emotions.* Cambridge: Cambridge University Press.

Gable, S., Gonzaga, G., & Strachman, A. (2006). Will you be there for me when things go right? Supportive responses to positive event disclosures. *Journal of Personality and Social Psychology, 91,* 904–917.

Gable, S. L., Reis, H. T., Impett, E. A., & Asher, E. R. (2004).What do you do when things go right? The intrapersonal and interpersonal benefits of sharing positive events. *Journal of Personality and Social Psychology, 87,* 228–245.

Graham, J., & Haidt, J. (2010). Beyond beliefs: Religions bind individuals into moral communities. *Personality and Social Psychology Review, 14,* 140–150.

Greeley, A. M. (1975). *Sociology of the paranormal: A reconnaissance.* Beverly Hills, CA: Sage.

Griskevicius, V., Shiota, M. N., & Nowlis, S. M. (2010). The many shades of rose-colored glasses: An evolutionary approach to the influence of different positive emotions. *Journal of Consumer Research, 37,* 238–250.

Hackney, C. H., & Sanders, G. S. (2003). Religiosity and mental health: A meta-analysis of recent studies. *Journal for the Scientific Study of Religion, 42,* 43–55.

Haidt, J. (2003). The moral emotions. In R. J. Davidson, K. R. Scherer, & H. H. Goldsmith (Eds.), *Handbook of affective sciences* (pp. 852–870). Oxford: Oxford University Press.

Harber, K. D., & Cohen, D. J. (2005). The emotional broadcaster theory of social sharing. *Journal of Language and Social Psychology, 24,* 382–400.

Herring, D. R., Burleson, M. H., Roberts, N. A., & Devine, M. J. (2011). Coherent with laughter: Subjective experience, behavior, and physiological responses during amusement and joy. *International Journal of Psychophysiology, 79,* 211–218.

Isen, A. (2000). Positive affect and decision making. In M. Lewis & J. Haviland (Eds.), *Handbook of emotions* (pp. 261–277). New York: Guilford.

Johnson, K. J., & Fredrickson, B. L. (2005). "We all look the same to me": Positive emotions eliminate the own-race bias in face recognition. *Psychological Science, 16,* 875–881.

Keltner, D., & Haidt, J. (2003). Approaching awe, a moral, spiritual, and aesthetic emotion. *Cognition and Emotion, 17,* 297–314.

Kim-Prieto, C., & Diener, E. (2009). Religion as a source of variation in the experience of positive and negative emotions. *Journal of Positive Psychology, 4,* 447–460.

Kirkpatrick, L. A. (2005). *Attachment, evolution, and the psychology of religion.* New York: Guilford.

Kirschner, S., & Tomasello, M. (2010). Joint music making promotes prosocial behavior in 4-year-old children. *Evolution and Human Behavior, 31,* 354–364.

Koenig, H., King, D., & Carson, V. B. (2012). *Handbook of religion and health* (2nd ed.). New York: Oxford University Press.

Konvalinka, I., Vuust, P., Roepstorff, A., & Frith, C. D. (2010). Follow you, follow me: Continuous mutual prediction and adaptation in joint tapping. *Quarterly Journal of Experimental Psychology, 63,* 2220–2230.

Lambert, N. M., Fincham, F. D., Braithwaite, S. R., Graham, S. M., & Beach, S. R. H. (2009). Can prayer increase gratitude? *Psychology of Religion and Spirituality, 1,* 139–149.

Langston, C. A. (1994). Capitalizing on and coping with daily-life events: Expressive responses to positive events. *Journal of Personality and Social Psychology, 67,* 1112–1125.

Laurenceau, J.-P., Feldman-Barrett, L., & Pietromonaco, P. R. (1998). Intimacy as an interpersonal process: The importance of self-disclosure, partner disclosure, and perceived partner responsiveness in interpersonal exchanges. *Journal of Personality and Social Psychology, 74,* 1238–1251.

Levenson, R. W. (2003). Blood, sweat and fears: The autonomic architecture of emotion. In P. Ekman, J. Campos, R. J. Davidson, & F. B. M. De Waal (Eds.), *Emotions inside out* (pp. 348–366). New York: New York Academy of Sciences.

McCullough, M. E., Emmons, R. A., & Tsang, J.-A. (2002). The grateful disposition: A conceptual and empirical topography. *Journal of Personality and Social Psychology, 82,* 112–127.

Malhotra, D. (2010). (When) are religious people nicer? Religious salience and the "Sunday effect" on pro-social behavior. *Judgment and Decision Making, 5,* 138–143.

Michael, S. T., Crowther, M. R., Schmid, B., & Allen, R. S. (2003). Widowhood and spirituality: Coping responses to bereavement. *Journal of Women and Aging, 15,* 145–165.

Miller, M. M., & Strongman, K. T. (2002). The emotional effects of music on religious experience: A study of the Pentecostal charismatic style of music and worship. *Psychology of Music, 30,* 8–27.

Nils, F., & Rimé, B. (2012). Beyond the myth of venting: Social sharing modes determine the benefits of emotional disclosure. *European Journal of Social Psychology, 42,* 672–681.

Otto, R. (1958). *The idea of the holy* (J. W. Harvey, Trans.). London: Oxford University Press. (Original work published 1917)

Paladino, M., Mazzurega, M., Pavani, F., & Schubert, T. W. (2010). Synchronous multisensory stimulation blurs self-other boundaries. *Psychological Science, 21,* 1202–1207.

Penman, J., & Becker, J. (2009). Religious ecstatics, "deep listeners," and musical emotion. *Empirical Musicology Review, 4*, 49–70.

Piedmont, R. L. (1999). Does spirituality represent the sixth factor of personality? Spiritual transcendence and the five-factor model. *Journal of Personality, 67*, 985–1013.

Philips-Silver, J., Aktipis, C. A., & Bryant, G. A. (2010). The ecology of entrainment: Foundations of coordinated rhythmic movement. *Music Perception, 28*, 3–14.

Privette, G. (1983). Peak experience, peak performance, and flow: A comparative analysis of positive human experiences. *Journal of Personality and Social Psychology, 45*, 1361–1368.

Rimé, B. (2009). Emotion elicits the social sharing of emotion: Theory and empirical review. *Emotion Review, 1*, 60–85.

Roederer, J. G. (1984). The search for a survival value for music. *Music Perception, 1*, 350–356.

Rudd, M., Vohs, K. D., & Aaker, J. L. (2012). Awe expands people's perception of time, alters decisionmaking, and enhances well-being. *Psychological Science, 23*, 1130–1136.

Saroglou, V. (2013). Religion, spirituality, and altruism. In K. I. Pargament, J. J. Exline, & J. W. Jones (Eds.), *APA handbook of psychology, religion and spirituality* (Vol. 1, pp. 439–457). Washington, DC: American Psychological Association.

Saroglou, V., Buxant, C., & Tilquin, J. (2008). Positive emotions as leading to religion and spirituality. *Journal of Positive Psychology, 3*, 165–173.

Sauter, D. (2010). More than happy: The need for disentangling positive emotions. *Current Directions in Psychological Science, 19*, 36–40.

Scherer, K. R., & Zentner, M. R. (2001). Emotional effects of music: Production rules. In P. Juslin & J. Sloboda (Eds.), *Music and emotion* (pp. 361–392). Oxford: Oxford University Press.

Schleiermacher, F. (1799). *On religion: Speeches to its cultured despisers*. London: Kegan Paul, Trench, Tribner.

Schnall, S., Roper, J., & Fessler, D. M. T. (2010). Elevation leads to altruistic behavior. *Psychological Science, 21*, 315–320.

Shiota, M. N., Keltner, D., & Mossman, A. (2007). The nature of awe: Elicitors, appraisals, and effects on self-concept. *Cognition and Emotion, 21*, 944–963.

Smith, B. W., Ortiz, J. A., Wiggins, K. T., Bernard, J. F., & Dalen, J. (2012). Spirituality, resilience, and positive emotions. In L. J. Miller (Ed.), *The Oxford handbook of psychology and spirituality* (pp. 437–454). New York: Oxford University Press.

Sosis, R. (2003). Why aren't we all Hutterites? Costly signaling theory and religious behavior. *Human Nature, 14*, 91–127.

Spilka, B., Hood, R. W., Jr., Hunsberger, B., & Gorsuch, R. (2003). *The psychology of religion: An empirical approach* (3rd ed.). New York: Guilford.

Todd, N. P. M., Lee, C. S., & O'Boyle, D. J. (2002). A sensorimotor theory of temporal tracking and beat induction. *Psychological Research, 66*, 26–39.

Tracy, J. L., & Robins, R. W. (2007). The nature of pride. In J. L. Tracy, R. W. Robins, & J. P. Tangney (Eds.), *The self-conscious emotions: Theory and research* (pp. 263–282). New York: Guilford.

van Baaren, R. B., Holland, R. W., Kawakami, K., & Vvan Knippenberg, A. (2004). Mimicry and prosocial behavior. *Psychological Science, 15*, 71–74.

van Cappellen, P. (2011). Un rituel collectif: Analyse de 1 Ch 15–16 selon le modèle de E. Durkheim [A collective ritual: Analysis of 1 Chr 15–16 from E. Durkheim's perspective]. *Scandinavian Journal of the Old Testament, 25*, 289–302.

van Cappellen, P. (2012). La fierté dans les Psaumes, ou le paradoxe de la glorification de soi en Dieu [Pride in the Psalms, or the paradox of self-glorification in God]. *Revue Théologique de Louvain, 43*, 341–362.

van Cappellen, P., & Saroglou, V. (2012). Awe activates religious and spiritual feelings and behavioral intentions. *Psychology of Religion and Spirituality, 4*, 223–236.

van Cappellen, P., Saroglou, V., & Cara, A. (2012). [Positive emotions and their effect on prosociality: A study among religious people]. Unpublished raw data.

van Cappellen, P., Saroglou, V., Iweins, C., Piovesana, M., & Fredrickson, B. (in press). Self-transcendent positive emotions increase spirituality through basic world assumptions. *Cognition and Emotion.*

van Cappellen, P., Saroglou, V., & Toth, M. (2011, August). *The place of positive emotions in the possible pathways from religion to well-being.* Paper presented at the International Association for Psychology of Religion Conference, Bari, Italy.

Wadlinger, H. A., & Isaacowitz, D. M. (2006). Fixing our focus: Training attention to regulate emotion. *Personality and Social Psychology Review, 15*, 75–102.

Waugh, C. E., & Fredrickson, B. L. (2006). Nice to know you: Positive emotions, self-other overlap, and complex understanding in the formation of a new relationship. *Journal of Positive Psychology, 1*, 93–106.

Wiltermuth, S. S., & Heath, C. (2009). Synchrony and cooperation. *Psychological Science, 20*, 1–5.

Wimberley, D. (1984). Socioeconomic deprivation and religious salience: A cognitive behavioral approach. *Sociological Quarterly, 25*, 223–238.

Zech, E., & Rimé, B. (2005). Is talking about an emotional experience helpful? Effects on emotional recovery and perceived benefits. *Clinical Psychology and Psychotherapy, 12*, 270–287.

Zinnbauer, B. J., & Pargament, K. I. (2005). Religiousness and spirituality. In R. F. Paloutzian & C. L. Park (Eds.), *Handbook of the psychology of religion and spirituality* (pp. 21–42). New York: Guilford.

Part II

Social Behavior, Morality, and Intergroup Relations

7 Religious Prosociality
Personal, Cognitive, and Social Factors

Jesse Lee Preston, Erika Salomon, and Ryan S. Ritter

Morality is a central theme in religion. Stories of gods in all religions and cultures suggest they are concerned with human morality and willing to punish or reward accordingly (Roes & Raymond 2003; Shariff, Norenzayan, & Henrich, 2009). All major world religions explicitly teach prosociality as a virtue, and share some version of the Golden rule—*treat others as you would want to be treated* (e.g., parable of the Good Samaritan, Luke 10: 25–37, King James Version; Baha"u'lla'h calling on his followers to "desire not for anyone the things you would not desire for yourselves," Gleanings from the Writings of Baha"u'lla'h, LXVI, Effendi, 1976; or Lao-Tzu's description of "true goodness," in the *Tao-Te Ching*; Lao Tzu, 2006). Given the close association between religious beliefs and moral issues, many argue that religion promotes prosociality and facilitates cooperation in large societies. But what are the true effects of religion on prosociality? The psychological literature reveals a complex relation between religious belief and moral action, leading to greater prosocial behavior in some contexts but not in others.

In this chapter, we provide an updated review of research and theory on religious prosociality. We focus primarily on *helping* behavior—that is, providing some personal assistance to a target, whether through direct actions or more indirect means such as donations, or volunteer work. However, we will also briefly discuss other behaviors generally related to morality, such as cheating and dishonesty (Randolph-Seng & Nielsen, 2007; Shariff & Norenzayan, 2011).

Some excellent reviews on religion and prosociality have been written and offer important organization and insight into the topic (Batson, Schoenrade, & Ventis, 1993; Galen, 2012; Norenzayan & Shariff, 2008; Preston, Ritter, & Hernandez, 2010). Studies on the effect of religion on prosociality are a favorite subject in the psychology of religion, and many studies have been conducted in the last few years. This constant stream of fresh findings makes the topic one that needs to be frequently examined and updated. In this review, we do not argue from any one theoretical perspective, rather we piece together the picture of religious prosociality from the evidence, by asking three basic questions: *Who* helps? *When* do people help? And *why* do people help? We hope to reveal a big picture of religious prosociality that is complex, but can be understood as an interaction between personal, cognitive, and social forces:

1. *Who* is prosocial? The first section of this chapter addresses the associations between personal factors and prosocial behavior. We review differences in religiosity that are associated with prosociality, but also discuss evidence that the kind of religious belief held may affect willingness to help.
2. *When* does religion increase prosociality? We review experimental studies investigating how religious cognition (e.g., by religious primes) can increase prosocial behavior.
3. *Why* would religion increase prosocial behavior? Although researchers agree that religion is connected to moral belief, the particular mechanisms underlying religious prosociality are hotly debated (cf. Graham & Haidt, 2010; Shariff et al., 2009). We compare several such theories and their ability to account for the existing evidence reviewed in the previous sections. We find that religious prosociality may be created through a concert of different cognitive and social mechanisms that each contribute to prosocial motivation.

Who is Prosocial? Individual Differences in Religiosity

Religious belief systems provide moral instruction for believers, whether through stories or in explicit laws. But do religious people behave more prosocially? Does the type of religious belief help also impact prosocial behavior? In this section, we examine the personal factors related to prosociality as we investigate the question: *Who helps?*

Are Religious People More Prosocial?

All religions prescribe laws for their followers to live by, including specific directives to help others. If religious followers truly internalize religious laws as their own moral values, religiousness should be associated with more prosociality. Self-report data suggest some support for these predictions. For example, religiosity and church attendance are associated with more volunteerism (Marris et al., 2000) and blood donations (St. John & Fuchs, 2005). Across many different cultures and nationalities, belief in God and the afterlife predicts other types of moral attitude towards specific behavior, for example adultery or cheating on taxes (Atkinson & Bourrat, 2011). And there is at least some evidence that religiosity impacts prosocial behavior by internalized prosocial values. A meta-analysis of 21 samples drawn from 15 countries revealed a weak but positive association between religiosity (as a general trait) and the value of benevolence, or concern for the welfare of others (Saroglou, Delpierre, & Dernelle, 2004). In a self-report survey of adolescents, religiosity predicted the prosocial value of *kindness*, which in turn predicted willingness to help others, especially when the help was anonymous and altruistic (i.e., the primary goal is to benefit others and not for self-gain) (Hardy & Carlo, 2005).

Still, other evidence suggests that any associations between religiosity and prosociality are due to extraneous factors or are otherwise extrinsically motivated. For example, religiosity sometimes predicts helping only close others (e.g., friend or neighbor) but not unknown others, suggesting a primary concern for prosocial reputation within a group or welfare of the ingroup (Saroglou, Pichon, Trompette, Verschueren, & Dernelle, 2005). In some cases, the relationship between religion and prosocial behavior may be circumstantial or indirect. For example, religious people made more donations and gave more blood following the Oklahoma City bombing, but this may have been because of the Church's facilitation of these donations, rather than the religiosity of the givers (St. John & Fuchs, 2005). Other data suggest that religion's apparent effect on prosocial behavior may be the result of other confounding demographic factors: When race and gender are controlled for, the benevolent effect of religiosity disappears (Gillum & Masters, 2010).

In sum, general religiosity shows some positive effect on prosocial behavior, but these effects are not always straightforward. In the following, we take a closer look at how different kinds of religiosity influence prosociality.

Kinds of Religious Belief

Correlational evidence suggests some relation between religiosity and prosociality. But these studies sometimes overlook differences in the kind of religious belief different people hold—not differences of affiliation (such as being a Catholic or Protestant), but differences in the style of religious belief or the general approach to religion. One of the first studied individual differences in religiosity is that between *intrinsic* and *extrinsic* religious orientations (Allport, 1966; Allport & Ross, 1967). Whereas intrinsically oriented believers view their religion as an end in itself (belief for its own sake), extrinsically oriented believers use religion as a means to gain other things, for example, social support from the group (Allport, 1966; Allport & Ross, 1967). Several studies suggest people with a stronger intrinsic religious orientation may be more prosocial than those with an extrinsic orientation. Intrinsically oriented people have more salient goals of social reward (e.g., praise), which, in turn, predicts volunteer behavior (Batson & Flory, 1990). Compared to extrinsically oriented believers, intrinsically oriented people are more empathetic toward others (Watson, Hood, Morris, & Hall, 1984), score higher on self-reported altruism (Chau, Johnson, Bowers, Darvill, & Danko, 1990), and are more charitable (Hunsberger & Platonow, 1986). In addition, intrinsic orientation also better predicts non-spontaneous helping behavior such as a recurring and long-term commitment to volunteering (Benson et al., 1980).

In addition to intrinsic and extrinsic religious orientations, Daniel Batson introduced a third orientation, *quest* religiosity (Batson, 1976). Believers with a quest orientation are focused on a search for existential meaning and an emphasis on questions over answers in the religious domain (Batson, 1976). Although both intrinsic and quest religiosity are associated with helping, researchers have found differences in *how* people with these orientations help others. Quest-oriented people prefer spontaneous forms of helping (e.g., helping someone pick up dropped papers), but intrinsically oriented people prefer non-spontaneous helping, such as volunteer work (Hansen, Vandenberg, & Patterson, 1995). Compared with intrinsic religiosity, quest religiosity has been associated with a more empathetic, universal form of prosociality (e.g., Batson & Gray, 1981). If they do initially offer help, those with an intrinsic orientation tend to be insistent on helping whether or not the target wants it. But people with a quest orientation offer tentative help, and do not persist if the target refuses the help (Batson, 1976; see also Batson & Gray, 1981). In addition, differences in intrinsic and quest religiosity are associated with differences in *whom* one helps. Intrinsic-oriented believers sometimes limit prosociality to like-minded others, for example, reduced helping towards those who violate one's religious values (e.g., homosexuality). In contrast, those with a quest orientation are often willing to help others with beliefs and values that oppose their own (Batson, Denton, & Vollmecke, 2008; Batson, Eidelman, Higley, & Russell, 2001; Batson, Floyd, Meyer, & Winner, 1999). Batson (1990) emphasizes that quest orientation is related to altruistic helping motivations (where the primary concern is for others), whereas intrinsic orientation is more strongly associated with egoistic helping motivations (primary concern for self or ingroup).

Overall, research on religious orientation supports the conclusion that one's motivations for being religious are related to both *whom* and *how* one helps. However, intrinsic, extrinsic, and quest orientations are not the only individual difference in kind of religious belief. For example, the belief that God is punishing (rather than forgiving) can impact moral actions by fear of supernatural punishment (Shariff & Norenzayan, 2011). Religious fundamentalism—characterized by stronger religious conviction and concern with the moral authority of religion (Altemeyer & Hunsberger, 1992)—is also related to reduced helping towards perceived outgroups (Blogowska & Saroglou, 2011), especially outgroups perceived as a moral threat (e.g., homosexuals and single mothers; Jackson & Esses, 1997). Given that fundamentalism is often negatively related to quest religiosity (Batson et al., 2008; Gold-fried & Miner, 2002), these findings are consistent with the conclusion that quest-oriented believers are more universally prosocial. However, other research suggests that the limited extent of religious prosociality may be a more general feature of religiosity not limited to orientation or fundamentalism.

Who Helps? The Bottom Line

Although some studies suggest that religious people help more than less religious people, this relationship is qualified by an understanding of individual differences in religion. Psychological variables, such as religious orientation and fundamentalism, have a profound impact on prosocial behavior. But it is also important to note that different types of religious belief (e.g., religious orientation) show different patterns of prosocial behavior depending on the target of help—e.g., a moral outsider/insider.

When Does Religion Help? Situational and Experimental Factors

Social psychologists are inherently interested in aspects of the situation that influence prosocial behavior. In addition to measuring one's religious disposition and correlating it with some measure of prosocial behavior, researchers have also experimentally manipulated whether or not people are thinking religious thoughts to observe their causal effect on prosociality. In this section, we examine some of the cognitive and social factors that activate religious prosociality. That is: *When does religion help?*

Does merely having religion on the mind make people more likely to help others? One of the most classic studies on the relation between religion and prosocial behavior suggests it is not. Following the logic of the parable of the Good Samaritan (Luke 10: 25–37), Darley and Batson (1973) reasoned that people who are thinking "religious and ethical" thoughts should be no more likely to stop and help a person in need than someone who is not thinking about religion. To test this prediction, Princeton seminary students were put in a situation similar to that in the parable of the Good Samaritan. They were asked to travel to another building on campus to give a talk, and, on the way, passed by a shabbily dressed confederate who coughed and groaned, and appeared to need help. The researchers manipulated two variables to assess their influence on helping behavior. First, some participants were told that they would be giving a short talk on the parable of the Good Samaritan itself (and thus had religion on their mind when they passed the groaning confederate) whereas other participants were told they would be giving a talk on a non-helping related topic. Second, some participants were asked to rush to the other building whereas others were not asked to rush. Participants who had religion on their mind were no more likely to stop and help the confederate. Rather, the other situational variable— time—had a huge impact: people who were in a hurry were significantly less likely to stop and help than people who were not in a hurry.

Although having religious thoughts on the mind did not influence helping behavior in this classic study, researchers have since used a variety of methods to activate religious concepts and measure their influence on prosocial behavior. For Christians, Sunday is set aside as a holy day— to attend Church and worship. If religion does have some association with prosocial behavior, we might expect this effect to be particularly robust on Sundays when Christians have just attended a church service and religious (prosocial) norms are highly salient. Indeed, this so-called "Sunday effect" hypothesis does have some support. In one study, people who regularly attended church were more likely than people who did not regularly attend church to respond to an appeal for prosocial behavior (by continuing to bid for a charitable cause), but only on Sundays (Malhotra, 2010). There was no difference between religious and non-religious participants on charitable bidding on the other six days of the week. In contrast to Darley and Batson's (1973) "Good Samaritan" study just examined, this finding suggests that situational factors that make religion more salient can have an important effect on prosocial behavior. But given these conflicting findings, it is clear that the effect of activating religious concept on prosocial behavior is not straightforward. Next we review more recent studies that have used a variety of methods to experimentally manipulate religious cognition.

Prosocial Intentions

As we have just seen, accessibility of religious thoughts can play an important role in the relation between religion and prosocial behavior. However, not all kinds of religious concept may be associated with prosocial behavior (Preston, Ritter, & Hernandez, 2010). Pichon, Boccato, and Saroglou (2007), for example, found that positive religious words (e.g., *bless, faith, baptism*) facilitated prosocial intentions, but neutral religious words (e.g., *monk, chapel, altar*) did not. In one study, participants who were first subliminally primed with positive religious primes were more likely to take charity pamphlets (containing information about an organization that provides food for disadvantaged people) to distribute to their friends. In a second study, participants primed with positive religious words showed increased accessibility of prosocial concepts, suggesting that *positive* religious words are more associated with prosocial behaviors (Pichon et al., 2007).

In addition to understanding the kinds of religious prime associated with prosocial intentions, a second important feature to consider is the target of behavior. That is, religious primes do not necessarily elicit universal prosocial behavior, but prosocial behavior toward specific persons or groups (Preston et al., 2010; Saroglou, 2006). Pichon and Saroglou (2009) used pictures to manipulate both the target and the religious context of prosocial behavior. Participants were presented with a picture of a homeless person or an illegal immigrant taken in front of a church or inside a gymnasium. Merely being exposed to the picture of the person-in-need in front of a church increased self-reported intention to help, but only for the homeless person, and not for the illegal immigrant, who was violating the law (Pichon & Saroglou, 2009). Other research has found that primes of "religion" increased cooperation and giving towards others, but only if the target shared the participants' religious background, whereas "God" primes increased prosociality towards religious outgroups (Preston, Ritter, & Hernandez, 2010). Thus, although religious primes are associated with increased prosociality, this is true only for *some* religious primes and only for *some* targets.

Moral Hypocrisy

When faced with someone in need of help, people do know what they *ought* to do. The golden rule is clear: Do unto others as you would have them do unto you. Yet people often fail to live up to this moral standard. That is, people often behave as moral hypocrites (Batson, Kobrynowicz, Dinnerstein, Kampf, & Wilson, 1997). One possible reason that activating religious concepts enhances prosocial behavior is that it increases the salience of moral standards, making it more difficult to engage in moral hypocrisy. Carpenter and Marshall (2009) addressed this question. Participants were told they were responsible for assigning themselves and another participant to a positive consequence task (i.e., entered into a raffle to win $30) or a neutral consequence task (i.e., no chance to win money). Participants could make this decision themselves or flip a coin to determine the assignment. A moral hypocrite, in this case, would admit that flipping the coin is the fair method to make the task assignment, but then assign themselves to the positive consequence task anyway (either by choosing not to flip the coin or flipping the coin until the desired outcome is obtained). Just before choosing the task assignments, however, half of the participants were asked to read a series of nine Bible verses whereas the other half were not asked to do so. Participants who read the Bible verses prior to making the task assignment behaved significantly less like moral hypocrites (i.e., were more likely to act in accordance with their moral values of fairness)—but only when they scored high on an intrinsic religiosity scale. In other words, the religious primes had no measurable effect on people who were not religious as an end-in-itself.

Cooperation

Cheating for the sake of selfish benefit—or "free riding"—is a threat to any cooperative community. Given the theoretical emphasis placed on religion's cultural-evolutionary role in reducing free riding and increasing cooperation (see "Theoretical Perspectives" section), the effect of activating religious thoughts on people's willingness to engage in either mutually beneficial cooperation with others or to cheat at others' expense has been an active area of research. Some of the most common methods to measure this behavior in the lab are through economic games such as the dictator game and the prisoner's dilemma. In the dictator game, participants are given a sum of money and may anonymously distribute the funds between themselves and another player. Participants can choose to distribute the money evenly, take it all, or give it all away (or anywhere in between). In the prisoner's dilemma, participants must decide to cooperate with or betray another player. Mutual cooperation provides the best-case outcome for both parties, but betrayal can lead to the best individual outcome without taking the risk of being betrayed. Critically, participants playing the prisoner's dilemma game must decide to cooperate or betray without knowing what the other player has decided.

Shariff and Norenzayan (2007) used the dictator game to examine the influence of implicit religious primes on prosocial behavior. Each participant was given $10 to distribute between themselves and another person, but just before making their decision some participants were primed with neutral words and others were primed with religious words (e.g., *spirit, divine, God, sacred, prophet*). Among all participants in an undergraduate student sample (Study 1), but only among theists in a wider community sample (Study 2), religious primes led to increased fairness in the distribution of the money relative to participants primed with neutral words. Further, a higher proportion of participants behaved selfishly (i.e., offered nothing) in the neutral prime condition than in the religious prime condition, whereas a higher proportion behaved fairly (i.e., offered exactly $5) in the religious prime condition than in the control condition (Shariff & Norenzayan, 2007). In a similar study, Ahmed and Salas (2011) primed participants with religious or neutral concepts immediately before they engaged in a dictator game and a prisoner's dilemma game with another player. Consistent with the results of Shariff and Norenzayan (2007), participants primed with religious concepts gave significantly more money to the other player in the dictator game (35% vs. 27%) and were significantly more likely to cooperate in the prisoner's dilemma (44% vs. 27%).

Decreased Anti-Social Behavior

Although the focus of this chapter is prosocial behavior, it is worth mentioning that religious priming can also decrease antisocial behavior such as cheating, presumably by activating feelings of being watched by a supernatural agent (Gervais & Norenzayan, 2012) and/or a desire to avoid supernatural punishment (Johnson & Bering, 2006). In one study, participants had the chance to cheat on a test of spatial reasoning by not dismissing answers that appeared on the computer screen before the questions (supposedly as part of a computer error; Bering, McLeod, & Shackelford, 2005). Just before completing the test, some participants were told that the task was created in memory of a recently deceased graduate student, and the experimenter mentioned that she had recently seen the deceased student's ghost roaming the laboratory. Participants who were primed to think of a ghost pressed the space-bar significantly faster than participants who were not so primed. A similar effect has been observed in children. Piazza, Bering, and Ingram (2011) demonstrated that children (ages 5–9) who were left alone in a room to complete a challenging task after being introduced to an invisible "Princess Alice" were significantly less likely to cheat—but only if they believed Princess Alice was real. Religious primes have also been shown to decrease antisocial attitudes toward outgroups. Ginges and colleagues (2009) found, for example, that Jewish Israeli settlers were significantly less likely to approve of suicide attacks against Palestinians if they were primed to think about how much they pray (6% approval) relative to participants who were not primed with any religious concept (15% approval). It is important to note, however, that participants primed to think of synagogue attendance at the beginning of the survey displayed the strongest approval of suicide attacks against Palestinians (23%). What this suggests is that the effects of religious primes are complex, causing decreased antisocial behavior in some contexts and an increase in antisocial behavior in others (see Chapter 8 in this volume).

Religiosity as a Moderator of Situational and Experimental Variables

Experimental priming studies have shown that activating religious cognition can increase prosocial behavior and intentions in a wide variety of tasks. Many of these priming studies also measure individual religiousness, which might be expected to moderate the effects of experimental manipulations. As reviewed in the previous section, religiosity does have some association with prosociality. But the effects of religiosity in experimental paradigms are mixed at best. Some studies do show an interaction between individual and experimental variables. Carpenter and Marshall (2009) found that when religiosity was primed, intrinsic religiosity predicted decreased moral hypocrisy. Tan and Vogel (2008) found that people in an economic game cooperated more with a partner who was known to be religious, especially if participants were religious themselves. Yet, other studies show mixed effects of religiousness, for example, Shariff and Norenzayan (2007) found in one study that religious primes increased giving in both religious and secular participants (Study 1), and in another study that the effect was found only in believers (Study 2). Still other studies show no effect of religiosity (e.g., Ahmed & Salas, 2011; Darley & Batson, 1973).

Religious priming studies examining behavior other than prosociality also show mixed effects of personal religiosity as a moderator (e.g., in the domain of self-control: Laurin, Kay, & Fitzsimons, 2012). While it is not clear why priming effects have worked well with nonbelievers alike, one possibility is that the moral associations tied to religion are also activated in nonbelievers, because of cultural exposure and shared knowledge of religious values. But as we reviewed earlier, prosociality is best predicted by the specific kind of religious belief a person holds (e.g., religious orientation), and also the target of help. These important differences in belief are often overlooked in priming studies, but perhaps future research may show that priming effects also interact with the kind of religious belief (or disbelief) a person holds.

When Does Religion Increase Prosociality? The Bottom Line

Overall, increasing the salience of religious concepts can increase prosociality. However, the causal influence of religious primes on prosocial behavior is not entirely straightforward. The efficacy of religious priming can depend on several important factors: the kind of religious concept being activated, the target of the prosocial behavior, and one's religiosity. In the following section, we examine different theoretical perspectives that have been advanced to explain the association between religion and prosociality.

Why Does Religion Increase Prosociality? Theoretical Perspectives

A variety of theoretical accounts have been formulated that predict a relationship between religion and prosociality. Most of these theories emphasize religion's ability to promote living in cooperative groups, but differ in the mechanisms they propose and in the scope of the prosocial behavior they predict. In this section, we discuss four such theories, beginning with the *supernatural punishment hypothesis* (e.g., Bering & Johnson, 2005; Johnson & Bering, 2006; Shariff et al., 2009), which argues that the felt presence of a watchful god is an adaptation that enables humans to live in large-scale cooperative groups. In contrast to the supernatural punishment hypothesis's emphasis on cheating behavior and cooperation, the *moral communities* perspective argues that religion's role in group cohesion stems from its emphasis on a broader, binding set of moral principles than only harm and fairness (Graham

& Haidt, 2010). The *costly signaling* theory holds that religiosity and its associated behavior communicate commitment to the ingroup and dedication to moral behavior (e.g., Irons, 1996, 2001; Sosis & Alcorta, 2003). Finally, the *self-regulation* account holds that religion, through its beliefs, practices, and associated community, promotes prosociality by strengthening one's ability to monitor and adjust one's behavior (McCullough & Willoughby, 2009).

Supernatural Punishment Hypothesis

Imagine that you see $20 fall out of a stranger's pocket onto the sidewalk. No one else is around, and the stranger, unaware of the loss, is walking away. You pick up the cash. Do you keep it or give it back? What if there were someone else around, who saw you take the money, and could also punish you for doing so; would this make you more likely to give the money back?

According to the supernatural punishment hypothesis (SPH), religious belief promotes prosocial behavior (i.e., returning the $20) by the self-conscious awareness of one's moral actions before the eyes of God (Bering & Johnson, 2005; Johnson & Bering, 2006; Shariff et al., 2009). Members of large-scale societies regularly face situations that allow for anonymous violations of moral rules, like the opportunity to take the stranger's money. When a group becomes too large to directly monitor who is good and who is bad, what keeps its members from free riding on the cooperation of others? This is the where fear of God (or gods) comes in. If you know that God will see you pick up the money, and that He will punish you for keeping it, you might be more likely not to steal at all or even to return the money to the stranger.

Critical to the supernatural punishment account is the capacity of humans to reason about the minds of others (Premack & Woodruff, 1978). This ability, called *theory of mind*, allows us to imagine the thoughts and intentions of other people and is essential to human social functioning. The ability to reason about the minds of others is also applied to the mind of God (Johnson & Bering, 2006; Shariff et al., 2009). For example, when you consider that God can see you take the stranger's money, you are engaging in theory of mind. If you also think that God would be *angry* about this behavior, then God becomes a moral audience for your actions.

Support for SPH comes from studies demonstrating that the (imagined) presence of a supernatural agent diminishes cheating (e.g., Bering et al., 2005; Piazza et al., 2011). In the "Princess Alice" study discussed earlier, there was no difference in cheating between children who were observed by a human confederate and those who believed they were watched by the imaginary princess (Piazza et al., 2011). This is evidence that imagining a supernatural being's mind has similar effects on anti-sociality to imagining a human's mind. Other evidence suggests that people who believe in a wrathful God are less likely to cheat than those who view God as forgiving (Shariff & Norenzayan, 2011), and across 67 countries, belief in Hell (but not Heaven) is associated with lower national crime rates (Shariff & Rhemtulla, 2012). However, it is not enough that supernatural punishment deters anti-sociality; it should also increase prosociality. Evidence from cross-sectional surveys suggests that this may be the case (Atkinson & Bourrat, 2011; Johnson, 2005), but experimental evidence would strengthen the causal inference that thinking about supernatural beings makes people more prosocial. Other research demonstrates that religious primes increase public self-awareness and socially desirable responding, especially among believers (Gervais & Norenzayan, 2012). However, no work has directly examined whether increased self-awareness mediates the effect of religious priming on prosociality.

There is some disagreement among proponents of the SPH about how beliefs in such punishing agents arose. Some argue for a genetic adaptationist account (Bering & Johnson, 2005), that belief in punishing gods was selected for at the genetic level because it contributed to cooperative living in larger societies. That is, someone who believes that a god knows his or her thoughts and behaviors has an evolutionary advantage because they will be more concerned about their reputation, get along better with other group members, and benefit more from their generosity and cooperation. In turn, groups containing many such members can expend fewer resources on enforcing cooperation and use them instead on productive and cooperative endeavors (Johnson & Bering, 2006). Others argue that the genetic evolutionary model is not adequate because (a) it lacks clarity regarding if or how such beliefs could be genetically encoded and (b) such beliefs are not present in all societies (Shariff et al., 2009). Instead, the cultural adaptationist account argues that religion was a cultural innovation that exploits biologically adapted cognitive mechanisms, such as theory of mind (Shariff et al., 2009). Groups that developed beliefs in punishing supernatural agents, and successfully enforced commitment to them, were able to outcompete other groups without such beliefs due to their increased cooperation and cohesion. Thus, religion was an adaptation of the *group* and not the individual. As groups espousing belief in punishing agents came to dominate, the adaptive cognitive mechanisms underlying this belief, such as theory of mind, necessarily became more common in the human genetic pool.

Self-Regulation

McCullough and Willoughby (2009) agree that belief in supernatural agents promotes self-monitoring, however they suggest that it is the resulting self-regulation that ultimately mediates the association between religion and prosociality. Perhaps what makes McCullough and Willoughby's (2009) account so interesting is its synthesis of existing literature and its consideration for the multiple facets of religion, from ritual practice to belief in the supernatural and from individual behavior to community. In doing so, they draw on research suggesting (a) that people scoring high in measures of self-control also score more highly on measures of religiosity (e.g., Bergin, Masters, & Richards, 1987; French, Eisenberg, Vaughan, Purwono, & Suryanti, 2008), (b) that the religious have children with greater self-control and less impulsiveness (e.g., Bartkowski, Xu, & Levin, 2008), and (c) that religiosity is negatively associated with many risky behaviors, such as gambling (e.g., Baier & Wright, 2001) and positively associated with many precautionary behaviors, such as higher age of first intercourse (e.g., Regnerus, 2007). They argue that religious communities act as moral audiences that constrain behavior and provide additional boosts to self-monitoring. Because religious settings are restrictive in terms of allowable behaviors, those who practice a religion will have more experience with self-monitoring. In addition, religious rituals, such as Buddhist meditation and Catholic confession, may serve as opportunities to increase self-regulatory control and to compare oneself to one's goals. McCullough and Willoughby (2009) additionally claim that goals positively related to self-regulation and prosociality (e.g., being polite) are promoted by religion. Likewise, goals negatively related to self-regulation and prosociality (e.g., personal gratification) are inhibited by religion. By sanctifying these self-regulatory goals, religion establishes their importance relative to other goals. Religious prosociality is, thus, a consequence of increased self-regulation under this hypothesis.

Moral Communities

Rituals such as weddings, baptism, bar mitzvahs, and Tawah, are vivid reminders of how religion brings people together for practice. Religion is fundamentally more than a set of beliefs in an individual's head; it is a community, a culture, a way of life. Graham and Haidt (2010) suggest that religion's contribution to group cohesion comes from its emphasis on what they call the "binding" moral foundations (p. 141). According to moral foundations theory (Haidt & Graham, 2007), three binding foundations form additional sources of moral concern to harm/care and fairness, the principles traditionally studied as comprising moral behavior (see Gilligan, 1982; Turiel, 1983). These foundations are ingroup/loyalty, which places moral value on respecting and acting favorably towards members of one's group; authority/respect, which places moral value on following authority and respecting community leaders and parents; and purity/sanctity, which places moral value on avoiding disgusting behaviors and striving for moral and spiritual cleanliness. These foundations bind group members together by imbuing group members and group activities with symbolic value. Religion strengthens ingroup moral intuitions through teachings that emphasize a sanctified community that is worthy of loyalty and whose members hold a special moral position relative to outgroup members. Respect for religious authority binds groups together through shared beliefs and practices derived from common sources. Many of these beliefs and traditions may focus on matters of cleanliness, purity, and sacredness, such as ritual washing, that, when imparted with symbolism, bind people into belief groups.

Graham and Haidt (2010) argue that religious prosociality is *not* driven by belief in the supernatural; rather, it is the result of the sense of social support and bonding that occurs when a community collectively values the three binding foundations. They interpret findings that both religious and civic primes decrease cheating (Shariff & Norenzayan, 2007) as evidence for the effect of a more general process of moral community building. Rather than supernatural observation, it is the emphasis of ingroup loyalty, respect for authority, and purity present in both religious and civic systems that makes individuals cooperative. Although this theory accords well with existing evidence (e.g., that religiosity is associated with social support; Koenig et al., 1997), it is a relatively new contribution to the field that remains to be tested.

Costly Signaling

Graham and Haidt (2010) are not the only theorists to suggest that community building is the primary advantage of religion. Alcorta and Sosis (2005; Sosis & Alcorta, 2003) propose that participating in religion is a way of communicating commitment to one's group. Their argument relies on *costly signaling theory* (Bleige Bird, Smith, & Bird, 2001), which proposes that seemingly onerous behaviors can serve as signs of adaptive fitness to potential mates. When applied to humans, this means that some behaviors, such as altruism, might not benefit an individual in the short term, but they have long-term benefits based on what they communicate to others. In the case of altruism, the initial cost of helping others without reward for the self is offset by an increased reputation, the communication that one has desirable traits such as generosity and compassion, and the communication that one has enough resources to give them away (Gintis, Smith, & Bowles, 2001). Participation in religion involves cooperative and ritual behavior that does not necessarily benefit an individual directly but instead increases his or her standing in the community and fosters trust among those who share the same practices.

According to Alcorta and Sosis (2005; also see Chapter 6, this volume), religious rituals that evoke positive emotions, such as the joy of a wedding, create communal empathy and associate religious symbols with rewards. Such rewarding experiences increase an individual's likelihood of engaging in religious rituals in future and bind the individual to other community members. In contrast, religious rituals that evoke negative emotional experiences impose a cost to participation in religion. This minimizes freeriding because those whose commitment is not genuine will be identifiable by their decreased participation in costly rituals. Consider the Catholic ritual of confession; the associated guilt and reparations entailed by confession impose a cost on participation in the Catholic faith. Participation in religious ritual thus constitutes a costly signal that one is committed to group cooperation.

Support for costly signaling theory comes from historical and correlational research into the role of religion in community development and cooperation. Sosis and Bressler (2003) found that of 83 communes in 19th-century United States, those that were bound together by religious principles were less likely to come to an end due to economic failure or internal disputes, suggesting that they were better able to solve collective action problems. When Sosis and Ruffle (2003) asked Israelis living in communes (*kibbutzim*) to participate in an anonymous economic game, men living in religious communes cooperated more than women living in religious communes and more than both men and women living in secular communes. They argue that the difference between men and women living in religious communes may be due to the fact that men in these communes participate more frequently in collective rituals, and collective ritual participation is what drives increased cooperation.

Why Does Religion Affect Prosociality? The Bottom Line

Many different theories predict that religious belief shapes prosocial behavior. But there is no one explanation that best predicts religious prosociality, neither are these theories mutually exclusive. Instead, the link between religion and prosociality likely arises from a number of cognitive and social mechanisms. Connections to cognitive factors, such as fear of supernatural punishment from gods that are a constant moral audience (Bering & Johnson, 2005; Shariff et al., 2009), can increase self-regulation that is needed for prosociality. Other social influences shape motivations to be prosocial, such as a sense of shared group identity and morality of the group (Graham & Haidt, 2010). Religious communities serve as ingroups that define and enforce moral rules, promote reciprocity, and reward participation in costly prosocial and ritual behavior (Alcorta & Sosis, 2005). These different forces each shape prosocial behavior by different routes, but all demonstrate the close association between morality and religion.

Conclusion

Connection between religion and prosocial behavior is predicted by many scholars, but an analysis of the research literature reveals a somewhat complex picture of religious prosociality. We see that there are general effects of religiosity in prosocial attitudes and charitable giving, but it is not known if these results are due to extraneous social factors. Furthermore, certain *types or styles* of religiosity (such as quest/intrinsic orientations) were stronger predictors of prosociality, depending on the context and target of help. We also reviewed evidence from a wide variety of studies that religious cognition can increase prosocial behavior (e.g., cooperation, sharing, and giving). These studies often use priming techniques to activate religious cognition, and although it is not entirely certain what kind of "religious cognition" is activated (i.e., the religious constructs being activated by words such as "God" or "church"), the preponderance of positive findings suggest that these concepts are tightly connected to prosocial concerns. Finally, we discussed several different theoretical accounts that predict religious prosociality, but differ in their emphasis of cognitive (Bering & Johnson, 2005; McCullough & Willoughby, 2009) and social mechanisms (Graham & Haidt, 2010; Sosis & Alcorta, 2003). But we see no reason why different theories are incompatible. Religion is a broad social institution that touches on moral, institutional, and interpersonal aspects of life, and so we should expect that different aspects of religious belief influence prosociality by different mechanisms.

To conclude, the picture of religious prosociality is rich and complex, and at first glance may seem to be too unclear to understand. But taking a step back, some things come into focus. Religion is interwoven with many different domains of life: personal, family, and institutional components that shape the effects of religion by personal, cognitive, and social forces. The multitude of connections between prosociality and religion in by different forces demonstrates the importance of morality as a dominant theme that pervades numerous domains of religious belief and practice.

References

Ahmed, A. M., & Salas, O. (2011). Implicit influences of Christian religious representations on dictator and prisoner's dilemma game decisions. *Journal of Socio-Economics, 40*, 242–246.

Alcorta, C. S., & Sosis, R. (2005). Ritual, emotion, and sacred symbols. *Human Nature, 16*, 323–359.

Allport, G. W. (1966). Religious context of prejudice. *Journal for the Scientific Study of Religion, 5*, 447–457.

Allport, G., & Ross, J. M. (1967). Personal religious orientation and prejudice. *Journal of Personality and Social Psychology, 5*, 432–443.

Altemeyer, B., & Hunsberger, B. (1992). Authoritarianism, religious fundamentalism, quest, and prejudice. *International Journal for the Psychology of Religion, 2,* 113–133.

Atkinson, Q. D., & Bourrat, P. (2011). Beliefs about God, the afterlife and morality support the role of supernatural policing in human cooperation. *Evolution and Human Behavior, 32,* 41–49.

Baier, C., & Wright, B. R. E. (2001). "If you love me, keep my commandments": A meta-analysis of the effect of religion on crime. *Journal of Research in Crime and Delinquency, 38,* 3–21.

Bartkowski, J. P., Xu, X., & Levin, M. L. (2008). Religion and child development: Evidence from the early childhood longitudinal study. *Social Science Research, 37,* 18–36.

Batson, C. D. (1976). Religion as prosocial: Agent or double agent? *Journal for the Scientific Study of Religion, 15,* 29–45.

Batson, C. D. (1990). Good Samaritans—or priests and Levites? Using William James as a guide in the study of religious prosocial motivation. *Personality and Social Psychology Bulletin, 16,* 758–768.

Batson, C. D., Denton, D. M., & Vollmecke, J. T. (2008). Quest religion, antifundamentalism, and limited versus universal compassion. *Journal for the Scientific Study of Religion, 47,* 135–145.

Batson, C. D., Eidelman, S. H., Higley, S. L., & Russell, S. H. (2001). "And who is my neighbor?" II: Quest religion as a source of universal compassion. *Journal for the Scientific Study of Religion, 40,* 39–50.

Batson, C. D., & Flory, J. D. (1990). Goal-relevant cognitions with helping by individuals high on intrinsic, end religion. *Journal for the Scientific Study of Religion, 29,* 346–360.

Batson, C. D., Floyd, R. B., Meyer, J. M., & Winner, A. L. (1999). "And who is my neighbor?": Intrinsic religion as a source of universal compassion. *Journal for the Scientific Study of Religion, 38,* 445–457.

Batson, C. D., & Gray, R. A. (1981). Religious orientation and helping behavior: Responding to one's own or to the victim's needs. *Journal of Personality and Social Psychology, 40,* 511–520.

Batson, C. D., Kobrynowicz, D., Dinnerstein, J. L., Kampf, H. C., & Wilson, A. D. (1997). In a very different voice: Unmasking moral hypocrisy. *Journal of Personality and Social Psychology, 72,* 1335–1348.

Batson, C. D., Schoenrade, P., & Ventis, W. I. (1993). *Religion and the individual: A social-psychological perspective.* New York: Oxford University Press.

Benson, P. L., Dehority, J., Garman, L., Hanson, E., Hochschwender, M., Lebold, C., et al. (1980). Intrapersonal correlates of nonspontaneous helping behavior. *Journal of Social Psychology, 110,* 87–95.

Bergin, A. E., Masters, K. S., & Richards, P. S. (1987). Religiousness and mental health reconsidered: A study of an intrinsically religious sample. *Journal of Counseling Psychology, 34,* 197–204.

Bering, J. M., & Johnson, D. (2005). "O Lord, You perceive my thoughts from afar": Recursiveness and the evolution of supernatural agency. *Journal of Cognition and Culture, 1,* 118–142.

Bering, J. M., McLeod, K., & Shackelford, T. K. (2005). Reasoning about dead agents reveals possible adaptive trends. *Human Nature, 16,* 360–381.

Bernt, F. M. (1989). Being religious and being altruistic: A study of college service volunteers. *Personality and Individual Differences, 10*, 663–669.

Bliege Bird, R., Smith, E., & Bird, D. (2001). The hunting handicap: Costly signaling in human foraging strategies. *Behavioral Ecology and Sociobiology, 50*, 9–19.

Blogowska, J., & Saroglou, V. (2011). Religious fundamentalism and limited prosociality as a function of the target. *Journal for the Scientific Study of Religion, 50*, 44–60.

Bushman, B. J., Ridge, R. D., Das, E., Key, C. W., & Busath, G. W. (2007). When God sanctions killing: Effect of scriptural violence on aggression. *Psychological Science, 18*, 204–207.

Carpenter, T. P., & Marshall, M. A. (2009). An examination of religious priming and intrinsic religious motivation in the moral hypocrisy paradigm. *Journal for the Scientific Study of Religion, 48*, 386–393.

Chau, L. L., Johnson, R. C., Bowers, J. K., Darvill, T. J., & Danko, G. P. (1990). Intrinsic and extrinsic religiosity as related to conscience, adjustment, and altruism. *Personality and Individual Differences, 11*, 397–400.

Darley, J. M., & Batson, C. D. (1973). "From Jerusalem to Jericho": A study of situational and dispositional variables in helping behavior. *Journal of Personality and Social Psychology, 27*, 100–108.

Fishbach, A., Friedman, R. S., & Kruglanski, A. W. (2003). Leading us not into temptation: Momentary allurements elicit overriding goal activation. *Journal of Personality and Social Psychology, 84*, 296–309.

French, D. C., Eisenberg, N., Vaughan, J., Purwono, U., & Suryanti, T. A. (2008). Religious involvement and the social competence and adjustment of Indonesian Muslim adolescents. *Developmental Psychology, 44*, 597–611.

Galen, L. W. (2012). Does religious belief promote prosociality? A critical examination. *Psychological Bulletin, 138*, 876–906.

Gervais, W. M., & Norenzayan, A. (2012). Like a camera in the sky? Thinking about God increases public self-awareness and socially desirable responding. *Journal of Experimental Social Psychology, 48*, 298–302.

Gilligan, C. (1982). *In a different voice: Psychological theory and women's development.* Cambridge, MA: Harvard University Press.

Gillum, F. R., & Masters, K. S. (2010). Religiousness and blood donation: Findings from a national survey. *Journal of Health Psychology, 15*, 163–172.

Ginges, J., Hansen, I., & Norenzayan, A. (2009). Religion and support for suicide attacks. *Psychological Science, 20*, 224–230.

Gintis, H., Smith, E. A., & Bowles, S. (2001). Costly signaling and cooperation. *Journal of Theoretical Biology, 213*, 103–119.

Goldfried, J., & Miner, M. (2002). Quest religion and the problem of limited compassion. *Journal for the Scientific Study of Religion, 41*, 685–695.

Graham, J., & Haidt, J. (2010). Beyond beliefs: Religions bind individuals into moral communities. *Personality and Social Psychology Review, 14*, 140–150.

Haidt, J., & Graham, J. (2007). When morality opposes justice: Conservatives have moral intuitions that liberals may not recognize. *Social Justice Research, 20*, 98–116.

Hansen, I. G., & Norenzayan, A. (2006). Between yang and yin and heaven and hell: Untangling the complex relationship between religion and intolerance. In P. McNamara (Ed.), *Where god and science meet: How brain and evolutionary studies alter our understanding of religion* (Vol. 3, pp. 187–211). Westport, CT: Greenwood Press/Praeger.

Hansen, D. E., Vandenberg, B., & Patterson, M. J. (1995). The effects of religious orientation on spontaneous and nonspontaneous helping behaviors. *Personality and Individual Differences, 19*, 101–104.

Hardy, S. A., & Carlo, G. (2005). Religiosity and prosocial behaviors in adolescence: The mediating role of prosocial values. *Journal of Moral Education, 34*, 231–249.

Henrich, J., & McElreath, R. (2006). Dual inheritance theory: The evolution of human cultural capacities and cultural evolution. In R. Dunbar & L. Barrett (Eds.), *Oxford handbook of evolutionary psychology* (pp. 555–570). Oxford: Oxford University Press.

Hood, R. W., Jr., Hill, P. C., & Spilka, B. (2009). *The psychology of religion: An empirical approach* (4th ed.). New York: Guilford.

Hunsberger, B., & Jackson, L. M. (2005). Religion, meaning, and prejudice. *Journal of Social Issues, 61*, 807–826.

Hunsberger, B., & Platonow, E. (1986). Religion and helping charitable causes. *Journal of Psychology, 120*, 517–528.

Irons, W. (1996). In our own self image: The evolution of morality, deception, and religion. *Skeptic, 4*, 50–61.

Irons, W. (2001). Religion as a hard-to-fake sign of commitment. In R. Nesse (Ed.), *Evolution and the capacity for commitment* (pp. 292–309). New York: Russell Sage Foundation.

Jackson, L. M., & Esses, V. M. (1997). Of scripture and ascription: The relation between religious fundamentalism and intergroup helping. *Personality and Social Psychology Bulletin, 23*, 893–906.

Johnson, D. D. P. (2005). God's punishment and public goods. *Human Nature, 16*, 410–446.

Johnson, D. D. P., & Bering, J. M. (2006). Hand of god, mind of man: Punishment and cognition in the evolution of cooperation. *Evolutionary Psychology, 4*, 219–233.

Johnson, M. K., Rowatt, W. C., & LaBouff, J. (2010). Priming Christian religious concepts increases racial prejudice. *Social Psychological and Personality Science, 1*, 119–126.

Koenig, H. G., Hays, J. C., George, L. K., Blazer, D. G., Larson, D. B., & Landerman, L. R. (1997). Modeling the cross-sectional relationships between religion, physical health, social support, and depressive symptoms. *American Journal of Geriatric Psychiatry, 5*, 131–144.

Lao Tzu (2006). *Tao Te Ching: A new English version* (S. Mitchell, Ed. and Trans.). New York: HarperCollins.

Laurin, K., Kay., A. C., & Fitzsimons, G. M. (2012). Divergent effects of activating thoughts of god on self-regulation. *Journal of Personality and Social Psychology, 102*, 4–21.

McCullough, M. E., & Willoughby, B. L. B. (2009). Religion, self-regulation, and self-control: Associations, explanations, and implications. *Psychological Bulletin, 135*, 69–93.

Malhotra, D. (2010). (When) are religious people nicer? Religious salience and the "Sunday effect" on pro-social behavior. *Judgment and Decision Making, 5*, 138–143.

Marris, J. S., Jagers, R. J., Hatcher, C. A., Lawhon, G. D, Murphy, E. J., & Murray, Y. F. (2000). Religiosity, volunteerism, and community involvement among African American men: An exploratory analysis. *Journal of Community Psychology, 28,* 391–406.

Norenzayan, A., & Shariff, A. F. (2008). The origin and evolution of religious prosociality. *Science, 322,* 58–62.

Piazza, J., Bering, J. M., & Ingram, G. (2011). "Princess Alice is watching you": Children's belief in an invisible person inhibits cheating. *Journal of Experimental Child Psychology, 109,* 311–320.

Pichon, I., Boccato, G., & Saroglou, V. (2007). Nonconscious influences of religion on prosociality: A priming study. *European Journal of Social Psychology, 37,* 1032–1045.

Pichon, I., & Saroglou, V. (2009). Religion and helping: Impact of target, thinking styles and just-world beliefs. *Archive for the Psychology of Religion, 31,* 215–236.

Premack, D., & Woodruff, G. (1978). Does the chimpanzee have a theory of mind? *Behavioral and Brain Sciences, 4,* 515–526.

Preston, J. L., Ritter, R. S., & Hernandez, J. (2010). Principles of religious prosociality: A review and reformulation. *Social and Personality Psychology Compass, 4,* 574–590.

Randolph-Seng, B., & Nielsen, M. E. (2007). Honesty: One effect of primed religious representations. *International Journal for the Psychology of Religion, 17,* 303–315.

Regnerus, M. D. (2007). *Forbidden fruit: Sex and religion in the lives of American teenagers.* New York: Oxford University Press.

Roes, F. L., & Raymond, M. (2003). Belief in moralizing gods. *Evolution and Human Behavior, 24,* 126–135.

Saroglou, V. (2006). Religion's role in prosocial behavior: Myth or reality? *Psychology of Religion Newsletter, 31,* 1–8.

Saroglou, V., Delpierre, V., & Dernelle, R. (2004). Values and religiosity: A meta-analysis of studies using Schwartz's model. *Personality and Individual Differences, 37,* 721–734.

Saroglou, V., & Galand, P. (2004). Identities, values, and religion: A study among Muslim, other immigrant, and native Belgian young adults after the 9/11 attacks. *Identity, 4,* 97–132.

Saroglou, V., Pichon, I., Trompette, L., Verschueren, M., & Dernelle, R. (2005). Prosocial behavior and religion: New evidence based on projective measures and peer ratings. *Journal for the Scientific Study of Religion, 44,* 323–348.

Shariff, A. F., & Norenzayan, A. (2007). God is watching you: Priming god concepts increases prosocial behavior in an anonymous economic game. *Psychological Science, 18,* 803–809.

Shariff, A. F., & Norenzayan, A. (2011). Mean Gods make good people: Different views of God predict cheating behavior. *International Journal for the Psychology of Religion, 21,* 85–96.

Shariff, A. F., Norenzayan, A., & Henrich, J. (2009). The birth of high gods: How the cultural evolution of supernatural policing agents influenced the emergence of complex, cooperative human societies, paving the way for civilization. In M. Schaller, A. Norenzayan, S. J. Heine, T. Yamagishi, &

T. Kameda (Eds.), *Evolution, culture, and the human mind* (pp. 119–136). New York: Psychology Press.

Shariff, A. F., & Rhemtulla, M. (2012). Divergent effects of beliefs in heaven and hell on national crime rates. *PLoS ONE, 7*(6): e39048.

Sosis, R., & Alcorta, C. (2003). Signaling, solidarity, and the sacred: The evolution of religious behavior. *Evolutionary Anthropology: Issues, News, and Reviews, 12,* 264–274.

Sosis, R., & Bressler, E. R. (2003). Cooperation and commune longevity: A test of the costly signaling theory of religion. *Cross-Cultural Research, 37,* 211–239.

Sosis, R., & Ruffle, B. J. (2003). Religious ritual and cooperation: Testing for a relationship on Israeli religious and secular kibbutzim. *Current Anthropology, 44,* 713–722.

St. John, C., & Fuchs, J. (2005). The heartland responds to terror: Volunteering after the bombing of the Murrah Federal Building. *Social Science Quarterly, 83,* 397–415.

Tan, J. H. W., & Vogel, C. (2008). Religion and trust: An experimental study. *Journal of Economic Psychology, 29,* 832–848.

Turiel, E. (1983). *The development of social knowledge: Morality and convention.* Cambridge: Cambridge University Press.

Watson. P. J., Hood, R. W., Jr., Morris, R. J., & Hall, J. R. (1984). Empathy, religious orientation, and social desirability. *Journal of Psychology, 117,* 211–216.

8 Religion, Prejudice, and Intergroup Relations

Wade C. Rowatt, Tom Carpenter, and Megan Haggard

This chapter reviews evidence for connections between religion, prejudice, and intergroup relations that comes from correlational studies and some experiments. The chapter is organized into three sections in which we 1) briefly review meta-analyses of correlational studies, 2) detail religious priming experiments from which causation can be inferred, and 3) discuss how several classic and contemporary psychological theories about intergroup attitudes and relations explain why religion and religiousness lead to some prejudices.

Broadly defined, we use the term *religion* to mean a set of beliefs, practices, and rituals that provides adherents with a sense of meaning, purpose, and value in life. We use the terms *religiousness* or *religiosity* in reference to a dimensional variable that represents the degree to which a person perceives the self to be a religious person and the degree to which s/he engages in religious behaviors (e.g., frequency of participation in religious services, prayer, and reading sacred texts). We define *prejudice* as a general negative evaluation of a person or group (Brown, 2010). *Intergroup relations* includes how members of a group think about or behave toward members of a different group (e.g., Christians–Muslims, Protestants–Catholics), but also how personal degree of religiosity, religious affiliation, or religious identity influences attitudes toward historically disadvantaged social groups or groups perceived to violate religious worldviews or norms (e.g., atheists, homosexuals). Social attitudes borne out of religious convictions could guide decisions about who to help, favor, shun, or avoid.

As we scoured the extant literature about prejudice and intergroup relations, we noticed that factors that capture the role of religion or religiousness were often absent. For example, the only mention of religion in Nelson's state-of-the science edited *Handbook of prejudice, stereotyping, and discrimination* was with regard to sexual prejudice (Herek, 2009; Stangor, 2009). In some situations or cases, religion or religious identity may not be relevant or salient enough to exert influence on thoughts, evaluative reactions, decisions, or behaviors (Chaves, 2010). However, when "religion" is activated cognitively (see Johnson, Rowatt,

& LaBouff, 2010), infused into existing intergroup disputes (Neuberg et al., 2012), or fused with other aspects of identity (see Swann, Gomez, Huici, Morales, & Hixon, 2010; Swann, Gomez, Seyle, Morales, & Guici, 2009), religion does account for unique variability in evaluative reactions, social judgments, and actions.

In an innovative study of over 190 pairs of groups at 97 sites around the world, Neuberg et al. (2012) found that increased conflict between groups was predicted independently and interactively by the degree to which religion was infused into a group's everyday life (i.e., religious infusion), resource–power differential, and value incompatibility. For example, only when religious infusion was high did value incompatibility predict intergroup prejudice. Evidence from many other correlational studies and well-controlled experiments supports the general conclusion that religiosity, religion, and prejudice are connected.

Religiosity and Prejudice: Clues from Meta-Analyses

Religion is a central component of the self for many people. Allport (1966) realized both prejudice and religion increase security and comfort in a social and natural world rife with imagined or real threats and dangers. In doing so, he theorized, religion or religiosity could create conditions in which prejudices develop and thrive. Two meta-analyses document correlations between religious dimensions and expressed racial and sexual prejudices (Hall, Matz, & Wood, 2010; Whitley, 2009). Hall et al. (2010) reported average weighted effect sizes between black–white racial prejudice and religious dimensions in American samples (n) as follows: extrinsic religiosity ($r = .17$, $k = 22$), religious fundamentalism ($r = .13$, $k = 14$), religious identification ($r = .12$, $k = 20$), religious orthodoxy ($r = -.04$, $k = 22$), intrinsic religiosity ($r = -.07$, $k = 21$), and quest religious orientation ($r = -.07$, $k = 10$). Across 17 independent samples comprising more than 5200 participants, Whitley (2009) found a mean effect size for the relation between religious fundamentalism and sexual prejudice that corresponded to a correlation of .45. Implicit religiousness/spirituality also predicts sexual prejudice above and beyond religious fundamentalism and right-wing authoritarianism (LaBouff, Rowatt, Johnson, Thedford, & Tsang, 2010). We review connections between religious fundamentalism and prejudices in more detail in another chapter (Rowatt, Shen, LaBouff, & Gonzalez, 2013).

Two recent correlational studies (Shen, Yelderman, Haggard, & Rowatt, 2013) investigated how different components of religiousness (i.e., belief in higher power; rigidity/flexibility of religious beliefs) covaried with self-reported attitudes toward racial and value-violating group members. Flexibility of religious beliefs correlated positively with racial tolerance, whereas degree of belief in a higher power correlated positively with prejudice toward atheists and gay men (Shen et al., 2013).

As will be presented later, controlled priming experiments also point to divergent associations between components of religion, social attitudes, and interpersonal behavior.

Religious Prosociality and Prejudice: Evidence from Priming Experiments

A handful of well-controlled experiments are beginning to tease apart potential causal effects of religion on prosociality and prejudices. Priming is a method of activating a concept in the mind (Bargh & Chartrand, 2000). Several research teams have applied supraliminal and subliminal priming methods to examine the effect of religious salience on social evaluations and behaviors (for summary tables, see Galen, 2012, and Preston, Ritter, & Hernandez, 2010).

In a typical experiment, the concept of God or religion is primed in some participants and not in others. Priming the concept of *God* appears to increase prosociality (Shariff & Norenzayan, 2007), especially among individuals with the 2- or 7-repeat alleles of the dopamine D4 receptor (DRD4) gene (Sasaki et al., 2013). Priming the concept of *religion*, by the same token, appears to increase the expression of racial and sexual prejudice among Christians (Johnson et al., 2010; Johnson, Rowatt, & Labouff, 2012; Ramsay, Pang, Shen, & Rowatt, 2013). Priming Buddhism also increased sexual prejudice among Buddhists in Singapore (Ramsay et al., 2013).

Reading a religious or sacred text may also prime components of religion. Blogowska and Saroglou (2012) found religious fundamentalists were less prosocial toward outgroup members after reading aggressive religious texts. This fits with earlier research indicating reading a passage in which God sanctioned violence increased aggression, particularly among religious believers (Bushman, Ridge, Das, Key, & Busath, 2007).

It is not completely clear why priming concepts of God and religion produce different patterns for ingroup prosociality and outgroup derogation, prejudice, and aggression. Research of this kind is in its infancy and multiple possible mechanisms for prime to behavior effects have been proposed (Wheeler & DeMarree, 2009). Preston, Ritter, and Hernandez (2010) posit priming the concept of God "activates moral concerns of virtue as a means of obedience to the supernatural agent as moral authority" (p. 584). If one thinks "God is watching," it is better to be charitable (Pichon, Boccato, & Saroglou, 2007; Shariff & Norenzayan, 2007) than cheat (Randolph-Seng & Nielsen, 2007). Preston et al. (2010) suggest priming religion, by way of contrast, "activates moral concerns for in-group protection" (p. 583). Priming religion increases submission to authority to take revenge, especially among submissive persons (Saroglou, Corneille, & Van Cappellen, 2009). Being close to or inside a religious building may be enough to activate this mechanism.

People in Western Europe near a religious building, for example, reported more ethnocentrism than people near a government building (LaBouff, Rowatt, Johnson, & Finkle, 2012). People expressed more conservative positions on issues in a religious building than a non-religious building (Rutchick, 2010).

Studies in which religion is primed in the lab or field are important, in part, because they provide a degree of experimental control not possible with correlational methods. However, priming religion with a photo, building, typed passage, scrambled sentence test, or lexical decision task is not as powerful or salient as religious group status or affiliation in some inter-religious conflicts around the world. In addition, it is not entirely clear from these studies why religion may relate to prejudice. In an attempt to better understand the nature of these relationships, we next turn to several social–personality theories of intergroup relations.

An Intergroup Perspective on Religion and Prejudice

In this section, we focus on religion, prejudice, and intergroup relations through the lens of several classic and contemporary social–personality theories, such as realistic group conflict, social identity, intergroup threat, and system justification. We also consider religion–prejudice connections from a broader evolutionary perspective. Our reviews are necessarily condensed and intended to bring basic social–personality psychology theory to the psychology of religion and prejudice. An overarching theme is that connections between religion, prejudice, and intergroup bias are due, in part, to basic social, cognitive, and affective mechanisms that aid humans in making sense of the world, solving basic adaptive problems, detecting and coping with real and symbolic threats, relating with diverse people and groups, and managing uncertainty or anxiety. For example, like almost any intergroup attitude, religious intergroup prejudices are fostered by realistic group conflict (i.e., competition for limited resources or value promotion), social identity processes that produce intergroup biases (Jackson & Hunsberger, 1999; Tajfel & Turner, 1986), and other basic processes that involve rapid social categorization, stereotyping, strengthened group identification, or system justification. We do not claim these basic social-cognitive-affective processes are unique to religious persons or groups. Groups formed for other purposes (e.g., athletic competition, political action, economic growth) often compete for limited resources (e.g., wins, votes, money) that produce heated rivalries (e.g., games, debates, elections, diplomatic negotiations, and trade or military wars) and other forms of healthy and unhealthy conflict. However, a consideration of basic biological, psychological, and social processes that involve rapid social categorization, emotional reactions, realistic group conflict, social identity, intergroup threat, system justification, and more can help illuminate religion–prejudice connections.

Social Categorization

To make sense of the social world, people categorize others according to essential qualities such as gender, race, and age. Categorical processing is fast, automatic, and may occur outside of awareness. For example, individuals react differently to ingroup and outgroup faces after approximately 250*ms* and may form evaluative judgments as early as 520*ms* (Dickter & Bartholow, 2007; Ito, Thompson, & Cacioppo, 2004). Although this rapid social categorization may have evolved to allow individuals to rapidly identify friends from foes (Neuberg & Cottrell, 2006), one consequence of social categorization appears to be stereotyping and prejudice (Allport, 1954; Tajfel, 1969).

Categorical processing of social information is efficient but engenders cognitive biases. Category labels bias perceptions, leading to exaggerated perceptions of similarity within groups and differences between groups (Tajfel & Wilkes, 1963). Category labels can also misguide perceptions of group members. For example, group members are inaccurately seen as possessing traits consistent with roles and functions of their social groups, even when presented with evidence to the contrary (Hoffman & Hurst, 1990). Ingroup and outgroup stimuli are also processed differently, with outgroup stimuli given less attentional resources (e.g., Dickter & Bartholow, 2007; Ito et al., 2004), recollected with decreased accuracy (e.g., Bernstein, Young, & Hugenberg, 2007), and seen as more homogenous (e.g., Mullen & Hu, 1989).

Presumably the process of categorization should be the same for religious and non-religious individuals. However, religion might interact with categorization in a number of ways. As with any social institution, religion provides a number of ingroup/outgroup distinctions. To date, little research has explored the possibility that individuals categorize their social world according to religious distinctions, such as creed, denominational affiliation, or perceived salvation status. Such differences are certainly not as visible as phenotypes such as gender and race (unless one wears religious clothing or jewelry such as a Star of David, cross, or pentagram). However, once known, they may provide meaningful categories that guide social perceptions, especially for individuals for whom these social distinctions are important.

Religion may also provide information that influences the attributes by which people are parsed into categories. Social categories are actively constructed; they are not objective maps of the social world. For instance, Wittenbrink, Hilton, and Gist (1998) asked participants to sort images of target individuals into groups. By subtly manipulating the background information available about the targets, they successfully influenced by which attributes individuals were grouped. Similarly, religion provides individuals with values and a worldview complete with explanatory models for social phenomena. Consequently, it could direct individuals to search for and prioritize specific attributes when forming social categories (e.g., sinner, saved, holy, worldly, humility, temperance). Given that individuals rely on social categories to infer traits about individuals (e.g., Hoffman & Hurst, 1990), the existence of categories such as "sinner" or "saved" could also have serious consequences for how individuals are perceived and evaluated.

Religion might also influence prejudice by changing the meaning ascribed to social categories. As argued by several theorists (Fox, 1992; Neuberg, 1992; Neuberg & Cottrell, 2006), social categorization and evaluation are adaptive and may exist so that friend can quickly be distinguished from foe, predator from prey. Religion, by way of contrast, may provide a meaning system by which some social categories could be seen as more or less threatening. Consequently, the way religion interplays with how individuals organize the world could have a strong influence on the religion–prejudice link.

Social Identity

Relatedness and belonging are fundamental human needs (Baumeister & Leary, 1995; Deci & Ryan, 2012). Inclusion in a religious group can satisfy belongingness needs. Unlike most other social identities, however, religious identity offers membership characterized by controllability, meaning, belonging, and well-being, making it more potent than less comprehensive worldviews (Ysseldyk, Matheson, & Anisman, 2010).

According to social identity theory (Brown, 2000; Tajfel & Turner, 1986), individuals work to maintain a positive social identity for their group via comparisons with other groups. As religious individuals are not immune to such forces, religious ingroup/outgroup biases are likely. Simple religious group identification could lead to ingroup favoritism and outgroup derogation (Hunsberger & Jackson, 2005; Johnson et al., 2012; Verkuyten, 2007; Verkuyten & Yildiz, 2007). This is especially true when religious identity is threatened by an outgroup, which can lead to retaliation in the forms of dehumanization, moral superiority, and even acts of terrorism (Schwartz, Dunkel, & Waterman, 2009).

If a certain group receives preferential treatment over time, it not only increases group identity salience, but can foster feelings of relative deprivation in minority groups. This can lead to negative comparisons between groups, especially for those who feel highly deprived. This is no exception for religious groups, as evidenced by Tripathi and Srivastava's (1981) findings that Muslims who felt highly deprived in India had more negative attitudes toward Hindus than Muslims who did not feel as deprived.

To complicate matters somewhat, multiple aspects of social identity—such as national, ethnic, and religious affiliation—are embedded within the self and group. Membership in more than one ingroup or outgroup, and one's role in the group, has predictable advantages and disadvantages, respectively. Double ingroups, for example, are evaluated most favorably and double outgroups are evaluated least favorably (Hewstone, Islam, & Judd, 1993). Strength of affiliation with a national, ethnic, or religious group affects intergroup attitudes (Verkuyten, 2007; Verkuyten & Yildiz, 2007). For example, Muslims who identified more strongly with their faith had lower national identification (Dutch) and higher intergroup bias than Muslims who identified less strongly with their religious social identity (Verkuyten & Martinovic, 2012). We speculate that prejudicial attitudes and intergroup conflicts are more likely when members of national/religious outgroups move to and occupy places populated by privileged and established double ingroups. When religious groups claim the same land as "holy land" or conceive of the religious or national group as a trans-generational entity, the stage is set for complex and enduring conflicts (Klar, Kahn, & Roccas, 2012).

Realistic Group Conflict and Intergroup Threat

Hunsberger and Jackson (2005) posited religious intergroup prejudice can be fostered not only by social identity processes or intergroup biases, but also realistic group conflict, such as competition for limited resources or value promotion. If group interests are compatible or complementary, cooperation between groups is likely. Increased contact that produces cross-group friendship would likely lead to more positive intergroup attitudes (Davies, Tropp, Aron, Pettigrew, & Wright, 2011). If group interests are incompatible, however, some intergroup conflict is likely. According to realistic group conflict theory (Duckitt, 1994; Sherif, 1966), competition between groups for limited resources generates feelings of threat and disliking between groups. For example, activating cognitions related to economic scarcity increased prejudice against ethnic minorities who were perceived as competing with white individuals for jobs (Butz & Yogeeswaran, 2011). Similarly, facets of the Israeli–Palestinian conflict center on land and water rights, and perceived conflicts of interest between denominations of Judaism have been shown to predict prejudice by some Jewish groups against ultraorthodox Jews in Israel (Struch & Schwartz, 1989, as cited in Hunsberger & Jackson, 2005).

Some religious groups may be in conflict for the attitudes, beliefs, and allegiance of third parties. This might be especially important among evangelical groups or groups that place a heavy emphasis on religious conversion. To our knowledge, no research has yet examined whether competition for church attendance, religious conversion, or evangelism amplifies religious intergroup tensions, yet such a possibility seems likely. Still another source of realistic intergroup conflict may be over epistemological claims of truth. For example, religious groups or churches sometimes feud and split over interpretation of sacred religious teachings. Similarly, the antipathy surrounding the social conflict in the United States over the acceptance and teaching of evolution (e.g., Miller, Scott, & Okamoto, 2006; Shortell, 2011) may partly reflect realistic conflict over claims of privileged access to the truth. Such realistic conflicts and the perceived threats they create provide important insights into intergroup prejudices associated with religion.

Intergroup Threat and Social Dominance

Intergroup threat occurs when members of one group perceive that another group may cause them physical or symbolic harm (Stephan, Ybarra, & Morrison, 2009). Realistic group threats involve potential loss of power, resources, or physical well-being. "Symbolic group threats are threats to a group's religion, values, belief system, ideology, philosophy, morality, or worldview" (Stephan et al., 2009, p. 45). As a facet of culture, religion–prejudice links could be due to intergroup threats, whether real or imagined. A gay man may pose a symbolic threat to a religious person who believes homosexuality is immoral or less psychologically essentialist but not to a person who believes sexual orientation is genetically determined (Dar-Nimrod & Heine, 2011). An Israeli Jew may pose a realistic threat to a Palestinian Muslim if the Jewish man's house occupies the site of the Muslim's ancestral home.

One possible source of symbolic threat is value violation. A handful of studies have documented that religiosity is associated with discrimination toward value-violating groups (e.g., Batson, Floyd, Meyer, & Winner, 1999; Duck & Hunsberger, 1999; Goldfried & Miner, 2002). Although religiosity is associated with a sense of proscription against prejudice toward some outgroups (e.g., African Americans), it is also associated with a sense of *prescription for* prejudice toward value-violating outgroups (e.g., homosexuals; Duck & Hunsberger, 1999). Some discrimination by religious individuals against value violators may represent attempts to prevent immoral behaviors from occurring and not always prejudice against value violators per se (Batson, Denton, & Vollmecke, 2008; Mak & Tsang, 2008).

Religion, like culture, also provides followers with a mindset through which they can interpret the actions of other groups. Research has shown that particular characteristics of religions may influence how often and in what way threats are perceived. For instance, religious groups with secure and dominant positions within society express more prejudice when faced with symbolic threats compared to realistic threats. This effect is reversed for more marginalized religious groups, who feel they are still fighting for resources and status (Tausch, Hewstone, & Roy, 2009). Other traits and experiences that can increase threat perception in groups include high-context communication, collectivism, high-group identification, prior negative relations with the outgroup, negative stereotypes, and uncertainty avoidance (Riek, Mania, & Gaertner, 2006; Stephan et al., 2009).

Given that some religious conflicts continue for generations, it is important to note that the nature of intergroup threat may change over time. Although hostility between Jews and Muslims in Israel may have originated in part as a realistic conflict (e.g., land), through the years it has also become symbolic. Contrariwise, differences between secular and religious Jews, which developed through disputes over symbolic interpretation, have transitioned into realistic threats as well (Shimoni & Schwarzwald, 2003).

Religious groups may also attract or foster different types of individual depending on whether they are monitoring for realistic or symbolic threats. Social dominance orientation, for example, is a belief that some groups are superior to others and should dominate (Pratto, Sidanius, & Levin, 2006; Pratto, Sidanius, Stallworth, & Malle, 1994), whereas right-wing authoritarianism indicates desire for social order (Altemeyer, 1981). Individuals with higher social dominance orientation are more prone to perceiving realistic threats, whereas those high in right-wing authoritarianism are more attuned to symbolic threats (Duckitt & Sibley, 2010). With regards to religious threats, Crowson (2009) examined social dominance, right-wing authoritarianism, and reactions to terrorism-related realistic threats (items such as "Terrorist networks are a threat to America's global standing") and symbolic threats ("Islamic radicalism is a challenge to traditional American values"). Results indicated that social dominance and right-wing authoritarianism only had an impact on symbolic terrorist threats.

Although social dominance orientation has historically been examined as a personality variable and is a strong predictor of prejudice (Pratto et al., 2006), it is also situationally malleable, tends to increase after reminders of the superiority of one's group (Guimond & Dambrun, 2002; Levin, 1996, as cited in Pratto et al., 2006) and is elevated among individuals who perceive greater status gaps between their groups and other groups (Levin, 2004). Notably, Levin (1996, as cited in Pratto et al., 2006) found that social dominance orientation increased after priming individuals with lower status groups.

Superiority and Relative Gratification

In contrast to threat-based theoretical perspectives, some perspectives emphasize the role of superiority, power, and status as an additional route to prejudice. According to Duckitt's (2001) dual-process model, prejudice can form as a result of either feelings of threat or a sense of superiority. At times the superiority effect can be even stronger than the threat effect. For example, Wann and Grieve (2005) found that sports fans whose teams win make more biased evaluations of others than fans of losing teams—despite the fact that fans of losing teams experience more threat. To the extent that religious individuals perceive their religious "teams" as winning spiritually, morally, epistemologically, socially, or theologically, they may make more biased and self-serving evaluations of other groups.

A similar pattern has been observed in recent research on relative gratification (Dambrun, Taylor, McDonald, Crush, & Méot, 2006; Guimond & Dambrun, 2002). Historically, theorists have focused on how the experience of disadvantage and injustice can foster prejudice (relative deprivation; see Smith & Ortiz, 2002), yet recent research has shown that prejudice is also formed following experiences of advantage. For example, experimentally reminding individuals of their economic advantage over others increases prejudice and support for discriminatory policies against minorities (Guimond & Dambrun, 2002). Similar findings have been observed in real-world contexts and appear to occur partly as a result of increased group identification (Dambrun et al., 2006), although the precise mechanisms underlying relative gratification remain unclear. To date, relative gratification has been examined primarily with respect to economic and social advantage, yet it seems plausible that it may occur in religious contexts as well. For example, beliefs that one's group has been specially chosen or favored by a higher power or deity or that one's group will live eternally might create a sense of relative gratification and foster outgroup derogation. Demoulin, Saroglou, and Van Pachterbeke (2008) suggested the supra-humanization of deities might, by comparison, help outgroups seem especially subhuman, exacerbating pre-existing tendencies to infra-humanize outgroups.

System Justification

A number of theories emphasize how prejudices are justified within a social or political system. According to system justification theory (Jost, Banaji, & Nosek, 2004; Jost & Hunyady, 2005), people are motivated to justify and rationalize, and therefore legitimize and maintain, the status quo. This is done by endorsing system-justifying ideologies, such as political conservatism, belief in a just world, the Protestant work ethic, social dominance orientation, and right-wing authoritarianism. For established groups in power, endorsement of system-justifying ideologies serves to justify their established position; for disadvantaged groups, endorsement leads to increased ingroup ambivalence and decreased support for the ingroup (e.g., Henry, Sidanius, Levin, & Pratto, 2005; Jost & Burgess, 2000; Jost et al., 2004; Kemmelmeier, 2005).

System justification legitimizes the status quo and removes impetus to reduce group-based disparities or inequities. For example, the belief that the world is just allows individuals to blame disparaged groups for their plights by maintaining that people get what they deserve and deserve what they get (e.g., Jost & Burgess, 2000). Similarly, endorsing the Protestant work ethic, which values hard work and equity over equality, allows individuals to disparage groups they see as less hard working (Christopher & Mull, 2006).

Although specific religious ideologies have not been implicated as system justifying per se, religiosity is associated with several system-justifying ideologies, such as political conservatism (Jones, Furnham, & Deile, 2010), right-wing authoritarianism (Mavor, Macleod, Boal, & Louis, 2009; Rowatt & Franklin, 2004), Protestant work ethic (Jones et al., 2010), just-world beliefs (Pichon & Saroglou, 2009), and need for closure (Brandt & Reyna, 2010). Also, as noted earlier, shared variance with system-justifying ideologies (e.g., right-wing authoritarianism) may help explain the link between religiosity and some forms of prejudice (e.g., Rowatt & Franklin, 2004). To date, however, little research has focused on how specific aspects of religious content can be system justifying. Historically, religion has been used as a source of both justification for and opposition toward prejudice and discriminatory social institutions (e.g., slavery). However, many world religions openly emphasize social justice and discourage prejudice. It appears that individuals have been able to draw on religious teachings to support both positions, making religion both system justifying and system challenging. For further insights into those forces and individual differences that influence the expression, suppression, and justification of prejudices, we next turn to the justification-suppression model of prejudice (Crandall & Eshleman, 2003).

Justification-Suppression Model of Prejudice

Prejudicial thoughts and feelings are not always overtly expressed. According to the justification-suppression model of prejudice (Crandall & Eshleman, 2003), initial affective reactions go through stages of modification before they are enacted in behavior and social responding. Suppression of automatic negative evaluations could lead to social displays of non-prejudice that mask underlying attitudes and reactions toward members of other groups. One central tenet of the justification-suppression model is that most individuals have varying degrees of automatic prejudicial responses that are either suppressed or justified.

Suppression is defined as any attempt to reduce the expression or awareness of prejudice, is an active process requiring cognitive effort, and may reflect desires to appear non-prejudiced to the self or others (Crandall & Eshleman, 2003; Plant & Devine, 1998). It is also motivated by factors such as norms, empathy, value systems, personal standards, and beliefs, all of which may be subject to religious influence. Such factors may account for the null or even negative relationship between intrinsic religiousness and prejudice (Hall et al., 2010). Although intrinsic religiosity is associated with less overt prejudice (Hall et al., 2010), research using covert behavioral measures—particularly behaviors that participants can attribute to non-prejudiced motivations—has found null associations between intrinsic religiosity and racial prejudice (Batson, Flink, Schoenrade, Fultz, & Pych, 1986; Batson, Naifeh, & Pate, 1978). This is consistent with Crandall and Eshleman's (2003) claims that values, beliefs, and social concerns do not change underlying affective reactions but may serve to regulate prejudiced responding when activated. However, it is still not entirely clear when religion may be used to explicitly justify prejudices and when religion may be used to suppress them.

Uncertainty-Identity Theory

How people deal with uncertainty, threat, and anxiety offers some clues about religion–prejudice connections. Uncertainty can be so uncomfortable and motivating that people affiliate or identify with a group (such as a religious group) to reduce self-uncertainty. Uncertainty-identity theory can explain why some people turn to religion but also intergroup prejudices, violence, or acts of extremism (Hogg, Adelman, & Blagg, 2010). Making uncertainty salient evokes increased anger and negative affect among religious persons when the religious worldview is threatened (Van den Bos, Van Ameijde, & Van Gorp, 2006). Hogg et al. (2010) review several experiments that show uncertainty increases intergroup conflict and religious extremism. An uncertainty-reducing motive for religion may therefore make individuals particularly prone to prejudices and intergroup biases.

Terror Management Theory

Similar to uncertainty-identity theory, terror management theorists posit people manage uncertainty or anxiety about death by immersion in a cultural worldview that provides a sense of meaning, purpose, and standards for behavior (Greenberg, Solomon, & Pyszczynski, 1997). Thoughts of death have a distinct influence beyond the effects of similar emotional states such as doubt, loneliness, loss, sadness, and pain (Vail et al., 2010). For some, religion operates as an existential buffer that imbues life with meaning and purpose that may thwart existential concerns. Most religions provide straightforward solutions to fears or uncertainties concerning death (e.g., the existence of an afterlife, ultimate meaning in chaos, and continuation of life in a different form). Across experiments, religiousness interacts with mortality salience to influence attitudes and behaviors. Jonas and Fischer (2006) showed that when mortality was salient, intrinsically religious persons experienced less death thought accessibility when their religious beliefs were affirmed than did less intrinsically religious persons. Religion does not simply buffer death anxiety, but can be bolstered by it, as individuals who endorse a belief in the afterlife report increased certainty in its existence after thinking about their own death (Osarchuk & Tatz, 1973).

Religion not only protects the individual from death anxiety but can serve as a reminder of the espoused beliefs of the worldview. This can lead to prosocial outcomes, such as increased benevolence, mainly directed toward ingroup members. For instance, among American college students with high religious fundamentalism scores who were primed with Biblical compassion (e.g., love your neighbor as yourself), those in a mortality salience condition expressed less support for extreme military action against an outgroup than those low in religious fundamentalism (Rothschild, Abdollahi, & Pyszczynski, 2009). Similarly, Schumann, Nash, McGregor, and Ross (2013) also found a simple religious prime (asking the participant "which religious belief system do you most identify with?") increased compassionate responses among participants in mortality salience conditions but not among participants not primed with a question about their religious identification.

However, the existence of several conflicting cultural worldviews, particularly those infused with religious beliefs, creates the uncertainty that one's worldview could be incorrect or faulty, therefore corrupting its meaning and purpose for reducing death anxiety. In order to eliminate this uncertainty, people may look for support from fellow believers or engage in antisocial behaviors toward those who endorse conflicting worldviews (Vail et al., 2010). This is measured by threatening or compromising an individual's religious worldview and either measuring responses to a mortality salience induction or assessing the accessibility of death thoughts. For example, if death-related thoughts associated with a terrorist threat are assuaged by beliefs in an afterlife, the spike in prejudice toward outgroups (e.g., Muslims and immigrants) is diminished following a threat (Kastenmuller, Greitemeyer, Ai, Winter, & Fischer, 2011). Similarly, after receiving a religion-related worldview threat, participants who received additional information that worldview-violating group members had perished in a plane crash experienced no increase in death thought accessibility compared to those who just received the religious threat (Hayes, Schimel, & Williams, 2008). In sum, these studies suggest that the existential anxiety reduction afforded by religiosity can foster prejudice as well as prosocial outcomes.

Evolutionary Perspectives

The variety and breadth of theories about prejudice and intergroup processes is impressive. An evolutionary theoretical perspective on the religion of the individual and religious groups within cultures provides additional clues about observed connections between religion and prejudice. Religion is not considered to have evolved as an independent mechanism, but rather as a byproduct of other adaptive psychological devices that led to the development, support, and maintenance of alliances with others who share similar beliefs (Kirkpatrick, 2005; Looy, 2005; Wilson, 1978). These coalitions are theorized to have led to reproductive success at the personal, familial, and group levels. The addition of perceived supernatural observation and, if necessary, punishment served to strengthen these bonds and utilize brain areas associated with behavior monitoring (Bering & Shackelford, 2004). Johnson and Kruger (2004) posited that religion contributed to the selection of cooperation throughout evolutionary history through: the establishment of laws, mores, and taboos specific to the ingroup; a threat of punishment that, regardless of enforcement, serves to increase adherence to group rules; and actual punishment (whether worldly or other-worldly) for those who do not follow the rules.

In order to transmit these cultural ideas from generation to generation, religious rituals were created as a tool to reaffirm cooperation within the group, to increase capacity for cultural learning and knowledge, and to spread beliefs to others. Groups with more intense and costly rituals foster more cohesion, more cultural learning, and, ultimately, more group members. Henrich (2009) details how the competition inherent in the creation of different religions has served to select religious groups with the most cohesion and capacity for cultural knowledge through cultural group selection.

Religion often strengthens group bonds and increases cohesion, which lead to prosociality toward the ingroup (see Preston, Salomon, & Ritter, Chapter 7, this volume), but also fosters hostility toward outgroup members who pose real or symbolic threats. Intergroup conflicts could arise when individuals in groups hold inconsistent beliefs and contend that only one can be correct. Heated dialogues and even violence could erupt as each side engages in worldview defense and value promotion. In these cases, religion operates as a component of social identity, which guides intergroup relations. Kirkpatrick (2005, p. 259) theorized that "our evolved psychology appears to contain a suite of mechanisms for distinguishing the good guys from the bad guys, or the in-group from the outgroup, and then giving preferential treatment to the good guys." Sosis and Ruffle (2003), for example, found group members who were more religious (as determined by attendance at religious services) were more willing to contribute their money to a community pot instead of keeping it compared to group members who were less religious. After interacting with another religious group member, religious people donated more money to the community pot than if they had interacted with a racial ingroup member.

Competition encouraged by the development of different religions due to varying selection pressures dictates that religion, in order to be carried into the next generation, must either eliminate other religious world-views or assimilate their members into the ingroup (Henrich, 2009). Ritter and Preston (2011) found participants who copied a rejected religious passage rated a drink to be more disgusting than those who copied an accepted religious passage. Some outgroup members may be rejected as impure or ostracized for fear of contagion, shown physically by the adoption of food rituals and rules by several world religions (Johnson, White, Boyd, & Cohen, 2011) or something far more deadly. Ginges, Hansen, and Norenzayan (2009) discovered individuals primed with religious service attendance were more supportive of a suicide bombing aimed at an opposing religious group than persons who were primed with prayer.

Although people feud in the name of religions, and religion has a coalitional nature, people from different religions and religious groups often interact peacefully and cooperatively. Forming and maintaining friendships or alliances with members of a religious outgroup should lead to more positive intergroup attitudes. A recent meta-analysis revealed positive attitudes increase (and prejudice declines) as people of different races, nationalities, sexual orientations, or religions form friendships with members of a different target group (Davies et al., 2011). With regard to religious affiliation for example, a positive association was observed between cross-group friendship and intergroup attitudes ($r = .30$). When components of right-wing authoritarianism are controlled, religiosity correlates positively with liking of members of racial and ethnic outgroups (Shen, Haggard, Strassburger, & Rowatt, under review).

As such, religion or religiosity in-and-of-itself is not the root of all prejudice or intergroup bias per se, but in some cases may create situations or activate social-cognitive mechanisms through which negative emotional evaluations could develop and flourish. Recall that when religion is infused into conflicts about incompatible values, intergroup prejudice ensues and amplifies (Neuberg et al., 2012). Increasing benevolent contact between members of religious groups (i.e., cross-group friendship), contrariwise, could reduce perceived threat and increase positive intergroup attitudes.

Conclusions and Future Directions

Understanding connections between religion, prejudice and intergroup relations requires conceptualizing religion both at broad historical, sociological, and cultural levels, and also at a psychological level within the self (i.e., religiosity). Evolutionary psychological perspectives provide much needed integration across disciplines and mid-level social–personality theories. Broadly, religions and denominations provide traditions, social systems, and networks that provide aid when faced with uncertainty or threat. Bringing people together in tight-knit social groups can provide security and protection. A potential byproduct is that religion, like other groups, can foster ingroup favoritism, outgroup derogation, and non-proscribed prejudices that could lead to discriminatory behavior or institutional systems that favor a majority group and disadvantage a minority group.

There are many instances, within the same religions, of religiosity/ religion increasing charity, peacemaking, and efforts to increase social justice. However, as meta-analytic studies reveal, religiosity correlates positively with prejudice. Priming experiments indicate something about religion when primed causes prejudices. Future experiments are needed to tease apart different aspects of religion being primed (e.g., religious agent, religious institution, spirituality; Preston, Ritter, & Hernandez, 2010), to test the duration of priming effects, and to investigate multiple possible prime-to-behavior mechanisms (Wheeler & DeMarree, 2009). Future researchers would be wise to supplement traditional survey and experimental methods with repeated measures of daily religious and spiritual practice (Kashdan & Nezlek, 2012). Longitudinal studies are also needed to investigate how changes, spurts, or lags in personal religiousness/spirituality affect stability or change in social evaluations (cf. Kashdan & Nezlek, 2012). Changes on a coalitional level (e.g., changing religions), on a devotional level (e.g., becoming religiously scrupulous), and when coping with physical or worldview threats will likely affect how people perceive and relate with others.

In closing, connections between religion and prejudice can be seen at individual, societal, and cultural levels. When activated, religion can be a powerful and motivating force for both antipathy toward and love of neighbor. Given most studies point to a religion–prejudice connection, a challenge for religiously motivated individuals is to recognize unjustified negative thoughts and feelings toward others and respond with charity. A charitable response is more likely to be consistent with core religious teachings than the alternative.

References

Allport, G. W. (1954). *The nature of prejudice*. Cambridge, MA: Addison-Wesley.
Allport, G. W. (1966). The religious context of prejudice. *Journal for the Scientific Study of Religion, 5*, 447–457.
Altemeyer, B. (1981). *Right-wing authoritarianism*. Winnipeg, Canada: University of Manitoba Press.
Bargh, J. A., & Chartrand, T. L. (2000). The mind in the middle: A practical guide to priming and automaticity research. In H. T. Reis & C. M. Judd (Eds.), *Handbook of research methods in social and personality psychology* (pp. 253–285). New York: Cambridge University Press.

Batson, C. D., Denton, D. M., & Vollmecke, J. T. (2008). Quest religion, anti-fundamentalism, and limited versus universal compassion. *Journal for the Scientific Study of Religion, 47*, 135–145.

Batson, C. D., Flink, C. H., Schoenrade, P. A., Fultz, J., & Pych, V. (1986). Religious orientation and overt versus covert racial prejudice. *Journal of Personality and Social Psychology, 50*, 175–181.

Batson, C. D., Floyd, R. B., Meyer, J. M., & Winner, A. L. (1999). "And who is my neighbor?": Intrinsic religion as a source of universal compassion. *Journal for the Scientific Study of Religion, 38*, 445–457.

Batson, C. D., Naifeh, S. J., & Pate, S. (1978). Social desirability, religious orientation, and racial prejudice. *Journal for the Scientific Study of Religion, 17*, 31–41.

Baumeister, R. F., & Leary, M. R. (1995). The need to belong: Desire for interpersonal attachments as a fundamental human motivation. *Psychological Bulletin, 117*, 497–529.

Bering, J. M., & Shackelford, T. K. (2004). The causal role of consciousness: A conceptual addendum to human evolutionary psychology. *Review of General Psychology, 8*, 227–248.

Bernstein, M. J., Young, S. G., & Hugenberg, K. (2007). The cross-category effect: Mere social categorization is sufficient to elicit an own-group bias in face recognition. *Psychological Science, 18*, 706–712.

Blogowska, J., & Saroglou, V. (2012). For better or worse: Fundamentalists' attitudes towards outgroups as a function of exposure to authoritative religious texts. *International Journal for the Psychology of Religion, 23*, 103–125.

Brandt, M. J., & Reyna, C. (2010). The role of prejudice and the need for closure in religious fundamentalism. *Personality and Social Psychology Bulletin, 36*, 715–725.

Brown, R. (2000). Social identity theory: Past achievements, current problems and future challenges. *European Journal of Social Psychology, 30*, 745–778.

Brown, R. (2010). *Prejudice: Its social psychology* (2nd ed.). Oxford: Blackwell.

Bushman, B. J., Ridge, R. D., Das, E., Key, C. W., & Busath, G. L. (2007). When God sanctions killing: Effect of scriptural violence on aggression. *Psychological Science, 18*, 204–207.

Butz, D. A., & Yogeeswaran, K. (2011). A new threat in the air: Macroeconomic threat increases prejudice against Asian Americans. *Journal of Experimental Social Psychology, 47*, 22–27.

Chaves, M. (2010). Rain dances in the dry season: Overcoming the religious congruence fallacy. *Journal for the Scientific Study of Religion, 49*, 1–14.

Christopher, A. N., & Mull, M. S. (2006). Conservative ideology and ambivalent sexism. *Psychology of Women Quarterly, 30*, 223–230.

Crandall, C. S., & Eshleman, A. (2003). A justification-suppression model of the expression and experience of prejudice. *Psychological Bulletin, 129*, 414–446.

Crowson, H. M. (2009). Predicting perceptions of symbolic and realistic threat from terrorists: The role of right-wing authoritarianism and social dominance orientation. *Individual Differences Research, 7*, 113–118.

Dambrun, M., Taylor, D. M., McDonald, D. A., Crush, J., & Méot, A. (2006). The relative deprivation-gratification continuum and the attitudes of South

Africans toward immigrants: A test of the V-curve hypothesis. *Journal of Personality and Social Psychology, 91,* 1032–1044.

Dar-Nimrod, I., & Heine, S. J. (2011). Genetic essentialism: On the deceptive determinism of DNA. *Psychological Bulletin, 137,* 800–818.

Davies, K., Tropp, L., Aron, A., Pettigrew, T. F., & Wright, S. C. (2011). Cross-group friendships and intergroup attitudes: A meta-analytic review. *Personality and Social Psychology Review, 15,* 332–351.

Deci, E. L., & Ryan, R. M. (2012). Self-determination theory. In P. A. M. Van Lange, A. W. Kruglanski, & E. T. Higgins (Eds.), *Handbook of theories of social psychology* (Vol. 1, pp. 416–437). Thousand Oaks, CA: Sage.

Demoulin, S., Saroglou, V., & Van Pachterbeke, M. (2008). Infra-humanizing others, supra-humanizing gods: The emotional hierarchy. *Social Cognition, 26,* 235–247.

Dickter, C. L., & Bartholow, B. D. (2007). Racial ingroup and outgroup attention biases revealed by event-related brain potentials. *Social Cognitive and Affective Neuroscience, 2,* 189–198.

Duck, R. J., & Hunsberger, B. (1999). Religious orientation and prejudice: The role of religious proscription, right-wing authoritarianism and social desirability. *International Journal for the Psychology of Religion, 9,* 157–179.

Duckitt, J. (1994). *The social psychology of prejudice.* Westport, CT: Praeger.

Duckitt, J. (2001). A dual-process cognitive-motivational theory of ideology and prejudice. In M. P. Zanna (Ed.), *Advances in experimental social psychology* (Vol. 33, pp. 41–112). San Diego, CA: Academic Press.

Duckitt, J., & Sibley, C. G. (2010). Right-wing authoritarianism and social dominance orientation differentially moderate intergroup effects on prejudice. *European Journal of Personality, 24,* 583–601.

Fox, R. (1992). Prejudice and the unfinished mind: A new look at an old failing. *Psychological Inquiry, 3,* 137–152.

Galen, L.W. (2012). Does religious belief promote prosociality?: A critical examination. *Psychological Bulletin, 138,* 876–906.

Ginges, J., Hansen, I., & Norenzayan, A. (2009). Religion and support for suicide attacks. *Psychological Science, 20,* 224–230.

Goldfried, J., & Miner, M. (2002). Quest religion and the problem of limited compassion. *Journal for the Scientific Study of Religion, 41,* 685–695.

Greenberg, J., Solomon, S., & Pyszczynski, T. (1997). Terror management theory of self-esteem and cultural worldviews: Empirical assessments and conceptual refinements. In M. P. Zanna (Ed.), *Advances in experimental social psychology* (Vol. 29, pp. 61–139). Orlando, FL: Academic Press.

Guimond, S., & Dambrun, M. (2002). When prosperity breeds intergroup hostility: The effects of relative deprivation and relative gratification on prejudice. *Personality and Social Psychology Bulletin, 28,* 900–912.

Hall, D. L., Matz, D. C., & Wood, W. (2010). Why don't we practice what we preach? A meta-analytic review of religious racism. *Personality and Social Psychology Review, 14,* 126–139.

Hayes, J., Schimel, J., & Williams, T. J. (2008). Fighting death with death: The buffering effects of learning that worldview violators have died. *Psychological Science, 19,* 501–507.

Henrich, J. (2009). The evolution of costly displays, cooperation and religion: Credibility enhancing displays and their implications for cultural evolution. *Evolution and Human Behavior, 30,* 244–260.

Henry, P. J., Sidanius, J., Levin, S., & Pratto, F. (2005). Social dominance orientation, authoritarianism, and support for intergroup violence between the Middle East and America. *Political Psychology, 26,* 569–583.

Herek, G. M. (2009). Sexual prejudice. In T. Nelson (Ed.), *Handbook of prejudice, stereotyping, and discrimination* (pp. 441–467). New York: Psychology Press.

Hewstone, M., Islam, M. R., & Judd, C. M. (1993). Models of crossed categorization and intergroup relations. *Journal of Personality and Social Psychology, 64,* 779–793.

Hoffman, C., & Hurst, N. (1990). Gender stereotypes: Perception or rationalization? *Journal of Personality and Social Psychology, 58,* 197–208.

Hogg, M. A., Adelman, J. R., & Blagg, R. D. (2010). Religion in the face of uncertainty: An uncertainty-identity account of religiousness. *Personality and Social Psychology Review, 14,* 72–83.

Hunsberger, B., & Jackson, L. M. (2005). Religion, meaning, and prejudice. *Journal of Social Issues, 61,* 807–826.

Ito, T. A., Thompson, E., & Cacioppo, J. T. (2004). Tracking the timecourse of social perception: The effects of racial cues on event-related brain potentials. *Personality and Social Psychology Bulletin, 30,* 1267–1280.

Jackson, L. M., & Hunsberger, B. (1999). An intergroup perspective on religion and prejudice. *Journal for the Scientific Study of Religion, 38,* 509–523.

Johnson, D., & Kruger, O. (2004). The good of wrath: Supernatural punishment and the evolution of cooperation. *Political Theology, 5,* 159–176.

Johnson, K. A., White, A. E., Boyd, B. M., & Cohen, A. B. (2011). Matzah, meat, milk, and mana: Psychological influences on religio-cultural food practices. *Journal of Cross-Cultural Psychology, 42,* 1421–1436.

Johnson, M. K., Rowatt, W. C., & LaBouff, J. (2010). Priming Christian religious concepts increases racial prejudice. *Social Psychological and Personality Science, 1,* 119–126.

Johnson, M. K., Rowatt, W. C., & LaBouff, J. P. (2012). Religion and prejudice revisited: In-group favoritism, out-group derogation, or both? *Psychology of Religion and Spirituality, 4,* 154–164.

Jonas, E., & Fischer, P. (2006). Terror management and religion: Evidence that intrinsic religiousness mitigates worldview defense following mortality salience. *Journal of Personality and Social Psychology, 91,* 553–567.

Jones, H. B., Furnham, A., & Deile, A. J. (2010). Religious orientation and the Protestant work ethic. *Mental Health, Religion and Culture, 13,* 697–706.

Jost, J. T., Banaji, M. R., & Nosek, B. A. (2004). A decade of system justification theory: Accumulated evidence of conscious and unconscious bolstering of the status quo. *Political Psychology, 25,* 881–920.

Jost, J. T., & Burgess, D. (2000). Attitudinal ambivalence and the conflict between group and system justification motives in low status groups. *Personality and Social Psychology Bulletin, 26,* 293–305.

Jost, J. T., & Hunyady, O. (2005). Antecedents and consequences of system-justifying ideologies. *Current Directions in Psychological Science, 14,* 260–265.

Kashdan, T. B., & Nezlek, J. B. (2012). Whether, when, and how is spirituality related to well-being? Moving beyond single occasion questionnaires to understanding daily process. *Personality and Social Psychology Bulletin, 38,* 1523–1535.

Kastenmuller, A., Greitemeyer, T., Ai, A. L., Winter, G., & Fischer, P. (2011). In the face of terrorism: Evidence that belief in literal immortality reduces prejudice under terrorism threat. *Journal for the Scientific Study of Religion, 50,* 604–616.

Kemmelmeier, M. (2005). The effects of race and social dominance orientation in simulated juror decision making. *Journal of Applied Social Psychology, 35,* 1030–1045.

Kirkpatrick, L. A. (2005). *Attachment, evolution, and the psychology of religion.* New York: Guilford.

Klar, Y., Kahn, D., & Roccas, S. (2012). *Conceiving the national group as an eternal entity and the willingness to sacrifice for a group.* Paper presented at the annual meeting of the Society for Experimental Social Psychology, Austin, Texas.

LaBouff, J. P., Rowatt, W.C., Johnson, M. K., & Finkle, C. (2012). Differences in attitudes towards out-groups in religious and non-religious contexts in a multi-national sample: A situational context priming study. *International Journal for the Psychology of Religion, 22,* 1–9.

LaBouff, J. P., Rowatt, W. C., Johnson, M. K., Thedford, M., & Tsang, J. A. (2010). Development and initial validation of an implicit measure of religiousness-spirituality. *Journal for the Scientific Study of Religion, 49,* 439–455.

Levin, S. (2004). Perceived group status differences and the effects of gender, ethnicity, and religion on social dominance orientation. *Political Psychology, 25,* 31–48.

Looy, H. (2005). The body of faith: Genetic and evolutionary considerations. *Journal of Psychology and Christianity, 24,* 113–121.

Mak, H. K., & Tsang, J. (2008). Separating the "sinner" from the "sin": Religious orientation and prejudiced behavior toward sexual orientation and promiscuous sex. *Journal for the Scientific Study of Religion, 47,* 379–392.

Mavor, K. I., Macleod, C. J., Boal, M. J., & Louis, W. R. (2009). Right-wing authoritarianism, fundamentalism, and prejudice revisited: Removing suppression and statistical artefact. *Personality and Individual Differences, 46,* 592–597.

Miller, J. D., Scott, E. C., & Okamoto, S. (2006). Public acceptance of evolution. *Science, 313,* 765–766.

Mullen, B., & Hu, I. (1989). Perceptions of ingroup and outgroup variability: A meta-analytic integration. *Basic and Applied Social Psychology, 10,* 233–252.

Neuberg, S. L. (1992). Evolution and individuation: The adaptiveness of nonstereotypical thought. *Psychological Inquiry, 3,* 178–180.

Neuberg, S. L., & Cottrell, C. A. (2006). Evolutionary bases of prejudices. In M. Schaller, J. A. Simpson, & D. T. Kenrick (Eds.), *Evolution and social psychology* (pp. 163–187). Madison, CT: Psychosocial Press.

Neuberg, S. L., Warner, C. M., Mistler, S. A., Berlin, A., Hill, E., Johnson, J. D. et al. (2012). *Religious infusion predicts enhanced resource- and values-linked intergroup conflict.* Manuscript submitted for publication.

Osarchuk, M., & Tatz, S. J. (1973). Effect of induced fear of death on belief in afterlife. *Journal of Personality and Social Psychology, 27*, 256–260.

Pichon, I., Boccato, G., & Saroglou, V. (2007). Nonconscious influences of religion on prosociality: A priming study. *European Journal of Social Psychology, 37*, 1032–1045.

Pichon, I., & Saroglou, V. (2009). Religion and helping: Impact of target thinking styles and just-world beliefs. *Archive for the Psychology of Religion, 31*, 215–236.

Plant, E. A., & Devine, P. G. (1998). Internal and external motivation to respond without prejudice. *Journal of Personality and Social Psychology, 75*, 811–832.

Pratto, F., Sidanius, J., & Levin, S. (2006). Social dominance theory and the dynamics of intergroup relations: Taking stock and looking forward. *European Review of Social Psychology, 17*, 271–320.

Pratto, F., Sidanius, J., Stallworth, L. M., & Malle, B. F. (1994). Social dominance orientation: A personality variable predicting social and political attitudes. *Journal of Personality and Social Psychology, 67*, 741–763.

Preston, J. L., Ritter, R. S., & Hernandez, J. I. (2010). Principles of religious prosociality: A review and reformulation. *Social and Personality Compass, 4*, 574–590.

Ramsay, J. E., Pang, J. S., Shen, M. J., & Rowatt, W. C. (2013). Rethinking value violation: Priming religion increases prejudice in Singaporean Christians and Buddhists. *International Journal for the Psychology of Religion*. Advance online publication.

Randolph-Seng, B., & Nielsen, M. E. (2007). Honesty: One effect of primed religious representations. *International Journal for the Psychology of Religion, 17*, 303–315.

Riek, B. M., Mania, E. W., & Gaertner, S. L. (2006). Intergroup threat and outgroup attitudes: A meta-analytic review. *Personality and Social Psychology Review, 10*, 336–353.

Ritter, R. S., & Preston, J. L. (2011). Gross gods and icky atheism: Disgust responses to rejected religious beliefs. *Journal of Experimental Social Psychology, 47*, 1225–1230.

Rothschild, Z. K., Abdollahi, A., & Pyszczynski, T. (2009). Does peace have a prayer? The effect of mortality salience, compassionate values, and religious fundamentalism on hostility toward out-groups. *Journal of Experimental Social Psychology, 45*, 816–827.

Rowatt, W. C., & Franklin, L. M. (2004). Christian orthodoxy, religious fundamentalism, and right-wing authoritarianism as predictors of implicit racial prejudice. *International Journal for the Psychology of Religion, 14*, 125–138.

Rowatt, W. C., Shen, M. J., LaBouff, J. P., & Gonzalez, A. (2013). Religious fundamentalism, right-wing authoritarianism, and prejudice: Insights from meta-analyses, implicit social cognition, and social neuroscience. In R. F. Paloutzian & C. L. Park (Eds.), *Handbook of psychology of religion and spirituality* (2nd ed., pp. 457–475). New York: Guilford.

Rutchick, A. M. (2010). Deus ex machina: The influence of polling place on voting behavior. *Political Psychology, 31*, 209–225.

Saroglou, V., Corneille, O., & Van Cappellen, P. (2009). "Speak, Lord, your servant is listening": Religious priming activates submissive thoughts and behaviors. *International Journal for the Psychology of Religion, 19,* 143–154.

Sasaki, J. Y., Kim, H. S., Mojaverian, T., Kelley, L. D. S., Park, I. Y., & Janusonis, S. (2013). Religion priming differentially increases prosocial behavior among variants of the dopamine D4 receptor (DRD4) gene. *Social Cognitive and Affective Neurosciences, 8,* 209–215.

Schumann, K., Nash, K. A., McGregor, I., & Ross, M. (2013). *Religious magnanimity: Religion primes supplant antagonistic with more compassionate reactions to threat.* Unpublished manuscript.

Schwartz, S., Dunkel, C. S., & Waterman, A. S. (2009). Terrorism: An identity theory perspective. *Studies in Conflict and Terrorism, 32,* 537–559.

Shariff, A. F., & Norenzayan, A. (2007). God is watching you: Priming God concepts increases prosocial behavior in an anonymous economic game. *Psychological Science, 18,* 803–809.

Shen, M., Haggard, M. C., Strassburger, D. C., & Rowatt, W. C. (2012). *Religiosity's association with positive attitudes toward ethnic/racial and value-violating out-groups.* Manuscript submitted for publication.

Shen, M. J., Yelderman, L., Haggard, M. C., & Rowatt, W. C. (2013). Disentangling the belief in God and cognitive rigidity/flexibility components of religiosity to predict racial and value-violating prejudice: A post-critical belief scale analysis. *Personality and Individual Differences, 54,* 389–395.

Sherif, M. (1966). *Group conflict and cooperation: Their social psychology.* London: Routledge & Kegan Paul.

Shimoni, M. T.-K., & Schwarzwald, J. (2003). Perceived threat and prejudice in three domains of inter-group tension in Israeli society. *Megamot, 42,* 549–584.

Shortell, T. (2011). The conflict over origins: A discourse analysis of the creationism controversy in American newspapers. *Mass Communication and Society, 14,* 431–453.

Smith, H. J., & Ortiz, D. J. (2002). Is it just me?: The different consequences of personal and group relative deprivation. In I. Walker & H. J. Smith (Eds.), *Relative deprivation: Specification, development, and integration* (pp. 91–115). New York: Cambridge University Press.

Sosis, R., & Ruffle, B. J. (2003). Religious ritual and cooperation: Testing for a relationship on Israeli religious and secular kibbutzim. *Current Anthropology, 44,* 713–722.

Stangor, C. (2009). The study of stereotyping, prejudice and discrimination within social psychology: A quick history of theory and research. In T. Nelson (Ed.), *Handbook of prejudice, stereotyping, and discrimination* (pp. 1–22). New York: Psychology Press.

Stephan, W. G., Ybarra, O., & Morrison, K. R. (2009). Intergroup threat theory. In T. D. Nelson (Ed.), *Handbook of prejudice, stereotyping, and discrimination* (pp. 43–59). New York: Psychology Press.

Swann, W. B., Gomez, A., Huici, C., Morales, J. F., & Hixon, J. G. (2010). Identity fusion and self-sacrifice: Arousal as a catalyst of pro-group fighting, dying, and helping behavior. *Journal of Personality and Social Psychology, 99,* 824–841.

Swann, W. B., Gomez, A., Seyle, D. C., Morales, J. F., & Guici, C. (2009). Identify fusion: The interplay of personal and social identities in extreme group behavior. *Journal of Personality and Social Psychology, 96,* 995–1011.

Tajfel, H. (1969). Cognitive aspects of prejudice. *Journal of Social Issues, 25,* 79–97.

Tajfel, H., & Turner, J. C. (1986). The social identity theory of intergroup behavior. In S. Worchel & W. G. Austin (Eds.), *Psychology of intergroup relations* (pp. 7–24). Chicago, IL: Nelson-Hall.

Tajfel, H., & Wilkes, A. L. (1963). Classification and quantitative judgment. *British Journal of Psychology, 54,* 101–114.

Tausch, N., Hewstone, M., & Roy, R. (2009). The relationships between contact, status and prejudice: An integrated threat theory analysis of Hindu–Muslim relations in India. *Journal of Community and Applied Social Psychology, 19,* 83–94.

Tripathi, R. C., & Srivastava, R. (1981). Relative deprivation and intergroup attitudes. *European Journal of Social Psychology, 11,* 313–318.

Vail, K. E., Rothschild, Z. K., Weise, D. R., Solomon, S., Pyszczynski, T., & Greenberg, J. (2010). A terror management analysis of the psychological functions of religion. *Personality and Social Psychology Review, 14,* 84–94.

Van den Bos, K., Van Ameijde, J., & Van Gorp, H. (2006). On the psychology of religion: The role of personal uncertainty in religious worldview defense. *Basic and Applied Social Psychology, 28,* 333–341.

Verkuyten, M. (2007). Religious group identification and inter-religious relations: A study among Turkish–Dutch Muslims. *Group Processes and Intergroup Relations, 10,* 341–357.

Verkuyten, M., & Martinovic, B. (2012). Social identity complexity and immigrants' attitude towards the host nation: The intersection of ethnic and religious group identification. *Personality and Social Psychology Bulletin, 38,* 1165–1177.

Verkuyten, M., & Yildiz, A. A. (2007). National (dis)identification and ethnic and religious identity: A study among Turkish–Dutch Muslims. *Personality and Social Psychology Bulletin, 33,* 1448–1462.

Wann, D. L., & Grieve, F. G. (2005). Biased evaluations of in-group and out-group spectator behavior at sporting events: The importance of team identification and threats to social identity. *Journal of Social Psychology, 145,* 531–545.

Wheeler, S. C., & DeMarree, K. G. (2009). Multiple mechanisms for prime-to-behavior effects. *Social and Personality Psychology Compass, 3,* 566–581.

Whitley, B. E., Jr. (2009). Religiosity and attitudes toward lesbians and gay men: A meta-analysis. *International Journal for the Psychology of Religion, 19,* 21–38.

Wilson, E. O. (1978). *On human nature.* Cambridge, MA: Harvard University Press.

Wittenbrink, B., Hilton, J. L., & Gist, P. L. (1998). In search of similarity: Stereotypes as naive theories in social categorization. *Social Cognition, 16,* 31–55.

Ysseldyk, R., Matheson, K., & Anisman, H. (2010). Religiosity as identity: Toward an understanding of religion from a social identity perspective. *Personality and Social Psychology Review, 14,* 60–71.

9   Values and Religiosity

Sonia Roccas and Andrey Elster

In this chapter, we discuss recent research on values and religiosity from a social psychological perspective. We focus on religion as a social identity (Hogg, Adelman, & Blagg, 2010; Ysseldyk, Matheson, & Anisman, 2010), and emphasize the aspects of religion that relate to group processes, such as norms, traditions, and common practices. We first describe what values are and how they have been conceptualized and studied. We then review research on the direct relationships between values and religiosity, and describe the consistent patterns of correlations found across cultures and religious groups. Next we discuss some of the implications of the relationship of values and religiosity: We show how understanding the value differences between religious and non-religious people offers a theoretical framework for investigating behavioral differences associated with religiosity. Finally, we discuss the implications of the relationships of values and religiosity for the management of multiple identities.

What Values Are

Values are abstract desirable goals that serve as guiding principles in people's lives (Kluckhohn, 1951; Rokeach, 1973; Schwartz, 1992). They are a core aspect of people's identity, and serve as standards or criteria that provide social justification for choices and behaviors across situations (Rokeach, 1973). Unlike needs and motives, which may be unconscious, values are represented cognitively in ways that enable people to think and communicate about them (Schwartz, 1992) Values are ordered by subjective importance, and thus form a hierarchy of value priorities. The relative importance of different values affects perception and interpretation (e.g., Sagiv, Sverdlik, & Schwarz, 2011; Sattler & Kerr, 1991; Van Lange & Liebrand, 1989), personal preferences and decisions (e.g., Adams, Licht, & Sagiv, 2011; Feather, 1995), emotions (e.g., Feather, Woodyatt, & McKee, 2012; Roccas, Klar, & Liviatan, 2004), daily actions (e.g., Bardi & Schwartz, 2003; Maio, Olson, Allen, & Bernard, 2001; Maio, Pakizeh, Cheung, & Rees, 2009), and long-term behavior (e.g., Gaunt, 2005; Sagiv & Schwartz, 2004). Thus, it is not surprising that values are closely related to religiosity.

In the last decade most of the research examining the direct relationships of values and religiosity was drawn on the Schwartz value theory (Schwartz, 1992; see reviews in Hitlin & Piliavin, 2004; Maio, 2010; Rohan, 2000). This theory is particularly useful for studying religiosity because it seeks to provide a comprehensive mapping of values according to the motivations that underlie them. Schwartz distinguishes between 10 motivational goals that are at the core of values: power, achievement, hedonism, stimulation, self-direction, universalism, benevolence, tradition, conformity, and security. These values are organized in a circular order according to two basic conflicts. *Self-enhancement values* (power and achievement) emphasize pursuit of self-interests, even at the expense of others. They conflict with *self-transcendence* values (benevolence and universalism), which emphasize concern for the welfare and interests of others, close and distant. *Openness to change values* (self-direction and stimulation) emphasize independent action, thought and feeling, and readiness for new experience. They conflict with *conservation* values (security, conformity, and tradition), which emphasize self-restriction, order, and resistance to change. *Hedonism* values share elements of both openness to change and self-enhancement and are in conflict with both self-transcendence and conservation values.

The circular structure of the motivations underlying values implies that the whole set of values relates to other variables in an integrated manner. Specifically, once the values most positively and most negatively correlated with religiosity are identified, one could expect correlations with other values to decrease monotonically in both directions around the circle from the most positively to the most negatively associated value. When the whole pattern of associations between values and religiosity is predicted, even non-significant associations provide meaningful information (Roccas, Sagiv, Schwartz, &, Knafo 2002; Sagiv & Schwartz, 1995).

Direct Relationships of Values and Religiosity

People believe that one's religious affiliation and the extent of one's commitment to religion conveys important information, and that it is a reliable source for assessment of a person's character and morality (e.g., Gervais, Shariff, & Norenzayan, 2011; Zuckerman, 2009). Are these beliefs true? Do people who differ in religious denomination or in the extent of their religiosity also differ in their values and their moral outlook? Extensive research sought to provide answers to these questions by examining the value priorities of people who differ in their religious denomination and in the extent of their religiosity. We first review these studies and then discuss the possible causes for the relationships between values and religiosity.

Compatibilities between the Motivational Goals of Values and Religiosity

In a seminal article, Schwartz and Huismans (1995) mapped the 10 values according to the extent to which they are consistent with religiosity, and examined these relationships in four religious groups. They reasoned that attributing high importance to *conservation* values is consistent with religiosity because the focus of these values on self-restriction, order, and resistance to change is highly compatible with religiosity. Tradition, in particular, is highly compatible with religiosity, because of its central goals of submission to transcendental authority and protecting individuals from uncertainty. In contrast, placing high importance on *openness to change* values is inconsistent with being strongly religious because these values conflict with accepting dogmas and resigning gratification of material desires. *Hedonism* values are highly incompatible with religiosity because, in addition to being a possible threat to existing social order, these values also directly oppose a primary function of religion—to temper self-indulgent tendencies. The relationship of *self-enhancement* values and religiosity is more complex: the self-interested focus of these values is opposed to religious teachings. Yet, self-enhancement values may serve to maintain the social order that is favored by religious institutions. Thus, the importance of these values for religious versus non-religious people is likely to vary according to the social context. For example, the association of self-enhancement values with religiosity is affected by policies of the state toward religion. Oppositional relations between church and state might hamper religious people from successfully pursuing power and achievement values, resulting in more negative relations of religiosity with self-enhancement (Roccas & Schwartz, 1997).

The role of *self-transcendence* values and religiosity is particularly intriguing. Universalism and benevolence values share the motivation of concern for others, but differ in the inclusiveness of the target of this concern: Benevolence values focus on close others; friends, neighbors, and ingroup members. Universalism values apply to all people, including members of outgroups. Schwartz and Huismans (1995) reasoned that religiosity is compatible with benevolence values because of the emphasis of religion on selflessness in relations with close others. However, religiosity is not necessarily compatible with universalism because of the particularism of religions.

During the last two decades an extensive body of research found support for this reasoning (see Saroglou, Delpierre, & Dernelle, 2004, for a meta-analysis). The studies varied in the cultural and religious groups they examined: Christians from the US (Dollinger, 2001); Buddhists from Belgium (Saroglou & Dupuis, 2006); Catholics from Mexico (Bilsky & Peters, 1999), Belgium (Fontaine, Luyten, & Corveleyn, 2000),

Italy, Portugal, and Spain (Roccas & Schwartz, 1997); Anglicans from the United Kingdom (Pepper, Jackson, & Uzzell, 2010); Protestants from the Netherlands and Germany (Schwartz & Huismans, 1995); Greek Orthodox from Greece (Schwartz & Huismans, 1995); Muslims from Belgium (Saroglou & Galand, 2004) and Turkey (Kusdil & Kagitcibasi, 2000); Jews from Belgium (Saroglou & Hanique, 2006) and Israel (Schwartz & Huismans, 1995; Roccas et al., 2002). The studies also differed in the demographic characteristic of the participants: secondary and high school students (Saroglou & Galand, 2004; Saroglou & Hanique, 2006), university students (Saroglou & Muñoz-García, 2008), working adults (Pepper et al., 2010), and so on. Finally, the studies differed in methodological aspects such as the measure of religiosity. In some studies religiosity was measured by a single item measuring self-rating of subjective religiosity (e.g., Roccas et al., 2002); in others religiosity was measured using multiple-items scales of religious commitment, or by self-reported frequency of church attendance (e.g., Pepper et al., 2010; Saroglou & Muñoz-García, 2008).

Overall, findings are very consistent. To exemplify the general pattern of correlations between values and religiosity across the different studies we averaged the correlations of each of the 10 values across 28 measures of religiosity derived from 24 samples (Figure 9.1).[1] We based this figure on studies included in the meta-analysis conducted by Saroglou and colleagues (2004), along with studies that were published later (see Pepper et al., 2010, for a similar figure based on the Saroglou et al., 2004,

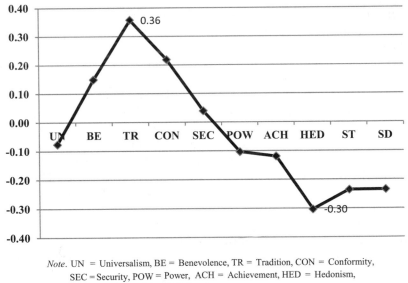

Note. UN = Universalism, BE = Benevolence, TR = Tradition, CON = Conformity,
SEC = Security, POW = Power, ACH = Achievement, HED = Hedonism,
ST = Stimulation, SD = Self-direction

Figure 9.1 Average correlations of values and religiosity across 24 samples.

meta-analysis). Consistent with the motivational value circle, the pattern of correlations forms a sinusoid curve. Correlations are most positive with tradition values and most negative with hedonism. The correlations with the rest of the values fall in between according to the circular order of the values.

Examining findings separately in each sample reveals that in all samples, religiosity is positively correlated with *conservation* values (in all samples with tradition and conformity values, and in 18 out of 28 with security values). Religiosity is negatively correlated with hedonism and *openness to change* values (in all samples with hedonism, in 26 with stimulation and in 27 with self-direction). The relationship between religiosity and *self-enhancement* values is generally negative (in 25 with power and in 26 with achievement). The correlations of religiosity with *self-transcendence* values are more complex: Correlations of religiosity with benevolence are generally positive (in 24 out of 28), while correlations with universalism were generally negative (in 21 out of 28).

Benevolence and universalism values are similar in that they express the motivation to care for the welfare of others. They differ, however, in the inclusiveness of the group of people who are at the focus of such concerns. Benevolence values focus on close others. The positive correlation of religiosity with benevolence values indicates that religiosity is associated with thinking that it is important to be devoted to the well-being of people with whom one has interpersonal relations. The target of the concern expressed in universalism values is all humanity. The negative correlation of religiosity with universalism values indicates that religiosity is associated with rejecting the belief that it is important to promote the welfare of all humankind. The contrasting relationships of religiosity with benevolence and universalism highlight the potential tension embedded in religion between being concerned about the well-being of close others who presumably share one's religious beliefs and being concerned about all humanity. Expressing concern for the whole of humankind implies that a religion is not an important dimension of categorization; that all people, irrespective of their religious category are targets of similar concern.

We examined the consistency of the structure of the relationship between values and religiosity by computing the pair-wise Spearman correlations between the orders of the correlations in the samples we used to produce Figure 9.1. For each sample we computed pair-wise Spearman correlations between the order of the correlations of religiosity with the 10 values found in that sample, and the order found in each of the other samples. This analysis resulted in 388 correlations that reflect the similarity of the relationship between values and religiosity across the pairs of samples. The higher the correlation the more similar is the pattern of relationship between the 10 value types and religiosity across the two samples. Overall, 88% of the Spearman correlations were higher than .50, and 46% were higher than .80. This indicates a remarkable similarity in the order of the correlations between religiosity and the 10 values across the different samples. In sum, people who define themselves as religious hold similar values, irrespective of the specific religious group they belong to. The same pattern is found among Catholics, Protestants, Greek Orthodox, Anglicans, Muslims, and Jews. Thus, in terms of values the main distinction is between people that differ in the extent of religiosity rather than between people that differ in their religious denomination (Schwartz, 2012).

It would seem that at least in the US there is growing awareness that the difference between people who differ in religiosity overshadows the differences between people who differ in their religious affiliation. Sociological analyses of religion in the US highlight the decrease of religiously based prejudice against Jews and Catholics in the last decades (Edgell, Gerteis, & Hartmann, 2006). Intolerance towards atheists, however, has changed at a much lower pace. For example, a large proportion of Americans would not vote for a presidential candidate who is atheist, whereas being Jewish or a Mormon does not seem to disqualify one from being president (Gervais, 2011). Thus, the convergence in values between religious people from different religion groups and the divergence in values between religious and non-religious is mirrored in a change in social categorization: The category of believer versus atheist has more social meaning than the category of Christian versus non-Christian.

We focused on studies that examined a unidimensional conceptualization of religiosity because this was the conceptualization adopted in most of the empirical studies on values and religiosity. People, however, can experience their religiousness in many ways, ranging from a focus on spirituality to a focus on public behavioral expressions of religion. The few studies examining the relationship between values and different dimensions of religiosity show the importance of distinguishing between the different dimensions.

Studies based on the distinction between exclusion versus inclusion of transcendence and a literal versus symbolic approach to religion (Wulff, 1991, 1997) show that the two dimensions are associated with different values (Muñoz-García & Saroglou, 2008). The dimension of exclusion versus inclusion of transcendence refers to the extent to which "the objects of religious interest are granted participation in a transcendent reality" (Fontaine, Duriez, Luyten, & Hutsebaut, 2003). This dimension is generally correlated with the conflict between hedonism, stimulation, and self-direction versus tradition and conformity values. The dimension of literal versus symbolic approach to religion refers to the extent to which "religion is interpreted literally versus symbolically" (Fontaine et al., 2003). It is generally correlated with the conflict between security and power versus universalism and benevolence values (Fontaine, Duriez, Luyten, Corveleyn, & Hutsebaut, 2005; Fontaine et al., 2000).

Values and Religiosity: Multiple Causal Pathways

Do values affect religiosity, or do religious people come to emphasize tradition, conformity, security, and benevolence values? The relationship of values and religiosity is probably due to mutual causation. Personal values are likely to affect the extent of religiosity because people are motivated to act in accordance to their values, and they choose groups, identities, and activities that are compatible with them (Gandal, Roccas, Sagiv, & Wrzesniewski, 2005; Schneider, 1987; Schneider, Goldstein & Smith, 1995). People who value conservation are likely to join religious groups and practice religiosity, because this enables the attainment of their important values. Emphasizing conservation values is likely to promote willingness to adhere to the norms prescribed by a religious group and the extent to which a person self-defines as religious.

The reverse causal pathway is also likely and membership in a religious group can shape value priorities. A core mission of religions is to shape people's values. Like other social institutions, religious institutions inculcate value priorities by encouraging compliance with behavioral patterns that are compatible with the values endorsed by religion (e.g., McCullough & Willoughby, 2009). Once a person is committed to a habitual set of behaviors, processes of self-perception and dissonance reduction are likely to lead to developing values that are compatible with one's behavior. Thus, religion can directly affect the development of values, through explicit and implicit value teaching and by encouraging behaviors that are consistent with the values endorsed by religion.

Values and religiosity are also related due to social factors that affect them simultaneously. A primary factor is family socialization. Parents' and children's religiosity are strongly correlated (e.g., Kim, McCullough, & Cicchetti, 2009; Landor, Simons, Simons, Brody, & Gibbons, 2011), and parents' religiosity predicts children's behavior: It enhances the likelihood of behaviors that are consistent with religion and reduces the likelihood of behaviors that are inconsistent with religion (Manlove, Logan, Moore, & Ikramullah, 2008; Udell, Donenberg, & Emerson, 2011). Parents also shape children's religiosity indirectly via the selection of social contexts compatible with their own religious attitudes, such as schools (Knafo, 2003; Knafo, Daniel, Gabay, Zilber, & Shir, 2012). Although the correlational nature of these studies could not answer the question whether parent–adolescent similarities in values promote trans-generational transmission of religious attitudes or the opposite is true, they provide significant evidence that both constructs are passing hand by hand through the generations (Dudley & Dudley, 1986; Hitlin, 2006).

Values, Religiosity, and Behavior

Religions explicitly prescribe the pursuit of certain behaviors (such as participation in religious rituals), and proscribe other behaviors (such as eating certain foods). Thus, it is not surprising that there are documented behavioral differences between religious and non-religious adolescences (see Rew & Wong, 2006, for a review; Cheung & Yeung, 2011, for a meta-analysis). However, religious and non-religious people also differ in behaviors in domains that are not explicitly related to religion such as smoking and alcohol use, and even the choice of academic field (e.g., Gross & Simmons, 2009). These differences are not readily understandable in terms of religion. We suggest that some of the behavioral differences between religious and non-religious people are derived from personal values rather than from religion. Thus, the associations of values and religiosity can broaden our understanding of the relationship between religiosity and behavior.

Values as Source of Behavioral Differences between Religious and Non-religious People

People are likely to act in ways that promote the attainment of their important values and refrain from acting in ways that block it (Feather, 1995; Feather, Norman, & Worsley, 1998; Sagiv & Schwartz, 1995). Values affect behavior directly because people view actions that are consistent with their values as more attractive than actions that contrast their values (Feather, 1988, 1995). Values also affect behavior indirectly through their effect on people's focus of attention (e.g., De Dreu & Boles, 1998), the way they interpret information (e.g., Sattler & Kerr, 1991; Van Lange & Liebrand, 1989), and the types of things they worry about (Schwartz, Sagiv, & Boehnke, 2000).

Behaviors can be classified according to the values that are most likely to guide them. Most behaviors that were found to be negatively correlated with religiosity can be classified as involving a violation of normative expectations such as excessive alcohol consumption, sexually permissive behaviors, and involvement in petty crimes (e.g., Cheung & Yeung, 2011; Li & Cohen, Chapter 10, this volume; Mullen & Francis, 1995; Rew & Wong, 2006). These behaviors are incompatible with conservation values and consistent with openness to change values. In contrast, religiosity was found to be positively correlated with behaviors such as helping, voluntary work, and involvement in civic activities (Furrow, King, & White, 2004; Kerestes, Youniss, & Metz, 2004; Trusty & Watts, 1999; for a review see Preston, Salomon, & Ritter, Chapter 7, this volume). These behaviors are compatible with benevolence values. The distinction between the relationships with benevolence versus universalism values also has behavioral manifestations: Religiosity is positively associated with willingness to help close others but is unrelated to the willingness to help unknown people (Saroglou, Pichon, Trompette, Verschueren, & Dernelle, 2005).

In sum, when focusing on behaviors that are not directly mandated by religion, the "behavioral profile" of the differences between religious and non-religious people mirrors the values associated with religiosity. People who are religious tend to behave in ways that are consistent with benevolence (but not universalism) values and tend to avoid behaviors that are inconsistent with conservation values.

So far, studies on behavioral differences between religious and non-religious people focused on a rather limited set of domains of behavior. On the basis of the relationships between values and religiosity, one can expect behavioral differences in additional domains. For example, people who attribute high importance to self-direction, stimulation, and universalism values and low importance to security, tradition, and conformity values were found more likely to behave creatively (e.g., Dollinger, Burke, & Gump, 2007; Kasof, Chen, Himsel, & Greenberger, 2007; Sousa & Coelho, 2011). Individuals who emphasize self-direction values are more likely to make suggestions for work improvement (Lipponen, Bardi, & Haapamäki, 2008) than people who attribute low importance to these values. Since these values are strongly correlated with religiosity it is possible that religious and non-religious people will differ also in these behavioral domains. In sum, understanding the underlying motivation of religiosity may help to understand differences in behavior between religious and non-religious people in domains that are not directly related to religion.

Religiosity, Self-Control, and the Relationship of Values and Behavior

In analyzing the direct relationships of values, religiosity, and behavior, we focused on the content of the behavior, and examined its compatibility with the motivations that underlie religiosity. Religiosity can also have a more general effect on behavior by moderating its relationship with personal values. People do not always act on their values. They may view a behavior as compatible with their values, but still do not engage in that behavior. Conversely, people may engage in a behavior even though it contrasts their values. How does religiosity affect the compatibility between values and behavior? Do religious people act on their values more or less than non-religious people? The relationship of values and behavior is moderated by two factors that are relevant to religion: the extent of social control and the extent of personal control over behavior. The lower the social control and the higher the personal control on behavior, the stronger the relationship of values and behavior.

Social control can be conceptualized in terms of "situational strength." Strong situations are social contexts that provide clear uniform expectations regarding appropriate behavior (Cooper & Withey, 2009; Mischel, 1977). When the situation is strong people act uniformly, regardless of their individual characteristics. Thus, in "strong situations", the effect of values on behavior is very limited. Values have a stronger effect on behavior in "weak situations," that do not clearly determine which specific action is the most desirable (e.g., de Kwaadsteniet, van Dijk, Wit, & de Cremer, 2006; see Roccas & Sagiv, 2010 for a review).

Religious environments engender "strong situations" with clear norms that regulate behavior. One of the core characteristics of religion is a strong community (Graham & Haidt, 2010; Ysseldyk et al., 2010). In religious communities people are raised to regulate their behavior more on the basis of social and religious expectations than on the basis of their own personal values and preferences. Consequently, among religious people, personal values are likely to have little effect on behaviors for which there are strong religious prescriptions. In contrast, among non-religious people such behaviors are likely to be affected by personal values. Consider, for example, the case of alcohol consumption among Muslims. Islam strictly proscribes the consumption of alcohol. Thus, among religious Muslims (the lack of) alcohol consumption is guided by religious imperatives, rather than by personal values. In contrast, among non-religious individuals values may affect alcohol consumption.

Many behaviors, however, are not subjected to strong religious prescriptions. When the religious community does not provide clear guidelines for behavior, behavior of both religious and non-religious individuals is subject to personal choices that are likely to be guided by values. There are several reasons to expect that for these behaviors the relationship between values and behavior is stronger among religious than among non-religious people. Religious individuals are likely to be more motivated to behave according to their values because religion sanctifies people's goals (Tix & Frazier, 2005). Attainment of values may be perceived by religious individuals as meritorious and even a moral obligation. In addition, religiosity is associated with higher self-control (e.g., Laird, Marks, & Marrero, 2011; Longshore, Chang, Hsieh, & Messina, 2004; for recent reviews see Geyer & Baumeister, 2005; McCullough & Willoughby, 2009). Often behaving according to one's values entails some measure of self-control: Value congruent behavior may be unpleasant and costly, and it might necessitate forgoing more tempting courses of action. For behaviors that necessitate self-control, religious people are more likely than non-religious to adhere to their values. In this context, the self-regulation habitual to religious people will ensure that they will not yield to temptations, and will act on their values.

In sum, we suggest that religiosity can have opposing effects on the extent to which values guide behavior. For behaviors that are strongly regulated by religion, religious people will act according to religious teaching, while non-religious people may be guided by their personal values. For behaviors that are not regulated by religion, both religious and non-religious will be guided by their values, but religious people are more likely to have the self-control needed to act on their values.

Values, Religiosity, and Multiple Identities

Religiosity does not exist in a social vacuum: People are simultaneously members of many groups and hold multiple social identities. Social identities consist of a variety of ascribed and achieved groups, such as one's national and ethnic group, one's profession and family. Groups facilitate the expression of certain values and hinder the expression of other values. For example, being a part of a mountain-climbing team enables expression and attainment of stimulation values but it hinders the attainment of security values. People tend to identify with groups that are compatible with their values (Roccas, Schwartz, & Amit, 2010). Thus, religious people are likely to choose to join and to identify with groups that allow the attainment of conservation values.

The nation is a prominent example of a group that is compatible with religion. Like religiosity, identification with the nation helps attaining conservation values and limits the attainment of openness to change values (Roccas et al., 2010). Consistently, the correlations of values with identification with the nation are very similar to those with religiosity. Like religiosity, identification with the nation is positively correlated with conservation values and negatively with openness to change values. Although correlations of benevolence and universalism with national identity are weak, they too are similar to the pattern found with religiosity: positive with benevolence and negative with universalism (Roccas et al., 2010). Not surprisingly, a religious identity is highly compatible with a national identity (e.g., Storm, 2011).

The occupational realm is one of the most important sources of social identities. How do people integrate between their religious and occupational identity? So far, research on religiosity and occupational choice is scarce, but it indicates that values can help understanding differences between the occupational choices of religious and non-religious people. Even in the limited realm of higher education, there are differences in religiosity among professors in different disciplines. For example, in a survey of US college and university professors, more than 63% of accounting professors reported that they have no doubt that God exists, while in psychology the percentage is much smaller (Gross & Simmons, 2009). This is compatible with studies examining the value preferences of people from different professions. Professions related to finance are associated with an emphasis on conservation values, while professions related to psychology are associated with a relatively high emphasis on self-direction values (Knafo & Sagiv, 2004). Sometimes, people are simultaneously members in groups that are perceived as holding different or even contrasting values. Consider, for example, the case of a religious physician. The two identities enable the attainment of benevolence values but they can differ with regards to other values. Thus, religious physicians can face strong conflicts between the two identities, especially in specializations that prescribe procedures that strongly contrast some religious prescriptions, such as providing access to birth contraceptives or to terminating pregnancies.

The potential value conflict between multiple identities necessitates the adoption of identity management strategies. All people may confront value driven conflicts between multiple identities; these conflicts are not unique to religion. However, value conflict between one's multiple identities may pose a special challenge for religious individuals, because of the high value they place on adherence to social expectations. In recent years, a growing body of research focuses on the different strategies individuals use to handle their multiple identities (Hong, Morris, Chiu, & Benet-Martinez, 2000; Miller, Brewer, & Arbuckle, 2009; Roccas & Brewer, 2002; Tadmor, Tetlock, & Peng, 2009). People manage multiple identities in a variety of ways that differ in their complexity (Roccas & Brewer, 2002; see Geller, Micco, Silver, Kolodner, & Bernhardt, 2009 for a detailed description of identity management strategies of genetic service providers who are religious). A religious doctor can form an exclusive and simple social identity in which there is a single ingroup identification based on the dominance of one identity over the other. She can identify primarily with her religion, and her actions, even in the professional domain, will be mainly guided by the religious values. Conversely, she can submit the religious identity to the professional identity, and be guided mainly by the values derived from the professional identity.

The conflict can also be managed by identifying with the intersection between the two identities. In this case, the primary ingroup includes only doctors that are also religious, in which case, she may focus on the properties that are shared by the two intersected identities. Her actions are guided by the values that are compatible with both the religious and professional identities. Both solutions create simple identities in the sense that one identifies with a single group: In the "dominance" example one identity is of supreme importance relatively to the other identity, and in the "intersection" example only the intersection between the two identities forms a meaningful ingroup.

Conversely, one can acknowledge and accept the distinctive aspects of each group and form an inclusive and complex social identity. One can compartmentalize the two identities by expressing the religious worldview only in the private sphere and adopting a secular–professional worldview at work. Some values could be attained and expressed in the professional setting while others could be attained and expressed in the religious identity. The most complex solution is represented when divergent group memberships are simultaneously recognized and included in their most inclusive form. Such social identity merges the two identities. In the case of a physician, she can draw on her faith to help coping with the difficult challenges of her profession in a way that is consistent with the tenets of the medical profession.

Values predict how people manage their multiple identities: The higher the importance of conservation values the simpler is the representation of one's identity (Roccas & Brewer, 2002). Thus, it is likely that religiosity will lead to the adoption of the simple identity management strategies in which the multiple identities are represented as a single group, either the "dominance" or "intersection" solution.

Conclusions

In this chapter, we have sought to tie together the psychology of religiosity and values. One's religious identity and one's values are closely intertwined, and religiosity and values are likely to affect each other. The close relationships between religiosity and values are apparent in the systematic pattern of correlations found between them across religious groups and cultures. Religiosity correlates positively with the importance attributed to values that emphasize self-restriction, order, and resistance to change, and correlates negatively with values that emphasize independence and readiness for new experience.

Integrating insights from research on values and research on religiosity contributes to achieving a better understanding of the motivational underpinnings of the behavioral differences between religious and non-religious people. They also lead us to expect differences between religious and non-religious individuals in the extent to which personal values guide behavior. Religious people are less likely than non-religious people to be guided by their personal values in pursuing behaviors that are strongly regulated by religion. They are more likely than non-religious people to be guided by their values in pursuing behaviors that are not regulated by religion and necessitate self-control.

Finally, values help achieving a better understanding of the compatibilities and conflicts between multiple identities. A religious identity is compatible with identities that allow and encourage the pursuit of conservation values, such as the national identity, but it may contrast with identities that emphasize autonomy and hedonism.

So far research on values and religiosity is based on cross-sectional surveys in which values and religiosity were observed at the same time. This methodology limits the type of questions that can be answered. For example, it does not allow for investigating the values associated with changes in religiosity (either from non-religious to religious or from religious to non-religious) and with conversion to a different religious denomination. Such profound changes in worldviews and belief system require openness to change, compatible with self-direction values. However, self-direction values contrast with religiosity leading to a paradoxical situation in which self-direction values are both compatible with religious conversion and incompatible with it.

Another important limitation of current studies is their cultural focus: Most of the studies that examined the relationships between values and religiosity were conducted in Western, individualistic cultures. These cultures endorse autonomy of thought and action and it is likely that the decision to be religious is driven more by personal values than by cultural norms. In contrast, it is possible that in collectivistic cultures, in which norms prescribe extensive domains of social behavior, the decision to be religious is driven more by cultural norms than by personal values. Thus, we expect that the relationship of values and religiosity may be higher in individualistic than in collectivistic cultures.

In conclusion, so far research on values and religiosity has focused on identifying the value difference between religious and non-religious and has successfully mapped these differences showing consistency across studies, cultural groups, and measures of religiosity. Research on the processes that lead to these differences and on their implications is much scarcer. We think that the robust findings on the relationship of values and religiosity made the field ready to broaden the scope of research of values and religiosity.

Note

1. In some samples, multiple measures of religiosity were used (e.g., religiousness and church attendance in Pepper et al., 2010 research). In this case, all measures (overall 28) were included in the analysis (the samples included in this analysis are indicated by * in the reference list).

References

Adams, R. B., Licht, A. N., & Sagiv, L. (2011). Shareholders and stakeholders: How do directors decide? *Strategic Management Journal, 32,* 1331–1355.

Bardi, A., & Schwartz, S. H. (2003). Values and behavior: Strength and structure of relations. *Personality and Social Psychology Bulletin, 29,* 1207–1220.

Bilsky, W., & Peters, M. (1999). Estructura de los valores y la religiosidad: Una investigacion comparada realizada en Mexico. *Revista Mexicana de Psicologia, 16,* 77–88.

*Burris, C. T., & Tarpley, W. R. (1998). Religion as being: Preliminary validation of the Immanence scale. *Journal of Research in Personality, 32,* 55–79.

Cheung, C., & Yeung, J. W. (2011). Meta-analysis of relationships between religiosity and constructive and destructive behaviors among adolescents. *Children and Youth Services Review, 33,* 376–385.

Cooper, W. H., & Withey, M. J. (2009). The strong situation hypothesis. *Personality and Social Psychology Review, 13*, 62–72.

De Dreu, C. K. W., & Boles, T. (1998). Share and share alike or winner take all?: The influence of social value orientation upon choice and recall of negotiation heuristics. *Organizational Behavior and Human Decision Processes, 76*, 253–267.

de Kwaadsteniet, E. W., van Dijk, E., Wit, A. P., & de Cremer, D. (2006). Social dilemmas as strong versus weak situations: Social value orientations and tacit coordination under resource size uncertainty. *Journal of Experimental Social Psychology, 42*, 509–516.

*Devos, T., Spini, D., & Schwartz, S. H. (2002). Conflicts among human values and trust in institutions. *British Journal of Social Psychology, 41*, 481–494.

*Dollinger, S. J. (2001). Religious identity: An autophotographic study. *International Journal for the Psychology of Religion, 11*, 71–92.

Dollinger, S. J., Burke, P. A., & Gump, N. W. (2007). Creativity and values. *Creativity Research Journal, 19*, 91–103.

Dudley, R. L., & Dudley, M. G. (1986). Transmission of religious values from parents to adolescents. *Review of Religious Research, 28*, 3–15.

Edgell, P., Gerteis, J., & Hartmann, D. (2006). Atheists as "Other": Moral boundaries and cultural membership in American society. *American Sociological Review, 71*, 211–234.

Feather, N. T. (1988). Values, valences, and course enrollment: Testing the role of personal values within an expectancy-valence framework. *Journal of Educational Psychology, 80*, 381–391.

Feather, N. T. (1995). Values, valences, and choice: The influence of values on the perceived attractiveness and choice of alternatives. *Journal of Personality and Social Psychology, 68*, 1135–1151.

Feather, N. T., Norman, M. A., & Worsley, A. (1998). Values and valences: Variables relating to the attractiveness and choice of food in different contexts. *Journal of Applied Social Psychology, 28*, 639–656.

Feather, N. T., Woodyatt, L., & McKee, I. R. (2012). Predicting support for social action: How values, justice-related variables, discrete emotions, and outcome expectations influence support for the Stolen Generations. *Motivation and Emotion, 36*, 516–528.

*Fontaine, J. R. J., Duriez, B., Luyten, P., Corveleyn, J., & Hutsebaut, D. (2005). Consequences of a multi-dimensional approach to religion for the relationship between religiosity and value priorities. *International Journal for the Psychology of Religion, 15*, 123–143.

Fontaine, J. R. J., Duriez, B., Luyten, P., & Hutsebaut, D. (2003). The internal structure of the Post-Critical Belief scale. *Personality and Individual Differences, 35*, 501–518.

Fontaine, J. R. J., Luyten, P., & Corveleyn, J. (2000). Tell me what you believe and I'll tell you what you want. Empirical evidence for discriminating value patterns of five types of religiosity. *International Journal for the Psychology of Religion, 10*, 65–84.

Furrow, J. L., King, P. E., & White, K. (2004). Religion and positive youth development: Identity, meaning, and prosocial concerns. *Applied Developmental Science, 8*, 17–26.

Gandal, N., Roccas, S., Sagiv, L., & Wrzesniewski, A. (2005). Personal value priorities of economists. *Human Relations, 58*, 1227–1252.

Gaunt, R. (2005). The role of value priorities in paternal and maternal involvement in child care. *Journal of Marriage and Family, 67*, 643–655.

Geller, G., Micco, E., Silver, R. J., Kolodner, K., & Bernhardt, B. A. (2009). The role and impact of personal faith and religion among genetic service providers. *American Journal of Medical Genetics Part C – Seminars in Medical Genetics, 151C*, 31–40.

Gervais, W. M. (2011). Finding the faithless: Perceived atheist prevalence reduces anti-atheist prejudice. *Personality and Social Psychology Bulletin, 37*, 543–556.

Gervais, W. M., Shariff, A. F., & Norenzayan, A. (2011). Do you believe in atheists? Distrust is central to anti-atheist prejudice. *Journal of Personality and Social Psychology, 101*, 1189–1206.

Geyer, A. L., & Baumeister, R. F. (2005). Religion, morality, and self-control: Values, virtues, and vices. In R. F. Paloutzian & C. L. Park (Eds.), *Handbook of the psychology of religion and spirituality* (pp. 412–432). New York: Guilford.

Graham, J., & Haidt, J. (2010). Beyond beliefs: Religions bind individuals into moral communities. *Personality and Social Psychology Review, 14*, 140–150.

Gross, N., & Simmons, S. (2009). The religiosity of American college and university professors. *Sociology of Religion, 70*, 101–129.

Hitlin, S. (2006). Parental influences on children's values and aspirations: Bridging two theories of social class and socialization. *Sociological Perspectives, 49*, 25–46.

Hitlin, S., & Piliavin, J. A. (2004). Values: Reviving a dormant concept. *Annual Review of Sociology, 30*, 359–393.

Hogg, M. A., Adelman, J. R., & Blagg, R. D. (2010). Religion in the face of uncertainty: Uncertainty-identity theory of religiousness and religious extremism. *Personality and Social Psychology Review, 14*, 72–83.

Hong, Y., Morris, M., Chiu, C, & Benet-Martinez, V. (2000). Multicultural minds: A dynamic constructivist approach to culture and cognition. *American Psychologist, 55*, 709–720.

Kasof, J., Chen, C., Himsel, A., & Greenberger, E. (2007). Values and creativity. *Creativity Research Journal, 19*, 105–122.

Kerestes, M., Youniss, J., & Metz, E. (2004). Longitudinal patterns of religious perspective and civic integration. *Applied Developmental Science, 8*, 39–46.

Kim, J., McCullough, M., & Cicchetti, D. (2009). Parents' and children's religiosity and child behavioral adjustment among maltreated and nonmaltreated children. *Journal of Child and Family Studies, 18*, 594–605.

Kluckhohn, C. (1951). Value and value orientations in the theory of action: An exploration in definition and classification. In T. Parsons & E. Shils (Eds.), *Toward a general theory of action* (pp. 388–433). Cambridge, MA: Harvard University Press.

Knafo, A. (2003). Contexts, relationship quality, and family value socialization: The case of parent-school ideological fit in Israel. *Personal Relationships, 10*, 371–388.

Knafo, A., Daniel, E., Gabay, S., Zilber, R., & Shir, R. (2012). Religion and the intergenerational continuity of values. In G. Trommsdorff & X. Chen (Eds.), *Values, religion, and culture in adolescent development* (pp. 370–390). New York: Cambridge University Press.

Knafo, A., & Sagiv, L. (2004). Values and work environment: Mapping 32 occupations. *European Journal of Psychology of Education, 19*, 255–273.

Kusdil, M. E., & Kagitcibasi, C. (2000). Tuerk oegretmenlerin deger yoenelimleri ve Schwartz deger kurami [Value orientations of Turkish teachers and Schwartz's theory of values]. *Turk Psikoloji Dergisi, 15*, 59–80.

Laird, R. D., Marks, L. D., & Marrero, M. D. (2011). Religiosity, self-control, and antisocial behavior: Religiosity as a promotive and protective factor. *Journal of Applied Developmental Psychology, 32*, 78–85.

Landor, A., Simons, L. G., Simons, R. L., Brody, G. H., & Gibbons, F. X. (2011). The role of religiosity in the relationship between parents, peers, and adolescent risky sexual behavior. *Journal of Youth and Adolescence, 40*, 296–309.

Lipponen, J., Bardi, A., & Haapamäki, J. (2008). The interaction between values and organizational identification in predicting suggestion making at work. *Journal of Occupational and Organizational Psychology, 81*, 241–248.

Longshore, D., Chang, E., Hsieh, S., & Messina, N. (2004). Self-control and social bonds: A combined social control perspective on deviance. *Crime and Delinquency, 50*, 542–564.

McCullough, M. E., & Willoughby, B.L.B. (2009). Religion, self-control, and self-regulation: Associations, explanations, and implications. *Psychological Bulletin, 135*, 69–93.

Maio, G. R. (2010). Mental representations of social values. In M. P. Zanna (Ed.), *Advances in experimental social psychology* (Vol. 42, pp. 1–43). New York: Academic Press.

Maio, G. R., Olson, J. M., Allen, L., & Bernard, M. M. (2001). Addressing discrepancies between values and behavior: The motivating effect of reasons. *Journal of Experimental Social Psychology, 37*, 104–117.

Maio, G. R., Pakizeh, A., Cheung, W.-Y., & Rees, K. (2009). Changing, priming, and acting on values: Effects via motivational relations in a circular model. *Journal of Personality and Social Psychology, 97*, 699–715.

Manlove, J., Logan, C., Moore, K. A., & Ikramullah, E. (2008). Pathways from family religiosity to adolescent sexual activity and contraceptive use. *Perspectives on Sexual and Reproductive Health, 40*, 105–117.

Miller, K. P., Brewer, M. B., & Arbuckle, N. L. (2009). Social identity complexity: Its correlates and antecedents. *Group Processes and Intergroup Relations, 12*, 79–94.

Mischel, W. (1977). The interaction of person and situation. In D. Magnusson & N. S. Endler (Eds.), *Personality at the crossroads: Current issues in interactional psychology* (pp. 333–352). Hillsdale, NJ: Lawrence Erlbaum.

Mullen, K., & Francis, L. J. (1995). Religiosity and attitudes towards drug use among Dutch school children. *Journal of Alcohol and Drug Education, 41*, 16–25.

Muñoz-García, A., & Saroglou, V. (2008). Believing literally versus symbolically: Values and personality correlates among Spanish students. *Journal of Beliefs and Values, 29*, 233–241.

*Pepper, M., Jackson, T., & Uzzell, D. (2010). A study of multidimensional religion constructs and values in the United Kingdom. *Journal for the Social Scientific Study of Religion, 49*, 127–146.

Rew, L., & Wong, Y. J. (2006). A systematic review of associations among religiosity/spirituality and adolescent health attitudes and behaviors. *Journal of Adolescent Health, 38*, 433–442.

Roccas, S., & Brewer, M. (2002). Social identity complexity. *Personality and Social Psychology Review, 6*, 88–106.

Roccas, S., Klar, Y., & Liviatan, I. (2004). Defensive cognitions, group identification and personal values as predictors of collective guilt among Jewish-Israelis. In N. R. Branscombe & B. Doosje (Eds.), *Collective guilt: International perspectives* (pp. 130–147). New York: Cambridge University Press.

Roccas, S., & Sagiv, L. (2010). Personal values and behavior: Taking the cultural context into account. *Social and Personality Psychology Compass, 4*, 30–41.

*Roccas, S., Sagiv, L., Schwartz, S. H., & Knafo, A. (2002). The Big Five personality factors and personal values. *Personality and Social Psychology Bulletin, 28*, 789–801.

*Roccas, S., & Schwartz, S. H. (1997). Church-state relations and the association of religiosity with values: A study of Catholics in six countries. *Cross-Cultural Research, 31*, 356–375.

Roccas, S., Schwartz, S. H., & Amit, A. (2010). Personal value priorities and national identification. *Political Psychology, 31*, 393–419.

Rohan, M. J. (2000). A rose by any name? The values construct. *Personality and Social Psychology Review, 4*, 255–277.

Rokeach, M. (1973). *The nature of human values*. New York: Free Press.

Sagiv, L., & Schwartz, S. H. (1995). Value priorities and readiness for out-group social contact. *Journal of Personality and Social Psychology, 69*, 437–448.

Sagiv, L., & Schwartz, S. H. (2004). Values, intelligence and client behavior in career counseling: A field study. *European Journal of Psychology of Education, 19*, 237–254.

Sagiv, L., Sverdlik, N., & Schwarz, N. (2011). To compete or to cooperate? Values' impact on perception and action in social dilemma games. *European Journal of Social Psychology, 41*, 64–77.

Saroglou, V., Delpierre, V., & Dernelle, R. (2004). Values and religiosity: A meta-analysis of studies using Schwartz's model. *Personality and Individual Differences, 37*, 721–734.

*Saroglou, V., & Dupuis, J. (2006). Being Buddhist in Western Europe: Cognitive needs, prosocial character, and values. *International Journal for the Psychology of Religion, 16*, 163–179.

*Saroglou, V., & Galand, P. (2004). Identities, values, and religion: A study among Muslim, other immigrant, and native Belgian young adults after the 9/11 attacks. *Identity: An International Journal of Theory and Research, 4*, 97–132.

*Saroglou, V., & Hanique, B. (2006). Jewish identity, values, and religion in a globalized world: A study of late adolescents. *Identity: An International Journal of Theory and Research, 6*, 231–249.

*Saroglou, V., & Muñoz-García, A. (2008). Individual differences in religion and spirituality: An issue of personality traits and/or values. *Journal for the Scientific Study of Religion, 47*, 83–101.

Saroglou, V., Pichon, I., Trompette, L., Verschueren, M., & Dernelle, R. (2005). Prosocial behavior and religion: New evidence based on projective measures and peer ratings. *Journal for the Scientific Study of Religion, 44*, 323–348.

Sattler, D. N., & Kerr, N. L. (1991). Might versus morality explored: Motivational and cognitive bases for social motives. *Journal of Personality and Social Psychology, 60*, 756–765.

Schneider, B. (1987). The people make the place. *Personnel Psychology, 40*, 437–454.

Schneider, B. Goldstein, H. W., & Smith, D. B. (1995). The ASA framework: An update. *Personnel Psychology, 48*, 747–773.

Schwartz, S. H. (1992). Universals in the content and structure of values: Theoretical advances and empirical tests in 20 countries. In M. P. Zanna (Ed.), *Advances in experimental social psychology* (Vol. 25, pp. 1–65). New York: Academic Press.

Schwartz, S. H. (2012). Universal and culture-specific functions of adolescent values and religion. In G. Trommsdorff & X. Chen (Eds.), *Values, religion, and culture in adolescent development* (pp. 97–122). New York: Cambridge University Press.

*Schwartz, S. H., & Huismans, S. (1995). Value priorities and religiosity in four western religions. *Social Psychology Quarterly, 58*, 88–107.

Schwartz, S. H., Melech, G., Lehmann, A., Burgess, S., Harris, M., & Owens, V. (2001). Extending the cross-cultural validity of the theory of basic human values with a different method of measurement. *Journal of Cross-Cultural Psychology, 32*, 519–542.

Schwartz, S. H., Sagiv, L., & Bochnke, K. (2000). Worries and values. *Journal of Personality, 68*, 309–346.

Sousa, C. M. P., & Coelho, F. (2011). From personal values to creativity: Evidence from frontline service employees. *European Journal of Marketing, 45*, 1029–1050.

Storm, I. (2011). "Christian nations"? Ethnic Christianity and anti-immigration attitudes in four Western European countries. *Nordic Journal of Religion and Society, 24*, 75–96.

Tadmor, C. T., Tetlock, P. E., & Peng, K. (2009). Acculturation strategies and integrative complexity: The cognitive implications of biculturalism. *Journal of Cross-Cultural Psychology, 40*, 105–139.

Tix, A. P., & Frazier, P. A. (2005). Mediation and moderation of the relationship between intrinsic religiousness and mental health. *Personality and Social Psychology Bulletin, 31*, 295–306.

Trusty, J., & Watts, R. E. (1999). Relationship of high school seniors' religious perceptions and behavior to education, career, and leisure variables. *Counseling and Values, 44*, 30–40.

Udell, W., Donenberg, G., & Emerson, E. (2011). Parents matter in HIV-risk among probation youth. *Journal of Family Psychology, 25*, 785–789.

Van Lange, P. A. M., & Liebrand, W. B. G. (1989). On perceiving morality and potency: Social values and the effects of person perception in a give-some dilemma. *European Journal of Personality, 3*, 209–225.

Wulff, D. M. (1991). *Psychology of religion: Classic and contemporary views.* New York: Wiley.

Wulff, D. M. (1997). *Psychology of religion: Classic and contemporary* (2nd ed.) New York: Wiley.

Ysseldyk, R., Matheson, K., & Anisman, H. (2010). Religiosity as identity: Toward an understanding of religion from a social identity perspective. *Personality and Social Psychology Review, 14*, 60–71.

Zuckerman, P. (2009). Atheism, secularity, and well-being: How the findings of social science counter negative stereotypes and assumptions. *Sociology Compass, 3*, 949–971.

10 Religion, Sexuality, and Family

Yexin Jessica Li and Adam B. Cohen

Most religions have much to say about sexuality, marriage, and family. For example, Biblical teachings contain several such themes—*sexual morality* (Colossians 3:5: "Put to death, therefore, whatever belongs to your earthly nature: sexual immorality, impurity, lust, evil desires"), *faithfulness to one's partner* (Hebrews 13:4: "Give honor to marriage, and remain faithful to one another in marriage. God will surely judge people who are immoral and those who commit adultery"), and *propagation* (Genesis 1:28: "Be fruitful and increase in number and fill the earth"). Over the last decade, much research has been done to examine whether and why religion leads to certain sexual attitudes and behaviors. Likewise, there is a growing literature on how religion influences marriage and childrearing.

In the current chapter, we first review literature on these topics. Then we present a new direction, informed by an evolutionary approach, for the study of religion, sexuality, and family. We contend that an evolutionary approach to religion and sexuality can help to answer some basic questions, such as why the links between religiosity and attitudes about sexuality are so strong and so common across cultural contexts.

Religion and Sexuality

Sexual Attitudes

Religious beliefs and behaviors have profound implications for a wide range of sexual attitudes. Most research has found a positive relationship between religiosity and sexual conservativeness. For example, even after controlling for important demographic variables such as age, gender, and ethnicity, religiosity was significantly related to negative attitudes toward premarital sexual intercourse (Pluhar, Frongillo, Stycos, & Dempster-McClain, 1998). Specifically, the authors found that religious attendance was correlated with more conservative attitudes toward premarital sex. Similarly, Lefkowitz, Gillen, Shearer, and

Boone (2004) found a positive correlation between conservative sexual attitudes and frequency of religious service attendance in the previous year. Religious attendance is also significantly positively correlated with negative views toward oral and anal sex (Davidson, Moore, & Ullstrup, 2004).

This relationship also appears to hold up cross-culturally. Schmitt (2002) found, across 52 cultures, a positive correlation between self-reported religiosity and self-described sexual restraint among both men ($n = 6982$; $r = .22$) and women ($n = 9763$; $r = .25$). The relation between religiosity and sexually restricted attitudes may be even stronger for older adults than adolescents. Le Gall, Mullet, and Shafighi (2002) looked at a sample of 800 French adults aged 18 to 87 and found that religious older adults were much less sexually permissive than religious younger adults, even after controlling for education level. Thus, the general finding that religiosity is associated with negative attitudes toward sexual permissiveness appears to be significant and robust.

There is also a relation between religious fundamentalism (the conviction that one's religion is uniquely and literally true; Altemeyer & Hunsberger, 1992) and sexual attitudes. For example, fundamentalism is positively correlated with endorsements of traditional feminine/masculine roles in female college students (Bang, Hall, Anderson, & Willingham, 2005). The authors claimed that fundamentalism is a stronger predictor of gender role expectations than are other kinds of religious commitment.

Recently, Lippa (2009) conducted a cross-cultural analysis of the effect of religion on gender differences in sex drive and sociosexuality (preferences for unrestricted sex versus restricted sex, which is to say sex without commitment versus sex only in the context of a committed relationship; Gangestad & Simpson, 2000). There were five main religious groupings in the 53 nations that Lippa studied: Catholic, Eastern Orthodox, Muslim, Protestant, and mixed Christian. Results revealed that Protestant and mixed Christian nations had the smallest gender differences in sociosexuality, while Eastern Orthodox and Moslem nations had the largest. One potential explanation for this is that the last two promote more conservative gender ideologies and social structures.

The relation between religiosity and sexual attitudes may depend on specific aspects of religiosity. For example, the positive correlation between religiosity and restricted sexual attitudes described earlier seems to be true more so for people who are intrinsically religious, while those who are more extrinsically religious are actually more likely to be sexually *unrestricted* (i.e., exhibiting increased sociosexuality and mate poaching, and decreased sexual restraint and relationship exclusivity) (Haerich, 1992; Rowatt & Schmitt, 2003).

Sexual Behaviors

Religiosity predicts not just sexual attitudes, but sexual behaviors. In general, religiosity is negatively correlated with sexually permissive behaviors. This may be unsurprising given the fact that celibacy or sexual restraint, in different forms and priesthood hierarchy levels, is valued across different religions. For instance, mandatory clerical celibacy in the Catholic Church has "traditionally enhanced institutional authority by investing a male priesthood with an aura of superior virtue and spiritual power" (Walker, 2004, p. 235). By extension, sexual restraint in nonclerical members is seen as spritual and righteous.

Much research has looked at the relation between religion and timing of sexual behaviors or coital delay. Rostosky, Wilcox, Wright, and Randall (2004) conducted a literature review on the causal effects of religion on sexual behaviors. After examining 10 peer-reviewed longitudinal studies, the authors concluded that religiosity delays the sexual behavior of adolescent females (but not necessarily adolescent males). Hardy and Raffaelli (2003) found a negative relation between religiosity and coital debut among 15 and 16 year olds. This result held for both males and females, and regardless of participant race. Jones, Darroch, and Singh (2005) used the 1995 National Survey of Family Growth (NSFG), a US nationally representative, cross-sectional sample of women aged 15–44 years, to look at the relation between religious experience and timing of first intercourse. They found that frequent attendance at religious services at age 14 has a strong delaying effect on the timing of first intercourse. Most recently, Hull, Hennessy, Bleakley, Fishbein, and Jordan (2011) found that religiosity delays onset of coitus among a longitudinal sample of 14–16 year old virgins.

It is important to note that, however, as Cahn and Carbone (2010) reviewed, greater religiousness does delay sexual activity, but even the most religious tend not to wait until marriage. In addition, Zaleski and Schiaffino (2000) argue that, while religiosity does delay sexual activity, it may not actually lead to safer sex practices. Indeed, the authors found that although religiosity is associated with less sexual activity, it is also associated with less condom use during sexual activity in first-year college students. Thus, religious students who are sexually active may actually be putting themselves at more risk when it comes to contracting sexually transmitted diseases and unwanted pregnancies than their atheist counterparts.

Several studies have investigated mechanisms by which religiosity delays sexual behavior in adolescents. For example, Hull et al. (2011) found that the effect of religiosity on delay of sexual intercourse is mediated by beliefs about the consequences of engaging in sex (e.g., the belief that having sex will result in sexually transmitted diseases or AIDS, or hurt one's relationship). In addition, Miller and Gur (2002) found a positive relation between religiosity (as measured by personal devotion and frequency of attendance of religious events) and perceived risk of sexual intercourse. Specifically, adolescent girls (with a mean age of 15.97 years) who were more religious were more likely to believe that they would contract HIV or become pregnant if they had sex. Similarly, Meier (2003) found that attitudes toward sex (i.e., how the adolescent would feel about having sexual intercourse at this time in his or her life) mediated the protective effects of religiosity on sexual behavior. In addition, Rostosky, Regnerus, and Wright (2003) used longitudinal data from 3691 adolescents to show that anticipation of negative emotions after coital debut reduced its likelihood. Instead of studying adolescents, Barkan (2006) used a sample of never-married adults. His findings show that religiosity reduces number of sexual partners, and that this relationship is partially mediated by moral disapproval of premarital sex. These data suggest that moral attitudes and beliefs about disease transmission are important mediators of the relationship between religiosity and sexual behavior.

Recently, there has been evidence showing greater perception of sexuality as sanctified (defined as an aspect of life having divine character and significance) predicts a host of positive sexually relevant traits, including sexual satisfaction and intimacy (Hernandez, Mahoney, & Pargament, 2011). The authors showed that this effect held even after controlling for general levels of religiosity and other demographic variables.

However, religiosity is not always positively correlated with chastity. Indeed, some theories of religion say that one benefit of being a religious leader is the ability to attract many mates. Buss (2002), for example, says that "religious leaders, typically men, not infrequently use their power, like many men in secular positions of power, to gain preferential sexual access to young, attractive, fertile women" (p. 202). Buss notes that there are many examples of polygamy in the Bible (King David, Solomon, etc.) From an evolutionary perspective (to which we will return later in the chapter), men are more likely to be in, and to take advantage of, positions of power (e.g., shamans, priests, rabbis) because women evolved to prefer high status males as mates (Buss, 2003). This creates what one may call a "religious hypocrisy" whereby religious leaders preach chastity and devotion to one's spouse and to their followers, yet engage in questionable sexual behaviors themselves.

Sexual Orientation

Religion often correlates with attitudes toward homosexuality and same-sex unions. Members of conservative religious denominations, frequent religious attenders, biblical literalists, and those with active or angry images of God tend to be the most condemning of homosexual behavior (Finlay & Walther, 2003; Olson, Cadge, & Harrison, 2006; Rowatt, LaBouff, Johnson, Forese, & Tsang, 2009). Along the same lines, religiously active individuals are less likely to support same-sex marriage and unions than people who are not active in their religion (Brumbaugh, Sanchez, Nock, & Wright, 2008; Haider-Markel & Joslyn, 2008; Olson, Cadge, & Harrison, 2006; Whitehead, 2010).

Whitley (2009) conducted a meta-analysis on 64 studies to examine how different forms of religiosity are associated with attitudes toward gay men and lesbians. He found that fundamentalism, frequency of attendance at religious services, endorsement of Christian orthodoxy, self-ratings of religiosity, and intrinsic religiosity were correlated with negative attitudes toward gay men and lesbians. Whitley hypothesized that religiosity would be related to prejudices that religions permit (e.g., those toward homosexuals) but not to those prejudices that religions proscribe (e.g., those toward racial/ethnic groups). He found that, indeed, frequency of attendance at religious services, endorsement of Christian orthodoxy, self-ratings of religiosity, quest orientation, and intrinsic religiosity all had small positive relationships with racial/ethnic tolerance.

Part of the reason religiosity is associated with negative attitudes toward homosexuality may be because religious individuals are more likely to believe that sexual orientation is a lifestyle choice rather than a genetically determined trait (Whitehead, 2010). Indeed, previous research shows that people who believe that homosexuality is a choice (non-biological) are less likely to endorse same-sex unions and gay rights (Herek & Capitanio, 1995). However, attributions of homosexuality are not enough to fully explain the link between religiosity and homosexual attitudes. Whitehead (2010) found that "religious behavior and belief continued to significantly predict negative attitudes toward same-sex marriage despite the presence of the attribution variable" (p. 71). Thus, religious prejudices against people with different sexual orientations or gender identities may be more complex than being just based on attributions for sexual orientations.

Another important factor to consider when studying the relationship between religiosity and attitudes toward homosexuality is disgust toward same-sex couples. Research suggests that feelings of disgust toward homosexual sexual activity are stronger among conservatives than liberals (Haidt & Hersh, 2001), and among highly religious individuals than less religious individuals (Johnson, Brems, & Alford-Keating, 1997; Rozin, Lowery, Imada, & Haidt, 1999). Olatunji (2008) found a complex relationship between disgust, religiosity, sexual attitudes, and attitudes toward gay and lesbian people. Specifically, he found that feelings of disgust lead to fear of sin, which then leads to conservative sexual attitudes and, finally, negative attitudes toward gay and lesbian people.

Thus, although there may be many possible reasons why highly religious people have negative attitudes toward gay and lesbian people, some of the factors that have been identified are: attribution of sexual orientation (e.g., whether homosexuality is a choice or genetically determined), fear of sin, and conservative sexual attitudes.

Religion and Family

Marriage

Research shows that religion tends to be associated with higher levels of marriage satisfaction and lower rates of divorce (Cahn & Carbone, 2010; Chatters & Taylor, 2005; Dollahite, Marks, & Goodman, 2004; Robinson, 1994). For example, Mahoney, Pargament, Tarakeshwar, and Swank (2001) conducted a meta-analysis on religion and marriage and found that greater religiousness was associated with marital functioning and slightly decreased the risk of divorce. Cutrona, Russell, Burzette, Wesner, and Bryant (2011) conducted a longitudinal study of African American midlife couples and found a positive relationship between religiosity and relationship stability through religion's associations with marriage, biological family status, and women's relationship quality. Recent longitudinal studies also find that higher religious attendance is associated with decreased rates of future divorce (Brown, Orbuch, & Bauermeister, 2008; Woods & Emery, 2002). However, personal importance of religion did not lead to less divorce (Woods & Emery, 2002). This suggests that integration into a spiritual community can help prevent divorce, but it is unclear whether this is due to the community's negative perception of divorce or to increased satisfaction and commitment between the married couple.

However, the relation between religiosity and marriage satisfaction is likely more complicated than it appears at first blush. Both spouses need to be similar in religiosity to enjoy its benefits. Spouses who have different levels of religious attendance or biblical interpretations actually argue more, particularly over money and housework (Curtis & Ellison, 2002). Also, while religiousness may relate to positive marital outcomes at the individual level, the opposite seems to be true at the state level. More religious states actually show higher divorce rates (Cahn & Carbone, 2010). In addition, Sullivan (2001) conducted a longitudinal study using 172 newlyweds and found that greater religiousness of newlywed husbands actually exacerbated marital distress if they were not psychologically well-adjusted. Furthermore, people's self-reported attitudes toward divorce and commitment did not predict observations of marriage interactions or self-reported marital quality.

Part of the reason that religion could promote greater relationship satisfaction and stability, at least at the individual level, may be because more religious individuals are better able to resist sexual temptation (McCullough & Willoughby, 2009). For example, Atkins and Kessel (2008) found that attendance at religious services decreased the likelihood of infidelity. In addition, research suggests that mere reminders of religion (via priming) can lead to increased temptation resistance and less sexual infidelity (Laurin, Kay, & Fitzsimons, 2012; Wolfinger & Wilcox, 2008). While only suggestive regarding sexual fidelity, Laurin et al. (2012) experimentally found that making people think about God (relative to a control prime) leads to better behavioral self-control (e.g., eating fewer cookies), especially for those people who believe God is omniscient.

In a similar vein, Dollahite and Lambert (2007) found that religious vows and involvement fortified marital commitment to fidelity, strengthened couples' moral values, and improved spouses' relationship with God, which encouraged them to avoid actions such as infidelity, which they believed would displease God. In a rare experimental test of these ideas, Fincham, Lambert, and Beach (2010) randomly assigned couples to do one of the following for four weeks: a) pray for their partner each day, b) engage in daily positive thoughts about their partner or c) a neutral activity. They found that participants who had prayed for their partner were less likely to have cheated on their partner than participants in the other conditions, and that perception of the relationship as sacred mediated the results. This is not to say that there are no exceptions. Atkins, Baucom, and Jacobson (2001), for example, found that religious attendance may not prevent infidelity for spouses who are unhappy with their relationship in the first place. Further, people who frequently attend church but do not feel close to God are more likely to have an affair than people who do not attend church or feel close to God (Atkins & Kessel, 2008).

The effects of religion on marital stability appear to be greatest when both partners are involved in religious activities together. Indeed, joint religious activities and perceptions regarding the sanctity of marriage were associated with greater global marital adjustment, more perceived benefits from marriage, less marital conflict, more verbal collaboration, and less use of verbal aggression and stalemate to discuss disagreements for both wives and husbands (Mahoney et al., 1999). Call and Heaton (1997), too, found that couples had the lowest risk of divorce when both spouses attended church together. Similarly, Fiese and Tomcho (2001) surveyed 120 couples and showed that marital satisfaction was related to the practice of religious holiday rituals, above and beyond that of general religiosity.

Recently, research has found that spirituality can have a positive influence, distinct from religiosity's effect, on marital stability. Fincham, Ajayi, and Beach (2011) asked 487 African American couples to answer questions about their marital satisfaction, religiosity, and spirituality.

They found that husbands' spirituality was particularly important in decreasing their negative evaluations of the marriage. Wives' spirituality was somewhat important for wives' positive evaluation of the marriage. Importantly, these results held after controlling for religiosity. The authors conclude that, "at an empirical level, spirituality and religiosity operated somewhat independently despite some conceptual overlap and their perceived covariation in the general population" (p. 265). Beach et al. (2011) also found that a relationship enhancement program focused on prayer is as effective as more traditional types of program, and may actually be more efficacious for wives, particularly in terms of its immediate effects from baseline to posttest.

It is not just level of religiousness or spirituality that predicts marital success. Another key variable may be the match of the couple's religious affiliation. Jewish culture and religion may provide one interesting case study of the importance of marrying within the faith. Jews strongly endorse endogamy, and marrying non-Jews is often strongly discouraged (Cohen, Gorvine, & Gorvine, 2013)—so much so that the parents of a child who is marrying a non-Jew may tear their clothes and sit *shiva* (observing Jewish mourning rituals, as when a close relative has died; see also Geffen, 2001). The reasons for this attitude are likely many, but may partly be because Judaism is a religion of "descent" (Cohen, Hall, Koenig, & Meador, 2005; Cohen & Hill, 2007; Morris, 1997). Religious affiliation in Judaism is a matter of heredity. Indeed, members of a Jewish community are about as genetically related to each other as fourth or fifth cousins (Atzmon et al., 2010; Behar et al., 2010). In fact, Jews are least likely among Jews, Catholics, Baptists, and Mormons to change their religion because of marriage (Musick & Wilson, 1995) and they are also historically unlikely to intermarry. Nevertheless, rates of intermarriage among Jews (in the US, for example), have vastly increased (between 1900 and 1920, only 2%; between 1966 and 1972, 32%; Reiss, 1976; and in the 1980s, rates may be as high as 60%; Spilka, Hood, Hunsberger, & Gorsuch, 2003), and attitudes may change as a result. Many synagogues have relaxed rules about recognition and participation of non-Jewish spouses, and the children resulting from these unions.

Major Aspects of Family Life

Research in the area of religion and parenting suggests parents with more conservative religious ideologies are more likely to believe in and use corporal punishment (e.g., spanking) (Day, Peterson, & McCracken, 1998; Ellison, Bartkowski, & Segal, 1996). One potential explanation for this is the fundamentalist belief that the Bible is always right and holds all the answers to life's questions; thus, anyone that goes against the Bible's teachings must be punished harshly (Ellison et al., 1996). In support of this, Gershoff, Miller, and Holden (1999) found that conservative Protestant parents attributed fewer negative consequences to corporal punishment than did parents of other religious affiliations. This suggests religious conservative parents believe corporal punishment to be an effective and ethical way to discipline children.

Even if some forms of religion might be related to harsher discipline, there is evidence that religion can have positive consequences on family process and youth competence. Brody, Stoneman, and Flor (1996), for example, found greater parental religiosity to be associated with "more cohesive family relationships, lower levels of interparental conflict, and fewer externalizing and internalizing problems" as well as greater self-regulation (p. 696) in a sample of African American youths living in the rural south. Christian and Barbarin (2001) found that African American children whose parents attended church consistently had fewer behavioral problems than children whose parents attended less frequently. Carothers, Borkowski, Lefever, and Whitman (2005) found that adolescent mothers high in religious involvement had "significantly higher self-esteem and lower depression scores, exhibited less child abuse potential, and had higher occupational and educational attainment than mothers classified as low in religious involvement" (p. 263). Perhaps as a result of this, children of religiously involved mothers had fewer internalizing and externalizing problems at 10 years of age.

In addition, Gunnoe, Hetherington, and Reiss (1999) found that parental religiosity was positively related to authoritative parenting and adolescent social responsibility. Authoritative parenting is defined as "the degree to which the parent behaves toward the child in an involved, affectionate, and responsive manner while setting reasonable controls on the child's behavior" (Hetherington, Hagan, & Eisenberg, 1992). Out of the four best-known parenting styles (authoritative, permissive, authoritarian, and neglectful), authoritative parenting generally elicits the most positive outcomes in youth (Steinberg, Lamborn, Darling, Mounts, & Dornbusch, 1994)

Religion, Evolution, Mating, and Family: A New Synthesis

As discussed earlier, religious individuals and groups have had much to say in regard to mate seeking, marriage and family—dictating with whom it is acceptable to mate (e.g., prohibitions against marrying close kin; arranged marriages), for whom it is acceptable to mate (e.g., Catholic priests must remain celibate), and how the act of mating should be practiced (e.g., with the goal of producing offspring or with the goal of experiencing pleasure). It might seem most intuitive that people learn their sexual and reproductive goals from religion. Vaas (2009) noted that religious people have more children, and asserted that this is because of religious doctrine (i.e., religiousness causes fertility), citing

God's commandment in Genesis to be fruitful and multiply (though Vaas does note other reasons, as well—social and psychological factors including "family bonding, social support, better coping with stress, a more trusted mate") (p. 31).

While it is certainly likely that people learn, to some extent, their sexual morals from religion, in this section, we discuss the possibility that religion may partly serve as a mating strategy and promote the passing down of genetic material. Thus, it is also possible that religion is a consequence (in addition to a cause) of people's sexual and family goals and behaviors. This perspective has already produced some interesting empirical findings (Li, Cohen, Weeden, & Kenrick, 2010; Weeden, Cohen, & Kenrick, 2008), and is a fruitful avenue for future research (Johnson, Li, & Cohen, under review).

Surprisingly, but predictably from an evolutionary approach, recent research suggests that people adjust their religiosity to support their current mating goals. First, attitudes about mating and sexuality are particularly strong correlates of adult religious attendance, and US rates of religious attendance diminish during peak mate-finding years and then rise when people are settling down—particularly when they are raising children (Weeden et al., 2008).

Weeden and colleagues (2008) proposed the "Reproductive Religiosity Model" to better understand the links between religiosity and sexual restrictedness. Their model, which takes an evolutionary approach to understanding religion and sexuality, theorizes that "a primary function of religious groups in the contemporary United States is to support low-promiscuity, marriage-centered, heterosexual, high-fertility sexual and reproductive strategies" (p. 327). Using a sample of over 900 college students, Weeden and colleagues found that sociosexual attitudes are more strongly linked to church attendance than other moral issues, including lying, stealing, and cheating. Indeed, after controlling for reproductive variables, the relationship between church attendance and these moral issues is non-significant. Weeden and colleagues speculated that this points to the centrality of sexual moral attitudes in religion, over and above other kinds of moral attitude.

Li and colleagues (2010) found further support for Weeden et al.'s model, by showing experimentally that mating prospects can influence religiosity. Both men and women reported greater religiosity (including belief in God) when they believed they were in a competitive, unfavorable mating pool with lots of attractive same-sex competitors. People's religiosity was not different from a control condition when they believed they were in a favorable mating pool with lots of attractive opposite-sex potential partners. These data suggest a counterintuitive yet robust link between sexual strategies and religiosity, such that religiosity can actually be deployed in strategic ways to address people's mating goals.

The moral attitudes religious people endorse should also vary according to their mating motivations, which depend on factors such as gender, fertility, and sociosexual orientation, all avenues for future research on religion and sexuality. Previous research has found links between testosterone and mating in both humans and non-human animals (e.g., Roney, Mahler, & Maestripieri, 2003). A high level of testosterone is correlated with increased mate seeking and short-term mating in both males and females, but particularly males. Thus, men might be especially likely to endorse religious codes that help them obtain mates or allow for more than one mate, but restrict such sexual opportunities for others.

Other research shows that men who are highly motivated to mate are more likely to conspicuously consume to show off their resources, whereas women are more likely to present themselves as nurturing and caring (Griskevicius et al., 2007). Thus, we would expect a mating motive to lead religious men to endorse messages of prosperity and to engage in rituals aimed at demonstrating their physical prowess or abundant resources, whereas religious women are expected to engage in religiously encouraged prosocial behaviors such as caring for others.

Individual differences in sociosexual orientation could also play a role in the type of religious affiliation people choose. Sociosexual orientation measures the degree to which people prefer a few relatively long-term, committed relationships (sexually restricted) or many short-term, uncommitted relationships (sexually unrestricted) (Simpson & Gangestad, 1991). From an evolutionary perspective, it is not functional for unrestricted individuals to find mates in a market that looks down on promiscuity and sex before marriage. Thus, people who are sexually unrestricted should be more likely to participate in religious groups that have less stringent rules regarding sex, or to stop identifying with being religious at all.

Finally, keeping mates poses a different set of challenges than acquiring mates. This "mate-retention" goal is theorized to shape moral and religious codes regarding the number of mates and/or divorce. Mate retention, unlike mate acquisition, involves maintaining the moral bond with one's partner. Research suggests people have strategies in place for preventing significant others from cheating. For instance, men whose partners are at the fertile phase of the menstrual cycle show robust mate-guarding behaviors (Haselton & Gangestad, 2006). They would be expected to endorse harsh punishments for adultery. Women with high mate value could potentially obtain resources for themselves and their offspring via short-term mating with high-status men. However, women are not as likely to gain genetic benefits by mating with multiple men. Thus women, more so than men, would be expected to use religion and the marriage dyad to enforce marital commitment.

Conclusion

There is much important psychological research in the area of religion, sexuality, and family. Most of the research in this area shows that religiosity is positively correlated with sexually conservative attitudes and behaviors. At the same time, religiosity leads to greater marriage satisfaction and lower divorce rates. Some research has been done to look at why such correlations exist, but almost all of the proposed mechanisms tend to be proximate explanations (e.g., perceived likelihood of getting a sexually transmitted disease, greater ability to control temptation). The exception is work done by Weeden, Cohen, Li, Kenrick and their colleagues, who propose an evolutionary approach to studying the link between religion and sexuality. They argue that religion serves an adaptive purpose—to support low-promiscuity, marriage-centered, heterosexual, high-fertility sexual and reproductive strategies. Individuals who use this reproductive strategy can gain genetic benefits from parenting multiple offspring and ward off threats from potential competitors.

The new perspective proposed here may be relevant for scholars in many disciplines, such as health psychologists, social workers, policy-makers, religious studies scholars, and cultural psychologists. In addition, this perspective can help researchers address important social issues such as condom usage, birth control, the spread of HIV and other sexually transmitted diseases, as well as hotly contested global and public policy matters such as the stoning of adulterers and same sex unions. For example, the theory that males value short-term mating opportunities more than women might lead to the hypothesis that men are more likely than women to take advantage of such opportunities, even if they do not have condoms or other forms of birth control on hand. This suggests that male-specific interventions designed to promote safe sex should be designed.

Along these same lines, the fundamental motivation of mate retention could lead to the endorsement of harsh punishments for adulterers. In societies where men have much of the social and economic power, this may translate into sanctions for female genital mutilation or capital punishment for promiscuous women. Thus, an evolutionary perspective can help us better understand why certain religious beliefs, practices, and regulations originated and why they are sometimes so resistant to change even in contemporary cultures.

References

Altemeyer, B., & Hunsberger, B. (1992). Authoritarianism, religious fundamentalism, quest and prejudice. *International Journal for the Psychology of Religion, 2*, 113–133.

Atkins, D. C., Baucom, D. H., & Jacobson, N. S. (2001). Understanding infidelity: Correlates in a national random sample. *Journal of Family Psychology, 15,* 735–749.

Atkins, D. C., & Kessel, D. E. (2008). Religiousness and infidelity: Attendance, but not faith and prayer, predict marital fidelity. *Journal of Marriage and Family, 70,* 407–418.

Atzmon, G., Hao, L., Pe'er, I., Velez, C., Pearlman, A., Palamara, P. F. et al. (2010). Abraham's children in the genome era: Major Jewish diaspora populations comprise distinct genetic clusters with shared Middle Eastern ancestry. *American Journal of Human Genetics, 86,* 850–859.

Bang, E., Hall, M. E. L., Anderson, T. L., & Willingham, M. M. (2005). Ethnicity, acculturation, and religiosity as predictors of female college students' role expectations. *Sex Roles, 53,* 231–237.

Barkan, S. E. (2006). Religiosity and premarital sex in adulthood. *Journal for the Scientific Study of Religion, 45,* 407–417.

Beach, S. R. H., Hurt, T. R., Fincham, F. D., Franklin, K. J., McNair, L. M., & Stanley, S. M. (2011). Enhancing marital enrichment through spirituality: Efficacy data for prayer focused relationship enhancement. *Psychology of Religion and Spirituality, 3,* 201–216.

Behar, D. M., Yunusbayev, B., Metspalu, M., Metspalu, E., Rosset, S., Parik, J. et al. (2010). The genome-wide structure of the Jewish people. *Nature, 466,* 238–242.

Brody, G. H., Stoneman, Z., & Flor, D. (1996). Parental religiosity, family processes, and youth competence in rural, two-parent African American families. *Developmental Psychology, 32,* 696–706.

Brown, F., Orbuch, T. L., & Bauermeister, J. A. (2008). Religiosity and marital stability among Black American and White American couples. *Family Relations, 57,* 186–197.

Brumbaugh, S. M., Sanchez, L. A., Nock, S. L., & Wright, J. D. (2008). Attitude toward gay marriage in states undergoing marriage law transformation. *Journal of Marriage and Family, 70,* 345–359.

Buss, D. M. (2002). Sex, marriage, and religion: What adaptive problems do religious phenomena solve? *Psychological Inquiry, 13,* 201–203.

Buss, D. M. (2003). *The evolution of desire: Strategies of human mating* (rev. ed.). New York: Basic Books.

Cahn, N., & Carbone, J. (2010). *Red families v. blue families: Legal polarization and the creation of culture.* New York: Oxford University Press.

Call, V. R., & Heaton, T. B. (1997). Religion influence on marital stability. *Journal for the Scientific Study of Religion, 36,* 382–392.

Carothers, S. S., Borkowski, J. G., Lefever, J. B., & Whitman, T. L. (2005). Religiosity and the socioemotional adjustment of adolescent mothers and their children. *Journal of Family Psychology, 19,* 263–275.

Chatters, L. M., & Taylor, R. J. (2005). Religion and families. In V. Bengtson, A. Acock, K. Allen, P. Dillworth-Anderson, & D. Klein (Eds.), *Sourcebook of family theory and research* (pp. 517–522). Thousand Oaks, CA: Sage.

Christian, M. D., & Barbarin, O. A. (2001). Cultural resources and psychological adjustment of African-American children: Effects of spirituality and racial attribution. *Journal of Black Psychology, 27,* 43–63.

Cohen, A. B., Gorvine, B. J., & Gorvine, H. (2003). The religion, spirituality, and psychology of Jews. In K. I. Pargament, J. J. Exline, & J. W. Jones (Eds.), *APA handbook of psychology, religion, and spirituality* (Vol. 1, pp. 665–679). Washington, DC: American Psychological Association.

Cohen, A. B., Hall, D. E., Koenig, H. G., & Meador, K. (2005). Social versus individual motivation: Implications for normative definitions of religious orientation. *Personality and Social Psychology Review, 9*, 48–61.

Cohen, A. B., & Hill, P. C. (2007). Religion as culture: Religious individualism and collectivism among American Catholics, Jews, and Protestants. *Journal of Personality, 75*, 709–742.

Curtis, K. T., & Ellison, C. G. (2002). Religious heterogamy and marital conflict: Findings from the national survey of families and households. *Journal of Family Issues, 23*, 551–576.

Cutrona, C. E., Russell, D. W., Burzette, R. G., Wesner, K. A., & Bryant, C. M. (2011). Predicting relationship stability among midlife African American couples. *Journal of Consulting and Clinical Psychology, 79*, 814–825.

Davidson, J. K., Moore, N. B., & Ullstrup, K. M. (2004). Religiosity and sexual responsibility: Relationships of choice. *American Journal of Health Behavior, 28*, 335–346.

Day, R. D., Peterson, G. W., & McCracken, C. (1998). Predicting spanking of younger and older children by mothers and fathers. *Journal of Marriage and the Family, 60*, 79–94.

Dollahite, D. C. (2003). Fathering for eternity: Generative spirituality in Latter-day Saint fathers of children with special needs. *Review of Religious Research, 44*, 339–351.

Dollahite, D. C., Marks, L. D., & Goodman, M. (2004). Families and religious beliefs, practices, and communities: Linkages in a diverse and dynamic cultural context. In M. J. Coleman & L. H. Ganong (Eds.), *The handbook of contemporary families: Considering the past, contemplating the future* (pp. 411–431). Thousand Oaks, CA: Sage.

Dollahite, D. C., & Lambert, N. M. (2007). Forsaking all others: How religious involvement promotes marital fidelity in Christian, Jewish, and Muslim couples. *Review of Religious Research, 48*, 290–307.

Ellison, C. G., Bartkowski, J. P., & Segal, M. (1996). Conservative Protestantism and the parental use of corporal punishment. *Social Forces, 74*, 1003–1028.

Fiese, B. H., & Tomcho, T. J. (2001). Finding meaning in religious practices: The relation between religious holiday rituals and marital satisfaction. *Journal of Family Psychology, 15*, 597–609.

Fincham, F. D., Ajayi, C., & Beach, S. R. H. (2011). Spirituality and marital satisfaction in African American couples. *Psychology of Religion and Spirituality, 3*, 259–268.

Fincham, F. D., Lambert, N. M., & Beach, S. R. H. (2010). Faith and unfaithfulness: Can praying for your partner reduce infidelity? *Journal of Personality and Social Psychology, 99*, 649–659.

Finlay, B., & Walther, C. S. (2003). The relation of religious affiliation, service attendance, and other factors to homophobic attitudes among university students. *Review of Religious Research, 44*, 370–393.

Gangestad, S. W., & Simpson, J. A. (2000). The evolution of human mating: Trade-offs and strategic pluralism. *Behavioral and Brain Sciences, 23*, 573–644.

Geffen, R. M. (2001). Intermarriage and the premise of American Jewish life. *Congress Monthly*, March–April, 6–8.

Gershoff, E. T., Miller, P. C., & Holden, G. W. (1999). Parenting influences from the pulpit: Religious affiliation as a determinant of parental corporal punishment. *Journal of Family Psychology*, 13, 307–320.

Griskevicius, V., Tybur, J. M., Sundie, J. M., Cialdini, R. B., Miller, G. F., & Kenrick, D. T. (2007). Blatant benevolence and conspicuous consumption: When romantic motives elicit strategic costly signals. *Journal of Personality and Social Psychology*, 93, 85–102.

Gunnoe, M. L., Hetherington, E. M., & Reiss, D. (1999). Parental religiosity, parenting style, and adolescent social responsibility. *Journal of Early Adolescence*, 19, 199–225.

Haerich, P. (1992). Premarital sexual permissiveness and religious orientation: A preliminary investigation. *Journal for the Scientific Study of Religion*, 31, 361–365.

Haider-Markel, D. P., & Joslyn, M. (2008). Understanding beliefs about the origins of homosexuality and subsequent support for gay rights: An empirical test of attribution theory. *Public Opinion Quarterly*, 72, 291–310.

Haidt, J., & Hersh, M. (2001). Sexual morality: The cultures and emotions of conservatives and liberals. *Journal of Applied Social Psychology*, 31, 191–221.

Hardy, S. A., & Raffaelli, M. (2003). Adolescent religiosity and sexuality: An investigation of reciprocal influences. *Journal of Adolescence*, 26, 731–739.

Haselton, M. G., & Gangestad, S. W. (2006). Conditional expression of women's desires and men's mate guarding across the ovulatory cycle. *Hormones and Behavior*, 49, 509–518.

Herek, G. M., & Capitanio, J. P. (1995). Black heterosexuals' attitudes toward lesbians and gay men in the United States. *Journal of Sex Research*, 32, 95–105.

Hernandez, K. M., Mahoney, A., & Pargament, K. I. (2011). Sanctification of sexuality: Implications for newlyweds' marital and sexual quality. *Journal of Family Psychology*, 25, 775–780.

Hetherington, E. M., Stanley Hagan, M., & Eisenberg, M. (1992). *Family interaction global coding system*. Charlottesville, VA: University of Virginia, Department of Psychology, The Remarriage Project.

Hull, S. J., Hennessy, M., Bleakley, A., Fishbein, M., & Jordan, A. (2011). Identifying the causal pathways from religiosity to delayed adolescent sexual behavior. *Journal of Sex Research*, 48, 543–553.

Johnson, K. A., Li, Y. J., & Cohen, A. B. (under review). *Fundamental social motives and the varieties of religious experience.*

Johnson, M. E., Brems, C., & Alford-Keating, P. (1997). Personality correlates of homophobia. *Journal of Homosexuality*, 34, 57–69.

Jones, R. K., Darroch, J. E., & Singh, S. (2005). Religious differentials in the sexual and reproductive behaviors of young women in the United States. *Journal of Adolescent Health*, 36, 279–288.

Laurin, K., Kay, A. C., & Fitzsimons, G. M. (2012). Divergent effects of activating thoughts of god on self-regulation. *Journal of Personality and Social Psychology*, 102, 4–21.

Lefkowitz, E. S., Gillen, M. M., Shearer, C. L., & Boone, T. L. (2004).

Religiosity, sexual behaviors, and sexual attitudes during emerging adulthood. *Journal of Sex Research, 41,* 150–159.

Le Gall, A., Mullet, E., & Shafighi, S. R. (2002). Age, religious beliefs, and sexual attitudes. *Journal of Sex Research, 39,* 207–216.

Li, Y. J., Cohen, A. B., Weeden, J., & Kenrick, D. T. (2010). Mating competitors increase religious beliefs. *Journal of Experimental Social Psychology, 46,* 428–431.

Lippa, R. A. (2009). Sex differences in sex drive, sociosexuality, and height across 53 nations: Testing evolutionary and social structural theories. *Archives of Sexual Behavior, 38,* 631–651.

McCullough, M. E., & Willoughby, B. L. B. (2009). Religion, self-regulation, and self-control: Associations, explanations, and implications. *Psychological Bulletin, 135,* 69–93.

Mahoney, A., Pargament, K. I., Jewell, T., Swank, A. B., Scott, E., Emery, E., & Rye, M. (1999). Marriage and the spiritual realm: The role of proximal and distal religious constructs in marital functioning. *Journal of Family Psychology, 13,* 321–338.

Mahoney, A., Pargament, K. I., Tarakeshwar, N., & Swank, A. B. (2001). Religion in the home in the 1980s and 1990s: A meta-analytic review and conceptual analysis of links between religion, marriage, and parenting. *Journal of Family Psychology, 15,* 559–596.

Meier, A. M. (2003). Adolescents' transition to first intercourse, religiosity, and attitudes about sex. *Social Forces, 8,* 1031–1052.

Miller, L., & Gur, M. (2002). Religiousness and sexual responsibility in adolescent girls. *Journal of Adolescent Health, 31,* 401–406.

Morris, P. (1997). Communities of assent and descent. *Massah; Journey. Journal of the New Zealand Council of Christians and Jews, 3,* 2–4.

Musick, M., & Wilson, J. (1995). Religious switching for marital reasons. *Sociology of Religion, 56,* 257–270.

Olatunji, B. O. (2008). Disgust, scrupulosity and conservative attitudes about sex: Evidence for a mediational model of homophobia. *Journal of Research in Personality, 42,* 1364–1369.

Olson, L. R., Cadge, W. & Harrison, J. T. (2006). Religion and public opinion about same-sex marriage. *Social Science Quarterly, 87,* 340–360.

Pluhar, E., Frongillo, E. A., Stycos, J. M., & Dempster-McClain, D. (1998). Understanding the relationship between religion and the sexual attitudes and behaviors of college students. *Journal of Sex Education and Therapy, 23,* 288–296.

Reiss, I. L. (1976). *Family system in America* (2nd ed.). New York: Holt, Rinehart, & Winston.

Robinson, L. C. (1994). Religious orientation in enduring marriage: An exploratory study. *Review of Religious Research, 35,* 207–218.

Roney, J. R., Mahler, S. V. & Maestripieri, D. (2003). Behavioral and hormonal responses of men to brief interactions with women. *Evolution and Human Behavior, 24,* 365–375.

Rostosky, S. S., Regnerus, M., & Wright, M. L. (2003). Coital debut: The role of religiosity and sex attitudes in the Add Health Survey. *Journal of Sex Research, 40,* 358–367.

Rostosky, S. S., Wilcox, B. L., Comer Wright, M. L., & Randall, B. A. (2004).

The impact of religiosity on adolescent sexual behavior: A review of the evidence. *Journal of Adolescent Research, 9,* 677–697.

Rowatt, W. C., LaBouff, J., Johnson, M., Froese, P., & Tsang, J. (2009). Associations between religiousness, social attitudes, and prejudice in a national random sample of American adults. *Psychology of Religion and Spirituality, 1,* 14–24.

Rowatt, W. C., & Schmitt, D. (2003). Associations between religious orientation and varieties of sexual experience. *Journal for the Scientific Study of Religion, 42,* 455–465.

Rozin, P., Lowery, L., Imada, S., & Haidt, J. (1999). The CAD triad hypothesis: A mapping between three moral emotions (contempt, anger, disgust) and three moral codes (community, autonomy, divinity). *Journal of Personality and Social Psychology, 76,* 574–586.

Schmitt, D. P. (2002). [Religious extremity and sexual restraint across 52 cultures.[Unpublished raw data.

Simpson, J. A., & Gangestad, S. W. (1991). Individual differences in sociosexuality: Evidence for convergent and discriminant validity. *Journal of Personality and Social Psychology, 60,* 870–883.

Spilka, B., Hood, R. W., Jr., Hunsberger, B., & Gorsuch, R. (2003). *Psychology of religion: An empirical approach* (3rd ed.). New York: Guilford.

Steinberg, L., Lamborn, S. D., Darling, N., Mounts, N. S., & Dornbusch, S. M. (1994). Over-time changes in adjustment and competence among adolescents from authoritative, authoritarian, indulgent, and neglectful families. *Child Development, 65,* 754–770.

Sullivan, K. T. (2001). Understanding the relationship between religiosity and marriage: An investigation of the immediate and longitudinal effect of religiosity on newlywed couples. *Journal of Family Psychology, 15,* 610–626.

Vaas, R. (2009). Gods, gains, and genes: On the natural origin of religiosity by means of bio-cultural selection. In E. Voland & W. Schiefenhövel (Eds.), *Biological evolution of religious mind and behavior* (pp. 25–49). New York: Springer.

Walker, G. (2004). Eunuchs for the kingdom of heaven: Constructing the celibate priest. *Studies in Gender and Sexuality, 5,* 233–257.

Weeden, J., Cohen, A. B., & Kenrick, D. T. (2008). Religious attendance as reproductive support. *Evolution and Human Behavior, 29,* 327–334.

Whitehead, A. L. (2010). Sacred rites and civil rights: Religion's effect on attitudes toward same-sex unions and the perceived cause of homosexuality. *Social Science Quarterly, 91,* 63–79.

Whitley, B. E. (2009). Religiosity and attitudes toward lesbians and gay men: A meta-analysis. *International Journal for the Psychology of Religion, 19,* 21–38.

Wolfinger, N., & Wilcox, W. (2008). Happily ever after? Religion, marital status, gender and relationship quality in urban families. *Social Forces, 86,* 1311–1337.

Woods, L. N., & Emery, R. E. (2002). The cohabitation effects on divorce: Causation or selection? *Journal of Divorce and Remarriage, 37,* 101–119.

Zaleski, E. H., & Schiaffino, K. M. (2000). Religiosity and sexual risk-taking behavior during the transition to college. *Journal of Adolescence, 23,* 223–227.

11 Religion and Domestic Political Attitudes around the World

Ariel Malka

For most of recorded history religious sentiment was inextricable from politics. Supernatural religious content infused the rules and procedures of social organization, and political leaders derived their legitimacy from religious belief systems.

Modernization has done much to change this state of affairs. According to secularization theory, religious sentiment and practice decline as societies reach higher stages of development. This may be because scientific and technological advance make religious beliefs seem implausible, secular institutions and organizations begin to fulfill formerly religious functions (such as promoting social order and regulating the distribution of resources), or security and material comfort make religious reassurance less necessary (e.g., Dobbelaere, 1985; Durkheim, 2001 [1912]; Martin, 1978; Norris & Inglehart, 2011; Weber, 2002 [1905]). Scholars fiercely debate secularization theory's validity and scope of applicability (e.g., Gill, 2001; Hadden, 1987; Stark, 1999). In defense of secularization theory, societal development is indeed negatively correlated with societal religiosity (Norris & Inglehart, 2011). But it is clear, nonetheless, that religion remains a factor in the contemporary political life of a great many nations (e.g., Esmer & Pettersson, 2007; Knutsen, 2004).

The focus of this chapter is one particular way in which religion and politics might nowadays be linked: Among ordinary people around the world, religious characteristics might display predictable relations with domestic political preferences. The domestic policy domains of present focus are the two most frequently discussed in terms of a right vs. left (or conservative vs. liberal) continuum—specifically, the "cultural" domain pertaining to issues such as abortion and homosexuality, and the "economic" domain concerning government intervention in economic life and redistributive social welfare provision. These attitude domains characterize differences between the political right and left across many societies, and they have implications for voting and other political behavior.

A focus on religious influences in these domains constitutes a departure from a primary area of concern within the political psychology of religion—specifically, the psychological elements of ethno-religious conflict, interfaith relations, and religiously based prejudice (e.g., Bar-Tal, Halperin, & Oren, 2010; Ginges, Atran, Medin, & Shikaki, 2007; Hammack, 2010; Rowatt, Carpenter, & Haggard, Chapter 8, this volume). But the relations of religious characteristics with domestic political preferences have social importance nonetheless. For one thing, religious group differences in political attitudes might impact relations across faith traditions. It is widely speculated, for example, that differences on cultural matters pertaining to sexuality and family hinder favorable relations between Muslim and Western societies. Religious differences in cultural preferences might have consequences for democratization within some societies (e.g., Inglehart, 2003), and religious differences in economic attitudes might produce variation in economic outcomes across religious groups (e.g., Guiso, Sapienza, & Zingales, 2003).

In addition to implications for interfaith relations, the present topic also has relevance to the structure of political conflict within societies. If religiosity naturally yields affinity for conservative preferences in both the cultural and economic domains, then there exists an important psychological constraint on the sociopolitical cleavages within societies. Under such circumstances, political disagreement is likely to be widely encompassing, characterized by conflict between two "teams" with diverging views on a wide range of political matters as well as diverging religious characteristics. Indeed, this assumption of widely encompassing conflict is reflected in the practice of including religious, economic, and cultural content within measures of "conservatism" (e.g., Wilson & Patterson, 1968). The present review can provide insight into whether such an assumption is tenable.

This chapter consists of four sections. In the first, I conceptually define the religious and political characteristics examined in the studies to be reviewed. In the second, I review research on the relation between *religious affiliation* and political preference, and, in the third, I review research on the relation between *religiosity* and political preference. In both the second and third sections, I primarily review cross-national evidence within a subsection entitled "Around the World." Then, because of the preponderance of data from American samples, and because of the unique (for a wealthy democratic nation) cultural importance of religion within the US (e.g., Norris & Inglehart, 2011), I briefly review evidence from American samples in a subsection entitled "Within the US." I then draw conclusions about the psychological and societal implications of overlap between religion and domestic political preference.

Religion and Domestic Political Preference: Definitions

Religion

How do people differ from one another religiously? The answer that would first come to mind for many is that people differ in terms of religious affiliation. But the conceptualization of religious affiliation is complicated by myriad historical and cultural considerations. Is there a single Christian category; do we categorize Christians as Catholic, Protestant, or Eastern Orthodox; or do we further decompose the last two categories into specific traditions or denominations? Does it make sense to speak of "Muslims," should we regard Sunni and Shiite Islam as separate religions, or should we further divide these categories into more specific ethno-religious groups?

These questions do not have single correct answers. The answers generated often reflect culturally rooted belief systems, and are subject to the preconceptions and biases associated therewith. Having offered this caveat, I review research that has operationalized religious affiliation in one of the following ways. First, religious affiliation is sometimes measured at the national level in terms of the "cultural zone" of an individual's nation (Huntington, 1996; Norris & Inglehart, 2002; Weber, 2002 [1905]; Welzel, Inglehart, & Klingemann, 2003). Cultural zones are groupings of nations based on their historically predominant religions and other pertinent cultural, institutional, demographic, and geographic characteristics (e.g., Protestant Western Zone, Formerly Communist Eastern European Orthodox Zone, Islamic Zone, Latin American Zone). Second, religious affiliation is sometimes measured at the national level in terms of the nation's currently predominant religion. For some nations, this differs from the historically predominant religion. Third, religious affiliation is sometimes measured at the individual level; specifically, the religious group with which the individual identifies. The categories of this type of indicator vary across studies (e.g., what are the Christian and Muslim categories?), and are sometimes linked with non-religious cultural attributes (e.g., black Protestantism and white Evangelical Protestantism in the US).

In addition to their religious affiliations, people also differ from one another in their levels of religiosity. This refers to individual-level variation in degree of behavioral and experiential commitment to one's religion. Indicators such as religious attendance, religious identity, and subjective importance of religion in one's life tend to converge on a superordinate "religiosity" construct (Layman & Green, 2005; Malka, Lelkes, Srivastava, Cohen, & Miller, 2012; Norris and Inglehart, 2011), although some research examines the unique effects of distinct religiosity indicators (e.g., Ginges, Hansen, & Norenzayan, 2009; Guiso et al., 2003; Hayward & Kemmelmeier, 2011). Other work distinguishes religiosity from "spirituality," which involves a subjective mystical feeling of self-transcendence (e.g., Hill & Pargament, 2003; Spilka, Hood, Hunsberger, & Gorsuch, 2003). Indeed, religiosity and spirituality may differentially impact some political attitudes (Hirsh, Walberg, & Peterson, 2013). More generally, a complex and multifaceted concept like religious devotion can be parsed in a great variety of ways. The present focus is on a "bare bones" formulation of religiosity, involving a sense of personal religious importance and conduct of religious behaviors. The World Values Survey (1981–2008), a large cross-national survey that has been fielded since the early 1980s, includes religiosity items along these lines; indicators that have relevance to a wide range of religious cultures. Many of the studies reviewed here use WVS data and, in general, this review summarizes research employing these types of religiosity indicator.

Political Attitudes

Elite political competition around the world is frequently conceptualized in terms of ideological differences between the political right (who espouse "conservatism") and the political left (who espouse "liberalism").[1] Because of the political importance of this dimension, and due to space limitations, I limit the present focus to domestic political attitudes that are widely viewed as relevant to this dimension. The two most common preference domains of this sort are cultural preferences—concerning traditional patterns of behavior as most often exemplified in the areas of sexuality, reproduction, and family –and economic preferences—regarding redistributive social welfare spending, public vs. private enterprise, and scope of government involvement in the economy (e.g., Shafer & Claggett, 1995).[2] These preference domains reflect two aspects of social organization in which societies face fundamental tradeoffs. Furthermore, an influential line of reasoning within political psychology posits that similar underlying psychological needs are served by religiosity, cultural conservatism, and economic conservatism (Adorno, Frenkel-Brunswik, Levinson, & Sanford, 1950; Jost, 2007; Rokeach, 1960; Wilson, 1973). In particular, needs for certainty, order, and security are said to drive people toward religious adherence and a broad-based conservative ideology, encompassing cultural *and* economic matters. Thus measures of "conservatism" often include overtly religious content, based on the ex ante assumption that religious adherence is an implicit part of a broad unidimensional conservative ideology. Consequently, in this review, I seek to critically evaluate this assumption. If religiosity relates to conservative positions in both the cultural and economic domains, then conceptualizing religiosity as part of a broad "conservative syndrome" may be justified. If religiosity does not relate to both forms of conservatism, then such a conceptualization provides a misleading portrait of the interplay among these constructs.

Religious Affiliation and Domestic Political Attitudes

When considering why religious groups might differ in political attitudes it is important to mind the distinction between the founding texts and prophetic messages of a religion, on the one hand, and what Weber (1963 [1922]) described as the "practical religion," on the other. The latter reflects the actual habits and patterns of behavior of religious adherents, which emerge from "the interaction between the original doctrine and the social, political, and economic conditions of the time" (Laitin, 1978, p. 571).

Today's major world religions contain ancient founding texts that prescribe conservative positions on cultural matters in the domain of sex and family (e.g., Norris & Inglehart, 2011). However, these founding texts send mixed messages about economic matters, in terms of personal vs. societal responsibility for gainful employment, redistributive provision for the needy, and private property (Guiso et al., 2003; Smith, 1971; Uppal, 1986). But sacred texts and prophetic messages cannot, by themselves, explain the impact of religion on domestic political attitudes. Rather, the attitudes of religious adherents are the product of the traditional teachings interacting with local political and institutional realities, at particular historical junctures. Because of this, explanations of contemporary religious group differences in terms of scriptural foundations may be risky (cf. Cohen & Rozin, 2001). Thus, I presently adopt the more descriptive goal of documenting findings in this domain; providing a summary of data that I hope will be useful for efforts to explain how scripture and social conditions interactively impact religious groups' political attitudes.

Around the World

Cultural Attitudes

Do religious groups around the world differ in their domestic political preferences? This question has frequently been addressed in the context of cultural attitudes concerning sex and family. The focus on cultural attitudes is understandable: Traditional religious doctrines have almost always offered prescriptions for these domains of life, and contemporary religious conservative movements tend to focus primarily on these types of issue.

One common assertion is that Catholics, because of the culturally traditional posture of their religious elite, are particularly culturally conservative. But a consistent lesson of public opinion research is that one should not infer opinions of ordinary people based on information about elite opinions (e.g., Converse, 1964; Fiorina, Abrams, & Pope, 2005). This consideration, coupled with attention to the distinction between theological discourse and "practical religion," should give pause to those who would extrapolate from elite findings to rank-and-file Catholics.

Indeed, cross-national evidence does not support the view that Catholics are an especially culturally conservative religious group. Adamczyk and Pitt (2009) analyzed data from a cross-national sample of 40 societies. On average, Catholics were less disapproving of homosexuality than were Muslims, Protestants, Hindus, Buddhists, and Orthodox Christians. Norris and Inglehart (2002) found that Western Christian societies were the most approving of homosexuality, and that Latin American and Central European societies (the other two cultural zones with substantial Catholic populations) were positioned in the middle of the nations analyzed. Western Christian, Central European and Latin American nations (cultural zones with substantial Catholic populations) were more approving of homosexuality than were nations in the Christian Orthodox, Sinic/Confucian, Sub-Saharan African, Hindu, and Islamic zones. As for abortion attitude, Western Christian and Central European nations were the most tolerant, whereas Latin American nations were among the least tolerant.

Using a cross-national sample of 15 (mostly Western) nations, Scheepers, Grotenhuis, and Van Der Slik (2002) did find that Catholics were more culturally conservative than non-Catholics on a composite of homosexuality, abortion, premarital sex, and extramarital sex. This effect was accounted for by the higher level of parental religious attendance among the Catholics. Similar findings using a nation-level measure of religion were obtained by Scott (1998a), who also found that, within most of the nations studied, being Catholic was unrelated to disapproval of homosexuality. Scott (1998b) found that in Britain and among German women, being Catholic was associated with opposition to abortion, but in the US, Ireland, Sweden, and Poland it was not. Yuchtman-Yaar and Alkalay (2007) found, within a sample of 36 nations, that Catholic nations were positioned between Protestant nations (most culturally liberal) and Muslim nations (most culturally conservative) on a composite of homosexuality tolerance, abortion tolerance, and respect for authority. Similarly, Norris and Inglehart (2011) found that Catholic nations were between Muslim nations and Protestant nations on disapproval of abortion. Thus the balance of evidence suggests that Catholics are not especially culturally conservative, although they may be somewhat less tolerant of abortion than are other Christian groups.

Are there particular religions whose adherents are especially culturally conservative? Yes, Islam and to a lesser extent prominent Eastern religions. The major social difference between contemporary Muslims and contemporary Westerners does not have to do with attitudes toward democracy (Diamond, 2008; cf. Huntington, 1996), but rather has to do with views of sexual liberalization. Norris and Inglehart (2002) found that Islamic and Hindu nations were consistently among the most conservative across the issues of gender equality, homosexuality, abortion, and divorce (see also Inglehart & Norris, 2011). Nations of the Sub-Saharan African Zone—which contains great numbers of Christians, Muslims, and adherents of traditional African religions—also tended to be culturally conservative across these issues, as did nations of the Sinic/ Confucian zone, which contains great numbers of Buddhists, Confucianists, and Taoists. But Inglehart and Norris (2002) found that much of the cultural conservatism of Hindu and Sub-Saharan African nations was accounted for by low levels of human and political development. This was not the case for Muslim nations; they were more culturally conservative than their national levels of development would predict. Similarly, Yuchtman-Yaar and Alkalay (2007) found that Islamic Zone nations were the least culturally liberal on an attitude composite consisting of homosexuality, abortion, and authority attitudes. Gallup polls conducted between 2006 and 2007 revealed that Muslim inhabitants of London, Paris, and Berlin were substantially more conservative than their non-Muslim counterparts on the matters of homosexuality and abortion (Nyiri, 2007).

Individuals with no religious affiliation tend to be the most culturally liberal, consistent with the finding (to be presented in the next section) that individuals low in religiosity tend to be culturally liberal. For example, using samples from seven European nations and the US, Hayes (1995) found that individuals with no religious affiliation were generally more tolerant of working women and abortion than were Protestants and Catholics. Adamczyk and Pitt (2009) found that individuals with no religious affiliation were more tolerant of homosexuals than were affiliates of each of the religions studied, with the exception of Jews.

Thus, regarding cultural matters, Muslims—and, to a lesser extent, Hindus and adherents of other Eastern religions—tend to be the most conservative, individuals with no religious affiliation tend to be the most liberal, and other religious groups, including the Christian groups, tend to be in between. However, Catholics show a conservative inclination on the abortion issue, Orthodox Christians are relatively opposed to homosexuality, and Christians from Sub-Saharan Africa might be quite culturally conservative.

Economic Attitudes

In comparison to cultural issues, economic issues are less frequently framed in religious terms. Perhaps for this reason there is less available evidence documenting religious group differences in economic attitudes. The most widely noted thesis concerning religious affiliation and economic preference is Weber's (2002 [1905]) classic and controversial view that Protestantism bears an inherent link with the norms and institutions of capitalism, some of which constitute conservative economic attitudes. The evidence concerning Protestants' economic conservatism is mixed.

Guiso et al. (2003) and Hayward and Kemmelmeier (2011) conducted large-scale cross-national analyses of religion and a broad set of capitalism-related attitudes, using WVS data. It is crucial to note that only some of the capitalism-related attitudes they studied may be conceptualized as economically conservative vs. liberal, in terms of directly pertaining to preferences regarding government economic involvement and redistributive social welfare provision. Other attitudes—such as valuing hard work, generally believing that competition brings out the best in people, supporting equal rights in work and education for women, trusting in institutions, and believing that the world contains a great deal of wealth—are not explicitly concerned with what the government should do in terms of economic intervention, although they may be empirically related to such attitudes.

Guiso et al. (2003) focused on the relation of *religiosity* indicators and capitalism-relevant attitudes. Although they reported how the relations of religiosity and such attitudes differ in magnitude and direction between those with no religious affiliation and those affiliating with each of the major world religions (p. 256), they did not report main effects of religious affiliation. Hayward and Kemmelmeier (2011), however, did, focusing on comparisons of Protestants with adherents of other religious traditions. They found that, with respect to opposing government promotion of economic equality, Protestants were not significantly more conservative than were members of other religious groups, with the exception of Jews. However, Protestants were significantly more conservative with respect to opposing government responsibility for social welfare than were the other religious groups (except Buddhists), and Protestants were more inclined to favor private rather than government business ownership than were the other religious groups (except Buddhists and Jews). This suggests that it is important to distinguish different forms of economic conservatism when evaluating how religious affiliation relates to this attitude domain. Consistent with this point, Norris and Inglehart (2011) found that the rank order of religious affiliations on economic attitudes differed substantially across the particular economic attitudes assessed. With respect to favoring economic incentives over economic equality, Muslims and Orthodox Christians were the most conservative. For the last, this might reflect a reaction to Communist rule. These groups were followed by Protestants, adherents of Eastern religions, and Catholics (with the last three being quite close together). However, with regard to favoring private ownership, Protestants were the most

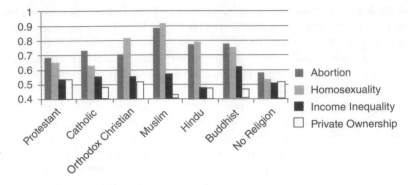

Figure 11.1 Differences across religious affiliations in conservative (vs. liberal) cultural and economic political preferences.

Note. World Values Survey wave 5 (2005–2008) data. Political preferences coded to range from 0 to 1 with higher scores signifying the conservative position. Respondents rated their views about whether or not abortion is justified and whether or not homosexuality is justified on a 1 ("Never justifiable") to 10 ("Always justifiable") scale. For income inequality, respondents rated their position on a 10-point scale ranging from "Incomes should be made more equal" to "We need larger income differences as incentives for individual effort". For private ownership, respondents rated their positions on a 10-point scale ranging from "Government ownership of business and industry should be increased" to "Private ownership of business and industry should be increased."

conservative, followed by Catholics. Orthodox Christians, Muslims, and adherents of Eastern religions were all quite close together, being less favorable to private ownership than both Protestants and Catholics. Thus Protestants are especially inclined to display some, but not other, forms of economic conservatism.

New Evidence and Summary

To further illustrate the empirical patterns reviewed earlier, I report the results of new analyses with the 5th wave of the WVS. In this wave, interviews were conducted with national samples from 57 nations between the years 2005 and 2008. Large numbers of Protestants, Catholics, Orthodox Christians, Muslims, Hindus, Buddhists, and individuals with no religious affiliation were interviewed. Figure 11.1 displays mean levels of abortion, homosexuality, income inequality, and private ownership attitudes among each of these seven religious affiliation groups. The political preferences are coded from 0 to 1, with higher scores representing more conservative positions (see, further, Figure 11.2).

Muslims are the most conservative on cultural matters of abortion and homosexuality, and individuals with no religious affiliation are the least culturally conservative. Catholics do not seem to be especially

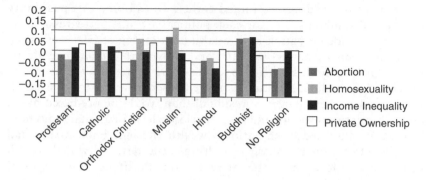

Figure 11.2 Differences across religious affiliations in conservative (vs. liberal) cultural and economic political preferences corrected for national and household wealth.

Note. World Values Survey wave 5 (2005–2008) data. Political preferences were first coded to range from 0 to 1 with higher scores signifying the conservative position and then regressed on the natural log of the respondent's nation's GDP per capita at purchasing power parity and the respondent's household income decile within his/her nation. The figure displays the residual scores from this analysis, representing the degree to which a religious group's political preference is higher vs. lower than predicted based on national and household wealth. For wording of political preference items, see the note at Figure 11.1.

culturally conservative, with slightly more conservative views on abortion and more liberal views on homosexuality in comparison to the other Christian groups. Hindus and Buddhists are more culturally conservative than the Christians (with the exception of Orthodox Christians on homosexuality), but they are less culturally conservative than Muslims. That Orthodox Christians are, on average, opposed to homosexuality might reflect lower levels of modernization within the societies in which they predominate (Štulhofer & Rimac, 2009).

As for economic preferences, the differences across the religious affiliations are far less pronounced and appear to bear no correspondence with religious differences in cultural attitudes. One finding of note is that Protestants do not stand out as especially economically conservative. Another finding of note is that while Muslims and Buddhists are the most tolerant of income inequality (although not by much), they are the least tolerant of private ownership (although, again, not by much). Hindus are the most consistently economically liberal. But, again, these religious differences are not large.

It is well known that wealth, both at the national level and at the household level, predicts liberal cultural attitudes, and that household wealth predicts conservative economic attitudes (e.g., Erikson & Tedin, 2010; Yuchtman-Yaar & Alkalay, 2007). Thus associations of religious affiliation with nation-level wealth and household wealth may account for some of the findings examined earlier. To examine this possibility I computed residual scores for each political attitude by regressing the political attitude on nation-level wealth (natural log of GDP per capita (purchasing power parity) in 2005) and individual-level income (decile within one's nation). Each respondent's score represents the degree to which his/her political attitude is more conservative (positive residual) vs. less conservative (negative residual) than would be predicted based on his/her nation's wealth and his/her relative level of annual household income. As expected, both national wealth and individual wealth had negative effects on conservative cultural attitudes, individual wealth had positive effects on conservative economic attitudes, and national wealth had small and inconsistent effects on conservative economic attitudes.

Muslims and Buddhists, especially the former, were more culturally conservative on both abortion and homosexuality than their national and household wealth would predict. Those with no religious affiliation were more culturally liberal than their national and household wealth would predict. As for Christians, Orthodox Christians were more dis-approving of homosexuality and Catholics were more approving of homosexuality and slightly less approving of abortion than national and household wealth would predict. As for economic preferences, the two strongest divergences from predicted values were for Hindus, who were less approving of income inequality than would be predicted, and for Buddhists, who were more approving of income inequality than would be predicted. These findings are difficult to explain. One might speculate that Hindu approval of redistributive intervention is somehow connected to contemporary concerns about the caste system. For example, a major-ity of Indians in a 2006 BBC poll reported belief that the caste system is an impediment to social harmony (GlobeScan Incorporated, 2006). As for Buddhism, one might speculate that a theological emphasis against material desire produces an aversion to government based redistribu-tion. But these are ad hoc conjectures. Their validity, and the validity of alternative explanations, should be subjected to careful empirical scru-tiny. In addition, Orthodox Christians were more favorable to private ownership (perhaps because of their Communist history) and Muslims were slightly more economically liberal than the wealth variables would predict.

Taken together, prior findings and the present analyses suggest that contemporary Muslims and Buddhists are the most culturally conser-vative religious affiliations and those with no religious affiliation are the most culturally liberal. Hindus are also quite culturally conservative but this might be fully accounted for by their low national and house-hold wealth. Other religious affiliations, including the major Christian groups, tend to be in between, although Orthodox Christians are quite conservative with respect to homosexuality, and Catholics display a conservative inclination on abortion. Finally, religious affiliation differences in economic preferences are small and inconsistent.

Within the US

Historically, religion has played a major role in American social and political organization (Layman, 2001). Many early English colonists were Calvinist Protestant separatists, and in the early years of the United States most of the non-slave citizens were Protestants whose lives were characterized by liturgical literalism, the experience of self-conversion, and in some cases beliefs that the United States' mission was to bring about the second coming of Christ. African Americans, mostly enslaved, developed their own Protestant traditions that were evangelical in nature but that focused on promoting justice and freedom.

From the mid-19th century until the 1920s the religious landscape changed (see Hunter, 1991; Layman, 2001; Putnam & Campbell, 2010). Large numbers of Catholics and Jews emigrated from Europe, and the forces of modernization brought about a theological split between "evangelical" and "mainline" Protestant denominations. Mainline Protestants came to support a less literal interpretation of scripture, less of a focus on orthodox religious beliefs, more interfaith tolerance, and greater engagement with the modern world (e.g., the "social gospel"). Evangelical Protestants continued to uphold the orthodox Protestant views that had historically characterized American religion. Similar traditional vs. progressive divisions developed within Catholicism and Judaism.

How do these religious groups differ on domestic political preferences? Not surprisingly, Evangelical Protestants tend nowadays to be the most culturally conservative on matters such as abortion and homosexuality (Guth, Kellstedt, Smidt, & Green, 2006; Layman, 1997; Layman & Green, 2005; Malka et al., 2012). This religious group has been the most strongly represented in the religious conservatism movement that took shape in the 1970s and 1980s. Their strong Democratic allegiance notwithstanding, black Protestants are not liberal on cultural attitudes but do not appear to be as culturally conservative as are white Evangelical Protestants (Guth et al., 2006; Malka et al., 2012). Catholics are not particularly culturally conservative (Newport, 2009), and neither are Mainline Protestants (Guth et al., 2006; Malka et al., 2012). Both groups are a good deal less culturally conservative than Evangelical Protestants but more culturally conservative than those with no religious affiliation and Jews. Latter-day Saints, the largest "non-traditional" Protestant denomination, are very culturally conservative (Guth et al., 2006). As for economic attitudes, Evangelical Protestants and Latter-day Saints tend to be conservative, black Protestants and Jews tend to be liberal, and those with no religious affiliation, mainline Protestants and Catholics tend to be in the middle (Guth et al., 2006; Malka et al., 2012).

Religiosity and Domestic Political Preference

Around the World

Within every major religious group, people vary in the degree to which they are committed to religious belief and practice. This is referred to as religiosity, and it is an individual difference variable that is often studied in the context of political attitudes. At the individual and the national level, subjective religious importance and religious attendance are strongly correlated (e.g., Layman & Green, 2005; Malka et al., 2012; Norris & Inglehart, 2011), justifying the formation of composite religiosity measures.

Cultural Preference

I first review evidence of the relation between religiosity and cultural political preferences. These characteristics would seem to bear an inherent organic relation; traditional religions almost invariably offer prescriptions for traditional behavior in the domains of family and sex. Indeed the evidence is strong and unequivocal that more religious people are more culturally conservative than are less religious people. Using cross-national data from 15 (mostly Western) samples, Scheepers et al. (2002) found that individuals holding religious worldviews were more conservative than their non-religious counterparts on a composite of abortion, homosexuality, premarital sex, and extra-marital sex. This same pattern replicated for parental religiosity (see also Scott, 1998a, 1998b). The effect of personal religiosity on cultural conservatism was stronger in more religious countries than in less religious countries. This may be because religious considerations are compartmentalized in less religious countries, and thus do not influence as strongly evaluations in all domains of life (Stark, 1999). Napier and Jost (2008) found, in a cross-national sample of 19 democracies, that subjective religious importance predicted a composite of opposition to divorce and opposition to homosexuality. Adamczyk and Pitt (2009) analyzed cross-national data from 40 nations and found that religiosity predicted disapproval of homosexuality both with and without controlling for religious affiliation dummy variables. Interestingly, they found that in countries characterized by an overwhelming concern with survival, disapproval of homosexuality was uniformly high and unrelated to religiosity, but in countries more concerned with self-expression than survival, religiosity robustly predicted opposition to homosexuality. This is consistent with the view that when post-materialist concerns are salient within a culture there is more room for individual-level variation in religious preference to impact political views (Inglehart, 1990; Layman & Carmines, 1997).

Cultural conservatism is sometimes construed as a form of moral intolerance, and it may be tempting to conclude that because religious people tend to be culturally conservative they also tend to be intolerant of, and supportive of violence against, members of outgroups. But the evidence on this front is not perfectly clear. Canetti, Hobfoll, Pedahzur, and Zaidise (2010) found that more religious Israeli Jews and Muslims were more inclined to support violence against the outgroup, and that this effect was completely accounted for by socioeconomic level and perceived discrimination. Ginges et al. (2009) found that religious attendance, but not religious devotion, predicted support of suicide attacks against the outgroup. But Tessler (2003) found that level of religiosity was uncorrelated with support of violence within Muslim societies. Similarly, Gallup polls from 130 countries conducted in 2008 and 2009 show that support of military and individual attacks on civilians do not differ between more and less religious people (Mogahed & Younis, 2011). Evidence from American samples suggests that religiosity actually relates to opposition to the death penalty and torture, despite being associated with a conservative self-identification (Malka & Soto, 2011; Malka et al., 2012; see also Blogowska & Saroglou, 2011). However, religiosity is often found to be correlated with intolerance on the basis of factors such as ethnicity or perceived deviance from norms (Guiso et al., 2003; Katnik, 2002; Napier and Jost, 2008; but see Arzheimer & Carter, 2009). And in Europe, extreme right-wing parties that promote ethnic and cultural intolerance often appeal to religion as a component of national identity, even though their current supporters are not particularly religious (Camus, 2007).

Economic Attitudes

What about economic preferences? Unlike cultural conservatism, there does not exist consistent evidence that religiosity predicts economic conservatism. Using WVS data from 66 countries from the early 1980s to the mid-1990s, Guiso et al. (2003) regressed capitalism-related attitude items on models containing nation-level fixed effects, demographic controls and the following binary religiosity indicators: atheism, attend religious services weekly vs. not, attend religious services at least once a year vs. not, and whether or not one was brought up religiously at home. As discussed earlier, some, but not all, of the capitalism-relevant items can be construed as economically conservative vs. liberal preferences. On these preferences, the authors found small and inconsistent effects. For example, having been raised religiously had small effects on *liberal* inequality and private vs. public ownership attitudes. However, attending weekly (as opposed to the comparison category of never attending) and being an atheist were associated slightly with conservative equality and private ownership preferences. However, these effects are somewhat difficult to interpret because multiple inter-correlated binary religiosity variables were entered together as predictors.

Hayward and Kemmelmeier (2011) used the most complete version of the WVS data to date, and simultaneously entered subjective religious importance and religious attendance as predictors of capitalism-related attitudes, controlling for several individual and nation-level variables. Three of these capitalism-relevant attitudes corresponded with economic conservatism vs. liberalism. Neither religiosity variable significantly predicted conservative position on private business ownership or government responsibility for social welfare provision. Religious importance, but not religious *attendance*, predicted conservative position on income inequality. Reporting findings separately for religious traditions, Protestants, Catholics, Buddhists, Hindus, Muslims, Orthodox Christians and even those with no religious affiliation displayed a relation between personal religious importance and conservative position on economic inequality. But not a single religious group displayed a significant relation between religious attendance and economic inequality attitude; in fact, religious attendance significantly predicted liberal position on economic inequality among Catholics and Orthodox Christians. Meanwhile, personal religiosity predicted liberal position on business ownership among Buddhists, Jews, Muslims, Orthodox Christians, and people of smaller religious groups. In general, there was a mix of positive and negative effects of religiosity variables on economic conservatism within religious groups.

Napier and Jost (2008) used a single religiosity indicator to predict political attitudes in samples from 19 nations, and the results of their analysis are thus relatively straightforward to interpret. As described already, religiosity predicted cultural conservatism and intolerance. Religiosity, however, was uncorrelated with economic conservatism. Overall, then, religiosity does not display reliable relations with economic conservatism in cross-national survey data.

If religiosity is associated with cultural conservatism, and cultural conservatism is correlated with economic conservatism, then why is it the case that religiosity does not correlate reliably with economic conservatism? The answer to this question may have to do with competing influences of religiosity on economic conservatism. On the one hand, some religious people may be driven by political discourse to adopt conservative economic positions in order to act consistently with their culturally based conservative identities. But, on the other hand, religiosity's link with prosocial values (e.g., Saroglou, Pichon, Tompette, Verschueren, & Dernelle, 2005; Shariff & Norenzayan, 2007; Smith & Stark, 2009; cf. Galen, 2012a; 2012b; Preston, Salomon, & Ritter, Chapter 7, this volume) may underlie a tendency of some religious people to move their economic preferences to the left. As discussed later, some evidence from American samples supports this competing pathways hypothesis.

Within the US

That ordinary Americans are involved in a bitter religiously based culture war has become conventional wisdom in some circles. This view is a sensationalized exaggeration of a real finding. There is indeed a "god gap" nowadays in American politics such that the more religious are more inclined to identify as conservative and to vote Republican than are the less religious (e.g., Putnam & Campbell, 2010). But this religious difference in political behavior is relatively new and is limited to particular issue domains.

How new is it? Prior to the religious conservatism movement that originated in the 1970s, level of religious commitment had not been much of a factor in American political life since the Prohibition era (Pew Forum on Religion and Public Life, 2005). But the rise of partisan division in cultural attitudes during the 1980s, 1990s, and 2000s somewhat restructured the mass partisan coalitions. Layman (1997) found that between 1980 and 1994, an effect of doctrinal orthodoxy on Republican self-identification and vote emerged, and the effect of religious commitment on Republican vote strengthened. Culture war rhetoric intensified in the early 1990s, and it appears that this was followed by an increase in the relation of religious attendance with both partisanship (Putnam & Campbell, 2010) and conservative self-identification (Malka et al., 2012). This was not entirely the result of Americans adjusting their politics to match their religion. Patrikios (2008) demonstrated that during the religiously divisive periods in the early 1990s and 2000s, Americans tended to adjust their religiosity levels to match their partisan and ideological self-identifications. Thus when culture war discourse intensified, the convergence of religious and political characteristics reflected bidirectional influence.

Does religiosity relate to both cultural and economic preferences? As in much of the world, religiosity predicts cultural conservatism in the United States. The more religious are more conservative on matters such as abortion and homosexuality, and religiosity is a relatively strong predictor of these preferences (e.g., Lecge & Kellstedt, 1993; Wilcox & Larsen, 2006; Wuthnow, 1988). Moreover, these effects are found consistently across all major religious denominations (Guth et al., 2006; Layman & Green, 2005; Malka et al., 2012).

The same is not true for economic preferences. First of all, Americans consider economic issues to be less religiously relevant than cultural issues (Guth et al., 2006; Pew Forum on Religion and Public Life, 2005). Within the US, religiosity's effects on economic attitudes tend to be small and inconsistent (e.g., Davis & Robinson, 1996; Jelen, 1990; Olson & Carroll, 1992; Tamney, Burton, & Johnson, 1989; Will & Cochran, 1995). This inconsistency may be the net outcome of competing effects across different segments of the population. For example, religiosity appears to have a relatively strong impact on economic conservatism among white Evangelical Protestants, effects that are weaker to non-existent among white mainline Protestants and white Catholics, and an effect on liberal economic preferences among black Protestants (Layman & Green, 2005; Malka et al., 2012). Also, the effect of religiosity on economic conservatism may be subject to competing influences via distinct psychological pathways. Malka, Soto, Cohen, and Miller (2011) found reliable support for a model in which religiosity triggers a pathway toward economic conservatism via culturally based conservative identity and a pathway toward economic liberalism via prosocial value orientation. Thus discursive messages may compel the religious to be economically conservative while a desire to help those in need may compel them to be economically liberal. That political discourse is a force linking religiosity and economic conservatism is consistent with findings that religiosity relates to economic conservatism among politically engaged Americans but that it does not among those who are relatively low in political engagement (Malka et al., 2012). And recent evidence suggests that any conflict regarding economic issues that religious conservatives might experience is sometimes dealt with by projecting their own political attitudes onto Jesus Christ (Ross, Lelkes, & Russell, 2012).

Psychological and Social Implications

The evidence reviewed in this chapter has both psychological and societal implications. One psychological implication has to do with the reasons for "constraint" across economic and cultural preferences. Constraint refers to the tendency to adopt an ideologically consistent configuration of attitudes (Converse, 1964). This tendency is not overwhelmingly strong within general publics, but it is substantially stronger among people who are highly politically engaged (e.g., Zaller, 1992). The findings reported here suggest that to whatever extent constraint does exist, religiosity does not appear to drive it. While religion is reliably linked with cultural conservatism, it is not so with economic conservatism. This should be kept in mind when evaluating claims and insinuations that unidimensional political ideology has a natural coherence with religious characteristics. It also casts skepticism on the practice of including religious content in broad measures of "conservatism."

However, evidence from American samples reveals that religiosity may relate to conservative economic and cultural preferences among people who are highly engaged with political discourse, but only to cultural preferences among those low in political engagement (Malka et al., 2012). This suggests the possibility of a discursively driven coherence between religiosity and conservative economic preferences among certain segments of the population. Religiosity may lead some people to economic liberalism via a desire to help others (e.g., Saroglou et al., 2005), but lead others to economic conservatism via a discursively driven pathway involving culturally based conservative identity (Malka et al., 2011). Regarding the latter pathway, some religious people may form ideological/partisan identities as a result of their cultural conservatism, and these identities may make them responsive to discursive cues in the economic domain (e.g., Cohen, 2003; Levendusky, 2009; Malka & Lelkes, 2010). Future research should explore the applicability of this process outside the US.

Another implication of the present review pertains to the social goals of promoting stability, democracy, and peace. In this regard, it is first of all important to acknowledge that the high level of cultural conservatism among Muslims does not mean that Muslims are opposed to democracy. In fact, overt support for democracy is as high in the Muslim world as it is in most of the rest of the world (Diamond, 2008; Inglehart, 2003). Democracy may indeed reflect a universal value for freedom and self-determination that is not specific to particular religious or cultural groups. However, the cultural conservatism of Muslims may have harmful implications for efforts to develop and consolidate democratic institutions in Muslim societies at a time when many of them are undergoing upheaval and transition. Inglehart (2003) reported evidence that a liberal societal view toward homosexuality is a far stronger predictor of sustained democratic institutions than is overt support for democracy. The explanation offered is that a mass cultural value of tolerance is necessary to uphold democratic institutions (e.g., Gibson, 1998; although see Muller & Seligson, 1994). As Inglehart (2003, p. 54) put it:

> Today, homosexuals constitute the most disliked group in most societies. Relatively few people express overt hostility toward other classes, races, or religions but rejection of homosexuals is widespread making attitudes toward them an effective litmus test of tolerance.

If it is true that dislike of homosexuals is the best way to gauge a society's tolerance, then a shift in cultural worldview may be necessary to bring about sustained democracy in the Muslim world.

Summary and Conclusion

There are pronounced differences in cultural political preferences across individuals of different religious affiliations and across individuals of different levels of religiosity. Muslims are more opposed to abortion and homosexuality than are members of other major religious groups and they are also more culturally conservative than one would predict on the basis of their national and individual wealth. Although Hindus and Buddhists are also relatively culturally conservative, new analyses with

WVS data suggest that, of these two, only Buddhists are more culturally conservative than what would be predicted based on their national and household wealth. Those without a religious affiliation show the opposite pattern; they are the most culturally liberal. That they are so is consistent with the reliable finding that those relatively high in religiosity are more culturally conservative than are those relatively low in religiosity. As for Christians, Catholics are somewhat conservative on abortion (but not homosexuality) whereas Orthodox Christians are conservative on homosexuality (but not abortion).

Religious affiliation differences in economic attitudes, having to do with redistributive social welfare policy and government intervention in the economy, are far less pronounced. The religious groups do not differ much in economic preferences. The new analyses do, however, suggest that Buddhists are relatively tolerant of income inequality, Hindus are economically liberal, and Muslims are relatively opposed to private ownership. Protestants seem to be more favorable to private ownership and individual responsibility for social welfare, but not more opposed to government efforts to promote economic equality. Effects of religiosity on economic preferences have been small and inconsistent. This may reflect competing influences of religious conviction on views about government's role in the economy.

The final point I make has to do with the claim that only religiously based cultural matters constitute "moral" issues whereas economic and other matters do not. This claim would be difficult to justify. Questions about the tradeoff between freedom and equality, and whether each is best promoted with or without an economically interventionist government, are most certainly moral matters. Moreover, religious conviction and moral conviction are not the same thing, and they can have independent influences on political viewpoints (Skitka, Bauman, & Lytle, 2009).

Nonetheless, the data show that issues concerning sex and family have more religious relevance to ordinary people than do economic issues. Why this is the case is not perfectly clear. It may have to do with specific traits and cognitive styles underlying both religiosity and cultural conservatism, but having little impact on economic attitudes (e.g., Crowson, 2009; Feldman & Johnston, in press). Or, it may reflect the contemporary tendency of elites to dwell on religion's cultural issue relevance while sidestepping or offering conflicting views about its economic relevance. This question is more than an intriguing theoretical matter; rather, it is one with implications for the nature and structure of social conflict.

Acknowledgments

Thanks to Yoel Epstein, Asher Lindenbaum, and Michael Silverstein for helpful comments on an earlier version of this chapter.

Notes

1 I do not refer here to liberalism in the classical sense, involving support of free markets and non-intervention of government in social life. Rather, I refer to liberalism as support of interventionist government in the economic domain and non-interventionist government in the social domain, the usage that currently predominates in the United States and other societies.

2 The cultural attitude domain, often called the "social" or "moral" domain, is often operationalized with indicators of sexual morality preferences, such as positions on abortion, homosexuality, and divorce (e.g., Baldassari & Gelman, 2008; Gerber, Huber, Doherty, Dowling, & Ha, 2010; Malka, Soto, Cohen, & Miller, 2011; Napier & Jost, 2008). In other studies, however, a broader cultural domain is assessed, that also includes positions on issues such as immigration and treatment of criminals and deviants (e.g., Treier & Hillygus, 2009). I focus on preferences concerning sexual morality because such attitudes have been widely studied in cross-national research on religion and political attitudes, tend to receive a strong emphasis in contemporary religious conservative movements, and may characterize a politically consequential fault line between societies (Norris & Inglehart, 2002). Readers interested in the effects of religion on other types of cultural attitude, particularly the complex effects of religion on prejudice, immigration attitudes, and crime attitudes are referred to Knoll, 2009; Malka & Soto, 2011; McDaniel, Nooruddin, & Shortle, 2010; Rowatt, Carpenter, & Haggard, Chapter 8, this volume; and Scheepers, Gijsberts, & Hello, 2002.

References

Adamczyk, A., & Pitt, C. (2009). Shaping attitudes about homosexuality: The role of religion and cultural context. *Social Science Research, 38*, 338–351.

Adorno, T. W., Frenkel-Brunswik, E., Levinson, D. J., & Sanford, R. N. (1950). *The authoritarian personality*. Oxford: Harpers.

Arzheimer, K., & Carter, E. (2009). Christian religiosity and voting for West European radical right parties. *West European Politics, 32*, 985–1011.

Baldassari, D., & Gelman, A. (2008). Partisans without constraint: Political polarization and trends in American public opinion. *American Journal of Sociology, 114*, 408–446.

Bar-Tal, D., Halperin, E., & Oren, N. (2010). Socio-psychological barriers to peace making: The case of the Israeli Jewish society. *Social Issues and Policy Review, 4*, 63–109.

Blogowska, J., & Saroglou, V. (2011, August). *Fundamentalism and authoritarianism: Global constructs, global relations?* Paper presented at the International Association for the Psychology of Religion Conference, Bari, Italy.

Camus, J. Y. (2007). The European extreme right and religious extremism. *Středoevropské Politické Studie [Central European Political Studies Review], 9*, 263–279.

Canetti, D., Hobfoll, S. E., Pedahzur, A., & Zaidise, E. (2010). Much ado about religion: Religiosity, resource loss, and support for political violence. *Journal of Peace Research, 47*, 575–587.

Cohen, A. B., & Rozin, P. (2001). Religion and the morality of mentality. *Journal of Personality and Social Psychology, 81*, 697–710.

Cohen, G. L. (2003). Party over policy: The dominating impact of group influence on political beliefs. *Journal of Personality and Social Psychology, 85*, 808–822.

Converse, P. E. (1964). The nature of belief systems in mass publics. In D. Apter (Ed.), *Ideology and discontent* (pp. 206–261). New York: Free Press.

Crowson, H. M. (2009). Are all conservatives alike? A study of the psychological correlates of cultural and economic conservatism. *Journal of Psychology: Interdisciplinary and Applied, 143*, 449–463.

Davis, N. J., & Robinson, R. V. (1996). Are the rumors of war exaggerated? Religious orthodoxy and moral progressivism in America. *American Journal of Sociology, 102*, 756–787.

Diamond, L. (2008). *The spirit of democracy: The struggle to build free societies throughout the world.* New York: Times Books.

Dobbelaere, K. (1985). Secularization theories and sociological paradigms: A reformation of the private–public dichotomy and the problem of social integration. *Sociology of Religion, 46*, 377–387.

Durkheim, E. (2001 [1912]). *The elementary forms of religious life.* New York: Oxford University Press.

Erikson, R. S., & Tedin, K. L. (2010). *American public opinion: Its origins, content, and impact* (8th ed.). New York: Pearson.

Esmer, Y., & Pettersson, T. (2007). The effects of religion and religiosity on voting behavior. In R. Goodin (Ed.), *The Oxford handbook of political behavior* (pp. 481–503). Oxford: Oxford University Press.

Feldman, S., & Johnston, C. D. (in press). Understanding the determinants of political ideology: Implications of structural complexity. *Political Psychology.*

Fiorina, M. P., Abrams, S. J., & Pope, J. (2005). *Culture war? The myth of a polarized America.* New York: Pearson Longman.

Galen, L. W. (2012a). Does religious belief promote prosociality? A critical examination. *Psychological Bulletin, 138*, 876–906.

Galen, L. W. (2012b). The complex and elusive nature of religious prosociality: Reply to Myers (2012) and Saroglou (2012). *Psychological Bulletin, 138*, 918–923.

Gerber, A. S., Huber, G. A., Doherty, D., Dowling, C. M., & Ha, S. E. (2010). Personality and political attitudes: Relationships across issue domains and political contexts. *American Political Science Review, 104*, 111–133.

Gibson, J. L. (1998). A sober second thought: An experiment in persuading Russians to tolerate. *American Journal of Political Science, 42*, 819–850.

Gill, A. (2001). Religion and comparative politics. *Annual Review of Political Science, 4*, 117–138.

Ginges, J., Altran, S., Medin, D., & Shikaki, K. (2007). Sacred bounds on rational resolution of violent political conflict. *Proceedings of the National Academy of Sciences, 104*, 7357–7360.

Ginges, J., Hansen, I., & Norenzayan, A. (2009). Religion and support for suicide attacks. *Psychological Science, 20*, 224–230.

GlobeScan Incorporated. (2006). *Indians proud of Country but worried caste system is holding country back.* BBC World Service. Retrieved from http://www.globescan.com/ news_archives/bbc_india/bbcindia.pdf.

Guiso, L., Sapienza, P., & Zingales, L. (2003). People's opium? Religion and economic attitudes. *Journal of Monetary Economics, 50,* 225–282

Guth, J. L., Kellstedt, L. A., Smidt, C. E., & Green, J. C. (2006). Religious influences in the 2004 presidential election. *Presidential Studies Quarterly, 36,* 223–242.

Hadden, J. (1987). Toward desacralizing secularization theory. *Social Forces, 65,* 587–611.

Hammack, P. (2010). *Narrative and the politics of identity: The cultural psychology of Israeli and Palestinian youth.* New York: Oxford University Press.

Hayes, B. C. (1995). The impact of religious identification on political attitudes: An international comparison. *Sociology of Religion, 56,* 177–194.

Hayward, R. D., & Kemmelmeier, M. (2011). Weber revisited: A cross-national analysis of religiosity, religious culture, and economic attitudes. *Journal of Cross-Cultural Psychology, 42,* 1406–1420.

Hill, P. C., & Pargament, K. I. (2003). Advances in the conceptualization and measurement of religion and spirituality: Implications for physical and mental health research. *American Psychologist, 58,* 64–74.

Hirsh, J. B., Walberg, M. D., & Peterson, J. B. (2013). Spiritual liberals and religious conservatives. *Social Psychological and Personality Science, 4,* 14–20.

Hunter, J. D. (1991). *Culture wars: The struggle to define America.* New York: Basic Books.

Huntington, S. P. (1996). *The clash of civilizations and the remaking of the world order.* New York: Simon & Schuster.

Inglehart, R. (1990). *Culture shift in advanced industrial society.* Princeton, NJ: Princeton University Press.

Inglehart, R. (2003). How solid is mass support for democracy—And how can we measure it? *Political Science and Politics, 36,* 51–57.

Jelen, T. G. (1990). Religious belief and attitude constraint. *Journal for the Scientific Study of Religion, 29,* 118–125.

Jost, J. T. (2007). Coda: After "The end of the end of ideology"— Reply to Glassman and Karno (2007) and Unger (2007). *American Psychologist, 62,* 1077–1080.

Katnik, A. (2002). Religion, social class, and political tolerance: A cross-national analysis. *International Journal of Sociology, 32,* 14–38.

Knoll, B. R. (2009). "And who is my neighbor?" Religion and immigration policy attitudes. *Journal for the Scientific Study of Religion, 48,* 313–331.

Knutsen, O. (2004). Religious denomination and party choice in Western Europe: A comparative longitudinal study from eight countries, 1970–1997. *International Political Science Review, 25,* 97–128.

Laitin, D. (1978). Religion, political culture, and the Weberian tradition. *World Politics, 30,* 563–592.

Layman, G. C. (1997). Religion and political behavior in the United States: The impact of beliefs, affiliations, and commitment from 1980 to 1994. *Public Opinion Quarterly, 61,* 288–316.

Layman, G. C. (2001). *The great divide: Religious and cultural conflict in American party politics.* New York: Columbia University Press.

Layman, G. C., & Carmines, E. G. (1997). Cultural conflict in American politics: Religious traditionalism, postmaterialism, and U.S. political behavior. *Journal of Politics, 59,* 751–777.

Layman, G. C., & Green, J. C. (2005). Wars and rumours of wars: The contexts of cultural conflict in American political behaviour. *British Journal of Political Science, 36*, 61–89.

Leege, D. C., & Kellstedt, L. A. (1993). *Rediscovering the religious factor in American politics*. New York: M. E. Sharpe Inc.

Levendusky, M. (2009). *The partisan sort: How liberals became democrats and conservatives became republicans*. Chicago, IL: University of Chicago Press.

McDaniel, E. L., Nooruddin, I., & Shortle, A. F. (2011). Divine boundaries: How religion shapes citizens' attitudes toward immigrants. *American Politics Research, 39*, 205–233.

Malka, A., & Lelkes, Y. (2010). More than ideology: Conservative-liberal identity and receptivity to political cues. *Social Justice Research, 23*, 156–188.

Malka, A., Lelkes, Y., Srivastava, S., Cohen, A. B., & Miller, D. T. (2012). The association of religiosity and political conservatism: The role of political engagement. *Political Psychology, 33*, 275–299.

Malka, A., & Soto, C. J. (2011). The conflicting influences of religiosity on attitude toward torture. *Personality and Social Psychology Bulletin, 37*, 1091–1103.

Malka, A., Soto, C. J., Cohen, A. B., & Miller, D. T. (2011). Religiosity and social welfare: Competing influences of cultural conservatism and prosocial value orientation. *Journal of Personality, 79*, 763–792.

Martin, D. (1978). *A general theory of secularization*. Oxford: Blackwell.

Mogahed, D., & Younis, A. (2011). Religion does not color views about violence. *Gallup*. Retrieved from http://www.gallup.com/poll/149369/religion-not-color-views-violence.aspx.

Muller, E. N., & Seligson, M. A. (1994). Civic culture and democracy: The question of causal relationships. *American Political Science Review, 88*, 635–652.

Napier, J. L., & Jost, J. T. (2008). The "antidemocratic personality" revisited: A cross national investigation of working-class authoritarianism. *Journal of Social Issues, 64*, 595–617.

Newport, F. (2009). Catholics similar to mainstream on abortion, stem cells: Catholics actually more liberal on some issues. *Gallup*. Retrieved from http://www.gallup.com/poll/117154/ catholicssimilarmainstream-abortion-stemcells.aspx.

Norris, P., & Inglehart, R. (2002). Islamic culture and democracy: Testing the "Clash of Civilizations" thesis. *Comparative Sociology, 1*, 235–263.

Norris, P., & Inglehart, R. (2011). *Sacred and secular: Religion and politics worldwide* (2nd ed.). New York: Cambridge University Press.

Nyiri, Z. (2007). Values questions set European Muslims apart. *Gallup*. Retrieved from http://www.gallup.com/poll/27397/values-questions-set-european-muslimsapart.aspx.

Olson, D. V. A., & Carroll, J. W. (1992). Religiously based politics: Religious elites and the public. *Social Forces, 70*, 765–786.

Patrikios, S. (2008). American Republican religion? Disentangling the causal link between religion and politics in the US. *Political Behavior, 30*, 367–389.

Pew Forum on Religion and Public Life (2005). *Religion and public life: A faith-based partisan divide*. Retrieved from http://pewforum.org/uploadedfiles/ Topics/Issues/ Politics_and_Elections/religion-and-politics-report.pdf.

Putnam, R., & Campbell, D. E. (2010). *American grace: How religion divides and unites us.* New York: Simon & Schuster.

Rokeach, M. (1960). *The open and closed mind.* Oxford: Basic Books.

Ross, L. D., Lelkes, Y., & Russell, A. G. (2012). How Christians reconcile their personal political views and the teachings of their faith: Projection as a means of dissonance reduction. *Proceedings of the National Academy of Science, 109,* 3616–3622.

Saroglou, V., Pichon, I., Trompette, L., Verschueren, M., & Dernelle, R. (2005). Prosocial behavior and religion: New evidence based on projective measures and peer ratings. *Journal for the Scientific Study of Religion, 44,* 323–348.

Scheepers, P., Gijsberts, M., & Hello, E. (2002). Religiosity and prejudice against ethnic minorities in Europe: Cross-national tests on a controversial relationship. *Review of Religious Research, 43,* 242–265.

Scheepers, P., Te Grotenhuis, M., & Van Der Slik, F. (2002). Education, religiosity and moral attitudes: Explaining cross-national effect differences. *Sociology of Religion, 63,* 157–176.

Scott, J. (1998a). Changing attitudes to sexual morality: A cross-national comparison. *Sociology, 32,* 815–845.

Scott, J. (1998b). Generational changes in attitudes to abortion: A cross-national comparison. *European Sociological Review, 14,* 177–190.

Shafer, B. E., & Claggett, W. J. (1995). *The two majorities: The issue context of modern American politics.* Baltimore, MD: Johns Hopkins University Press.

Shariff, A. F., & Norenzayan, A. (2007). God is watching you: Priming God concept increases prosocial behavior in an anonymous economic game. *Psychological Science, 18,* 803–809.

Skitka, L. J., Bauman, C. W., & Lytle, B. L. (2009). Limits on legitimacy: Moral and religious convictions as constraints on deference to authority. *Journal of Personality and Social Psychology, 97,* 567–578.

Smith, B. G., & Stark, R. (2009). Religious attendance relates to generosity worldwide: Religious and the secular more charitable if they attend services. *Gallup.* Retrieved from http://www.gallup.com/poll/122807/religious-attendance-relates-generosity-worldwide.aspx.

Smith, D. E. (1971). *Religion, politics, and social change in the third world.* New York: Free Press.

Spilka, B., Hood, R. W., Jr., Hunsberger, B., & Gorsuch, R. (2003). *The psychology of religion: An empirical approach* (3rd ed.). New York: Guilford.

Stark, R. (1999). Secularization, R.I.P. *Sociology and Religion, 60,* 249–273.

Štulhofer, A., & Rimac, I. (2009). Determinants of homonegativity in Europe. *Journal of Sex Research, 46,* 24–32.

Tamney, J. B., Burton, R., & Johnson, S. D. (1989). Fundamentalism and economic restructuring. In T. G. Jelen (Ed.), *Religion and political behavior in the United States* (pp. 67–82). New York: Praeger.

Tessler, M. (2003). Arab and Muslim political attitudes: Stereotypes and evidence from survey research. *International Studies Perspectives, 4,* 175–181.

Treier, S., & Hillygus, D. S. (2009). The nature of political ideology in the contemporary electorate. *Public Opinion Quarterly, 73,* 679–703.

Uppal, J. S. (1986). Hinduism and economic development in South Asia. *International Journal of Social Economics, 13,* 20–33.

Weber, M. (1963). *The sociology of religion.* Boston, MA: Beacon Press. (Original work published 1922)

Weber, M. (2002). *The Protestant ethic and the spirit of capitalism.* New York: Penguin Group. (Original work published 1905)

Welzel, C., Inglehart, R., & Klingemann, H. (2003). The theory of human development: A cross-cultural analysis. *European Journal of Political Research, 42,* 341–379.

Wilcox, C., & Larson, C. (2006). *Onward Christian soldiers? The religious right in American politics.* Boulder, CO: Westview Press.

Will, J. A., & Cochran, J. K. (1995). God helps those who help themselves? The effects of religious affiliation, religiosity, and deservedness on generosity toward the poor. *Sociology of Religion, 56,* 327–338.

Wilson, G. D. (1973). *The psychology of conservatism.* London: Academic Press.

Wilson, G. D., & Patterson, J. R. (1968). A new measure of conservatism. *British Journal of Social and Clinical Psychology, 7,* 264–269.

World Values Survey 1981-2008 Official Aggregate. (2009). *World Values Survey Association.* Retrieved from http://www.wvsevsdb.com/wvs/WVSData.jsp.

Wuthnow, R. (1988). *The restructuring of American religion: Society and faith since World War II.* Princeton, NJ: Princeton University Press.

Yuchtman-Yaar, E., & Alkalay, Y. (2007). Religious zones, economic development and modern value orientations: Individual versus contextual effects. *Social Science Research, 36,* 789–807.

Zaller, J. (1992). *The nature and origins of mass opinion.* Cambridge: Cambridge University Press.

12 Religion, Mental Health, and Well-Being

Social Aspects

R. David Hayward and Neal Krause

Psychologists have been interested in the capacity of religion to affect happiness and mental health since William James first articulated the distinction between the religion of the "healthy minded" and "sick souled" in his *Varieties of religious experience* (1902). Yet only relatively recently has a sizeable body of empirical evidence developed to substantiate the relationship between religion and well-being, and to begin to delineate the specific factors by which it operates. As recently as 1993, in their landmark volume on the social psychology of religion, Batson, Schoenrade, and Ventis were able to remark on the basis of their review of the literature that "the relationship between religious involvement and mental health seems weak, but, if anything, appears to be *negative* rather than positive" (p. 240, emphasis in original). In the intervening years, the research landscape has changed dramatically. The volume of research addressing both the positive and negative aspects of this relationship has multiplied many times over, and there is strong evidence that religious involvement has, on average, a modest but robust relationship with lower incidence and severity of mental illness, and with greater psychological well-being overall (see Koenig, King, & Carson, 2012 for a comprehensive review). Meta-analyses have estimated an average effect of magnitude $r = -0.09$ between religiousness and depression (Smith, McCullough, & Poll, 2003), and $r = 0.11$ between religiousness and general psychological well-being (Hackney & Sanders, 2003). At the same time, there are elements of religion that have deleterious effects, and the understanding of this "dark side" of religion has also expanded (see Ellison & Lee, 2010). Consequently, recent research has turned to the task of uncovering the mechanisms by which these relationships operate.

Ever since psychologists first began to study religion, a number of researchers have maintained that religion is an inherently social phenomenon. For example, James Mark Baldwin, an early president of the American Psychological Association, maintained that: "The fact is constantly recognized that religion is a social phenomenon. No man is religious by himself, nor does he choose his god, nor devise his offerings, nor enjoy his blessings alone" (1902, p. 325). Religion is a complex and multifaceted set of phenomena, but the interface of group and individual processes cuts across many of these facets. Religion is to an overwhelming extent transmitted and performed within the context of organizations, and thus these groups' structures, norms, and social networks exert a profound influence on what their members take away from participating. At the same time, it is central to religion that it entails particular ways of perceiving and thinking about the world, which have their primary impact at the level of individual psychology: on cognition, perception, and affect. Group and individual elements have reciprocal influence, as groups act to teach and reinforce the beliefs that reflect their norms and values, while the group exists through particular instances of individual interaction. There is a wealth of empirical evidence supporting both group-mediated and psychosocial pathways connecting religion with mental health. A smaller, but growing, body of research concerns aspects of the interface between the group and the individual. In particular, the potential role of religious identity as a mediator between group processes and individual mental health consequences has become a recent subject of investigation from a social psychological perspective.

This chapter is organized around these three general approaches to explaining the connection between religion and mental health: social resources that come from belonging to a religious community, psychological resources that come from having religious beliefs, and social identity resources that come from categorization as a member of a religious group. We focus on empirical studies addressing the social pathways of mediation between religion and mental health. There is a far broader body of literature consisting of studies measuring the relationship between religion and mental health without directly assessing its mediation, or focusing on personality, clinical, or physiological elements connecting them. A number of excellent recent volumes provide valuable reviews on topics related to religion and mental health that fall outside the scope of this chapter (e.g., Koenig et al., 2012; Paloutzian & Park, 2013; Pargament, 2013).

Challenges in the Study of Religion and Mental Health

A few methodological issues pose challenges that must be explicitly addressed in attempting to create a coherent picture of the literature in the area of religion and mental health. Perhaps most important is the question of conceptualization and measurement. Both religion and mental health represent broad categories, and the decisions researchers make in terms of how to measure each of them may profoundly impact the results they produce. Mental health and well-being may be conceived in a number of ways, but the most common approaches are to examine either the presence of positive attributes (e.g., happiness, satisfaction with life), or the absence of negative attributes (e.g., depressed affect, diagnosis of psychiatric illness). A subset of the latter approach involves focusing specifically on the severity or course of mental illness among individuals suffering from specific disorders.

There is even greater diversity in approaches to measuring religion (see Hall, Meador, & Koenig, 2008). Key elements of religion that are used because of their inclusion in a wide variety of broader studies are organizational behavior (e.g., frequency of attendance at public worship), non-organizational behavior (e.g., frequency of prayer or scripture reading), and measures of the subjective importance of religion (e.g., "religiosity," religious salience). Research designed with religion as a primary subject of study typically includes more detailed measures tailored to some of its specific elements, such as congregational support and religious coping. One conflict that must be assessed when interpreting these studies is that of specificity versus generality: different religious traditions may in some cases vary greatly in terms of core beliefs and their psychosocial consequences. Thus the choice must sometimes be made between a measure that is highly relevant to members of one religious tradition but of questionable value when applied to another, and one that is more universal but fails to capture important processes at work within specific groups. This is an issue that can be addressed by careful interpretation of a study's findings. More problematic is maintaining conceptual clarity in distinguishing between religious and mental health-related constructs, an issue that has been clearly articulated by Koenig (2008). In brief, certain measures of religious constructs may be conflated with positive psychological states, artificially inflating their correlation with well-being.

A related consideration is the impact of culture (see Johnson & Cohen, Chapter 15, this volume). Most research regarding religion and well-being has been conducted in Western, Christian-dominated populations, and within that group North America is overrepresented in comparison to Europe. In addition to differences among religious traditions in terms of beliefs and structure, there is considerable evidence that these populations are generally unrepresentative of the rest of the world (see Henrich, Heine, & Norenzayan, 2010 for a thorough summary). The generalizability of these findings to contexts defined by different cultural and religious histories is thus not yet established. Results from the few major single-country studies outside of the West show mixed results (Brown & Tierney, 2009; Kim, 2003; Krause et al., 2010; Suhail & Chaudhry, 2004). Cross-national analyses have found that there are differences in the relationship between some religious and well-being factors that may be partially due to other attributes that differ between countries, such as the general level of religiosity in the population (Gebauer, Sedikides, & Neberich, 2012; Okulicz-Kozaryn, 2010), and to the extent of government regulation of religion (Elliott & Hayward, 2009).

Finally, because the majority of the research in this area is cross-sectional and correlational, the question of directionality remains an important concern. Assuming that there is a correlation between religion and better mental health, it is equally possible to account for this in terms of individuals with better mental health tending to participate more in religion as it is to assume that participating in religion leads to better mental health. This point has been made by notable critics of the study of religion and health more generally (e.g., Sloan, 2008), and there is some empirical evidence that selection effects may play a role in the observed relationship. For example, one study using longitudinal epidemiological data found that women who experienced early onset of depression were more likely than their non-depressed age peers to drop out of religious participation in early adulthood, and thus associations between religious participation and low depression incidence later in life may have been spurious (Maselko, Hayward, Hanlon, Buka, & Meador, 2012). The majority of the studies reviewed in this chapter are based on cross-sectional data, but a growing body of longitudinal research has also begun to address the question of directionality more carefully. Additionally, a growing body of laboratory-based experimental and quasi-experimental research has begun to explicate some of the potential causal mechanisms linking manipulable elements, such as priming with religious symbols, with immediate changes in outcomes influencing well-being.

Group Resources: Religion as Belonging

The first general category of religious elements that may have an impact on mental health and well-being are those that stem directly from belonging to a religious group. While there is great diversity between religious traditions in the use and structure of organized religious communities, it is common for groups of some sort to regularly gather for the purposes of worship and mutual spiritual support. In some cases, these congregations[1] may influence their members' psychological well-being directly by providing access to mental health care resources, but the bulk of their effects are probably indirect, resulting from participation in formal and informal social networks, or as the byproduct of compliance with group religious practices.

Formal Mental Health Services

One way in which congregations may benefit their members' well-being through organizational means is by acting as a nexus for the provision of and referral to formal mental health care services. A significant amount of research into the scope and effectiveness of formal congregation-based programs of this type resulted from changes in law and public policy in the US during the early 2000s that sought to encourage government funding for these activities (Chaves & Tsitsos, 2001). Studies aimed at quantifying congregational social services have produced a mixed picture of their formal role as mental health care providers. In their nationally representative sample of congregations in the US, Chaves and Tsitsos (2001) found that while a majority of congregations provided at least one formal social service, only 7% offered health or substance abuse services, although their study did not distinguish between mental health and other health services. In a study focused specifically on mental health services provided by congregations in the southern US, Blank, Mahmood, Fox, and Guterbock (2002) found that African American congregations were substantially more likely to provide programs of this type, but also that these programs were relatively rare overall.

However, religious factors may also contribute to the apparent neglect of mental health among congregational services, as there may be real or perceived conflicts between theological and medical or psychological explanations of mental illness, particularly among members of more conservative religious groups, that discourage cooperation (Trice & Bjorck, 2006; Wesselmann & Graziano, 2010). The implications of this situation for the effectiveness of the formal programs that do exist is not clear; a comprehensive review of evaluations of congregation-based social services found that only two mental health programs had been evaluated, each with small samples (DeHaven, Hunter, Wilder, Walton, & Berry, 2004).

Pastoral Care and Support from Clergy

Although only a minority of congregations provide formal mental health care services, pastoral care is a nearly universal feature of religious groups. A large study of data from the US National Comorbidity Survey found that about a quarter of those diagnosed with a mental disorder consulted a member of the clergy before seeking professional treatment, although the proportion appeared to have decreased over the course of several decades (Wang, Berglund, & Kessler, 2003). Other studies have found that those most likely to seek help with mental health problems from clergy include members of underserved categories (Ellison, Vaaler, Flannelly, & Weaver, 2006). The impact of this pattern of support is ambiguous, given that clergy members may lack appropriate training to address serious mental health problems (Weaver, 1995) and that, at least among African Americans, it appears that seeking support from clergy may serve to discourage seeking support from other sources (Neighbors, Musick, & Williams, 1998).

The influence of more general forms of emotional support from religious leaders has received less empirical evaluation, but one study focusing on older adults found that receiving emotional support from clergy members was associated with better self-esteem among African Americans, but not among whites (perhaps reflecting the greater salience of clergy as community leaders in the African American church), while negative interaction with the clergy was associated with lower self-esteem in both groups (Krause, 2003a). A longitudinal study in the same population found that older adults received more emotional support from the clergy after experiencing stressful life events, and that those receiving more support subsequently experienced increased hope (Krause & Hayward, 2012a). One qualitative study conducted among clergy members in the UK suggests a broadly similar situation, with religious leaders commonly being called on for support with mental health issues (Leavey, Loewenthal, & King, 2007).

Social Support and Interaction with Other Group Members

The beneficial relationship between social support—the tangible and socioemotional support received from one's social ties—and well-being has long been established (e.g., Cohen & Wills, 1985). One approach to researching social support in the context of religious groups is thus to treat it as functionally the same as secular forms of social support, from sources like neighborhoods and families. Religious congregations serve to embed their members in a network of enduring social relationships, so active religious participants should have larger support networks, from which they should receive greater benefit. Several large studies based on representative surveys of the population of the US have demonstrated that more frequent religious group participation is related to general forms of social support. In a regional sample of older adults in New England, Idler (1987) found that more frequent worship attendance was related to having a greater number of social ties overall, as well as to greater intimacy with members of one's social network. Ellison and George (1994) examined another regional sample, representing adults of all ages in a single southern community, with similar results: frequency of religious participation was related to having both a larger number of non-family social ties, and to greater frequency of contact with them.

The case for a directional relationship, in which religious participation has an impact on social ties, is bolstered by a study of longitudinal data from a representative sample of the adult population of a California county, which found that people who were attending religious services at least weekly in 1965 were much more likely to see their social network size increase by 1994, and less likely to see it shrink, compared with less frequent attenders (Strawbridge, Shema, Cohen, & Kaplan, 2001). In addition to the amount of participation, a congregation's character may also have an impact on the degree of social support that its members exchange; a study matching members' social support with separately collected data on organizational characteristics of the congregation found that people experienced less support in groups that were very large, and that offered few opportunities for social interaction (Ellison, Krause, Shepherd, & Chaves, 2009).

But while there is clear evidence that participating in a religious group is related to better social integration overall, it is less clear the extent to which this alone serves to mediate its relationship with mental health. For example, Idler's (1987) study of older adults found that none of the salutary relationship between religious participation and depression symptoms was explained by the fact that more religious individuals had larger social networks. Several more recent studies have sought to articulate the role of general social support, both inside and outside the church, in this relationship using more detailed measures in more restricted samples, with mixed results. For example, studies of depression in medical patients have found that higher levels of social support do not account for a significant amount of the relationship between frequent religious participation and the initial severity (Hayward, Owen, Koenig, Steffens, & Payne, 2012a) or time to remission (Koenig, 2007). However, both of these studies used relatively simple designs, modeling single outcomes. Several studies examining more complex structural equation models of the factors mediating the religion–mental health relationship have found that while more frequent religious participation does have an indirect relationship with fewer depression symptoms via that path of general social support, it also has an equal or greater direct relationship among Korean immigrant older adults (Park, Roh, & Yeo, 2012), and longitudinally among cardiac patients (Ai, Park, Huang, Rodgers, & Tice, 2007) and psychiatric patients (Hayward, Owen, Koenig, Steffens, & Payne, 2012b).

In contrast to those studies focused on total social support as an element of the religion–mental health relationship, many researchers have focused specifically on support processes within the congregation, and particularly on ways in which religious support may differ from that received in secular settings. There is empirical support for both the hypotheses that the high salience and self-centrality of the religious groups serves to enhance the impact of congregational support on well-being, and that there are certain qualitative differences between congregational and secular support that confer additional well-being benefits. A number of studies have found a beneficial association of congregational support with key outcomes including psychological distress (Walls & Zarit, 1991), depression symptoms (Nooney & Woodrum, 2002), and risk of a range of psychiatric diagnoses (Kendler et al., 2003). Further studies have found evidence of a differential impact of this congregational support, accruing particularly strongly for the most highly involved members. Krause, Ellison, and Wulff (1998), examining a representative sample of Presbyterian church members and leaders in the US, found that clergy and elders not only received more emotional support from the congregation, compared with more peripherally involved lay members, but that this support also had a stronger impact on their reported affect. In a sample more broadly representing the population of the US, Lim and Putnam (2010) found that while the size of one's congregational friendship network was related to greater life satisfaction, this effect became stronger in proportion to the centrality of the congregation to one's identity. Thus, to the extent that religion's cultural and existential importance make the congregation an especially salient social group, it is likely that congregational support has a more pronounced impact on well-being than support received in more peripherally important settings.

In addition to these ways in which the congregational setting may enhance the impact of general social support, there is evidence that congregational support has unique elements that may further increase these effects. In particular, Krause, Ellison, Shaw, Marcum, and Boardman (2001) found evidence using second-order factor analysis that "spiritual support," a construct encompassing specifically religious elements such as discussing one's religious experiences with others and receiving support in following religious principles, was conceptually distinct from both emotional and tangible support received in religious settings. They also found that receiving spiritual support was more strongly related with use of religious coping strategies than was receiving church-based emotional and tangible support. Subsequent research using this construct has found that receiving spiritual support from a religious congregation is related cross-sectionally to greater optimism (Krause, 2002) and sense of closeness to God (Krause & Hayward, 2013b), and longitudinally to lower religious doubt (Krause & Ellison, 2009) and stronger sense of god-mediated control (Krause, 2007). Although no direct effect of spiritual support on mental health outcomes has been established, each of these outcomes has been related to well-being benefits, and thus an indirect effect appears plausible.

As is the case in any group, not all social relationships within the congregation are supportive. Negative interaction, including feelings that other members are too demanding, judgmental, or excluding, is reported by qualitative studies of church experiences to be an intense topic of concern and discussion (Krause, Chatters, & Meltzer, 2000). Several quantitative studies in the US have also substantiated the deleterious relationship between negative interaction in the congregation and worse mental health, including among adolescents (Pearce, Little, & Perez, 2003), medical patients (Cohen, Yoon, & Johnstone, 2009), Mexican American older adults (Krause & Hayward, 2012b), and longitudinally in the general adult population (Ellison, Zhang, Krause, & Marcum, 2009). In tandem with their finding that emotional support was more beneficial for those holding congregational leadership roles, Krause et al. (2001) found that leaders also suffered the greatest harm from negative interaction. Thus the generally beneficial impact of the religious group as a source of social support appears to be significantly tempered.

Psychosocial Resources: Religion as Believing

The second general set of processes that have been investigated as mediators of the relationship between religion and health are psychological factors. Religious groups may encourage their members to adopt a variety of particular beliefs that, when internalized, may influence cognitive processes and thus, in turn, have an impact on mental health and well-being outcomes. Three key ways in which religious beliefs may influence mental health and well-being, and which have received significant attention from researchers, are by providing cognitive tools for coping with stressful life events, by providing means to reduce existential uncertainty and the anxiety associated with it, and by providing ways of enhancing the sense of control.

Religious Coping Resources

When faced with stressful and traumatic events, the methods used to cope can have a dramatic impact on the ability to minimize psychological distress and maintain a sense of well-being (Lazarus & Folkman, 1984). Systems of religious belief often entail views of the world that help believers to reframe negative life events in such a way as to cope with them more effectively. A recent study based on representative survey data from the US found that use of religious faith and practices to cope with stress is highly prevalent overall, although its use varies substantially by race and religious background, with 67% of non-Hispanic whites, but 90% of African Americans reporting that prayer was a "very important" method of coping with stress (Chatters, Taylor, Jackson, & Lincoln, 2008). Another study conducted immediately after the terrorist attacks of September 11, 2001, found that 90% of adults in the US reported "turning to prayer, religion, or spiritual feelings" as a means of coping with stress related to the event (Schuster et al., 2001). Other studies examining groups undergoing specific forms of stress find that religious coping is often an important element of dealing with life events including hospitalization (Koenig, Pargament, & Nielsen, 1998), serious mental illness (Tepper, Rogers, Coleman, & Malony, 2001), and bereavement (Park & Cohen, 1993). A number of studies outside of the US, for example in the UK (Bhui, King, Dein, & O'Connor, 2008), Japan (Krause et al., 2010), and Pakistan (Khan & Watson, 2006) have also indicated that religious coping is a common method of dealing with stress.

Pargament and his colleagues have articulated a detailed taxonomy of religious coping techniques, including 21 specific methods, such as reappraising the situation to see it as part of God's plan, or seeking a closer spiritual connection with God (Pargament, Koenig, & Perez, 2000). This general framework for understanding religious coping processes has been adopted in numerous subsequent studies. Use of certain types of religious coping to deal with stressful events appears to have a generally beneficial association with well-being, as demonstrated by a major meta-analysis finding an overall effect size of $r = 0.32$ between positive religious coping and positive adjustment, and of $r = -0.12$ between positive religious coping and negative adjustment (Ano & Vasconcelles, 2005).

Most studies examining the impact of religious coping and mental health outcomes have focused on groups undergoing specific stressful life events. One study with a broader focus, using longitudinal survey data representative of the population of the US (Schnittker, 2001), found that individuals who engaged in more religious coping also suffered from more symptoms of depression. However, in the same study, use of religious coping was also associated with a reduced subsequent impact of stressful life events on depression symptoms, suggesting that religious coping may increase as a response to stress, and then has a partial buffering effect. In this vein, several major studies have found that pre-operation use of religious coping strategies predicts lower post-operation distress and greater well-being in patients undergoing major surgery (Ai, Pargament, Kronfol, Tice, & Appel, 2010; Ai et al., 2007). Similar relationships between religious coping and well-being have also been reported cross-sectionally among war refugees (Ai, Peterson, & Huang, 2003), family members of murder victims (Thompson & Vardaman, 1997), and college students coping with the death of a friend (Park & Cohen, 1993), and longitudinally among victims of a major flood (Smith, Pargament, Brant, & Oliver, 2000), and recently divorced individuals (Krumrei, Mahoney, & Pargament, 2011).

In addition to its immediate stress-buffering effects, positive religious coping may have an impact on long-term well-being by facilitating stress-related growth, which in turn bolsters well-being through social and emotional pathways (Park, Cohen, & Murch, 1996). Support for this view was found in a study of more than 500 medical patients showing that more use of religious coping, on a variety of specific subscales, was related to greater stress-related growth, and furthermore that these relationships were stronger than those connecting non-religious forms of coping with stress-related growth (Koenig et al., 1998). Two smaller studies of bereavement similarly found that individuals using positive religious coping to a greater extent were more able to derive personal growth in the wake of the death of a child (Maton, 1989) or friend (Park & Cohen, 1993). Along similar lines, Maltby, Day, and Barber (2004), in a study of British adults, found that those using religious coping techniques were more likely to make challenge-based appraisals of stressful events, suggesting greater potential for successful growth.

Not all forms of religious coping are adaptive, however. Negative religious coping includes those aspects that exacerbate stressful events either by placing emphasis on anxiety-inducing elements such as sin and fear of divine punishment, or by encouraging deferral of other active forms of coping, for example, by waiting for God to resolve the problem (Pargament et al., 2000). Ano and Vasconcelles' (2005) meta-analysis found that negative religious coping had an overall relationship with effect size $r = 0.22$ on negative stress adjustment, although its relationship with positive adjustment was not significant. Elaborating on this basic relationship, in a nationally representative sample in the US, McConnell, Pargament, Ellison, and Flannelly (2006) found that the deleterious relationship between negative coping and mental health was more severe among individuals suffering from the stress of a recent illness, compared with those who were healthy. Among those coping with a recent divorce, negative coping was related to worse depression after one year, an effect which was exacerbated by the belief that divorce represented an act of religious desecration (Krumrei et al., 2011).

Existential Certainty Reduction

Another psychosocial pathway by which religion may influence well-being is by reducing existential uncertainty (Hogg, Adelman, & Blagg, 2010; Vail et al., 2010). Religious beliefs often provide a way to answer potentially anxiety-inducing questions about the meaning of life, the significance of the individual in the universe, and what happens after death. Moreover, participation in a religious community consisting of others holding the same beliefs serves to reinforce the perception of consensus, providing a further sense of certainty, and forming the basis of what Berger (1967) called the "sacred canopy." In keeping with this view, analysis of social network data indicates that religious attendance is most beneficial for those with highly religiously homogeneous friendship networks (Brashears, 2010).

Several recent studies have demonstrated the connection between religion and existential certainty from the perspective of Terror Management Theory (Vail et al., 2010). Norenzayan and Hansen (2006) found that mortality salience caused experimental participants to rate themselves as more religious and as believing more strongly in God (Studies 1 and 2), as well as causing religious participants to report stronger beliefs in supernatural agency, even outside the context of their own faith (Studies 3 and 4). Taking up the next step in the process, three studies have shown that religious beliefs can go on to moderate the impact of existential uncertainty on other psychological outcomes. Jonas and Fischer (2006) found that when they had the opportunity to affirm their religious beliefs, participants who were high in intrinsic religiosity did not react with defense against mortality salience (Studies 1 and 2), and that this was attributable to a buffering effect against heightened availability of death-related thoughts among the highly religious (Study 3). Norenzayan, Dar-Nimrod, Hansen, and Proulx (2009) found that self-identified "religious" and "not religious" participants differed in terms of their reactions to mortality salience priming; religious individuals did not react with worldview defense, although in this case they did experience increased death-thought availability (Study 2). Similarly, Friedman and Rholes (2008) found that mortality salience did not prompt worldview defense among individuals scoring highly on a scale of fundamentalism, and additionally found evidence that this was partially due to greater prevalence of positive attitudes towards death among highly fundamentalist participants. Taken together, these results suggest that one way in which religion may serve to improve well-being is by effectively buffering against some of the anxiety associated with existential uncertainty; mortality salience activates the religious belief system, which, in turn, moderates the impact of that anxiety.

Results of several survey research studies also provide empirical support for the connection between holding specific religious beliefs that provide existential certainty, and enhanced well-being. In a study of older adults, Krause (2003b) found that those who derived a stronger sense of meaning in general from their religious faith enjoyed more self-esteem and satisfaction with life. In a longitudinal diary study that tracked daily spirituality and well-being in a sample of 87 participants over the course of two weeks, Kashdan and Nezlek (2012) found that higher self-rated spirituality on one day was associated with greater self-esteem and positive affect on the next day, and that this association was mediated by higher next-day sense of meaning in life. Other studies have focused on specific beliefs that may enhance existential certainty. Several studies have found belief in an afterlife to be related to lower anxiety (Ellison, Burdette, & Hill, 2009), less psychological distress in the face of hardship (Bradshaw & Ellison, 2010), and less incidence of a range of mental illnesses (Flannelly, Koenig, Ellison, Galek, & Krause, 2006). Viewing God as taking an active and positive role in one's life also appears to be related to better well-being. Having an image of God as loving and close is related to lower incidence of mental illness (Bradshaw, Ellison, & Flannelly, 2008), and believing that God can be trusted to answer one's prayers is related cross-sectionally to a reduced impact of lifetime trauma on symptoms of depression in late life (Krause, 2008), and longitudinally to increased life satisfaction over time (Krause & Hayward, 2013a).

By the same token, some religious beliefs may serve to undermine existential certainty. In general, religious doubt has been linked cross-sectionally to anxiety and depression in the general population of the US (Galek, Krause, Ellison, Kudler, & Flannelly, 2007), and longitudinally to declining life satisfaction among older adults (Krause, 2006) and longer and more severe experience of depressive symptoms following bereavement (Hayward & Krause, in press). Negative views of God have been related to worse mental health outcomes in samples of college students (Exline, Yali, & Lobel, 1999) and the general population (Bradshaw et al., 2008). In a large study of coping in a national sample of Presbyterian Church members in the US, negative views of God were found to exacerbate the impact of stressful life events on well-being (Bradshaw, Ellison, & Marcum, 2010). Using longitudinal data, Exline, Park, Smyth, and Carey (2011) explicated how generally positive views of God (e.g., that he is powerful and intervenes in one's life) can lead to anger towards God; when these beliefs are combined with the experience of negative events, they can contribute to attributions of cruelty on the part of God (Study 4), which in turn contributes to worse distress in the face of traumatic events (Study 5).

Enhanced Sense of Control

The perception of being in control of one's environment has important implications for well-being (Ross & Sastry, 1999). The theoretical impact of religion on control may be complex. Religious beliefs may provide an enhanced sense of control by providing the perception of an orderly universe that can be influenced through religious practice. However, it may also inhibit the sense of control if those beliefs inculcate the view that events are entirely caused by the will of an all-powerful God, with little room for human beings to have any impact. Indeed, evidence from large population surveys suggests a mixed relationship between religion and the overall sense of personal control. In a sample representative of the Canadian population, Schieman, Nguyen, and Elliott (2003) found that higher religiosity was related to a weaker sense of control among those with low levels of education, but with stronger personal control among the highly educated. Ellison and Burdette (2012) examined a range of dimensions of religiousness and their relationship with control in a sample from the US, and found that while attendance, prayer, and belief in an afterlife were related to stronger sense of control, biblical literalism, and a belief in sin were related to weaker control.

Several studies have focused specifically on the role of religion in the sense of control during older adulthood, because the sense of general control is known to decline during later life (Mirowsky, 1997), with distinct effects emerging depending on the type of religious control examined. One of these approaches conceptualizes "divine control" in terms of the belief that the course of one's life is determined by God (Schieman, Pudrovska, & Milkie, 2005). Studies in the US show that the implications of divine control appear to differ by culture and socio-economic status; in one case, it was shown to be related to lower sense of mastery among older whites, but to higher self-esteem among African American women (Schieman et al., 2005). In another, having a sense of divine control was related to higher anxiety among low socioeconomic status whites, but with lower anxiety among low socioeconomic status African Americans (Schieman, Pudrovska, Pearlin, & Ellison, 2006). An alternative approach examines the construct of "god-mediated control," which focuses on the belief that God provides assistance and support in pursuing one's own goals. Again in a sample of older adults, Krause (2005) found god-mediated control to be related to better life satisfaction, self-esteem, optimism, and lower death anxiety. God-mediated control was also found to be longitudinally related to better coping with financial strain, via a pathway of gratitude to God (Krause, 2009).

Social Identity Resources: Religion as Being

The final general set of processes with potential implications for the relationship between religion and well-being are those involving social identity. The perception of social category membership plays a central role in defining the self-concept (Turner, Hogg, Oakes, Reicher, & Wetherell, 1987), and a strong sense of group belonging of all kinds is associated with better mental health (Haslam, Jetten, Postmes, & Haslam, 2009). As Ysseldyk, Matheson, and Anisman (2010) have argued, religion may represent a uniquely powerful source of social identity, because it ties together a strong and salient social category with a set of morally authoritative beliefs and affectively compelling experiences. Several empirical studies have found support for the hypothesis that strength of identification with the religious group is related to better well-being. In one study of older adults, religious identity strength was more strongly related to low depression in older adults than worship attendance or religiosity (Keyes & Reitzes, 2007). In studies analyzing large surveys of the population of the US, Greenfield and Marks (2007) found that religious identity strength was related to life satisfaction and affect, and accounted for most of the positive association of frequency of group participation in these outcomes, while Lim and Putnam (2010) found that having a strong congregational support network was related to better life satisfaction only among those with a strong religious social identity. Studies conducted with smaller non-probability samples suggest that religious identity strength is related to the ability to access religious coping (Elliott & Hayward, 2007), and to the sense of meaning derived from religion (Furrow, King, & White, 2004).

Studies of Specific Identity Processes

While the empirical literature regarding the impact of religious social identity on well-being remains underdeveloped in comparison to other group and psychosocial processes, a few studies have addressed specific hypotheses about this relationship from a social identity perspective. For example, group cohesion should contribute to the existence of a clear and consensual social identity, and thus members of more cohesive groups should have the potential to benefit more from their social identities. Results from a study of congregational support networks among older adults support this hypothesis, finding that members' perceptions of their groups' cohesiveness were strongly related to the amount of support they received, to their sense of optimism (Krause, 2002), and to life satisfaction (Krause & Hayward, 2012c).

Based on the social attraction hypothesis, according to which individuals are perceived by themselves and others as members of a social category in proportion to the extent to which they exemplify its norms and ideals (Hogg, Hardie, & Reynolds, 1995), other studies have examined the role of group prototype fit in religious group members' well-being. In keeping with this view, Hayward and Elliott (2009) found, in a large representative study of religious congregations in the US and their members, that it was the most prototypical among them, as measured by low deviance from group norms on a variety of measures of belief and practice, who reported getting the most spiritual satisfaction and help with coping from the group. A follow-up study in a smaller sample articulated a model by which both being and perceiving oneself to be a prototypical group member are related to life satisfaction (Hayward & Elliott, 2011). In a similar vein, multiple studies have shown that religious processes have a differentially stronger impact on well-being among clergy and lay leaders, who act as social category exemplars, compared with rank and file members (Krause et al., 1998; Park & Cohen, 1993).

Religious social identification may also contribute to well-being by acting to extend positive perceptions of the group to the self. Blaine and Crocker (1995) examined the relationship between religion and well-being in a sample of college students, and found that African Americans in particular derived a sense of collective self-esteem from religious group identification, which partially accounted for the apparent benefits of religion for psychological well-being. Also in relation to the role of positive group perception, studies of older African Americans have found that those members who had more positive views of the historical role of the African American church enjoyed better life satisfaction (Krause, 2004), and experienced more improvement in self-esteem over time (Krause & Hayward, 2012d).

However, religious social identity may also have negative implications for well-being, particularly in situations marked by intergroup conflict (see Rowatt, Carpenter, & Haggard, Chapter 8, this volume), or by perceived conflict among different social categories salient to one's identity. Strong religious social identity was found to exacerbate the impact of perceived discrimination on psychological distress in a study of Muslim women in New Zealand (Jasperse, Ward, & Jose, 2012). Similarly, high religiosity was related to worse depression among Belgian Muslims, mediated by perceived discrimination by and hostility towards the dominant culture (Friedman & Saroglou, 2010). This contrasts with research generally finding that religion can serve as a buffer against the experience of discrimination in minority members (e.g., Bierman, 2006). Experimental results reported by Ysseldyk, Matheson, and Anisman (2011) may help to explain this discrepancy, finding that while more religious participants reacted to identity threat directed at a non-religious identity with less distress and more adaptive coping, they also suffered more when facing a specifically religious identity threat.

Conclusion and Directions for Future Research

While the last two decades have seen great strides in our understanding of the social processes by which religion influences mental health and well-being, much more remains to be resolved. One fact evident from this review is that research in this area remains heavily slanted toward the US. A growing number of large survey studies have assessed the extent to which the basic relationship between religion and well-being exists in a variety of settings, including Europe (Braam et al., 2001; Denny, 2011), Australia (Francis & Kaldor, 2002), Pakistan (Suhail & Chaudhry, 2004), China (Brown & Tierney, 2009), South Korea (Kim, 2003), Japan (Krause et al., 2010), Kuwait (Abdel-Khalek, 2007), and Saudi Arabia (Abdel-Khalek, 2009). However, these studies have largely lacked the capacity to directly assess the specific social mediators, like social support and religious coping, that have frequently been examined in studies conducted in the US. The experimental literature in this area has been more international in character, but remains relatively small. A growing number of cross-national studies underscore the difficulties in making generalizations based on studies from a single cultural context, suggesting that group-level social environment may moderate the relationship between religion and well-being. For example, in places where social norms are more religious, individual religiousness tends to be more strongly related to self-enhancement (Sedikides & Gebauer, 2010), as well as to life satisfaction (Gebauer et al., 2012; Okulicz-Kozaryn, 2010), and in places where the government regulates religion more severely, the otherwise generally positive association between religion and life satisfaction may weaken and even become negative (Elliott & Hayward, 2009).

By the same token, the current body of research remains focused overwhelmingly on Christians. The literature linking religion with mental health among members of other groups has grown rapidly in recent years, including a number of studies in Jewish (Levin, 2012; Rosmarin, Pargament, & Mahoney, 2009; Rosmarin, Pirutinsky, Pargament, & Krumrei, 2009) and Muslim (Abdel-Khalek, 2007, 2009; Suhail & Chaudhry, 2004) populations, but there has been less direct assessment of the social pathways that may mediate this relationship. While it is often tacitly assumed that the basic social functions of religion are largely the same across specific traditions, some studies have found differences between groups in the elements of religion that have the greatest impact. For example, Cohen (2002) found that well-being was related to behavioral aspects of religion, including congregational support and organizational participation, among Jewish and Christian samples alike, whereas psychological elements including strength of belief and use of religious coping were related to well-being only among Christians. Another study found that the deleterious relationship of spiritual struggles with mental health among Jews contrasted with findings among Christians, in that their impact appeared to decrease at higher levels of religiosity (Rosmarin, Pargament, & Flannelly, 2009). Both findings are consistent with the idea that the emphasis on elements of religious practice in the Jewish tradition, in contrast to the Christian emphasis on orthodoxy of belief, may lead to different specific pathways acting as mediators on mental health outcomes among members of these groups, implying that conclusions drawn from Christians samples only may be at least partly culturally bound. Again, the situation calls for expanding the scope of the populations examined in the research.

Another major avenue for innovation in the coming years will be the integration of our understanding of the social aspects of religion and well-being with its biological underpinnings. Recent research has related religious factors to moderation of stress hormones (Ai et al., 2010), activation of control and reward centers in the brain (Inzlicht & Tullett, 2010; Schjødt, Stødkilde-Jørgensen, Geertz, & Roepstorff, 2008), and long-term changes in brain structures implicated in depression (Hayward, Owen, Koenig, Steffens, & Payne, 2011; Owen, Hayward, Koenig, Steffens, & Payne, 2011). Other research suggests that not only are there genetic components predisposing later religiousness (Bradshaw & Ellison, 2008), but that religion can interact with genotype and culture in its relationship with depression (Sasaki, Kim, & Xu, 2011).

In short, while the study of religion and mental health has undergone dramatic development in recent decades, much more remains to be done to extend these findings, and to integrate the many mechanisms that have been examined in relative isolation. The social psychological approach remains a key tool in this process, helping to articulate the complex interactions between group and individual facets of religion and their impact on well-being. Beyond contributing to an academic understanding of the social and psychological phenomena comprising religion, elaborating the processes by which it may both improve and detract from individual well-being holds out the potential of contributing to interventions designed to improve the mental health of the religiously inclined. We hope that this chapter represents a modest step toward turning the inherent promise in research on religion and mental health into a reality.

Note

1 While the term is specific to certain forms of Christianity, for the purposes of this chapter we use the term "congregation" to refer to similar groups regardless of religious tradition for the sake of brevity and clarity.

References

Abdel-Khalek, A. M. (2007). Religiosity, happiness, health, and psychopathology in a probability sample of Muslim adolescents. *Mental Health, Religion & Culture, 10,* 571–583.

Abdel-Khalek, A. M. (2009). Religiosity, subjective well-being, and depression in Saudi children and adolescents. *Mental Health, Religion & Culture, 12,* 803–815.

Ai, A. L., Pargament, K. I., Kronfol, Z., Tice, T. N., & Appel, H. (2010). Pathways to postoperative hostility in cardiac patients: mediation of coping, spiritual struggle and interleukin-6. *Journal of Health Psychology, 15,* 186–195.

Ai, A. L., Park, C. L., Huang, B., Rodgers, W., & Tice, T. N. (2007). Psychosocial mediation of religious coping styles: A study of short-term psychological distress following cardiac surgery. *Personality and Social Psychology Bulletin, 33,* 867–882.

Ai, A. L., Peterson, C., & Huang, B. (2003). The effect of religious-spiritual coping on positive attitudes of adult Muslim refugees from Kosovo and Bosnia. *International Journal for the Psychology of Religion, 13,* 29–47.

Ano, G. G., & Vasconcelles, E. B. (2005). Religious coping and psychological adjustment to stress: A meta-analysis. *Journal of Clinical Psychology, 61,* 461–480.

Baldwin, J. M. (1902). *Fragments in the philosophy and science of being: Collected essays and addresses.* New York: Charles Scribner's Sons.

Batson, C. D., Schoenrade, P., & Ventis, W. L. (1993). *Religion and the individual: A social-psychological perspective.* New York: Oxford University Press.

Berger, P. L. (1967). *The sacred canopy.* New York: Random House.

Bhui, K., King, M., Dein, S., & O'Connor, W. (2008). Ethnicity and religious coping with mental distress. *Journal of Mental Health, 17,* 141–151.

Bierman, A. (2006). Does religion buffer the effects of discrimination on mental health? Differing effects by race. *Journal for the Scientific Study of Religion, 45,* 551–565.

Blaine, B., & Crocker, J. (1995). Religiousness, race, and psychological well-being: Exploring social psychological mediators. *Personality and Social Psychology Bulletin, 21*, 1031–1041.

Blank, M. B., Mahmood, M., Fox, J. C., & Guterbock, T. (2002). Alternative mental health services: The role of the Black church in the south. *American Journal of Public Health, 92*, 1668–1672.

Braam, A. W., Van Den Eeden, P., Prince, M. J., Beekman, A. T. F., Kivelä, S.-L., Lawlor, B. A. et al. (2001). Religion as a cross-cultural determinant of depression in elderly Europeans: Results from the EURODEP collaboration. *Psychological Medicine, 31*, 803–814.

Bradshaw, M., & Ellison, C. G. (2008). Do genetic factors influence religious life? Findings from a behavior genetic analysis of twin siblings. *Journal for the Scientific Study of Religion, 47*, 529–544.

Bradshaw, M., & Ellison, C. G. (2010). Financial hardship and psychological distress: Exploring the buffering effects of religion. *Social Science and Medicine, 71*, 196–204.

Bradshaw, M., Ellison, C. G., & Flannelly, K. J. (2008). Prayer, God imagery, and symptoms of psychopathology. *Journal for the Scientific Study of Religion, 47*, 644–659.

Bradshaw, M., Ellison, C. G., & Marcum, J. P. (2010). Attachment to God, images of God, and psychological distress in a nationwide sample of Presbyterians. *International Journal for the Psychology of Religion, 20*, 130–147.

Brashears, M. E. (2010). Anomia and the sacred canopy: Testing a network theory. *Social Networks, 32*, 187–196.

Brown, P. H., & Tierney, B. (2009). Religion and subjective well-being among the elderly in China. *Journal of Socio-Economics, 38*, 310–319.

Chatters, L. M., Taylor, R. J., Jackson, J. S., & Lincoln, K. D. (2008). Religious coping among African Americans, Caribbean Blacks and Non-Hispanic Whites. *Journal of Community Psychology, 36*, 371–386.

Chaves, M., & Tsitsos, W. (2001). Congregations and social services: What they do, how they do it, and with whom. *Nonprofit and Voluntary Sector Quarterly, 30*, 660–683.

Cohen, A. B. (2002). The importance of spirituality in well-being for Jews and Christians. *Journal of Happiness Studies, 3*, 287–310.

Cohen, D., Yoon, D. P., & Johnstone, B. (2009). Differentiating the impact of spiritual experiences, religious practices, and congregation support on the mental health of individuals with heterogeneous medical disorders. *International Journal for the Psychology of Religion, 19*, 121–138.

Cohen, S., & Wills, T. A. (1985). Stress, social support, and the buffering hypothesis. *Psychological Bulletin, 98*, 310–357.

DeHaven, M. J., Hunter, I. B., Wilder, L., Walton, J. W., & Berry, J. (2004). Health programs in faith-based organizations: Are they effective? *American Journal of Public Health, 94*, 1030–1036.

Denny, K. J. (2011). Instrumental variable estimation of the effect of prayer on depression. *Social Science and Medicine, 73*, 1194–1199.

Elliott, M., & Hayward, R. D. (2007). Religion and well-being in a church without a creed. *Mental Health, Religion & Culture, 10*, 109–126.

Elliott, M., & Hayward, R. D. (2009). Religion and life satisfaction worldwide: The role of government regulation. *Sociology of Religion, 70*, 285–310.

Ellison, C. G., & Burdette, A. M. (2012). Religion and the sense of control among US adults. *Sociology of Religion, 73*, 1–22.

Ellison, C. G., Burdette, A. M., & Hill, T. D. (2009). Blessed assurance: Religion, anxiety, and tranquility among US adults. *Social Science Research, 38*, 656–667.

Ellison, C. G., & George, L. K. (1994). Religious involvement, social ties, and social support in a Southeastern community. *Journal for the Scientific Study of Religion, 33*, 46–61.

Ellison, C. G., Krause, N., Shepherd, B. C., & Chaves, M. A. (2009). Size, conflict, and opportunities for interaction: Congregational effects on members' anticipated support and negative interaction. *Journal for the Scientific Study of Religion, 48*, 1–15.

Ellison, C. G., & Lee, J. (2010). Spiritual struggles and psychological distress: Is there a dark side of religion? *Social Indicators Research, 98*, 501–517.

Ellison, C. G., Vaaler, M. L., Flannelly, K. J., & Weaver, A. J. (2006). The clergy as a source of mental health assistance: What Americans believe. *Review of Religious Research, 48*, 190–211.

Ellison, C. G., Zhang, W., Krause, N., & Marcum, J. P. (2009). Does negative interaction in the church increase psychological distress? Longitudinal findings from the Presbyterian Panel Survey. *Sociology of Religion, 70*, 409–431.

Exline, J. J., Park, C. L., Smyth, J. M., & Carey, M. P. (2011). Anger toward God: Social-cognitive predictors, prevalence, and links with adjustment to bereavement and cancer. *Journal of Personality and Social Psychology, 100*, 129–148.

Exline, J. J., Yali, A. M., & Lobel, M. (1999). When God disappoints: Difficulty forgiving God and its role in negative emotion. *Journal of Health Psychology, 4*, 365–379.

Flannelly, K. J., Koenig, H. G., Ellison, C. G., Galek, K., & Krause, N. (2006). Belief in life after death and mental health: Findings from a national survey. *Journal of Nervous and Mental Disease, 194*, 524–529.

Francis, L. J., & Kaldor, P. (2002). The relationship between psychological well-being and Christian faith and practice in an Australian population sample. *Journal for the Scientific Study of Religion, 41*, 179–184.

Friedman, M., & Rholes, W. S. (2008). Religious fundamentalism and terror management. *International Journal for the Psychology of Religion, 18*, 36–52.

Friedman, M., & Saroglou, V. (2010). Religiosity, psychological acculturation to the host culture, self-esteem and depressive symptoms among stigmatized and nonstigmatized religious immigrant groups in Western Europe. *Basic and Applied Social Psychology, 32*, 185–195.

Furrow, J. L., King, P. E., & White, K. (2004). Religion and positive youth development: identity, meaning, and prosocial concerns. *Applied Developmental Science, 8*, 17–26.

Galek, K., Krause, N., Ellison, C. G., Kudler, T., & Flannelly, K. (2007). Religious doubt and mental health across the lifespan. *Journal of Adult Development, 14*, 16–25.

Gebauer, J. E., Sedikides, C., & Neberich, W. (2012). Religiosity, social self-esteem, and psychological adjustment: On the cross-cultural specificity of the psychological benefits of religiosity. *Psychological Science, 23*, 158–160.

Greenfield, E. A., & Marks, N. F. (2007). Religious social identity as an explanatory factor for associations between more frequent formal religious participation and psychological well-being. *International Journal for the Psychology of Religion, 17,* 245–259.

Hackney, C. H., & Sanders, G. S. (2003). Religiosity and mental health: A meta-analysis of recent studies. *Journal for the Scientific Study of Religion, 42,* 43–55.

Hall, D., Meador, K., & Koenig, H. G. (2008). Measuring religiousness in health research: Review and critique. *Journal of Religion and Health, 47,* 134–163.

Haslam, S. A., Jetten, J., Postmes, T., & Haslam, C. (2009). Social identity, health and well-being: An emerging agenda for applied psychology. *Applied Psychology, 58,* 1–23.

Hayward, R. D., & Elliott, M. (2009). Fitting in with the flock: Social attractiveness as a mechanism for well-being in religious groups. *European Journal of Social Psychology, 39,* 592–607.

Hayward, R. D., & Elliott, M. (2011). Subjective and objective fit in religious congregations: Implications for well being. *Group Processes and Intergroup Relations, 14,* 127–139.

Hayward, R. D., & Krause, N. (in press). How religious doubt moderates depression symptoms following older adult bereavement. *Death Studies.*

Hayward, R. D., Owen, A. D., Koenig, H. G., Steffens, D. C., & Payne, M. E. (2011). Associations of religious behavior and experiences with extent of regional atrophy in the orbitofrontal cortex during older adulthood. *Religion, Brain & Behavior, 1,* 103–118.

Hayward, R. D., Owen, A. D., Koenig, H. G., Steffens, D. C., & Payne, M. E. (2012a). Religion and the presence and severity of depression in older adults. *American Journal of Geriatric Psychiatry, 20,* 188–192.

Hayward, R. D., Owen, A. D., Koenig, H. G., Steffens, D. C., & Payne, M. E. (2012b). Longitudinal relationships of religion with posttreatment depression severity in older psychiatric patients: Evidence of direct and indirect effects. *Depression Research and Treatment, 2012,* Article ID 745970, 8 pages.

Henrich, J., Heine, S. J., & Norenzayan, A. (2010). The weirdest people in the world? *Behavioral and Brain Sciences, 33,* 61–83.

Hogg, M. A., Adelman, J. R., & Blagg, R. D. (2010). Religion in the face of uncertainty: An uncertainty-identity theory account of religiousness. *Personality and Social Psychology Review, 14,* 72–83.

Hogg, M. A., Hardie, E. A., & Reynolds, K. J. (1995). Prototypical similarity, self-categorization, and depersonalized attraction: A perspective on group cohesiveness. *European Journal of Social Psychology, 25,* 159–177.

Idler, E. L. (1987). Religious involvement and the health of the elderly: Some hypotheses and an initial test. *Social Forces, 66,* 226–238.

Inzlicht, M., & Tullett, A. M. (2010). Reflecting on God: Religious primes can reduce neurophysiological response to errors. *Psychological Science, 21,* 1184–1190.

James, W. (1902). *The varieties of religious experience: A study in human nature.* New York: The Modern Library.

Jasperse, M., Ward, C., & Jose, P. E. (2012). Identity, perceived religious discrimination, and psychological well-being in Muslim immigrant women. *Applied Psychology, 61,* 250–271.

Jonas, E., & Fischer, P. (2006). Terror management and religion: Evidence that intrinsic religiousness mitigates worldview defense following mortality salience. *Journal of Personality and Social Psychology, 91,* 553–567.

Kashdan, T. B., & Nezlek, J. B. (2012). Whether, when, and how is spirituality related to well-being? Moving beyond single occasion questionnaires to understanding daily process. *Personality and Social Psychology Bulletin, 38,* 1523–1535.

Kendler, K. S., Liu, X.-Q., Gardner, C. O., McCullough, M. E., Larson, D., & Prescott, C. A. (2003). Dimensions of religiosity and their relationship to lifetime psychiatric and substance use disorders. *American Journal of Psychiatry, 160,* 496–503.

Keyes, C. L. M., & Reitzes, D. C. (2007). The role of religious identity in the mental health of older working and retired adults. *Aging and Mental Health, 11,* 434–443.

Khan, Z. H., & Watson, P. J. (2006). Construction of the Pakistani religious coping practices scale: Correlations with religious coping, religious orientation, and reactions to stress among Muslim university students. *International Journal for the Psychology of Religion, 16,* 101–112.

Kim, A. E. (2003). Religious influences on personal and societal well-being. *Social Indicators Research, 62–63,* 149–170.

Koenig, H. G. (2007). Religion and remission of depression in medical inpatients with heart failure/pulmonary disease. *Journal of Nervous and Mental Disease, 195,* 389–395.

Koenig, H. G. (2008). Concerns about measuring "spirituality" in research. *Journal of Nervous and Mental Disease, 196,* 349–355.

Koenig, H. G., King, D. E., & Carson, V. B. (2012). *Handbook of Religion and Health* (2nd ed.). New York: Oxford University Press.

Koenig, H. G., Pargament, K. I., & Nielsen, J. (1998). Religious coping and health status in medically ill hospitalized older adults. *Journal of Nervous and Mental Disease, 186,* 513–521.

Krause, N. (2002). Church-based social support and health in old age. *Journals of Gerontology Series B: Psychological Sciences and Social Sciences, 57,* S332–S347.

Krause, N. (2003a). Exploring race differences in the relationship between social interaction with the clergy and feelings of self-worth in late life. *Sociology of Religion, 64,* 183–205.

Krause, N. (2003b). Religious meaning and subjective well-being in late life. *Journals of Gerontology Series B: Psychological Sciences and Social Sciences, 58,* S160–S170.

Krause, N. (2004). Common facets of religion, unique facets of religion, and life satisfaction among older African Americans. *Journals of Gerontology: Series B: Psychological Sciences and Social Sciences, 59B,* S109–S117.

Krause, N. (2005). God-mediated control and psychological well-being in late life. *Research on Aging, 27,* 136–164.

Krause, N. (2006). Religious doubt and psychological well-being: A longitudinal investigation. *Review of Religious Research, 47,* 287–302.

Krause, N. (2007). Social involvement in religious institutions and God-mediated control beliefs: A longitudinal investigation. *Journal for the Scientific Study of Religion, 46,* 519–537.

Krause, N. (2008). Lifetime trauma, prayer, and psychological distress in late life. *International Journal for the Psychology of Religion, 19,* 55–72.

Krause, N. (2009). Religious involvement, gratitude, and change in depressive symptoms over time. *International Journal for the Psychology of Religion, 19,* 155–172.

Krause, N., Chatters, L. M., & Meltzer, T. (2000). Negative interaction in the church: Insights from focus groups with older adults. *Review of Religious Research, 41,* 510–533.

Krause, N., & Ellison, C. G. (2009). The doubting process: A longitudinal study of the precipitants and consequences of religious doubt in older adults. *Journal for the Scientific Study of Religion, 48,* 293–312.

Krause, N., Ellison, C. G., Shaw, B. A., Marcum, J. P., & Boardman, J. D. (2001). Church-based social support and religious coping. *Journal for the Scientific Study of Religion, 40,* 637–656.

Krause, N., Ellison, C. G., & Wulff, K. M. (1998). Church-based emotional support, negative interaction, and psychological well-being: Findings from a national sample of Presbyterians. *Journal for the Scientific Study of Religion, 37,* 725–741.

Krause, N., & Hayward, R. D. (2012a). Informal support from a pastor and change in hope during late life. *Pastoral Psychology, 61,* 305–318.

Krause, N., & Hayward, R. D. (2012b). Negative interaction with fellow church members and depressive symptoms among older Mexican Americans. *Archive for the Psychology of Religion, 34,* 149–171.

Krause, N., & Hayward, R. D. (2012c). Emotional expressiveness during worship services and life satisfaction: Assessing the influence of race and religious affiliation. *Mental Health, Religion & Culture.* Advance online publication.

Krause, N., & Hayward, R. D. (2012d). Awareness of the historical role of the church and change in self-esteem among older African Americans. *Applied Psychology: Health and Well-Being, 4,* 240–260.

Krause, N., & Hayward, R. (2013a). Prayer beliefs and change in life satisfaction over time. *Journal of Religion and Health, 52,* 674–694.

Krause, N., & Hayward, R. D. (2013b). Older Mexican Americans and God-mediated control: Exploring the influence of Pentecostal/Evangelical affiliation. *Mental Health, Religion & Culture, 16,* 319–333.

Krause, N., Liang, J., Bennett, J., Kobayashi, F., Akiyama, H., & Fukaya, T. (2010). A descriptive analysis of religious involvement among older adults in Japan. *Ageing and Society, 30,* 671–696.

Krumrei, E. J., Mahoney, A., & Pargament, K. I. (2011). Spiritual stress and coping model of divorce: A longitudinal study. *Journal of Family Psychology, 25,* 973–985.

Lazarus, R. S., & Folkman, S. (1984). *Stress, appraisal, and coping.* New York: Springer.

Leavey, G., Loewenthal, K., & King, M. (2007). Challenges to sanctuary: The clergy as a resource for mental health care in the community. *Social Science and Medicine, 65,* 548–559.

Levin, J. (2012). Religion and mental health among Israeli Jews: Findings from the SHARE-Israel Study. *Social Indicators Research*. Advance online publication.

Lim, C., & Putnam, R. D. (2010). Religion, social networks, and life satisfaction. *American Sociological Review, 75*, 914–933.

McConnell, K. M., Pargament, K. I., Ellison, C. G., & Flannelly, K. J. (2006). Examining the links between spiritual struggles and symptoms of psychopathology in a national sample. *Journal of Clinical Psychology, 62*, 1469–1484.

Maltby, J., Day, L., & Barber, L. (2004). Forgiveness and mental health variables: Interpreting the relationship using an adaptational-continuum model of personality and coping. *Personality and Individual Differences, 37*, 1629–1641.

Maselko, J., Hayward, R. D., Hanlon, A., Buka, S., & Meador, K. (2012). Religious service attendance and major depression: A case of reverse causality? *American Journal of Epidemiology, 175*, 576–583.

Maton, K. I. (1989). The stress-buffering role of spiritual support: Cross-sectional and prospective investigations. *Journal for the Scientific Study of Religion, 28*, 310–323.

Mirowsky, J. (1997). Age, subjective life expectancy, and the sense of control: The horizon hypothesis. *Journals of Gerontology Series B: Psychological Sciences and Social Sciences, 52B*, S125–S134.

Neighbors, H. W., Musick, M. A., & Williams, D. R. (1998). The African American minister as a source of help for serious personal crises: Bridge or barrier to mental health care? *Health Education & Behavior, 25*, 759–777.

Nooney, J., & Woodrum, E. (2002). Religious coping and church-based social support as predictors of mental health outcomes: Testing a conceptual model. *Journal for the Scientific Study of Religion, 41*, 359–368.

Norenzayan, A., Dar-Nimrod, I., Hansen, I. G., & Proulx, T. (2009). Mortality salience and religion: Divergent effects on the defense of cultural worldviews for the religious and the non-religious. *European Journal of Social Psychology, 39*, 101–113.

Norenzayan, A., & Hansen, I. G. (2006). Belief in supernatural agents in the face of death. *Personality and Social Psychology Bulletin, 32*, 174–187.

Okulicz-Kozaryn, A. (2010). Religiosity and life satisfaction across nations. *Mental Health, Religion & Culture, 13*, 155–169.

Owen, A. D., Hayward, R. D., Koenig, H. G., Steffens, D. C., & Payne, M. E. (2011). The association between religious factors and hippocampal atrophy in late life. *PLoS ONE, 6*, e17006.

Paloutzian, R. F., & Park, C. L. (Eds.). (2013). *Handbook of the psychology of religion and spirituality* (2nd ed.). New York: Guilford.

Pargament, K. I. (Ed.). (2013). *APA Handbook of psychology, religion, and spirituality* (2 vols.). Washington, DC: American Psychological Association.

Pargament, K. I., Koenig, H. G., & Perez, L. M. (2000). The many methods of religious coping: Development and initial validation of the RCOPE. *Journal of Clinical Psychology, 56*, 519–543.

Park, C. L., & Cohen, L. H. (1993). Religious and nonreligious coping with the death of a friend. *Cognitive Therapy and Research, 17*, 561–577.

Park, C. L., Cohen, L. H., & Murch, R. L. (1996). Assessment and prediction of stress-related growth. *Journal of Personality, 64*, 71–105.

Park, J., Roh, S., & Yeo, Y. (2012). Religiosity, social support, and life satisfaction among elderly Korean immigrants. *The Gerontologist, 52,* 641–649.

Pearce, M. J., Little, T. D., & Perez, J. E. (2003). Religiousness and depressive symptoms among adolescents. *Journal of Clinical Child and Adolescent Psychology, 32,* 267–276.

Rosmarin, D. H., Pargament, K. I., & Flannelly, K. J. (2009). Do spiritual struggles predict poorer physical/mental health among Jews? *International Journal for the Psychology of Religion, 19,* 244–258.

Rosmarin, D. H., Pargament, K. I., & Mahoney, A. (2009). The role of religiousness in anxiety, depression, and happiness in a Jewish community sample: A preliminary investigation. *Mental Health, Religion & Culture, 12,* 97–113.

Rosmarin, D. H., Pirutinsky, S., Pargament, K. I., & Krumrei, E. J. (2009). Are religious beliefs relevant to mental health among Jews? *Psychology of Religion and Spirituality, 1,* 180–190.

Ross, C. E., & Sastry, J. (1999). The sense of personal control: Social-structural causes and emotional consequences. In C. S. Aneshensel & J. C. Phelam (Eds.), *Handbook of the sociology of mental health* (pp. 369–394). New York: Klewer/Plenum.

Sasaki, J. Y., Kim, H. S., & Xu, J. (2011). Religion and well-being: The moderating role of culture and the oxytocin receptor (OXTR) gene. *Journal of Cross-Cultural Psychology, 42,* 1394–1405.

Schieman, S., Nguyen, K., & Elliott, D. (2003). Religiosity, socioeconomic status, and the sense of mastery. *Social Psychology Quarterly, 66,* 202–221.

Schieman, S., Pudrovska, T., & Milkie, M. A. (2005). The sense of divine control and the self-concept. *Research on Aging, 27,* 165–196.

Schieman, S., Pudrovska, T., Pearlin, L. I., & Ellison, C. G. (2006). The sense of divine control and psychological distress: Variations across race and socioeconomic status. *Journal for the Scientific Study of Religion, 45,* 529–549.

Schjødt, U., Stødkilde-Jørgensen, H., Geertz, A. W., & Roepstorff, A. (2008). Rewarding prayers. *Neuroscience Letters, 443,* 165–168.

Schnittker, J. (2001). When is faith enough? The effects of religious involvement on depression. *Journal for the Scientific Study of Religion, 40,* 393–411.

Schuster, M. A., Stein, B. D., Jaycox, L. H., Collins, R. L., Marshall, G. N., Elliott, M. N. et al. (2001). A national survey of stress reactions after the September 11, 2001, terrorist attacks. *New England Journal of Medicine, 345,* 1507–1512.

Sedikides, C., & Gebauer, J. E. (2010). Religiosity as self-enhancement: A meta-analysis of the relation between socially desirable responding and religiosity. *Personality and Social Psychology Review, 14,* 17–36.

Sloan, R. P. (2008). *Blind faith: The unholy alliance of religion and medicine.* New York: St. Martin's Griffin.

Smith, B. W., Pargament, K. I., Brant, C., & Oliver, J. M. (2000). Noah revisited: Religious coping by church members and the impact of the 1993 midwest flood. *Journal of Community Psychology, 28,* 169–186.

Smith, T. B., McCullough, M. E., & Poll, J. (2003). Religiousness and depression: Evidence for a main effect and the moderating influence of stressful life events. *Psychological Bulletin, 129,* 614–636.

Strawbridge, W. J., Shema, S. J., Cohen, R. D., & Kaplan, G. A. (2001). Religious attendance increases survival by improving and maintaining good health behaviors, mental health, and social relationships. *Annals of Behavioral Medicine, 23*, 68–74.

Suhail, K., & Chaudhry, H. R. (2004). Predictors of subjective well-being in an eastern Muslim culture. *Journal of Social and Clinical Psychology, 23*, 359–376.

Tepper, L., Rogers, S. A., Coleman, E. M., & Malony, H. N. (2001). The prevalence of religious coping among persons with persistent mental illness. *Psychiatric Services, 52*, 660–665.

Thompson, M. P., & Vardaman, P. J. (1997). The role of religion in coping with the loss of a family member to homicide. *Journal for the Scientific Study of Religion, 36*, 44–51.

Trice, P. D., & Bjorck, J. P. (2006). Pentecostal perspectives on causes and cures of depression. *Professional Psychology: Research and Practice, 37*, 283–294.

Turner, J. C., Hogg, M. A., Oakes, P. J., Reicher, S. D., & Wetherell, M. S. (1987). *Rediscovering the social group: A self-categorization theory.* New York: Blackwell.

Vail, K. E., Rothschild, Z. K., Weise, D. R., Solomon, S., Pyszczynski, T., & Greenberg, J. (2010). A terror management analysis of the psychological functions of religion. *Personality and Social Psychology Review, 14*, 84–94.

Walls, C. T., & Zarit, S. H. (1991). Informal support from Black churches and the well-being of elderly Blacks. *The Gerontologist, 31*, 490–495.

Wang, P. S., Berglund, P. A., & Kessler, R. C. (2003). Patterns and correlates of contacting clergy for mental disorders in the United States. *Health Services Research, 38*, 647–673.

Weaver, A. J. (1995). Has there been a failure to prepare and support parish-based clergy in their role as frontline community mental health workers: A review. *Journal of Pastoral Care, 49*, 129–147.

Wesselmann, E. D., & Graziano, W. G. (2010). Sinful and/or possessed? Religious beliefs and mental illness stigma. *Journal of Social and Clinical Psychology, 29*, 402–437.

Ysseldyk, R., Matheson, K., & Anisman, H. (2010). Religiosity as identity: Toward an understanding of religion from a social identity perspective. *Personality and Social Psychology Review, 14*, 60–71.

Ysseldyk, R., Matheson, K., & Anisman, H. (2011). Coping with identity threat: The role of religious orientation and implications for emotions and action intentions. *Psychology of Religion and Spirituality, 3*, 132–148.

Part III

Religion in Context

Age, Gender, and Culture

13 Religion and Cognitive, Emotional, and Social Development

Pehr Granqvist

"I've met Jesus!"

(2-year old Stella at her great grandmother's funeral)

Many branches of science have had enough of some particular ways of thinking. Developmental psychology, including its literature on religious and spiritual development, is no exception. This branch of science has had enough of stage models describing how highly domain-general aspects of development unfold, whether it be all-purpose cognition as in Piaget's theory (e.g., 1930), psychosocial adaptation as in Erikson's theory (e.g., 1997), or any of their multiple applications to religious and spiritual development (for reviews, see Hood, Hill, & Spilka, 2009; Oser, Scarlett, & Bucher, 2007). The problems with these models can be formulated succinctly: Psychological development is never that domain general and rarely unfolds in discrete stages.

Therefore, an increasing number of developmental psychologists have shifted their focus to other kinds of models. In particular, and influenced by evolutionary considerations, normal development is increasingly viewed as an expression of domain-specific spurts in evolved mechanisms (or "systems" or "modules" or "programs") during age/maturity periods associated with the functional utility of those mechanisms (e.g., Bowlby, 1982 [1969]; Brown & Bjorklund, 1998; Geary & Bjorklund, 2003). For example, people tend to become markedly interested in sex following reproductive maturation. As religious and spiritual development is likely to build on such domain-specific developmental spurts, developmental psychologists and cognitive scientists of religion have increasingly shifted their focus accordingly (e.g., Barrett, 2004; Bering & Parker, 2006; Boyer, 2001; Kirkpatrick, 2005). However, much of the literature on how the development of evolved mechanisms is reflected in religious and spiritual development is top heavy on theory. Also, most such treatises have focused on one particular (or a few) evolved mechanism(s) without any large-scale theoretical integration of the pieces. In addition, the interplay among such mechanisms and the influence of that interplay on religious and spiritual development are as of yet largely unexplored questions. Therefore, time is regrettably not ripe to base this chapter on an exhaustive understanding of the development of evolved mechanisms, and their interplay, as involved in religious/spiritual development.

The aim with this chapter is considerably more modest. Using a chronological approach, the chapter will highlight the major dimensions of cognitive, emotional, and social development believed to be especially important for understanding religious and spiritual development within each major life period. The chapter contains four main sections, divided by developmental period. In each developmental period, I emphasize key aspects of development, and then illustrate how they are involved in religious/spiritual development. Both normative/typical developmental trends and notable individual differences of relevance for religious/spiritual development are addressed. As is common in developmental psychology, particular emphasis is placed on the early years, where development takes place rapidly and across most foundational domains. Also, one chapter devoted to development over the entire lifespan necessitates a highly selective review. To save space, and in realization that other chapters concern mostly adulthood, adult development is downplayed by comparison. As theoretical anchor points in the review, the topics and approaches that have been supported in empirical research on religious/spiritual development are emphasized. And this includes not only domain-specific developmental models (e.g., attachment theory and the notion of "core" cognition underlying most cognitive science of religion research) but also research literature that is typically viewed as more domain general, including imitation, socialization, parenting styles, and other cognitive strands of literature.

Throughout the chapter, the terms "religious" and "spiritual" are used in a conventional way, where both religious (organized, collective components) and spiritual (private components) include reference to (an) invisible other(s) likely to be viewed as divine at some point in life (cf. Pargament, 2003). "Development" refers to the unfolding of that process, the psychological stuff involved in its unfolding, and the transformations (changes) occurring at later points in the lifecycle.

Infancy and Toddlerhood (0–2 Years)

Basics of Development

One useful, general way of understanding development is in terms of increases in complexity, differentiation, *and* integration of physical and psychological components (Bowlby, 1982 [1969]; Carlson, Yates, & Sroufe, 2009). Due to the marked immaturity and plasticity of the human newborn's brain, much of these increases take place during the first two years of life. This reflects the maturation of genetically based neural systems, part of which is accomplished by environmental "calibration" (cf. "nurture") of those systems.

Taking cognitive development as a first illustration of increases in complexity, differentiation, and integration, Piaget (1930) argued that the infant initially develops cognitive schemas from highly concrete sensorimotor exploration. Through the acquisition of an understanding that things not currently perceived continue to exist (i.e., object permanence) and an increasing reliance on mental representation in the second year of life, the toddler is capable of more complex but still highly concrete ways of understanding and representing the world, partly due to an increasingly sophisticated integration of schemas.

Developmental "core" cognition theorists (see, e.g., Wellman & Gelman, 1992) have made a compelling case that infants come equipped with a genetic preparedness for acquiring knowledge especially rapidly and following even minimal environmental input in certain core domains (i.e., domains linked with inclusive fitness in our environments of evolutionary adaptation). For example, infants have an intuitive understanding of elementary physics (e.g., gravity). Also, they convey an implicit understanding of language pragmatics and soak up words at such a pace and with sufficient cross-cultural commonality to suggest that language is another core domain (e.g., Pinker, 1994).

Development of the self is a suitable second example. In the first months of life, infants possess an implicit sense of the self as distinct from their surroundings (i.e., self-awareness; e.g., Rochat & Hespos, 1997), but more than a year typically elapses before they gain an explicit understanding of their selves (i.e., self-recognition; e.g., Harter, 1999).

The development of emotions provides a good third example. From the newborn's highly general states of distress and positive interest, more differentiated emotional states of anger, fear, and joy (i.e., basic emotions) gradually emerge during the first year of life (e.g., Camras, 1992). Following the development of self-recognition, the toddler's emotional repertoire also becomes increasingly complex, reflecting an integration of self-relevant information with emotional states, expressed in self conscious emotions of guilt, shame, pride, and envy. Like language for explicit social communication, emotion is our principal mode of implicit social communication; emotions function as important social signals. Consequently, early emotional development contains an increasing ability to "read" others' emotional states. For example, the 6- to 12-month-old can distinguish between emotional expressions in others, and uses such information as safety-vs.-danger cues for his or her own exploration (i.e., social referencing; e.g., Stenberg, 2003).

Imitation is yet another important example. Very shortly after birth, infants are capable of imitating not just emotional expressions (i.e., emotional contagion; e.g., Stern, 1985) but also other forms of simple overt behaviors, probably reflecting the operation of a mirror neuron system

(Iacoboni & Dapretto, 2006). Due to concomitant cognitive advancements, such as longer memory-recognition intervals, the infant gains an increasing ability for delayed imitation, and may now also imitate more complex behavioral sequences (e.g., Barr, Muentener, & Garcia, 2007). Although the likelihood that any given behavior will be imitated may be variable (see later), imitation is an important general tool that increases the offspring's social adaptation, and thereby possibly its inclusive fitness (e.g., Bjorklund, 1997).

Finally, the development of attachment, as an evolved behavioral system, is a crown jewel illustrator of increased complexity, differentiation, and integration (cf. Bowlby, 1982 [1969]). Indeed, as the development of attachment illustrates, integration does not really take place in the development of cognitive, self, emotion, and learning components separately. In fact, those components are never truly separate to begin with. Integration takes place at the level of functional systems. Taking attachment as the example, in the process of developing selective attachments to caregivers ("attachment figures"), the infant moves from a kind of socially "promiscuous" responsiveness (e.g., smiling, an emotional expression) to whomever that happens to interact with him or her during the first few months of life to an increasingly salient preference for the familiar caregivers, coupled with separation anxiety (following object permanence, i.e., a cognitive component) and increased mobility (e.g., crawling, i.e., a motor component) during the second half of the first year. The toddler will then increasingly use the attachment figure as a secure base for exploration (e.g., by means of social referencing, using emotional expressions as a cue) and as a safe haven when alarmed (e.g., frightened) by danger cues.

A direct implication of this process for emotional development is that pleasant emotional states will be increasingly experienced when the infant is in contact with attachment figures, especially with attachment figures who are sensitive to the infant's needs, whereas unpleasant states will be increasingly associated with strangers as well as with caregivers who fail to meet the infant's/toddler's needs.

Regarding the self component, sensitive caregiving helps to define the self as worthy of care and leads to a strong and resourceful sense of self (e.g., Goodvin, Meyer, Thompson, & Hayes, 2008). As for additional cognitive components, early interactions with the attachment figure are generalized into a set of internal working models (i.e., relationship-related mental representations) concerning self and others, which are at the core of individual differences in attachment security (Ainsworth, Blehar, Waters, & Wall, 1978). As the development of attachment illustrates, the components just discussed are not only integrated, but the functional nature of their integration remains invisible until we shift focus from the components themselves to the level of evolved systems.

Religious and Spiritual Development

Development in infancy and toddlerhood has a clearly paradoxical relation to religious and spiritual development. On the one hand, infants/toddlers are sufficiently absorbed by the world of their senses, indeed for most part happily unaware of any invisible world, that this phase of development is best viewed as pre-religious and pre-spiritual. Although ideally basking in the love of their caregivers, their caregivers can be seen, heard, smelled, tasted, and are associated with concrete tactile stimulation. Infants' and toddlers' mental representations (including language comprehension and use) similarly concern concrete objects, people, and situations, although they may become puzzled and attentionally drawn to counterintuitive material (e.g., an object violating the laws of gravity; Baillargeon & DeVos, 1991). To the extent that they direct attachment behaviors towards inanimate, surrogate others (e.g., following separation from attachment figures), those objects are highly concrete, including blankets, dolls, pacifiers, teddybears, and other adults (Bowlby, 1982 [1969]). The use of such "transitional" objects tends to increase in importance as a function of increased autonomy when the growing toddler makes his or her way into the outer worlds of daycare, strangers, and playmates.

On the other hand, development in infancy and toddlerhood is probably unparalleled in importance for what is, at a later stage in development, to emerge as religious and spiritual development. Although difficult to empirically substantiate due to insufficient variance in children's developmental contexts, it seems plausible to assume, for example, that if no caregiver has allowed an attachment relationship (whether secure or insecure) to develop during the first years of life (e.g., no experience from physical interaction or consolation), it is likely that the child will not only be at a disadvantage for developing attachments to other humans (e.g., Zeanah, Smyke, Koga, & Carlson, 2005), but also (by extension) to direct attachment bids to symbolic attachment targets (e.g., God; see later) in later development. This is because the attachment system would be chronically underdeveloped due to insufficient environmental calibration of the system in a sensitive phase of development. Put differently, there would be no relevant interaction history as the basis for attachment-related working models of self and others to develop, let alone generalize from. Similarly, if the child were never to have any experience of objects re-appearing from having been out of sight (touch, smell, and so on), he or she would probably not develop object permanence, and thus not gain an understanding that things (e.g., God) may exist even if not perceived. For another example, if the child were never to perceive an object in motion (e.g., falling), he or she would probably not gain an understanding of elementary physics (e.g., gravity), and thus the child would presumably never come to wonder about "ultimate" causation (cf. the cosmological argument for God's existence).

These are merely a few examples in a potentially much longer list of developmental acquisitions in infancy whose importance for later religious and spiritual development is easy to overlook simply because there is almost no variation in their occurrence. However, lack of variation should not be confused with lack of importance; on the contrary, most truly substantive parameters of development (including contexts of development) have been "canalized" into one (or very few) outcomes (Bowlby, 1982 [1969]; Waddington, 1957). As a notable example, almost all newborns have at least one caregiver at their disposal.

Although I have argued that infancy and toddlerhood represent pre-religious and pre-spiritual phases of development, this contention is largely informed (or, perhaps, constrained) by the definition of "religious" and "spiritual" used in this chapter (i.e., as referring to some sense of invisible others). Scholars with a more inclusive understanding of these terms might come to very different conclusions. For example, the new born's entire psychological state might well be viewed as "all-spiritual" or perhaps "proto-spiritual." Indeed, the newborn is bathing in the love of caregivers, incapable of visual acuity, and without a clear, explicit sense of the world's physical layout (e.g., limited depth perception), time–space relations, and of his/her own distinct self. In sum, the newborn may experience the world somewhat "psychedelically" (cf. Freud's, 1961 [1930], notion of an "oceanic feeling").

My argument that "religious" and "spiritual" have somewhat different connotations than this converges with how some developmental scholars have approached the dissociation construct; dissociation (i.e., a disintegration of the self) becomes a useful term only at ages associated with most children having developed an integrated sense of self (Carlson et al., 2009). Likewise, "religious" and "spiritual" become useful terms only at ages associated with most children having achieved sufficient complexity, differentiation, and integration of relevant psychological components. For example, and likely presuming the acquisition of object permanence, symbolic thinking and the development of attachment, "spiritual" is a useful term to denote the sense of being loved and cared for by something that cannot be perceived with one's ordinary sense modalities (e.g., God, spirits). Similarly, "spiritual (or mystical) experience" is a useful term only at ages associated with most individuals having achieved explicit self-recognition and a clear sense of time–space relations and of the world's "linear" layout. Such experiences represent the very sense of these basic acquisitions being (re-) brought to disdain; indeed, unless these experiences contrasted with those acquisitions, they would probably not be experienced as "spiritual" or "mystical."

Early and Middle Childhood (2–11 Years)

Basics of Development

Although most matters of development have been solidly set in motion during the first two years, many core acquisitions underlying religious and spiritual development unfold during early childhood. This is the case particularly for cognitive aspects of development. Entering what Piaget (1930) described as the preoperational period (roughly ages 2 to 6), the child is now capable of representing the world symbolically (e.g., in language). The world has moved inside the mind of the child, which is increasingly relying on its own mental representations of the world in exploring it. This is typically manifested in pretend play, such as when a 2-year-old is acting out its representation of a phone conversation, with a block held to his/her ears, chatting with a pretend conversationalist. Although Piaget noted such advancements, he focused his attention on the limitations of preoperational thought.

As is often the case in Piaget's theory, he gravely underestimated the cognitive capacities of children at these ages. Relatedly, evolutionary developmental psychologists (e.g., Geary & Bjorklund, 2003) have suggested that mind-related knowledge (or a "mentalizing" capacity) is a core cognitive domain, because some knowledge of others' minds has been pivotal for social communication (e.g., cooperation) and acceptance, which have in turn been essential for survival and reproduction (i.e., inclusive fitness) in our environments of evolutionary adaptation. An important argument in favor of a core interpretation of mentalizing capacities is that we never observe the mental operations of others; we just observe their behaviors. Nevertheless, a seed for mentalizing capacities develops already during the first year of life (e.g., an implicit understanding of joint attention and that others are intentional beings), makes headway during the second to third years (e.g., understanding that other's perspectives may differ from one's own, starts using mind-related concepts), and this capacity climaxes in a full-blown "theory of mind" roughly by four years (Wellman, Cross, & Watson, 2001). Thus, the child now typically understands that the knowledge possessed by their own mind may not necessarily be the knowledge possessed by another mind (e.g., certain beliefs may be false).

Building on these aspects of cognitive maturation, the child's attachment relationships are typically transformed to "goal-corrected partnerships" (Bowlby, 1982 [1969]). Due to an increasing capacity to represent their attachment figures symbolically and to understand the intentions of their attachment figures, children are able to withstand longer separations from their attachment figures. Relatedly, children at these ages are often satisfied by visual or verbal contact, or eventually by mere knowledge of an attachment figure's whereabouts (Bretherton, 1987). Similar observations led Sroufe and Waters (1977) to suggest that "felt security" (rather than physical proximity, as in infancy) is the set goal of the attachment system in older individuals. Similarly, a consideration of these cognitive abilities was an important part of the so-called "move to the level of representation" (Main, Kaplan, & Cassidy, 1985) that has influenced attachment research for more than a quarter of a century. In my view, these cognitive maturations and focal shifts within attachment theory have also opened the door to considering the possibility of imagined attachments to unseen others.

These advancements in symbolic and mentalizing capacities, along with the concomitant maturation of attachment, are reflected in children's seemingly spontaneous elaboration with unseen others. Thus, as children experience themselves thinking and planning, and imagine the intentions of their social interaction partners, they may start to apply their increasingly sophisticated mentalizing capacities to abstract, symbolic (yet typically highly anthropomorphized) others. For example, the child starts to elaborate and interact with imaginary companions. Although not the typical scenario, in some children's minds, especially children experiencing low levels of psychological well-being (Hoff, 2005), these imaginary companions seem to take on quite a concrete existence and may well be viewed as some of the principal relationship partners in the child's mind. Thus, whereas toddlers would use a concrete object such as a teddybear or blanket as an "attachment surrogate" (Ainsworth, 1985), preschool children may now start to direct their attachment-related thoughts/behaviors to unseen others, which is, of course, particularly likely when their primary attachment figures are, for whatever reason, unavailable. Other examples of unseen others populating preschool children's minds, are ghosts, monsters, trolls, and witches, who function as diabolical objects of fears and nightmares rather than as attachment surrogates.

Many of these imaginary figures exit from children's minds as rapidly as they entered, at least in the contemporary Western world. Most have passed their due dates by middle childhood, though they may on occasion make nightly visits in children's dreams. Piaget attributed their exit from children's minds to cognitive maturation; as egocentrism is outgrown, so are animistic thinking and imaginary figures. The child's thinking has now shifted to concrete operations (i.e., logical thinking in relation to concrete material). However, this analysis needs to be qualified. First, children's somewhat elevated tendencies for animistic or magical thinking are partially explained by incomplete object knowledge rather than animistic thinking per se (e.g., Jipson & Gelman, 2007). Second, as illustrated by mythology, folk beliefs, and religion, animistic/magical thinking is seldom fully outgrown, but rather becomes focused on new entities that, for whatever reason, have found acceptance in the cultural milieu and historical era surrounding the individual (cf. Boyatzis, 2005).

This illustrates another well-known shortcoming in Piaget's theory, which is almost equally applicable to some (but by no means all) core cognition proposals (see Jensen, 2009); the child's representation of the world is not a solitary undertaking, but is heavily influenced by other members of the child's culture (Boyatzis, 2005; Tomasello, Kruger, & Ratner, 1993; Vygotsky, 1978), especially by the testimonies of those viewed as stronger and wiser by the child (e.g., attachment figures) and, somewhat later, by others holding a respected position in the child's culture. Another way to say this is that the child's representation of the world, including unseen others, is built from the child's own core cognitions ("intuitive ontologies") *in combination with* the cultural "calibration" of those cognitions/ontologies. Two simple tools by which that calibration may be accomplished are through imitation of and instruction from important models (Tomasello et al., 1993). If the model's behavior/instruction accords well with the child's core cognitions, then all the more likely it should be to be imitated. For example, a model's testimonies about unseen others who possess some anthropomorphic (e.g., mind) attributes will probably fall on more attentive ears than a model's testimonies about purely abstract entities. Thus, presumably, children abandon certain unseen others partly because they are discouraged by natural authorities in the child's life, and yet maintain or come to embrace certain other ones because they accord with children's intuitive ontologies *and* natural authorities model affirmative behaviors.

Apart from a diminished crowd of unseen characters in the child's mind, middle childhood, from age 6 onwards, is marked by an ever increasing focus on the outer (i.e., extra-familial) world of peers, school, and leisure activities. Indeed, presuming that no cause of distress is present, children of these ages typically prefer to spend time with their peers over their parents (Zeifman & Hazan, 2008). In particular, peer relations come to take on a new important role in the form of friendships, marked by trust and companionship (Hartup, 1996). As their attachment systems are also less easily activated, attachment often appears to take on a subordinate role for the child (Bowlby, 1982 [1969]). However, this does not imply that attachment becomes obsolete. For example, children who fail to develop any friendships and who receive low levels of support and engagement from parents, often start to experience a painful sense of loneliness (Cassidy & Berlin, 1999), defined by Weiss (1973) as the perceived absence of a satisfying emotional bond with an attachment figure.

Along with previous experiences from interactions with caregivers, how well the child manages to navigate in relation to the wider horizon of developmental challenges facing the school-aged child is an important source of individual differences in self-esteem (e.g., Harter, 1999).

Finally, starting already in early childhood, children should typically find their parents engaged less in caregiving behaviors but more in socializing behaviors than previously in development. Parents now set limits for appropriate conduct, including tactics of discipline if necessary, they monitor and engage themselves in their children's leisure activities, and they model important social attitudes and behaviors (e.g., Baumrind, 1971). Like caregiver sensitivity at earlier child ages, authoritative parenting, marked by a combination of warmth/acceptance, moderate control, and appropriate levels of autonomy granting, bode well for many important aspects of subsequent child development (ibid.). For example, children of such parents tend to develop high self-esteem, are relatively resilient to stress, and are inclined to agree and identify with the parent's social attitudes and behaviors (e.g., Ainsworth, Bell, & Stayton, 1974; Baumrind, 1971).

Religious and Spiritual Development

The seemingly "wild" (i.e., overgeneralized) application of symbolic thinking and mentalizing attributions that is characteristic of early childhood makes this a developmental period of spirituality in the making. Relatedly, Rizzuto (1979) has suggested that this period gives birth to the "living God"; thus, God ultimately takes the throne as a living mental representation in the child's cast of unseen characters, whereas other characters have been dethroned and may eventually be entirely abandoned. Supportive research for this conclusion comes from cognitive science of religion studies on children's use of religious concepts as well as from studies informed by attachment theory (for a recent review, see Richert & Granqvist, in press).

Cognition, Supernatural Agents, and Religious Thinking

Much of the cognitive science of religion research has focused on the relationship between developing social cognition (e.g., theory of mind) and agency attributions (including hyperactive agency "detection"; Barrett, 2004), on the one hand, and children's understanding of religious concepts, on the other. This shift in focus from previous Piagetian stage conceptions was largely driven by hypotheses about social cognition and agency detection as core cognitive mechanisms underlying the representation of supernatural agents (e.g., Barrett, 2004; Bering, 2006; Boyer, 2001). More specifically, and heightening their memorability, supernatural beings tend to be viewed as persons but with some minimal counterintuitive properties (e.g., Boyer, 2001). For example, researchers have found that around the age when children master theory of mind (i.e., comprehend that people may have false beliefs), they do not attribute the same false beliefs to God (e.g., Barrett, Richert, & Driesenga, 2001; Knight, Sousa, Barrett, & Atran, 2004).

However, whereas adults tend to anthropomorphize certain fictional beings (e.g., fairies, zombies) more than God, children at these young ages attribute at least as many human-like psychological, physical, and biological properties to God as they do to those fictional beings (e.g., Shtulman, 2008). These findings illustrate a common observation made also in previous Piagetian stage models of religious development (see Hood et al., 2009; Oser et al., 2007), namely that childhood conceptions of God are very concrete. For example, at these ages, God is particularly likely to be described and drawn as a person (Heller, 1986). Yet, another Piaget-reeking conceptualization of an undifferentiated magical or fairytale stage (i.e., reflecting the child's presumed failure to distinguish between reality and fantasy, see Hood et al., 2009, for a review) seems misguided (e.g., Woolley, 1997). Notably, children in early childhood are less concerned with questions of ontology/existence than older individuals and therefore *may appear* incapable of distinguishing between fantasy and reality (ibid.). However, already at these ages, God and other religious entities will typically start to part company with (other) fictional beings; the latter, unlike the former, are typically viewed as pretend figures even in early childhood (e.g., Shtulman, 2008).

Another area of interest illustrating the development of religious thinking in childhood concerns children's explanations of origins. Again reflecting a reliance on anthropomorphic thinking (as expressed in "naïve biology"; Hatano & Inagaki, 1994), children as young as 4 years of age demonstrate a preference for teleological explanations (explanations in terms of a purpose) over physical explanations of biological properties, and this preference persists throughout most of early and middle childhood (e.g., Kelemen, 1999). Thus, not surprisingly, children (aged 5 to 13) tend to prefer creation (i.e., God's direct work) as an explanation for the origins of species and the earth over evolutionary explanations (Evans, 2001).

An appealing feature of many religions is that they grant (at least some) humans (and at least some "parts" of them) continued existence after death. Yet adults, whether religious or not, also understand that death means "shop is closed," at least as far as bodily and mind-related functions are concerned. The notion of a "soul" or "spirit," however, at least holds some prospect for the hereafter. Thus, the development of afterlife and associated dualistic beliefs has been of interest to cognitive scientists of religion. Researchers have argued that by the end of middle childhood, children hold two conceptions of death in mind: one scientific and one religious (Harris & Giménez, 2005). Prior to that, in early childhood, children may attribute certain mind-related properties (such as emotions, desires, knowledge) as continuing after we die (Bering,

2006). During middle childhood, children come to make clearer distinctions between properties of the soul, on the one hand, and those of the body and mind, on the other; the soul has spiritual (but not cognitive or physical) functions, it remains stable, it connects people to God and it goes to heaven when people die (Richert & Harris, 2006).

Religious and Spiritual Attachments

Other anthropomorphic themes observed by Heller (1986) in his study of children's images of God, included "God, the therapist" ("an all-nurturant, loving figure"), "intimacy" (feelings of closeness to God), and "omnipresence" (God is "always there"). By way of contrast, God was also described as inconsistent and distant by some children. Such a human-like representation of God presumably aids developmentally in making God viable as a symbolic attachment figure that is, though, stained by the child's attachment-related internal working models. Thus, on top of its more purely cognitive components (typically studied by cognitive scientists), children's representation of God carries an affective load that is influenced by (generalized from) the child's interaction history with attachment figures.

Research on children's use of God as a symbolic attachment figure has focused both on attachment normative (or typical) processes and aspects related to individual differences in attachment security. Regarding attachment normative processes, empirical data from early childhood onwards indicate that God is perceived as an available safe haven in times of stress. For example, Tamminen (1994) found that 40% of Finnish 7- to 12-year-olds reported that they felt close to God particularly during loneliness and emergencies (e.g., escaping or avoiding danger, dealing with death or sorrow). In addition, using a quasi-experimental and semi-projective setup, a study of American pre- and elementary-school children found that they placed a God symbol closer to a fictional child when the fictional child was in attachment-activating situations than when the fictional child was in situations that would be less clear-cut as activators of the attachment system (Eshleman, Dickie, Merasco, Shepard, and Johnson, 1999). These findings have since been conceptually replicated in three additional studies of children in early to middle childhood from Italy, Sweden, and the US (Cassibba, Granqvist, & Costantini, 2013; Dickie, Charland, & Poll, 2005; Granqvist, Ljungdahl, & Dickie, 2007).

Regarding individual differences in attachment security, several child studies have shown that children's view of God is likely to mirror that of their other attachment figures, supporting a notion of generalizing internal working models (i.e., the IWM aspect of the correspondence hypothesis; Granqvist & Kirkpatrick, 2008). For example, a study with

4- to 11-year-old American Protestant children showed that children who perceived their parents as nurturing (cf. sensitive, a predictor of security) also perceived God as nurturing (Dickie et al., 1997). In addition, a study with 5- to 7-year-old Swedish children showed that secure (compared with insecure) children placed a God symbol closer to a fictional child when the fictional child was in attachment-activating situations (e.g., sick and in hospital) and farther from the fictional child when the fictional child was in attachment-neutral situations (e.g., bored, in a bad mood; Granqvist, Ljungdahl, & Dickie, 2007). Thus, just as in Ainsworth and colleagues' (1978) strange situation procedure, secure, but not insecure, children's attention shifted to attachment (in this case closeness to God) specifically when the attachment system should be activated. Moreover, Cassibba and colleagues (2013) have recently extended parts of these findings in an Italian sample. They showed that, just as attachment security tends to be transmitted from mother to child, mothers' attachment security predicted a higher degree of proximity in their children's placements of a God symbol vis-à-vis the fictional child. These findings suggest that experiences with secure versus insecure mothers generalize to the offspring's sense of the availability of another (symbolic) figure (i.e., God) than the mother herself.

The Calibrating Influence of Contextual Factors and the Transition from Early to Middle Childhood

The research reviewed in the earlier sections converges in illustrating how certain core psychological domains (e.g., mentalization, naïve biology, attachment) find a clear anthropomorphized expression in children's developing understanding of religious concepts, including their representation of God. In these reviews, I volitionally put a blind eye to the calibrating influence of contextual factors, which is highly visible even in some of the very same studies. For example, although Evans (2001) clearly observed a preference for creationist over evolutionary origin explanations among younger children from secular schools and with non-fundamentalist parents, she also found moderating roles of age and school/home context, such that children with increasing age came to mirror the explanations favored by their parents and other authority figures. Similarly, although Swedish children from secular homes placed a God symbol closer to a fictional child in attachment-activating than in attachment-neutral situations, children from religious (compared to secular) homes placed the God symbol closer across both types of situation (Granqvist et al., 2007).

These examples illustrate the important role that aspects of socialization may have in coaching or calibrating (e.g., amplifying or weakening) the expression of core domains/cognitive components on religious outcomes over the course of children's development. How this calibration works more precisely is a matter of speculation. For example, do elements of socialization (merely) "fill in" the core cognitive structures with specific religious content (Kelemen, 2004) or do they play a more fundamental role in shaping also the structure of children's cognition (Vygotsky, 1978)? Whatever the case may be, the socializing influence on specific beliefs and ways of thinking with regard to God/religion probably becomes increasingly visible with increasing child ages, from early to middle childhood. Put another way, religiousness gradually emerges from spirituality, and the transition from early to middle childhood represents a key period of that development.

Notably, this understanding of socialization-as-calibrator does *not* represent an approach to the child as a tabula rasa or a sponge, soaking up whatever happens to be modeled (cf. Kirkpatrick, 2005). Yet what is modeled is variable—from one family to the other, and from one historical period to another—and as long as the modeled behavior accords with the child's intuitive ontologies, the variability in modeled behavior presumably helps explain why one unseen other is ultimately embraced at the expense of others. Thus, it is not surprising that children in the Western world, like little Stella (who was quoted at the outset of this chapter),[1] might entertain encounters with Christ whereas children from India are more inclined to entertain encounters with Krishna (or perhaps Ganesh).

It has already been noted that parental sensitivity and authoritative parenting tend to increase the offspring's receptivity to parental social attitudes and behavior (e.g., securely attached children are generally more well-socialized than insecurely attached children; e.g., Ainsworth et al., 1974). However, although reliably supported in relation to religious outcomes in adolescent and adult studies (below), support for such an idea of "social correspondence" is absent in the childhood studies (see De Roos, 2006; Granqvist et al., 2007). Thus, it presumably takes additional years of autonomy development until secure and insecure children show *differential* susceptibility to their parents as religious models.

In middle childhood, as children enter school and move even farther from their parents' immediate care, their God representations become somewhat less anthropomorphic, although at the same time God is typically viewed as personally closer (i.e., more of an attachment figure) than in early childhood (Eshleman et al., 1999; Tamminen, 1994). Presumably, spirituality also becomes increasingly religiously framed for children raised in religious homes, whereas other children may leave their unseen others behind as unbelievable relics of early childhood fantasies, and yet other children may anthropomorphize nature or cosmos without giving them more precise framing.

Adolescence and Emerging Adulthood (12–25 Years)

Basics of Development

The two most pronounced themes of adolescent and early adult development coincide: maturation of the reproductive system goes in tandem with increasing autonomy strivings and a transfer of principal attachment figures from parents to age mates, typically romantic partners (sometimes close friends) (e.g., Zeifman & Hazan, 2008). It is not difficult to imagine that this developmental transformation has been selected for (i.e., adaptive). Besides surviving until adolescence, the offspring may now also pass their parents' genes on to the next generation. Moreover, in a species such as ours, where offspring are immature and dependent on high parental investment for a very long period, genetic reproduction has not sufficed; parents have also had to stick together for mutual investment in the next generation. Attachment may serve here as the emotional "glue" that binds prospective parents together. Thus, evolution has presumably co-opted the attachment system for use also in the context of reproductive relationships and other close relationships in adulthood (ibid.).

As straightforward as this puberty-to attachment transfer process may seem, it is of course in reality a long and crooked path—many fall by its side and others hit numerous deadends before the appearance of succeeding has realized itself, only to then wind up in a heart-wrenching separation, and then start all over again, in some cases *ad infinitum*. The transfer of attachment components from parents to peers is initiated already in childhood (i.e., preferential proximity to friends over parents in normal circumstances), it climaxes in mid- to late adolescence (i.e., overt autonomy-related conflicts with parents, preferentially starts using age mates as safe havens), and it is typically not concluded until early adulthood (i.e., preferentially starts using an age mate as a secure base) (Fraley & Davis, 1997; Friedlmeier & Granqvist, 2006).

Regarding the crookedness of this developmental process, and of adolescent development in general, there are important individual differences to consider. Security, unlike insecurity, of attachment is associated with generally favorable developmental outcomes, such as constructiveness of conflict resolution with parents, social competence with peers, and a relative absence of aggression and risk behaviors (e.g., heavy drug and alcohol consumption, sexual promiscuity) as well as of anxiety and depression-related problems (for a review, see Allen, 2008). In addition, insecure adolescents tend to make a premature transfer of attachment (Friedlmeier & Granqvist, 2006), and yet are less likely to build close, trusting, and satisfactory peer relations (Allen, 2008). Thus, the path may be particularly crooked for insecurely attached adolescents who may be left in a state wherein felt security cannot be derived either by turning to parents or to peers for support.

Erikson (1997) emphasized similar themes in his lifecycle theory of psychosocial development. The adolescent faces the challenge of exploring and then establishing a stable sense of personal identity, a process for which some measure of autonomy from parents is required. Identity formation is often facilitated by adolescents' experimentation with looks, drugs, sex, music, and subcultural "gangs" of various sorts. Thus, even though this period is marked by increasing autonomy (from parents) it typically coincides with increasing, and perhaps seemingly inappropriate, dependence on peers. However, identity formation by no means requires a period of intense storm and stress, neither does it entail separation from parents and a desperate seeking of a personal identity completely apart from parents. In contrast, the continued ability to use parents as a secure base for exploration fosters continuity of adaptation throughout adolescence, and this applies to identity formation as well (Lapsley, Rice, & Fitzgerald, 1990). Using Erikson's (1997) terminology, a few years later, the young adult faces the challenge of establishing intimacy with others, typically age mates (e.g., reproductive partners). In Erikson's (1997) view, individuals who fail to acquire these developmental tasks (identity and intimacy) run the risk of remaining directionless and confused about themselves, and of experiencing isolation from others.

Regarding cognitive development, a capacity for formal operational thinking (Piaget, 1930) brings with it new avenues of understanding. Many adolescents and adults are less dependent on concrete material and more appreciative of abstract principles and rules (e.g., hypothetical reasoning, if–then constructions) than previously in development.

Religious and Spiritual Development

A century of research indicates that adolescence to young adulthood represents an age period that is, at least for some people, associated with notable increases in aspects of spirituality and religiousness (e.g., Argyle & Beit-Hallahmi, 1975; Hood et al., 2009). As William James (1985 [1902]) observed, there is something with religion that appeals to adolescents' sentiment, such that although the cognitive machinery required for a belief in unobservable agents is set in motion already in early childhood, it is typically not until adolescence that the emotional fuel required for deep religious feelings is poured into that machine.

Not surprisingly, adolescence and early adulthood are the life periods most intimately associated with sudden religious conversions and other significant changes in one's relationship with God (e.g., Argyle & Beit-Hallahmi, 1975; Hood et al., 2009). However, adolescence to early adulthood is also generally associated with a decline in institutional religious involvement (Benson, Donahue, & Erickson, 1989) and with apostasy (e.g., Roof & McKinney, 1987; Tamminen, 1994). Thus, in this life period, some adolescents seem to decide, temporarily or permanently, *not* to accept parents as religious models.

There are probably multiple reasons for why adolescence to early adulthood represents such a religious/spiritual transitional period. Consequently, depending on one's theoretical persuasions, one may suggest the involvement of very different psychological components. For example, there could be links to puberty and sexual instincts (e.g., Coe, 1916). For another example, formal operational thinking may challenge one's previously anthropomorphized conceptions, such that God comes to lose some of the personal attributes that could make God appealing as a relational partner. In exchange, of course, religious thought may eventually become increasingly complex and differentiated (Hood et al., 2009). For yet another example, adolescents' search for an identity may include that of a religious (or non-religious) identity. As religion is often associated with parental and other forms of conservation values, whereas many identity seeking adolescents tend to endorse openness values, it is not surprising that identification with religion tends to decrease in adolescence (cf. Saroglou, 2012). For a fourth example, self-awareness often becomes painfully pronounced for many adolescents, and with that comes increased mortality salience, one defense to which might be spiritual awareness (Rothbaum, Wang, & Cohen, 2012). For a fifth example, in order to explain the religious re-affirmations that sometimes occur during adolescence to early adulthood, often after a period of doubting, socialization researchers have focused on this period as an important period of re-socialization processes (e.g., Hood et al., 2009; Ozorak, 1989).

Without denying that such processes and components may be involved, the co-occurrence of attachment transfer is presumably also an important reason for the religious/spiritual transitions observed during adolescence to early adulthood (see also Granqvist, 2012). According to Weiss (1973), relinquishing one's parents as attachment figures leads to a vulnerability for loneliness. At such a time, adolescents may turn to God as a substitute symbolic attachment figure. Thus, attachment components may not only be transferred to peers, but also to God. However, as adolescence also signifies a growing pressure of autonomy from parents and their values (including religious values), attachment transfer also leads some adolescents to shy away from God and religion.

Thus, the critical theoretical question in relation to adolescence/early adulthood as religious/spiritual transitional periods becomes one of individual differences: why do some adolescents/young adults become increasingly "attached to God," whereas others shun God and religion? This question has been at the forefront of attachment research in the psychology of religion, with largely converging results across studies.

First, several adolescent to early adult studies have supported the notion that religiosity in the case of insecure attachment develops from attachment-related distress regulation strategies, where God functions as a surrogate, symbolic attachment figure (the "compensation hypothesis"; Granqvist & Kirkpatrick, 2008). For example, attachment insecurity and parental insensitivity have been linked to religious instability; religiosity characteristically waxes and wanes over time for these individuals (Granqvist, 2002). Regarding its waxing, religiousness tends to increase specifically during stress, such as upon romantic relationship dissolution (Granqvist & Hagekull, 2003). These conclusions were corroborated in a meta-analysis of sudden religious conversions, which included nearly 1500 participants, most of whom were adolescents and young adults. In the meta-analysis, insecurity (as compared to security) with parents was overrepresented among the sudden converts (9% vs. 5%, respectively) but not among gradual converts or non-converts (Granqvist & Kirkpatrick, 2004). Similarly, in a recent US Young Life Evangelical summer camp study (Schnitker, Porter, Emmons, & Barrett, 2012), late adolescent summer camp staff members whose relationship narratives suggested insecure parental attachment were significantly more likely (38%) to have experienced a sudden religious conversion when they attended camp themselves, compared to those whose relationship narratives suggested secure parental attachment (10%). Regarding its waning, follow-up analyses of an adolescent sample documented that religiosity decreases for some insecure adolescents, typically following the formation of other close relationships (Granqvist & Hagekull, 2003).

As the findings from the meta-analysis of sudden conversions indicate, such conversion experiences are typically rare even among insecure adolescents. Indeed, since the early days of the psychology of religion, parts of the world—and especially European "Welfare States"—have seen traditional, institutionalized religion take on a marginalized role in society (e.g., Gill & Lundsgaarde, 2004). Perhaps not coincidentally, more privatized and self-centering forms of spirituality have increased, especially among adolescents and young adults (e.g., Houtman & Aupers, 2007). Research has confirmed an association between such a "new age" orientation, on the one hand, and attachment insecurity, on the other (Granqvist & Hagekull, 2001; Granqvist, Ivarsson, Broberg, & Hagekull, 2007).

Second, several adolescent to adult studies have also supported the social learning aspect of the "correspondence hypothesis," that is, the notion that religiosity in the case of secure attachment reflects receptivity to the calibrating influence of a sensitive caregiver's religious modeling (Granqvist & Kirkpatrick, 2008). For example, attachment security with parents and peers has been linked to a comparatively high degree of parent–adolescent similarity in religiousness (Granqvist, 2002). In other words, these adolescents tended to affirm (and possibly re-affirm) the faith or lack of faith of their parents. Moreover, in the same study, security was associated with religious stability. However, when these adolescents nevertheless experienced a prospective increase in religiousness, the change tended to be gradual (Granqvist, 2002) and to occur in the context of a positive influence from others, such as a new romantic relationship partner (Granqvist & Hagekull, 2003). Some of these results were conceptually replicated in the recent Young Life summer camp study, which showed that secure attachment with parents prospectively predicted an at-camp re-affirmation of the faith one had been brought up with (Schnitker et al., 2012). Finally, several studies informed by the socialization and parenting styles literatures have shown not only that parental religiousness remains a solid predictor of offspring religiousness during adolescence and young adulthood but also that its predictive power is especially pronounced when the parent–adolescent relationship is marked by warmth and acceptance (i.e., parts of authoritative parenting; for a review, see Hood et al., 2009).

Thus, adolescence to early adulthood appears as a religious and spiritual junction, where two relatively distinct developmental pathways to religion and spirituality emerge. One of these goes via insecure attachment and compensatory distress regulation strategies, winding up as a conversion-based path to religion and spirituality (cf. James's 1985 [1902] description of the twice-born religion of the "sick soul"). The other one goes via experiences with sensitive, religious caregivers, and winds up as a socialization-based path to religion and spirituality (cf. James's 1985 [1902] description of the once-born religion of the "healthy-minded"). Yet another path goes "from the fold," which tends to be the case for apostates, often adolescents raised by religious but insensitive/non-authoritative caregivers. Finally, it should be borne in mind that many individuals, especially those brought up sensitively by non-religious parents in highly secular countries, will pass through adolescence and young adulthood without either turning to or away from religion and spirituality.

Middle Adulthood and Aging (beyond 25 Years)

Basics of Development

Over the course of adulthood, development becomes increasingly heterogeneous (Nelson & Dannefer, 1992), implying that individual, cultural, and sub-cultural differences make it difficult to characterize normative (or typical) adult development. As implied already by Freud (1961

[1930]), though, two major themes stand out as important characteristics of a psychologically healthy adult life, namely love and work. This converges with Erikson's (1997) emphasis on generativity as the positive resolution of the developmental "crisis" facing middle-aged adults. And evolutionary theorists concur; reproduction brings with it an enormous parental investment task (Trivers, 1972): to care for one's children and spouse (i.e., "love") as well as to provide necessary resources for the family (i.e., through "work").

With children, in particular, another experiential domain of love (i.e., bonding love) is thus given birth, and one which is likely more emotionally profound than any other one in the adult's life. The very signs of immaturity with which infants come equipped (e.g., the disproportionately big skull, the characteristic facial features, the unmasked social smile) tend to disarm most adults, make them hooked to the child, and activate a disposition to engage in behaviors governed by the adult's evolved caregiving system, and to do so for quite a long period of time (George & Solomon, 2008). And those 20 years or so certainly are not just characterized by love, but also by sleep deprivation, frustration, worry, and anger. The combination of work, caregiving, and spousal investments effectively keeps many middle-aged adults highly busy, and typically with mundane matters, often making this a period marked by a "resurrection of the concrete."

Further increases in heterogeneity in late adulthood makes it difficult to arrive at a normative yet non-stereotypical conceptualization of the development of the elderly (Nelson & Dannefer, 1992). Nevertheless, most elders acquire lessened sensory acuity, information processing speed, and working memory capacity (Hedden & Gabriele, 2004). All in all, this may lead to a restriction of engagement in activities that were formerly enjoyable. Consequently, the elderly report lower self-efficacy, more loneliness and depressive symptoms, and a smaller social network (e.g., Kramer, Kapteyn, Kuik, & Deeg, 2002).

Apart from physical and sensory impairments the losses through death of loved ones, such as spouses or close friends, are clearly overrepresented among the elderly. Thus, a psychologically painful process of grief or mourning is very common among the elderly, in particular following the death of a spouse (i.e., typically one's principal adult attachment figure; Bowlby, 1980). Loss of a principal attachment figure is a powerful stressor, indeed a potentially traumatic event, in part because it is a stressful event in itself, and in part because it eliminates the availability of the person to whom one would otherwise have been likely to turn for support in a stressful situation. Consequently, spousal bereavement is associated with depression and elevated risks for suicide (Rosenzweig, Prigerson, Miller, & Reynolds, 1997).

Research and theorizing on development during aging has documented that some elders also have profoundly positive experiences. For example, research relating to Erikson's idea (1997) of "ego integrity" (or wisdom) indicates that some elderly report high levels of psychological wellbeing (e.g., an upbeat mood, self-acceptance, and marital satisfaction; James & Zarrett, 2007). Relatedly, the term "gerotranscendence" (Tornstam, 1997) has been coined in the literature to characterize states of inner calm and serenity, of peace-of-mind when engaging in quiet reminiscence, which characterizes favorable development in the very final stages of life. This somewhat mysticism-reeking term denotes a cosmic/transcendent perspective, directed beyond the individual's self.

Religious and Spiritual Development

William James (1950 [1890], p. 121) noted that "Habit is ... the enormous fly-wheel of society, its most precious conservative agent." In middle adulthood, as people are busy with mundane tasks related to caregiving and work, religiosity typically takes the form of consolidating such a habit, at least when compared to the religious/spiritual developments that occur during the other major life periods discussed in this chapter (cf. Dillon, 2007; Krause, 2006). Moreover, the "religious habit" may become an important component of what is to be transmitted to the next generation as part of children's socialization (cf. Hood et al., 2009). In that regard, religion may also become a conserving "agent" (cf. Saroglou, 2012); a question of "going to Church on Sunday" and of socializing and forming protective alliances with a community of like-minded people.

However, there are, as always, notable exceptions to the stability implied in the notion of religion as habit. One of those is the experience of initially becoming a parent, which may engender the formation of religious faith (e.g., Palkovitz & Palm, 1998). Another exception is the experience of marital discord and breakup. Research suggests that religiousness may increase following the separation from loved ones, but this may be the case exclusively for people with insecure attachments, for whom the separation may set a compensatory religious conversion process in motion (Granqvist & Hagekull, 2003). For others, religiousness may decrease following separations (ibid.; Lawton & Bures, 2002).

Aging brings with it a multitude of situations which should both activate the elderly's attachment system and function as death reminders that effectively increase mortality salience (e.g., illnesses, physical ailments, losses, and loneliness). For these reasons alone, it is not surprising that religion and spirituality tend to gain increased importance for some elderly (Dillon, 2007; Krause, 2006), often making aging a period of spiritual and religious "reawakening." For example, and illustrating the role filled by the loss of a spouse, Brown, Nesse, House, and

Utz (2004) found that elders who were destined to suffer bereavement during the course of their longitudinal study experienced a prospective increase in the importance of their religious beliefs following bereavement compared to the non-bereaved (cf. Cicirelli, 2004). This study also showed that grief over the loss decreased as a function of the increased significance of the bereaved individual's religious beliefs. Importantly, none of those effects was obtained when church attendance rather than religious beliefs was used as the outcome (or predictor) variable, indicating that it may be a private, attachment-related component of religiousness that is activated in such situations and contributes to a more favorable outcome.

Relatedly, Bowlby (1980) noted that to proceed favorably in terms of promoting adaptation to a life without the loved one's physical accessibility, the mourning process requires that bereaved individuals eventually accommodate information regarding the permanence of the person's death into their representational world. Otherwise, the individual is at risk of remaining unresolved or disorganized with respect to the loss; for example, they may display continued searching for the lost person and slip into dissociated states of disbelief regarding the person's physical death. Available evidence indicates that the proportion of unresolved/disorganized loss is somewhat lower in religious samples (Cassibba et al., 2008; Cassibba et al., 2013; Granqvist, Ivarsson, et al., 2007) than in a non-clinical meta-analytic sample (Bakermans-Kranenburg & van IJzendoorn, 2009). As noted by Cassibba and colleagues (2008), religion may promote mental resolution of loss via offering a prospect of reunion with deceased loved ones in the hereafter. In addition, the bereaved individual's attachment to God may serve as a surrogate bond assisting the individual in distress regulation (e.g., grief work) in lieu of the inaccessibility of a lost attachment figure (Granqvist & Kirkpatrick, 2008).

Finally, religious beliefs and interpretations may offer additional benefits to the states experienced by some elders. For example, elders who are capable of gerotranscendence in the very final stages of life may, through religion and spirituality, gain an increased sense of the interrelatedness of all things, of life and death as meaningful, and of security with God. If not before, then at the very end of the day, death may definitely lose its sting (Vaillant, 2002).

Conclusions

As made clear in this chapter, the story of lifespan spiritual and religious development is one with multiple beginnings, several peaks and dead-ends, and with many endings. In fact, one might conceivably argue that it's not *a* story, but several stories. In view of the multifaceted nature of human development in general and the fact that spiritual and religious development builds on that, this conclusion should not come as a surprise. Needless to say, however, it has been necessary for the purposes of this chapter to turn a blind eye to some true sources of additional complexity. Consequently, the chapter as a whole has told an unrealistically uniform story, for most part leaving out cultural, historical, and societal considerations, although such considerations would have provided important macro-level contexts within which development, after all, takes place.

No matter how many parameters that are reflected in development in general, and spiritual and religious development in particular, I maintain that it is, at least in principle, possible to arrive at the general organizing principles needed to achieve some level of conceptual integration of the pieces. This brings us back to the introduction of the chapter. I have argued that religious and spiritual development builds on the adaptive, domain-specific spurts that characterize development in general. Understanding the timing of those spurts is typically straightforward, as it depends on the functional utility of the evolved systems that operate in any given domain. It is more challenging to settle on exactly which systems and domains that most importantly manifest themselves in the spiritual and religious realms. In this chapter, particular emphasis was placed on certain core cognitive domains and the attachment system, along with associated internal working models of attachment, but additional systems warrant further research attention (see Kirkpatrick, 2005).

In addition, it is a challenge to be clear about the exact factors that serve to calibrate those systems, and how a specific form of calibration affects religious and spiritual outcomes. In this chapter, modeling and other aspects of social learning have been emphasized as domain-general tools that may serve to calibrate several pertinent systems, essentially tweaking them to find expression in the religious and spiritual realm. Needless to say, other environmental calibrators should be entertained as well. Attachment theorists (e.g., Ainsworth et al., 1978; Bowlby, 1982 [1969]) typically conceive of the attachment figure's characteristic behaviors as an important calibrator of the offspring's attachment systems, causing individual differences (cf. parameter adjustments in the system) in attachment to develop. In comparison, cognitive science models have typically given less explicit attention to the issue of environmental calibration, which represents an important topic of potential theoretical improvement for those models.

Nevertheless, by replacing stage models and highly domain-general ways of understanding development with the general organizing principles of evolutionary and cognitive science, our understanding of religious and spiritual development has made significant progress, and largely so during the last decade. By continuing to build on and further refine these organizing principles, our understanding of religious and spiritual development has the potential to flourish further.

Notes

1　The encounter with Christ to which 2-year-old Stella referred was tellingly (for her age) concrete; just before her great grandmother's funeral, her mother had read her a passage about Jesus from the children's Bible, and when the priest then mentioned Jesus during the funeral, Stella just happened to get the lingo right.

References

Ainsworth, M. D. S. (1985). Attachments across the life span. *Bulletin of the New York Academy of Medicine, 61,* 792–812.

Ainsworth, M. D. S., Bell, S. M., & Stayton, D. J. (1974). Infant–mother attachment and social development: "Socialization" as a product of reciprocal responsiveness to signals. In M. P. M. Richards (Ed.), *The integration of a child into a social world* (pp. 99–137). Cambridge: Cambridge University Press.

Ainsworth, M. D. S., Blehar, M. C., Waters, E., & Wall, S. (1978). *Patterns of attachment: A psychological study of the strange situation.* Hillsdale, NJ: Lawrence Erlbaum.

Allen, J. P. (2008). The attachment system in adolescence. In J. Cassidy & P. R. Shaver (Eds.), *Handbook of attachment theory and research* (2nd ed., pp. 419–435). New York: Guilford.

Argyle, M., & Beit-Hallahmi, B. (1975). *The social psychology of religion.* London: Routledge & Kegan Paul.

Baillargeon, R., & DeVos, J. (1991). Object permanence in young infants: Further evidence. *Child Development, 62,* 1227–1246.

Bakermans-Kranenburg, M. J., & van IJzendoorn, M. H. (2009). The first 10,000 Adult Attachment Interviews: Distributions of attachment representations in clinical and non-clinical groups. *Attachment and Human Development, 11,* 223–263.

Barr, R., Muentener, P., & Garcia, A. (2007). Age-related changes in deferred imitation from television by 6- to 18-month-olds. *Developmental Science, 10,* 910–921.

Barrett, J. L. (2004). *Why would anyone believe in God?* Lanham, MD: AltaMira Press.

Barrett, J. L., Richert, R.A., & Driesenga, A. (2001). God's beliefs versus mother's: The development of nonhuman agent concepts. *Child Development, 72,* 50–65.

Baumrind, D. (1971). Current patterns of parental authority. *Developmental Psychology Monographs, 4*(1), 2.

Benson, P. L., Donahue, M. J., & Erickson, J. A. (1989). Adolescence and religion: A review of the literature from 1970 to 1986. *Research in the Social Scientific Study of Religion, 1,* 153–181.

Bering, J. M. (2006). The folk psychology of souls. *Behavioral and Brain Sciences, 29,* 453–498.

Bering, J. M., & Parker, B. D. (2006). Children's attributions of intentions to an invisible agent. *Developmental Psychology, 42,* 253–262.

Bjorklund, D. F. (1997). The role of immaturity in human development. *Psychological Bulletin, 122,* 153–169.

Bowlby, J. (1982). *Attachment and loss: Vol. 1. Attachment* (2nd ed.). New York: Basic Books. (Original work published 1969)

Bowlby, J. (1980). *Attachment and loss: Vol. 3. Loss.* New York: Basic Books.

Boyatzis, C. J. (2005). Religious and spiritual development in childhood. In R.F. Paloutzian & C. L. Park (Eds.), *Handbook of the psychology of religion and spirituality* (pp. 123–143). New York: Guilford.

Boyer, P. (2001). *Religion explained: The evolutionary origins of religious thought.* New York: Basic Books.

Bretherton, I. (1987). New perspectives on attachment relations: Security, communication, and internal working models. In J. D. Osofsky (Ed.), *Handbook of infant development* (2nd ed., pp. 1061–1100). New York: Wiley.

Brown, R. D., & Bjorklund, D. F. (1998). The biologizing of cognition, development, and education: Approach with cautious enthusiasm. *Educational Psychology Review, 10,* 355–373.

Brown, S. L., Nesse, R. M., House, J. S., & Utz, R. L. (2004). Religion and emotional compensation: Results from a prospective study of widowhood. *Personality and Social Psychology Bulletin, 30,* 1165–1174.

Camras, L. A. (1992). Expressive development and basic emotions. *Cognition and Emotion, 6,* 267–283.

Carlson, E. A., Yates, T. M., & Sroufe, L. A. (2009). Dissociation and development of the self. In P. Dell & J. A. O'Neil (Eds.), *Dissociation and the dissociative disorders: DSM V and beyond* (pp. 39–52). New York: Routledge.

Cassibba, R., Granqvist, P., & Costantini, A. (2013). Mothers' security of attachment predicts their children's sense of God's closeness. *Attachment and Human Development, 15,* 51–64.

Cassibba, R., Granqvist, P., Costantini, A., & Gatto, S. (2008). Attachment and God representations among lay Catholics, priests, and religious: A matched comparison study based on the Adult Attachment Interview. *Developmental Psychology, 44,* 1753–1763.

Cassidy, J., & Berlin, L. J. (1999). Understanding the origins of childhood loneliness: Contributions of attachment theory. In K. J. Rotenberg & S. Hymel (Eds.), *Loneliness in childhood and adolescence* (pp. 34–55). New York: Cambridge University Press.

Cicirelli, V. G. (2004). God as the ultimate attachment figure for older adults. *Attachment and Human Development, 6,* 371–388.

Coe, G. A. (1916). *Psychology of religion.* Chicago, IL: University of Chicago Press.

De Roos, S. A. (2006). Young children's God concepts: Influences of attachment and religious socialization in a family and school context. *Religious Education, 101,* 84–103.

Dickie, J. R., Charland, K., & Poll, E. (2005). *Attachment and children's concepts of God.* Unpublished manuscript, Hope College, Holland, MI.

Dickie, J. R., Eshleman, A. K., Merasco, D. M., Vander Wilt, M., & Johnson, M. (1997). Parent–child relationships and children's images of God. *Journal for the Scientific Study of Religion, 36,* 25–43.

Dillon, M. (2007). Age, generation, and cohort in American religion and spirituality. In J. A. Beckford & N. J. Demerath III (Eds.), *The SAGE handbook of the sociology of religion* (pp. 526–546). London: Sage.

Erikson, E. H. (1997). *The life cycle completed. Extended version with new chapters on the ninth stage by Joan M. Erikson.* New York: Norton.

Eshleman, A. K., Dickie, J. R., Merasco, D. M., Shepard, A., & Johnson, M. (1999). Mother God, father God: Children's perceptions of God's distance. *International Journal for the Psychology of Religion, 9*, 139–146.

Evans, E. M. (2001). Cognitive and contextual factors in the emergence of diverse belief systems: Creation versus evolution. *Cognitive Psychology, 42*, 217–266.

Fraley, R. C., & Davis, K. E. (1997). Attachment formation and transfer in young adults' close friendships and romantic relationships. *Personal Relationships, 4*, 131–144.

Freud, S. (1961). *Civilization and its discontents* (J. Strachey, Trans.). New York: Norton. (Original work published 1930)

Friedlmeier, W., & Granqvist, P. (2006). Attachment transfer among German and Swedish adolescents: A prospective longitudinal study. *Personal Relationships, 13*, 261–279.

Geary, D. C., & Bjorklund, D. F. (2003). Evolutionary developmental psychology. *Child Development, 71*, 57–65.

George, C., & Solomon, J. (2008). The caregiving system: A behavioral systems approach to caregiving. In J. Cassidy & P. R. Shaver (Eds.), *Handbook of attachment theory and research* (2nd ed., pp. 833–856). New York: Guilford.

Gill, A., & Lundsgaarde, E. (2004). State welfare spending and religiosity: A cross-national analysis. *Rationality and Society, 16*, 399–436.

Goodvin, R., Meyer, S., Thompson, R.A., & Hayes, R. (2008). Self-understanding in early childhood: Associations with child attachment security and maternal negative affect. *Attachment and Human Development, 10*, 433–450.

Granqvist, P. (2002). Attachment and religiosity in adolescence: Cross-sectional and longitudinal evaluations. *Personality and Social Psychology Bulletin, 28*, 260–270.

Granqvist, P. (2012). Attachment and religious development in adolescence: The implications of culture. In G. Trommsdorff & X. Chen (Eds.), *Values, religion, and culture in adolescent development* (pp. 315–340). New York: Cambridge University Press.

Granqvist, P., & Hagekull, B. (2001). Seeking security in the new age: On attachment and emotional compensation. *Journal for the Scientific Study of Religion, 40*, 529–547.

Granqvist, P., & Hagekull, B. (2003). Longitudinal predictions of religious change in adolescence: Contributions from the interaction of attachment and relationship status. *Journal of Social and Personal Relationships, 20*, 793–817.

Granqvist, P., Ivarsson, T., Broberg, A. G., & Hagekull, B. (2007). Examining relations between attachment, religiosity, and New Age spirituality using the Adult Attachment Interview. *Developmental Psychology, 43*, 590–601.

Granqvist, P., & Kirkpatrick, L. A. (2004). Religious conversion and perceived childhood attachment: A meta-analysis. *International Journal for the Psychology of Religion, 14,* 223–250.

Granqvist, P., & Kirkpatrick, L. A. (2008). Attachment and religious representations and behavior. In J. Cassidy & P. R. Shaver (Eds.), *Handbook of attachment: Theory, research, and clinical applications* (2nd ed., pp. 906–933). New York: Guilford.

Granqvist, P., Ljungdahl, C., & Dickie, J. R. (2007). God is nowhere, God is now here: Attachment activation, security of attachment (SAT), and God proximity among 5–7 year-old children. *Attachment and Human Development, 9,* 55–71.

Harris, P. L., & Giménez, M. (2005). Children's acceptance of conflicting testimony: The case of death. *Journal of Cognition and Culture, 5,* 143–164.

Harter, S. (1999). *The construction of self: A developmental perspective.* New York: Guilford.

Hartup, W. W. (1996). The company they keep: Friendships and their developmental significance. *Child Development, 67,* 1–13.

Hatano, G., & Inagaki, K. (1994). Young children's naive theory of biology. *Cognition, 50,* 171–188.

Hedden, T., & Gabriele, D. E. (2004). Insights into the ageing mind: A view from cognitive neuroscience. *Nature Reviews Neuroscience, 5,* 87–97.

Heller, D. (1986). *The children's God.* Chicago, IL: University of Chicago Press.

Hoff, E.V. (2005). Imaginary companions, creativity, and self-image in middle childhood. *Creativity Research Journal, 17,* 167–180.

Hood, R. W., Jr., Hill, P. C., & Spilka, B. (2009). *The psychology of religion: An empirical approach* (4th ed.). New York: Guilford.

Houtman, D., & Aupers, S. (2007). The spiritual turn and the decline of tradition: The spread of post-Christian spirituality in 14 Western countries, 1981–2000. *Journal for the Scientific Study of Religion, 46,* 305–320.

Iacoboni, M., & Dapretto, M. (2006). The mirror neuron system and the consequences of its dysfunction. *Nature Reviews Neuroscience, 7,* 942–951.

James, J. B., & Zarrett, N. (2007). Ego integrity in the lives of older women. *Journal of Adult Development, 13,* 61–75.

James, W. (1950). *The principles of psychology* (2 vols.). New York: Dover. (Original work published 1890)

James, W. (1985). *The varieties of religious experience.* New York: Longmans, Green. (Original work published 1902)

Jensen, J. S. (2009). Religion as the unintended product of brain functions in the "standard cognitive science of religion model": On Pascal Boyer, Religion Explained (2001) and Ilkka Pyysiäinen, How Religion Works (2003). In M. Stausberg (Ed.), *Contemporary theories of religion* (pp. 129–155). London: Routledge.

Jipson, J. L., & Gelman, S. A. (2007). Robots and rodents: Children's inferences about living and non-living kinds. *Child Development, 78,* 1675–1688.

Kelemen, D. (1999). Why are rocks pointy? Children's preference for teleological explanations of the natural world. *Developmental Psychology, 35,* 1440–1452.

Kelemen, D. (2004). Are children "intuitive theists"? Reasoning about purpose and design in nature. *Psychological Science, 15,* 295–301.

Kirkpatrick, L. A. (2005). *Attachment, evolution, and the psychology of religion.* New York: Guilford.

Knight, N., Sousa, P., Barrett, J. L., & Atran, S. (2004). Children's attributions of beliefs to humans and God: Cross-cultural evidence. *Cognitive Science, 28,* 117–126.

Kramer, S. E., Kapteyn, T. S., Kuik, D. J., & Deeg, D. J. (2002). The association of hearing impairment and chronic diseases with psychosocial health status in older age. *Journal of Aging and Health, 14,* 122–137.

Krause, N. (2006). Religion and health in late life. In J. E. Birren & K. W. Schaie (Eds.), *Handbook of the psychology of aging* (6th ed., pp. 499–518). San Diego, CA: Academic Press.

Lapsley, D. K., Rice, K. G., & Fitzgerald, D. P. (1990). Adolescent attachment, identity, and adjustment to college: Implications for the continuity of adaptation hypothesis. *Journal of Counseling and Development, 68,* 561–565.

Lawton, L.E., & Bures, R. (2002). Parental divorce and the "switching" of religious identity. *Journal for the Scientific Study of Religion, 40,* 99–111.

Main, M., Kaplan, N., & Cassidy, J. (1985). Security in infancy, childhood, and adulthood: A move to the level of representation. In I. Bretherton & E. Waters (Eds.), Growing points of attachment theory and research, *Monographs of the Society for Research in Child Development, 50* (1–2, Serial No. 209), 66–104.

Nelson, E. A., & Dannefer, D. (1992). Aged heterogeneity: Fact or fiction? The fate and diversity in gerontological research. *The Gerontologist, 32,* 17–23.

Oser, F. K., Scarlett, W. G., & Bucher, A. (2007). Religious and spiritual development throughout the life span. In W. Damon & R. L. Lerner (Eds.), *Handbook of child psychology, Vol. 1: Theoretical models of human development* (6th ed., pp. 942–998). Hoboken, NJ: Wiley.

Ozorak, E. W. (1989). Social and cognitive influences on the development of religious beliefs and commitment in adolescence. *Journal for the Scientific Study of Religion, 28,* 448–463.

Palkovitz, R., & Palm, G. (1998). Fatherhood and faith in formation: The developmental effects of fathering on religiosity, morals, and values. *Journal of Men's Studies, 7,* 33–51.

Pargament, K. I. (2003). Advances in the conceptualization and measurement of religion and spirituality: Implications for physical and mental health research. *American Psychologist, 58,* 64–74.

Piaget, J. (1930). *The child's conception of the world.* New York: Harcourt, Brace, & World.

Pinker, S. (1994). *The language instinct: How the mind creates language.* New York: HarperCollins.

Richert, R., & Granqvist, P. (in press). Religious and spiritual development in childhood. In R. F. Paloutzian & C. L. Park (Eds.), *Handbook of the psychology of religion and spirituality* (2nd ed.). New York: Guilford.

Richert, R. A., & Harris, P. L. (2006). The ghost in my body: Children's developing concept of the soul. *Journal of Cognition and Culture, 6,* 409–427.

Rizzuto, A. M. (1979). *The birth of the living God: A psychoanalytical study.* Chicago, IL: Chicago University Press.

Rochat, P., & Hespos, S. J. (1997). Differential rooting responses by neonates: Evidence for an early sense of self. *Early Development and Parenting, 6,* 105–112.

Roof, W.C., & McKinney, W. (1987). *American mainline religion: Its changing shape and future.* New Brunswick, NJ: Rutgers University Press.

Rosenzweig, A., Prigerson, H., Miller, M. D., & Reynolds, C. F. (1997). Bereavement and late-life depression: Grief and its complications in the elderly. *Annual Review of Medicine, 48,* 421–428.

Rothbaum, F., Wang, J. Z., & Cohen, D. (2012). Cultural differences in self-awareness in adolescence: Pathways to spiritual awareness. In G. Trommsdorff & X. Chen (Eds.), *Values, religion, and culture in adolescent development* (pp. 66–96). New York: Cambridge University Press.

Saroglou, V. (2012). Adolescents' social development and the role of religion: Coherence at the detriment of openness. In G. Trommsdorff & X. Chen (Eds.), *Values, religion, and culture in adolescent development* (pp. 391–423). New York: Cambridge University Press.

Schnitker, S. A., Porter, T. J., Emmons, R. A., & Barrett, J. L. (2012). Attachment predicts adolescent conversions at Young Life religious summer camps. *International Journal for the Psychology of Religion, 22,* 216–230.

Shtulman, A. (2008). Variation in the anthropomorphization of supernatural beings and its implications for cognitive theories of religion *Journal of Experimental Psychology: Learning, Memory, and Cognition, 34,* 1123–1138.

Sroufe, L. A., & Waters, E. (1977). Attachment as an organizational construct. *Child Development, 48,* 1184–1199.

Stenberg, G. (2003). Effects of maternal inattentiveness on infant social referencing. *Infant and Child Development, 12,* 399–419.

Stern, D. (1985). *The interpersonal world of the infant.* New York: Basic Books.

Tamminen, K. (1994). Religious experiences in childhood and adolescence: A viewpoint of religious development between the ages of 7 and 20. *International Journal for the Psychology of Religion, 4,* 61–85.

Tomasello, M., Kruger, A. C., Ratner, H. H. (1993). Cultural learning. *Behavioral and Brain Sciences, 16,* 495–552.

Tornstam, L. (1997). Gero-transcendence: A reformulation of disengagement theory *Aging, 1,* 55–63.

Trivers, R. L. (1972). Parental investment and sexual selection. In R. B. Campbell (Ed.), *Sexual selection and the descent of man: 1871–1971* (pp. 136–179). Chicago, IL: Aldine.

Vaillant, G. F. (2002). *Aging well.* Boston, MA: Little, Brown.

Vygotsky, L. S. (1978). *Mind in society: The development of higher psychological processes.* Cambridge, MA: Harvard University Press.

Waddington, C. H. (1957). *The strategy of the genes.* London: Allen & Unwin.

Weiss, R. S. (1973). *Loneliness: The experience of emotional and social isolation.* Cambridge, MA: MIT Press.

Wellman, H., Cross, D., & Watson, J. (2001). Meta-analysis of theory of mind development: The truth about false-belief. *Child Development, 72,* 655–684.

Wellman, H. M., & Gelman, S. A. (1992). Cognitive development: Foundational theories of core domains. *Annual Review of Psychology, 43,* 337–375.

Woolley, J. D. (1997). Thinking about fantasy: Are children fundamentally different thinkers and believers from adults? *Child Development, 68,* 991–1011.

Zeanah, C. H., Smyke, A. T., Koga, S. F., & Carlson, E. (2005). Attachment in institutionalized and community children in Romania. *Child Development*, 76, 1015–1028.

Zeifman, D., & Hazan, C. (2008). Pair bonds as attachments: Reevaluating the evidence. In J. Cassidy & P. R. Shaver (Eds.), *Handbook of attachment theory and research* (2nd ed., pp. 436–455). New York: Guilford.

14 Gender Differences in Religion

Leslie J. Francis and Gemma Penny

In their classic review of empirical research in the social psychology of religion, Argyle and Beit-Hallahmi (1975) concluded that:

> The differences between men and women in their religious behaviour and beliefs are considerable ... This is one of the most important of the statistical comparisons to be made in this book. (p.71)

Two decades later, Francis (1997) confirmed Argyle and Beit-Hallahmi's assessment of the existing literature, but also raised serious questions about the consistency and generalizability of the evidence (especially outside the Christian tradition) and about the adequacy of the theoretical explanations offered to account for these findings. The present chapter brings the assessment up to date by examining six themes: contemporary evidence from Christian (or post-Christian) and other religious traditions; classic sociological theories (gender role socialization and structural location); new sociological theories (risk aversion and power control); classic psychological theories (depth psychology and gender differences theories); new psychological theories (gender orientation and personality); and the universal nature of religious gender differences. The present chapter will focus predominantly on the findings of empirical studies exploring the question of religious gender differences generated within a Christian (or post-Christian) context, since, comparatively, empirical studies exploring religious gender differences generated within the context of other religious faiths (e.g., Judaism, Islam, Hinduism, Buddhism, or Sikhism) remain limited. Where the developing literature exists and is relevant, findings from the latter will be included throughout the text.

Empirical Evidence

Recent empirical evidence generated from a Christian (or post-Christian) context continues to indicate that women are more religious than men.

The empirical evidence in terms of gender differences in church attendance is consistent across many different locations, including: Africa
(Akinyele & Akinyele, 2007), Australia (Moxy, McEvoy, & Bowe, 2011),
Canada and the USA (Eagle, 2011; Maselko & Kubzansky, 2006), and
Western Europe (Crockett & Voas, 2006; Pollak & Pickel, 2007). The
empirical evidence for women being more religious than men within
a Christian context is consistent across a range of other indicators of
religiosity in addition to church attendance, including: attitude toward
religion (Francis, Ispas, Robbins, Ilie, & Iliescu, 2009), denominational
membership (Smith, Denton, Faris, & Regenerus, 2002), religious belief
(Bartkowski & Hempel, 2009), religious experience and spiritual connection with God (Anthony, Hermans, & Sherkat, 2010; Baker, 2008).
Empirical evidence for women being more religious than men has also
been demonstrated within the context of other religious faiths including
studies generated within the Islamic tradition (Hassan, 2007), the Jewish tradition (Kalstein & Power, 2008), and the Hindu tradition (Firth,
1997).

While the empirical evidence supporting the claim that women are
more religious than men has remained stable from the time of Argyle
and Beit-Hallahmi's (1975) classic review to the end of the first decade
of the 21st century, considerable change has taken place in the weight
given to different theories for explaining this difference between men
and women. In the 1970s sociological theories dominated the field, but
by the 2000s psychological theories came more into prominence.

Classic Sociological Theories

In the mid-1990s, Francis (1997) distinguished between two prominent
classic sociological theories advanced to account for gender differences
in religiosity, named gender role socialization theories, and structural
location theories.

Gender Role Socialization Theories

Gender role socialization theories maintain that gender difference in
religiosity can be attributed to different experiences of socialization
among males and females. According to this theory, males are socialized in terms of accomplishment and aggressiveness, which are ideals
congruent with secular culture. By contrast, females are socialized in
terms of conflict resolution, submission, gentleness, and nurturance,
which are ideals congruent with religious emphases. This position was
supported by Nelsen and Potvin (1981), who argued that both gender
role socialization and parent–child interaction generally place more
weight on religiousness and conformity for girls than for boys. Against
this perspective, Francis (1997) argued that the strength of gender role

socialization theories to account for gender difference in religiosity has been eroded by societal trends that encourage treating boys and girls in similar ways.

Structural Location Theories

Structural location theories argue that greater religiosity among women can be attributed to their position in society. There are two main forms of structural location theory: those that focus on the family role of women, and those that focus on women's place in the workforce.

The first form of structural location theory advances the view that the childrearing role of women leads to greater religiousness. Arguments in favor of this view have suggested that women, as the prime caregivers and socializers of children, participate in religious activities to encourage religious behaviors and moral development in their children (Nelsen & Nelsen, 1975), or that gender differences in religion can be explained by the division of labor in the home (Iannaccone, 1990). Empirical research testing this form of structural location theory has found ambiguous results. In support of this theory, empirical studies have shown that mothers are more likely to attend church than childless women (De Vaus, 1982). Against this theory, empirical studies have shown little difference in church attendance among mothers and fathers (Ploch & Hastings, 1998), and that childrearing is a weak predictor of religious behavior among men and women (Tilley, 2003). Other empirical studies have shown that family formation influences men and women's religious involvement in different ways. Becker and Hofmeister (2002), for example, found that having children had no direct impact on women's religious involvement, whereas having children had the direct effect of increasing religious involvement among men.

The second form of structural location theory advances the view that greater religiosity among women can be attributed to the different place of women in the workforce. Arguments in favor of this view have suggested that, because women are less likely to work outside the home, they are less likely to be influenced by secularization (Luckman, 1967), more likely to seek social support from religion (Yinger, 1970), and are more likely to have time for religious involvement (Glock, Ringer, & Babbie, 1967). This would suggest that employment decreases religiosity among women, and narrows gender differences in religiosity between men and women (De Vaus, 1984). Empirical research testing this form of structural location theory has found ambiguous results. In support of this theory, empirical studies have shown that full-time employment decreases religious activity among both men and women (Cotter & Song, 2009). Against this theory, empirical studies have shown that, even when the influence of employment is controlled for, women are still more likely to attend church than men (De Vaus, 1984). Other empirical studies have shown that full-time employment influences men's and women's religious involvement in different ways. Becker and Hofmeister (2002), for example, found no statistically significant associations in the relationship between full-time employment and religious involvement among women. Among men full-time employment was associated with higher levels of religious involvement.

A further group of studies argue that the relationship between levels of religiosity and labor participation among women may be explained by the view that women who are more committed to religion should be less willing to enter the workforce, preferring traditional family roles. For example, empirical studies have shown that regular religious activity has a negative impact on women's decision to enter the labor force (Heineck, 2004).

Francis (1997) argued that the strength of structural location theories to account for gender difference in religiosity has been diminished by societal trends that encourage providing similar opportunities for males and females. Empirical studies supporting this claim suggest that living in an advanced industrial economy may increase individualism among women and decrease willingness to assume traditionally gendered roles that have historically been associated with religiosity (Becker, 2000; Christiano, 2000). This suggests that the account of gender differences in religiosity advanced by structural location theories may be more applicable in societies that continue to uphold traditional gendered roles.

In sum, classic sociological theories of religious gender differences have attempted to account for greater religiosity among women in terms of gender role socialization theories and structural location theories. Gender role socialization theories argue that religious gender differences are the result of different socialization experiences among males and females. On this basis, females are socialized in terms of ideals that are more compatible with a religious outlook (i.e., nurturance, gentleness, submissiveness). Structural location theories argue that religious gender differences can be explained by women's position in society. On this basis, experience of a family-centered role or different experience of workforce participation (compared with men) encourages a religious outlook among women. The ability of classic sociological theories to explain religious gender differences has diminished in recent years due to social trends that emphasize the egalitarian treatment of males and females, and equal opportunities in the workforce.

New Sociological Theories

The classic sociological theories designed to account for gender differences in religiosity and named by Francis (1997) gender role socialization theories and structural location theories were formulated quite independently of psychological or biological consideration. More recent sociological theories that have come into prominence to account for gender differences in religiosity hold a much closer connection with ideas shaped by psychology, to the point that debate and controversy arises between sociological and psychological interpretation of the data. The new sociological theories of particular significance can be named risk-aversion theories and power-control theories.

Risk-Aversion Theories

The sociological perspective on risk aversion posits that women are socialized to be more risk averse than men. This theory was brought into the debate on gender differences in religiosity by Miller and Hoffmann (1995) who argued that the acceptance of religion is a risk-averse strategy since those who reject religion place themselves at the risk of eternal judgment. Since women perceive greater risks than men in many aspects of life, and since men tend to be greater risk takers than women, men are less likely than women to be religious because they are more willing to risk the prospect of eternal damnation. This hypothesis was tested on a national sample of high school students from the US, using a general measure of risk preference (self-reported attraction to risk and to danger). Data from the study supported the theory and suggested that risk preference attenuates gender differences in religiosity and is a significant predictor of religiosity within each gender. Miller and Hoffmann (1995) concluded that greater religiosity among women could, therefore, be accounted for by the idea that women are socialized to be more risk averse than men. Miller (2000) also found support for the association between risk preferences and religiosity, particularly in Western societies. Analyzing data from the 1990 to 1993 World Values Survey, Miller (2000) explored the hypothesis that the connection between risk and religion would only exist in Western (e.g., Christian and Muslim) societies, as these traditions emphasize exclusivity in religious practices, beliefs, and affiliation which provide comfort for the believer. However, since Eastern (e.g., Hindu and Buddhist) societies tend to be non-exclusive and emphasize independent personal behaviors, in such societies not participating in organized religious practices does not necessarily constitute a risk-taking behavior. Findings of the study which compared the risk preferences of Christian and Muslim societies (US, Italy, and Turkey) with Hindu and Buddhist societies (India and Japan) found evidence to support the association between risk preference and religiosity in Western but not Eastern societies.

When Stark (2002) and Miller and Stark (2002) continued to develop risk-aversion theory, they challenged the adequacy of socialization theories to account for differences in risk aversion between men and women. Stark (2002) argued that risk preferences develop from biological functioning (mainly the central nervous and endocrine systems), and thus, greater or lesser religiosity can be attributed to hormonal differences that affect an individual's willingness to risk punishment in the afterlife. Using data from the 1995 to 1997 World Values Survey and the American General Social Survey, Miller and Stark (2002) attempted to test the strength of socialization theories by examining: whether gender differences in religiosity were smaller among people with traditional sex role attitudes; and whether gender differences in religiosity were larger in societies where traditional sex roles predominate and women's roles are family oriented. Risk aversion theory was tested by an item which assessed belief in life after death. Results of the study showed no relationship between traditional gender attitudes and gender differences in religious beliefs and behavior (leading to rejection of socialization theories), and supported the theory that women are more religious than men to the extent that being irreligious constitutes a risk-taking behavior (Miller & Stark, 2002). This finding was supported in 'high-risk religions' (e.g., Christianity, Islam and Orthodox Judaism) as well as in different cultural contexts (America and Japan).

Miller and Stark's (2002) rejection of socialization explanations has been challenged by Collett and Lizardo (2009) who identify two main problems with Miller and Stark's dismissal of socialization explanations. First, their operationalization of socialization theory is too narrow and relies on a battery of gender-related attitudinal items. Second, their analysis fails to take into account variation in gender differences across different populations or groups, wrongly dismissing socialization theories on the basis that, if such a factor were to exist, it would exercise the same influence on all individuals.

In a similar vein, Roth and Kroll (2007) argue that Miller's (2000) and Miller and Stark's (2002) operationalization of religious risk is inadequate because it limits risk to "other worldly" reward and punishment. This assumes that *all* individuals perceive or calculate the costs and rewards of religious involvement. However, being irreligious is not risky unless the individual believes that punishment in the afterlife is actually possible (Roth & Kroll, 2007). Using the same data as Miller (2000), and Miller and Stark (2002), Roth and Kroll (2007) tested the hypothesis that when belief in an afterlife (and belief in hell) is taken into account: women who perceive a risk of punishment after death should be more religious than men who perceive such risk; and among nonbelievers in an afterlife (who perceive no risk), men and women should exhibit similarly low rates of religious participation because there is no risk of eternal damnation to motivate differences in religiosity. Findings of the study suggested that women were still more religious than men, but that the gender gap is bigger among nonbelievers than among believers in an afterlife. This contradicts risk-preference theory, which assumes that the gender gap should be bigger among believers.

The data demonstrated that women who do not believe in hell participate in religious activity more than men who do not believe in hell. Therefore, women's slightly higher tendency to believe in life after death does not explain their greater religiosity. The findings also suggest that men respond more strongly to belief in an afterlife than women, and that male and female believers in hell are more similar in their religiousness than male and female nonbelievers.

Freese and Montgomery (2007) also highlight the importance of accounting for individual belief in heaven or hell when assessing the utility of risk-preference theory. Analyzing data from the 1990 to 1995 World Values Survey and the 1998 International Social Survey Program, Freese and Montgomery (2007) demonstrate that, while overall women are generally more religious than men, gender differences in religiosity are not confined only to those whose belief in an afterlife includes hell. In line with the findings of Roth and Kroll's (2007) study, gender differences were actually larger among those who believe in both heaven and hell. Overall, findings reported by Roth and Kroll (2007) and Freese and Montgomery (2007) question Miller and Stark's risk-aversion theory because they demonstrate that aversion to hell is not the only factor influencing gender differences in religion.

Further to this, Freese's (2004) re-analysis of Miller's (2000) data shows that the empirical measure of risk preference used by Miller (2000) fails to account for the sex differences in religiosity observed in the original study. This draws attention to the fact that Miller's (2000) classification of Western (Christian and Muslim) societies and Eastern societies (Hindu and Buddhist) does not reflect the true religious diversity in the data analyzed from the selected countries. Similarly, Miller's (2000) argument that affiliation to Christian and Islamic traditions can be understood as a risk-averse behavior is based on the view that these religions emphasize exclusive affiliation and proscriptive religious practices that generate comfort. This is too narrow a description of the functions served by religiosity among both men and women, and (incorrectly) assumes that these aspects of religiosity are experienced in the same way for both men and women (see the section in this chapter regarding *universality*).

Sullins (2006) questions Stark's (2002) argument that differences in risk preference are physiologically based. Following this assumption, gender differences in religiosity should be considered universal since biological sex differences cannot vary culturally. However, as Sullins (2006) maintains, the premise of a physiological basis for religious differences in sex can be disproved if it can be shown that in some cultures male religious participation is the same or higher than female religiosity. Drawing on data from the 1995 to 1997 World Values Survey, Sullins (2006) proceeds to demonstrate that, worldwide, Jewish men report significantly higher rates of synagogue attendance and belief in life after death than do Jewish women, although there are no other sex differences in religiousness among Jews. Similarly, Muslim men also report much higher mosque membership and attendance than women (although this may represent institutional barriers to women's participation that are standard to the Islamic tradition).

Power-Control Theories

The sociological perspective on power control posits that there is a link between socially structured power relations outside the household and variations in the social control of sons and daughters within the household. For example, Collett and Lizardo (2009) suggest that in patriarchal households sons are encouraged to develop a stronger preference for risky behaviors, whereas daughters will be more constrained in their orientation toward risk taking due to the high propensity of mothers to attempt to control their daughter's behavior. By contrast, in more egalitarian households, where the socioeconomic status of mothers and fathers is similar, the difference between risk preference among sons and daughters should be smaller. Application of this theory to the question of gender differences in religiosity assumes that, if risk-averse individuals are more religious, gender differences in religiosity should be stronger for those who grow up in patriarchal households, and weaker for those who grow up in more egalitarian households. Collett and Lizardo (2009) tested this hypothesis on data from the 1994 to 2004 General Social Survey. In support of power-control theory, the findings suggest that gender differences in religiosity are stronger among respondents raised in patriarchal households (measured by socioeconomic status of mothers) than among respondents raised in egalitarian households. Furthermore, daughters of mothers with high socioeconomic status (higher earners) tend to be more irreligious than daughters of mothers with low socioeconomic status (lower earners). This demonstrates the importance of including socialization explanations into the examination of gender differences in religion. In this case, a mother's class position narrows the gender gap in religiosity among men and women.

Collett and Lizardo's (2009) theory of power control as an explanation of gender differences in religiosity has been subject to criticism. Hoffmann (2009) argues that the finding that daughters of high-status mothers tend to be less religious than daughters of low-status mothers renders the reliance on risk preferences and risk perceptions unnecessary. A simpler explanation might suggest that high-status mothers, being less religious, socialize these qualities to their daughters, leading them to also be less religious (Hoffmann, 2009). Bradshaw and Ellison (2009) maintain that Collett and Lizardo's (2009) study, which purports to challenge Miller and Stark's (2002) physiological explanation for gender differences in risk preference, does not measure anything biological.

This prevents Collett and Lizardo's (2009) study from ruling out biology altogether and means that the findings cannot account for potential confounding variables such as biological influences.

In sum, new sociological theories of religious gender differences have attempted to account for greater religiosity among women in terms of risk-aversion theories and power-control theories. Risk-aversion theories argue that women are less inclined toward risk-taking behaviors than men and so are more likely to accept religiousness (a risk-averse strategy) because it diminishes the chance of eternal damnation. Power-control theories accept that risk aversion accounts for the finding that women are more religious than men, but argue that male and female risk preferences are shaped by different experiences of the social control structures which exist within a household. Criticisms of new sociological theories highlight that, while risk preference may have some impact on religious gender differences, the relationship between religion and gender is too complex to be accounted for by risk preference alone. For this reason, the new sociological perspectives, named as risk-aversion theories and as power-control theories, may prove to be no more enduring than the classic sociological perspectives.

Classic Psychological Theories

In the mid-1990s, Francis (1997) distinguished between two prominent classic psychological theories advanced to account for gender differences in religiosity, namely depth psychology theories and personality theories. Recent developments to this area of research suggest that the latter may have been better named gender differences theories.

Depth Psychology Theories

Freud's (1950 [1913]) psychoanalytic perspective of parental projection is one of the best documented psychological theories advanced to account for gender differences in religion. According to Freud (1950 [1913]), God is in every case modeled after the father, and our personal relation to God is dependent on our relation to our physical father. Psychoanalytic theory concerning infantile sexuality (the Oedipus complex) proposes that boys emerge from the Oedipal age with ambivalent feelings towards their fathers, whereas girls emerge with a positive attachment to their father. When these feelings are projected onto God, it follows that women should be more attracted to God and religion.

One strand of empirical research that tests aspects of this Freudian-based theory compares images of God with images of male and female parents (Vergote & Tamayo, 1981). The findings from this strand of research are far from consistent or conclusive. In support of this theory, empirical studies have shown that both boys and girls are more likely to empathize with a paternal image of God (Gibson, 1994), and that the relation between God and father is pre-eminent in women (Deconchy, 1968). Against this theory, empirical studies have shown that women hold a more feminine image of God than the image held by men (Nelsen, Cheek, & Au, 1985), or that God images do not fall primarily into masculine or feminine factors, but rather loving, controlling, and permissive factors (Steenwyk, Atkins, Bedics, & Whitley, 2010).

A second strand of research has examined the conceptualization of God images and their relation to paternal projections. This approach suggests that, if women identify with God as father, they are more likely to see God as benevolent, loving, and nurturing. Thus, women are likely to be more religious than men if they live in a culture that supports an image of God as male (Beit-Hallahmi, 2003). In support of this perspective, empirical studies have generally shown that girls are more likely to view God as loving, nurturing, and feeling, whereas boys are more likely to view God as authoritarian, controlling, and judging (Dickie, Ajega, Kobylak, & Nixon, 2006; Foster & Babcock, 2001).

Gender Differences Theories

A second strand of psychological theory has its roots in the wider study of gender differences theories. Arguments from this area of research have maintained that women are more religious than men because they possess certain psychological characteristics that predispose them to seek the psychological support offered by religion (Argyle & Beit-Hallahmi, 1975). Empirical studies have provided evidence to suggest that religion acts as a mechanism for dealing with heightened levels of guilt, frustration, fear, anxiety, shame, and dependency found among women (Helm, Berecz, & Nelson, 2001). Other empirical studies have argued that gender differences in religiosity are linked to more fundamental differences in gender role ideology and that generational shifts in gender role ideology (the prior psychological variable) can account for changes in levels of religiosity.

In sum, classic psychological theories of religious gender differences have attempted to account for greater religiosity among women in terms of depth psychology theories and gender differences theories. Depth psychology theories employ Freud's (1950 [1913]) psychoanalytic framework to argue that females empathize with a paternal image of God and are more likely to perceive God as benevolent, loving, and nurturing than males. Gender differences theories argue that women seek psychological support from religion, which helps them to deal with the presence of certain psychological characteristics such as guilt, fear, and dependency. The classic psychological theories designed to account for gender differences in religiosity have received less attention during the past two decades. In their place, psychologists of religion have given more attention to two schools of thought that can best be named as personality-based theories and gender-orientation theories.

New Psychological Theories

Personality-based theories propose the existence of a range of stable and enduring psychological constructs that consistently differentiate between men and women. Gender-orientation theories focus specifically on the psychological constructs of masculinity and femininity that are also considered as stable and enduring aspects of personality among both men and women. Personality-based theories and gender-orientation theories have recently been brought into the debate on gender differences in religiosity.

Personality-Based Theories

Three personality-based models in particular have been employed within the context of religious gender differences: the *three-dimensional model of personality* proposed by Eysenck (see Eysenck & Eysenck, 1991) and operationalized through the Eysenck Personality Questionnaire (Eysenck & Eysenck, 1975), and the Eysenck Personality Questionnaire Revised (Eysenck, Eysenck, & Barrett, 1985); the *big five-factor model* proposed by Costa and McCrae (1985) and subsequently operationalized through a range of instruments; and *the model of psychological type* originally proposed by Jung (1971 [1921]) and operationalized through the Myers-Briggs Type Indicator (Myers & McCaulley, 1985), the Keirsey Temperament Sorter (Keirsey & Bates, 1978), and the Francis Psychological Type Scales (Francis, 2005a).

The three-dimensional model of personality proposed by Eysenck maintains that individual differences can be most adequately and economically summarized in terms of the three higher order factors defined by the high scoring poles as extraversion, neuroticism, and psychoticism. Two of these factors have recorded significant and stable sex differences over time and across cultures. From the early development of the three-dimensional model, higher psychoticism scores were associated with being male (Eysenck & Eysenck, 1976), on a continuum from tendermindedness, through toughmindedness, to psychotic disorder. By way of contrast, higher neuroticism scores have been associated with being female (see Francis, 1993), on a continuum from emotional stability, through emotional lability, to neurotic disorder.

In terms of empirical evidence, a series of studies (see Francis, 2009a, for a review) have demonstrated that, within a Christian context, psychoticism scores comprise the dimension of personality fundamental to individual differences in religiosity, *and that neuroticism scores are unrelated to individual differences in religiosity after controlling for sex differences.* Recent studies have also reported similar results within the context of the Jewish faith (Francis, Katz, Yablon, & Robbins, 2004), and Hindu faith (Francis, Robbins, Santosh, & Bhanot, 2008). These findings would account for gender differences in religiosity in terms of basic differences between men and women in levels of psychoticism.

Further support for this view, drawing on Eysenck's three-dimensional model of personality is provided by a series of studies exploring the personality profile of male clergy. These studies routinely have suggested that male clergy display a characteristically feminine profile (see Robbins, Francis, Haley, & Kay, 2001, for a review).

The model of personality proposed by the big five-factor model identifies five higher order factors defined by the high scoring poles as neuroticism, extraversion, openness, agreeableness, and conscientiousness. Two of these factors have recorded significant and stable sex differences over time and across cultures. Higher neuroticism scores are consistently associated with being female (see Costa & McCrae, 1992), where this relationship is particularly shaped by high scores on the anxiety, vulnerability, and self-consciousness facets of the neuroticism factor. Higher agreeableness scores are consistently associated with being female (see Schmitt, Realo, Voracek, & Allik, 2008), where this relationship is particularly shaped by high scores on the tendermindedness and trust facets.

In terms of empirical evidence, a series of studies have found evidence to support the view that agreeableness and conscientiousness are the personality factors fundamental to individual differences in religiosity (see Saroglou, 2010, for a review). Relatively few studies employing the five-factor model of personality have been designed to deal specifically with the question of gender differences in religiosity, although Saroglou (2010) argues that low psychoticism, according to the Eysenck model, is comparable to a blend of agreeableness and conscientiousness in the five-factor model (Goldberg & Rosolack, 1992; McCrae & Costa, 2003), and is likely to be related to religiousness in a similar way.

Findings among studies that have included gender in the question concerning the relationship between the five-factor model and religiosity are somewhat mixed and less definitive than those demonstrated by empirical studies employing Eysenck's model of personality. For instance, Saroglou's (2010) meta-analyses across 55 nations demonstrated that gender had no significant impact on the relationship between religiosity, agreeableness, and conscientiousness. Yet, empirical studies that have explored the relationship between religiosity and the five-factor model before and after taking sex differences into account have demonstrated that sex does have a hand in shaping this relationship (see Adamovova & Striženec, 2004; Cramer, Griffin, & Powers, 2008; Galen & Kloet, 2011). These studies, in addition to others, demonstrate that agreeableness emerges as the strongest predictor of religiosity even when sex differences are controlled for (see also Robbins, Francis, McIlroy, Clarke, & Pritchard, 2010; Saroglou & Fiasse, 2003). This appears to suggest that gender differences in religiosity could be accounted for in terms of basic differences between men and women in levels of agreeableness.

The model of personality proposed by psychological type theory identifies four aspects of psychological functioning that are explored in two contrasting ways: two orientations (introversion or extraversion), two perceiving functions (sensing or intuition), two judging functions (thinking or feeling), and two attitudes (judging or perceiving). Introverts draw energy from their inner world, and extraverts from their outer world. Sensing types form their perceptions on the basis of detailed information, and intuitive types on larger theories. Feeling types form their evaluations on the basis of interpersonal concerns, and thinking types on objective analysis. Judging types take an organized approach to the outer world, and perceiving types a flexible approach. One of these aspects of psychological functioning has recorded significant and stable sex differences over time and across cultures. Population studies have demonstrated that men are more likely to prefer thinking and that women are more likely to prefer feeling: in the UK 65% of men prefer thinking and 70% of women prefer feeling (Kendall, 1998); in the US 56% of men prefer thinking and 76% of women prefer feeling (Myers, McCaulley, Quenk, & Hammer, 2003).

In terms of empirical evidence, a series of studies has demonstrated that, among male religious professionals, the proportion preferring feeling is much closer to the population norms for women than to the population norms for men. For example, among clergymen serving in the church in Wales, Francis, Payne, and Jones (2001) found that 69% preferred feeling. This finding has been replicated in studies conducted among Anglican, Roman Catholic, Methodist, and Presbyterian clergymen (see Francis, 2009b, for review). These findings would account for gender differences in religiosity in terms of basic differences between men's and women's preferences within the judging process between thinking and feeling.

Gender-Orientation Theory

Gender-orientation theory has its roots in the theory and measurement proposed by Sandra Bem (1981) through the Bem Sex Role Inventory. According to this conceptualization, masculinity and femininity are not bipolar descriptions of a unidimensional construct, but two orthogonal personality dimensions. Empirically the Bem Sex Role Inventory demonstrates considerable variations in both femininity and masculinity among both men and women. The Bem Sex Role Inventory assesses gender orientation through a number of feminine and masculine characteristics that are represented in the scale. Respondents are asked to rate themselves according to each characteristic on a scale ranging from 1 "never or almost true" through to 7 "always or almost always true". Characteristics associated with a feminine orientation include: affectionate, gentle, or understanding. Characteristics associated with a masculine orientation include: ambitious, independent, or forceful.

This theory was brought into the debate on gender differences in religiosity by Thompson (1991). Using this theory, Thompson (1991) argued that individual differences in religiosity should be affected more by gender orientation than by being male or female. According to this approach, being religious is a consonant experience for *people* with a feminine orientation, while men as well as women can have a feminine orientation. Thompson (1991) formulated two hypotheses concerning the relationship between gender orientation and individual differences in religiosity between men and women. The first hypothesis was that, if being religious is a gender type attribute related to women's lives in general, then multivariate analyses that control for the personality dimensions of masculinity and femininity should demonstrate that being female continues to have a significant effect in predicting religiosity. The second hypothesis was that, if being religious is a function of gender orientation, then multivariate analyses that control for the personality dimensions of masculinity and femininity should result in no additional variance being explained by being female. Thompson's analysis of data from a sample of 358 undergraduate students in the US, who completed the Bem (1981) Sex Role Inventory alongside five measures of religiosity, supported the hypothesis that being religious is a function of gender orientation.

In terms of empirical evidence, studies have demonstrated that higher femininity scores are associated with higher levels of religiosity within a Christian context (Mercer & Durham, 1999; Smith, 1990) and within the context of the Islamic faith (Abu-Ali & Reisen, 1999). More specifically, studies that have controlled for gender orientation have demonstrated that sex has no additional impact on individual differences in religiosity (Francis, 2005b; Francis & Wilcox, 1996, 1998). This demonstrates, in agreement with Thompson's hypotheses, that higher levels of religiosity are a function of gender orientation rather than a function of being female.

Another strand of research supporting the view that gender orientation is fundamental to religiosity is concerned with the personality profile of male clergy. For example, Francis, Jones, Jackson, and Robbins (2001) found that male Anglican clergy in England, Ireland, Scotland and Wales scored lower on the masculinity scale of the Eysenck Personality Profiler (Eysenck, Wilson, & Jackson, 1999).

Criticisms of gender-orientation theory relate to the constructs of masculinity and femininity operationalized by the Bem Sex Inventory.

Characteristics comprising the inventory were developed in the 1970s and were defined as feminine or masculine according to whether they were judged to be more desirable in Western society for one sex than for the other (Bem, 1981). Wilcox and Francis (1997) have argued that the femininity and masculinity constructs are in need of updating. The incompatibility of these constructs with modern perceptions of femininity and masculinity may be what is being observed with regard to changes in the factor structure of the scale reported by a number of recent studies (see Choi, Fuqua, & Newman, 2008, for a review).

In sum, new psychological theories of religious gender differences have attempted to account for greater religiosity among women in terms of personality-based theories and gender-orientation theories. Personality-based theories argue that differences in certain psychological constructs can explain gender differences in religiosity. According to the model of personality proposed by Eysenck, empirical studies have shown that differences in the personality dimension of psychoticism can account for gender differences in religiosity. According to the five-factor model of personality, empirical studies have shown that differences in the personality dimensions of agreeableness and conscientiousness can account for gender differences in religiosity. According to the model of personality proposed by psychological type theory, differences between men's and women's preferences within the judging process between thinking and feeling can account for gender differences in religiosity. Gender-orientation theories argue that differences in the psychological constructs of masculinity and femininity can explain gender differences in religiosity. Empirical studies have shown that gender differences in religiosity are linked to higher levels of femininity. Taken together, empirical studies employing personality-based theories and gender-orientation theories provide firm evidence to support the view that gender differences in religiosity may be most adequately conceptualized in terms of personality differences.

At present, however, there are no empirical studies examining whether gender differences in religiosity persist after gender differences in Eysenck's model of personality, the five-factor model of personality, and psychological type have been controlled for. Future empirical research in this area is needed to provide a clearer picture of the strength of the association between gender differences in personality and gender differences in religiosity.

Universal Gender Differences?

Within the empirical study of gender differences in religion, the finding that women are more religious than men, as Stark (2002) and Sullins (2006) highlight, is so taken for granted that it comes close to a universally accepted truth. However, a growing body of empirical and theoretical research has developed that questions the consistency and generalizability of this finding. The view that women are more religious than men has been questioned from three angles.

First, a number of studies have examined the consistency of gender differences in religiosity by comparing findings from a variety of religious traditions in a range of cross-cultural contexts. These studies demonstrate that, while in Christian contexts it may generally be the case that women are more religious than men, within the context of the Hindu, Jewish, and Islamic traditions men are generally found to be more *religiously active* than women (see Kamal & Loewenthal, 2002; Loewenthal, MacLeod, & Cinnirella, 2002). These findings are most clearly observed within large-scale comparative studies such as those reported by Sullins (2006), which incorporate data from the General Social Survey, and the World Values Survey (including 51 nations). Sullins (2006), for instance, demonstrates that when a distinction is made in religious measures between *affective* (personal piety) and *active* (organizational participation) religiosity, in one-third of nations, women are no higher than men in active religiousness. Further to this, across all nations, Jewish men were higher than women in both active and affective religiousness. Muslim men were also found to be significantly higher than women in active religiousness.

Greater religiosity among men can also be observed by empirical studies generated specifically within the context of the Jewish tradition (Francis & Katz, 2007; Ruffle & Sosis, 2007), and the Islamic tradition (Gonzalez, 2011; Momtaz, Hamid, Yahaya, & Ibrahim, 2010; Sahin & Francis, 2002). Empirical studies generated specifically within the context of the Hindu tradition demonstrate no significant differences in religiosity between men and women (Francis, Santosh, Robbins, & Vij, 2008; Tiliopoulos, Francis, & Slattery, 2010).

Second, the consistency of gender differences in religiosity has been questioned according to geographical location. For example, Sullins (2006) demonstrates that the gender gap in religiosity is highest in countries that are more secular, with particular focus on Western Christian cultures. Further to this, multivariate analysis from the study demonstrated that much of the gender disparity in active religiousness in Western Christian cultures (e.g., the US) can be explained by a combination of social factors *and* personality factors. This would tend to suggest that gender differences in religiosity may be larger or smaller in certain geographical locations because the factors that shape these differences are themselves influenced by cultural variations. For example, Sullins (2006) highlights that the social factors specifically related to the gender disparity in active religiousness in Western Christian cultures are linked to structural (hours worked) and network-related (amount of friends in the religious congregation) reasons.

From the perspective of personality psychology, this would also cohere with recent empirical research demonstrating how gender differences in the five-factor model of personality are larger in secular, prosperous, and egalitarian cultures (see for example McCrae & Terracciano [with 78 co-authors], 2005). For example, Schmitt et al.'s (2008) analysis of data from a cross-cultural study among 55 nations revealed that variations in men's personality traits were the primary cause of sex difference variation across cultures, where men are becoming less agreeable and less conscientious in Western countries. Schmitt et al. (2008) speculate that the personality traits of men and women living in developed nations are able to diverge naturally because they are less constrained by the impact of social and economic conditions. This might suggest, for instance, that men in Western cultures are less likely to be religious than men in non-Western cultures because they experience lower levels of agreeableness and conscientiousness, which are the key predictors of religiosity according to the five-factor model of personality.

Third, the consistency of gender differences has also been questioned according to how religion is measured. As Sullins (2006) highlights, a key problem for the empirical study of gender differences in religiosity is that men and women may conceptualize their experience of religiousness differently. This creates gender differences that vary according to the dimension of religiosity measured. For example, a number of studies have observed that a larger gender gap exists when religion is measured according to personal prayer and personal belief, than when religion is measured according to religious attendance (Beit-Hallahmi & Argyle, 1997; Freese, 2004; Sullins, 2006). This highlights that caution should be taken in the interpretation of findings from empirical studies that employ inconsistent measures of religiosity in examination of the relationship between religion and gender.

In sum, empirical and theoretical literature exploring the universality of religious gender differences has demonstrated that, while it may generally be the case that women are more religious than men in Christian (or post-Christian) contexts, this is not necessarily the case among other religious traditions (most notably Islam and Judaism) where men are often found to be more religious than women (in terms of religious service attendance and public religious activities). Similarly, gender differences in religiosity can also vary according to the type of religiosity measure employed in empirical studies. Women are, for example, often found to score more highly on measures of internal religiosity (i.e., such as private prayer or personal belief) than men. This may account for some of the findings of empirical studies conducted within the context of the Jewish, Islamic, and Hindu faith traditions (see studies cited earlier in this chapter in the *empirical evidence* section), which have found that women are more religious than men. Gender differences in religiosity can also vary according to geographical context, where larger gender differences are observed in Western cultures.

Conclusion

Consideration of empirical and theoretical research associated with gender differences in religion reveals four main conclusions.

First, while it is *generally* the case that women are found to be more religious than men, it is not *always* the case. This confirms the limitations of constructing an empirical psychology of religion within just one religious tradition and highlights the need for further empirical research among non-Christian faiths and cross-cultural contexts so that an accurate picture of religious gender differences can be developed.

Second, consideration of the sociological arguments put forward to explain gender differences in religiosity demonstrates that, while social factors can be shown to have some impact on the relationship between gender and religiosity, this influence cannot be attributed to any one factor. Empirical studies have shown that there are a wide range of social factors capable of shaping religious gender differences (e.g., family formation, workforce participation, risk aversion, power control, or socioeconomic status) and that these factors may be working together to influence differences in religiosity among men and women (see Sullins, 2006). The range of social factors influencing this relationship are also context specific, which means that some theoretical explanations are better equipped to explain religious gender differences in certain contexts than others (see, for example, structural location theories). Criticisms of sociological theories reveal a tendency in empirical research to limit the question of gender differences in religiosity to a unitary explanation, creating a fragmented view of how a number of isolated social factors impact on religious gender differences in specific contexts. This highlights the need for further cross-cultural comparative empirical research that explores how a range of social factors and the interaction between them are capable of influencing religious gender differences in a variety of different contexts.

Third, consideration of the psychological arguments put forward to explain gender differences in religiosity demonstrates that psychological theories focusing on psychologically-shaped gender differences provide the strongest family of explanations. Compared with sociological arguments, this form of empirical research (based on Eysenck's model of personality, the five-factor model of personality, Jung's psychological type model and gender-orientation theory) presently provides the most convincing argument of religious gender differences. This is because gender differences in the personality characteristics, known to shape the relationship between personality and religiosity, can be observed over time, across cultures, and within the context of other religious faiths.

This is most clearly demonstrated among empirical studies that have employed Eysenck's personality model to show that basic differences in psychoticism between men and women can account for gender differences in religiosity.

However, some findings of empirical research employing different personality models are better established than others. For example, cross-cultural empirical research employing the five-factor model of personality, Jung's psychological type model and gender-orientation theory is currently limited. Future empirical research is required in this area to gain a clearer picture of whether the association between gender differences in personality (according to each model) and gender differences in religiosity persist within different cultural contexts and different religious faiths. This is necessary because recent empirical studies exploring gender differences in the five-factor model across different cultures have observed changes to the personality characteristics typically associated with men and women (see Schmitt et al., 2008). If it is the case that personality characteristics can vary according to cultural context, this may, in turn, have an impact on which personality characteristics predict the relationship between gender and religiosity. Future empirical studies are also needed to examine whether gender differences in religiosity persist after gender differences in personality are taken into account. Without empirical studies of this type, it is difficult to get a view of how *exactly* the relationship between gender differences and religiosity is shaped by gender differences in personality.

Finally, empirical research exploring the impact of sociological and psychological factors on religious gender differences together (see Sullins, 2006) has demonstrated that both have a hand in shaping the relationship between religion and gender. This may promote the benefits of working toward an integrative and reflexive model of religious gender differences which can account for the full complexity of the question.

References

Abu-Ali, A., & Reisen, C. A. (1999). Gender role identity among adolescent Muslim girls living in the US. *Current Psychology: A Journal for Diverse Perspectives on Diverse Psychological Issues, 18,* 185–192.

Adamovova, L., & Striženec, M. (2004). Personality-structural correlates of cognitive orientation to spirituality. *Studia Psychologica, 46,* 317–325.

Akinyele, S., & Akinyele, T. (2007). Gender differences and church member satisfaction: An appraisal. *Gender and Behavior, 5,* 1433–1442.

Anthony, F. V., Hermans, C. A. M., & Sherkat, C. (2010). A comparative study of mystical experience among Christian, Muslim, and Hindu students in Tamil Nadu, India. *Journal for the Scientific Study of Religion, 49,* 264–277.

Argyle, M., & Beit-Hallahmi, B. (1975). *The social psychology of religion.* London: Routledge & Kegan Paul.

Baker, J. O. (2008). An investigation of the sociological patterns of prayer frequency and content. *Sociology Review*, 69, 169–185.

Bartkowski, J. P., & Hempel, L. M. (2009). Sex and gender traditionalism among conservative Protestants: Does the difference make a difference? *Journal for the Scientific Study of Religion*, 48, 805–816.

Becker, P. E. (2000). Boundaries and silences in post-feminist sociology. *Sociology of Religion*, 62, 315–335.

Becker, P. E., & Hofmeister, H. (2002). Work, family, and religious involvement for men and women. *Journal for the Scientific Study of Religion*, 40, 707–722.

Beit-Hallahmi, B. (2003). Religion, religiosity, and gender. In C. R. Ember & M. Ember (Eds.), *Encyclopedia of sex and gender* (pp. 117–129). New York: Kluwer Academic.

Beit-Hallahmi, B., & Argyle, M. (1997). *The psychology of religious behaviour, belief and experience*. London: Routledge.

Bem, S. L. (1981). *Bem Sex Role Inventory: Professional manual*. Palo Alto, CA: Consulting Psychologists Press.

Bradshaw, M. E., & Ellison, C. (2009). The nature–nurture debate is over, and both sides lost! Implications for understanding gender differences in religiosity. *Journal for the Scientific Study of Religion*, 48, 241–251.

Choi, N., Fuqua, D. R., & Newman, J. L. (2008). The Bem Sex-Role Inventory: Continuing theoretical problems. *Educational and Psychological Measurement*, 68, 881–900.

Christiano, K. (2000). Religion and the modern family in American culture. In S. Houseknecht & J. Pankhurst (Eds.), *Family, religion and social change in diverse societies* (pp. 43–78). New York: Oxford University Press.

Collett, J. L., & Lizardo, O. (2009). A power control theory of gender and religiosity. *Journal for the Scientific Study of Religion*, 48, 213–231.

Costa, P. T., & McCrae, R. R. (1985). *The NEO Personality Inventory*. Odessa, FL: Psychological Assessment Resources.

Costa, P. T., & McCrae, R. R. (1992). *Revised NEO Personality Inventory and NEO Five Factor Inventory: Manual*. Odessa, FL: Psychological Assessment Resources.

Cotter, D. A., & Song, Y. (2009). The religious time bind: US work hours and religion. *Social Indicators Research*, 93, 209–214.

Cramer, R. J., Griffin, M. P., & Powers, D. V. (2008). A five-factor analysis of spirituality in young adults: Preliminary evidence. *Research in the Social Scientific Study of Religion*, 19, 43–57.

Crockett, A., & Voas, D. (2006). Generations of decline: Religious change in 20th-century Britain. *Journal for the Scientific Study of Religion*, 45, 567–584.

Deconchy, J. P. (1968). God and the parental images. In A. Godin (Ed.), *From cry to word* (pp. 85–94). Brussels: Lumen Vitae Press.

De Vaus, D. A. (1982). The impact of children on sex related differences in church attendance. *Sociological Analysis*, 43, 145–154.

De Vaus, D. A. (1984). Workforce participation and sex differences in church attendance. *Review of Religious Research*, 25, 247–256.

Dickie, J. R., Ajega, L. V., Kobylak, J. R., & Nixon, K. M. (2006). Mother, father, and self: Sources of young adults' God concepts. *Journal for the Scientific Study of Religion, 45,* 57–71.

Eagle, D. (2011). Changing patterns of attendance at religious services in Canada, 1986–2008. *Journal for the Scientific Study of Religion, 50,* 187–200.

Eysenck, H. J., & Eysenck, S. B. G. (1975). *Manual of the Eysenck Personality Questionnaire.* London: Hodder & Stoughton.

Eysenck, H. J., & Eysenck, S. B. G. (1976). *Psychoticism as a dimension of personality.* London: Hodder & Stoughton.

Eysenck, H. J., & Eysenck, S. B. G. (1991). *Manual of the Eysenck Personality Scales.* London: Hodder & Stoughton.

Eysenck, S. B. G., Eysenck, H. J., & Barrett, P. (1985). A revised version of the psychoticism scale. *Personality and Individual Differences, 6,* 21–29.

Eysenck, H. J., Wilson, G. D., & Jackson, C. J. (1999). *Manual of the Eysenck Personality Profiler.* Guildford: PSI Press.

Firth, S. (1997). *Dying, death and bereavement in the Hindu community.* Leuven: Peters.

Foster, R. A., & Babcock, R. L. (2001). God as a man versus God as a woman: Perceiving God as a function of the gender of God and the gender of the participant. *International Journal for the Psychology of Religion, 11,* 93–104.

Francis, L. J. (1993). The dual nature of the Eysenckian neuroticism scales: A question of sex differences? *Personality and Individual Differences, 15,* 43–59.

Francis, L. J. (1997). The psychology of gender differences in religion: A review of empirical research. *Religion, 27,* 81–96.

Francis, L. J. (2005a). *Faith and psychology: Personality, religion and the individual.* London: Darton, Longman & Todd.

Francis, L. J. (2005b). Gender role orientation and attitude toward Christianity: A study among older men and women in the United Kingdom. *Journal of Psychology and Theology, 33,* 179–186.

Francis, L. J. (2009a). Comparative empirical research in religion: Conceptual and operational challenges within empirical theology. In L. J. Francis, J. Astley, & M. Robbins (Eds.), *Empirical theology in texts and tables: Qualitative, quantitative and comparative perspectives* (pp. 127–152). Leiden: Brill.

Francis, L. J. (2009b). Psychological type theory and religious and spiritual experience. In M. De Souza, L. J. Francis, J. O'Higgins-Norman, & D. G. Scott (Eds.), *International handbook of education for spirituality, care and wellbeing* (pp. 125–146). Dordrecht: Springer.

Francis, L. J., Ispas, D., Robbins, M., Ilie, A., & Iliescu, D. (2009). The Romanian translation of the Francis Scale of Attitude toward Christianity: Internal reliability, re-test reliability and construct validity among undergraduate students within a Greek Orthodox Culture. *Pastoral Psychology, 58,* 49–54.

Francis, L. J., Jones, S. H., Jackson, C. J., & Robbins, M. (2001). The feminine personality profile of male Anglican clergy in Britain and Ireland: A study employing the Eysenck Personality Profiler. *Review of Religious Research, 43,* 14–23.

Francis, L. J., & Katz, Y. J. (2007). Measuring attitude toward Judaism: The internal consistency reliability of the Katz-Francis Scale of Attitude toward Judaism. *Mental Health, Religion and Culture, 10,* 309–324.

Francis, L. J., Katz, Y. J., Yablon, Y., & Robbins, M. (2004). Religiosity, personality and happiness: A study among Israeli male undergraduates. *Journal of Happiness Studies, 5,* 315–333.

Francis, L. J., Payne, V. J., & Jones, S. H. (2001). Psychological types of male Anglican clergy in Wales. *Journal of Psychological Type, 56,* 19–23.

Francis, L. J., Robbins, M., Santosh, R., & Bhanot, S. (2008). Religion and mental health among Hindu young people in England. *Mental Health, Religion and Culture, 11,* 341–347.

Francis, L. J., Santosh, R., Robbins, M., & Vij, S. (2008). Assessing attitude toward Hinduism: The Santosh-Francis Scale. *Mental Health, Religion and Culture, 11,* 609–621.

Francis, L. J., & Wilcox, C. (1996). Religion and gender orientation. *Personality and Individual Differences, 20,* 119–121.

Francis, L. J., & Wilcox, C. (1998). Religiosity and femininity: Do women really hold a more positive attitude toward Christianity? *Journal for the Scientific Study of Religion, 37,* 462–469.

Freese, J. (2004). Risk preferences and gender differences in religiousness: Evidence from the World Values Survey. *Review of Religious Research, 46,* 88–91.

Freese, J., & Montgomery, J. (2007). The devil made her do it: Evaluating risk preference as an explanation of sex differences in religiousness. In S. J. Correll (Ed.), *Advances in group processes. Vol. 24: The social psychology of gender* (pp. 187–230). Greenwich, CT: Elsevier Ltd./JAI Press.

Freud, S. (1950). *Totem and taboo.* London: Routledge & Kegan Paul. (Original work published 1913)

Galen, L. W., & Kloet, J. (2011). Personality and social integration factors distinguishing nonreligious from religious groups: The importance of controlling for attendance and demographics. *Archiv für Religionspsychologie [Archive for the Psychology of Religion], 33,* 205–228.

Gibson, H. M. (1994). Adolescents' images of God. *Panorama, 6,* 105–114.

Glock, C. Y., Ringer, B. B., & Babbie, E. R. (1967). *To comfort and to challenge.* Berkeley, CA: University of California Press.

Goldberg, L. R., & Rosolack, T. K. (1992). The big five-factor structure as an integrative framework: An empirical comparison with Eysenck's P-E-N model. In C. F. Halverson, G. A. Kohnstamm, & R. P. Martin (Eds.), *The developing structure of temperament and personality from infancy to adulthood* (pp. 7–35). Hillsdale, NJ: Lawrence Erlbaum.

Gonzalez, A. L. (2011). Measuring religiosity in a majority Muslim context: Gender, religious salience, and religious experience among Kuwaiti college students—A research note. *Journal for the Scientific Study of Religion, 50,* 339–350.

Hassan, A. (2007). On being religious: Patterns of religious commitment in Muslim societies. *The Muslim World, 97,* 437–478.

Heineck, G. (2004). Does religion influence the labor supply of married women in Germany? *Journal of Socio-economics, 33,* 307–328.

Helm, H. W., Berecz, J. M., & Nelson, E. A. (2001). Religious fundamentalism and gender differences. *Pastoral Psychology, 50,* 25–37.

Hoffmann, J. P. (2009). Gender, risk, and religiousness: Can power control provide the theory? *Journal for the Scientific Study of Religion, 48,* 232–240.

Iannaccone, L. R. (1990). Religious practice: A human capital approach. *Journal for the Scientific Study of Religion, 29,* 297–314.

Jung, C. G. (1971). *Psychological types: The collected works. Vol. 6.* London: Routledge & Kegan Paul. (Original work published 1921)

Kalstein, S., & Power, R. (2008). The Daily Spiritual Experiences Scale and well-being: Demographic comparisons and scale validation with older Jewish adults and a diverse internet sample. *Journal of Religion and Health, 48,* 402–417.

Kamal, Z., & Loewenthal, K. M. (2002). Suicide beliefs and behavior among young Muslims and Hindus in the UK. *Mental Health, Religion and Culture, 5,* 111–118.

Keirsey, D., & Bates, M. (1978). *Please understand me.* Del Mar, CA: Prometheus Nemesis.

Kendall, E. (1998). *Myers-Briggs type indicator: Step 1 manual supplement,* Palo Alto, CA: Consulting Psychologists Press.

Loewenthal, K. M., MacLeod, A. K., & Cinnirella, M. (2002). Are women more religious than men? Gender differences in religious activity among different religious groups in the UK. *Personality and Individual Differences, 32,* 133–139.

Luckman, T. (1967). *The invisible religion.* New York: Macmillan.

McCrae, R. R., & Costa, P. T., Jr. (2003). *Personality in adulthood: A five-factor theory perspective* (2nd ed.). New York: Guilford.

McCrae, R. R., & Terracciano, A. (with 78 members of the Personality Profiles of Cultures Project) (2005). Universal features of personality traits from the observer's perspective: Data from 50 cultures. *Journal of Personality and Social Psychology, 88,* 547–561.

Maselko, J., & Kubzansky, L. D. (2006). Gender differences in religious practices, spiritual experiences and health: Results from the US General Social Survey. *Social Science and Medicine, 62,* 2848–2860.

Mercer, C., & Durham, T. W. (1999). Religious mysticism and gender orientation. *Journal for the Scientific Study of Religion, 38,* 175–182.

Miller, A. S. (2000). Going to hell in Asia: The relationship between risk and religion in a cross-cultural setting. *Review of Religious Research, 42,* 5–18.

Miller, A. S., & Hoffmann, J. P. (1995). Risk and religion: An explanation of gender differences in religiosity. *Journal for the Scientific Study of Religion, 34,* 63–75.

Miller, A. S., & Stark, R. (2002). Gender and religiousness: Can socialization explanations be saved? *American Journal of Sociology, 107,* 1399–1423.

Momtaz, Y. A., Hamid, T. A., Yahaya, N., & Ibrahim, R. (2010). Religiosity among older Muslim Malaysians: Gender perspective. *Journal of Muslim Mental Health, 5,* 210–220.

Moxy, A., McEvoy, M., & Bowe, S. (2011). Spirituality, religion, social support and health among older Australian adults. *Australasian Journal on Ageing, 30,* 82–88.

Myers, I. B., & McCaulley, M. H. (1985). *Manual: A guide to the development and use of the Myers-Briggs Type Indicator.* Palo Alto, CA: Consulting Psychologists Press.

Myers, I. B., McCaulley, M. H., Quenk, N. L., & Hammer, A. L. (2003). *Manual: A guide to the development and use of the Myers-Briggs Type Indicator.* Palo Alto, CA: Consulting Psychologists Press.

Nelsen, H. M., Cheek, N. H., & Au, P. (1985). Gender differences in images of God. *Journal for the Scientific Study of Religion, 24,* 396–402.

Nelsen, H. M., & Nelsen, A. K. (1975). *Black church in the sixties.* Lexington, KY: University Press of Kentucky.

Nelsen, H. M., & Potvin, R. H. (1981). Gender and regional differences in the religiosity of Protestant adolescents. *Review of Religious Research, 22,* 268–285.

Ploch, D. R., & Hastings, D. W. (1998). Effects of parental church attendance, current family status, and religious salience on church attendance. *Review of Religious Research, 39,* 309–320.

Pollak G., & Pickel, D. (2007). Religious individualization or secularization? Testing hypotheses of religious change—the case of Eastern and Western Germany. *British Journal of Sociology, 58,* 603–632.

Robbins, M., Francis, L. J., Haley, J. M., & Kay, W. K. (2001). The personality characteristics of Methodist ministers: Feminine men and masculine women? *Journal for the Scientific Study of Religion, 40,* 123–128.

Robbins, M., Francis, L., McIlroy, D., Clarke, R., & Pritchard, L. (2010). Three religious orientations and five personality factors: An exploratory study among adults in England. *Mental Health, Religion and Culture, 13,* 771–775.

Roth, L. M., & Kroll, J. C. (2007). Risky business: Assessing risk preference explanations for gender differences in religiosity. *American Sociological Review, 72,* 205–220.

Ruffle, B. J., & Sosis, R. (2007). Does it pay to pray? Costly ritual and cooperation. *BE Journal of Economic Analysis and Policy, 7,* 30–50.

Sahin, A., & Francis, L. J. (2002). Assessing attitude toward Islam among Muslim adolescents: The psychometric properties of the Sahin-Francis Scale. *Muslim Education Quarterly, 19,* 35–47.

Saroglou, V. (2010). Religiousness as a cultural adaption of basic traits: A five-factor model perspective. *Personality and Social Psychology Review, 14,* 108–125.

Saroglou, V., & Fiasse, L. (2003). Birth order, personality, and religion: A study among young adults from a three-sibling family. *Personality and Individual Differences, 35,* 19–29.

Schmitt, D. P., Realo, A., Voracek, M., & Allik, J. (2008). Why can't a woman be more like a man? Sex differences in the big five personality traits across 55 cultures. *Journal of Personality and Social Psychology, 94,* 168–182.

Smith, C., Denton, M. L., Faris, R., Regenerus, M. (2002). Mapping American adolescent participation. *Journal for the Scientific Study of Religion, 41,* 597–612.

Smith, R. D. (1990). Religious orientation, sex-role traditionalism, and gender identity: Contrasting male and female responses to socializing forces. *Sociological Analysis, 51,* 377–385.

Stark, R. (2002). Physiology and faith: Addressing the "universal" gender difference in religious commitment. *Journal for the Scientific Study of Religion, 41,* 495–507.

Steenwyk S. A. M., Atkins, D. C., Bedics, J. D., & Whitley, B. E. (2010). Images of God as they relate to life satisfaction and hopelessness. *International Journal for the Psychology of Religion, 20*, 85–96.

Sullins, D. P. (2006). Gender and religiousness: Deconstructing universality, constructing complexity. *American Journal of Sociology, 112*, 830–880.

Thompson, E. H. (1991). Beneath the status characteristics: Gender variations in religiousness. *Journal for the Scientific Study of Religion, 30*, 381–394.

Tiliopoulos, N., Francis, L. J., & Slattery, M. (2010). The internal consistency reliability of the Santosh-Francis Scale of Attitude toward Hinduism among Bunts in South India. *North American Journal of Psychology, 12*, 185–190.

Tilley, J. (2003). Secularization and aging in Britain: Does family formation cause greater religiosity? *Journal for the Scientific Study of Religion, 42*, 269–278.

Vergote, A., & Tamayo, A. (1981). *The parental figure and the representation of God*. The Hague: Mouton.

Wilcox, C., & Francis, L. J. (1997). Beyond gender stereotyping: Examining the validity of the Bem Sex Role Inventory among 16–19 year old females in England. *Personality and Individual Differences, 23*, 9–13.

Yinger, J. M. (1970). *The scientific study of religion*. New York: Macmillan.

15 Religious and National Cultures

Kathryn A. Johnson and Adam B. Cohen

The interaction of religious and national cultures has long been recognized in the humanities, anthropology, sociology, and political science (for reviews of theoretical perspectives, see Pals, 1996; Thrower, 1999). Recently, psychologists have also begun to investigate the ways in which religious and national cultures and the identities of their constituents may be related (Belzen, 2010; Belzen & Lewis, 2010; Johnson, Hill, & Cohen, 2011; Saroglou, 2003; Saroglou & Cohen, 2011; Tarakeshwar, Stanton, & Pargament, 2003).

In this chapter, we consider the relation between religious and national cultures from five perspectives: (1) religion as a kind of culture, (2) religious culture as a subset shaped by a dominant national culture, (3) national culture as a subset shaped by a dominant transnational religious culture, (4) religious and national (secular) cultures in conflict, and (5) the effects of globalization on religion (i.e., familiarity with multiple national and religious cultures).

Religion as Culture

First, religion can be considered a kind of culture (Cohen, 2009). Culture can be defined as "a socially transmitted or socially constructed constellation consisting of such things as practices, competencies, ideas, schemas, symbols, values, norms, institutions, goals, constitutive rules, artifacts, and modifications of the physical environment" (Fiske, Kitayama, Markus, & Nisbett, 2002, p. 85). Like national cultures, religious cultures have shared beliefs, special vocabularies or languages, moral codes, ultimate goals, values, community structures, and unique behaviors, as well as symbolic and artistic artifacts and physical structures. Indeed, anthropologist Clifford Geertz (1973) referred to religion as a cultural system and sociologists such as Durkheim (1995 [1912]) and Weber (1993 [1922]) have viewed religion and the social world as inextricably linked. Moreover, religion has mostly been studied in the social sciences as culture with special attention given to postcolonial theory (e.g., changes in indigenous religious culture due to colonialization), social power disparities (e.g., differences between the doctrines of religious traditions and popular religious beliefs), and identity formation (Waggoner, 2009).

Religious cultures are unique, however, in the sense that members of religious cultures generally endorse metaphysical beliefs about the involvement of immaterial or supernatural non-human agents in human affairs (Ysseldyk, Matheson, & Anisman, 2010). These shared beliefs about non-human agents are, in turn, associated with particular worldviews regarding causality, ultimate goals, values, social norms, community structures, reproductive strategies, and other aspects of worldview (Atran & Norenzayan, 2004; Johnson et al., 2011; Koltko-Rivera, 2004). However, as we discuss in later sections of this chapter, religious beliefs may also reflect a person's idiosyncratic or syncretic interpretation of traditional religious beliefs (Bellah, Madsen, Sullivan, Swidler, & Tipton, 1985).

Importantly, the multidimensionality of religion has been recognized by many and various taxonomies of religion have been proposed (Atran & Norenzayan, 2004; Boyer, 2001; Sosis, 2006). Most recently, Saroglou (2011) has reconciled these taxonomies, proposing four broad components of religious culture that are of primary interest to psychologists: beliefs, rituals, communities, and moral attitudes and behaviors. These four components are theorized to be linked with distinct cognitive, emotional, social, and moral psychological processes, respectively. The components of religious culture may differ and change in content (e.g., specific beliefs or unique religious rituals may be instituted) and may also vary in importance between and within religious groups as different psychological process become activated or more salient.

We contend that national cultures present an important influence on religious culture—an influence that shapes the components of religious culture. Likewise, the religious beliefs and practices of a group of people may shape different aspects of national culture. In the following sections, we discuss instances of the potentially bidirectional influences of religious and national cultures. When we say that religious and national cultures are mutually influential, we mean that the various aspects of religious and/or national cultures are changed in some way. In other words, the thoughts, feelings, behaviors, communities, vocabularies, symbols, physical artifacts, or worldviews of religious adherents and/or cultural constituents—any or all of the different aspects of culture—may be altered in their content or importance.

The Influence of the Dominant National Culture on Religious Culture(s)

Religion is often investigated and conceptualized as a subculture located within a dominant national culture (see Figure 15.1), sometimes as a

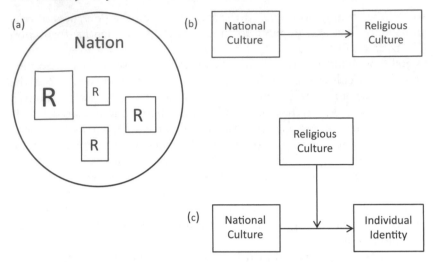

Figure 15.1 Religion(s) conceptualized as a subset within a dominant national culture (a). Religions are represented within the nation by the letter "R." At the group level, national culture may influence religious culture (b). At the individual level, religious culture moderates the influence of the national culture on individual psychological outcomes (c).

minority and sometimes as the majority religion. For example, Hindus are one of many religious groups situated within the larger context of Indian (80% Hindu) national culture, Buddhists are situated within US (77% Christian) national culture, Coptic Christians are situated within the larger Egyptian (90% Muslim) national culture, and Muslims are situated within the larger Chinese (officially atheist) national culture. These relations suggest at least three possible associations between religious cultures and the host national culture: (1) the religious group is the majority or dominant religious group within the national culture, (2) the religious group is an accepted or tolerated minority religious group within the national culture, or (3) the religious group is restricted, regulated, or persecuted in the national culture.

Religious Culture as a Majority

There are many aspects of the national culture that converge to shape the different components of a religious culture including (but not limited to) socioeconomic conditions, real or perceived threats to national security, and cultural innovations such as technological advances, mass media, and entertainment. In times of national economic uncertainty, for example, the authoritarian nature of God tends to be emphasized (McCann, 1999; Sales, 1972) and people are more likely to defend the legitimacy of governmental and religious institutions (Kay, Gaucher,

Napier, Callan, & Lauren, 2008). Religion can also be a powerful coping mechanism (Pargament, 1997) and, not surprisingly, researchers found that the importance of religiosity increased significantly in the US researchers have found following the attacks of September 11 (Seirmarco et al., 2012).

As Diamond (1997) has elaborated, the local ecology (available resources, types of food, water, predictable weather patterns, topography, etc.) and the prevalence of disease also afford threats and opportunities at the national level. Religious cultures may institute various moral codes, rituals, and social norms to deal with conditions in the local ecology, such as level of disease threat (Schaller & Duncan, 2007). Johnson, White, Boyd, and Cohen (2011) have argued that certain kinds of disease avoidance strategies may have led to a preponderance of religious cultural food practices such as the avoidance of meat (e.g., some Hindus are vegetarian), avoidance of certain *kinds* of meat (e.g., Jews and Muslims do not eat pork), the institution of religious rules for ritual washings (e.g., Muslim hand washing), or regulations regarding the cleansing of food and food preparation items (e.g., kosher food regulations in Judaism). These kinds of disease avoidance strategies often result in religious group exclusivity, as they also differentiate members of the religious culture from uninitiated individuals in the national culture.

Psychologists have identified other national cultural characteristics that may influence religious cultures. For example, apparitions of the Virgin Mary occur most frequently in Catholic-majority nations with a strong sexual domination of women by men (Carroll, 1983). Differing degrees of emphasis on individual freedom and unique self-expression versus allegiance to one's group and traditional group values (individualism vs. collectivism; Markus & Kitayama, 1991) or differences in egalitarian, horizontal social structures versus authoritarian, vertical social structures (Triandis & Gelfand, 1998) may also influence religious cultures. For example, Protestantism is often associated with individualism and the values of self-expression and prosperity (Weber, 1993 [1922]); yet, these values appear to be less important in communist national cultures (Roccas & Schwartz, 1997).

National cultures can also moderate the effects of religious culture on individual identity formation. Eastern and Western national cultures differ in many ways including variation in perceptions of the self (Easterners are less independent), cognition (Easterners are more likely to think in holistic rather than analytic terms), emotional expression (Easterners are less likely to express emotions) (Heine, 2010; Henrich, Heine, & Norenzayan, 2010; Kitayama & Cohen, 2007; Nisbett, 2003; Nisbett, Choi, Peng, & Norenzayan, 2001). Thus, Eastern versus Western national cultural context might moderate the effects of religious cultures. For instance, Sasaki and Kim (2011) found that religious coping was associated with personal control for Euro- but not Asian Americans, and that egocentric themes (e.g., spiritual growth, appreciation of diversity) were more common on US church websites, whereas sociocentric themes (e.g., close relationships within the church, social events) were more frequent on Korean church websites. Similarly, Stark (2001) found that, in Western cultures, religion has an effect in sustaining moral order only in so far as religious beliefs center on a powerful, active, morally concerned deity. However, this was not the case in Eastern national cultures (e.g., India, Japan, China; cf. Liu, 2010; Miller, 2000; Young, Morris, Burrus, Krishnan, & Regmi, 2011).

Religious Culture as an Accepted Minority

Power differentials in existing political and social structures are another source of influence on religious culture. Importantly, the minority status of a religious culture *and* the degree to which the religious culture, be it a minority or not, is tolerated by the dominant national culture is a key predictor of the type of national cultural influence on the religious culture. Elliott and Hayward (2009) investigated 65 countries in the World Values Survey and found that the degree of life satisfaction for religious adherents depended on the degree to which the government allowed religious freedoms; that is, the more restrictive the government, the lower the association between religiosity and life satisfaction.

One important goal in the study of the intersection of religious and national cultures is to understand how being affiliated with a particular religious culture may mitigate—or exacerbate—the stresses of individuals in minority religious populations, such as those who are voluntary immigrants (Cadge & Ecklund, 2007; Kivisto, 2007; Plüss, 2009). A key problem for immigrants is to negotiate between the heritage and the new culture (Hong, Wan, No, & Chiu, 2007). The heritage national culture may often involve religious cultural worldviews that were prevalent in the culture of origin but are not well accepted in the new one.

Berry (1997) proposed a two dimensional acculturation process in which immigrants may: (1) assimilate into the dominant culture, and (2) retain an allegiance to their heritage culture. Four acculturation strategies have been proposed relative to these two underlying dimensions. *Integrated* individuals develop a cultural identity that is comprised of elements of both the heritage and the new culture; *separated* individuals are less strongly identified with the new culture and more strongly identified with the heritage culture; *assimilated* individuals are, conversely, less strongly identified with the heritage culture and more strongly identified with the new culture; and *marginalized* individuals are characterized by weak identification with both the heritage and the new culture (Berry, 1994, 1997; Sam & Berry, 1995).

Systematic quantitative studies of how religious cultures relate to the process of acculturation have only recently begun. However, current research shows that the religious identity of first- and second-generation immigrants is often positively linked with one's ethnic identity and attachment to the heritage culture. As examples, Asian Americans and African Americans in the US (Ghorpade, Lackritz, & Singh, 2006), Christian European women married to Muslim Arabs in Israel (Abu-Rayya, 2007), Jews living in Belgium (Saroglou & Hanique, 2006), Turkish Muslims in the Netherlands (Verkuyten & Yildiz, 2007), and Muslims in the US (Sirin et al., 2008) have all been shown to retain aspects of their religious cultural heritage even in the context of the new national culture where the dominant religious group may differ.

Importantly, the identification with the heritage religious culture appears to play a positive role in the mental health of immigrants by enhancing self-esteem or self-control (Viladrich & Abraído-Lanza, 2009, for a review). One reason is that religious beliefs appear to buffer the effects of perceived discrimination on psychological distress (e.g., among African Americans in the US; Bierman, 2006; Ellison, Musick, & Henderson, 2008). Thus, it seems to be important for immigrants to maintain links and develop social relations with others from the heritage religious culture (Amer & Hovey, 2007; Kivisto, 2007; Plüss, 2009).

However, retaining one's heritage religious culture can also moderate the acculturation process, hindering the development of one's identification with the new national culture (Friedman & Saroglou, 2010; Verkuyten & Yildiz, 2007) and thus increasing the deleterious effects of discrimination (Awad, 2010; Ellison, Finch, Ryan, & Salinas, 2009; Friedman & Saroglou, 2010). In the case of minority immigrants, life satisfaction may increase through connections with the heritage religious culture, yet life satisfaction has also been shown to decrease due to perceived discrimination (Verkuyten, 2008).

Religious Culture as a Restricted Minority

Religious freedoms are withheld from nearly 70% of the world's population (Pew Forum on Religion & Public Life, 2011). Further, minority religious groups often represent a particular ethnic heritage or race that differs from the dominant national cultural group. These ethnic, racial, and religious differences have often led to misunderstandings, real and perceived threats, and outright prejudice and discrimination towards members of minority religious cultures (see Rowatt, Carpenter, & Haggard, Chapter 8, this volume).

How do minority religious groups cope with intolerance, prejudice, and discrimination? Procter and Hornsby-Smith (2003) found evidence in the European Values Study that Catholics tend to develop a restrictive sexual strategy and emphasize collectivistic values—evidences of exclusivity—when living in countries in which Protestantism is the dominant religious culture. This is consistent with studies showing that people who are chronically concerned with physical harm or in constant competition for resources are also increasingly distrustful of outgroup members (Roes & Raymond, 2003) and may be more likely to institute secretive religious rituals that serve as costly signals of commitment to the religious group (Sosis & Alcorta, 2003).

It is estimated, however, that over 250 million people endure more horrific kinds of cultural, ethnic, or religious group persecution that often include torture, death, and even genocide (White & Marsella, 2007). Moreover, crises in China, Tibet, Sudan, Iraq, Serbia, and Egypt have produced millions of refugees from nearly every religious cultural group (Shea, 2008). The need is great for psychologists to begin to address ways to treat and restore the mental health of those who have been persecuted, tortured, or displaced for their faith.

The national cultural context can exert a powerful influence on religious culture(s) particularly in regard to minority religious cultures. However, it is important to recognize that even minority religious cultures sometimes shape or continue to influence the dominant national culture. For instance, Inglehart and Baker (2000) analyzed data from 60 countries and found that, although the socioeconomic development of a national culture predicts a shift from traditional religious values to secular ones in nearly all national cultures, individualistic values emphasizing self-expression, subjective well-being, and self-esteem were still more prevalent in national cultures that were historically Protestant. Further, Nepstad and Williams (2007) point to labor struggles in the US in the early 1900s, the human rights movement in El Salvador, and the conflict over racial apartheid in South Africa as examples of the role that religious beliefs and practices have played in instigating social movements, ultimately influencing national culture.

Transnational Religious Culture as an Influence on National Culture(s)

National cultures can also be conceptualized as subcultures of large, transnational religious cultures (Figure 15.2) —such as Protestant Christianity, Catholicism, Judaism, or Islam. Historically, there have also been demonstrations of the transformative impact of these transnational religious cultures on national cultures. For example, the Protestant Reformation initiated a cascade of broad political changes in Europe that ultimately led to the colonization of the Americas. Spanish conquistadors—and the Franciscan friars who followed—introduced Catholicism to Central and South America, and Muslims extended the Ottoman Empire to colonize the nations in West Asia and Africa. In the more recent past, a number of religious beliefs have also contributed to an increasingly vitriolic and polarized political landscape in, for instance, the US (see Malka, Chapter 11, this volume). These religious cultural

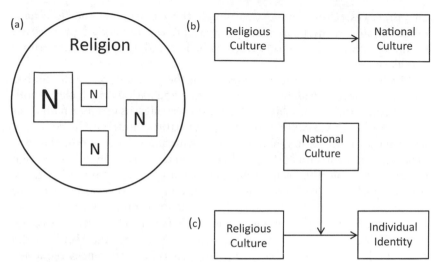

Figure 15.2 Nations conceptualized as a subset of a transnational religious culture (a). Individual nations are represented by the letter "N." At the group level, religious culture may influence national culture (b). At the individual level, national culture moderates the influence of the religious culture on individual psychological outcomes (c).

influences include, for example, the Vatican's well-known and strong stance against abortion and artificial birth control, the rise of religious conservatism among Protestant Evangelicals, and the leanings of mainline Protestants toward a more liberal worldview of social justice and civil rights (Putnam & Campbell, 2010).

Religion can change a nation. However, transnational religious cultures may also interact with national cultures to produce syncretic forms of religiosity. A considerable amount of research has been conducted regarding how religion has been used in negotiating the power differential between colonists and colonizers (e.g., Asad, 1993; King, 1999; Mignolo, 2006). Even when their conquerors' religious culture is publically adopted, individuals in colonized nations often hold religious beliefs or participate in religious rituals that are quite different from those of the colonizers. In Mexico, for example, the story of Juan Diego and the Virgin of Guadalupe has become, for some, an integral symbol and narrative tradition unique to Mexican Catholicism (see Beatty, 2006). This narrative contains traditional Catholic elements (e.g., the Virgin Mary) as well as important Aztec symbols (e.g., the sun and the crescent moon) (Gruzinski, 1995; Lafaye, 1976). Indigenous religions (e.g., African, Meso-American, or American Indian) and Haitian Voodoo (Pierre, 1977) are also replete with instances of syncretic beliefs and rituals that provide evidence of Muslim, Pentecostal Christian, or Roman Catholic influence but incorporate popular metaphysical beliefs and practices. Consequently, although the elements of the dominant religious culture may be readily apparent, the impact of preexisting national cultural or religious cultural beliefs and practices is sometimes just as evident.

Much of the cross-cultural research in the psychology of religion has focused, however, on identifying and comparing nations in which Catholicism, Protestantism, or Islam is the dominant religious group. An analysis of psychological variables from more than 100 countries (Georgas, van de Vijver, & Berry, 2004) showed that, controlling for economic factors, Protestant and Muslim countries do differ in terms of individualism (high versus low), subjective well-being (high versus low), and power distance (low versus high). Protestant and Catholic countries also varied in regard to secular authority (high versus low) and uncertainty avoidance (low versus high). Although some associations between religiosity and values were similar between Catholics, Protestants, Muslims, and Hindus, data from the World Values Survey showed that other differences remained (Guiso, Sapienza, & Zingales, 2003). For example, whereas Muslims and Hindus have a negative attitude towards economic competition, Catholics and Protestants have a positive attitude towards competition and the value of private property—values that have been described as the Protestant work ethic in Western nations (Weber, 1988 [1958]).

Differences between predominantly Muslim, Catholic, and Protestant nations are important and meaningful. However, there is a paucity of research considering how transnational religions might differ in beliefs and practices in diverse national contexts. For example, studies in the US have consistently shown a positive association between religiosity, health and longevity (McCullough, Hoyt, Larson, Koenig, & Thoresen, 2000) where the dominant religion is Christianity. As another example, there may be differences in religious coping and bereavement in different national contexts. In Euro-American national culture, relinquishing emotional and physical bonds with deceased family members is generally expected; however, in Pakistani culture, maintaining those bonds through talking to or dreaming about the deceased may be encouraged instead (Suhail, Jamil, Oyebode, & Ajmal, 2011). How, then, might bereavement practices (and counseling) differ for an American versus a Pakistani Muslim?

We have provided here only a few examples of differences that may occur within a transnational religious culture when individual members are located within distinct national cultures. There are surely a host of other religious beliefs and practices including attitudes toward women, rates of prosocial behavior (Dekker & Halman, 2003), values (Schwartz & Huismans, 1995), and definitions of mental health (Loewenthal, 2007), that may be reinterpreted or expressed somewhat differently—in both content and importance—depending upon the national culture.

Religious and National Cultural Conflict

So far, we have discussed the interaction of national and religious cultures in which either the national or the religious culture is most salient or clearly dominant. However, an important interaction also occurs when powerful religious and national cultures (and the corresponding worldviews of their constituents) conflict—an area underexplored in social psychology (Eidelson & Eidelson, 2003). These conflicts may occur on a global scale (e.g., secularization vs. fundamentalism), within a nation (e.g., pro-life vs. pro-choice), or even between nations (e.g., Iran vs. Israel).

One source of conflict between national and religious cultures has been secularization (Juergensmeyer, 1993; Norris & Inglehart, 2004). Although many social scientists had predicted that industrialization and scientific positivism would lead to the demise of religion (e.g., Durkheim, 1995 [1912]; Freud, 1961 [1927]), the world saw a resurgence of religious culture in the 20th century – particularly in fundamentalist forms (Halman & Riis, 2003; Hood, Hill, & Williamson, 2005). Fundamentalism has been observed in nearly every world religion (Altemeyer & Hunsberger, 1992; Marty & Appleby, 1991), and is characterized by dualism (black and white evaluations of good vs. evil), obedience to authority (all meaning found in certain sacred books and leaders), selectivity (privileging certain beliefs, practices or groups to the exclusion of others), millennialism (eschatological beliefs of a perhaps imminently coming cosmic order), and reactivity (hostility toward secularism and modernity) (Herriot, 2007). The individual motivation to preserve the religious group's exclusivity and concomitant religious worldview becomes particularly salient in times of threat, often eliciting reactive attitudes and behaviors that may serve to further isolate religious individuals, thereby fostering a continued sense of distinctiveness and conflict (Ysseldyk, Matheson, & Anisman, 2010, 2011).

Another related source of conflict is the perceived clash between the religious and scientific worldviews (Barbour, 1998; Nelson, 2009). In US national surveys, for instance, belief in a personal God (rather than a distant, impersonal deity) has been shown to be associated with diminished support for funding scientific research, the opposition to stem-cell research, and a rejection of evolutionary accounts of human origins (Froese & Bader, 2010; Pew Forum on Religion & Public Life, 2008). The conflict runs in both directions. These researchers also found that 51% of atheists, but only 11% of those who professed belief in God, said that religion and science were ultimately incompatible. Atheists' estimations appear to be more accurate regarding the incompatibility of religious and secular worldviews, however. In an experimental design, Preston and Epley (2009) found that using either religion or science as causal explanations typically elicited opposition to explanations in the other domain.

Groups that are highly distinctive or antagonistic in respect of the dominant national or religious culture will draw increasing discrimination and social stress, eventually leading to high rates of attrition. By the same token, groups that fail to satisfy the motives for religious participation will also diminish in number as members seek out other religious groups. Following work by Niebuhr (1929) and Troeltsch (1931), Finke and Stark (2001) have argued that, in a free market, religious groups will predictably shift the content or importance of their beliefs, rituals, community structures, and values to appeal to religious "consumers." Described as church–sect theory, churches that are inclusive and whose beliefs and structure accommodate those of the dominant national and/ or religious culture thrive precisely because they conform to the broader national and religious cultural norms. Thus, along a hypothetical bell curve of tension between the religious and national culture, ultraliberal and ultraconservative religious groups are expected to adjust their beliefs and practices to conform to the needs of their constituents yet also to the norms of the national culture. The official renunciation of polygamy by Mormon leaders (Quinn, 1993), the ostracism of snake handlers in the Church of God (Williamson & Hood, 2004), and the switching of young adults to churches with more mainstream social norms (Sherkat, 2001) can all be seen as examples of church–sect conflict resolution.

Although some progress has been made, the social consequences of religious cultural extremes (whether antireligious or religious extremists), secularism, fundamentalism and their related values, ultimate goals, and ideologies demand more concentrated research programs aimed at understanding how differences in religious and national cultural worldviews might be predicted (Appleby, 2000; Johnson, Hill, & Cohen, 2011; Silberman, Higgins, & Dweck, 2005). Eidelson and Eidelson (2003) have proposed five belief domains that may lead to religious conflict—feelings of superiority, injustice, vulnerability, distrust, and helplessness. Ginges, Hansen, and Norenzayan (2009) subsequently found that, across six national contexts, frequent attendance at religious services—but not regular personal prayer—was associated with outgroup hostility and the endorsement of suicide terror attacks. Consistent with research on intergroup conflict in other domains (Yzerbyt, Judd, & Corneille, 2004), Ginges and his colleagues suggest that frequent attendance enhances strong coalitional commitments that, depending on the religious group's discourse, may lead to the justification of religious violence.

Understanding the sources of religious and religious/national conflict may also shape strategies for peace and conflict resolution. It has been argued that the prosocial values inherent in nearly every religious culture (e.g., sanctity of life, moral obligation to care even for strangers, empathy, humility, self-control, and the benevolent nature of the divine) may also be emphasized to inspire peace and aid in conflict resolution (e.g., Gopin, 2000; see also Preston, Salomon, & Ritter, Chapter 7, this volume).

Religion and Culture in a Multinational (Globalization) Context

We have discussed religious and national cultures in this chapter as being institutions and nation states, respectively—that is, individuals in groups with obvious membership and clear social and conceptual boundaries. However, people do not always "stay put" and group boundaries are not always clear. Beginning in the late 20th century, the communication of diverse beliefs and practices has been made possible through increased migration in the forms of tourism, international trade, acceptance of interethnic and interracial marriages, the media, and the internet. People everywhere are now increasingly exposed to foods, clothing, music, architecture, social norms, and, importantly, novel ideas, philosophies, perspectives, and technological innovations (all the things that constitute and reflect culture) from other religious and national cultures. Thus, some sociologists have argued that whereas the age of modernity was characterized by nationalism and secularism versus traditionalism, the current epoch can be characterized as one of globalization and radical individualism, which, in turn, have fostered the development of novel, pluralistic, diversified, and localized forms of religious expression (Beyer, 2007; Bouma & Ling, 2009). Along these same lines, Heelas, Lash and Morris (1996) have argued that a kind of ethic of humanity has emerged that draws on, and yet supersedes, the moral codes of traditional religious cultures.

Historically, changes in either a nation or a transnational religious tradition have created broad, sweeping changes in the other domain. This raises a novel question: What will be the effects of globalization on transnational religious cultures? On the one hand, increased participation in religious culture has been clearly linked with increased national pride (Juergensmeyer, 1996). This suggests that religious people may be more resistant to the influences of other national and religious cultures (i.e., resistant to globalization). Indeed, nationalism and religious orthodoxy share some common values (Duriez, Luyten, Snauwaert, & Hutsebaut, 2002), and people who are nationalists tend to value social cohesion, social order, and security as do religious traditionalists. Therefore, it is not surprising that religiosity is also generally unrelated to the value of universalism, and is even negatively related with universalism in countries with a dominant religious culture (e.g., Catholicism in Italy, Judaism in Israel, or Islam in Turkey; Saroglou, Delpierre, & Dernelle, 2004).

On the other hand, it has been suggested that as the products, information, and religious beliefs and practices from different cultures become increasing accessible (that is, as globalization increases in a particular locality), individual religious identities will also become more eclectic and less traditional. The globalization hypothesis finds some confirmation in other studies showing that ethnocentrism can also be *un*related to young adults' religiosity, is low among atheists, and even low among Protestants in some European countries (Bréchon, 2003; Strabac & Listhaug, 2008).

In another empirical confirmation of this hypothesis, Halman and Pettersson (2003) created indices of globalization for 15 European nations and the US and found that increased globalization was negatively correlated with religious heterogeneity. In this same vein, it is estimated that over half of US Christians today attend more than one church—many having allegiance to none (Pew Forum on Religion & Public Life, 2009). Further, approximately 25% of US Christians hold eclectic worldviews that typically blend Eastern philosophies, ancient Native American or pagan traditions, astrology, and personal interpretations of scriptural texts with a sense of connectedness to all humanity (Figure 15.3).

Thus, there appears to be some consensus that the effects of globalization, coupled with the radical individualism evident in the late 20th century, has resulted in religious identity as a *bricolage*—the idiosyncratic cobbling together of a variety of beliefs and practices drawn from a

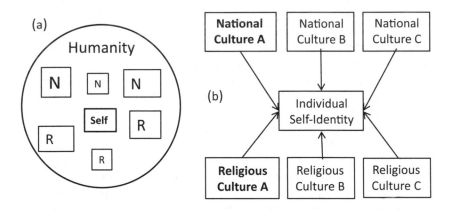

Figure 15.3 The individual conceptualizes the self as a unique individual connected to all of humanity, open to (nearly) all human beliefs and practices (a). Such an individual's identity and psychological outcomes are shaped by a dominant national and religious culture (in bold), but also subject to the multi-cultural influences of other national and religious cultures (b).

multitude of national and religious cultures (Beyer, 2007; Heelas, 1996; Luckmann, 1996). One example of these changes in religious identity is the increasing number of people reporting religious affiliation as spiritual but not religious. In a recent survey of 1334 college students, 23% of religious students born in the US reported being spiritual but not religious; somewhat similar percentages occur for international students (46%) and multiracial students (35%) (Johnson & Cohen, 2011). Again, in support of the globalization hypothesis, being spiritual but not religious often implies a value of universalism (Saroglou & Muñoz-García, 2008) and a sense of connectedness with all humanity (Piedmont, Kennedy, Sherman, Sherman, & Williams, 2008; Saroglou & Galand, 2004; Saroglou & Hanique, 2006).

A challenge for future research will be to better understand the changes in national and transnational religious identities brought about by multiculturalism and globalization. For example, do such changes intensify previously identified processes or create new situations to be understood (see Saroglou, 2006)? As discussed earlier, psychologists have discovered a wide range of psychosocial differences in the cognitive and relational styles of Eastern vs. Western individuals. In light of globalization and the increasingly eclectic religious views of Westerners, one intriguing line of research will be to understand how Eastern philosophical and religious worldviews may begin to exert subtle changes in Western culture. For example, as people shift from Western, anthropomorphic concepts of God to, say, more naturalistic concepts of God as the universe or an energetic force (or to atheistic philosophies like Buddhism), how will religious coping strategies change? Might we expect loneliness to increase (Epley, Waytz, Akalis, & Cacioppo, 2008) or moral judgments to change (Morewedge & Clear, 2008; Shariff & Norenzayan, 2011) as the concept of a personal God is replaced with the idealization of humanity or the universe as the transcendent "other" (see also Heelas, 1996)? What will be the social consequences for individuals who creatively link disparate religious beliefs and practices—but who lack the social support of the national culture or religious community?

Conclusion

The attention devoted to understanding religion as culture—and understanding the interaction of religious and national cultures—has varied among social scientists and across time. Sociologist James Beckford points out that the ordination of women, the participation of Japanese government officials in Shinto ceremonies, and Hindu nationalism are all exemplars of the bidirectional influences of religious and national culture, and the ongoing "changes in the conceptualization and regulation of what counts as religion" (2003, p. 2).

There are multiple ways to conceptualize the relation between religious and national cultures (Johnson, Hill, & Cohen, 2011; Saroglou & Cohen, 2011). Viewing religion as a subset of a national culture highlights the ways in which religious beliefs and practices may reflect political, ecological, economic, or demographic changes in the broader national cultural context. One important set of questions for future research will be to develop counseling strategies for members of religious minorities in order to cope with discrimination and, sometimes, persecution by the majority religious or national cultural group.

Conversely, transnational religious cultural groups (e.g., Catholicism, Protestant Christianity, Islam) may impact national cultures. These effects have been seen most clearly as missionaries, conquerors, and colonizers have brought—and continue to bring—their particular religious cultural beliefs, practices, values, and artifacts to new lands.

The bidirectional influences of religious and national cultures can lead to sweeping changes in human social attitudes and behavior, and those changes do not always occur without intense conflict. One promising area of social psychological research is in regard to conflict resolution and the identification of strategies for shifting the discourse in religious (and national) cultures from distrust and superiority to one of benevolence and coalition formation.

Religious and national cultures are constantly in a state of flux, sometimes almost imperceptibly and sometimes more obviously in the case of revolution, perceived revelation, or migration. As we continue to observe the migration of individuals and ideas around the globe in the 21st century, social scientists will want to remain acutely aware of potential shifts in the religious cultural landscape.

References

Abu-Rayya, H. M. (2007). Acculturation, Christian religiosity, and psychological and marital well-being among the European wives of Arabs in Israel. *Mental Health, Religion, and Culture, 10*, 171–190.

Altemeyer, B., & Hunsberger, B. (1992). Authoritarianism, religious fundamentalism, quest, and prejudice. *International Journal for the Psychology of Religion, 2*, 113–133.

Amer, M. M., & Hovey, J. D. (2007). Socio-demographic differences in acculturation and mental health for a sample of 2nd generation/early immigrant Arab Americans. *Journal of Immigrant and Minority Health, 9*, 335–347.

Appleby, R. S. (2000). *The ambivalence of the sacred: Religion, violence, and reconciliation.* Lanham, MD: Rowman & Littlefield.

Asad, T. (1993). *Genealogies of religion: Discipline and reasons of power in Christianity and Islam.* Baltimore, MD: Johns Hopkins University Press.

Atran, S., & Norenzayan, A. (2004). Religion's evolutionary landscape: Counterintuition, commitment, compassion, communion. *Behavioral and Brain Sciences, 27*, 713–779.

Awad, J. H. (2010). The impact of acculturation and religious identification on perceived discrimination for Arab/Middle Eastern Americans. *Cultural Diversity and Ethnic Minority Psychology, 16,* 59–67.

Barbour, I. B. (1998). *Religion and science: Historical and contemporary issues.* London: SCM Press Ltd.

Beatty, A. (2006). The pope in Mexico: Syncretism in public ritual. *American Anthropologist, 108,* 324–335.

Beckford, J. A. (2003). *Social theory and religion.* Cambridge: Cambridge University Press.

Bellah, R., Madsen, R., Sullivan, W., Swidler, A., & Tipton, S. M. (1985). *Habits of the heart: Individualism and commitment in American life.* Berkeley, CA: University of California Press.

Belzen, J. A. (2010). *Towards cultural psychology of religion: Principles, approaches, applications.* New York: Springer.

Belzen, J. A., & Lewis, C. A. (Eds.). (2010). Cultural psychology of religion [Special issue]. *Mental Health, Religion, and Culture, 13,* 327–328.

Berry, J. (1994). Acculturation and psychological adaptation: An overview. In A. M. Bouvy, J. R. Van de Vijver, P. Boski, & P. Schmitz (Eds.), *Journeys into cross-cultural psychology* (pp. 129–141). Amsterdam: Swets & Zeitlinger.

Berry, J. (1997). Immigration, acculturation and adaptation. *Applied Psychology: An International Review, 46,* 5–68.

Beyer, P. (2007). Globalization and glocalization. In J. A. Beckford & N. J. Demerath III (Eds.), *The Sage handbook of the sociology of religion* (pp. 98–117). Los Angeles, CA: Sage.

Bierman, A. (2006). Does religion buffer the effects of discrimination on mental health? Differing effects by race. *Journal for the Scientific Study of Religion, 45,* 551–566.

Bouma, G. D., & Ling, R. (2009). Religious diversity. In P. B. Clarke (Ed.), *The Oxford handbook of the sociology of religion* (pp. 507–522). New York: Oxford University Press.

Boyer, P. (2001). *Religion explained: The evolutionary origins of religious thought.* New York: Basic Books.

Bréchon, P. (2003). Integration into Catholicism and Protestantism in Europe: The impact on moral and political values. In L. Halman & O. Riis (Eds.), *Religion and secularizing society: The Europeans' religion at the end of the 20th century* (pp. 114–161). Leiden: Brill.

Cadge, W., & Ecklund, E. H. (2007). Immigration and religion. *Annual Review of Sociology, 33,* 359–379.

Carroll, M. P. (1983). Visions of the Virgin Mary: The effect of family structures on Marian apparitions. *Journal for the Scientific Study of Religion, 22,* 205–221.

Cohen, A. B. (2009). Many forms of culture. *American Psychologist, 64,* 194–204.

Dekker, P., & Halman, L. (Eds.). (2003). *The values of volunteering: Cross-cultural perspectives.* New York: Kluwer Academic/Plenum Publishers.

Diamond, J. (1997). *Guns, germs, and steel: The fates of human societies.* New York: W. W. Norton & Company.

Duriez, B., Luyten, P., Snauwaert, B., & Hutsebaut, D. (2002). The importance of religiosity and values in predicting political attitudes: Evidence for the continuing importance of religiosity in Flanders (Belgium). *Mental Health, Religion, and Culture, 5*, 35–54.

Durkheim, E. (1995). *The elementary forms of religious life.* New York: Free Press. (Original work published 1912)

Eidelson, R. J., & Eidelson, J. I. (2003). Danger ideas: Five beliefs that propel groups toward conflict. *American Psychologist, 58*, 182–192.

Elliott, M., & Hayward, R. D. (2009). Religion and life satisfaction worldwide: The role of government regulation. *Sociology of Religion, 70*, 285–310.

Ellison, C. G., Finch, B. K., Ryan, D. N., & Salinas, J. J. (2009). Religious involvement and depressive symptoms among Mexican-origin adults in California. *Journal of Community Psychology, 37*, 171–193.

Ellison, C. G., Musick, M. A., & Henderson, A. K. (2008). Balm in Gilead: Racism, religious involvement, and psychological distress among African American adults. *Journal for the Scientific Study of Religion, 47*, 291–309.

Epley, N., Waytz, A., Akalis, S., & Cacioppo, J. T. (2008). When we need a human: Motivational determinants of anthropomorphism. *Social Cognition, 26*, 143–155.

Finke, R., & Stark, R. (2001). The new holy clubs: Testing church-to-sect propositions. *Sociology of Religion, 62*, 175–189.

Fiske, A., Kitayama, S., Markus, H., & Nisbett, R. (2002). The cultural matrix of social psychology. In D. Gilbert, S. Fiske, & G. Lindzey (Eds.), *Handbook of social psychology* (4th ed., Vol. 2, pp. 915–981). Boston, MA: McGraw-Hill.

Friedman, M., & Saroglou, V. (2010). Religiosity, psychological acculturation to the host culture, self-esteem and depressive symptoms among stigmatized and nonstigmatized religious immigrant groups in Western Europe. *Basic and Applied Social Psychology, 32*, 185–195.

Freud, S. (1961). *The future of an illusion* (J. Strachey, Trans.). New York: W. W. Norton & Company. (Original work published 1927)

Froese, P., & Bader, C. (2010). *America's four gods: What we say about God—& what that says about us.* New York: Oxford University Press.

Geertz, C. (1973). Religion as a cultural system. In C. Geertz, *The Interpretation of cultures* (pp. 87–125). New York: Basic Books.

Georgas, J., van de Vijver, F. J. R., & Berry, J. W. (2004). The ecocultural framework, ecosocial indices, and psychological variables in cross-cultural research. *Journal of Cross-Cultural Psychology, 35*, 74–96.

Ghorpade, J., Lackritz, J. R., & Singh, G. (2006). Intrinsic religious orientation among minorities in the United States: A research note. *International Journal for the Psychology of Religion, 16*, 51–62.

Ginges, J., Hansen, I., & Norenzayan, A. (2009). Religion and support for suicide attacks. *Psychological Science, 20*, 224–230.

Gopin, M. (2000). *Between Eden and armageddon: The future of world religions, violence, and peacemaking.* New York: Oxford University Press.

Gruzinski, S. (1995). Images and cultural Mestizaje in Colonial Mexico. *Poetics Today, 16*, 53–77.

Guiso, L., Sapienza, P., & Zingales, L. (2003). People's opium? Religion and economic attitudes. *Journal of Monetary Economics, 50*, 225–282.

Halman, L., & Pettersson, T. (2003). Globalization and patterns of religous belief systems. In L. Halman & O. Riis (Eds.), *Religion in a secularizing society: The Europeans' religion at the end of the 20th Century* (pp. 185–204). Leiden: Brill.

Halman, L., & Riis, O. (Eds.). (2003). *Religion and secularizing society: The Europeans' religion at the end of the 20th century*. Leiden: Brill.

Heelas, P. (1996). On things not being worse, and the ethic of humanity. In P. Heelas, S. Lash, & P. Morris (Eds.), *Detraditionalization: Critical reflections on authority and identity* (pp. 200–222). Cambridge, MA: Blackwell.

Heelas, P., Lash, S., & Morris, P. (Eds.). (1996). *Detraditionalization: Critical reflections on authority and identity*. Cambridge, MA: Blackwell.

Heine, S. I. (2010). Cultural psychology. In S. T. Fiske, D. T. Gilbert, & G. Lindzey (Eds.), *Handbook of social psychology* (5th ed., Vol. 2, pp. 1423–1464). New York: Wiley.

Henrich, J., Heine, S. J., & Norenzayan, A. (2010). The weirdest people in the world? *Behavioral and Brain Sciences, 33*, 61–83.

Herriot, P. (2007). *Religious fundamentalism and social identity*. New York: Routledge.

Hong, Y., Wan, C., No, S., & Chiu, C. (2007). Multicultural identities. In S. Kitayama & D. Cohen (Eds.), *Handbook of cultural psychology* (pp. 323–345). New York: Guilford.

Hood, R. W., Hill, P. C., & Williamson, W. P. (2005). *The psychology of religious fundamentalism*. New York: Guilford.

Inglehart, R., & Baker, W. E. (2000). Modernization, cultural change, and the persistence of traditional values. *American Sociological Review, 65*, 19–51.

Johnson, K. A., & Cohen, A. B. (2011). [Spiritual but not religious college students in the U.S.] Unpublished raw data.

Johnson, K. A., Hill, F. D., & Cohen, A. B. (2011). Integrating the study of culture and religion: Toward a psychology of worldview. *Social and Personality Psychology Compass, 5*, 137–163.

Johnson, K. A., White, A. E., Boyd, B. M., & Cohen, A. B. (2011). Matzah, meat, milk, and mana: Psychological influences on religious food practices. *Journal of Cross-Cultural Psychology, 42*, 1421–1436.

Juergensmeyer, M. (1993). *The new cold war? Religious nationalism confronts the secular state*. Berkeley, CA: University of California Press.

Juergensmeyer, M. (1996). The worldwide rise of religious nationalism. *Journal of International Affairs, 50*, 1–20.

Kay, A. C., Gaucher, D., Napier, J. L., Callan, M. J., & Lauren, K. (2008). God and the government: Testing a compensatory control mechanism for the support of external systems. *Journal of Personality and Social Psychology, 95*, 18–35.

King, R. (1999). *Orientalism and religion: Postcolonial theory, India, and "The Mystic East"*. New York: Routledge.

Kitayama, S., & Cohen, D. (Eds.). (2007). *Handbook of cultural psychology*. New York: Guilford.

Kivisto, P. (2007). Rethinking the relationship between ethnicity and religion. In J. A. Beckford & N. J. Demerath III (Eds.), *The Sage handbook of the sociology of religion* (pp. 490–510). London: Sage.

Koltko-Rivera, M. E. (2004). The psychology of worldviews. *Review of General Psychology, 8*, 3–58.

Lafaye, J. (1976). *Quetzalcoatl and Guadalupe: The formation of Mexican national consciousness, 1531–1813*. Chicago, IL: University of Chicago Press.

Liu, E. Y. (2010). Are risk-taking persons less religious? Risk preference, religious affiliation, and religious participation in Taiwan. *Journal for the Scientific Study of Religion, 49*, 172–178.

Loewenthal, K. (2007). *Religion, culture and mental health*. Cambridge: Cambridge University Press.

Luckmann, T. (1996). The privatization of religion and morality. In P. Heelas, S. Lash, & P. Morris (Eds.), *Detraditionalization: Critical reflections on authority and identity* (pp. 72–86). Cambridge, MA: Blackwell.

McCann, S. J. (1999). Threatening times and fluctuations in American church memberships. *Personality and Social Psychology Bulletin, 25*, 325–336.

McCullough, M. E., Hoyt, W. T., Larson, D. B., Koenig, H. G., & Thoresen, C. (2000). Religious involvement and mortality: A meta-analytic review. *Health Psychology, 19*, 211–222.

Markus, H. R., & Kitayama, S. (1991). Culture and the self: Implications for cognition, emotion, and motivation. *Psychological Review, 98*, 224–253.

Marty, M. E., & Appleby, R. S. (1991). *Fundamentalisms observed*. Chicago, IL: University of Chicago Press.

Mignolo, W. D. (2006). *The darker side of the Renaissance: Literacy, territoriality, and colonization* (2nd ed.). Ann Arbor, MI: University of Michigan Press.

Miller, A. S. (2000). Going to hell in Asia: The relationship between risk and religion in a cross cultural setting. *Review of Religious Research, 42*, 5–18.

Morewedge, C. K., & Clear, M. E. (2008). Anthropomorphic god concepts engender moral judgment. *Social Cognition, 26*, 182–189.

Nelson, J. M. (2009). Science, religion, and psychology. In J. M. Nelson, *Psychology, religion, and spirituality* (pp. 43–75). New York: Springer.

Nepstad, S. E., & Williams, R. H. (2007). Religion in rebellion, resistance, and social movements. In J. A. Beckford & N. J. Demerath III (Eds.), *The Sage handbook of the sociology of religion* (pp. 419–437). Los Angeles, CA: Sage.

Niebuhr, H. R. (1929). *The social sources of denominationalism*. New York: Holt, Rinehart & Winston.

Nisbett, R. E. (2003). *The geography of thought: How Asians and Westerners think differently and why*. New York: Free Press.

Nisbett, R. E., Choi, I., Peng, K., & Norenzayan, A. (2001). Culture and systems of thought: Holistic versus analytic cognition. *Psychological Review, 108*, 291–310.

Norris, P., & Inglehart, R. (2004). *Sacred and secular: Religion and politics worldwide*. Cambridge: Cambridge University Press.

Pals, D. L. (1996). *Seven theories of religion*. New York: Oxford University Press.

Pargament, K. I. (1997). *The psychology of religion and coping: Theory, research, practice*. New York: Guilford.

Pew Forum on Religion & Public Life. (2008). *U.S. religious landscape survey: Religious beliefs and practices: Diverse and politically relevant*. Washington, DC: Pew Research Center.

Pew Forum on Religion & Public Life. (2009). *Many Americans mix multiple faiths: Eastern, New Age beliefs widespread.* Retrieved October 18, 2010: http://www.pewforum.org/Other-Beliefs-and-Practices/Many-Americans-Mix-Multiple-Faiths.aspx#1.

Pew Forum on Religion & Public Life. (2011). *New Pew Forum report analyzes religious restrictions around the world.* Retrieved April 15, 2012: http://www.pewforum.org/Press-Room/Press-Releases/New-Pew-Forum-Report-Analyzes-Religious-Restrictions-Around-the-World.aspx.

Piedmont, R. L., Kennedy, M. C., Sherman, M. F., Sherman, N. C., & Williams, J. E. (2008). A psychometric evaluation of the assessment of spirituality and religious sentiments (ASPIRES) scale: Short form. *Research in the Social Scientific Study of Religion, 19,* 163–181.

Pierre, R. (1977). Caribbean religion: The voodoo case. *Sociological Analysis, 38,* 25–36.

Plüss, C. (2009). Migration and the globalization of religion. In P. B. Clarke (Ed.), *The Oxford handbook of the sociology of religion* (pp. 491–506). New York: Oxford University Press.

Preston, J., & Epley, N. (2009). Science and God: An automatic opposition between ultimate explanations. *Journal of Experimental Social Psychology, 45,* 238–241.

Procter, M., & Hornsby-Smith, P. (2003). Individual religiosity, religious context and values in Europe and North America. In L. Halman & O. Riis (Eds.), *Religion and secularizing society: The Europeans' religion at the end of the 20th century* (pp. 92–113). Leiden: Brill.

Putnam, R. D., & Campbell, D. E. (2010). *American grace: How religion divides and unites us.* New York: Simon & Schuster.

Quinn, D. M. (1993). Plural marriage and Mormon fundamentalism. In M. E. Marty & R. S. Appleby (Eds.), *Fundamentalism and society* (pp. 240–293). Chicago, IL: University of Chicago Press.

Roccas, S., & Schwartz, S. H. (1997). Church-state relations and the association of religiosity with values: A study of Catholics in six countries. *Cross-Cultural Research, 31,* 356–375.

Roes, F. L., & Raymond, M. (2003). Belief in moralizing gods. *Evolution and Human Behavior, 24,* 126–135.

Sales, S. M. (1972). Economic threat as a determinant of conversion rates in authoritarian and nonauthoritarian churches. *Journal of Personality and Social Psychology, 23,* 420–428.

Sam, D., & Berry, J. (1995). Acculturative stress among immigrants in Norway. *Scandinavian Journal of Psychology, 36,* 10–24.

Saroglou, V. (2003). Trans-cultural/religious constants vs. cross-cultural/religious differences in psychological aspects of religion. *Archive for the Psychology of Religion, 25,* 71–87.

Saroglou, V. (2006). Religious bricolage as a psychological reality: Limits, structures and dynamics. *Social Compass, 53,* 109–115.

Saroglou, V. (2011). Believing, bonding, behaving, and belonging: The big four religious dimensions and cultural variation. *Journal of Cross-Cultural Psychology, 42,* 1320–1340.

Saroglou, V., & Cohen, A. B. (Eds.). (2011). Psychology of culture and religion: Introduction to the *JCCP* special issue. *Journal of Cross-Cultural Psychology, 42*, 1309–1319.

Saroglou, V., Delpierre, V., & Dernelle, R. (2004). Values and religiosity: A meta-analysis of studies using Schwartz's model. *Personality and Individual Differences, 37*, 721–734.

Saroglou, V., & Galand, P. (2004). Identities, values, and religion: A study among Muslim, other immigrant, and native Belgian young adults after the 9/11 attacks. *Identity: An International Journal of Theory and Research, 4*, 97–132.

Saroglou, V., & Hanique, B. (2006). Jewish identity, values, and religion in a globalized world: A study of late adolescents. *Identity: An International Journal of Theory and Research, 6*, 231–249.

Saroglou, V., & Muñoz-García, A. (2008). Individual differences in religion and spirituality: An issue of personality traits and/or values. *Journal for the Scientific Study of Religion, 47*, 83–101.

Sasaki, J. Y., & Kim, H. S. (2011). At the intersection of culture and religion: A cultural analysis of religion's implications for secondary control and social affiliation. *Journal of Personality and Social Psychology, 101*, 401–414.

Schaller, M., & Duncan, L. A. (2007). The behavioral immune system: Its evolution and social psychological implications. In J. P. Forgas, M. G. Haselton, & W. von Hippel (Eds.), *Evolution and the social mind: Evolutionary psychology and social cognition* (pp. 293–307). New York: Psychology Press.

Schwartz, S. H., & Huismans, S. (1995). Value priorities and religiosity in four Western religions. *Social Psychology Quarterly, 58*, 88–107.

Seirmarco, G., Neria, Y., Insel, B., Kiper, D., Doruk, A., Gross, R. et al. (2012). Religiosity and mental health: Changes in religious beliefs, complicated grief, posttraumatic stress disorder, and major depression following the September 11, 2001 attacks. *Psychology of Religion and Spirituality, 4*, 10–18.

Shariff, A. F., & Norenzayan, A. (2011). Mean gods make good people: Different views of God predict cheating behavior. *International Journal for the Psychology of Religion, 21*, 85–96.

Shea, N. (2008). The origins and legacy of the movement to fight religious persecution. *Review of Faith and International Affairs, 6*, 25–31.

Sherkat, D. E. (2001). Investigating the sect-church-sect cycle: Cohort specific attendance differences across African-American denominations. *Journal for the Scientific Study of Religion, 40*, 221–233.

Silberman, I., Higgins, E. T., & Dweck, C. S. (2005). Religion and world change: Violence and terrorism versus peace. *Journal of Social Issues, 61*, 761–784.

Sirin, S. R., Bikmen, N., Mir, M., Fine, M., Zaal, M., & Katsiaficas, D. (2008). Exploring dual identification among Muslim-American emerging adults: A mixed methods study. *Journal of Adolescence, 31*, 259–279.

Sosis, R. (2006). Religious behaviors, badges, and bans: Signaling theory and the evolution of religion. In P. McNamara (Ed.), *Where God and science meet: How brain and evolutionary studies alter our understanding of religion: Vol. 1: Evolution, genes, and the religious brain* (pp. 61–86). Westport, CT: Praeger.

Sosis, R., & Alcorta, C. (2003). Signaling, solidarity, and the sacred: The evolution of religious behavior. *Evolutionary Anthropology, 12*, 264–274.

Stark, R. (2001). Gods, rituals, and the moral order. *Journal for the Scientific Study of Religion, 40*, 619–636.

Strabac, Z., & Listhaug, O. (2008). Anti-Muslim prejudice in Europe: A multilevel analysis of survey data from 30 countries. *Social Science Research, 37*, 268–286.

Suhail, K., Jamil, N., Oyebode, J., & Ajmal, M. A. (2011). Continuing bonds in bereaved Pakistani Muslims: Effects of culture and religion. *Death Studies, 35*, 22–41.

Tarakeshwar, N., Stanton, J., & Pargament, K. I. (2003). Religion: An overlooked dimension in cross-cultural psychology. *Journal of Cross-Cultural Psychology, 34*, 377–394.

Thrower, J. (1999). *Religion: The classical theories*. Washington, DC: Georgetown University Press.

Triandis, H. C., & Gelfand, M. J. (1998). Converging measurement of horizontal and vertical individualism and collectivism. *Journal of Personality and Social Psychology, 74*, 118–128.

Troeltsch, E. (1931). *The social teachings of the Christian churches* (2 vols., O. Wyon, Trans.). New York: Macmillan.

Verkuyten, M. (2008). Life satisfaction among ethnic minorities: The role of discrimination and group identification. *Social Indicators Research, 89*, 391–404.

Verkuyten, M., & Yildiz, A. A. (2007). National (dis)identification, and ethnic and religious identity: A study among Turkish-Dutch Muslims. *Personality and Social Psychology Bulletin, 33*, 1448–1462.

Viladrich, A., & Abraído-Lanza, A. F. (2009). Religion and mental health among minorities and immigrants in the U.S. In S. Loue & M. Sajatovic (Eds.), *Determinants of minority mental health and wellness* (pp. 149–174). New York: Springer.

Waggoner, M. (2009). Culture and religion. In P. B. Clarke (Ed.), *The Oxford handbook of the sociology of religion* (pp. 210–225). New York: Oxford University Press.

Weber, M. (1988). *The Protestant ethic and the spirit of capitalism* (T. Parsons, Trans.). Gloucester, MA: P. Smith. (Original work published 1958)

Weber, M. (1993). *The sociology of religion* (E. Fischoff, Trans.). Boston, MA: Beacon Press. (Original work published 1922)

White, J. D., & Marsella, A. J. (2007). *Fear of persecution: Global human rights, international law, and human well-being*. Lanham, MD: Lexington Books.

Williamson, W. P., & Hood, R. W. (2004). Differential maintenance and growth of religious organizations based upon high-cost behavior: Serpent handling within the Church of God. *Review of Religious Research, 46*, 150–168.

Young, M. J., Morris, M. W., Burrus, J., Krishnan, L., & Regmi M. P. (2011). Deity and destiny: Patterns of fatalistic thinking in Christian and Hindu cultures. *Journal of Cross-Cultural Psychology, 42*, 1030–1053.

Ysseldyk, R., Matheson, K., & Anisman, H. (2010). Religiosity as identity: Toward an understanding of religion from a social identity perspective. *Personality and Social Psychology Review, 14*, 60–71.

Ysseldyk, R., Matheson, K., & Anisman, H. (2011). Coping with identity threat: The role of religious orientation and implications for emotions and action intentions. *Psychology of Religion and Spirituality, 3,* 132–148.

Yzerbyt, V., Judd, C. M., & Corneille, O. (Eds.). (2004). *The psychology of group perception: Perceived variability, entitativity, and essentialism.* New York: Psychology Press.

16 Conclusion
Understanding Religion and Irreligion

Vassilis Saroglou

Understanding religion psychologically means being able to deal with and answer three kinds of question. First, what are the psychological—cognitive, emotional, moral, and social—functions of religion in contemporary individuals' lives? Second, provided that at least some of these functions may be universal, why are there important inter-individual differences in attitudes regarding religion? Finally, can the historical presence of religion in the human species be explained as having served some basic adaptive needs and the corresponding psychological mechanisms? The first question is typically a matter of social psychology; the second, of personality psychology; and the third, of evolutionary psychology.

The three questions are partially interdependent. For instance, it may be that the functions of religion as studied today in peoples' lives are ones to which religious people are more sensitive than the non-religious, and are ones that have some meaningful evolutionary psychological past. But the three questions are also partially independent from one another. Religion may influence cognitions, feelings, and behavior regardless of whether individuals are religious or not, and religion's role in human psychology may be independent from strictly evolutionary adaptive needs. Orthogonal to these questions is the issue of the extent to which religion's psychological functioning is universal and to what extent it is culture sensitive.

The main objective of this chapter is to offer an integrative synthesis of the psychological functions of religion on the basis of the accumulated empirical evidence of the last years reviewed in this volume's chapters. Attention will be paid to distinguish between the universal—for both believers and nonbelievers—character of the psychological needs addressed within religion and the specific ways through which these needs are addressed within a religious context, for instance compared to irreligion. An integrative view of the origins of individual differences on religiousness will also be provided. The emphasis will be on a social and personality psychological understanding of religion, while not neglecting some insight from evolutionary psychology. Finally, the chapter ends with considerations for future research on personal religiousness as an individual differences construct to be studied principally in interaction with several contextual factors.

The Multiple Functions of Religion and Some Specifics

As shown through the various chapters of the present volume, religion, as a multifaceted reality, i.e., including the four "B" dimensions of believing, bonding, behaving, and belonging, has not a sole but rather multiple functions at the intra-individual, interpersonal, and social levels (see Figure 16.1 for an integrative view). These may be cognitive, emotional, moral, and social or may be rather transversal, i.e., for the individual and social self as a whole. Interestingly, none of these psychological functions seems unique, specific to religion, compared to other domains of human activity; they are universal, i.e., concern human beings in general, be they religious or not. Following Fiske's (2010) model of five major social motives, as psychologists we can argue that religion is mainly based on panhuman motives: understanding, controlling, and trusting (oneself, others, and the world), as well as self-enhancing, and belonging. However, religion implies several specifics in the way these universal motives work within a religious context and/ or among religious participants. Later in the chapter, I will focus on key characteristics and specifics that make religion to be both (1) built upon universal psychological motives and (2) distinct from irreligion

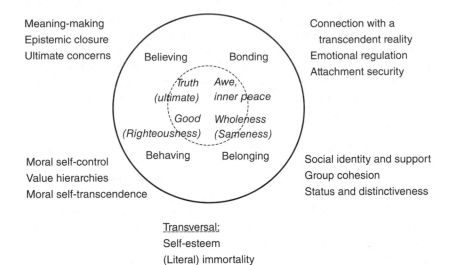

Figure 16.1 Cognitive, emotional, moral, and social functions of religion (individual level).

as well as from other, proximal to religion, domains of human activity (e.g., art, paranormal beliefs, ideologies, morality, cultural/ethnic groups).

As will be shown later, a key specificity of religion comes from the fact that the four basic components of religion (beliefs, ritualized experiences, norms, and groups) and the corresponding cognitive, emotional, moral, and social mechanisms are interdependent, mutually supportive, and delimitating of one another. This is especially the case with religions that have become historically dominant and large in membership.

Religion is Not Simply a Meaning-Making System

Religion functions, to some extent, as a meaning-making system. It includes worldviews and beliefs, influences appraisal of internal and external events, and impacts attributions and causal inferences about the physical world, the self, others, and life in general. Thus, religious functions also intervene on decision making and the justification of thoughts, feelings, and acts. Correlational, biographical, historical, longitudinal, experimental, and neuropsychological evidence converges to show that religiousness is activated—mostly increases, sometimes decreases, or serves as a coping mechanism—when meaning and related self-control and self-esteem are threatened (see in this volume: Hayward & Krause, Chapter 12; Sedikides & Gebauer, Chapter 3). These threats cover a wide spectrum of situations and events: loneliness, ostracism, frustration, mortality salience, illness, death or loss of loved ones, uncertainty, loss of control, economic distress, natural disasters, and terrorist attacks. Through meaning making and related mechanisms, religion exerts some empowerment on people's lives, thus contributing to some extent to various aspects of well-being and mental health (Park, 2007).

However, compared to other meaning-making systems, religion is distinguished by several particularities (Saroglou, 2011). Religiousness implies intense investment on meaning making and strong beliefs in the meaningfulness of one's own life and the world. Moreover, religion provides distal, God-related, attributions when proximal (e.g., physical, psychological) explanations of unexplained events are missing. However, the core interest of religion is on the very distal causes of human existence. Therefore, it provides answers—more literal than symbolic—to the big existential enigmas, i.e., beliefs about specific transcendent entities, narratives about the origin of the world, and promises of literal immortality to face death-related anxiety. In fact, religion has *vacuum horror*: it prefers a world having plenty of meaning over the experience of emptiness. Not surprisingly, therefore, religious conversion and spiritual transformation mainly constitute a transition from subjective meaninglessness to subjective meaningfulness (Paloutzian, 2005).

Related to this is the fact that religiousness implies a particular way of meaning making that is animated by the epistemic needs for order, structure, and closure—at least in monotheistic religions (Saroglou, 2002a). Interestingly, the increase of self-uncertainty and frustration leads to the radicalization of religious conviction; and conversely, people may de-radicalize after self-certainty has been re-established (Hogg, Adelman, & Blagg, 2010; McGregor, Nash, & Prentice, 2012). Consequently, even if well-being is a typical outcome of religious meaning making in general, to the extent to which it is mobilized by a high need for closure and a reduction of uncertainty, religion also leads to prejudice against various outgroups (Rowatt, Carpenter, & Haggard, Chapter 8, this volume; see also Brandt & Reyna, 2010). Note that modern spirituality, although equally motivated by a search for meaning, seems to evade traditional religiosity's temptation for epistemic closure and prejudice (Saroglou, 2002a, 2013).

The psychological functions of religion related to beliefs and meaning making are not isolated from other functions; they are importantly qualified by the co-presence of the three other religious dimensions, i.e., emotional, moral, and social. For instance, in religious conversion, emotional and relational factors play an equally, if not more, important role as the cognitive factors and meaning-making processes. Moreover, religious beliefs are mostly moral in nature and implications rather than simple cognitive elaborations built, for instance, on the need for cognition to understand the world. Believing that God is the creator of the world, that Jesus was born to a virgin mother, or that a messiah will come to establish a new world, are moral affirmations rather than pure cognitions. In addition, religious and spiritual cognitions constitute shared beliefs within a group or community—even a virtual one—and they are subject to authority or tradition—even in the case of symbolic religiousness or non-religious spirituality. Finally, the fragile, unverifiable and, more importantly, counterintuitive character of many religious beliefs incites regular re-affirmation of these beliefs through emotional, ritualized, especially collective experiences and endorsement by a relatively homogenous group of numerous co-believers.

Religious beliefs in supernatural agents in general, and in Gods in particular, exemplify the fact that religion is built on common psychological mechanisms while at the same time implies a specific combination of psychological constructs and processes. Beliefs in supernatural entities should be understood as being based on common social cognition: they presuppose the acquisition of mentalizing capacities (mind perception or theory of mind) to infer the mental states of others, as well as of mind–body dualism (the perception of minds working differently from bodies) and teleology (the belief that there is some intentionality in nature and objects) (Gervais, Chapter 4, this volume; Norenzayan &

Gervais, 2012). At the same time, the most successful, in terms of cultural transmission, supernatural entities (Gods) are human-like beings perceived as possessing several specific counterintuitive *suprahuman* qualities. These qualities span four levels: cognitive (full knowledge and memory; Barrett, 2012; Boyer, 2001), emotional (the existence of secondary, human-specific emotions but not primary, animal-specific, ones Demoulin, Saroglou, & Van Pachterbeke, 2008), moral (higher, compared to the self, levels of moral personality traits; Saroglou, 2010; see also Oishi, Seol, Koo, & Miao, 2011, Table 2), and social (the capacity to relate with all human beings and nature).

In sum, although religion functions like other meaning systems, and religious cognitions are built on general mechanisms of social cognition, religious meaning making is specific in direction (affirmation of meaningfulness), content (specific religious beliefs), nature (several literal answers), extent (inferences, from the smallest personal event to the afterlife), validation source and means (community, tradition, authority, rituals), and underlying epistemic motives (order, certainty, and closure). All these make religion partly distinct from other meaning-making systems such as art, philosophical systems, political or moral ideologies, and paranormal beliefs.

Religious doubters, agnostics, or atheists are, of course, also concerned with the universal need for meaning making in general, and facing existential anxiety in particular. However, they seem to adopt, to some extent, different, if not opposite, pathways for exploring and creating meaning. Autonomy/nonconformity, skepticism, analytic rather than intuitive and holistic thinking, open mindedness, and intelligence tend to overall characterize nonbelievers (Aarnio & Lindeman, 2007; Caldwell-Harris, 2012; Gervais, Chapter 4, this volume; Streib & Klein, 2013).

Religion is Not Only a Haven to Face Adversity

Religion also serves psychological functions related to emotions that are universal. However, like for beliefs and meaning making, it does so with some particularities; and the interaction with the other three dimensions—cognitive, moral, and social—impacts the emotional functioning of religion.

Religion provides means to cope with negative emotions and experiences and foster self-regulatory skills; and it provides practices—mainly rituals and especially prayer/meditation—and symbols that contribute psychologically, physiologically, and neurologically to emotional regulation, in particular for persons with a negative emotionality profile (Burris & Petrican, Chapter 5, this volume). Religion's regulatory role may encompass the whole spectrum of negative emotions, be they basic such as anger, fear, sadness, and disgust, or secondary and self-conscious such as envy, contempt, guilt, and shame (Watts, 2007). Experimental induction of various negative affects in the laboratory increases individual religiousness (Sedikides & Gebauer, Chapter 3, this volume). Similarly, God serves as a substitute attachment figure in the context of prior attachment insecurity in childhood or adulthood (Granqvist, Chapter 13, this volume).

However, religion is not only a haven to face adversity. Religious experience also generates positive emotions not aimed at compensating for previous vulnerability. Religion may involve all kinds of positive emotion ranging from the basic such as joy, amusement, and interest to the moral and/or complex such as pride, compassion, gratitude, enthusiasm, awe, and admiration (Emmons, 2005). More importantly, positive emotions not only result from religious experiences but may cause or facilitate them. Complementing previous evidence on religion as a way to compensate for adversity and deprivation, a series of recent experiments show that positive emotions are also capable of increasing spirituality and religiousness and related feelings and behaviors (Van Cappellen & Rimé, Chapter 6, this volume). Similarly, there is a bidirectional causal link between attachment security and religiousness: secure attachment generalizes to all kinds of relationships, including that with God, and trust in God consolidates relational quality (Granqvist, Chapter 13, this volume).

What is specific about religion regarding its emotional functioning? Scholars agree that there exists no specifically religious emotion. Religion involves common, universal emotions and related psychological processes. (This parallels the idea that religious beliefs about supernatural agents are built on common social cognition.) However, historical and empirical evidence suggests some affinities between religion and certain emotions. These are the so-called moral emotions, be they negative or positive.

For instance, religion both instills and helps one to face things such as existential anxiety (over death), guilt (over sins), shame (of being unworthy of the love of God), and moral disgust (against outgroups perceived to threaten religious values). Similarly, positive moral emotions, also called self-transcendent emotions, such as awe, elevation, admiration, and gratitude, but not self-focused positive emotions such as joy, pride, and especially amusement, have the power to activate or heighten spirituality (Van Cappellen & Rimé, Chapter 6, this volume). Music styles that reflect emotions such as awe, love, and compassion are preferred by religious and spiritual people, whereas music styles that reflect energy, activation, and amusement are unrelated to religiousness (Saroglou, Prade, & Rodriguez, 2012). Finally, in a series of studies, religiousness was found to predict low appreciation and use of several humor styles, and even low spontaneous humor creation as a way to cope with life's everyday difficulties (at least in a cultural context influenced by Catholicism; Saroglou, 2002b, 2003a, 2004).

Overall, one gets the impression that William James (1985 [1902]) was right when affirming that religiousness implies a tonality of seriousness in life and gravity in human existence. It appears that religion favors emotional self-transcendence and inner peace but not simple changes of the reference framework (humor) or emotional energy. Note that "spiritual joy" is not quite the same thing as happiness or pleasure; and "spiritual laughter" is something different from sex jokes and sick humor (Saroglou & Anciaux, 2004).

Religion provides rituals that help one to experience emotions in a specific way, i.e., aesthetically (search for the sublime), in an artistically hieratic way (with self-mastery), and extraordinarily (outside of life's everyday routine), but still familiarly (repetition of established behavior patterns). Moreover, within rituals, emotions translate bodily expressions into religious ideas and, in turn, consolidate them, thus heightening religious memory. Finally, like beliefs, emotions within a religious context have both moral and social identity orientations. As argued by Burris and Petrican (Chapter 5, this volume), religious emotional self-regulation is a moral issue and is linked to one's identity as a religious person and as a member of a specific religious community that values, legitimizes, or condemns certain emotions. Emotional regulation thus serves to preserve and promote individuals' religious identity.

Empirical psychological research on religion, emotions, and rituals is somehow comparatively less developed than research investigating the cognitive and moral functions and consequences of religion. It is thus difficult to extrapolate on irreligion and make assumptions regarding the specifics in the way agnostics and atheists experience universal self-transcendent and moral emotions. There may be differences in the elicitors of the later emotions: for instance, science and not only nature elicit awe among the non-religious (Caldwell-Harris, Wilson, LoTempio, & Beit-Hallahmi, 2011). Also, as far as mental health is concerned, non-religious persons may evade religious sources of negative emotions such as beliefs and rituals that possibly induce fear, guilt, or shame. At the same time, they may also lack some of the self-regulatory resources that aid in coping with adversity, depression, and death anxiety. Currently, empirical research gives a modest but consistent advantage to the religious, regarding many emotional and regulatory aspects of mental health and well-being (Hayward & Krause, Chapter 12, this volume; Koenig, King, & Carson, 2012). Some argue, however, for a curvilinear relation with both the very religious and irreligious, compared to the moderately religious, being high on some aspects of well-being (Galen, 2012; Streib & Klein, 2013).

Religion is Not the Source of Universal Morality

A common idea is that religion serves as an important source of morality for humans. However, accumulated research using a variety of method-ologies, including priming studies, shows that this is only partly true and needs to be importantly nuanced. Morality—moral emotions and values—emerges rather universally in early childhood and does so inde-pendently from (religious) teachings and socialization; children may question adults' behavior, including religious norms, as being immoral (Turiel, 2006). Among adults, religious conviction may be in conflict with moral conviction (Skitka, Bauman, & Lytle, 2009). Nevertheless, an important function of religion is to sustain a sense of righteousness. Religious righteousness overlaps to some extent with what humans uni-versally consider to be moral, i.e., care- and justice-based morality, but not always.

There are, in fact, a number of specifics to keep in mind when one con-siders the role of religion with respect to morality. Religiousness implies, consistently across the major religions, a specific hierarchy between uni-versal human values with an emphasis on values denoting primarily con-servation and secondarily some self-transcendence (benevolence), and a low consideration of the values of autonomy and hedonism (Roccas & Elster, Chapter 9, this volume). Modern spirituality shifts the priority to valuing extended self-transcendence (universal prosocial concerns) while neglecting the values of power and hedonism (Saroglou & Muñoz-García, 2008). Moreover, religion explicitly emphasizes the importance of coherence between value hierarchy and behavior (Roccas & Elster, Chapter 9, this volume). This may activate and increase honesty, or decrease dishonesty, as has been shown in several experiments (Preston, Salomon, & Ritter, Chapter 7, this volume), but also renders more prob-lematic the presence of religious moral hypocrisy. Witnessing the last is a major predictor of religious doubting and apostasy (Altemeyer, 2004; Saroglou, 2012a).

Another characteristic of religion is that it seems to encourage a double extension in the moral domain. On the one hand, through specific reli-gious ideas (e.g., an omniscient and all-controlling supernatural agent, family-related metaphors) and collective practices (e.g., costly rituals that indicate fellows to trust), religion enhances prosocial behavior. In doing so, it has contributed to a cultural evolution from kinship-based altruism to an extended altruism in large societies disposing of moralizing Gods (Preston et al., Chapter 7, this volume). On the other hand, in addition to interpersonal morality, which is founded on the universal principles of care and justice, religion is also concerned with non-interpersonal morality based primarily on purity (avoidance of moral disgust) and secondarily on group/society-related principles of loyalty and respect to authority (Graham & Haidt, 2010). The last three principles are more strongly endorsed in collectivistic societies and by conservative individuals. This may explain the extension of religion's moralizing effects on other domains such as sexuality (restriction of), family (commitment to), and political preferences (cultural conservatism) (see in this volume: Li & Cohen, Chapter 10; Malka, Chapter 11).

The co-existence in religion of prosocial interpersonal morality with moral concerns for the preservation of social order and individual purity does not imply a simple extension of moral domains. In fact, conservative religiousness corresponds to excessive moralism—like excessive meaningfulness, as far as the religious meaning-making process is concerned—attested through moralization in all domains of life (e.g., Nucci & Turiel, 1993). Moreover, whereas in spirituality the extended prosocial values come first, in traditional religiosity, sexuality-, family- and purity-related concerns are predominant (Weeden, Cohen, & Kenrick, 2008; see also Malka, Chapter 11, this volume). More broadly, when in conflict, deontological moral judgment takes priority over consequentialism and prosocial concerns among traditionally religious people (Piazza, 2012) and authoritarians primed with religious ideas (Van Pachterbeke, Freyer, & Saroglou, 2011). Conservative, non-interpersonal moral principles may importantly limit prosocial religious tendencies (Saroglou, 2013). Similarly, religious prejudice against value-threatening individuals (homosexuals, atheists, members of other religions; Rowatt et al., Chapter 8, this volume) may be explained as resulting from deontological concerns that neutralize religious prosocial tendencies and the hypothetical support of the "sin–sinner" distinction. Note that, conversely, religious prosocial concerns may attenuate the antisocial effects of religious moral conservatism (Arzheimer & Carter, 2009; Malka, Chapter 11, this volume).

The moral functions of religion are reinforced by the co-presence of beliefs, rituals, practices, and the community. Religious moral tendencies—either prosocial or impersonal, deontological—are cognitively justified by religious beliefs, theological arguments, and narratives with key religious figures playing the roles of moral exemplars (Oman, 2013; Saroglou, 2006b). These tendencies are amplified by emotions experienced in collective and private rituals (Van Cappellen & Rimé, Chapter 6, this volume). Religious practices such as fasting and meditation, together with beliefs and collective rituals, provide channels for fostering self-control. Self-control thus becomes a "moral muscle" that acts across a variety of domains of human activity and allows for the control of impulsivity, the resistance to temptations, the capacity to postpone gratification, and the perseverance to accomplish one's goals (Baumeister & Exline, 1999; Burris & Petrican, Chapter 5, this volume; McCullough & Willoughby, 2009). Furthermore, the religious group legitimizes norms, rewards morality, punishes immorality, and defines the frontiers within which cultural altruism applies.

Finally, religion encourages the pursuit of high, possibly excessively high, moral standards. This concerns interpersonal morality, since sacrificial altruism has often been motivated by religious motives. It also concerns a strict deontological non-interpersonal morality that denotes excessive self-control to the detriment of hedonism—a kind of religious masochism.

Are agnostics and atheists low in prosociality and morality in general? There is currently a hot debate on whether this is simply a stereotype or may reflect truth (Galen, 2012; Myers, 2012; Saroglou, 2012c). No doubt, agnostics and atheists dispose of a huge variety of secular, non-religious sources of, and motives for, moral action—all, in fact, of the cognitive, emotional, and social common determinants of morality. Nevertheless, as argued elsewhere (Saroglou, 2012c, 2013), the existing evidence suggests that agnostics and atheists may be overall less inclined to show prosocial tendencies and act prosocially. However, when prosociality occurs among the non-religious, it may be more autonomous than dependent on religious authority and norms, more altruistically than egoistically motivated, and more universal than ingroup-oriented. In addition, among the non-religious, morality seems to be focused on interpersonal aspects and less on concerns of purity, conservation of social order, and the development of a "moral muscle."

Religion is Not Simply Belonging to an Ingroup

Religion also implies some identification, be it weak or strong, with a group of coreligionists, thus serving common psychological functions relative to many social groups. These are mainly the need to belong, collective identity, social self-esteem, and social support. Additional functions include attachment to an ingroup, delimitation from outgroups, coalition formation for achieving various goals, disposing of a common culture (beliefs, norms, symbols, practices, and leisure activities), finding friends, professional acquaintances, and mating partners, and contracting marriages under public commitment (Gebauer & Maio, 2013; Johnson & Cohen, Chapter 15, this volume; Kirkpatrick, 2005; Li & Cohen, Chapter 10, this volume; Ysseldyk, Matheson, & Anisman, 2010). Many of these are known to contribute to mental health and well-being; this is also the case with religious groups (Hayward & Krause, Chapter 12, this volume).

However, religious groups are characterized by series of particularities. First, following theory on entitative social groups in general (Kruglanski, Pierro, Mannetti, & De Grada, 2006; Yzerbyt, Judd, & Corneille, 2004), one can argue that religions—from world religions to small religious communities—are groups with high entitativity, homogeneity, and essentialism. This is because religious groups (1) are perceived as "real entities," are particularly stable in time, and have fixed boundaries; (2)

include members of similar beliefs, values, and goals, whereas inter-individual variability is considered unimportant or secondary; and (3) are perceived as natural-like entities with a common essence rather than simply cultural networks. The last is facilitated by the geographical proximity and the distribution of the major world religions into few large zones of civilization (see Pew Research Center, 2012). The high need for sameness within religious groups can explain why the history of religions is replete with schisms and fights against heresies.

Second, religious groups satisfy not only motives for communion, social integration, and social cohesion, but also the agentic need for distinctiveness from the encompassing society, especially when that society is secular (Sedikides & Gebauer, Chapter 3, this volume). Religious identification is greater in religious groups of small size, a fact that suggests a need for optimal distinctiveness (Hoverd, Atkinson, & Sibley, 2012). The strength, especially under conditions of discrimination, of religious identification among immigrants, can be understood as resulting from, among other things, such a need for optimal distinctiveness (see Verkuyten & Martinovic, 2012).

Third, contrary to other social identities such as ethnic, professional, or those related to leisure, which may be multiple and accumulative, religious social identities are mostly unique and exclusive. For the highly religious, religious identity is superior to all others. Additionally, religious identities are enhanced by an attachment to common beliefs, the practice of collective rituals where the group acts as a homogeneous whole, and the self-perception as moral and righteous; they thus serve to reduce feelings of uncertainty (Hogg et al., 2010). Not only does this increase the strength of the ingroup versus outgroup distinction, but it may render extremely difficult the creation of superordinate common ingroup identities (e.g., "world believers"). The last identities are known to constitute one possible solution for overcoming intergroup conflict (Dovidio & Gaertner, 2010). Subsequently, competition between religious groups to increase membership and social status and power may be particularly high, especially given the affinities between religion, physical territory, and political influence.

Fourth, religious groups are particular in that they are perceived by their members as eternal and glorious, much more so, in fact, than ethnic and national groups (Saroglou, 2011; Ysseldyk et al., 2010). The majority of world religions have their (glorious) origin situated in a very distant past—often earlier than the creation of modern nations—and promote the belief that they will survive as communities after the end of the world. This is an incredibly powerful source of collective self-esteem and a factor that contributes to an underestimation of believers regarding the dark sides of the religious group's past and present.

Finally, religious groups have a hierarchical structure, with authority figures and instances (texts, persons, and institutions), leaders, and followers. These imply asymmetric relations as well as deliberate or subtle mechanisms leading to submission to authority, conformity to the majority, and social influence by religious peers and other sources. Religious authorities exert various forms of power: reward based, coercive, expert, legitimate, and/or charismatic. Overall, one can distinguish between experts, i.e., ministers who are supposed to manipulate contact with the sacred, and models, such as saints and spiritual figures, who are admired as prototypes of the group's values. Note also that religious ministers in many societies are professionals who have succeeded to be paid by the society, like doctors, teachers, and functionaries and unlike artists, poets, philosophers, and astrologists who may also help, in their own way, people in meaning making and self-transcendence.

These characteristics may be particularly appealing for individuals with high dispositional submissiveness (see, for instance, some theories on gender difference in religion: Francis & Penny, Chapter 14, this volume). In a series of seven experiments, religious subliminal priming or explicit stimulation increased several relevant behaviors among participants with dispositional submissiveness/authoritarianism. These behaviors included accessibility to submission-related concepts and submission to the experimenter's suggestion to take revenge (Saroglou, Corneille, & Van Cappellen, 2009), conformity to peer informational influence (Van Cappellen, Corneille, Cols, & Saroglou, 2011), rigid deontological moral decisions at the detriment of the well-being of proximal others (Van Pachterbeke et al., 2011), and prosocial or antisocial tendencies depending on the prosocial versus violent nature of the biblical text participants were exposed to (Blogowska & Saroglou, 2013).

An intriguing question is whether the social functions of religion are less relevant for modern spirituality, to the point that spirituality is rather independent from religious institutions. It is reasonable, on one hand, to conceive modern spirituality as being independent from traditional forms of religious organizations' effects on power, conformity, and social influence. On the other hand, there may exist a feeling of belonging to a broad worldwide spiritual human community, which, additionally, is to be distinguished from nihilist and materialist individuals. There also exist new forms of spiritual groups consisting, for instance, of virtual networks. Research is needed on this issue, but one can expect self-identification as spiritual and as belonging to a spiritual world community to play a similar role with regard to the basic psychological functions mentioned earlier in this section: satisfaction of the need to belong, social self-esteem, and social support. Furthermore, even if marked by a spirit of autonomy, modern spiritual quest is made with a marked interest in the spiritual teachings of traditional religions—this is not necessarily the case for people who identify as "non-religious and non-spiritual."

As far as the non-religious and non-spiritual are concerned, one might expect them to satisfy their social psychological needs through many non-religious/spiritual sources of community and belonging. It is also reasonable to expect agnostics and atheists to evade the characteristics and consequences of belonging to entitative and hierarchical religious groups—even if at the cost of some additional contributors to well-being like identifying with an eternal glorious group. However, attachment to alternative ideologies (e.g., secular humanism, laicism) or to organized groups (e.g., active atheist groups) may not be exempt from the respective risks for dogmatism and outgroup derogation. Nevertheless, the existing empirical evidence suggests that, overall, the non-religious are low, compared to the religious, on prejudice against various outgroups (ethnic and religious groups, minorities, and low-status groups), and that their possible ideological "ethnocentrism" and derogation of believers is weaker than the ideological "ethnocentrism" of the religious and their derogation of atheists (Altemeyer, 2010; Beit-Hallahmi, 2010; Gervais, Shariff, & Norenzayan, 2011; Hunsberger & Altemeyer, 2006; Zuckerman, 2009).

Conclusion: Religion and the Pyramids of Needs

The many cognitive, emotional, moral, and social functions of religion cover a large array of human psychological needs. Although these needs, within a religious context, are addressed through the many specific ways that were described earlier, they are universal needs. Following the classic pyramid of needs elaborated by Maslow (1968; Figure 16.2, left), it

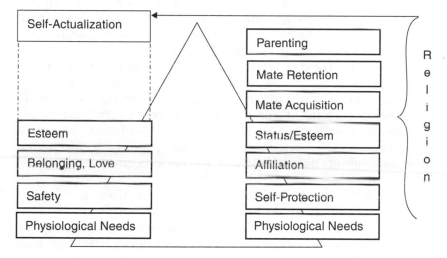

Figure 16.2 Religion and the pyramids of needs, following Maslow's (1968) humanistic psychological perspective (left), and Kenrick et al.'s (2010) evolutionary psychological perspective (right).

is often argued that religion satisfies principally the highest need in this pyramid, i.e., self-actualization, also referred to as a "being" need. This need is defined as the desire for self-fulfillment through actualization of one's own potential and can be accomplished in a variety of ways, including intellectual, moral, and spiritual self-transcendence. However, as detailed by Batson and Stocks (2004) and as illustrated in this chapter, people seek religion to also satisfy almost all of the basic, so-called "deficiency," needs of Maslow's pyramid. These include self-esteem, love and belonging, safety, and even physiological needs. Regarding the physiological needs, Batson and Stocks (2004) note that people may pray to God for food—or rain to guarantee food—and physical health, as well as for issues related to sexual needs, for instance to find a convenient sexual partner, to resist sexual desires, or to sublimate them.

In a recent revision of Maslow's pyramid of needs from an evolutionary psychology perspective (Kenrick, Griskevicius, Neuberg, & Schaller, 2010; see Figure 16.2, right), three major developments were made. First, from a strictly evolutionary perspective, the need for self-actualization is no longer part of the pyramid as it does not constitute an evolutionarily adaptive need. Second, the need for sex is no longer included in the primary physiological needs but has become a need for mate acquisition that occurs later in human development. Third, the satisfaction of each need of the pyramid is no longer a *sine qua non* condition for the higher needs to emerge; each need concurrently exerts its influence on humans' lives.

Subsequently, religion can be conceived as serving both psychological needs that are strictly evolutionarily adaptive, and other needs, located under the broad umbrella of "self-actualization," that may be psychologically important today without having had an evolutionary past. Some functions of religion can thus be seen as responding, or as a past response, to evolutionarily fundamental needs, i.e., survival and reproductive motives. These are: (1) fertility, parenting, and protection of the offspring; (2) careful—often homo-religious—mate selection; and (3) efforts for mate retention through marriage and commitment; (4) reputation as being worthy of trust and establishment of status-based social hierarchies; (5) affiliation, reciprocity, and coalition formation; and, to some extent, (6) self-protection (e.g., hygienic religious rules and norms, belief on divine providence); and (7) physiological needs (e.g., control of hunger and thirst through religious fasting) (see also Kirkpatrick, 2005; Li & Cohen, Chapter 10, this volume; Preston et al., Chapter 7, this volume). Note also that, on the basis of the revised evolutionary pyramid of needs, religion should no longer be seen as something that emerges only to address some superior needs after more primary needs have been satisfied.

A final important distinction to be made is that between several evolutionarily adaptive needs that can be addressed within a religious context—as they can be addressed within non-religious contexts—and religion itself as a system. Regarding the latter, there is a relative consensus today among evolutionary psychologists that religion may be a byproduct of psychological mechanisms (see the seven mentioned earlier) that evolved for their own adaptive purposes, i.e., before religion appeared. Religion thus resembles, for instance, art or sport, i.e., human activities that are not necessary outcomes of natural evolution, even if they imply psychological mechanisms that have been themselves selected for evolutionary reasons.

Religion and the Search for Unity

The force of religion lies not only in the multiplicity of the involved psychological functions, but also in the fact that the cognitive, emotional, moral, and social dimensions are organized into a coherent set. This is the case at least in the contemporary major world religions (Hinde, 2009). Of course, from an evolutionary psychological perspective, one should understand the different aspects of religion as corresponding to distinct psychological mechanisms (e.g., attachment, power structures, coalitions, mating) that are each domain specific and organized into functional systems with respective adaptive functions—like a body's organs and systems (see Figure 16.2, right). This view is preferred to that of the brain/mind as an all-purposed computer that operates on a small number of general principles in the service of only few broad motivations (Kirkpatrick, 2005). Nevertheless, the integration under one umbrella of a very specific pattern of different aspects of religion and their corresponding psychological functions, and the relative success of the major religions that have accomplished such integration, is an intellectually fascinating issue. For instance, adding a moralizing dimension to personal high Gods, rather than venerating natural objects and impersonal transcendent entities, has had numerous individual, collective, and cross-cultural implications (Stark, 2001; see also Shariff, Norenzayan, & Henrich, 2010).

I argue that the possible strength of the religious integration of such various aspects and psychological mechanisms into a unique set may lie in the fact that, in that way, religion fulfills straightforwardly a universal human search for unity and wholeness. Such a need may have been culturally present, possibly but not necessarily, as part of the motivation for self-actualization. Like self-actualization, the need for unity should not be perceived as having strictly an adaptive value, if we follow the revision of Maslow's (1968) hierarchy of needs from an evolutionary psychology perspective (Kenrick et al., 2010; see also Figure 16.2).

Theoretical and empirical evidence favors the idea that religion notably addresses a human search for unity, which reflects a broader need encompassing the more specific ones for epistemic order, connection with the world, moral exhaustiveness, and the need to belong (Saroglou, 2006a). Humans often have the subjective experience that their internal world, as well the external world, is divided and fragmented—in many respects. This concerns the subjective experience of many divisions such as those between: mind and body, cognitions and emotions, intentions and behavior, the ideal and real self, men and women, three times (past, present, and future), the self and the others, humans and the world, as well as our world and the cosmos. Religion, while affirming the distinctiveness of each of these poles from their opposites, at the same time offers for all of these divisive experiences the subjective perception of unity. It thus emphasizes the following ideas which are fostered through rituals: humans are psychosomatic beings; cognitions and emotions, intentions and behaviors, and the different parts of the self in general, are unified in the spiritual life. Similarly, manhood and womanhood are two sides of unique humanness; divisions between past, present, and future are illusions, with the very end being in fact a return to the very origins. Finally, the self and others are co-included in an encompassing religious brotherhood and family; humans are just part of a broad world with a transcendent entity having also some relation with non-human beings and non-living entities; and our world is just part of a more global cosmos.

Note that the notion of "oceanic feeling," popularized—although criticized—by Freud (1961 [1927]), qualifies the very essence of religious experience by pointing out this subjective experience of unity and wholeness. Similarly, magical thinking and holistic thinking, present in religious cognition (Gervais, Chapter 4, this volume), directly imply the perception of a common invisible essence across many distinct entities in the world and the importance of having a global, not fragmented, perception of things. From a perspective of embodied social cognition, this unity can metaphorically be represented through a horizontal axis of being (co-inclusion of all beings in a encompassing whole), but also a vertical axis that creates the subjective experience of order by locating all beings on a hierarchical chain. This chain spans from Gods through half-gods and humans to animals and further on to demons. The first axis reflects prosocial concerns, sameness (within a religious ingroup or a spiritual universe), and horizontal self-transcendence. The second axis points to the religion's role in favoring vertical self-transcendence, but also hierarchy, status, and prejudice toward outgroups. Interestingly, religion's strength is that it invests in both axes and creates a unity between them, even if there may exist inter-individual and cultural variability in the emphasis given to one axis over the other. (For the moral significance of the vertical chain of being and/or the social significance of the horizontal axis, see Brandt & Reyna, 2011; Haidt & Algoe, 2004.)

To use a Freudian wording, one can say that the promise to fulfill such a search for unity is an "illusion." Probably religion's utopia, or "positive illusion" like meaning, self-esteem, and optimism (Taylor & Brown, 1994), is to make people believe and feel that the world is a united whole. It may be an illusion, but it is built on the grounds of humans' common social cognition. Although it is objectively known that "true" is in fact distinct from "beautiful," that both are distinct from "good," and that all three are distinct from "me/us," humans implicitly perceive these four as interrelated to some extent. Empirical research shows, for instance, that people tend to perceive honest individuals as nice (Brambilla, Sacchi, Rusconi, Cherubini, & Yzerbyt, 2012) and beautiful (Paunonen, 2006); and perceive beautiful persons as also being skilled in interpersonal qualities (Lemay, Clark, & Greenberg, 2010). People also overestimate their own qualities and those of their friends, i.e., think that "I" and "we" are good (Taylor & Brown, 1994). Philosophy, from *Bhagavad Gita* through Plato and up to Hegel, has conceived truth, goodness, and beauty as constituting the three major qualities of the transcendence (see also Gardner, 2011, for a modern essay; see Changeux, 2012, for a neuroscientific approach). For the Christian medieval thought, in God, the three are united into one. Note also that Jesus affirmed that he is "the way *and* the truth *and* the life" (John 14:6), thus blending into one the objectives of religious behaving, believing, and experiencing.

Just-world beliefs constitute another category of beliefs that, although universal, are particularly present in religion and foster a sense of unity. Substantial research attests that religiousness, across several countries, relates positively to just-world beliefs, i.e., the beliefs that one gets what one deserves, and that the way we behave determines what we get (Saroglou, 2003b, for a review). The world thus appears as having an implicit internal unity. Interestingly, intrinsic or symbolic religiousness is found to positively relate to believe in ultimate justice (justice is not to be found here but later in another world) and outgroup tolerance, whereas extrinsic or orthodox religiousness relates to just-world belief for others (victims are responsible for their problems) and to victim derogation (Pichon & Saroglou, 2009; VanDeursen, Pope, & Warner, 2012). Related to the just-world belief are the problems of theodicy, i.e., why good people suffer, and unmerited gain, i.e., it is immoral to gain too much without having worked for it, both of which have received particular attention within religious traditions. Both situations threaten the perception of the world as ordered.

In sum, studying separately the multiple functions of religion without also trying to understand what makes religion a unique combination of various aspects and corresponding psychological functions may leave part of the picture unexplained. The encompassing character of the many distinct psychological domains and the "utopia" of a unity that embraces a large spectrum of human issues may be what makes religion's presence so pervasive across history. To slightly extend Freud's (1961 [1927]) classic assertion, one can say that the force of religion is not only the strength of the underlying human needs religion is supposed to address, but also the extent of these needs.

Being Religious or Not: Understanding Individual Differences

The synthesis of the multiple psychological functions of religion made in this chapter and the portrayal of religion's specifics can facilitate the work of those who think of religion and irreligion in terms of (psychological) costs and benefits. It also raises the question of the origins of individual differences on religiousness: some people may be more oriented to the benefits of religion; others to the benefits of irreligion. This begs the question of the possible adaptive role of being religious or irreligious.

Religion and Irreligion: Costs and Benefits

Overall, and with the risk of extreme oversimplification, the global picture from existing research is that religion facilitates or reinforces— more precisely than "causes"—a sense of meaning, self-control, self-esteem, individual coherence and stability, well-being, prosociality, and social cohesion within group barriers. At the same time, it facilitates or reinforces—again, more precisely than "causes" —inflexibility in ideas, conservatism in many life domains (from sexuality and family to politics), rigid moral deontology, system justification, and intergroup conflict. Thus religion does not seem to contribute to optimal maturation, a process that implies autonomy and openness and leads to social change and possibly global peace.

The benefits and costs of religion are not fully orthogonal to each other; they are interdependent to some extent. Religion is helpful when facing situations of "under-control," but at the same time it may be detrimental by leading to "over-control" (Gartner, 1996). Following the analysis made in the present chapter, this means that religion's positive role with respect to meaning making, emotional regulation, morality, and group belongingness includes the risk for, respectively, over-interpretation, hyper-emotionality, moralization, and heightened group entitativity. Regarding mental health, religion makes people "feel happy, but lack autonomy" (Buxant & Saroglou, 2008), at least in contexts where previous vulnerability pushes some to join small-size religious groups offering a haven of safety. Similarly, from a social developmental perspective, the effects of religion point to "coherence at the detriment of openness" (Saroglou, 2012a). Again at the risk of extreme oversimplification, but for the convenience of a synthesis, one can reasonably conclude that the benefits and costs of religion are respectively the costs and benefits of irreligion, at least as far as agnosticism and indifferent (not militant, organized) atheism are concerned.

From a strict rational choice theory perspective, one could expect people to weigh the costs and benefits and to make decisions with regard to existential attitudes and endorsement or not of religious systems. However, from an individual differences psychological perspective, being religious or irreligious is not only a matter of choice; important determinisms also play a role.

The Origins of Individual Differences on Religiousness

Why are some people religious and others not? Existing research points to the coexistence of, and possibly interaction between, three kinds of source: genetic influences, common environmental factors, and personal experiences (Ashton & Lee, Chapter 2, this volume; Hood, Hill, & Spilka, 2009; Saroglou, 2012b).

Religiousness, or lack thereof, is rather stable across age periods when we consider differences *between* individuals. Changes (conversion, apostasy, change of religious affiliation, radicalization, de-radicalization) *within* individuals also occur and are important to understand psychologically. However, these changes are less important in size than the overall lifespan "rank-order" stability when comparing between the high, the moderate, the low, and the non-religious. *Socialization* seems to be the most important predictor not only of religious affiliation but also of individual differences on religiousness: family, in particular, but also peers and other sources of socialization, play a key role in transmitting religious beliefs, emotions, practices, and identities; or transmitting indifference to religion and atheism (Hood et al., 2009; Norenzayan & Gervais, 2012).

However, there are also *genetic influences* on religiousness. These influences are rather minimal in childhood and adolescence, when family impact is strong, but become important in early adulthood when young adults gain autonomy (Ashton & Lee, Chapter 2, this volume). The more plausible way to explain these differences—but which is still in need of empirical confirmation—is that genetic influences on religiousness are to some extent mediated by genetic influences on basic personality traits. In fact, agreeableness and conscientiousness (as well as honesty within the HEXACO model), which are heavily influenced by heritability, typically characterize religiousness and have been found to longitudinally predict it. Thus, people who are genetically predisposed to be agreeable and conscientious may become or remain religious if religious ideas and practices are available in their own social environment. People who are not high in agreeableness and conscientiousness may be more willing to break the continuity of a religious family environment; or to be uninterested in religion if they were raised as non-religious (Saroglou 2010, 2012b). Moreover, high versus low openness to experience, another basic personality trait, predisposes one for respectively modern spiritual versus fundamentalist forms of religiousness. Note also that explanations of religiousness in terms of genetically influenced personality predispositions may help to explain, to some extent, gender differences in religiousness (Francis & Penny, Chapter 14, this volume).

Finally, *personal experiences* add a third source of inter-individual variability to religiousness. Often negative life events that touch the self, but also self-transcendent positive experiences, facilitate the emergence or intensification of religious quests—although negative experiences may also, under some conditions, facilitate religious doubt and apostasy (Hood et al., 2009; Van Cappellen & Rimé, Chapter 6, this volume). Attachment history seems to be a particularly powerful source of variety in trajectories related to religion or irreligion (Granqvist, Chapter 13, this volume). In addition, education and intelligence (Ashton & Lee, Chapter 2, this volume), cognitive styles (Gervais, Chapter 4, this volume) and cognitive, moral, and social development, especially in adolescence and young adulthood (Granqvist, Chapter 13, this volume), may provide opportunities and tools for religious doubting. Indeed, this age period implicates a questioning of religion because of perceived counterintuitiveness of religious beliefs, moral incoherence in some religious attitudes and behaviors, and social irrelevance of various religious aspects. Adolescence is thus a "sensitive" period for religious doubt and atheism (Saroglou, 2012a). These factors may, on the contrary, also provide opportunities for spiritual development (Good & Willoughby, 2008).

The impact of each piece of this puzzle on religiousness or irreligion (heritability, personality traits, thinking style, socialization, other environmental influences, life events, quality of family relations, and social development) has now received important empirical confirmation. However, there is still a need for studies that will empirically investigate how the interaction between these factors influences religiousness or irreligion. In particular, it is important to study the interaction between personality, socialization, and developmental factors; or between genetic influences, environmental influences, and specific personal experiences.

Religiousness and Irreligion: Both Adaptive?

An intriguing question is why religiousness has overall been more prevalent than irreligion across most societies. A related question is why there has consistently been an important minority of irreligious, be they atheists opposing religion, agnostics, persons indifferent to religion or, more recently, persons socialized as atheists. On the basis of the personality characteristics of religiousness and the comparable or divergent social attitudes and practices (e.g., authoritarianism, paranormal beliefs, creativity, rebel ideologies), it has been argued that, overall, both religiousness and irreligion may have been adaptive for different reasons (Saroglou, 2010). Religiousness "clearly expresses, as a cultural adaptation of personality traits [agreeableness and conscientiousness], a human concern for personal and social stability and moral self-transcendence but not the human needs for playfulness, personal growth, and social change" (p. 119–120). The last are expressed by extraversion and openness to experience, personality traits whose "cultural adaptations (e.g., artistic interests, atheist orientations, contesting ideologies) provide entertainers, creators, rebels, and revolutionaries" (p. 120).

From an evolutionary psychology perspective that tries to understand the possible adaptiveness—or indifference with regard to adaptive functions—of individual differences, it can be speculated that variation between believers and nonbelievers may follow general evolutionary mechanisms proposed to explain individual differences. These are mainly (1) *frequency-dependent selection* (a balance between religiousness and atheism is optimal, if one of the two becomes too rare, evolution will increase its numeric presence); (2) *fluctuating optimum* (religiousness or atheism outperforms the other pole depending on what it is optimal under specific conditions in specific contexts); and (3) *contingency on other traits* (religiousness or irreligion is indirectly selected depending on the co-occurrence of other traits/characteristics (see also Johnson, 2012). The evolutionary understanding of personality and individual differences is an emerging dynamic field of research (Buss & Hawley, 2011). Interpretations of individual differences in religiousness may be developed in the future, possibly in parallel with developments on the evolutionary understanding of the variation in basic personality traits (see Ashton, 2013; Nettle, 2011).

Understanding How Religiousness Works: Emerging Issues

Throughout the different chapters of the present volume, the contributors have proposed future research questions for the respective topics. In the present concluding chapter, I have also provided additional questions for future investigation. In concluding the chapter, it is of interest to focus on some methodological and theoretical issues that specifically regard individual religiousness and its consequences. These issues are important to keep in mind for future research. They concern the way individual religiousness interacts with (1) the activation of religious ideas, for instance in priming studies, (2) the induction of emotions and mood, and (3) the presence of cultural factors at the individual and the group levels, thus predicting divergent outcomes.

As stated in the previous section, religiousness can be regarded as an individual difference that is rather stable across lifespan, with stability being more pronounced than possible changes. However, changes exist in religiousness and its psychological consequences as a function of several factors. Important typical moderators of religiousness and its effects are age and gender (see in this volume, respectively: Granqvist, Chapter 13; and Francis & Penny, Chapter 14), as well as global societal changes impacting "cohorts," i.e., generations of people who were born in the same date range (Dillon, 2007; Schwadel, 2010, 2011). Recent social experimental and cross-cultural psychological research on religion urges us to consider some key additional moderators: religious context, emotional states, and cultural factors. I will comment on each of these in what follows.

Individual Religiousness as Interacting with Religious Stimulation

Does individual religiousness parallel the effects of religion, i.e., the effects of the activation of religious ideals and symbols? This is often the case but is not consistent. For instance, series of priming studies show that (devotional) religious ideas activate prosocial concepts and behavior; and that (coalitional) religious ideas activate prejudice against outgroups. These effects parallel those of individual religiousness and its forms, i.e., devotional versus coalitional (see in this volume, Preston et al., Chapter 7; Rowatt et al., Chapter 8). However, in many priming studies the religious activation of prosociality was independent from individual religiousness, i.e., it occurred for both religious and non-religious participants (Galen, 2012, for review). The religious priming was thus not more appealing for those participants for whom religion was a central theme in their life, and was successful even for participants for whom religion was irrelevant in their life. However, other studies show that, whereas individual religiousness alone may not have the expected social effects (prosocial or antisocial, depending on the target and the religious dimension involved), it does so only after some activation of religious ideas and norms (Blogowska & Saroglou, 2013; Malhotra, 2010; Rothschild, Abdollahib, & Pyszczynski, 2009).

From an individual differences perspective, this implies that individual religiousness may not consistently function as a miraculous predictor of all kinds of social attitude and behavior. Some "arousal," i.e., stimulation from relevant religious ideas and values is needed to activate or strengthen the consequences of individual religiousness. One can thus better understand why for centuries, across religions and societies, people regularly participated in religious services, listened to sermons, and read holy texts that repetitively evoked similar, if not the same ideas. This also suggests that the effects of religious activation may not necessarily be long lasting. (Note that, until now, studies have examined only immediate effects of religious priming.)

Religiousness as a State, Not Only a Trait

The outcomes of religiousness also become more visible after some emotional arousal. For instance, associations of religiosity/spirituality with relevant outcomes (feelings of closeness with others, spiritual behavioral intentions, prosocial behavior, meaning of life) were confirmed or strengthened after participants were experimentally induced with self-transcendent emotions such as awe, admiration, or elevation (Van Cappellen & Rimé, Chapter 6, this volume).

More fundamentally, religiousness, including spirituality, may not only be a *trait*, i.e., an individual disposition that is stable across time and situations, but also a *state*, i.e., a momentary feeling that, although influenced by a trait disposition, may show within-person daily variability, as a function of personal and contextual factors. Following college students for two weeks and collecting daily data on spirituality and other measures, Kashdan and Nezlek (2012) found significant within-person daily variability on all measures, including spirituality. Moreover, present day spirituality increased the next day's meaning in life—although the present day's meaning in life did not predict the next day's spirituality. Furthermore, for people high in trait spirituality, present day negative affect predicted greater spirituality the next day.

Religiousness across Religions, Cultures, and Nations

Individual religiousness may function, to some extent, differently across (1) religions—be it in the same or different nations, (2) cultures—be it with the same or different religions, and (3) nations—be it for the same, different, or multiple religious groups (Johnson & Cohen, Chapter 15, this volume; Saroglou & Cohen, 2013). As shown in various chapters of the present volume, when studying the psychological characteristics of religiousness, cultural, cross-religious, and cross-national sensitivity lead to fascinating findings across a variety of research domains: personality and the self (Sedikides & Gebauer, Chapter 3), emotions (Burris & Petrican, Chapter 5), values (Roccas & Elster, Chapter 9), politics (Malka, Chapter 11), gender differences (Francis & Penny, Chapter 14), and mental health (Hayward & Krause, Chapter 12; see also Loewenthal, 2007). This is also the case regarding cognition (Hommel, Colzato, Scorolli, Borghi, & van den Wildenberg, 2011; Li et al., 2012), human development (Holden & Vittrup, 2010; Trommsdorff & Chen, 2012), ritual (Atkinson & Whitehouse, 2011), morality (Cohen, Malka, Rozin, & Cherfas, 2006; Cohen & Rozin, 2001), and prosocial behavior and prejudice (Clobert, Saroglou, Hwang, & Soong, 2013; Clobert & Saroglou, 2013).

It is important for future psychological research on religion to be sensitive to cultural influences and distinguish between different causal factors besides such influences in the analyses, both at the individual and the group level. Note that how religion works at the collective level may parallel—showing thus *isomorphism*—or be in contrast with how it works at the individual level (Saroglou & Cohen, 2013). A first source of difference is religious affiliation (individual level), religious dominant tradition (in a given country), or religious/civilizational area (across nations). A second source of difference is the mean level of religiousness (how religious or secular a study's sample or a country is) and the predominance of a given religious form (e.g., fundamentalism versus religious quest) at the individual and the collective levels. Third, at both levels, factors indicating socioeconomic and sociocultural development are important moderators, and sometimes mediators, of the psychological characteristics, predictors or outcomes, of individual religiousness. Fourth, at the country level, historical or current societal characteristics such as church–state relations or religious diversity have been found to be interesting moderators. Finally, there is a need to better take into account the influences of broad cultural, transnational differences on the way religiousness works within and across religious groups, for instance by comparing Western and Eastern Buddhists to Western and Eastern Catholics or Protestants. These influences may result from deep cultural psychological specifics in personality, cognitions, emotions, social relationships, and moral thinking, or may stem from even further factors having to do with the natural environment and ecology such as those involving geography, climate, food, water, diseases and mortality, natural threats, and types of economy.

To conclude, a full understanding of the cognitive, emotional, moral, and social functions of religion and religiousness benefits from taking into account within-person, between-religion, and between-culture variability. Religion is one of the complex means humans have developed to address and transcend universal psychological needs that are deeply rooted in the physical, social, and cultural environment.

Acknowledgments

The writing of this chapter benefited from Grant ARC08/13-013 from the Communauté Française de Belgique. I am grateful to Wade C. Rowatt for very helpful comments on an earlier version of the chapter.

References

Aarnio, K., & Lindeman, M. (2007). Religious people and paranormal believers: Alike or different? *Journal of Individual Differences, 28*, 1–9.

Altemeyer, B. (2004). The decline of organized religion in Western civilization. *International Journal for the Psychology of Religion, 14*, 77–89.

Altemeyer, B. (2010). Atheism and secularity in North America. In P. Zuckerman (Ed.), *Atheism and secularity: Vol. 2. Global experiences* (pp. 1–21). Santa Barbara, CA: Praeger.

Arzheimer, K., & Carter, E. (2009). Christian religiosity and voting for West European radical right parties. *West European Politics, 32*, 985–1011.

Ashton, M. C. (2013). *Individual differences and personality* (2nd ed.). San Diego: Academic Press.

Atkinson, Q. D., & Whitehouse, H. (2011). The cultural morphospace of ritual form: Examining modes of religiosity cross-culturally. *Evolution and Human Behavior, 32*, 50–62.

Barrett, J. L. (2012). *Born believers: The science of children's religious belief.* New York: Free Press.

Batson, C. D., & Stocks, E. L. (2004). Religion: Its core psychological functions. In J. Greenberg, S. L. Koole, & T. Pyszczynski (Eds.), *Handbook of experimental existential psychology* (pp. 141–155). New York: Guilford.

Baumeister, R. F., & Exline, J. J. (1999). Virtue, personality, and social relations: Self-control as the moral muscle. *Journal of Personality, 67*, 1165–1194.

Beit-Hallahmi, B. (2010). Morality and immorality among the irreligious. In P. Zuckerman (Ed.), *Atheism and secularity: Vol. 1. Issues, concepts, and definitions* (pp. 113–148). Santa Barbara, CA: Praeger.

Blogowska, J., & Saroglou, V. (2013). For better or worse: Fundamentalists' attitudes towards outgroups as a function of exposure to authoritative religious texts. *International Journal for the Psychology of Religion, 23*, 103–125.

Boyer, P. (2001). *Religion explained: Evolutionary origins of religious thought.* New York: Basic Books.

Brambilla, M., Sacchi, S., Rusconi, P., Cherubini, P., & Yzerbyt, V. (2012). You want to give a good impression? Be honest! Moral traits dominate group impression formation. *British Journal of Social Psychology, 51*, 149–166.

Brandt, M. J., & Reyna, C. (2010). The role of prejudice and the need for closure in religious fundamentalism. *Personality and Social Psychology Bulletin, 36*, 715–725.

Brandt, M. J., & Reyna, C. (2011). The chain of being: A hierarchy of morality. *Perspectives in Psychological Science, 6*, 428–446.

Buss, D. M., & Hawley, P. H. (Eds.). (2011). *The evolution of personality and individual differences.* New York: Oxford University Press.

Buxant, C., & Saroglou, V. (2008). Feeling good, but lacking autonomy: Closed-mindedness on social and moral issues in new religious movements. *Journal of Religion and Health, 47*, 17–31.

Caldwell-Harris, C. L. (2012). Understanding atheism/non-belief as an expected individual-differences variable. *Religion, Brain and Behavior, 2*, 4–23.

Caldwell-Harris, C. L., Wilson, A. L., LoTempio, E., & Beit-Hallahmi, B. (2011). Exploring the atheist personality: Well-being, awe, and magical thinking in atheists, Buddhists, and Christians. *Mental Health, Religion, and Culture, 14,* 659–672.

Changeux, J.-P. (2012). *The good, the true, and the beautiful: A neuronal approach.* New Haven, CT: Yale University Press.

Clobert, M., & Saroglou, V. (2013). Intercultural non-conscious influences: Prosocial effects of Buddhist priming on Westerners of Christian tradition. *International Journal for Intercultural Relations, 37,* 391–398.

Clobert, M., Saroglou, V., Hwang, K.-K., & Soong, W.-L. (2012). *Eastern religious tolerance: A myth or a reality? Empirical investigations of religious prejudice in East Asian societies.* Manuscript submitted for publication.

Cohen, A. B., Malka, A., Rozin, P., & Cherfas, L. (2006). Religion and unforgivable offenses. *Journal of Personality, 74,* 85–118.

Cohen, A. B., & Rozin, P. (2001). Religion and the morality of mentality. *Journal of Personality and Social Psychology, 81,* 697–710.

Demoulin, S., Saroglou, V., & Van Pachterbeke, M. (2008). Infra-humanizing others, supra-humanizing gods: The emotional hierarchy. *Social Cognition, 26,* 235–247.

Dillon, M. (2007). Age, generation, and cohort in American religion and spirituality. In J. A. Beckford & N. J. Demerath III (Eds.), *The Sage handbook of the sociology of religion* (pp. 526–546). London: Sage.

Dovidio, J. F., & Gaertner, S. L. (2010). Intergroup bias. In S. T. Fiske, D. T. Gilbert, & G. Lindzey (Eds.), *Handbook of social psychology* (Vol. 2, pp. 1084–1121). New York: Wiley.

Emmons, R. A. (2005). Emotion and religion. In R. F. Paloutzian & C. L. Park (Eds.), *Handbook of the psychology of religion and spirituality* (pp. 235–252). New York: Guilford.

Fiske, S. T. (2010). *Social beings: Core motives in social psychology* (2nd ed.). New York: Wiley.

Freud, S. (1961). *The future of an illusion* (J. Strachey, Trans.). New York: Norton. (Original work published 1927).

Galen, L. W. (2012). Does religious belief promote prosociality? A critical examination. *Psychological Bulletin, 138,* 876–906.

Gardner, H. (2011). *Truth, beauty, and goodness reframed: Educating for the virtues in the age of truthiness and twitter.* New York: Basic Books.

Gartner, J. (1996). Religious commitment, mental health, and prosocial behavior: A review of the empirical literature. In E. P. Shafranske (Ed.), *Religion and the clinical practice of psychology* (pp. 187–214). Washington, DC: American Psychological Association.

Gebauer, J. E., & Maio, G. R. (2012). The need to belong can motivate belief in God. *Journal of Personality, 80,* 465–501.

Gervais, W. M., Shariff, A. F., & Norenzayan, A. (2011). Do you believe in atheists? Distrust is central to anti-atheist prejudice. *Journal of Personality and Social Psychology, 101,* 1189–1206.

Good, M., & Willoughby, T. (2008). Adolescence as a sensitive period for spiritual development. *Child Development Perspectives, 2,* 32–37.

Graham, J., & Haidt, J. (2010). Beyond beliefs: Religions bind individuals into moral communities. *Personality and Social Psychology Review, 14,* 140–150.

Haidt, J., & Algoe, S. (2004). Moral amplification and the emotions that attach us to saints and demons. In J. Greenberg, S. L. Koole, & T. Pyszczynski

(Eds.), *Handbook of experimental existential psychology* (pp. 322–335). New York: Guilford.

Hinde, R. A. (2009). *Why gods persist: A scientific approach to religion* (2nd ed.). London: Routledge.

Hogg, M. A., Adelman, J. R., & Blagg, R. D. (2010). Religion in the face of uncertainty: An uncertainty-identity theory account of religiousness. *Personality and Social Psychology Review, 14,* 72–83.

Holden, G. W., & Vittrup, B. (2010). Religion. In M. H. Bornstein (Ed.), *Handbook of cultural developmental science* (pp. 279–295). New York: Psychology Press.

Hommel, B., Colzato, L. S., Scorolli, C., Borghi, A. M., & van den Wildenberg, W. P. M. (2011). Religion and action control: Faith-specific modulation of the Simon effect but not stop-signal performance. *Cognition, 120,* 177–185.

Hood, R. W., Jr., Hill, P. C., & Spilka, B. (2009). *The psychology of religion: An empirical approach* (4th ed.). New York: Guilford.

Hoverd, W. J., Atkinson, Q. D., & Sibley, C. G. (2012). Group size and the trajectory of religious identification. *Journal for the Scientific Study of Religion, 51,* 286–303.

Hunsberger, B., & Altemeyer, B. (2006). *Atheists: A groundbreaking study of America's nonbelievers.* Amherst, NY: Prometheus Books.

James, W. (1985). *The varieties of religious experience: A study in human nature.* Cambridge, MA: Harvard University Press. (Original work published 1902).

Johnson, D. (2012). What are atheists for? Hypotheses on the functions of non-belief in the evolution of religion. *Religion, Brain and Behavior, 2,* 48–99.

Kashdan, T. B., & Nezlek, J. B. (2012). Whether, when, and how is spirituality related to well-being? Moving beyond single occasion questionnaires to understanding daily process. *Personality and Social Psychology Bulletin, 38,* 1523–1535.

Kenrick, D. T., Griskevicius, V., Neuberg, S. L., & Schaller, M. (2010). Renovating the pyramid of needs: Contemporary extensions built upon ancient foundations. *Perspectives on Psychological Science, 5,* 292–314.

Kirkpatrick, L. A. (2005). Evolutionary psychology: An emerging new foundation for the psychology of religion. In R. F. Paloutzian & C. L. Park (Eds.), *Handbook of the psychology of religion and spirituality* (pp. 101–119). New York: Guilford.

Koenig, H., King, D., & Carson, V. B. (2012). *Handbook of religion and health* (2nd ed.). New York: Oxford University Press.

Kruglanski, A. W., Pierro, A., Mannetti, L., & De Grada, E. (2006). Groups as epistemic providers: Need for closure and the unfolding of group-centrism. *Psychological Review, 113,* 84–100.

Lemay, E. P., Jr., Clark, M. S., & Greenberg, A. (2010). What is beautiful is good because what is beautiful is desired: Physical attractiveness stereotyping as projection of interpersonal goals. *Personality and Social Psychology Bulletin, 36,* 339–353.

Li, Y. J., Johnson, K. A., Cohen, A. B., Williams, M. J., Knowles, E. D., & Chen, Z. (2012). Fundamental(ist) attribution error: Protestants are dispositionally focused. *Journal of Personality and Social Psychology, 102,* 281–290.

Loewenthal, K. M. (2007). *Religion, culture, and mental health.* Cambridge: Cambridge University Press.

McCullough, M. E., & Willoughby, B. L. B. (2009). Religion, self-regulation, and self-control: Associations, explanations, and implications. *Psychological Bulletin, 135,* 69–93.

McGregor, I., Nash, K., & Prentice, M. (2012). Religious zeal after goal frustration. In M. A. Hogg & D. L. Blaylock (Eds.), *Extremism and the psychology of uncertainty* (pp. 147–164). Hoboken, NJ: Wiley-Blackwell.

Malhotra, D. (2010). (When) are religious people nicer? Religious salience and the "Sunday effect" on pro-social behavior. *Judgment and Decision Making, 5,* 138–143.

Maslow, A. H. (1968). *Toward a psychology of being* (2nd ed.). New York: Harper & Row.

Myers, D. G. (2012). Reflections on religious belief and prosociality: Comment on Galen (2012). *Psychological Bulletin, 138,* 913–917.

Nettle, D. (2011). Evolutionary perspectives in the five-factor model of personality. In D. M. Buss & P. H. Hawley (Eds.), *The evolution of personality and individual differences* (pp. 5–28). New York: Oxford University Press.

Norenzayan, A., & Gervais, W. M. (2012). The origins of religious disbelief. *Trends in Cognitive Sciences, 17,* 20–25.

Nucci, L., & Turiel, E. (1993). God's word, religious rules, and their relation to Christian and Jewish children's concepts of morality. *Child Development, 64,* 1475–1491.

Oishi, S., Seol, K. O., Koo, M., & Miao, F. F. (2011). Was he happy? Cultural difference in conceptions of Jesus. *Journal of Research in Personality, 45,* 84–91.

Oman, D. (2013). Spiritual modeling and the social learning of spirituality and religion. In K. I. Pargament, J. J. Exline, & J. W. Jones (Eds.), *APA handbook of psychology, religion and spirituality* (Vol. 1, pp. 187–204). Washington, DC: American Psychological Association.

Paloutzian, R. F. (2005). Religious conversion and spiritual transformation: A meaning-system analysis. In R. F. Paloutzian & C. L. Park (Eds.), *Handbook of the psychology of religion and spirituality* (pp. 331–347). New York: Guilford.

Park, C. L. (2007). Religiousness/spirituality and health: A meaning systems perspective. *Journal of Behavioral Medicine, 30,* 319–328.

Paunonen, S. V. (2006). You are honest, therefore I like you and find you attractive. *Journal of Research in Personality, 40,* 237–249.

Pew Research Center. (2012). *The global religious landscape: A report on the size and distribution of the world's major religious groups as of 2010.* The Pew Forum on Religion and Public Life. Retrieved from: http://www.pewforum.org/global-religious-landscape-exec.aspx.

Piazza, J. (2012). "If you love me keep my commandments": Religiosity increases preference for rule-based moral arguments. *International Journal for the Psychology of Religion, 22,* 285–302.

Pichon, I., & Saroglou, V. (2009). Religion and helping: Impact of target, thinking styles and just-world beliefs. *Archive for the Psychology of Religion, 31,* 215–236.

Rothschild, Z. K., Abdollahib, A., & Pyszczynski, T. (2009). Does peace have a prayer? The effect of mortality salience, compassionate values, and religious fundamentalism on hostility toward out-groups. *Journal of Experimental Social Psychology, 45*, 816–827.

Saroglou, V. (2002a). Beyond dogmatism: The need for closure as related to religion. *Mental Health, Religion, and Culture, 5*, 183–194.

Saroglou, V. (2002b). Religiousness, religious fundamentalism, and quest as predictors of humor creation. *International Journal for the Psychology of Religion, 12*, 177–188.

Saroglou, V. (2003a). Humor appreciation as function of religious dimensions. *Archive for the Psychology of Religion, 24*, 144–153.

Saroglou, V. (2003b). Trans-cultural/religious constants vs. cross-cultural/religious differences in psychological aspects of religion. *Archive for the Psychology of Religion, 25*, 71–87.

Saroglou, V. (2004). Being religious implies being different in humor: Evidence from self- and peer-ratings. *Mental Health, Religion, and Culture, 7*, 255–267.

Saroglou, V. (2006a). Quête d'unité: Spécificité religieuse d'une fonction non nécessairement religieuse [Quest for unity: Religious specifics of a universal psychological function]. *Archives de Psychologie, 72*, 161–181. English version retrieved from http://www.uclouvain.be/cps/ucl/doc/psyreli/documents/QuestForUnity.pdf.

Saroglou, V. (2006b). Saints et héros: Vies parallèles et psychologies spécifiques [Saints and heroes: Parallel lives and distinct psychologies]. *Revue Théologique de Louvain, 37*, 313–341.

Saroglou, V. (2010). Religiousness as a cultural adaptation of basic traits: A five-factor model perspective. *Personality and Social Psychology Review, 14*, 108–125.

Saroglou, V. (2011). Believing, bonding, behaving, and belonging: The big four religious dimensions and cultural variation. *Journal of Cross-Cultural Psychology, 42*, 1320–1340.

Saroglou, V. (2012a). Adolescents' social development and the role of religion: Coherence at the detriment of openness. In G. Trommsdorff & X. Chen (Eds.), *Values, religion, and culture in adolescent development* (pp. 391–423). Cambridge: Cambridge University Press.

Saroglou, V. (2012b). Are we born to be religious? Genes and personality influence our attitudes toward religion. *Scientific American Mind, 23*(2), 52–57.

Saroglou, V. (2012c). Is religion not prosocial at all? Comment on Galen (2012). *Psychological Bulletin, 138*, 907–912.

Saroglou, V. (2013). Religion, spirituality, and altruism. In K. I. Pargament, J. J. Exline, & J. W. Jones (Eds.), *APA handbook of psychology, religion and spirituality* (Vol. 1, pp. 439–457). Washington, DC: American Psychological Association.

Saroglou, V., & Anciaux, L. (2004). Liking sick humor: Coping styles and religion as predictors. *Humor: International Journal of Humor Research, 17*, 257–277.

Saroglou, V., & Cohen, A. B. (2013). Cultural and cross-cultural psychology of religion. In R. F. Paloutzian & C. L. Park (Eds.), *Handbook of the psychology of religion and spirituality* (2nd ed., pp. 330–353). New York: Guilford.

Saroglou, V., Corneille, O., & Van Cappellen, P. (2009). "Speak, Lord, your servant is listening": Religious priming activates submissive thoughts and behaviors. *International Journal for the Psychology of Religion, 19*, 143–154.

Saroglou, V., & Muñoz-García, A. (2008). Individual differences in religion and spirituality: An issue of personality traits and/or values. *Journal for the Scientific Study of Religion, 47*, 83–101.

Saroglou, V., Prade, C., & Rodriguez, N. (2012, July). Music preferences of religious people and the role of related personality and emotions. In V. Saroglou & G. J. Lewis (Chairs), *Religion and personality: From genes to behavior*. Symposium conducted at the 16th European Conference on Personality, Trieste, Italy.

Schwadel, P. (2010). Period and cohort effects on religious nonaffiliation and religious disaffiliation: A research note. *Journal for the Scientific Study of Religion, 49*, 311–319.

Schwadel, P. (2011). Age, period, and cohort effects on religious activities and beliefs. *Social Science Research, 40*, 181–192.

Shariff, A. F., Norenzayan, A., & Henrich, J. (2010). The birth of high gods: How the cultural evolution of supernatural policing influenced the emergence of complex, cooperative human societies, paving the way for civilization. In M. Schaller, A. Norenzayan, S. Heine, T. Yamagishi, & T. Kameda (Eds.), *Evolution, culture, and the human mind* (pp. 119–136). New York: Psychology Press.

Skitka, L. J., Bauman, C. W., & Lytle, B. L. (2009). Limits on legitimacy: Moral and religious convictions as constraints on deference to authority. *Journal of Personality and Social Psychology, 97*, 567–578.

Stark, R. (2001). Gods, rituals, and the moral order. *Journal for the Scientific Study of Religion, 40*, 619–636.

Streib, H., & Klein, C. (2013). Atheists, agnostics, and apostates. In K. I. Pargament, J. J. Exline, & J. W. Jones (Eds.), *APA handbook of psychology, religion and spirituality* (Vol. 1, pp. 713–728). Washington, DC: American Psychological Association.

Taylor, S. E., & Brown, J. D. (1994). Positive illusions and well-being revisited: Separating fact from fiction. *Psychological Bulletin, 116*, 21–27.

Trommsdorff, G., & Chen, X. (Eds.). (2012). *Values, religion, and culture in adolescent development*. Cambridge: Cambridge University Press.

Turiel, E. (2006). The development of morality. In W. Damon & R. M. Lerner (Series Eds.) & N. Eisenberg (Vol. Ed.), *Handbook of child psychology: Vol. 3. Social, emotional, and personality development* (6th ed., pp. 789–857). Hoboken, NJ: Wiley.

Van Cappellen, P., Corneille, O., Cols, S., & Saroglou, V. (2011). Beyond mere compliance to authoritative figures: Religious priming increases conformity to informational influence among submissive people. *International Journal for the Psychology of Religion, 21*, 97–105.

VanDeursen, M. J., Pope, A. R. D., & Warner, R. H. (2012). Just world maintenance patterns among intrinsically and extrinsically religious individuals. *Personality and Individual Differences, 52*, 755–758.

Van Pachterbeke, M., Freyer, C., & Saroglou, V. (2011). When authoritarianism meets religion: Sacrificing others in the name of abstract deontology. *European Journal of Social Psychology, 41*, 898–903.

Verkuyten, M., & Martinovic, B. (2012). Social identity complexity and immigrants' attitude toward the host nation: The intersection of ethnic and religious group identification. *Personality and Social Psychology Bulletin, 38,* 1165–1177.

Watts, F. (2007). Emotion regulation and religion. In J. J. Gross (Ed.), *Handbook of emotion regulation* (pp. 504–520). New York: Guilford.

Weeden, J., Cohen, A. B., & Kenrick, D. T. (2008). Religious attendance as reproductive support. *Evolution and Human Behavior, 29,* 327–334.

Ysseldyk, R., Matheson, K., & Anisman, H. (2010). Religiosity as identity: Toward an understanding of religion from a social identity perspective. *Personality and Social Psychology Review, 14,* 60–71.

Yzerbyt, V., Judd, C. M., & Corneille, O. (Eds.). (2004). *The psychology of group perception: Perceived variability, entitativity, and essentialism.* New York: Psychology Press.

Zuckerman, P. (2009). Atheism, secularity, and well-being: How the findings of social science counter negative stereotypes and assumptions. *Sociology Compass, 3,* 949–971.

Author Index

Subject Index